The Church, Marriage, and the Family

Other Titles in the Series

THE CHURCH, MARRIAGE, AND THE FAMILY

Proceedings from the 27th Annual Convention of the Fellowship
of Catholic Scholars, September 24-26, 2004
Pittsburgh, Pennsylvania

Including a Tribute:
In Memoriam: Rev. Msgr. George A. Kelly, 1916-2004
Founder of the Fellowship of Catholic Scholars

Edited by Kenneth D. Whitehead

ST. AUGUSTINE'S PRESS

South Bend, Indiana
2007

Manufactured in the United States of America.

1 2 3 4 5   12 11 10 09 08 07

Library of Congress Cataloging in Publication Data
Fellowship of Catholic Scholars. Convention (27th : 2004 :
Steubenville, Ohio)
The church, marriage, and the family : proceedings from the 27th
Annual Convention of the Fellowship of Catholic Scholars : including
a tribute, In memoriam, Rev. Msgr. George A. Kelly, 1916-2004,
founder of the Fellowship of Catholic Scholars / Kenneth D.
Whitehead, editor.
p. cm.
Includes bibliographical references.
ISBN 1-58731-153-4 (paperbound : alk. paper)
1.. Marriage – Religious aspects – Catholic Church – Congresses. 2.
Family – Religious aspects – Catholic Church – Congresses. 3. Sex –
Religious aspects – Catholic Church – Congresses. 4. Kelly, George
Anthony, 1916–2004 – Congresses. 5. Catholic Church – Doctrines –
Congresses. I. Whitehead, K. D. II. Title.
BX2250.F45 2004
261.8'358 – dc22   2006016535

∞ *The paper used in this publication meets the minimum requirements of the American National Standard for Information Sciences – Permanence of Paper for Printed Materials, ANSI Z39.48-1984.*

St. Augustine's Press
www.staugustine.net

CONTENTS

Session III: Catholic Marriage and Feminism

Concurrent Sessions
Session A: Psychological Insights on Chastity and
the Dignity and Affirmation of the Person

Session B: Raising Catholic Children in a Secular Culture

Session C: The Cultural Battle for the Family
in Contemporary Society

Introduction to the Convention Program

WILLIAM L. SAUNDERS, PROGRAM CHAIRMAN

Good morning, and welcome to the Fellowship of Catholic Scholars' 2004 27th annual convention. My name is Bill Saunders, of the Family Research Council. I am a member of the Board of Directors of the Fellowship, and the program chairman for this year's convention. I want to thank the other members of the program committee, Elizabeth Fox-Genovese and Msgr. Stuart Swetland, for all their hard work in putting this program together.

2004 was designated by the United Nations as the "International Year of the Family Plus 10." This rather odd and amusing UN terminology refers to the fact that the first International Year of the Family was observed in 1994, ten years ago. It was during that year, in solidarity with most of those who wanted a "Year of the Family," that the Holy Father, Pope John Paul II, issued, in 1994, an important papal document, his "Letter to Families." This letter of the Holy Father's is mentioned and cited by a number of our speakers and it also forms the centerpiece of the reflections of the president of the Pontifical Council on the Family, Cardinal Alfonso Lopez-Trujillo, who could not, unfortunately, be with us in person, as he had originally planned, but whose remarks will be distributed later (and printed in the volume of conference speeches). In his absence, we are thrilled that Congressman Chris Smith of New Jersey, who is the recipient this year, along with his wife, Marie, of the Cardinal O'Boyle Award, will deliver a Keynote Address this evening on "Pro-Family Prospects in the Next Congress."

The Fellowship board chose the theme of the "International Year of the Family" for this year's convention to coincide with all the interest generated by the UN designation. Our aim over the next few days is to focus upon, and to reflect upon, the state of marriage and the family today, in the year 2004. Our speakers will consider the issue from many perspectives – philosophical, theological, demographic, historical, and scriptural – and both domestically in the United States as well as internationally. On the international front, by the way, we are especially pleased that members of the Fellowship's chapter in Australia, including Bishop Anthony Fisher, will be among these speakers.

For the first time at a Fellowship convention, we will be holding concurrent sessions. These sessions include speakers who responded to a special "call for papers" for this convention and whose contributions were selected from among a number of worthy entries. They will take place on Saturday morning. We believe these concurrent sessions will give some younger members of the Fellowship an opportunity to present their ideas and to develop them in dialogue with other FCS members. We urge you to attend as many of these sessions as you can.

We are also beginning this year with a Friday morning session. We particularly wanted to do this in order to feature scholars from nearby Franciscan University of Steubenville, an institution which has been a very generous friend of the Fellowship throughout the years. These first two speakers belong to what I am calling the "Steubenville All-Stars," Professors Stephen Miletic and John Crosby. With them, we begin this year's convention, which is star-studded with talent across the board, as you will see with each successive speaker. Both the concurrent sessions and the extra Friday morning session make for a fuller and longer program than has been usual, but we believe you will find it to be eminently worth it.

Also, this is our first convention since the death of our founder, Msgr. George A. Kelly. Several voices will pay tribute to Msgr. Kelly in the course of the convention, and we also plan to publish a number of memorial reminiscences of him and his inimitable presence in the life of the Fellowship in the volume of the "Proceedings" that has customarily issued from each Fellowship convention.

Thank you all for attending.

Keynote Address
Chapter 1: Pro-Family Prospects in the Congress

REPRESENTATIVE CHRISTOPHER H. SMITH (R.- N. J.)

On behalf of my wife Marie and I, let me offer a very special thank you to the Fellowship of Catholic Scholars for honoring us with the Cardinal O'Boyle Award. I especially want to thank you for recognizing a remarkable, unsung hero in the cause of life – my wife, Marie. Thirty years ago, Marie and I met in the pro-life movement while in college – she was on the Trenton State College Pro-Life Committee. A teacher by profession, Marie began her work in the movement in the early 1970s. Today, she is a great mother to our four kids and my best friend on earth.

Marie currently serves as the International Director of Feminists for Life, and passionately believes we need to be more pro-active than we have been in helping to protect women, unborn children, and the family overseas. The purveyors of death are on the march worldwide seeking – to paraphrase St. Peter – whom they can devour.

In the Lord's Prayer Jesus told us to pray: "Our Father, who art in heaven, hallowed be thy Name. Thy kingdom come, thy will be done on earth as it is in heaven…" Have you ever thought how reassuring it is to know that God's will is perfectly adhered to in heaven? At least there, in heaven, there is unending joy, love, peace, happiness and kindness.

But, of course, that is not enough. God wants His will known and enthusiastically embraced here on earth as well. Amazingly, God has entrusted the awesome responsibility of *proclaiming the good news* – the Gospel – to His Church and to every believer. Whatever our walk of life, we are all missionaries; we are all ambassadors of Christ. And to the scholars here tonight, let me just say that because of your knowledge, insight, and wisdom, you can impact disproportionately on our society for the good.

In the Gospels, our Lord gives us the key to a meaningful and abundant life – when he instructs us to seek first the Kingdom of Heaven and

God's righteousness; and if we do that, there is a promise that all else shall be added unto us. Yet, God's incredible offer of unbridled joy in the here and in the hereafter often goes unclaimed, like a winning million-dollar lottery ticket collecting dust in a drawer. Jesus says that He knocks on the door of our souls – but it is we who must open the door. Indeed, we all run the risk of missing out on the gift of eternal bliss due to laziness, indifference, or slavery to sin.

Someone once told me: if you say you don't have time for something, you haven't stated a fact, you've stated a priority. If seeking God and His will is the priority – you and I will have the time to do whatever God calls us to do.

It was stated long ago that as Catholic men and women who have the gift of faith, heaven expects much from us. As scholars, I suspect God expects even more from you. Hey, better you than me! Not only are we expected to walk in a way worthy of our calling, but to take the brilliant light of Christ to an increasingly lost and morally obtuse world – to share the Good News; to bear witness to the truth even when there is a cost. You and I are called by Jesus to be "the salt of the earth." Salt not only mitigates corruption, but also enhances taste. In like manner, Catholics and others of good will should lessen society's corruption and decay and make society more moral, sane, and compassionate.

After 24 years in Congress, I can attest to the fact that any serious attempt to be of service in accomplishing "His will on earth" requires persistent prayer, an immense amount of sacrifice, fasting, and hard work. And good intentions are not enough – we must be as our Lord said – wise as serpents, gentle as doves! We have to work harder and be smarter than the opponents of life. When you dig in your heels to fight for the family – especially its littlest member, the unborn child – you can rest assured that hefty amounts of scorn, libel, and slander will come your way. You can be assured that the *New York Times*, the *Washington Post*, and Dan Rather will attack, mock, and ridicule you.

Counting it as all joy and as "light affliction," however, we are urged by St. Paul to run with endurance the race set before us with our eyes firmly fixed on the Lord, the author and perfecter of faith. Quitting is never an option. Even discouragement is a luxury we can ill afford. God's grace will refresh and renew our spirits, minds, and bodies – if we only ask and trust in him.

No one in the world has more faithfully or more courageously defended human life than Pope John Paul II, by the way. The pope's *Gospel of Life*, his incisive homilies – contrasting the culture of life with the culture of death – his holy persistence, his personal example of joyous piety, and his global trekking and leadership have all combined to make him the greatest champion of human rights alive today – or any day, for that matter.

The pope's bold calls for universal justice, Christ-like mercy, compassion, and inclusion of the disenfranchised and forgotten – especially the unborn – all these things inspire us to live Matthew 25:40, where Jesus said: "As you did it to one of the least of these my brethren, you did it to me."

Elected officials, judges, and bureaucrats need to recognize their obligation to be faithful to all that God commands; they need to recognize that we have a responsibility that is not easily satisfied to promote genuine human rights and justice. You can help raise up a new generation of lawmakers and bureaucrats who will put God first and see public service as a ministry. Far too many politicians and their handlers, however, have personalized their faith so as to render it meaningless in the public square. At home they believe one thing. At work, say, in Congress, their actions are motivated by polls, focus groups, big donors, and re-election. Today, many politicians, judges, and scholars are in league with the fringe – misguided radical pro-abortionists, oneworlders at the UN, and the shrewd manipulators in the news and entertainment media. A powerful anti-family coalition has emerged that must be challenged.

Abortion is violence against children. It is a "weapon" no less lethal than an Uzi, in the hands of a terrorist. Peace begins in the womb.

Part of what you asked me to address this evening is the outlook for pro-life prospects in the next Congress. To this request I must say: it depends. It depends on who wins the presidency, the House, and the Senate. But it especially depends on who goes to the White House. If John Kerry wins, the family will lose big time, and it will be *déjà vu* all over again – just as it was in the case of President Clinton.

Despite the fact that a recent Zogby poll clearly shows that a significant majority of Americans reject abortion in most circumstances. This majority includes women (56%), African Americans (62%), Hispanics (79%), and young adults (61%). Senator Kerry nevertheless continues to make it absolutely clear that he desperately wants to be the "abortion president." So if he wins, we clearly will be on the defensive. The whole ship of state will shift to a *pro-death* orientation.

On the Larry King Live show, Senator Kerry proclaimed that if elected President the first thing he will do is reverse the pro-life Mexico City Policy, thereby forcing taxpayers to give money to groups that promote abortion overseas. Make no mistake: millions are at risk. As you know, anti-life strategies which rely on the deception and hyperbole honed so effectively in the United States and other Western countries are now being deployed with a vengeance in the developing world to promote abortion on demand. In the early 1990s, every country affiliate of the International Planned Parenthood Federation based in London agreed to "Vision 2000," a strategic battle plan to make war on the unborn child using legislative action, case law, and executive branch fiats. Three weeks ago they and other Non-Governmental Organizations (NGOs) met in London in order to hatch an action plan of new and expanded schemes to impose abortion and the other elements of the culture of death on the world; this plan is called "Countdown 2015." Week after week, Planned Parenthood, joined by Marie Stopes International and several Fortune 500 foundations, employ the same tactics they used to enlist the support of pliable media here to amplify their agenda. As a result, pro-life laws in Ireland, Poland, Northern Ireland, the Phillipines, Nigeria, Kenya, Uganda, and every country in Latin America are today at risk.

The abortionists and their allies in the European Union, Canada, and the UN have already succeeded in establishing pro-abortion laws in more than 100 countries, including South Africa, Romania, Croatia, Bosnia, Nepal, and Cambodia. Let us not be under any false illusions; the abortionists are aggressive to a fault, and they will campaign without ceasing to establish an unfettered global right to abortion. No expense has been spared to promote abortion. For example, George Soros, worth roughly $4 billion, established the Program on Reproductive Health and Rights. This organization has given tens of millions to pro-abortion causes, including paying for the litigation to keep partial-birth abortion legal here in the United States.

Bill Gates, valued at $76 billion, has given $57 million to the United Nations Population Fund, almost $14 million to International Planned Parenthood, $4 million to the Population Council, and $400,000 to the initiative in California to kill embryos for their stem cells. And he has given millions more to other related causes. Ted Turner earmarked $1 billion from 1997 to 2007 for UN health and population control efforts. The David and Lucille Packard Foundation, worth $13 billion, is almost exclusively concerned with population control and similar issues. Warren Buffet, worth $28 billion, plans to dedicate almost his entire fortune to "population control." In one year alone, the Buffet Foundation committed $20 million to IPAS (International Project Assistance Services), makers of the hand-held abortive suction pump called a Manual Vacuum Aspirator. $2 million more went to Family Health

International whose president, Willard Cates, once presented a paper called "Abortion as a Treatment for Unwanted Pregnancy – the Number Two Sexually Transmitted 'Disease.'" The Buffet Foundation gave an additional $1.4 million to Planned Parenthood. The Foundation also has intimate ties with the Population Council, the inventors of NORPLANT and holders of the US patent rights to the RU-486 abortifacient drug.

I believe that as weapons against the family go, population control is the equivalent of nuclear weapons. It causes massive destruction. However, it is cloaked in "sheep's clothing." Population Control is something you rarely hear about in the newspapers, but its horrific impact on the family has been without equal. According to today's prevailing junk science, elitists would have us believe there are just too many people on earth. Some of the leading environmental organizations have now joined the population control fanatics. This represents a dangerous escalation. Now, with breathtaking ease, the mantra of "sustainable development" is plausibly invoked to impose draconian population control initiatives in order to "thin the human herd." Of course, these elites volunteer others – mostly Africans, Asians and Latinos – to do the dying.

The brutal population control policies of the People's Republic of China are the direct consequence of the same anti-family weapons and the same kind of junk science. China – the land of forced abortion and forced sterilization, and the land where only one child is permitted per family – is a place where brothers and sisters are illegal. If a pregnant woman does not have explicit government permission to have her one single child, or if she is pregnant for a second or third time – which is against the law – she is fined up to eight times her annual salary unless she "consents" to an abortion. The impact on women's health has been horrifying.

A recent US State Department human rights report noted that one of the direct results of coercive population control in China is that 500 Chinese women commit suicide each and every day. The suicide rate among young Chinese women is five times that of any other country in the world, yet the UN continues to heap praise and money on China for its one child policy. If you want to know where the elitists want to take us, just look at China. Government imposed-policies of one-child-per-family are the nightmarish vision in store for us, if Planned Parenthood and the UN have their way.

On the subject of "human embryo stem-cell research," Senator Kerry wants to force you and me to subsidize the killing of tens of thousands of human embryos. He will also promote human cloning – clone and kill for research is practically his motto.

This past Wednesday, I was at an event sponsored by the Family Research Council in the Capitol. The room was filled with children who had been frozen embryos; they were several months, even years, old, who then went on to be adopted (implanted in an adoptive mother's womb). The stories of these "adopted embryos," with names now like Kate and Mike, are compelling. We know of at least sixty children who had once been cryogenically frozen but have now gone on to be adopted. There is an adoption program called the Snowflakes adoption agency that has been promoting this loving adoption option. This underscores the reason why we need to protect these newly created human beings, and not steal their stem cells for use in research. Notwithstanding the ethical problem inherent in *in-vitro* fertilization, we are faced with the moral dilemma of what to do with 400,000 frozen embryos. The answer is clear: Adopt them! The term "spare embryos" conveniently invoked in connection with embryonic stem cell research is an oxymoron. There is no such thing as a spare embryo. These human lives can be adopted; they are being adopted; and they turn out to be just like any other little boy or girl.

For years several of us in Congress have argued that we should steer our research dollars into adult stem cell research and cord blood stem cell research. This research has no ethical downside. And it has worked. That is where the real breakthroughs are occurring each and every day. Heart repair and myriad other advances are occurring not from embryonic, but from adult and cord blood stem cells.

As you know, the Scott Peterson trial is now winding down to a close. A new law called the Unborn Victims of Violence Act (opposed by Senator Kerry, by the way) – or the "Laci and Connor Law" – was signed by President Bush on February 26, 2004. This Unborn Victims of Violence Act established a new penalty in law for those who do violence to both a woman and her unborn child. A mugger or killer does not have an unfettered right to maim or kill an unborn child. The mother's amniotic sac is a protective covering over an unborn child, but it is not made of Kevlar. Those sacs are easily pierced by a knife or bullet. Unborn children feel pain when they are shot or beaten. They bleed and they bruise easily. Unborn children are as vulnerable as their mothers to an assailant wielding a knife, a gun, or a steel pipe.

A few weeks ago, I introduced a new bill in the House. Senator Sam Brownback introduced the same bill in the Senate. It is the Unborn Child Pain Awareness Act. It is an informed consent bill, and would require that a woman would have to be told that her child experiences pain during an abortion. If George W. Bush wins, it will be signed. If John Kerry wins, it will be vetoed. In expert testimony provided to the Northern District of the US District Court in California on April 15, during the partial birth abortion trials, Dr. Sunny Anand, director of the Pain Neurobiology Laboratory at the Arkansas Children's Hospital Research Institute, explained the following: "The human fetus possesses the ability to experience pain from 20 weeks of gestation, if not earlier, and the pain perceived by a fetus is possibly more intense than that perceived by term newborns or older children."

Dr. Anand further described before the court that the "highest density of pain receptors per square inch of skin in human development occurs *in utero*" – that is, while still in the womb – "from 20 to 30 weeks gestation. During this period, the epidermis is still very thin, leaving nerve fibers closer to the surface of the skin than in older neonates and adults." He went on to explain that the pain inhibitory mechanisms, in other words, fibers which dampen and modulate the experience of pain, do not begin to develop until 32 to 34 weeks of gestation. Thus, Dr. Anand concluded, a fetus at 20 to 32 weeks of gestation would experience a much more intense pain than older infants or children or adults when these groups are subjected to similar types of injury.

Dr. Anand points out on the question of fetal consciousness that more than three decades of research show that preterm infants are actively perceiving, learning, and organizing information, and they are constantly striving to regulate themselves, their environment, and their experiences. All preterm infants actively approach and favor experiences that are developmentally supportive and they actively try to avoid experiences that are disruptive.

Americans are now beginning to recognize another truth: *Abortion exploits women.* Abortion hurts and harms women physically, emotionally, and psychologically, and there is also mounting evidence that abortion can increase the chance of breast cancer. Women deserve better than abortion.

There is a new powerful voice of women called "Silent No More." These women speak of their personal abortion tragedies. They deeply regret that they believed the big lie – that abortion was a benign option, a reasonable choice, rather that an act of violence.Women wounded by abortion like actress Jennifer O'Neill, singer Melba Moore, and civil rights activist Dr. Alveda King, niece of Dr. Martin Luther King, have called on us to listen to their heart-wrenching stories and take seriously our moral duty to protect women and children from the predators who ply their lethal trade in abortion mills throughout the land. These brave wounded women are the new champions of life.

Marie and I heard several women wounded by abortion tell their stories on the steps of the Supreme Court this past January 22nd, and at a forum we sponsored on Capitol Hill, Dr. Alveda King said the following about abortion: "How can the Dream survive if we murder the children?" Dr. King said more: "[We] can no longer sit idly by and allow this horrible spirit of murder to cut down, yes, cut out, and cut away our unborn…This is the day to choose life. We must live and allow our babies to live. If the dream of Dr. Martin Luther King is to live, our babies must live."

One woman told how as her abortion was underway, the abortionist paused and said, "It's trying to get away." Shocked and remorseful, the partially sedated mother suddenly wanted to leave – but it was too late. But now she and hundreds of others like her have refused to be silent any longer. They care too deeply about other women and their children, and they want others to be spared the anguish they have endured. And to the millions of women who have aborted, these courageous women are uniquely equipped to convey the breathtaking message of love, healing, and reconciliation that God provides to those who ask. Please keep them in your prayers and support them every way you can.

As a member of the United States House of Representatives from New Jersey, the Honorable Christopher H. Smith has championed the rights and interests of many – from children forced to toil in sweatshops to women kidnapped and sold into lives of prostitution – but, especially, unborn children whose very chance to live is constantly threatened by legalized abortion. Congressman Chris Smith has dedicated his entire life to helping the world's most vulnerable human beings, and thus the Fellowship of Catholic Scholars was honored that he agreed to keynote our 27th annual convention. We were happy to honor him and his wife Marie in turn by the presentation to them of the 2004 Cardinal O'Boyle Award.

Congressman Smith has represented the citizens of New Jersey's Fourth Congressional District since 1981, when he was sworn into office at the age of 27. Throughout his twenty-four years of service, he has established himself as one of the hardest working, most compassionate, and dedicated members of the House of Representatives. A resident of Hamilton, New Jersey, Congressman Smith and his wife Marie have four children.

Chapter 2: Message from the Pontifical Council for the Family on the 10th Anniversary of the Holy Father's "Letter to Families"

HIS EMINENCE CARDINAL ALFONSO LÓPEZ TRUJILLO
PRESIDENT OF THE PONTIFICAL COUNCIL
FOR THE FAMILY

Ten years ago, in 1994, the Year of the Family was convoked by the United Nations, after some unexpected events and opposition from certain nations and groups. The Holy Father immediately saw the importance of such an event and with great interest welcomed the initiative. The Year of the Family in the Church, as we know, was celebrated with great jubilation, dynamism, and hope. The Holy See not only made itself present in the various stages of the United Nations' preparations and in the different programs that were being put on, but also, within the Church, encouraged numerous activities in many episcopal conferences, dioceses, parishes, apostolic movements, non-government organizations, and so on. The Holy See commissioned the Pontifical Council for the Family to plan extensively for theological reflections and pastoral animations that would have wide repercussions.

The United Nations was grateful for all the Church's support. The Holy Father's close attention was continuous, and his efforts constituted a unique stimulus and inspiration for all. It was furthermore necessary to emphasize certain concepts and directions in the case of an event that was without doubt historical, but which was also challenging, given that certain tendencies showed the need for fundamental clarifications regarding the very concept of the family itself, founded on marriage; the family ran the risk of losing its core and its meaning. We could not ignore certain themes that kept coming up, especially during the preparations for the Cairo Conference on Population and Development. One problem that constantly came up from the beginning of the preparations for the Year of the Family was the attempt to talk about *families*, in the plural, and to avoid the use of simply the *family*, in the singular. The aim of this plural usage was to impose an unacceptable interpretation that altered the model of the family as willed by God – a natural institution that should have been recognized without any reluctance, along with all of the consequences that follow from such a recognition, as the basic unit of society.

The use of the plural, *families*, opened the door to diverse and capricious concepts of what were supposed to be "families," dissipating the truth about *the* family. In certain parliaments and institutions new tendencies were surfacing which, over the last ten years, would introduce remarkable new conceptual ambiguities into the very idea of the family, and this in turn would give rise to serious confusion in the philosophical, juridical, anthropological, and cultural realms – the effects of which are now only too evident.

In broad strokes, this was the context that the Church wanted to underline. The Year of the Family was in itself a positive event; but it required particular attention and reflection, since in certain milieus, even within the Church, there were signs of less profound insight and lack of understanding and coherence regarding the real truths about the family.

This was the context, I think, in which the Holy Father thought out and formulated his "Letter to Families." It represented a special gift for the Church. It carried the date of February 2, 1994. It was a privileged occasion to echo with great force the proclamation of the good news, the Gospel, the "splendid news," about the family.

It would be good to say something about the literary *genre* of this most important document, which should have great impact, and which is part of the radiant triptych of John Paul II's magisterium on the family, which consists of three major titles: the apostolic exhortation *Familiaris Consortio* (1981), the "Letter to Families" (1994), and the encyclical *Evangelium Vitae* (1995).

I would have thought that a document of similar value and depth could well have been an encyclical. The Holy Father wanted it to be a letter, however, one which we now call by its Latin title *"Gratissimam Sane"*; in it he knocks with fatherly hope on the doors of our homes. The Letter begins thus: "Dear Families! The celebration of the Year of the Family gives me a welcome opportunity to knock at the door of your home, eager to greet you with deep affection and to spend time with you."

The first document of the triptych that I have just mentioned was the apostolic exhortation, *Familiaris Consortio*. It was among the first major documents of John Paul II's pontificate, and stemmed from and corresponded to the Bishops' Synod on the Family. The literary *genre* "apostolic exhortation" has been used for documents based on the Bishops' Synods: the Holy Father gathers the propositions presented to him by the bishops, and, after careful elaboration and profound study, he presents them to the Church. Perhaps – and this is just my personal perception – the Holy Father did not wish to use the *genre* "encyclical" because the immense value of the document would thereby be sort of diffused. Thus he preferred to call it a "letter." The designation "encyclical" was used for *Evangelium Vitae*, however, out of consideration for the desire of the cardinals who originally requested the document that the proclamation and defense contained in it would have a special significance, due to the special meaning and transcendence of its theme. The Holy Father has also called other important documents "letters," however.

In this regard, we may also take note of the apostolic letter *Mulieris Dignitatem* on the Dignity of Women dated August 15, 1988. To a very great extent, this particular letter tackles the theme of "woman" – who is spouse, mother, daughter, and sister; and who thus performs an important task in society. The idea of woman should be integrated into the vocation to which she is fittingly called. Her eminent dignity should be acknowledged and fully respected.

Also during the Year of the Family, on December 13, 1994, the Holy Father wrote by way of a simple dialogue his "Christmas Letter to All Children," *Ad Paucos Deis* – brief and full of love and tenderness towards those who are the center of the home, and objects of the tenderness and care of their parents. Then, on June 29, 1995, he wrote the "Letter to Women of the Whole World," *A Ciascuna di Voi* ("To each one of you").

And with the date of October 22, 1983, we have the Charter of the Rights of the Family. It had been requested during the Synod dedicated to the family. It is a valuable instrument of dialogue which considers the family as a subject in which all other members are integrated, with their rights and duties, and in which the family is given due recognition due by the state.

The Holy Father only later formulated the "Letter to Families," then, the importance of which was much appreciated. Being closely related to *Familiaris Consortio*, but without in the least being a repetition of it, he treats questions of great importance, with the focus, experience, and richness that has characterized his work in the Church as a whole. Summarizing the historical challenges faced by the family, which he would later call the "patrimony of humanity," John Paul II profoundly reflects on the "splendid news" of its identity found in the reciprocal gift that spouses exchange in their total self-giving to each other. Explaining the demands of this reciprocal self-giving by the spouses in marriage, which is the foundation of the family – and in the context of the characteristic values dealt with in Paul VI's 1968 encyclical *Humanae Vitae* – the pope reflects on the subject of conjugal love, which is faithful, exclusive, lasting until death, and open to the gift of life. The "Letter to Families" not only penetrates into questions of greater relevance today, but also by dealing with the issue of openness to life, it adequately prepares and treats basic themes related to the proclamation and respect for life which anticipate the historical 1995 encyclical *Evangelium Vitae*.

Some thought that a new document would no longer be necessary, since the "Letter to Families" had completely covered serious questions such as abortion and other contemporary attacks against human life that were increasing at an alarming rate. Luckily the successor of Peter did not listen to such suggestions, however, even as he formulated his rich teachings and defenses against today's anti-life abuses that had been explicitly requested from him by the cardinals in the Extraordinary Consistory that took place from April 4 to 7, 1991. Their vote was unanimous; they asked him "to reaffirm with the authority of the successor of Peter the value of human life and its inviolability, in the light of present circumstances and attacks threatening it today" (EV #5).

What I have called a triptych of John Paul II's magisterium on the family abundantly shows how family and life are inseparable, and how the domestic Church is, at the same time, the sanctuary of life and its cradle – and also how human procreation forms an essential part of the mission of marriage. This explains why in the pastoral field the Pontifical Council for the Family normally participates with Commissions on Family and Life in the episcopal conferences. In another domain, the Pontifical Academy for Life and the Pontifical Council for the Family also work closely with each other, each in its own sphere, in the service of the successor of Peter.

Let us now look at some aspects of the "Letter to Families" that have particular importance. I do not, however, wish to expend too much time on this occasion such as might be required to make a more complete presentation.

I would like to point out once more, though, the great value of *Gratissimam Sane,* which has notably nourished the reflections of theologians and pastoralists, not only in the various commissions in episcopal conferences and dioceses, but also in parishes and apostolic movements that work with great zeal and dynamism.

Gratissimam Sane has an anthropological depth which is notable. Its reflections reveal the profound value of the concept of the truth about man, marriage, and the family. It has contributed a great deal to contemporary thought regarding the value and meaning of conjugal love, beginning with the reciprocal self-giving of the spouses and the demands that arise from this. The brilliance of the treatment stems from the teachings of the Second Vatican Council, and, more concretely, from the Pastoral Constitution *Gaudium et Spes*, as well as from Pope John Paul II's apostolic exhortation *Familiaris Consortio*. It was also influenced by the pope's 1993 encyclical *Veritatis Splendor*. But it is squarely based on the chapter in *Gaudium et Spes* entitled "Fostering the Nobility of Marriage and the Family" (Part II, Chapter I). The conciliar passage which is without doubt cited most often in the magisterium of the Holy Father, and which appears often in the "Letter to Families," is the following: "Man...is the only creature on earth which God willed for itself"; and he "cannot fully find himself except through a sincere gift of himself" (*GS* #24). There follow the Holy Father's reflections on "the gift," on the reciprocation of the spouses in offering or giving themselves; on the children, who are God's gifts, and who are the most precious of gifts, to the parents, to the family, and society.

The concept of the Church as the family of God, and of human society as the family of peoples – concepts that have characterized the continental Synods, especially the Synod on Africa – find in this Letter a rich inspiration (cfr., especially, *Ecclesia in Africa* #6, *Ecclesia in Asia* #13, *Ecclesia in America* #32).

The "Letter to Families" assumes and qualifies the uneasy dimensions of the challenges that both family and life face, without forgetting the progress made in the different fields and the great number of marriages that give living witness to the truth of all this. An atmosphere of hope dominates in the face of today's crisis – that is nevertheless presented in all its objectivity.

That the divine plan for marriage and the family – the latter being the fundamental pillar of society and of the Church – should aim to found a "civilization of love" is in stark contrast to the destructive anti-civilization that is manifested in so many other tendencies and situations today, which, in fact, threaten "a kind of cultural uprooting." This is the greatest of dangers and it should be exposed. There has been a kind of progressive *dehumanization* in the name of "modernization" which is supported by today's secularism bordering on neo-paganism.

The crisis that has been increasing in the last decade is manifested in evil laws, which reveal the attitude of not a few members of various legislatures. Such phenomena point to a crisis: "Who can deny that our age is marked by a *great crisis*, which appears above all as a profound *'crisis of truth'"* (*Grat. San.*, #13)? Romano Guardini long ago warned us about this phenomenon, which he described as a disease of the soul, precisely because the soul without the truth is sick and gives rise to an inhuman man. The pope's diagnosis is realistic about this: "A crisis of truth means, in the first place, *a crisis of concepts*" (*Grat. San.* #13). John Paul II continues: "Do the words *'love,' 'freedom,' 'sincere gift,'* and even *'person'* and *'rights of the person,'* really convey their essential meaning?" (*Ibidem*). In an effort to respond to such grave confusion, the Pontifical Council for the Family has come up with its *Lexicon: Ambiguous and Discussed Terms on Family, Life and Ethical Questions.* This *Lexicon* has been published in Italian and Spanish, and will soon be out in French; steps have also recently been initiated for the publication of an English edition. It states the truth that has been imprisoned by a "culture" that, having lost its values, leads to a defeat in terms of true humanity. This obliges in us a passion for the *truth*. The encyclical *Veritatis Splendor* examined the foundations of moral truth. Not a few allow themselves to be seduced by today's false science and think that they serve the Church by surrendering to all sorts of pressures and ignoring the true demands of the day. Have we not seen such behavior in the ethical relativism that slips into the "adjusted interpretations" not only of *Humanae Vitae*, but also of the concepts of contraception and "contragestation"? The definitions of family and life are changed thereby. The pope's "Letter to Families" warns that today we must consider that man, unique and unrepeatable, cannot be separated from the family. Man comes into the world through the family and "owe[s] to the family the very fact of his existing as an individual" (*Grat. San.* #2). Thus, "when he has no family, the person coming into the world develops an anguished sense of pain and loss, one which will subsequently burden his whole life" (*Ibidem).* This is something that cannot be hidden: only through the family can man integrally humanize himself. The family is an irreplaceable institution. That is why "the Church considers serving the family to be one of her essential duties" (*Ibidem*). One must go to what is central and essential. Otherwise one may be ruined. To remain silent, not to announce the Gospel of the family and of life, or to soften it through incoherent political positions, is to contribute to the defeat of man, whose future would then be lost to hope. The family is and has always been considered to be the first and fundamental expression of the social nature of man himself. Its essential nucleus has not been changed, not even today. The family constitutes the smallest as well as the primordial human community (cfr. *Grat. San.* #7).

A number of the clarifications that have now been incorporated into the habitual language of theologians and pastoralists in this priority action of the Church in defense of the family come from *Gratissimam Sane*.

We have emphasized and reflected upon the truths of the Gospel and of life. Now we must be on our guard, in line with *Familiaris Consortio*, with regard to new problems that have been seriously burdening the crumbling of the structure and identity of the family. These have encountered great hostility arising from certain tendencies manifesting the torment of the cultural uprooting described above and include: forgetting about the existence of a natural law and of its demands; and the eclipse of any concept of the dignity of the person, which in turn brings about a certain dismantling of what should be a *community of persons,* and thus the primary unit of human society itself (cfr. *Grat. San.* #7). This stable community of love and life, built upon the pact of marriage, "is brought to completion in a full and specific way with the procreation of children: the 'communion' of the spouses gives rise to the 'community' of the family (*Ibidem*). The personal communion of the "I" and "you" opens itself up through human procreation towards the most noble task of paternity and maternity, which is brought about through permanent fidelity in mutual self-giving. Conjugal love brings along with it "the truth of the person," a rational and free being, eminently an image of God that is rooted in and is deduced from the mystery of the Trinitarian "We." "The family, which originates in the love of man and woman, ultimately derives from the mystery of God. This conforms to the innermost being of man and woman, to their innate and authentic dignity as persons" (*Grat. San.* #8). In conjugal love, uniting themselves in "one flesh," their union takes place "in truth and love" (*Ibidem*). Man is called from conception and birth, as a new being, to regard himself as a person, and is destined to express the plenitude of his humanity (cfr. *Grat. San.* #9).

The family fulfills itself in the process of conjugal love from which new life arises as a common good of the same family and of humanity (cfr. *Grat. San.* #11). There is not even a minimal opposition between love among spouses, a love that is due reciprocally, and being instruments of God's love in procreation. The children's new life is not limited to a merely biological level, but implies an integral procreation that demands the true education of children. This is far from a minimalist vision, or from the sort of alteration that transforms integral human *procreation* into *production*. In almost technical language, this latter kind of alteration does not fail to hide the fact that a person is being conceived as an object, as a thing, and that a personal loving encounter is being subjected to a technical mediation with the illicit modes of "assisted fecundity." In this way the self-giving and encounter of bodies and spirits are replaced by dehumanizing technical "advances," as is seen in the drama of those who desire a child, as if it were a right, and at any cost.

And how far from what we really are is the concept of *de facto* unions as encountered today. A merely *de facto* union is a juridical fiction which robs marriage of its true identity. How can we conceive of the family apart from a genuine concept of "gift"? The family is indeed – more than any other human reality – the place where an individual can exist "for himself" through "the sincere gift of self" (*Grat. San.* #11). What some attempt to introduce in its place remains a caricature, a profound dehumanization, sustained by a false concept of law and by a new form of discrimination, namely, that flowing from the ideology of so-called "gender."

It is a bitter surprise to see God's plan thus changed. The complementarity between man and woman is changed through this odd new idea that was never before known in the various cultures and religions of the world. How can we explain why some government leaders and legislators see a progress, a gain, of freedom and democracy, in accepting a superficial hypothesis that does not contemplate man and woman as they really are and as how God has wanted them to be. A document from the Congregation for the Doctrine of the Faith recently became urgently necessary in this regard.. I refer to the recent "Letter to the Bishops of the Catholic Church on the Collaboration of Men and Women in the Church and in the World," dated May 31 of this year (2004). The concepts of "opposition between men and women," and of course, of "gender," have as a consequence introduced a "harmful confusion regarding the human person, which has its most immediate and lethal effects in the structure of the family" (#2). As for the ideology of "gender": "The obscuring of the difference or duality of the sexes has enormous consequences on a variety of levels" (*Ibidem*). "Its deeper motivation must be sought in the human attempt to be freed from one's biological conditioning. According to this perspective, human nature in itself does not possess characteristics in an absolute manner: all persons can and ought to constitute themselves as they like, since they are free from every predetermination linked to their essential constitution" (#3). Thus, social influence, cultural evolution, and an arbitrary concept of freedom, would replace the plan of God as far as the complementarity of the sexes is concerned. This more recent document cites the "Letter to Families" several times.

A community of persons lies at opposite poles from the inhuman "community" of things; the latter entails the destruction of the whole concept of what marriage is.

Meanwhile, we are victims of ethical relativism, of the kind of utilitarianism denounced in the encyclical *Veritatis Splendor:* "*Utilitarianism* is a civilization of production and of use, a civilization of '*things*' and not of '*persons*,' a civilization in which persons are used in the same way as things are used. In the context of a civilization of use, woman can become an object for man, children a hindrance to parents, the family an institution obstructing the freedom of its members" (*Grat. San.* #13). The situation could not be more alarming: "It is evident that in this sort of a cultural situation that the family cannot fail to feel threatened, since it is endangered at its very foundations" (*Grat. San.* #13).

Sex made banal, sex education with models that give rise to a false anthropology, love converted into egoism – are all these things not a tremendous threat to society? Yet these are the ways of life that many wish to impose! To work for the family is to liberate society from a profound dehumanization. "Within a similar anthropological perspective…man…ceases to live as a person and a subject. Regardless of all intentions and declarations to the contrary, he becomes merely an object" (*Grat. San.* #19). Since "modern rationalism does not tolerate mystery," (*Ibidem*), man becomes a reality unknown to himself, an incognito, and rushes to his ruin.

Another aspect that is of a certain originality in the "Letter to Families" is the deepening of the meaning of the subject in the community of the family. The family can be atomized, or separated, into the members composing it. This is characteristic of an individualistic form of thinking and leaves its traces in some legislation. It is the doubt raised in the United Nations Convention of the Rights of the Child itself, which in some points does not remove such conditioning. The family is not taken as a whole, truly as a community, but rather children are considered separately from the parents. This is a temptation which arises when one removes children from the environment of their parents in their sexual education, for example, or when one considers their problems without relying on those who have given them life.

Furthermore, in the relationship between the family and the state, the respect due to the family, along with its relative independence, is lost; and thus the family is invaded, is "colonized." This is well-known in totalitarianisms and in the phenomena of privatization, considered elsewhere (see my article, "*Familia y Privatización*, in *Lexicón. Términos ambiguous y discutidos sobre familia, vida y cuestiones éti-*

cas "). The family is no longer an institution of great public interest, protected by laws, but rather becomes a phenomenon reduced to the private sphere, to the whims of the spouses. Its public and political dimensions, central in social life, thus have to be preserved. The family "expects a recognition of its identity and an acceptance of its status as a subject in society" (*Grat. San.* #17). "As a community of love and life, the family is a firmly grounded social reality. It is also, in a way entirely its own, a sovereign society, albeit conditioned in certain ways" (*Ibidem).*

At this point the "Letter to Families" treats of the 1983 Charter of the Rights of the Family, which maintains its ardent relevance. Formulated by the Holy See, its great importance for dialogue and for legislation has been proven. Some rights refer to the family, others to life (cfr. *Ibidem*). It consolidates the family institution in national and international communities, with an "almost organic" link.

The family contributes to the nation's cultural patrimony, and from it emanates its own culture and language, which helps the family and the nation find its spiritual sovereignty.

As we have indicated earlier, this "Letter to Families" is a cry and a protest against today's attacks against the dignity of human life and is an anticipation of the encyclical *Evangelium Vitae.*

The family is in the midst of a decisive combat for the future of humanity. It has a face that is, we repeat, human. "The history of mankind, the history of salvation, passes by way of the family…The family is placed at the center of the great struggle between good and evil, between life and death…To the family is entrusted the task of striving, first and foremost, to unleash the forces of good, the source of which is found in Christ the Redeemer of man"(*Grat. San.* #23).

Just a few more words, before concluding these lines. In this historical combat the family maintains a strong current of energy, which is seen in the millions and millions of homes that splendidly bear their witness to its nature and importance.

There should be an immense effort to give a soul to the world and form the faith properly, for the sake of the family, which is the source of humanization.

The Holy Father insistently invites us to prayer, and for this reason he addresses himself to all families, regardless of the diversity and complexity of the cultures (cfr. *Grat. San.* #4), in order to ask for a new sending of the Spirit, so that the Spirit's love may be infused into the hearts of all (cfr. *Ibidem*).

John Paul II invites us to discover the Lord in ourselves. To this end the pope dedicates the whole of the second chapter of the "Letter to

Families," "*The Bridegroom Is with You*." This splendid truth about the family moves us to announce it joyfully to the world, thus sowing the hope of life and of the family in the Lord, who is ever victorious.

His Eminence Cardinal Alfonso López Trujillo is the president of the Pontifical Council for the Family. A native of Columbia, he was born in 1935 and ordained a priest in 1960. He taught at a major seminary, and in 1970 was ordained an auxiliary bishop of Bogota. He served as secretary of the Latin American Bishops' Conference (CELAM) between 1972 and 1978. Named archbishop of Medellin in 1979, he was president of CELAM between 1979 and 1983. He was named a cardinal in 1983, and became the president of the Pontifical Council for the Family in 1990. He is world renowned as a defender of F.M.Cap., Diocese of Pittsburgh.

Chapter 3: Sacred Scripture and Sexual Identity

STEPHEN F. MILETIC, PH.D.[1]

Introduction

The Church faces a number of challenges as it enters into the 21st Century. Perhaps one of its most serious tasks is to effectively proclaim anew its supernatural identity and mission in and through the Gospel. Of the many issues to be addressed, human sexuality has emerged as a complex and multifaceted social, political, philosophical, theological, and even an economic force requiring serious attention. In particular, institutions of learning at all levels have developed curriculum and engage learners in a variety of points of view on sexual identity, that is, in gender theory. An even deeper challenge that we all face is the fragmentation of our Western view of the world, or reality. There is now no dominant narrative that holds together a collective memory/experience or understanding of the human person, let alone the nature of human sexuality.[2] Clearly we are in the midst of an intellectual and cultural disintegration that feels more like a massive tidal wave.

In this presentation I would like to reflect on Genesis 1 & 2 and Ephesians 5, texts about human sexuality and marriage in order to explore what they might have to say about human sexual identity. The thesis I would like to advance is that the texts of Genesis contain and mediate an understanding of humanity and human sexuality which establishes ontological, existential, and teleological aspects of human sexuality which are then transformed into an eschatological context focusing on ecclesiology, Christology, and soteriology. The text of Ephesians 5, then, represents a significant development of these three elements by applying Genesis 2:24 first to the Christ/Church relationship (Eph 5:31–32) and only secondly to the wife/husband relationship. The net effect of the argument below holds that human sexuality within Christian marriage, while intrinsic to human existence (ontological), functions as a living soteriological sign of Christ's ongoing work of redemption. That is, any understanding of the fundamental structure of human sexuality must understand human sexuality first for its own intrinsic merit and goodness, but also in terms of its fundamental ability to bear witness to and mediate Christ's saving work.

In summary, then, we turn to ancient, very sophisticated texts to learn something about the origins and final fulfillment of our own identity as human, sexual beings and so draw once more on that divine wellspring of understanding and light mediated by these texts as we face an ancient challenge resurfacing in "modern" or post-modern garb.[3]

Methodological Considerations

Before I proceed to the analysis of the texts let me establish an interpretative framework for this presentation.

Gender Theory and Scripture. In spite of this presentation's title and the general theme of this conference, I will not engage gender theories directly.[4] In principle, gender theory constructs draw their data from social science and their assumptions, premises, etc., are rooted in philosophical thought. This presentation will serve as an attempt to extract a *theorea* or vision about human nature, about its universal qualities and attributes, about its origins and about its ultimate ends. While Scripture does not engage in explicit construct building, it does contain religious, symbolic, and very real language which prompts a great deal of reflection about its seen and unseen referents.[5]

As we shall see below, the contents of both Genesis and Ephesians relate to gender theory in that they speak of the origins and ultimate ends of human sexuality.

The Relationship between Genesis and Ephesians. The relationship between the two books is not difficult to establish. First, Genesis 1–11 and the whole Epistle to the Ephesians stand respectively at the very beginning (Genesis) and end (Ephesians) of what their human authors take to be historical reality, what in subsequent theological language we call salvation history.[6] Second, the first two chapters of Genesis contain a type of poetic language[7] with liturgical qualities[8] not unlike other ancient Near Eastern texts that scholars identify as myth. However, Genesis 1 is not ancient Near Eastern myth.[9] The text of Genesis places the reader "in the beginning" of creation, including history. Other terms for this are primeval history,[10] *Uhrzeit*, protological time.[11] Since it addresses absolute beginnings, all of Genesis 1–11 is foundational not just to the narrative we call the Pentateuch, but for the whole of Sacred Scripture. Third, the author of Ephesians writes from a perspective of a partially realized eschatology – at the "other end" of time. This is the time of redemption completed in Christ's resurrection but not fully realized within the pilgrim Church. The new creation is united with Christ (Eph 2:15–16); the Church is united to Christ the savior (Eph 5:23c) within a "one flesh" union (Eph 5:31–33). And yet, the Church continues to strive to reach that reality of union with Christ.[12] We may call this time *Endzeit* or the final days of salvation. The text of Ephesians 5 transposes the husband/wife relationship of Genesis 1–2 into a new key, rooted in a particular understanding of eschatological reality.[13] Fourth and finally, Genesis 2:24 is quoted at Ephesians 5.31 and then directly applied to the Christ/Church relationship (5:32–33). Clearly the author of Ephesians takes the first two chapters of Genesis as an essential frame of reference for his interpretation of the Christ/Church and husband/wife relationships.

Given that both texts treat the husband/wife relationship, address this theme from a universal perspective (e.g., at the two polar ends of salvation history), that they share thematic and linguistic similarities, they can and ought to be interpreted together. Both are quite pertinent to discussions of gender or sexual identity. Given that they share vocabulary and thematic material related to human nature, sexuality and marriage, they will be interpreted in light of each other.[14]

Analysis of Texts

Exegetical Notes on Gen 1:1–2:4a.[15] The text of Genesis 1–2 contains an account of how the whole of creation comes into existence (Gen 1:1–2:4a), followed by an account of how aspects of that whole, in particular man and woman, come into existence (Gen 2:4b–25). This movement (from "whole" to "particular") is common in ancient Near Eastern creation accounts[16] and generally intends that what is said of the whole applies to the particular.

The application of the broad cultural ancient Near Eastern pattern to Genesis 1–2 is as follows. What is said of "the whole" (Gen 1) is applicable to "the particular" (Gen 2). That is, Genesis 1 is the primary source for establishing the meaning of God as creator, God's relationship to creation and especially to humans, and, the meaning of gender identity. Therefore, Genesis 1 functions are a frame of reference for interpreting Genesis 2. Our first principle of interpretation, then, is to interpret the text in the light of its historical and cultural context.[17]

The following exegetical summary establishes the divine intent for creation as a whole and for the first human couple in particular. For the purposes of this presentation, we may distinguish between the narratives of Genesis 1 and 2.[18]

The key verses in Genesis 1 are 26–27, where God creates humanity in his image, male and female. An excessively literal translation reads as follows:

1:26 Then said Elohim, "Let us make adam in our image, in our likeness [so that][19] they may rule over the fish of the sea, and over the bird of the air and over the livestock and over all of the earth and over every crawler, the one crawling upon the earth."

1:27 So He [Elohim] created the adam in the image of Him, in the image of Elohim He created him male and female Elohim created them

The exegetical summary below has two goals: establish how the text articulates the divine intent for creation and how this intent shapes an understanding of sexual identity. Our *focii* will be the pattern of creation and the following key terms from Gen. 1:26: "Let us make" (*na seh*) "in our image and likeness" (*b salmenu kidmutenu*) "so that they may rule" (*w yirdu*). The first phase of the argument will be to establish that the text does advance a catechesis about divine intent towards creation in general and for human sexuality in particular. The second phase of the argument will focus on what the above terms either explicate or imply in terms of the ontological, existential, and teleological meanings of human sexuality.

Intent through the Pattern of Creation. An examination of the pattern of creation highlights divine intent for creation. Within the pattern of creation we note seven distinctive moments:[20] (i) intent to create; (ii) divine creative acts; (iii) the injunction to be fruitful and to exercise dominion over the earth and all living things; (iv) the divine colloquy between God and Adam; (v) the narrator's observation that creation came into existence just as God had commanded; (vi) God's approval over all that was done; and (vii) the consecration of the seventh day as Sabbath. To the above I would add the observation that there appears to be an ascent by level of importance – an hierarchy if you will – moving from the cosmological environment (e.g., sun, moon, stars, etc.), to the earthly environment, to the creation of man and women, and then the establishment of the Sabbath.

First, the divine pattern of creation suggests that God intended to create a cosmos that could be described as a well-ordered existence. The movement from "formless void"[21] to an ordered, created reality organized into seven days of creating (with the seventh set aside for worship) confirms intent for a structured existence with a particular teleology – the worship of God. Second, the creation of a life-sustaining environment leading to the creation of life and then humanity itself implies that ordered existence is to be sustained (creation is not for an occasion or a series of occasions). Further, by ordering cosmological bodies towards the marking of time (days, nights, seasons, etc.),with no indication of their role as celestial powers within the hierarchy of divine powers, the author completely eliminates them as legitimate objects of worship.[22] Such a disposition implies that God is the ultimate authority over and is beyond creation. Third, the narrator's proclamation that God "sees" [23] that creation as good[24] implies that God's "sight" is in effect synonymous with a true and sure knowledge about created reality. Fourth, God blesses[25] what is made, suggesting a divine beneficence towards created reality.

The above exegetical comments permit the following observations about God's intent towards creation. The divine acts of creation appear to intend a created order which sustains a kind of life that has an essential goodness within it. That is, the pattern of intent (found in creative act and narratological description) suggests an ontological focus (the essential goodness of things created) with a particular teleology – the worship of the one true God. One might take another step based on the sequence of Genesis 1, namely, the goodness of created reality is the first step toward the worship of the Creator.

The intent for goodness is further underscored by the tendency towards fertility, towards a fullness of existence not immediately seen in the actual act of creating.[26] In effect, creation has a particular ontological structure, namely, its "goodness." This particular ontological configuring has a teleological focus, namely, to expand, grow, and prosper. The above summary establishes a general interpretive frame of reference for analysis of the key vocabulary below. The following analysis makes more precise the divine intent for human sexuality.

Key Vocabulary. The teleological intent that the good creation should extend in life giving activity beyond its initial existence ("be fruitful and multiply")[27] continues with the creation of humanity. As we shall see, an additional element comes into play with the creation of humanity, namely, the existential.

The plural "Let us make humanity," *adam*[28] in "our image, as our likeness" should be taken as divine self-deliberation[29] and not necessarily as an address to a divine court.[30] The reader is introduced to a particular creative intent. The divine intent to create humanity in the divine image and likeness establishes a foundational understanding for human sexual identity. A careful examination of "image" will show that it signifies a relational existence that mediates an essential goodness, requires further development and signifies a type of divine presence.

The term *selem b salmenu,* lit. "in our own image") articulates a broad semantic range.[31] It can refer to divine image,[32] the image of God made in human likeness,[33] etc. Its most significant use is in representing the divine image.[34] The author of Genesis 1 does not apply this term to any other living being. The term is applied only to *adam* (meaning humanity). By applying this term to only *adam* and by making "image and likeness" the key focus in creating the first human, the author unfolds a type of ontological catechesis – "humanity" consists of, at least, the human reflection of God's image and likeness. One clear implication is that humanity is to be sharply distinguished from the rest of "all living things." By its very nature (e.g., ontologically), human existence is structured in direct relationship with God.

There is another aspect of humanity's dignity suggested by this term. Scholars note that a bilingual (Akkadian/Aramaic) 9th century B.C. inscription found at Tell Fekheyre (Syria) is placed on a statue of Hadadyisi (King of Guzan). The Akkadian term referencing the statue is *salmu* ("image") that translates into Aramaic twice as *salma* (Hebrew, *selem*) and twice as *demuta* ("likeness"). The statue was erected to establish the king's authority over that particular region, almost as an extension of royal presence, power and dignity. The inference we may make is that the term's semantic content was such that its use would immediately signal some notion of a royal presence or dignity resident within humanity, representing not a monarch but the Creator. The application of "image and likeness" to humans in light of the above strongly suggests that part of the structure of humanity (i.e., ontology) is that humans embody, represent an "image" of God and perhaps even mediate something of God's presence.[35] A strong implication is that humans are the royal, monarchical representatives of God.[36]

The above prompts the following observations. The term establishes or at least suggests a specific ontological structure to human existence – as divine representation and perhaps mediation. The ontological structure of human existence necessarily implies a relational quality between *adam* and God. The creative narrative in Genesis 2 extends and explores this relational quality between male and female.

The intent to create man and women in God's image and likeness does carry an explicit intent, namely, "so that they may rule."[37] The verb "so that they may rule" can be taken as *waw* plus the jussive verb form.[38] Thus we have an "indirect volitive" which should be rendered "so that they may rule".[39] The theme of rulership would be consistent with what we have just seen as the ontological structure of humanity – being in the image and likeness of God means that humans at least represent if not mediate God's presence to the rest of creation. The implication is that God intends to be present to and to govern all of creation not solely based on the fact of divine existence but also as mediated through human stewardship over creation. A second implication is that human authority mediates a vision or view of creation drawn from God.[40] In summary, the ontological element ("image and likeness") drives the teleological elements (representational, mediational, governmental) and creates a unique existential element (*adam*'s "personal" relationship with the Creator).

Exegetical Notes On Gen. 2.4b–25. To the two key analytical elements of ontology and teleology can be added the existential, which unfolds in Genesis 2. The existential element is more obvious when we evaluate the meaning of "intimacy" suggested by the text.

Genesis 2 makes clear that God's intimate contact with humanity (e.g., breathing life directly into the nostrils of the first human being) highlights the distinctive relationship between God and humans previously articulated in Genesis 1 ("image and likeness"; "so that they might have dominion"). In Genesis 2 divine/human intimacy is expanded or extended to human/human intimacy via the creation of woman. God takes a rib from the man and in his response to her we see the intimacy – she is bone of his bone and flesh of his flesh, for the woman (*issa*) was taken from the man (*is* and not *adam* or *ha'adam*). Several observations are possible from these simple facts of the text.

The woman's existence is from living, human flesh. There can be no mistake, the two are of the same material essence, as a direct result of God's (not the male's) creative work. The intimacy suggested by the narrative cannot be missed. Adam's response to Eve contains a specific meaning for this first experience of human intimacy – specifically as this relates to covenantal communion, as will be noted below. But there is an existential moment, namely, there is a joy of discovery. Adam's response to the woman is unique in comparison to his response to the animals (2:18–20). That is, by contrast, the first male's response to the first female is one of discovering meaning in one like himself, and there is joy! The existential moment is the coming of knowledge, to a consciousness of a fulfillment of a deeply human need, a *communio*. This development of knowledge and understanding is, for lack of a better term, an "existential" moment of consciousness – there is another like him, not the same, with whom he may commune, as we are about to see.[41]

Four critical moments in the text unfold the mystery of the divine intent for creating woman, namely, the meaning of "good" (*tob*), of "to be alone" (*l baddo*), of a "fitting helpmate" (*ezer k negdo*) and the covenantal implications within Adam's specific response to Eve.

According to Genesis 2:18, God declares: "It is not good that the man should be alone. I will make him a helper fit for him" (Gen 2:18 [RSV]). Given the use of "good" in Genesis 1 (vv. 4, 10, 12, 18, 21, 25), it is striking first that prelapsarian creation could contain something "not good" and second that such is declared to be the case by the Creator![42] Being alone is not good – human are not meant for solitude; put positively, humans are made for community. What is clear from the immediate context is that the lower animal kingdom is not adequate for this community.[43] What is "good" is that *ha'adam* must have a complement, a fitting counterpart. Animals are, apparently, not adequate. The catechesis on humanity unfolds as follows: humans are not created for isolation.[44]

What is intended, then, by "fitting helpmate"[45]? The term "helpmate" (*ezer*) has an interesting semantic range. The majority of texts with this term refer to help which comes from God (e.g., Dt 33:26; Hos 13:9; Ps 20:3; 89:20; 121:1–2; 124:8; Dn 11:34). It is sometimes used as a title for God (e.g., Ex 18:4; Dt 33:7, 29; Ps 33:20; 70:6; 115:9–11; 146:5). One notes that its negative use (Is 30:5; Ez 12:14) tends to emphasize a life or death crisis, for which "help" will not be forth coming. The context of Genesis 2 suggests a meaning similar to the above. First, it is not good for "man" to be alone. The animal kingdom does not present the potential for *communio*. Even the "man's" communion with God is not totally complete. "Man" must be rescued from isolation, must be delivered and saved from that which is "not good." That is, one could state that the "helpmate" is one who, like God, saves from a life and death context. Another, equally important, sense of meaning lies in the preposition "fitting" (*k negdo*). The construct can be translated variously but resulting with the same basic sense: "a helper like himself," "one who corresponds to him," "one who has a similar nature," "One who stands face to face to him." All of these get at the same idea – this next human will be the first human's corresponding opposite.[46]

We see a confirmation of this sense that the woman is to be the "correspondence to the man" in the man's response to her very existence; that response is nuanced in covenantal language[47] at Genesis 2:23–24. The Revised Standard Version renders the text as follows:

[23] Then the man said, "This at last is bone of my bones and flesh of my flesh; she shall be called Woman, because she was taken out of Man."

[24] Therefore a man leaves his father and his mother and cleaves to his wife, and they become one flesh.

The covenantal qualities within and around this passage are as follows. God casts a "deep sleep" (Gen 2:21: *tardema*) upon the first male before the woman is created. This specific kind of sleep is present just prior to revelation (e.g., Job 4:12; 33:15), and Abraham falls into a *tardema* just prior to his encounter with God, which is followed by the solemn ratification of a covenant (see Gen 15:21 and context). At v.22 we note that God presents the woman to the man, reminiscent of ancient Near Eastern nuptial practices where the father presents the bride to the husband.[48] And finally, the language of "bone of my bone and flesh of my flesh" is strongly reminiscent of covenantal language.[49] This is the kind of language that articulates allegiance, loyalty, friendship, and sameness in kind – it is kinship and covenant bound together.[50] This language expresses the reality of their physical, emotional and spiritual bond. In v. 24 the language is clearly an expression of sexual union between the first couple, a nuptial reality that is at the heart of the covenant bond they share.[51]

Clearly Genesis 2 extends and develops the story of humanity's beginnings by unfolding the existential, personal dimension to human, sexual identity.

Summary for Genesis

We might gather the above comments into the following very brief summary statements.

Genesis 1 offers a catechesis on the divine intent for created matter based on the ordering of creation which places humans at the highest point within an hierarchy, linking all of this work to the Sabbath and then inviting humans to join God in that Sabbath. The nature of human life is that it is physical ("from clay"), spiritual ("image and likeness"), and the direct result of God's creative power ("let us make"). The text will permit us to conclude that human sexuality is to be fertile ("be fruitful and multiply"), both physical and spiritual, that its spiritual quality is dependent on God's imparting of his image and likeness to both male and female humanity, and that this sexual identity is essentially good.

Genesis 2 further develops details on the creation of the first human couple at an existential level. As "helpmate" she is his complement in the sense of standing opposite to him, face to face. She is his equal and the only other suitable part of creation which can join with him to form a *communio*. It is within this sense of solidarity, unity, and communion that only she may rescue him from the desolation of isolation. They share a covenantal, nuptial bond with each other ("bone of my bone …") and with God.

This potential for human community through intimacy is rooted in a fundamental, ontological bond – they are both of the same "stuff" (yet not identical); both are a "living being" (*l nepes hayya*);[52] *issa* (woman or female) was taken from the '*is* (man or male) and so both share the same breath of God; and, within the context of Genesis 1–2, both are made in God's "image and likeness." Here we have the fundamental meaning of gender distinction. That is, gender distinction is based in the nature of their beings – sexual identity is rooted in an essential ontological unity of matter/spirit that shares in God's "breath of life" and his "image and likeness." From this substantial oneness emerges the plurality of male and female.

Exegetical Notes on Ephesians. 5:21–33. The Letter to the Ephesians (Eph) presents a unique teaching on wives and husbands (Eph 5:21–33), one that radically transforms the meaning of Genesis 1–2 in the light of Christian revelation. The key text for interpreting the whole of Ephesians 5:21–33 is the quotation of Genesis 2:24 at Ephesians 5:31. As we shall see below, this text is full of striking features which signal that the husband/wife relationship reflects something grander than simply a Christianized view of Genesis.

Strikingly, the quotation from Genesis 2:24 – a text about the primal unity between husband and wife – is not applied directly to the wife/husband relationship but to the Christ/Church relationship. The text of 5:32 states that "this mystery" (*to mysterion touto)* applies first to Christ and the Church. This application is striking because it is based on the passage's literary form which intends to address wives (5:22–24) and husbands (5:25–30, 33). Within such a context, one would think a more "natural" application of Genesis 2:24 would be to the wife/husband relationship.[53]

That the author does not apply Genesis 2:24 directly to the husband/wife relationship is not surprising when one considers the logical structure of the passage. In both addresses (wives and husbands), the defining moments begin "from above" and moves "below." That is, the heavenly reality defines the earthly one. As we shall see immediately below, the Christ/Church relationship is the interpretive key for understanding what is intended for the husband/wife relationship.

For example, the injunction to be subordinate (5:22) is grounded in the Church's horizontal mutual subordination to each other (5:8–21),[54] the wife's vertical relationship to the Lord (5:22), and, the Church's vertical subordination to Christ (5:24b). On the other hand, the injunction to the husband to love his wife (5:25–29) is directly informed by Christ's love for the Church (5:25). The grammatical and logical structure of the text leads the reader to understand that the eschatological reality of the Christ/Church relationship redefines or transforms the meaning of marriage, now in Christ, in terms of its participation within the new creation.[55]

The application of Genesis 2.24 to the Christ/Church relationship, then, is quite consistent with the logical structure of the address to wives and husbands prior to it. Within the context of Ephesians 5.21–33, Genesis 2.24 does not refer primarily to Adam and Eve. Rather, the new creation relationship of Christ and the Church now signals a new, deeper meaning for that Old Testament text. In essence, by quoting and interpreting Genesis 2.24 at Ephesians 5.31–32, the reality of the "one flesh" union between Adam and Eve now has a new meaning found in the Christ/Church relationship. The term "one flesh" now refers to an eschatological reality seen in the Christ/Church relationship. This new "one flesh" is the first fruits, so to speak, of Christ's work of the cross which destroys enmity and the deepest alienation between God and humanity, and, between Jew and Gentile.[56] This unity is a creative one, redeeming and making anew what was distorted and fragmented as seen in Genesis 3; it is the "one new humanity" of Christ which he shares with the Church.[57]

We many now turn to the meaning of this unique application of Genesis 2.24 at Eph. 5.32 in light of Genesis 1 and 2, especially in terms of ontology, teleology, and existentialism.

Genesis 1–2 establishes the ontological structure of all human life – it is material and spiritual ("image and likeness") with concomitant elements of direct communication with God and the mutual mediation of the divine presence between the first couple and through them to the rest of creation (through divinely appointed stewardship). Within this context, the divinely intended teleology of human sexuality (Genesis 2.18–24) is towards *communio*, fruitfulness, which are grounded in the implied mandate to extend God's good creation beyond what God has accomplished.

The teleological intent of Genesis 1–2 for human marriage and sexuality finds its fullest realization within the eschatological "one flesh" unity of Christ and the Church, in the heavenly places (Eph 2). What is from above defines what is from below, the Church's subordination defines that of the wife. The author accomplishes this in two ways. First, the verb *hypotassomeno* (Eph 5.21 [*hypotassomenoi*], 24 [*hypotassetai*]) is never applied directly to the wife (5.22, 24). The ellipsis of the verb forces the reader to "fill-in" the main verbal idea from the prior sentence. That is, at both 5.22 ("Wives, [ellipsis of the verb] to your own husbands as to the Lord") and 5.24 ("so also wives [ellipsis of the verb] to your own husbands in everything) the reader is forced to first consider both the vertical and horizontal ecclesial examples of subordination as the main way of understanding what then is intended for the wife's subordination.[58]

In effect, what was intended for the husband and wife in Genesis 1–2 but not expressed there is now revealed or unveiled in light of Christ and the Church. That is, the teleological intent for husband and wife is now more fully realized in the eschatologically determined Christ/Church relationship.

The existential moment for Christian marriage is that their covenantal, sexual union, in Christ and in and as the Church, is a revelation of Christ's "one flesh" union with the Church, which is redemptive (Eph 5.23c: "he savior of the body"). That is, the husband and wife, through their chaste sexual love, make present Christ's redemptive work of the Cross, which takes away sin, communicates divine life and creates the "one new humanity" (Eph 2). This makes Christian marriage an extremely important participant in and witness to the mystery of redemption. In this redemptive sense, then, Christian marriage is a *mysterion* or mystery, or, sacrament.

Concluding Reflections

The existential moment for human sexual activity is the discovery of love, communication, friendship and respect. Christian marriage is the broadest, deepest, healthiest, holiest, and definitive context in which this discovery and committed human development can take place. It is within this matrix of ontology, teleology, existentialism, ecclesiology, and soteriology that the human discovers himself or herself as being in communion with the other and with God.

Stephen F. Miletic, Ph.D., is a Professor of Scripture and Catechetics in the Theology Department of the Franciscan University of Steubenville, Ohio. He has taught both Scripture and catechetics at the graduate and undergraduate levels in the United States and Canada. Formerly he was the Director of the National Office of Religious Education for the Canadian Conference of Catholic Bishops; then, Provost and Academic Dean of the Notre Dame Institute in Virginia (which later became the Notre Dame Graduate School of Christendom College); and then Dean of the Faculty at the Franciscan University of Steubenville. His books include *One Flesh: Marriage and the New Creation* (Rome: Pontifical Biblical Institute Press, 1985). Dr. Miletic is married to Joyce, and they have four children and two grandchildren.

Bibliography

Allen, Prudence. *The Concept of Woman. Volume 2, the Early Humanist Reformation*, 1250–1500. Grand Rapids, Mich.: W.B. Eerdmans Pub., 2002.

———. *The Concept of Woman: The Aristotelian Revolution, 750 BC – AD 1250*. 1st ed. Montreal: Eden Press, 1985.

———. "Integral Sex Complementarity and the Theology of Communion." *Communio: International Catholic Review* 17, no. Winter (1990): 523–544.

Brueggemann, Walter. "Of the Same Flesh and Bone." *Catholic Biblical Quarterly* 32 (1970): 532–542.

Catechism of the Catholic Church. 2nd ed. Vatican City/Washington, D.C.: Libreria Editrice Vaticana; [distributed by United States Catholic Conference], 2000.

Commission, The Pontifical Biblical. *The Interpretation of the Bible in the Church*. Boston, Mass.: Pauline Books & Media, 1993.

Cross, Frank Moore. *Canaanite Myth and Hebrew Epic; Essays in the History of the Religion of Israel*. Cambridge, Mass.: Harvard University Press, 1973.

Gilbert, Maurice. "Une Seule Chair (Gen 2,24)." *Nouvelle Revue Théologigue* 100 (1978): 66–89.

Grabowski, John S. *Sex and Virtue: An Introduction to Sexual Ethics, Catholic Moral Thought*. Washington, D.C.: Catholic University of America Press, 2003.

II, John Paul. *Original Unity of Man and Woman: Catechesis on the Book of Genesis*. Boston, Mass.: St. Paul Editions, 1981.

Jenson, Robert W. "How the World Lost Its Story." *First Things* October (1993): 19–26.

Joüon, Paul. *Grammaire De L'hebreax Biblique*. Deuxième édition anastatique corrigée ed. Roma: Editrice Pontificio Istituto Biblico, 1947.

Maley, Eugene M. "Genesis." In *The Jerome Biblical Commentary*, 7–46. Englewood Cliffs, N.J.: Prentice-Hall, 1968.

Martin, Fr. Francis. "The New Feminism: Biblical Foundations and Some Lines of Development." In *Women in Christ: Towards a New Feminism*, edited by Michele M. Schumacher, 141–168. Grand Rapids, Mich.: Wm. B. Eerdmans Pub., 2004.

Martin, Francis. "Male and Female He Created Them: A Summary of the Teaching of Genesis Chapter One." *Communio: International Catholic Review* 20, no. Summer (1993): 240–265.

Miletic, Stephen Francis. *"One Flesh" – Eph. 5.22–24, 5.31: Marriage and the New Creation.* Vol. 115. Roma: Editrice Pontificio Istituto Biblico, 1988.

Rad, Gerhard von. *Genesis: A Commentary, Old Testament Library.* Philadelphia: Westminster Press, 1961.

Schumacher, Michele M. *Women in Christ: Toward a New Feminism.* English ed. Grand Rapids, Mich.: W.B. Eerdmans Pub., 2004.

Ska, Jean-Louis. "'Je Vais Lui Faire Un Allie Qui Soit Son Homologue' (Gen. 2, 18) a Propos Du Term 'Ezer – 'Aide'." *Biblica* 65 (1984): 233–238.

Verbum, Dei. Dogmatic Constitution on Divine Revelation of Vatican Council Ii, Promulgated by Pope Paul Vi, November 18, 1965. Commentary and Translation by George H. Tavard. Glen Rock, N.J.,: Paulist Press, 1966.

Westermann, Claus. *Genesis 1–11: A Commentary.* Translated by John J. Scullion. Minneapolis: Augsburg Pub. House, 1984.

Notes

1. I would like to thank the following colleagues for reading drafts of this presentation and for offering valuable criticisms: Dr. Andew Minto and Dr. John Bergsma of the Franciscan University of Steubenville; and Dr. Gregory Vall of Ave Maria University. I am responsible for all remaining defects.

2. In terms of intellectual currents in Western Civilization, this point is well developed by Robert W. Jenson, "How the World Lost Its Story," *First Things* October (1993): 19–26. For a recent commentary on the kind of confusion now prevalent, see the recent article "Key West, Suddenly Shy, Puts Pasties on Its Party," by Nick Madigan, *New York Times* October 20, 2004 (follow the link nytimes.com).

3. The turn to Divine and human wisdom to address the deepest issues of human identity is not new in the Church. For an excellent, brief, study of the history of the philosophy of sex identity, see Prudence Allen, "Integral Sex Complementarity and the Theology of Communion," *Communio: International Catholic Review* 17, no. Winter (1990). For an in depth study of the issues see her other two works Prudence Allen, *The Concept of Woman: The Aristotelian Revolution, 750 Bc – Ad 1250*, 1st ed. (Montreal: Eden Press, 1985); and Prudence Allen, *The Concept of Woman. Volume 2, the Early Humanist Reformation, 1250–1500* (Grand Rapids, Mich.: W.B. Eerdmans Pub., 2002). For an example of how ancient wisdom may inform contemporary discourse on sexual ethical theory, see John S. Grabowski, *Sex and Virtue: An Introduction to Sexual Ethics, Catholic Moral Thought.* (Washington, D.C.: Catholic University of America Press, 2003), 156.

4. There are a number of excellent studies on this particular topic. See the bibliography in note 3 and especially the whole volume edited by Michele M. Schumacher, *Women in Christ: Toward a New Feminism*, English ed. (Grand Rapids, Mich.: W.B. Eerdmans Pub., 2004).

5. On the symbolic and real sense of biblical language, see The Pontifical Biblical Commission, *The Interpretation of the Bible in the Church* (Boston, Mass.: Pauline Books & Media, 1993), II, A, 1. For illustrations of how this principle works, see *Catechism of the Catholic Church*, 2nd ed. (Vatican City/Washington, D.C.: Libreria Editrice Vaticana; [distributed by United States Catholic Conference], 2000).

6. One could also organize human history according to three fundamental states of human existence. Following the work of John Paul II, see Fr. Francis Martin, "The New Feminism: Biblical Foundations and Some Lines of Development," in *Women in Christ: Towards a New Feminism*, ed. Michele M. Schumacher (Grand Rapids, Mich.: Wm. B. Eerdmans Pub., 2004), 141–142.

7. The poetic quality of Genesis 1 has long been acknowledged. There are a number of recurring phrases which mark off various units (e.g., "and God said" at Gen 1.2, 6, 9, 11, 14, 20, 24, 28, 29; the five-fold refrain of "and God saw that it was good" at Gen 1.19, 12, 18, 21, 25). The repetitions are consistent with liturgical refrains found within communal prayer. Each period (or "day") occurs in strophe-like style creating a strong impression of rhythm to the reader. Cf. Claus Westermann, *Genesis 1–11: A Commentary*, trans. John J. Scullion (Minneapolis: Augsburg Pub. House, 1984), 90–91.

9. The essential differences between ancient Israelite creation accounts and those of other ancient Near Eastern cultures could be summarized as follows. Mythological narratives articulate absolute origins and pre-origins (of all kinds) using historical, time bound language. Mythology speaks of timeless realities in historicized language perhaps to make the central points intelligible and perhaps to stabilize social order. Ancient Israelite or Hebrew epic, on the other hand, speaks of historical realities with vocabulary similar to ancient Near Eastern mythology. For an excellent summary of this discussion see Westermann, *Genesis 1–11*, 19–47. On the distinction between ancient Near Eastern myth and ancient Hebrew Epic see Frank Moore Cross, *Canaanite Myth and Hebrew Epic; Essays in the History of the Religion of Israel* (Cambridge, Mass.: Harvard University Press, 1973), viii.

10. *CCC#* 390.

11. The term "protological" refers to the absolute beginning of historical time.

12. The moral exhortations found in the last three chapters of Ephesians (the verbs are in the imperative) make it clear that while the unity with Christ is fully realized in the heavenly places, the pilgrim Church has not yet fully realized this unity on earth.

13. One might even say that the hope for man and woman in Genesis, at the beginning of time, is recovered and developed in Christ and the Church at the end of time.

14. *Dei Verbum, Dogmatic Constitution on Divine Revelation of Vatican Council Ii, Promulgated by Pope Paul Vi, November 18, 1965. Commentary and Translation by George H. Tavard* (Glen Rock, N.J.,: Paulist Press, 1966), §12.

15. Given the limitations of space a full exegesis is not possible for this presentation.

16. See Westermann, *Genesis 1–11*, 22–25.

17. *DV* §12 states: "... due attention must be paid to the customary and characteristic styles of feeling, speaking, and narrating which prevailed at the time of the sacred writer, and to the patterns men normally employed at that period in their everyday dealings with one another ..."

18. It is not commonplace to assume that the editor of Genesis 1 (so-called Priestly author [P]) is necessarily responsible for bringing together that text with the older account of Genesis 2 (so-called Yahwist author [J]). However, this position is tenable and will be assumed in this paper. Genesis 1 and 2 contain two different traditions which an editor has placed within their current setting and so has created meaning by their canonical associating. A summary of the distinguishing differences includes the following. In Genesis 1 God is creator of and not subordinate to creation. Other ancient Near Eastern creation accounts generally include God or some level of deity as part of the created (spiritual or materials) order. The gap between God and creation cannot be mistaken. God's ability to acknowledge or pronounce creation as good signifies God's authentic, true knowledge of reality – God correctly names reality. God creates through the mediation of speech, majestic commands which always come to completion. God's speech, word, or command is all powerful, creative and distinguishable for the creation it effects. God creates what is good. In sharp contrast, chapter. 2 depicts God through anthropocentric imagery. The reader has the impression that God fashions the clay of Adam's body personally, directly, with physical hands. Further, God breathes the breath of life directly into the nostrils of the inanimate body of clay, transforming inanimate material in a living being. The transcendent God of chapter 1 is the immanent one in chapter 2, intimately – one is tempted to say almost physically – present to what is created. Divine presence, intimacy, creation's dependency on God for sustained life and especially the implied relational qualities that emerge are dominant attributes depicting God. On the basis of the image of God, we may distinguish these two chapters. Turning to the exercise of divine power, in chapter 1 God's creative power is mediated through power speech: (i) God creates "from a distance" (transcendence); (ii) God shares knowledge of creation's goodness and names created reality. In Genesis 2, God exercises divine power more directly (presence). God (i) directly fashions

the clay and (ii) breaths life's breath directly into Adam's nostrils; (iii) God's power is exercised through intimate contact. Clearly Genesis 1 establishes God as the central figure whose power, knowledge and goodness are fundamental to God. In summary, chapters 1 and 2 may be distinguished based on the above material considerations.

19. See the discussion on "so that they may rule" below on for the arguments supporting this translation.

20. Following Martin with some modifications, see Francis Martin, "Male and Female He Created Them: A Summary of the Teaching of Genesis Chapter One," *Communio: International Catholic Review* 20, no. Summer (1993): 244.

21. Genesis 1.2: hay ta tohu wabohu.

22. No doubt the author of Genesis 1 was familiar with many ancient Near Eastern creation accounts. For a convenient reconstruction of pre- and extra-biblical parallels see Westermann, *Genesis 1–11*, 19–53.

23. Cf. Gen. 1.4, 10, 12, 18, 21, 25, 31 (*wayyar'*} "and he saw").

24. Cf Gen. 1.4, 10, 12, 18, 21, 25 (*tob* "good").

25. Cf. Gen. 1.22, 28, 2.3 (*way barek* "and he blessed").

26. As a side point to this analysis I should point out what is implied about the relationship between God and creation. There is an insurmountable gap between the creator and the created. Only God – not planetary bodies, not nature, not divine or semi-divine figures – may be worshipped. God is not part of creation, even its highest point. Rather, God is "beyond" creation since God created it.

27. Gen. 1.28: *way barek 'otam' lohim wayyo'mer lahem lohim p ru ur'bu umil'u 'et-ha'ares*. One might also argue that "to rule over" has within it an extension of the divine creative act itself, in the sense that cultivation of the fields and the production of offspring ("be fruitful and multiply…") is a new level of created order now under the creative work of Adam and Eve. This line of interpretation is at least suggested by Genesis 2.7–9 – the details of God's creative action seems to be consistent with verse 15, where humanity now participates in extending created order through agricultural labor.

28. The term is generic, referring to humanity as a whole. Due to technical limitations, the transliterations of Hebrew are in the simplest possible form.

29. See Martin, "Male and Female," 244–225. See also Paul Jouüon, *Grammaire De L'hebreax Biblique*, Deuxieème édition anastatique corrigeée ed. (Roma: Editrice Pontificio Istituto Biblico, 1947).

30. The two other examples for the use of this term as divine self deliberation are Genesis 11.7 and Psalms 2.3. Several other examples for humans (same grammatical form) exist, see Joüon, *Grammaire*, esp. §114e and §136d for a fuller discussion of the texts. Scholarly opinion varies on this point. See the standard treatment by Gerhard von Rad, *Genesis: A Commentary*, *Old Testament Library*. (Philadelphia: Westminster Press, 1961), 57 ff.

31. The term occurs 17 times in the Old Testament. It may refer to images such as idols (10X), to depleted human existence as with a shadow or vapor (2X), and, as a term of reference between Adam and his son Seth (Gen. 5.3).

32. E.g., Ez. 7.20; Amos 5.26; Num. 33.52.

33. E.g., Ez. 16.17; 23.14; 1 Sam. 6.5, 11.

34. Westermann, *Genesis 1–11*.

35. Perhaps this presence is concretely realized through the couple's fertility – life-giving self donaton – and through their prophetic stewardship over creation. If the statue is equivalent to the royal scepter – a symbol of royal authority – then its effect is not to establish the existence of the monarch but His presence in symbol and thus his authority. I am grateful to Dr. Minto for the conversation leading to this point.

36. See Martin, "The New Feminism," 144.

37. At Genesis 1:26 *na'aseh* can be taken as a cohortative based on syntax and not morphology. The form is ambiguous because it is a III-yodh/he class verb, meaning, it is a "direct volitive" (="let us make").

38. The form here is ambiguous and could be taken as a simple imperfect.

39. I am grateful to Dr. Gregory Vall of Ave Maria University for his kind assistance in the technical matters of morphology and syntax.

40. Of course this has enormous implications for keeping the planet and its inhabitants in "good order" and is the principle foundation for environmental issues.

41. John Paul II, *Original Unity of Man and Woman: Catechesis on the Book of Genesis* (Boston, Mass.: St. Paul Editions, 1981), 47.

42. Others have noted this as well. On the exegetical data see Martin, "The New Feminism," p.147.

43. For example, it is only after God creates all sorts of animals and presents them to Adam for naming that the narrator indicates the need for "a suitable helper (helpmate)" (Gen 2.22).

44. At this point in the narrative I one could render *levaddu* ("to be alone") as something like "to be in isolation from other humans" without reference to the creation of woman. A number of commentators use the term "solitude," e.g., see II, *Original Unity*, 43–49 and Ska, 1984 , Jean-Louis Ska, "'Je Vais Lui Faire Un Allie Qui Soit Son Homologue' (Gen 2, 18) a Propos Du Term 'Ezer – 'Aide'," *Biblica* 65 (1984): 237, Westermann, *Genesis 1–11*, 227. Others simply avoid the term and describe the necessity of human community, e.g., see Ska, "Je Vais Lui Faire," 233–238. I would resist using the term "solitude" because today it can have the connotation of communion with God, carrying with it the sense of *contemplatio*.

45. For the literature, see Westermann, *Genesis 1–11*, 225–229. For a briefer treatment, see Eugene M. Maley, "Genesis," in *The Jerome Biblical Commentary* (Englewood Cliffs, N.J.: Prentice-Hall, 1968), 7–46, esp. 12. For examples of translations into European languages, see Ska, "Je Vais Lui Faire," 233–234. Cf. Martin, "The New Feminism," pp.146–151.

46. Of the 488 times this preposition occurs in the Masoretic Text, it has the meaning of "in front of" or "opposite" 151 times. This is the meaning found in Genesis 2.28; 20; 21.16; 31.32, 37; 33.12; 47.15. In the case of Genesis 2.20, 28, the term does not apply to the animals.

47. A brief summary of the essential exegetical points can be found in Grabowski, *Sex and Virtue*, pp.32–48, 98–107. For an exegetical reflection on the covenantal nature of Genesis 2.24 as applied in Ephesians 5.31–32, see Stephen Francis Miletic, *"One Flesh" – Eph. 5.22–24, 5.31: Marriage and the New Creation*, vol. 115 (Roma: Editrice Pontificio Istituto Biblico, 1988), 99–111.

48. See Rad, *Genesis*, 82. For more details, see Walter Brueggemann, "Of the Same Flesh and Bone," *Catholic Biblical Quarterly* 32 (1970): 535–538.

49. For examples of such language, see 2 Samuel 5:1, 1 Chronicles 11:1.

50. Brueggemann, "Flesh and Bone," 533–535, 539.

51. On the nuptial, sexual and covenantal nature of v. 24 see Maurice Gilbert, "Une Seule Chair (Gen 2,24)," *Nouvelle Revue Théologigue* 100 (1978): 66–89.

52. It is also possible to translate *l nepes hayya* as "living soul" or even "a living life."

53. For a detailed examination of the logical structure of this text see Miletic, *One Flesh*, 25–43.

54. The ellipsis of the verb at 5.22 is resolved by reading the middle/passive from the previous sentence, which is the fifth of five participles which unpack the meaning of "be filled in the spirit." That is, the Church's mutual subordination directly, grammatically speaking, informs the wife's subordination to the husband. I have worked this out in greater detail elsewhere Ibid. See also Martin, "The New Feminism," pp.161–168.

55. For a discussion of the theological and anthropological implications of the position taken in this paper, see Miletic, *One Flesh*.

56. See Ephesians. 2.1–10, 15–16.

57. See esp. Ephesians. 2.14–15.

58. I have worked this out in greater detail elsewhere, see Miletic, *One Flesh*, 25–43.

Chapter 4: John Paul II on the Complementarity of Man and Woman

JOHN F. CROSBY, PH.D.

When we hear the proposal to open the institution of marriage even to homosexual couples, we are at first at a loss how to respond, for something utterly fundamental to our understanding of human existence has been called into question. Chesterton somewhere describes what it is like to be challenged to explain why civilization is better than barbarism. Our first reaction, he says, as I recall, is to stammer something about the benefits of having policemen, an observation that we know misses the mark; but we are at first too disoriented by the radicality of the challenge to say anything that really meets it. The proposal to let homosexual couples marry is similarly disorienting for us. It forces us to stop taking man and woman for granted and to ask, as if for the first time, what is the man-woman difference? How deep does it go? What kind of complementarity exists between man and woman? There is a certain loss of innocence that goes with asking these questions and with struggling to find answers to them. But we have no alternative; we can in this day no longer remain in the innocence of taking man and woman for granted.

Fortunately we Catholics have a rich new resource for encountering the radical challenges to the meaning of man and woman: we have the teaching of John Paul II, who has surely thought more profoundly about sex and gender than any previous pope. I will leave for another day the task of formulating a Christian response to the proposal of homosexual marriage; my task for today is to take up the preliminary work of examining with John Paul the fundamental meaning of man and woman, and especially the complementarity of man and woman. I want to begin with his original teaching on the image of God in man and woman, and then proceed to his equally original teaching on the "genius" of woman. I might of course have also dealt with John Paul's "theology of the body," but that is becoming so well known in the Catholic world, and certainly among the members of the Fellowship, that I have chosen some rich themes in John Paul that are not as well known.

The Image of God in Man and Woman

We all know that passage from *Gaudium et Spes*, #24, that the pope has quoted thousands of times. Here it is again: "The Lord Jesus, when he prayed to the Father 'that all may be one...as we are one,' opened up vistas closed to human reason. For he implied *a certain likeness* between the union of the divine Persons and the union of God's children in truth and charity. This likeness reveals that man, who is the only creature on earth which God willed for its own sake, cannot fully find himself except through a sincere gift of self." This passage implies an important development in the theology of the image of God in man, for the Council is teaching here that we find an image of the Trinitarian God in human persons whenever they encounter each other in love. This means that God is not only imaged in solitary persons, that is, in the spiritual faculties of each finite person, but that He is also imaged in interpersonal relations, in persons loving each other. By discerning the image of God in interpersonal relations, we discern it in a new place, a place where it had been neglected because of a certain individualistic focus of the earlier theology of the image of God. I image the Trinitarian God not only by displaying some triad in the inner makeup of my own being but also in and through existing in relation with other persons to whom I make some gift of my self. In fact, in this latter way I image God more perfectly than in the former, according to John Paul, who says, "Man becomes the image of God not so much in the moment of solitude as in the moment of communion."[1]

Notice how the pope is here challenging the many exaggerated notions of the autonomy of human persons. The divine persons who make up the one God are not centers of autonomy but rather are what they are through their relations to each other; it follows that if we exist in their image we exist for and towards one another. This compels even us Christians to give up certain idols of autonomy that we may have grown attached to. These idols make themselves constantly felt in discussions of man and woman, and they constantly interfere with an adequate understanding of the way man and woman are ordered to each other.

Now in his apostolic letter from 1988, *Mulieris Dignitatem* #7, John Paul takes a further step; he sees the man-woman difference in the light of our vocation to interpersonal sharing; he sees our existing as man and woman as being "the first, and in a sense, the fundamental"[2] way in which we are called out of ourselves and into an existence of self-giving. Thus the image of the Trinitarian God that can be detected in our general call to interpersonal sharing, can in a particular way be detected in our existing as man and woman.

You might say that there is nothing new in seeing an image of God in man and woman, since the first chapter of Genesis already speaks of such an image: "God created man in his own image, in the image of God he created him; male and female he created them" (Gen 1:27). But John Paul takes care to avoid reducing the teaching of this text to the teaching that all human beings image God, men as well as women, women no less than men, and he makes a point of drawing out of this text the further teaching that the man-woman couple images God just by the fact that each is turned towards the other and is called to live as gift for the other.[3]

This further teaching seems to follow very naturally from affirming the radical way in which human persons, as we just said, exist for each other. Once our fundamental vocation to interpersonal sharing comes to light, it seems only natural to think of man and woman as partaking in this vocation in a particular way. One would think that we have only to cast down those idols of autonomy and the way is clear for discerning an eminent image of God in the man-woman relation.

But the way is not clear, and in fact a large obstacle still encumbers the way. For many Christians think that the man-woman difference deserves no "special mention" in connection with our vocation to interpersonal sharing and thus no special mention in connection with our existing in the image of God. They typically say that the man-woman difference is a purely contingent fact about human beings, a mechanism devised by nature for propagating the species, that it can be meaningfully studied only by the empirical sciences, that it ranks in significance with the racial differences that have emerged among human beings. They also typically say that, if you go beyond the biological into deeper and richer notions of the masculine and the feminine, you still remain in the realm of the contingent, only this time the contingent facts are sociological and not just biological facts; you have just replaced the contingent products of nature with the contingent products of culture. What they deny is any properly spiritual or personal significance to the man-woman difference, as well as any morally normative significance to it. They secularize the human body, as it were, they de-numinise it. Since they are not pagans but Christians they quite acknowledge our vocation to interpersonal sharing, but they say that it is simply *as persons* that we are called to share something of ourselves with others and not also *as men and women*. They might go on to say that man-woman friendships and loves have no advantage over same-sex friendships and loves. They might point out that Aristotle in his memorable discussion of friendship made no mention of an eminent form of friendship that exists only between man and woman (he was probably thinking of friendship existing most properly between two worthy adult men). If these dualistic Christians are right – and I call them dualistic because of the extreme dualism of spiritual person and biological body that they hold – then it would follow that the man-woman difference has no distinct interpersonal significance of its own and hence no distinct power of its own to show forth God in the visible world.

The first thing that these dualistic Christians have to recover is a sense of the sacramental capacity of the human body, that is, its capacity to provide a medium for things of the spirit and to render them visible. This sacramental capacity of the body is the very thing that gets lost in the overly secularized view of the body. They need to learn from John Paul about the nuptial meaning of the bodies of man and of woman, that is, they need to learn from him how man and woman are through their bodies capacitated for a certain kind of human love. They need to learn anew from Christian revelation about our condition as embodied persons, and indeed about the dignity of the material. If they can begin to see how un-Christian their person-body dualism is, then John Paul can as it were argue with them about the image of God in man and woman.

Here is one way in which he might argue with them. Let us go back to that rich early work of Karol Wojtyla, *Love and Responsibility*, and in particular to the wonderful characterization that he gives there of the love that is proper to man and woman and that is in fact possible only between man and woman.[4]

Here is what Wojtyla says about this kind of love. Man and woman surrender themselves to each other in a way in which they do not surrender themselves in even the most intimate friendship. This self-surrender in fact goes so far that Wojtyla is at first puzzled at the fact that persons can hand themselves over to each other in this spousal way without doing violence to their personhood. For the elementary self-possession in which each person stands could seem to be annulled by a man or a woman making himself or herself belong to another in a distinctly spousal way. In the end Wojtyla marvels at the paradoxical interpenetration of self-possession and self-abandonment that he finds in spousal love.[5] Wojtyla proceeds to clarify with great precision the relation of spousal self-surrender to sexual self-surrender. On the one hand he says that the spousal self-surrender is enacted in an incomparable way in the one-flesh union of man and woman; this bodily enactment even reveals something to us about the full meaning of spousal self-surrender, and also about the different way in which it is lived by man and by woman. But on the other hand he makes a point of saying that the spousal self-surrender cannot be reduced to or simply identified with sexual union. He says that the spousal self-surrender "validates" the sexual, and this implies that it in some sense precedes the sexual. In this way he emphasizes that it is not just sexual union that presupposes man and woman – a fact that is not difficult to grasp – but that it is a certain type of personal love that presupposes man and woman.

Now the argument here is this: *if the man-woman difference is presupposed for a classical type or category of love, making that category of love possible at all, then this difference does indeed merit a special mention in any discussion of the interpersonal vocation and capacity of human persons. And if we image the Trinitarian God through our interpersonal vocation, then we image Him distinctly and particularly through our existing as man and woman.*

Of course, the debate does not end here; the dualists will have their responses. For example, they might say that the real personal substance of the love between man and woman is simply friendship – friendship of the kind that can just as well as exist between two men or two women. They might say that what we call spousal love is nothing other than a combination of a friendship between a man and a woman together with a sexual relationship. This would mean that at the level of personal love there is nothing in so-called spousal love that really presupposes the man-woman difference. John Paul would respond that friends do not surrender to each other in a spousal way, nor do they make themselves belong to each other in a spousal way. The spousal self-surrender is so total, he argues, that it is possible only towards one other person of the other sex; but the bond between me and my friend, and even if I am ready to die for him, does not limit me to this one friend and does not close the possibility of other deep friendships at the same time. Thus the interpersonal core of the love between man and woman cannot be reduced to friendship; it is a kind of love all its own, with its own genius. And the sexual enactment of spousal love is not just extrinsically connected with a friendship; it empowers the man and the woman to enact their spousal love in and through their bodies. Thus John Paul persists in seeing in spousal love a kind or category of love that is possible only between man and woman. And this is why he persists in seeing a distinct image of God in the man-woman difference.

But we cannot discern this image of God if we think of ourselves as autonomous selves, or if we remain beholden to the person-body dualism. Only by avoiding these errors can we see with John Paul how the man-woman difference serves a unique kind of human love, and only then does the image of God in man and woman appear.

The Genius of Woman

I mentioned that the dualists typically say that masculine and feminine are nothing but cultural constructs built on the biological basis of male and female. They deny that there is any masculinity that is proper to man prior to all such constructs, or that there is any femininity that is proper to woman prior to them. But John Paul sees more in masculinity and femininity; and his teaching on the complementarity of man and woman presupposes that there is more. We could express his idea in the language of St. Edith Stein like this: in a man there is not only a male body but also a masculine soul, and in a woman there is not only a female body but also a feminine soul.[6] John Paul has tried to show this in the case of woman in his profound meditations on the "genius" of woman.

In one of these meditations he wrote: "Woman is endowed with a particular capacity for accepting the human being in his concrete form."[7]

In another one he developed the thought in this way: "Perhaps more than men, women *acknowledge the person*, because they see persons with their hearts. They see them independently of various ideological or political systems."[8] He means that women are not as liable as men to lose persons in abstractions and stereotypes. He also means that they are not as liable as men to see persons in terms of their achievements; women tend more readily to see past the doing and making of persons to the very being of persons.

This is why John Paul elsewhere says that the presence of women is needed in all those areas of society where human activity is organized in terms of efficiency and productivity. Women's sense for the concrete person will counteract the dehumanizing tendencies of these forms of social and economic life; in fact, he says that women can in a particular way be agents of the "civilization of love" in the contemporary world. Thus in one place he says: "In our own time, the successes of science and technology make it possible to attain material well-being to a degree hitherto unknown. While this favors some, it pushes others to the margins of society. In this way, unilateral progress can also lead to a gradual *loss of sensitivity for man, that is, for what is essentially human*. In this sense, our time in particular *awaits the manifestation* of that 'genius' which belongs to women, and which can ensure sensitivity for human beings in every circumstance..."[19]

What John Paul here characterizes as the genius of woman has recently appeared in the writings of the "difference" feminists as the "feminine voice" in the moral life. One author recently surveyed the writings of these feminists and summed up their thought on the feminine voice like this: "The feminine voice in ethics attends to the particular other, thinks in terms of responsibilities to care for others, is sensitive to our interconnectedness, and strives to preserve relationships. It contrasts with the masculine voice, which speaks in terms of justice and rights, stresses consistency and principles, and emphasizes the autonomy of the individual and impartiality in one's dealings with others."[10]

It is not difficult to recognize in this feminine voice John Paul's genius of woman with its special sensitivity to concrete persons. This author brings out the feminine voice by means of a contrast that John Paul does not use, as far as I know, though he might well have used it; I mean the contrast with the typically masculine concern for impartiality and consistent moral principles. It seems to be quite true that one can be so concerned with being impartial and with respecting universal principles that one loses one's close contact with concrete persons and their concrete claims. A Kantian, for example, who is more concerned with acting on a maxim that can be universalized than with relieving the need of the particular other towards whom he acts, is living his moral life with a particular masculine emphasis. So is the person who in practicing impartiality makes a point of being "blind" to the particular persons towards whom he acts impartially, so that he treats them as he would treat anyone else who had the same kind of claim. But there is a way of giving more attention to concrete persons in the moral life, and this is the way of the feminine voice. For example, there is a certain partiality that we rightly feel at certain moments for our friends or children, an entirely legitimate partiality that just expresses our special relationship with them and can be just as morally positive as the impartiality of blind justice. Those speaking in the feminine voice will be more sensitive to such partiality to particular persons.

One might object to the teaching of John Paul on the "genius of women" by saying that men too can acknowledge concrete persons and can prefer them to achievements and products, and can avoid sacrificing persons to universals; and that in fact some men can do these things better than some women. This would mean that John Paul has not found anything that can count as distinctly womanly. The objection does not exactly contest that there is a feminine voice, but it says that this voice has no special tie to women, that it expresses a sensitivity that men can have as well as women. This means that if John Paul had spoken simply of the "feminine genius" he would not have provoked this objection; what provoked it was his talk of the "genius of women." Sometimes the objection is elaborated by using terms introduced by Sr. Prudence Allen: it is too "fractional" a view of man and woman to think that each has something that the other lacks, as if there were a fullness in the man-woman union that is not possible in man alone or in woman alone; we have to take the more "integral" view of man and woman according to which a man can be feminine as well as masculine and that a woman can be masculine as well as feminine.[11]

This objection is commonly supported by different reasons, two of which I will consider here. First, when women are thought to have their own excellence or genius, it usually happens that their genius turns out to be much inferior to the distinctly masculine genius, so that the equality of men and women is undermined. And secondly, it does not cohere with the nature of man and woman as persons to think of them in fractional terms. Persons are not mere parts, as already St. Thomas teaches; each is his or her own whole, each is a world for himself or herself. We can best respect this wholeness of persons, as well as the equality of all human persons, by letting men be capable of all that women are capable of and letting women be capable of all that men are capable of. Let us consider first the objection itself and then each of these supporting reasons.

Though I am not aware of the pope ever posing exactly this objection, he would respond to it by saying that woman's affinity for the personal is understandably rooted in something that men do not have, namely the capacity for conceiving and bearing a child. He writes in *Mulieris Dignitatem*: "Motherhood involves a special communion with the mystery of life, as it develops in the woman's womb...This unique contact with the new human being developing within her gives rise to an attitude toward human beings, not only toward her own child but every human being, which profoundly marks the woman's personality. It is commonly thought that *women* are more capable than men of paying attention *to another person*, and that motherhood develops this predisposition even more."[12] With this consideration the pope underlines the connection of the feminine voice with women and so justifies his talk of this voice in terms of the "genius of women."

But there is something else that we can say in response to the objection that men can attend to the personal just as well as women. Even if John Paul does not exactly make this response, he suggests it, and would certainly recognize it as being along the line of his thought. Let us just consider what results when men have it all their way, acting together with each other and without receiving anything from the genius of woman. Where can we see such an exclusive predominance of men and of the masculine? It is commonly said that the socio-economic order of North America and Western Europe is based on the masculine principle run amuck; that the obsession with productivity and efficiency and competition is nothing other than an excess of the masculine principle. This was the view of Emmanuel Mounier, who said that "our social world is one that man has made for men, and that the resources of feminine being are among those which humanity still largely neglects."[13]

If women were in charge of our socio-economic order, it would surely lack some of the brutal and depersonalized aspects that it in fact presents. It would of course have other problems of its own, for the feminine has its characteristic distortions no less than the masculine. But the characteristic distortion of the masculine that we can see in our socio-economic system shows that the feminine voice does not belong to men in the way in which it belongs to women.

Furthermore, John Paul mitigates somewhat the fractionality of his teaching on the genius of woman by holding that woman can teach man, and is in fact called to teach man about sensitivity to concrete persons. She does not keep her genius for herself but shares it with man, who is protected from certain excesses natural to himself by his encounter with the genius of woman. But even when he is enriched by this encounter he retains his own genius, different from that of woman. Thus the position of man and woman is still not exactly the one envisioned by the "integral" approach to their complementarity.

Finally, John Paul would say that this objection is infected with the person-body dualism mentioned above. He would say that to let a woman be female in her body but androgynous in her soul is to fail to do justice to the unity of body and soul in woman. Such a conception may have a place within the Platonic view of body and soul, but certainly no place within the Aristotelian-Thomistic-hylomorphic view. A woman is a woman in body and in soul; she has what St. Edith Stein called a *Frauenseele*, or soul of a woman. Thus John Paul would invoke general considerations about the unity of body and soul in human beings in support of his claim that the feminine genius is also the genius of women.

Let us now consider the two reasons given in support of this objection. To the first he might respond that, whatever might be said of other accounts of the genius of woman, his own account could not possibly be taken as implying any inferiority of woman. For the genius of woman is for him nothing other than a particular excellence in living out the vocation proper to all persons. All persons are called to interpersonal sharing, as *Gaudium et Spes* 24 teaches; this vocation is blocked whenever some people see other people too much in terms of achievement and productivity, or too much in terms of abstract principle and stereotype. Women live this vocation in an eminent way insofar as they avoid these depersonalized modes of seeing and thus know how to get at the being of other persons, at their concrete identity. Their genius is simply to have a particular gift for doing something that all human persons are called to do. If anything, one would have to go away from the pope's account of the genius of woman thinking that there is some deficiency in the genius of man!

As for the second reason supporting the objection (namely that a fractional view of the genius of woman does not befit the personhood of woman), I would agree to this extent, that the primary unit of mankind is not the man-woman couple, but rather individual men and women. It is not as if individual men and women were only halves of larger wholes, as Aristophanes teaches in Plato's *Symposium*; no, each one, being a person, is a whole human being. But we certainly do not have to hold the position of Aristophanes when we hold that each sex has its own genius, and that the complementarity of the sexes is based on each having something of its own. And I can certainly not see in this fractionality anything inconsistent with men and women existing as persons. For I see the same fractionality not only on the level of gender but also on the level of individual persons. That is, each person, being unrepeatable, has something of his own, something that cannot be repeated in any other person. When persons come together they enrich each other with their unrepeatable selves, each contributing what only he or she can contribute and each receiving from others what only they can contribute. All together they help to constitute a larger whole of humanity, which contains treasures that cannot be recapitulated in any one human person but that can exist only as spread among the many human persons. Now if we have this fractionality on the level of individual persons, what prevents us from acknowledging a kind of fractionality on the level of man and woman? If the former fractionality does not interfere with human beings being persons, why does the latter have to interfere with men and women being persons?[14]

I might add that the fear of a fractional account of the genius of man or woman is understandable if one defines each genius in terms that describe simply what every human being ought to be. For example, if I describe the feminine genius in terms of "receptivity" and the masculine genius in terms of "creativity," then it is natural to protest that these excellences are equally open to men and women, and natural to say that otherwise men would be seriously deprived by their lack of receptivity and women seriously deprived by their lack of creativity. But John Paul describes the genius of woman with such nuance and care that he does not play into this fear of the fractional.

And so I can find no objectionable fractionality in the idea that woman has that genius described by John Paul, or in the idea, implied but not elaborated by him, that man has his own genius. The genius of woman, as portrayed by the pope, seems to belong to a psycho-spiritual makeup proper to woman, surpassing her biological identity as a female, but grounded in it and analogous to it.

Professor John F. Crosby is a Professor of Philosophy at the Franciscan University of Steubenville in Ohio where he has been since 1990. Previously he taught at the University of Dallas, the University of Salzburg, and the International Academy of Philosophy in Liechtenstein. He has published numerous articles on such subjects as the thought of John Henry Newman and the Christian personalism of Pope John Paul II. His most recent book is *Personalist Papers* (Catholic University of America Press, 2004). He studied philosophy under Dietrich von Hildebrand, and he holds a B.A. from Georgetown University and a Ph.D. from the University of Salzburg in Austria. He and his wife Pia have six children.

Notes

1. John Paul II, General Audience Address of Nov. 14, 1979, in *The Original Unity of Man and Woman* (Boston: St. Paul Editions, 1981), 73–74.

2. John Paul II, *On the Dignity and Vocation of Women* (Boston: St. Paul Books, 1996), 27.

3. See I*bidem*, #26, for a passage in which John Paul avoids this reduction and makes this point.

4. Karol Wojtyla, *Love and Responsibility* (New York: Farrar, Straus, and Giroux, 1981), 95–100.

5. *Ibid.*, 96–98.

6. Edith Stein, *Woman* (Washington DC: ICS Publications, 1987), the section entitled "Woman's Soul," 87–97.

7. John Paul II, *The Genius of Women* (Washington, DC: United States Catholic Conference, Inc., 1997), #28.

8. *Ibid.*, 58.

9. John Paul II, *On the Dignity and Vocation of Women*, Section 30, *op. cit.*, 101–102.

10. Celia Wolf-Devine, "Abortion and the 'Feminine Voice,'" in *Life and Learning: Proceedings of the Third University Faculty for Life Conference*

(Washington DC: University Faculty for Life, 1993), 47–48. In this brilliant article the author brings out the contradiction between defending abortion and speaking with the feminine voice.

11. See her discussion of the terms "fractional" and "integral" in her paper, "Integral Sex Complementarity and the Theology of Communion," in *Communio* 17 (Winter, 1990). I do not mean that Sr. Prudence has criticized John Paul for holding a too fractional position on the genius of woman, but she has criticized as too fractional the view of St. Edith Stein, who is very close to John Paul on woman.

12. *Ibid.*, section 18, p. 66.

13. Emmanuel Mounier, Personalism (Notre Dame: University of Notre Dame Press, 1952), 109.

14. We have to take care that the fear of the fractional does not betray us into exaggerating the autonomy of persons.

Session II: Public and Personal Goods of Marriage

Chapter 5: The Public Goods of Marriage; Or, Why Church and State Should Protect and Support Real Marriage

MOST REVEREND ANTHONY FISHER, O.P.

Introduction

The year is 2024. The revolution is over. The legal and social under-standings of marriage, family, and sexuality have been stretched to a point unimagined only a few decades ago. There is a sexual free-for-all and rates of sexual activity are at an all-time high; courts and govern-ments have held that even children have a right to sex without interfer-ence from parents or social workers.[1] Some even advocate sex with domestic pets.[2] While sex rates are on the up-and-up, marriage rates have hit an all-time low, with fewer and fewer people marrying at all.[3] This is the case despite the fact that many jurisdictions now allow men to marry men, women to marry women,[4] transsexuals to marry people of either sex,[5] live people to marry dead people[6] and to have children with them.[7] No marriage need last more than a year, after which its extension is optional.[8] With serial polygamy widespread for so long, concurrent polygamy is coming.[9]

It is 2024 and what Peter Berger called 'the war against the family' and Pat Buchanan dubbed 'the suicide of the West' have been consum-mated.[10] Despite all the varieties of marriage and the sheer quantity of sex, birth rates are in free fall, well below demographic replacement level.[11] Many of those now getting married decide from the beginning to have no children or at most one or two. Pregnancy rates remain surpris-ingly high, despite widespread sex-education, contraception and infertil-ity. Abortion is what keeps down the birthrate and so no real brakes have been put on that practice for decades. Over-the-counter abortifacients have successfully blurred the line between contraception and abortion, and have helped hide the real abortion rate.[12] Those who *do* have children often do so as a kind of life-style project, and then only with the aid of considerable technology, first to avoid and later to achieve conception, as well as to quality test along the way.[13] It is increasingly rare for children, once born, to grow up with both their parents married to each other and living in the same home as them. All in all, marriage and family as they were known in former times are disappearing.

Will 2024 really be like that? I don't know. What I do know is that 2004 already is. We are now forced to rethink and re-articulate the case for marriage and the marriage-based family against the background of a culture that is no longer even sure what these things are, let alone whether it wants them. When we do this hard thinking and talking, we are portrayed as fundamentalists and enemies of anyone who does not fit in to the *Little House on the Prairie*. Yet I believe we can make a reasoned case for marriage and family as traditionally understood, without demeaning other friendships or people. We may also be charged with idealizing heterosexual marriage and the nuclear family and running down everyone else: but we do not pretend that all married people make good spouses and parents or that all unmarried people make bad friends or parents. We may be accused of denying the heroism of people who support children without the aid of a spouse or who struggle against inclination to live according to God's plan for the human person, sexuality, marriage, and the family: but the Church has long been in the forefront of helping just such people and opposing all unjust discrimination.[14]

When Christians deny that same-sex relationships are equivalent to marital ones, or that homosexual acts are equivalent to conjugal ones, or that the manufacture of laboratory children for single or same-sex parents is equivalent to procreation through genuinely marital acts, we are not discriminating unjustly: we are recognizing relevant differences.

How Did We Get Here?

Marriage and the family have over the past four decades been the subjects of radical social experimentation, led and fed by four revolutions:

Stage 1 was *the sex-on-demand revolution* of the 1960s in which the me-generation denied that sex has any intrinsic meaning or limits, let alone any marital significance. With the rapid adoption of a contraceptive-abortion mentality and practice, the West was able to sustain a copulation explosion at the same time as a population implosion. This denied even Christians the traditional boundary notions that "sex is for marriage" and "marriage is for family."

Stage 2 was *the divorce-on-demand revolution* of the hedonistic 1970s which cast to the wind the notion of life-long commitments and the attendant self-sacrifice, except as a sentimental ideal for the newly-wed or the religious. From the 1970s on the divorce rate in Western countries spiralled, robbing spouses and children of the experience of permanence and even Christians of the "for life" horizon for marriage and family.

Stage 3 was *the children-on-demand revolution* of the 1980s which built on the contraceptive-abortion mentality of the previous two decades and now saw the laboratory manufacture and quality-testing of children as if they were commodities. No longer need there be any connection between children and marriage, or even with marital acts. Both fertility and infertility technologies were now used not merely to space children but also to prevent them altogether for a new generation of "DINKs" ("Double Income, No Kids"). Paul VI's 1968 prophesy of a radical break between love-making and life-making, sex and children, came to its fulfillment as even Christians were denied a sense of the mystery and givenness of fertility and children.

Stage 4 is *the "marriage"-and-"family"-on-demand revolution* which began even before the 1990s with the recognition of 'de facto' marriages in law. From the 1990s on other relationships such as same-sex ones have increasingly been put on an equal footing with and even called marriage; and various domestic arrangements have been equated with the marriage-based family in law and society. Everyone has a "right" to marry, and to marry whomever they wish, without being bound to any expectations such as heterosexuality, openness to children, or permanence; everyone has a right to manufacture a family by whatever means and with whomever they please. The notions of marriage and family are being expanded to the point of triviality. This has robbed even many Christians of a coherent understanding of what marriage and family are and of the special treatment their marriages and families deserve.

These several developments are much more radical than they seem to us because, like kangaroos hypnotized by oncoming car headlights, we often fail to notice what is happening until it is too late for us to protest, let alone hop out of the way! All four revolutions continue to unfold themselves and feed each other and, in the process, contribute to the breakdown of many marriages and families. Recent rewriting of history by activists notwithstanding, "marriage" has almost always been understood as *the union of a man and a woman to the exclusion of all others, voluntarily entered into for life, whereby they undertake to live sexually and otherwise as husband and wife with a view to family.*[15]

Despite cultural variations, "family" has consistently meant *a communi-ty of two or more generations related by blood, law and affections, based on marriage and sharing a domestic life.*[16] The desire of many people who do not fit the traditional understanding of marriage and family to share in those titles and attendant privileges might be thought to repre-sent a kind of reverence for traditional marriage and family. Yet as I will argue today, far from honoring marriage and family, mimicking them and extending their benefits to others only adds to the widespread con-fusion about what marriage and family are, dilutes further the precious little marriage-specific support there still is, and threatens what are already fragile institutions. The future of those institutions – and so of the societies that receive great public goods through them – will require greater clarity about what marriage and family are and a greater willing-ness to give them some preferential treatment. For the rest of this lecture I want to unpack some of these public goods of marriage, especially in view of recent trends and controversies.

The Public Goods of Marriage

Marriage, then, is the union of a man and a woman to the exclusion of all others, voluntarily entered into for life whereby they undertake to live sexually and otherwise as husband and wife. When Catholics talk about a "vocations crisis" they usually mean a shortage of priests and religious. Yet there is a worse vocations crisis at the moment in the Western world: it is the crisis in marriage. Fewer and fewer people get married at all and of those who do, fewer stay married. The marital breakdown rate and divorce rate are now so high in the West that it has raised in some theologians' minds the possibility that for the first time in history a significant proportion of people *cannot* validly marry. The reason: because in their heart of hearts they believe that marriage is only for as long as it "works." The divorce option is now so deeply ingrained in us that it is hard for any young person today to engage in the sort of total self-giving that true marriage requires. Divorce, the "Get Out of Jail Free" card, can always be played when the going gets tough. In the meantime, years of "living together" and other experiences have habitu-ated would-be spouses to a debilitating non-commitment.[17]

It is not that people are selfish, precisely, though many no doubt are. Rather, it is that in our culture nothing is forever, nothing for keeps any more, whether relationships, work, housing, causes, beliefs, morals. All is transient, revisable, renegotiable. Paradoxically, we maintain the hope for life-long near-perfect relationships, though without compromise of anyone's will and without total commitment on either side. If marriage, family, priesthood, and consecrated life are to have a future, we must sacrifice some of our Western "autonomania," and learn again how to commit, for life, heart, and soul, persevering even when the going gets tough, even when the warm feelings are missing. We must rediscover what it means "to love, honor and obey till death do us part".

On the classical account marriage is not only *for life* but also *for a man and a woman*, i.e., two people (not one or three or more), of adult age (that is, rational, sexually mature beings able to commit to and live a marriage), who are free to marry, of opposite sex, and both alive and consenting at the time. Those who argue for same-sex marriage (as has been permitted in some parts of North America and Northern Europe, and is soon to be introduced even in "Catholic" Spain), marriage to a corpse (as has been permitted in France[18]), and other exotic variants, either do not understand marriage or do not understand other relationships. Not all friendships are marriage and not all people are marriageable. Homogenising marital and non-marital friendships devalues both; trying to force the non-marital into a marital mould and *vice versa* is a losing game and creates inappropriate expectations on both sides. But children apart, what is the relevance to spouses that they are of opposite sex?

First, on any sound anthropology of the sexes, there are real differences between men and women. Much has been said about this throughout the history of law and politics, science and the arts, psychology and sociology. Despite the confusions of the contemporary world, most Freudians, feminists, and popular writers on men being Martians and women Venetians, agree that there are essential differences between men and women, and that these go beyond genitalia. In theology this point has been richly developed by the current pontiff whose deep insights into the theology of the body has spawned a whole industry.[19] Now if these many traditions are right about the essential differences between the sexes, marriage presents a unique challenge to human beings: to deal with the otherness of a spouse whose sexuality one will never fully understand. Only the male-female relationship allows the discovery and expression of both the similarities and the differences, especially the complementarities, of temperaments and rôles of both sexes in that relationship. Same-sex couples commit instead to someone more like another self, psychosexually speaking. This has important social consequences for the understanding and the relationships between the sexes.

Secondly, marriage and family life generally require both husband and wife to give up much of their same sex world (e.g. "going out with the boys") for the sake of their new family; those who cohabit, however, more often continue as before. Only genuine marriage (and family) seems to have the power to draw forth the kind of self-sacrificial commitment needed for marriage and family and to change all the relationships that the couple had individually with others before the marriage.

Thirdly, marriage is a place where the "eros" of the two is tamed, enriched, and directed to the service of vocation and the common good, and where human life and love will most easily be understood as "gifts" or trusts received rather than "projects" chosen. In marriage we learn to be spouses and parents, children and siblings, and to subordinate sexual and other desires to the common good of the marriage and the family.

Fourthly, marriage is a school of intimacy and community for persons of the opposite sex. In the contemporary world "intimates" have been reduced to "partners" – with all the impersonality this business terminology suggests – or to short-term "compatibles," meaning: "I take you on my terms." What Pope John Paul II, on the other hand, has dubbed "the nuptial gift of the self," promotes certain crucial values such as decisiveness, fidelity, generosity, trust, hope, and forgiveness. Other relationships are unlikely to cultivate such virtues so effectively and may even encourage contrary vices. The loss of this primal experience of community and of this school for certain virtues is potentially very damaging not just for the spouses and their families, but also for society. It is very difficult to "build community" with people who have never been schooled in the qualities of character it requires or where their most fundamental relationships have been reduced to autonomy, compatibility, and contract.

Fifthly, marriage is the place where the roles of husband and wife are learnt and enacted. Yet it is more difficult in 2004 than at any time in history to write the job description for a "husband" or a "wife." To the extent that there are real differences between the sexes there will be real differences in the ways they espouse and in turn the ways they parent. It would be naïve to imagine that the roles of both husband and wife (and so of father and mother) are entirely interchangeable or can readily be performed by persons of either sex without loss to themselves or others, or without very considerable supplementation.[20]

Marriage Is Good for the Spouses Themselves

Philosophers have identified marriage (and the marriage-based family) as one of the *basic goods of human flourishing*.[21] It is the purpose (or end or for-the-sake-of) which explains an enormous range of human choices, activities, commitments, institutions and policies. Marriage is self-evidently and intrinsically choice-worthy: no further explanation is needed as to why people do many of the things that they do than that it is "for the sake of their marriage," their spouse, their family, or someone else's, or the very institutions themselves. Marriage is something we enjoy "for its own sake," irreducible to other goods or ends, even if it is also a means to other goods such as friendship and life, work and leisure. That marriage is a good of human beings is something "given" in our nature rather than merely a preference of individuals or communities. It is an aspect of every person's flourishing – even those who are unmarried – and one of that range of goods in which everyone seeks to participate, within the confines of their own nature, circumstances, and commitments. Most people find their vocation and happiness in being married, thereby making it a central life commitment, the goal of many of their day-to-day choices, and the structuring principle of their identity or "narrative unity." Any life-course so crucial to individual fulfilment will of course also be essential to the common good and any community worth the name will enable and support such a course of life to come to fruition.

To say that marriage (and the marriage-based family) is a basic human good is *not* to say that participation in it is reasonably to be pursued by everybody, at all times, by whatever means. If that were so, nuns would be required to jump the convent walls, the monogamous to try polygamy, and everyone to have as many children as physically possible. But some means of participating in marriage and family are unreasonable (such as adulterous seduction or abduction or IVF); and there are other important values which might preclude marriage and family for a particular person. Marriage does not trump all other goods in our choices. So while there is always a good reason to pursue marriage and family, whether for ourselves or for others, there may well concurrently be good reasons *not* to do so, such as our other proper goals or responsibilities.

Of course there are many ways of participating in the good of marriage. As a son of good parents, a sibling and uncle, and a friend of many married people I have personally benefited enormously from participating in the good of (other peoples') marriage. As a consecrated celibate and priest, I do so by preparing people for marriage, both remotely and proximately, by celebrating their marriages liturgically and assisting them thereafter with counselling and other support, by preaching, teaching, and lobbying about marriage and the family, by mediating for the married at the altar of God and in the rest of my prayer-life, and by being invited by them to share in their family lives in various ways. Yet I will never be married myself, except in the spiritual sense of being, as a

Christian, part of Christ's bride the Church; as a priest, one who acts *in persona Christi* as a husband to that bride and father to her children; and, as a religious, as an eschatological sign of the ultimate marriage – that of the Lamb, at the consummation of all things. But I am not literally married, and that could be instructive to those who think the only way to dignify a state in life is to call it marriage or that the only way to honour a person is to call him married.

People today focus a lot of their energy and their personal wealth on *houses*. Yet they are often at a loss as to how to make their house a *home* and they often underestimate the real value of a home even as they over-estimate the value of a house. Leon Kass has written of the home (or domestic household) as

> ...that nest and nursery of humanity – private, intimate and vulner-able. Though its roots are the needs of bodily life – nurture, protec-tion, reproduction, and then protection and nurture of the young – it provides for more than the body. A richly woven fabric of nature and convention, it is established by law to nurture our nature. It is sustained by customs that humanize the human animal, engender-ing love and friendship, speech and education, choice and aware-ness, and shared beliefs and feelings...[22]

Thus while houses are what we make them, homes have certain given meanings and responsibilities. Before we can extend the notion of a home and a family to various strangers and make various metaphorical and extended uses of those terms, we need first to experience a home and a family into which we can invite others and treat them "as family," where they too can be "at home." There is much more that could be said philosophically and theologically about why marriage is good for people and what the implications of this are for personal morality and public policy. There is also a huge weight of sociological evidence on the importance of marriage for home-building and for the fulfilment of the spouses. Put simply, it says: married people are generally healthier and happier than their divorced, never-married, cohabiting or same-sex coun-terparts.[23] They live longer and better; they are less likely to engage in "problem drinking" or other high risk behaviors, and more likely to engage in responsible, healthy behaviors; they are less likely to experi-ence sexual dysfunction or STDs and are more likely to be sexually sat-isfied; they have lower rates of depression and other psychological and psychiatric disorders, and cope better with stressful events; they are more socially productive and less alienated from their work; they have lower rates of suicide and fatal accidents; they are more likely to invest emotionally in their relationships and develop partner-specific relational skills; they are on average more physically, emotionally, and spiritually satisfied; and they report that marriage gives their life a sense of meaning and purpose. There is no evidence that pseudo-marriages yield all these public and private benefits.

The future of marriage and the family will crucially depend upon a continuing clear understanding of marriage as an exclusive and life-long commitment of a man and a woman to live sexually and otherwise as husband and wife. To extend the notion of marriage by excluding one of these elements is to risk undermining personal and social conceptions of this relationship and weakening existing marriages. Put baldly: if everyone is married, no-one is. And given the public goods which marriage and family provide, this is a highly dangerous course for any society.

Marriage Is Intergenerational and Includes Children

As noted above, marriage is also a commitment with a view to a *family* – a domestic community of two or more generations related by blood, law and affections which is good for the children

The traditional notion that marriage is a commitment with a view to – or at least openness to – family has been challenged since the sexual revolution and the children-on-demand revolution which I treated earlier in this paper. The effects have been dramatic. Most Western countries now have birthrates well below replacement level of 2.1 babies per woman and about half the birthrate of four decades ago. Principally for this reason the median age in most Western countries will rise sharply in the next few decades. This worries governments and economists, and there are lots of proposals about stemming the tide. Yet there are powerful forces operating for our demographic demise.

Of course there are still some married people who want children, some who are even open to more than one. And then there are yuppies who postpone them but would still expect to have one some day. And there are some "gay couples" who want them, perhaps with a bit of laboratory help, surrogacy, or adoption. And there are plenty of single mothers who have children who are "fatherless" in practical terms, often from birth. But is it really irrelevant to children whether their parents are of each sex, related to them and to each other? Is a single parent or two parents of the same sex just as good? For several reasons it is desirable that a child's parents, where possible, be a man and a woman, married to each other:

* The male-female relationship that constitutes marriage enables children to come to be, through procreation; any other relationship

requires artifice to achieve pregnancy, often at some risk to the child, and is likely to yield fewer if any children.

* The natural bonds between spouses, between parents, and between generations, are bonds not just of choice, but also bodiliness, emotions, instinct, and genealogy; such bonds strengthen each other and normally draw forth from all concerned great generosity and self-sacrifice in the care of each other; other relationships lack such strong natural bonds and effects.

* The presence of a male and a female parent allows children to experience and model masculinity and femininity, husbanding and wifing, fathering and mothering; single and same-sex parenting denies children some of these important experiences and models.

* The permanence which comprises marriage as a long-haul commitment is also crucial for the security of family members, especially for children who are dependent for many years; a non-permanent relationship endangers the economic and personal security and identity of the members.

* The commitment and self-sacrifice which constitute marriage are also a great advantage to the children, not only as the principal beneficiaries of much of the parents' commitment and self-sacrifice, but also as learners of these same virtues; the love and care which the marriage-based family should provide is also by far the most emotion-ally stable and economically secure arrangement for child rearing.

* The clear family lines which marriage and the marriage-based family provide go to the heart of people's sense of identity, roles, and how to relate to each other; other kinds of 'family' relationship complicate these for all the family members, especially for children.

* In addition to children, the marriage-based family commonly provides for other dependents, such as the elderly and handicapped, because it builds an environment of care upon the sense of continuity with past generations, of belonging in the present, and of aspirations for the future.

No alternative family arrangement, no bureaucracy, business, or agency can fully substitute for the marriage-based family as the ideal place for personal formation, education in relating, and schooling in virtue for children. This is probably also true for adults.

Psychological and sociological experience backs up these philosophical claims.[24] Studies have found that children who grow up in "families" not based on marriage: are more likely to suffer economic, geographic, emotional, and educational deprivation of various sorts, with attendant disadvantages to child development, and expectancy of health, life and happiness; are on average less well socialized and more likely to suffer disorientation, depression, anger, values bewilderment, delinquency, or an inability to commit; are more likely to engage in substance abuse, violence, suicide and other risky behaviours; report significantly lower-quality relationships both as children and as adults; are much more likely to engage in early sexual activity, be sexually promiscuous and have unwanted pregnancies, abortions and ex-nuptial children; and are much less likely to marry and have children themselves.[25] The lack of a father has been demonstrated to increase the risk of various "deficiencies in well-being," such as: felt and expressed "father hunger"; compromised learning by modelling about sexual differences, masculinity, fatherhood and relating; diminished learning in other areas, such as certain sporting, craft, intelligence quotient and academic skills; increased rates of accidents, unemployment, criminal activity and imprisonment; and much greater risk of suffering physical or sexual abuse.

Yet again, human experience and sociology back the philosophical and theological arguments for the proposition that the family is not just a social construct for which a married mother and father are an optional extra but nature's nursery for children providing essential public goods. Notions such as "spouse," "husband," "wife," "parent," "mother," "father," "family," "household," and "home" are natural realities which transcend social variations and private preferences, and all these terms relate to children. Yet it is striking how little attention the welfare of children (and our relationship to them) has received in the four stage cultural revolution I identified at the beginning of this paper. The focus of each stage has been decidedly on the immediate desires of adults.[26] Were we to recover a sense of "the paramount interests of the child" we would quickly realize how important marriage and the marriage-based family really are and how much our children's future depends on them.

Public Recognition and Support

Marriage and the family are good for (or essential to) the wider community and so deserving of public recognition and support. The Second Vatican Council described the marriage-based family as "the first and vital cell of society."[27] Pope John Paul II calls it "the primordial and, in a certain sense, 'sovereign' society" and, following St Thomas Aquinas, he has argued that the very legitimacy of the state rest upon their support for life and for families.[28] Aquinas followed Aristotle in arguing that: "Man is by nature more inclined to live as a couple than to associate politically, since the family is something that precedes and is more necessary than the state."[29] Many other thinkers have made a similar point.[30]

Throughout this paper I have outlined many benefits of marriage and the marriage-based family not only for the individuals concerned but for the community as a whole. The public recognition and regulation of human sexuality and the promotion of healthy marriage and family life are essential for the common good as the ordinary vehicles by which societies provide for the generation, nurture, education, moral formation, housing, healthcare and welfare of their younger citizens. They are also fundamental to employment, commerce, culture and politics. Society therefore has a compelling interest in promoting, sustaining, and preferring marriage and the marriage-based family, especially in times when they are under particular pressure or especially fragile.[31]

Good marriages and families don't just happen. They require enormous commitment and need to be supported by an appropriate cultural, economic and political-juridical context. The social significance of "gay couples" and others who cohabit is very different from that of marriage: such arrangements last for one generation only; they do not provide the same benefits or require same self-sacrifice for the couple themselves, the next generation or the community as a whole and so do not require the same social regulation or merit the same social support. The state has in the past wisely part-compensated genuinely married couples for the sacrifices which they make in order to get and stay married and raise a family, and has "privileged" the institution by recognizing it as a civil reality, not easily dissolved, forbidding incest and bigamy, protecting family property by pension, superannuation, and inheritance laws, providing various tax breaks or endowments to support marriage and family, and so on.

Marriage, Family, and Salvation

Marriage and the family are good for the salvation of those concerned and so deserving of ecclesial support. So far in this paper I have focussed largely on those elements of marriage as it has been understood by most major religions, philosophies and cultures to date, and why I think our society's future depends upon these elements being respected and protected. In this sense, marriage as a natural institution has been described by Pope John Paul II as "the primordial sacrament." But for Catholics there are additional reasons to want to protect and support fully *sacramental* marriage. Many of the aspects of natural marriage are healed and heightened and have a new significance under the New Law.

The fact that the spouses are of opposite sexes and complement each other as husband and wife and are fruitful in raising up a new generation makes their relationship iconic of Christ's "spousal" relationship with the Church in a way that no other relationship is.[32] By the power of that sacrament their bodies, minds and wills are united indissolubly and fruitfully in the service of each other and the wider Church. Marriage thus points them and us back to the original blessedness of that first marriage when Adam and Eve were at ease with God in Paradise.[33] And it also points them and us forward to that ultimate marriage, when Paradise Lost will be regained, and when all the saved shall be perfectly united to each other and to God in the marriage feast of the Lamb.[34]

The love told in sacramental marriage and family is not just the sentimental love of the great classics of Western romance such as *Days of Our Lives* and *Friends:* sacramental love is cross-shaped rather than heart-shaped, the persevering love told better in Easter cards than Valentine's Day cards. Marriage understood in this self-sacrificial way will be family-focussed and God-focussed, not in a way that demeans the intimacy and personal fulfilment proper to spouses, but in a way which finds much of that intimacy and fulfilment precisely in that most concrete enfleshment of their love in the sacrament of children.

This is about more than just "preserving the species" and "keeping the vows": bearing children of God, raising saints within a domestic church, and accepting responsibility for others makes married love not only iconic of Christ's union with the Church but also of the open-ended love of the Trinity. The grace of the sacrament strengthens and sanctifies the couple for this ministry of spouse and parent, so that they mediate divine love and energy to each other not only on their wedding day when they are first "priests" to each other, but also thereafter. Other relationships, vocations, and ministries may confer some of these responsibilities and benefits but not all: only marriage and the marriage-based family are this distinctive path to holiness, service and salvation.

To what extent the spiritual benefits of marriage might count as public goods of which the state should take account is contentious. It may not be the state's role to get us to heaven, but minimally it should not provide obstacles by cooperating in cultural revolutions which are undermining people's understanding of and inoculating them against living this most crucial spiritual as well as secular institution.

Conclusion

Imagine the year is 2024. The revolution is over. Having looked over the precipice at the prospect of the complete breakdown of the institutions of marriage and family, demographic suicide, and multiple personal and social sequelæ, marriage and family are in recovery mode – just as happened in the past with baby-booms after plagues, wars and economic depressions had decimated families. Even in the dark days of the late 20th and early 21st centuries, despite all the confusion about the meaning of marriage and family, most people thought being a good spouse (of the old-fashioned husband and wife kind) and being a good parent (of the old-fashioned two parents married to each other and caring for their kids kind) was the most important element of human happiness. Despite the best efforts of cultural elites in the courts, academies, and media, the overwhelming majority of people and their political representatives still honored genuine marriage and the marriage-based family and wanted church and state to support their continued existence.[35] The classical definition of marriage ultimately won the day, and laws were clarified and strengthened on that basis. But no one imagined that achieving or maintaining sound legal definitions and social policies in this area would be enough: the wider evangelical and educational challenge of 2004 was seen for what it was and embraced with enthusiasm by Catholic scholars and others.

What was the cause of this turnaround by 2024? Partly it was the strange grace which the four revolutions of the late 20th and early 21st centuries provided in challenging each and every aspect of marriage and the family as traditionally understood. This forced Christians and others to re-examine what marriage and family truly are, why they matter so much, and how they might be protected and strengthened. No longer could we smugly assume that secular society understands or cares. At that very time of crisis the world had also been blessed with the papacy of Karol Józef Wojtyla. By 2024 he has been dead – a few years! – but he is already honored as a saint. His legacy has been successfully to equip a new generation of Catholic scholars and evangelists to recover the truth of God's plan for the human person, marriage and the family.[36] Paradoxically, the 21st century survival of some of the most basic human instincts and natural institutions ultimately depended upon the supernatural instinct for God and the divine institution of the Church.

The Most Reverend Anthony Fisher is a Dominican friar who was ordained as Auxiliary Bishop of Sydney, Australia, in 2003, where he serves as Episcopal Vicar for Life and Health and Archdiocesan Director of Vocations. He has degrees in history, law, philosophy, and theology, with a doctorate in bioethics from the University of Oxford. His academic life has included lecturing in several countries, and extensively throughout Australia, as well as publishing many books and articles on bioethics and morality. He is a member of the Australian Bishops' Committees for Doctrine and Morals and Family and Life and is also a member of the Pontifical Academy for Life. He is the youngest Catholic bishop in Australia.

Notes

I acknowledge with gratitude the assistance of Hayden Ramsay, Bill Muehlenberg and Brett Doyle.

1. A few weeks ago Judge J. Thomas Merten in the U.S. District Court in Kansas held that mandatory reporting of sexual abuse of minors was unconstitutional because children have a right to sexual self-expression and to privacy: "Kansas judge blocks sex reporting law," *Reuters* July 26 2004. Recently the U.K. Health Department likewise decided to allow children as young as 14 to have abortion without parental consent or even notification: Peter Hitchens, "State of decay," *The Spectator* 7 August 2004, 23.

2. Peter Singer, "Heavy Petting," nerve.com, reviewing Midas Dekkers, *Dearest Pet: On Bestiality* (trans. Paul Vincent, London: Verso, 1994); cf. Kathryn Lopez, "Peter Singer Strikes Again: This could be your kid's teacher," *National Review* 5 March 2001.

3. David Popenoe & Barbara Dafoe Whitehead, *The State of Our Unions: The Social Health of Marriage in America* (Rutgers NJ: National Marriage Project, 2004).

4. Though this has recently been resisted by the Australian Federal Parliament and the California Supreme Court, it has at the time of writing this paper already been allowed by the governments or courts of Holland, Belgium, British Columbia, Manitoba, Massachusetts, Ontario, Quebec, Washington state and Yukon province; local officials have also conducted or permitted same-sex 'marriages' in California, Alaska and DC and by courts in and state. Civil unions have been recognized for same-sex couples in much of Scandinavia and in several states/provinces of North America. The Spanish Government plans to introduce same-sex 'marriage' later this year. On the day I read this paper the courts in Nova Scotia declared in favour of same-sex 'marriage'.

5. In *Re Kevin (validity of marriage of transsexual)* [2001] FamCA 1074 Chisholm J in the Family Court of Australia held that for the purposes of marriage law a transsexual man who is 'socially' a woman could be the wife in a marriage.

6. A few months ago a 35-year-old Frenchwoman, Christelle Demichel, married her dead boyfriend, becoming by fiat of the French President both married and widowed in the one act: Associated Press, 11 February 2004.

7. In several places children have been conceived with the sperm of dead men, sometimes extracted as the man was dying or soon after his death.

8. Since the passage of 'no fault' divorce laws in most countries all that is commonly required is that the spouses live apart for a year and the contract can then be broken.

9. It is hard to see on what basis polygamy can be resisted once de facto marriage, gay marriage, and easy divorce have been allowed. Two years ago the Law Commission of Canada produced a report on adult relationships which stated that the Commission could see no reason in principle to limit registration of relationships to two people.

10. Brigitte Berger & Peter Berger, *The War Over the Family* (Garden City NY: Anchor Press/Doubleday, 1983) and Patrick Buchanan, *The Death of the West* (New York: St Martin's Griffin, 2002). Bill Muehlenberg, *Deconstructing the Family* (Melbourne: Australian Family Association, 2004) helpfully lists the following titles addressing the modern campaign against the family: Philip Abbott, *The Family on Trial* (University Park: Pennsylvania State UP, 1981); William Bennett, *The Broken Hearth* (New York: Doubleday, 2001); Bryce Christensen, *Utopia Against the Family* (San Francisco: Ignatius Press, 1990); William Gairdner, *The War Against the Family* (Toronto: Stoddart, 1992); George Grant, *The Family Under Siege* (Minneapolis: Bethany House, 1994); Sylvia Ann Hewlett & Cornell West, *The War Against Parents* (New York: Houghton Mifflin, 1998); Rita Kramer, *In Defense of the Family* (New York: Basic Books, 1983); Christopher Lasch, *Haven in a Heartless World: The Family Besieged* (New York: W.W. Norton, 1977); Dana Mack, *The Assault on Parenthood* (San Francisco: Encounter Books, 1997); James Q. Wilson, *The Marriage Problem: How Our Culture Has Weakened Families* (New York: Harper Collins, 2002). See also Maggie Gallagher, *The Abolition of Marriage: How We Destroy Lasting Love* (Washington DC: Regnery, 1996).

11. Buchanan, *The Death of the West*. US birthrates have not yet fallen as drastically as those in Europe and Australia, but are likely to continue to fall.

12. While the USFDA has not yet allowed over-the-counter provision of the 'morning-after pill' without doctor's prescription, many other countries have done so, such as the U.K. and Australia. Behind the campaign for ready access to so-called 'emergency' contraception is the notion that new children are intruders, the enemy, something nasty to be warded off at all costs, even with hazardous drugs. Their appearance – indeed the very thought of them – sounds emergency alarm bells. Instead of being socialized to love our lives, our marriages and our children we are increasingly being taught by our culture to fear our fertility, to withhold it even from our spouses, to drug-bomb it out of existence. Instead of being encouraged to be generous toward the future, we are rewarded for living only for today. The Western world is becoming sterile in the process and it is doing its level best to infect the rest of the world with a similar infertility.

13. *cf.* Donald De Marco, *Biotechnology and the Assault on Parenthood* (San Francisco: Ignatius Press, 1991).

14. The Catholic Church teaches that "men and women with homosexual ten-

dencies must be accepted with respect, compassion, and sensitivity. Every sign of unjust discrimination in their regard should be avoided." Congregation for the Doctrine of the Faith, *On the Pastoral Care of Homosexual Persons* (1986); Pontifical Council for the Family, *Family, Marriage and "De Facto" Unions* (2000); Congregation for the Doctrine of the Faith, *Considerations regarding Proposals to give Legal Recognition to Unions between Homosexual Persons* (2003).

15. Hayden Ramsay, "Philosophy of the Family," *Lexicon: Termini ambigui e discussi su famiglia, vita e questioni etiche* (Rome, 2002); Bill Muehlenberg, *The Historicity and Universality of the Natural Family* (Melbourne: Australian Family Association, 2004). Kingsley Davis, in *Contemporary Marriage: Perspectives on a Changing Institution* (New York: Russell Sage, 1985), 19, notes that: "compared to most other aspects of human society, marriage has changed surprisingly little. As an institution, contemporary wedlock bears an indubitable likeness to marriage three centuries or three millennia ago. It still has the same essential character that it had then." Wilson, *The Marriage Problem*, 54: "Marriage, broadly defined, is a universal feature of all societies and apparently has been since records first were kept."

16. Moira Eastman, "Myths of Marriage and Family," in David Popenoe, Jean Bethke Elshtan, & David Blankenhorn (Eds), *Promises to Keep* (Rowman & Littlefield, 1996), 38, points out that "the fact that family has varied from time to time and place to place does not prove that family is a recent historical invention, or that it has not existed in all societies." Wilson, *The Marriage Problem*, 24, concurs: "In every community and for as far back in time as we can probe, the family exists and children are expected, without exception, to be raised in one. By a family I mean a lasting, socially enforced obligation between a man and a woman that authorizes sexual congress and the supervision of children. Its style and habits will vary greatly, of course, but nowhere do we find a place where children are regularly raised by a mother who has no claims on the father." Ferdinand Mount, *The Subversive Family* (London: Jonathan Cape, 1982), 153: "The family is not an historical freak. If the evidence we have put together is correctly interpreted, the family as we know it today – small, two-generation, nuclear, based on choice and affection...is neither a novelty nor the product of unique historical forces. The way most people live today is the way most people have preferred to live when they had the chance." Michael Levin, *Feminism and Freedom* (New Brunswick NJ: Transaction Books, 1987), 283–84: "Human beings have always been reared within 'traditional' families. It is true that in many cultures children are raised after infancy by communal groups, but these groups are generally composed of mothers who know each other. Not only has there never been an open, democratic society not based on the family, there has never been any society of any sort not based on the family. In every society a child's upbringing has been the responsibility of close blood relations, with his daily care a female task and

his protection a male task." See Muehlenberg, *Deconstructing the Family*.

17. Steven Nock, "A Comparison of Marriages and Cohabiting Relationships," *Journal of Family Issues* 16 (1995), 53–76; Ronald Rindfuss & Audrey Van den Heuvel, "Cohabitation: a Precursor to Marriage or an Alternative to Being Single?" *Population and Development Review* 16(4) (Dec 1990), 702–26.

18. See note 6 above.

19. John Paul II, *Familiaris Consortio: Apostolic Exhortation on the Family* (1981) and *The Theology of the Body: Human Love in the Divine Plan* (Boston: Books & Media, 1997). *Cf.* Donald Asci, *The Conjugal Act as a Personal Act* (San Francisco: Ignatius, 2002); John Kippley, *Sex and the Marriage Covenant* (Cincinnati: Couple to Couple League, 1991; Richard Hogan & John LeVoir, *Covenant of Love: Pope John Paul II on Sexuality, Marriage and Family in the Modern World* (New York: Image Books, 1984); Mary Shivanandan, *Crossing the Threshold of Love: A New Vision of Marriage* (Edinburgh: T & T Clark, 1999); Vincent Walsh, *Pope John Paul II's Theology of the Body: A Simplified Version* (Merion: Key of David, 2002); Christopher West, *Good News about Sex and Marriage: Answers to Your Honest Questions about Catholic Teaching* (Ann Arbor MI: Servant Publications, 2000); Christopher West, *Theology of the Body Explained: A Commentary on John Paul II's "Gospel of the Body"* (Boston: Pauline Books, 2003). See also the recent Vatican document: Congregation for the Doctrine of the Faith, *On the Collaboration of Men and Women in the Church and in the World* (2004).

20. Vatican Council II, *Lumen Gentium: Dogmatic Constitution on the Church* (1964), §§31–35; Vatican Council II, *Gaudium et Spes: Pastoral Constitution on the Church in the Modern World* (1965) §§47–52; John Paul II, *Familiaris Consortio: Apostolic Exhortation on the Family* (1981); John Paul II, *Christifideles Laici: Apostolic Exhortation on the Vocation and the Mission of the Lay Faithful in the Church and in the World* (1988); John Paul II, *Letter to Families* (1994); Congregation for the Doctrine of the Faith, *On the Pastoral Care of Homosexual Persons* (1986); Congregation for the Doctrine of the Faith, *Considerations regarding Proposals to Give Legal Recognition to Unions between Homosexual Persons* (2003); Congregation for the Doctrine of the Faith, *On Some Questions Regarding the Participation of Catholics in Political Life* (2003); Congregation for the Doctrine of the Faith, *On the Collaboration of Men and Women in the Church and in the World* (2004); Pontifical Council for the Family, *Family, Marriage and "De Facto" Unions* (2000). Dan Cere notes that the "current debates over sexual difference, love and marriage have generated conflicts that are deep and fundamental," raising dilemmas which are "painful and often personal" ("Justice, gender, and love: liberal and communitarian perspectives on the domestic church", *Église et Théologie*, 26 (1995), 225–252). The question of gender or sexual difference is, according to Luce Irigaray, "the issue" of our age and accordingly "the issue in our time which

could be our 'salvation' if we thought it through": *An Ethic of Sexual Difference* (Ithaca NY: Cornell UP, 1993), 5. Much of the debate is driven philosophically and Cere usefully examines its theoretical antecedents. He notes how the protagonists align themselves around two normative poles. The first group (after Rousseau) views marriage, sexual difference and spousal relations from the standpoint of shared meaning, love, complementarity and intimacy. The second (after Woolstonecraft) views these relationships from the standpoint of liberal principles of justice, liberty, equality, and impartiality. Both exercise considerable sway over our allegiances.

21. See especially the writing of Germain Grisez, John Finnis, Robbie George. and Bill May.

22. Leon Kass, *Toward a More Natural Science: Biology and Human Affairs* (New York: Free Press, 1985), 237.

23. See the following surveys and the sources therein: Katherine Anderson, Don Browning and Brian Boyer (Eds), *Marriage: Just a Piece of Paper?* (Grand Rapids: Eerdmans, 2002); National Marriage Coalition, *Why Marriage Matters: Twenty-one Reasons* (Melbourne: National Marriage Coalition, 2004): this is an update of Center of the American Experiment *et al, Why Marriage Matters: Twenty-one Conclusions from the Social Sciences* (New York: Institute for American Values, 2002); Bryce Christensen (Ed), *When Families Fail... The Social Costs* (University Press of America, 1991); Robert Coombs, "Marital Status and Personal Well-being: a Literature Review," *Family Relations* 40 (1991), 97–102; E Mavis Hetherington & John Kelly, *For Better or For Worse: Divorce Reconsidered* (New York: W. W. Norton, 2002); Joyce Jacobsen, "The Household as an Economic Unit," in Joyce Jacobsen, *The Economics of Gender* (Oxford: Blackwell, 1998), 67–79; Bill Muehlenberg, *The Benefits of Marriage* (Melbourne: Australian Family Association, 2004); David Popenoe *et al* (Eds), *Promises To Keep* (Lanham: Rowman & Littlefield, 1996); Steven Stack and J Ross Eshleman, "Marital Status and Happiness: a 17-Nation Study," *Journal of Marriage and the Family* 60 (1998), 527–36; Glenn Stanton, *Why Marriage Matters: Reasons to Believe in Marriage in Postmodern Society* (Colorado Springs: Pinon, 1997); Linda Waite, "Does Marriage Matter?" *Demography* 32 (1995), 431–53; Linda Waite & Maggie Gallagher, *The Case for Marriage: Why Married People are Happier, Healthier, and Better Off Financially* (New York: Doubleday, 2000); Linda Waite *et al* (Eds), *The Ties that Bind: Perspectives on Marriage and Cohabitation* (New York: Aldine de Gruyter, 2000).

24. See the following surveys and the sources therein: Paul Amato & Alan Booth, *A Generation at Risk: Growing Up in an Era of Family Upheaval* (Cambridge MA: Harvard UP, 1997); David Blankenhorn, *Fatherless America: Confronting Our Most Urgent Social Problem* (New York: Basic Books, 1995); Bryce Christensen (Ed), *When Families Fail... The Social Costs* (University Press of America, 1991); Nicholas Davidson, "Life without Father: America's Greatest Social Catastrophe," *Policy Review* (Winter

1990); David Demo & Alan Acock, "The Impact of Divorce on Children," *Journal of Marriage & the Family* 50 (August 1988); Norman Dennis & George Erdos, *Families Without Fatherhood* (Institute of Economic Affairs, 1992); Mary Eberstadt; "Home-alone America," *Policy Review* 107 (June 2001); Maggie Gallagher, *The Age of Unwed Mothers* (Institute for American Values, 1999); House of Representatives Standing Committee on Legal and Constitutional Affairs (Australia), *To Have and to Hold: A Report of the Inquiry into Aspects of Family Services* (June 1998); Francis Ianni, *The Search For Structure: A Report on American Youth Today* (New York: Free Press, 1989); Gay Kitson & Leslie Morgan, "The Multiple Consequences of Divorce: a Decade Review," *Journal of Marriage & the Family* 52 (November 1990); Sara McLanahan & Gary Sandefur, *Growing up with a Single Parent: What Hurts, What Helps* (Cambridge MA: Harvard UP, 1994); Bill Muehlenberg, *The Case for the Two-Parent Family* (Melbourne: Australian Family Association, 2004); Bryan Rodgers, "Social and Psychological Well-being of Children from Divorced Families: Australian research findings," *Australian Psychologist*, 31(3) (November 1995), 174–82; Alice & Peter Rossi, *Of Human Bonding: Parent-Child Relations Across the Life Course* (New York: Aldine de Gruyter, 1990); Judith Wallerstein, Julia Lewis & Sandra Blakeslee, *The Unexpected Legacy of Divorce* (Hyperion Books, 2000); Lenore Weitzman & Mavis Maclean (eds), *Economic Consequences of Divorce* (OUP, 1992).

25. Paul Amato & Bruce Keith, "Parental Divorce and Adult Well-being: a Meta-analysis," *Journal of Marriage & the Family* 53 (February 1991); William Aquilino, "Impact of Childhood Family Disruption on Young Adults' Relationships with Parents," *Journal of Marriage & the Family* 56 (1994), 295–313; Bob Birrell (2001); Dan Brubeck & John Beer, "Depression, Self-esteem, Suicide Ideation, Death Anxiety, and GPA in High School Students of Divorced and Non-divorced parents," *Psychological Reports* 71 (1992); Teresa Cooney, "Young Adults' Relations with Parents: the Influence of Recent Parental Divorce," *Journal of Marriage & the Family* 56 (1994), 45–56; William Doherty & Richard Needle, "Psychological Adjustment and Substance Use among Adolescents before and after a Parental Divorce," *Child Development* 62 (1991); Sanford Dornbusch *et al*, "Single Parenthood," *Society* 30 (July 1, 1996); Robert Flewelling & Karl Bauman, "Family Structure as a Predictor of Initial Substance Use and Sexual Intercourse in Early Adolescence," *Journal of Marriage & the Family* 52 (February 1990); William Galston, "Causes of Declining Well-being among U.S. Children," in David Estlund & Martha Nussbaum (eds), *Sex, Preference, and Family* (OUP, 1997); Nadia Garnefski & Rene Diekstra, "Adolescents from One Parent, Step-parent and Intact Families; Emotional Problems and Suicide Attempts," *Journal of Adolescence* 20 (1997), 201–208; Michael Gurian, *The Good Son: Shaping the Moral Development of our Boys and Young Men* (New York: Jeremy Tarcher, 1999); T Hanson *et al*, "Windows on Divorce: Before and After," *Social Science Research* 27 (1998), 329–349; Lingxin Hao,

"Family Structure, Private Transfers, and the Economic Well-being of Families with Children," *Social Forces* 75 (1996), 269–292; William Heyes, "The Effects of Several of the Most Common Family Structures on the Academic Achievement of Eighth Graders," *Marriage & Family Review* 30 (1/2) (2000), 73–97; John Hoffman, "The Effects of Family Structure and Family Relations on Adolescent Marijuana Use*," International Journal of the Addictions* 30 (1995), 1207–1241; Sara McLanahan & Karen Booth, "Mother-only Families: Problems, Prospects and Politics," *Journal of Marriage & the Family* 51 (August 1989); Wendy Manning & Kathleen Lamb, "Adolescent Well-being in Cohabiting, Married, and Single-parent Families," *Journal of Marriage & Family.* 65(4) (November 2003), 876–893; Wendy Manning & Daniel Lichter, "Parental Cohabitation and Children's Economic Well-being," *Journal of Marriage & the Family* 58 (1996), 998–1010; Leslie Margolin, "Child Abuse by Mothers' Boyfriends: Why the Overrepresentation*?" Child Abuse & Neglect* 16 (1992); Donna Morrison & Amy Ritualo, "Routes to Children's Economic Recovery after Divorce," *American Sociological Review* 65 (Aug 2000), 560–80; Nicholas Zill *et al*, "Long-term Effects of Parental Divorce on Parent-child Relationships, Adjustment and Achievement in Young Adulthood," *Journal of Family Psychology* 7(1) (1993), 91–103; Karl Zinsmeister, "Do Children Need Fathers? The Murphy Brown question," *Crisis* (October 1992).

26. Mary Ann Glendon, "For Better or for Worse?" *Wall Street Journal* February 25 2004.

27. Vatican Council II, *Gaudium et Spes* §§42ff.

28. John Paul II, *Mulieris Dignitatem: Apostolic Letter on the Dignity of Women* (1988) §29; *cf.* John Paul II, *Familiaris Consortio*; John Paul II, *Letter to Families*; John Paul II, *Address to the ad limina of the US Bishops Region X* (27 June 1998); CDF, *On the Duties of Catholic Politicians*.

29. Aristotle, *Nicomachean Ethics* VIII, 12; cf. Muehlenberg, "Deconstructing the Family", 3.

30. Robert Nisbet, *The Twilight of Authority* (OUP, 1975), 260: "It should be obvious that family, not the individual, is the real molecule of society, the key link in the social chain of being. It is inconceivable to me that either intellectual growth or social order or the roots of liberty can possibly be maintained among a people unless the kinship tie is strong and has both functional significance and symbolic authority. On no single institution has the modern political state rested with more destructive weight than on the family. From Plato's obliteration of the family in his Republic, through Hobbes, Rousseau, Bentham, and Marx, hostility to family has been an abiding element in the West's political clerisy." *cf.* Wilson, *The Marriage Problem,* 66: "The family is not only a universal practice, it is the fundamental social unit of any society."

31. Davis, "The Meaning and Significance of Marriage," 5: "The unique trait of what is commonly called marriage is social recognition and approval ... approval of a couple's engaging in sexual intercourse and bearing and rearing offspring".

32. e.g. *Ephesians* Ch. 5.
33. *Genesis* Chs 1 & 2. See John Paul II's extraordinary exegesis in his *Theology of the Body,* note 19.
34. *Revelation* ch. 22
35 Katherine Seelye & Janet Elder, "Strong Support Found for Ban on Gay Marriage", *New York Times* December 21 2003.
36. Even before he was pope, as a young priest and bishop, ministry to families was Karol Wojty³a's No. 1 priority. As an artist-scholar he wrote *Love and Responsibility*, poems and plays specifically about relationships; as pope he has devoted so many words to family life ever since *Familiaris Consortio* (1981) and his catecheses on the *Theology of the Body*. In his diocese of Cracow he established an Institute for Marriage and the Family to prepare a new generation of leaders and servants of the family, through study and research in philosophy, theology, social science and pastoral care; this was the precursor of the worldwide John Paul II Pontifical Institute for Studies on Marriage and the Family which he began soon after his election and which now has about ten campuses around the world. John Paul's pontificate has also been marked by listening to families and about families on their home turf or at various meetings in central locations. His first synod of bishops was on the family (1980) and it led to the establishment of the Pontifical Council for the Family (1981). Also as a result of his Synod on the Family and constant prompting either personal or though the curia, there is now a network of family support services, marriage and sex education programs and other initiatives being undertaken at a local level by the Church throughout the world.

Chapter 6: The "Good of the Spouses" and Marriage as a Vocation to Holiness

William E. May, Ph.D.

Introduction

Long ago St. Augustine distinguished three cardinal goods of marriage: the *bonum prolis*, or the good of offspring who are to be begotten lovingly, nurtured humanely, and educated religiously; the *bonum fidei*, or the good of steadfast fidelity between husband and wife; and the *bonum sacramenti*, which entails both the *sacramentum vinculum* or holy bond of indissoluble unity and the *sacramentum signum*, a good found only in Christian marriages and the good of the sacrament in the strict sense as the good pointing to and inwardly participating in Christ's bridal union with his spouse, the Church.[1]

Subsequent Catholic tradition made these goods its own, constantly affirming them; in fact, Pope Pius XI structured his 1930 encyclical *Casti Connubii* around these three Augustinian goods.[2] These goods are quite familiar, and much theological literature has been devoted to them.[3]

Among these goods we do not find the "good of the spouses" (the *bonum coniugum*). Nonetheless, the very first canon on marriage in the 1983 *Code of Canon Law* declares: "The matrimonial covenant, by which a man and a woman establish between themselves a partnership for the whole of life, is by its nature ordered toward the *good of the spouses* and the procreation and education of offspring."[4] The *Catechism of the Catholic Church* reaffirms this in its opening number devoted to the sacrament of matrimony.[5] Thus the Church today identifies as the principal *ends* of marriage both the procreation and education of children and what she calls the "good of the spouses," the *bonum coniugum*, and in fact the Church names this end first.

The expression "good of the spouses," however, is very recent and was first used to designate an *end* of marriage in the revised *Code of Canon Law* in 1983. It was *not* explicitly identified as such either by

Vatican Council II[6] or by Pope John Paul II in his 1981 apostolic exhortation *Familiaris Consortio,* which he himself has described as a *"summa"* of Church teaching on marriage and the family.[7] Nor have theologians given much thought to the meaning of this good.[8] Canon lawyers, however, have debated its meaning to considerable extent. In fact, a doctoral study in canon law by Dominic Kimengich offers a helpful summary, analysis, and critique of the positions taken by canon lawyers regarding the nature of the *bonum coniugum.*[9] Kimengich offers a tentative formulation of the essential content of this good. According to him, it consists in:

> ...the growth and maturing of the spouses as persons, through the aids, comforts, and consolations, but also through the demands and hardships, of conjugal life, when lived according to God's plan. The full view of the scope and content of the "good of the spouses" emerges when we recall that the spouses are called to eternal life, which is the one definitive bonum of the spouses.[10]

Kimengich here suggests that the *bonum coniugum* is, in the last analysis, found in the sanctification of the spouses. I believe that this is true, and thus I will try to show that the "good of the spouses" ultimately consists in the holiness that husbands and wives are meant to attain precisely in and through their married life, and that the teaching of Pope Pius XI in his 1930 encyclical *Casti connubii* is central in understanding this. I will then consider the *means,* i.e., the human acts, that spouses must choose in order to achieve this primary and essential end of marriage, considering as well the indispensable *conditions* needed if spouses are to be capable of choosing these means. The principal conditions, I believe, are the sexual complementarity of husband and wife, their mutual respect for one another, and the virtue of fidelity required to overcome the inevitable difficulties that they encounter, and the contribution that overcoming these difficulties makes to the attainment of the "good of the spouses." I will conclude with the beautiful "marriage exhortation" used in the United States prior to Vatican Council II, insofar as I consider this to be an eloquent description of what the "good of the spouses" entails.

The Vocation to Holiness and the "Good of the Spouses"

To show the intimate, indeed essential bond between the "good of the spouses" and the vocation of husband and wife to holiness *precisely insofar as they are husband and wife*, it is imperative to consult the "sources" for canon 1055, where the "good of the spouses" was first identified as an essential end of marriage. The Pontifical Commission for the Interpretation of the Code in its annotated version of the new Code in 1989 enumerated these sources. In my opinion, the most central of these sources, as noted already, is the teaching of Pius XI in *Casti Connubii*.[11] But before looking at the thought of Pius XI, however, let us look at the other sources which the Commission identified. Three are passages from Vatican Council II, and these passages are also very important in showing that the "good of the spouses" ultimately consists in their sanctification. The first is the chapter of its Dogmatic Constitution on the Church, *Lumen Gentium*, devoted to the theme, "The Universal Call to Holiness."[12] The second is from the same Constitution identifying marriage as a *specific* vocation to holiness.[13] The third is found in the Council's presentation of the dignity of marriage and the family in the Pastoral Constitution on the Church in the Modern World, *Gaudium et Spes*, where it is declared that husbands and wives "increasingly further their own perfection and their mutual sanctification" by fulfilling their conjugal and family roles.[14]

Another source is a passage from Pope Pius XII's 1951 Address to the Italian Union of Midwives in which he spoke of the "personal perfecting of the spouses" as a *"secondary* end" of marriage.[15] Finally, the Commission referred to the passage in Pius XI's *Casti Connubii*, where he declared that married love "demands not only mutual aid but must have as *its primary purpose* (emphasis added) that man and wife help each other day by day *in forming and perfecting themselves in the interior life* (emphasis in original), so that through their partnership in life they may advance ever more and more in virtue, and *above all that they may grow in true love* toward God and their neighbor."[16] I believe that this statement of Pius XI, together with one immediately following it, is the major source of the teaching that the "good of the spouses" is an essential end of marriage.

Surprisingly, the Pontifical Commission did *not* call attention to the paragraph in *Casti Connubii* immediately following this citation. This is surprising because this text is of utmost importance in understanding the *bonum coniugum* as an end of marriage and how this end is intrinsically related to the spouses' vocation to holiness precisely as spouses. In it Pope Pius XI declared:

> ...[t]his inward molding of husband and wife, this determined effort to perfect each other, can in a very real sense, as the *Roman Catechism* teaches, be said to be the *chief reason* and *purpose of*

matrimony, provided matrimony be looked at *not in the restricted sense* as instituted for the proper conception and education of the child, but *more widely* as the blending of life as a whole and the mutual interchange and sharing thereof.[17]

The text of *Roman Catechism* (popularly known as *The Catechism of the Council of Trent*) to which Pius refers reads as follows: "The first reason to marry is the instinctive mutual attraction of the two sexes to form a *stable companionship* of the two persons, as a basis for *mutual happiness* and *help* amid the trials of life extending even to sickness and old age."[18] Comparing this text with Pius's statement, we can see that the pope has in reality provided us with a gloss, and a most important one, on this text. I think that from what has been said thus far we can conclude that Pius XI is here, in effect, speaking of what the 1983 *Code* will call the "good of the spouses," and that he identifies it as a primary *end* of marriage. Pius XI clearly shows that this end consists in the endeavor of the spouses, rooted in their unique and exclusive love for one another, to help each other perfect themselves and grow in *holiness.* In short, a married person's path to the holiness God wants him to have has a name: his or her spouse.

Means to Achieve the "Good of the Spouses" and the Indispensable Conditions Required

If the spouses are to attain the "good of the spouses," a primary end toward which their marriage is by its very nature ordered, and to which they commit themselves when they marry, they must choose the means necessary for attaining that end. These means are the human acts that spouses are supposed to freely choose, i.e., the acts "proper and exclusive" to spouses. And to be able to do these things, indispensable conditions are required. Here I will first consider the human acts that spouses must freely choose as means of attaining the "good of the spouses," then the indispensable conditions required if they are to choose these means.

The Means Necessary: the Acts "Proper and Exclusive" to Spouses

These acts are the following: (1) freely to choose to "give" themselves to one another and to "receive" on another, i.e., to give and received conjugal or marital love; (2) freely to choose to engage in the conjugal or marital act; and (3) freely to choose to cooperate with God in giving life to new human persons and to "welcome that life lovingly, nurture it humanely, and educate it in the love of service of God and neighbor."

1. "Giving" and "Receiving" One Another: Conjugal Love

An act necessary as a chosen means for attaining the "good of the spouses" is the act whereby husbands and wives "give" themselves to one another and "receive" one another so that they become "one." In fact, a man and a woman establish their marriage only when, forswearing all others, they freely choose to "consent" to marry one another. Through this act of "irrevocable personal consent,"[19] they "give" themselves to each other and "receive" one another and by doing so make themselves to be husband and wife, spouses. They freely give to themselves a new identity: this man becomes this woman's husband, and this woman becomes this man's husband, and together they become spouses. In short, by irrevocably "giving" themselves to one another and "receiving" one another in marriage, a man and a woman capacitate themselves to do what married persons are supposed to do, and first of all to give and receive conjugal or marital love, which is unique and proper to spouses.[20] Moreover, through this act they commit themselves to "give and receive" one another throughout their entire married lives.

2. Choosing to Engage in the Conjugal or Marital Act as Unitive

Non-married men and woman can choose to engage in genital sex, but they cannot choose to engage in the conjugal act. Genital sex between non-married men and women is *not* an act that *unites* two irreplaceable and non-substitutable persons, but is rather an act that simply *joins* two persons who are in principle replaceable, substitutable, and disposable. The conjugal or marital act, on the contrary, *unites two persons who are irreplaceable, non-substitutable, and non-disposable.* And the reason why these persons, husbands and wives, are such is that they have freely chosen to make each other irreplaceable, non-substitutable, and non-disposable by irrevocably "giving" and "receiving" one another in marriage. This shows that the marital act is not simply a genital act between a man and a woman who happen to be married. It is in truth an act that inwardly participates in their marital union; it is an act of "giving" and "receiving." It is an act honoring the "unitive" meaning of human sexuality.

3. Choosing to Engage in the Conjugal Act as Procreative

Non-married men and women have the natural capacity, by virtue of their sexuality and endowment with sexual organs, to engage in genital sex and through it to generate human life. But they do not have the capacity to *generate human life* lovingly, nourish it humanely, and educate it in the love and service of God and neighbor, as St. Augustine so well expressed matters centuries ago. They do not have this capacity because they have failed to choose to make themselves *fit* to give new human life the *home* to which it has right, the home where it can take root and grow as God wants it to grow.[21] But husbands and wives, precisely because they have irrevocably given themselves to one another in marriage, have made themselves *fit* for this noble task. Pope Paul VI brought this out beautifully in his encyclical *Humanae Vitae* when he wrote: "because of its intrinsic nature the conjugal act, while uniting husband and wife in the most intimate of bonds, also *makes them fit [eos idoneos facit]* to bring forth new life according to the laws written in their very nature as male and female" (no. 12, par. 2). In other words, husbands and wives, by irrevocably giving and receiving one another in marriage have capacitated themselves to honor the unitive and procreative meanings of human sexuality and the conjugal act; they have made themselves, obviously with God's help, to use the means necessary for attaining the "good of the spouses."

The Church (cf. canon 1055, par. 1 and *The Catechism of the Catholic Church,* no. 1601) recognizes that the procreation and education of children is an *end* of marriage distinct from the end identified as the "good of the spouses." Nonetheless, the two ends are inherently interrelated. Openness to the end of procreating and educating children is essential if spouses are to attain the "good of the spouses." This is true even of couples who are naturally sterile. When such couples unite in the conjugal act, they do nothing to "close" it to the gift of new human life. Their conjugal act is and remains the *kind of human act "per se" apt for the generation of human life according to laws inscribed into the very being of man and woman.*

Indispensable Conditions Required to Engage in the Means Necessary to Attain the "Good of the Spouses."

I now turn to consider the indispensable condition making it possible for spouses to "give" and "receive" one another. These indispensable conditions are their sexual complementarity and the virtue of fidelity which includes "respect" for the personhood of the spouses.

1. The Sexual Complementarity of Husband and Wife

Husbands and wives, while equal in their dignity as persons, are complementary in their sexuality, and I will explore the nature of this complementarity. It is obviously a vast topic.[22] It is this complementarity, however, that enables them to "give" themselves to one another and to "receive" one another as well as to carry out responsibilities as spouses and parents in the light of John Paul II's "theology of the body."[23]

A. The Nuptial Meaning of the Body and the "Gift" of the Man Person to the Female Person and Vice Versa

John Paul II offers profound reflections on the first man's cry of joy on awakening from the "sleep" into which the Lord God had cast him when, discovering the woman who had been fashioned from his rib, he cried out: "This at last is bone of my bone and flesh of my flesh..." (Gen 2.24). John Paul II says that these words express "the subjectively beatifying beginning of man's existence in the world" (14.4). Man now emerges, the Holy Father continues:

> ...in the dimension of the mutual gift, the expression of which – and for that very reason the expression of his existence as a person – is the human body in all the original truth of its masculinity and feminity...Masculinity-femininity – namely sex – is the original sign of a creative donation and of an awareness on the part of man, male-female, of a gift lived so to speak in an original way. Such is the meaning with which sex enters the theology of the body. That beatifying "beginning" of man's being and existing, as male and female, is connected with the revelation and discovery of the meaning of the body, which can be called "nuptial" (14.3–4).

In short, the male's body, precisely because of its *sexual* character, its masculinity, is a sign of the gift of the male person to the female person and vice versa. This nuptial meaning, moreover, is intimately linked to the "blessing of fertility." "Genesis 2.24," John Paul says, "speaks of the finality of man's masculinity and femininity in the life of the spouses-parents. Uniting with each other so closely as to become 'one flesh,' they will subject, in a way, their humanity to the blessing of fertility, namely, 'procreation, of which the first narrative speaks (Gen 1.28)" (14.6). In addition, the pope continues:

> The human body, with its sex, and its masculinity and femininity seen in the very mystery of creation...includes right "from the beginning" the "nuptial" attribute, that is, the capacity of expressing love: that love precisely in which the man-person becomes a gift and – by means of this gift – fulfills the very meaning of his being and existence...it is indispensable that man may be able to "give himself," in order that he may become a gift, in order that he will be able to "fully discover his true self" in a "sincere giving of himself" [see *Gaudium et Spes*, 24] (15.1–2).

John Paul II himself develops the meaning of "gift" in later cycles of his "theology of the body" addresses, in particular those devoted to the meaning of marriage as a sacrament. I will not here go into detail by presenting John Paul II's further developments of the meaning of "gift." It is, however, most important to reflect on (1) a passage exceptionally significant for showing the "complementarity" of male and female precisely as "gifts" to each other in their bodily, sexual union, and (2) on the way he shows that openness to the gift of fertility and to motherhood and fatherhood deepen the body's nuptial meaning. A passage I consider of special importance for understanding how male and female complement each other as "gifts" is the following:

> ...If the woman, in the mystery of creation, is the one who was "given" to the man, the latter, on his part, in receiving her as a gift in the full truth of her person and femininity, thereby enriches her, and at the same time he, too, is enriched. The man is enriched not only through her, who gives him her own person and femininity, but also through the gift of himself. The man's giving of himself, in response to that of the woman, is an enrichment of himself. In fact, *there is in it*, as it were, *the specific essence of his masculinity, which, through the reality of the body and of sex, reaches the deep recesses of the "possession of self," thanks to which he is capable both of giving himself and of receiving the other's gift.* The man, therefore, not only accepts the gift, but at the same time is received as a gift by the woman, in the revelation of the interior spiritual essence of his masculinity, together with the whole truth of his body and sex...Subsequently, this acceptance, in which the man finds himself again through the "sincere gift of himself," becomes in him the source of a new and deeper enrichment of the woman. The exchange is mutual, and in it the reciprocal effects of the "sincere gift," and of the "finding oneself again," are revealed and grow (17.6; emphasis added).

I have emphasized the passage in which the pope says that the specific essence of man's masculinity enables him to *give himself* and *to receive the other's gift*. I do so because I believe that this passage shows that John Paul II, while recognizing that both the male person and the woman person are called to "give" and to "receive," suggests that the man is the one who emphatically *gives in a receiving way*, whereas the woman is the one who emphatically *receives in a giving way*.[24]

This can be illustrated if we reflect on the conjugal or spousal act, whereby husband and wife literally become "one flesh," as a "giving" and a "receiving." In the marital act, husband and wife "give" themselves to one another and "receive" one another. Yet they do so in strikingly different and complementary ways, for it is an act made possible precisely by reason of their sexual differences and the nuptial meaning of the body. The wife does not have a penis; therefore, in this act of marital union she cannot enter the body, the person, of her husband, whereas he can and does personally enter into her body-person. He gives himself to her and by doing so he receives her. On the other hand, she is uniquely capable of receiving her husband personally into her body, her self, and in so doing she gives herself to him. The wife's receiving of her husband in a giving sort of way is just as essential to the unique meaning of this act as is her husband's giving of himself to her in a receiving sort of way. The husband cannot, in this act, give himself to his wife unless she gives herself to him by receiving him, nor can she receive him in this self-giving way unless he gives himself to her in this receiving way.[25] As the philosopher Robert Joyce says: "The man does not force himself upon the woman, but gives himself in a receiving manner. The woman does not simply submit herself to the man, but receives him in a giving manner."[26]

Moreover, the God whom male and female image in complementary ways is both transcendent, the "wholly other," the superabundant giver of good gifts, and immanent, the One who is within us, sustaining us in our being and longing to welcome us into our heavenly home and give our hearts refreshment and peace. The wondrous mystery of God's transcendence-immanence, otherness-closeness has, I believe, been beautifully expressed by Henry Van Dyck in the lyrics to the hymn, "Joyful, Joyful, We Adore Thee," where he addresses God as "the wellspring of the joy of living and the ocean depth of happy rest." Both men and women are called upon to image God as the "wellspring of the joy of living and the ocean depth of happy rest." But the man, in his way of imaging God, emphasizes his transcendent, superabundant goodness, his glory as the "wellspring of the joy of living," whereas the woman, in her way of imaging God, emphasizes his immanence, his "withinness," his glory as the "ocean depth of happy rest." The wife/mother, who receives human life in a giving sort of way, welcomes her children and her husband within herself, giving them happy rest, whereas the husband/father is the one who should bring to his wife and children the "good things" of creation; he is called to be, within the family, the "wellspring of the joy of living."

I will return to this asymmetrical complementarity of male and female later, in considering their distinctive roles as mothers and fathers. But first I want to call attention to some texts in which John Paul II shows how openness to fertility and to motherhood and fatherhood deepen our understanding of the "nuptial meaning" of the body and male-female complementarity.

In Genesis 4.1–2 we read: "Adam knew Eve his wife, and she conceived and bore Cain, saying, 'I have gotten a man with the help of the Lord.' And again, she bore his brother Abel (Gen 4.1–2). Commenting on this text John Paul II affirms that the "knowledge" spoken of by Genesis 4.1 reveals to us both the *mystery of both femininity and masculinity*. The pope brings this out very clearly:

> …According to Genesis 4.1, the one who knows is the man, and the one who is known is the woman-wife, as if the specific determination of the woman, through her own body and sex, hid what constitutes the very depth of her femininity…It should be noted that in the "knowledge" of which Genesis 4.1 speaks, *the mystery of femininity is manifested and revealed completely by means of* motherhood…The woman stands before the man as a mother, the subject of the new human life that is conceived and develops within her, and from her is born into the world. Likewise, *the mystery of man's masculinity, that is, the generative and "fatherly" meaning of his body, is also thoroughly revealed* (21.2; emphasis added).

To put matters another way, the conjugal act, through which husband and wife become literally one flesh when the husband gives himself to his wife in a receiving way and she receives him in a giving way, opens the spouses up to the gift of fertility and to a new revelation of the mystery of their complementary sexuality, namely, their capacity for motherhood and fatherhood.

B. Spouses as mothers and fathers

Among the means necessary if spouses are to attain the "good of the spouses" is their responsible exercise of motherhood and fatherhood. The complementary differences of men and women noted already are manifested in their social behavior, as numerous studies point out.[27] As a whole, women tend to respond to situations as entire persons, with their minds, bodies, and emotions integrated, whereas men tend to respond in a more diffuse and differentiated manner. On the whole, women are more oriented toward caring for personal needs, whereas men, on the whole, are more inclined to formulate and pursue long-range goals and to reach objectives that they have set for themselves. These major tendencies seem to correspond to the view that the man emphasizes otherness and differentiation, exteriority, and transcendence, superabundance, while the woman emphasizes sameness and withinness, interiority, depth, and rest.

The Congregation for the Doctrine of the Faith, reflecting on the truth that women are oriented toward caring for persons and their needs, offers a helpful insight women's sexuality and the importance of feminine values for the life of society. In its 2004 "Letter to the Bishops of the Catholic Church on the Collaboration of Men and Women in the Church and in the World" The CDF declared:

> Among the fundamental values linked to women's actual lives is what has been called a "capacity for the other"...This intuition is linked to women's physical capacity to give life. Whether lived out or remaining potential, this capacity is a reality that structures the female personality in a profound way. It allows her to acquire maturity very quickly, and gives a sense of the seriousness of life and its responsibilities. A sense and a respect for what is concrete develop within her, opposed to abstractions which are so often fatal for the existence of individuals and society. It is women, in the end, who even in very desperate situations, as attested by history past and present, possess a singular capacity to persevere in adversity, to keep life going even in extreme situations, to hold tenaciously to the future, and finally to remember with tears the value of every human life.[28]

These tendencies are reflected in their roles within the family, as we can see by considering the woman as mother and the man as father, following John Paul II's lead.

(1) Woman as Mother. When new human life comes to be in and through the marital act, it comes to be *within* the wife/mother. This new life, like every human life is, as John Paul II says, entrusted "to each and every other human being, but in a special way the human being is entrusted to woman."[29] The mother, the pope says elsewhere:

> ...accepts and loves as a person the child she is carrying in her womb. This unique contact with the new human being developing within her gives rise to an attitude toward human beings – not only towards her own child but every human being – which profoundly marks the woman's personality. It is commonly thought that women are more capable than men of paying attention to another person and that motherhood develops this predisposition even more. The man – even with his sharing in parenthood – always remains "outside" the process of pregnancy and the baby's birth; in many ways he has to *learn* his own *"fatherhood" from the mother...*[30]

Note how, in motherhood, the woman's sexuality as a "receiving in a giving way" and as symbolizing the withinness of being and God as the "ocean depth of happy rest" is manifested. She receives the child in a giving way and her body is, as it were, the ocean depth of happy rest where the child finds his or her first home. Moreover, what the pope has to say here about the woman's "unique intuition" and "understanding" of what is going on within her fits in well with what we have seen about the psychic-spiritual life of women. A woman is, precisely because of her sexuality and her way of imaging God, uniquely prepared to receive new human life lovingly and give it the care it needs to take root and grow. Indeed, the biologically determined relationship between mother and child, whom she nurtures in her womb and suckles at her breast seems to "shape those qualities usually associated with mothering: unconditional availability, receptivity, and tenderness."[31]

(2) Man as Father. A woman becomes a mother more or less "naturally." As one contemporary writer puts it, "simply stated, an adult female will be naturally transformed into a social mother when she bears a child." But the same author goes on to say, "there is no corresponding natural transformation for a male."[32] A father, as Pope John Paul II himself notes in a passage cited above (*Mulieris Dignitatem,* 18) has to "learn his own 'fatherhood'" – and, he says, he learns this from the mother; and, I would add, from his own father. But the wife-mother has to let her husband *be* a father by allowing him to become involved with his own children. Their own well-being requires his loving presence.

The husband-father, John Paul II emphasizes, has the glorious mission of "revealing and reliving on earth the very Fatherhood of God" (cf. Eph 3.15); and, as such, has a leadership role in the family insofar as he is "called upon to ensure the harmonious and united development of all the members of the family."[33] His own masculinity serves to prepare him to do so. He is to give himself in a receiving way both to his wife and to his children, and as the one who must make himself welcome into the communion of mother and child he is the one who should be the wellspring of the joy of life.

Moreover, as we have seen already, men tend to be more differentiated than women in their responses to persons and situations, to be more goal-oriented; their sexual identity depends to a much greater extent than does a woman's on what they do. While a woman nurtures, a man, as Benedict Ashley, O.P., puts it, "tends to *construct,* i.e., to impose an order on things, whether it is the simple physical fact of initiating pregnancy, providing the home as shelter and protection, or the more spiritual tasks of disciplining the children physically and mentally, or undertaking the work of the wider social order. Where the woman *allows* a child to grow, the father *causes* the child to grow."[34]

Like the mother, the father has an indispensable role to play in the education of his children, a role complementary to hers. Precisely because of the characteristics that define a mother as a woman (interiority, withinness, depth of being, tranquility or peacefulness as the "ocean depth of happy rest") she has a predominant role to play in educating her children when they are very young and when their personal needs are of such paramount importance. The father, too, has great responsibility here in caring for them and treating them with tenderness and affection. But his role in their education becomes more and more central as they mature and enter into their teens. He must help introduce them to the external world of work; he must watch over their friends; he must help them avoid being corrupted by seductive hedonists. As his sons mature and grow in strength, they will (ordinarily) soon be much stronger than their mother and their sisters – and their father as well. They may be tempted to abuse their strength by seeking to dominate their mother and sisters; hence they must be taught, and taught by their father, that men who are true to their vocation do not tyrannize women or lord it over them because of superior physical strength. They must be disciplined, and the father is the one chiefly responsible for doing this. And a father's daughters need to have a man – their father – affirm them in their femininity and show them, by his faithful love of their mother, that they must treasure themselves as female persons and not allow males to exploit them for their sexual values.

2. The Need for Fidelity and Respect

Overcoming marital difficulties contributes to the "good of the spouses," but there is need for fidelity and respect. In a memorable and very wise passage, Pope Pius XII nicely articulated *one major key* to happiness in marriage. This Pontiff declared that:

> ...Some would like to maintain that happiness in married life is in direct ratio to the mutual enjoyment of marital relations. This is not so. On the contrary, happiness in married life is in direct ratio to the respect that husband and wife have for each other, even in the intimate act of marriage. Not that they should regard what nature offers them and God has given them as immoral and refuse it, but because the respect and mutual esteem which arise from it are one of the strongest elements of a love which is all the more pure because it is the more tender.[35]

Mutual respect is central to happiness in marriage to achieving the *bonum coniugum*. Nothing is so destructive of marital friendship and unity as the "putting down" of one's spouse – a temptation that is perhaps more frequent for husbands than for wives. Both the equal dignity of husband and wife as persons and the "good of the spouses" require this mutual respect.

In order to maintain mutual respect in marriage and to have the strength to keep going in the midst of difficulties and disappointments, the virtue of marital fidelity is indispensable. This is one of the basic ingredients of the "good of the spouses." Fidelity in marriage is analogous to the virtue of theological faith. That virtue, which, as Germain Grisez has said, is "the foundation of the Christian life," and entails "openness to God who remains hidden from us even as he reveals and communicates himself to us. It is for the sake of maintaining openness to God that faith must also take the form of a steadfast conviction of the truthfulness and trustworthiness of the divine Truth who promises us intimate knowledge of himself in the unending joy of heavenly intercourse." Similarly, marital fidelity is a "commitment of one's whole life to the true self of another. In this commitment one opens oneself to the reality of one's husband and wife, a reality which can never be known in advance. As God remains a mystery to us, so in a way does our marital partner remain mystery to us, for we remain mystery even to ourselves."[36]

Our spouse, like ourselves, is a human person and, as such, is imperfect here and now. His or her defects and limitations, like our own, are obvious. And if our love was not perfect to begin with – and whose love ever is? – the one we once found so charming and attractive will inevitably disappoint us again and again. For, as Grisez also says, "in every love, to the extent that it is an imperfect love, I ask another to treat me as if I were God. No one can satisfy such a demand, and no one should try to satisfy it. And so every imperfect love disappoints" and one is tempted to infidelity and/or to resentment and hostility toward one's spouse.[37]

But fidelity endures when romantic love, which tends to idealize the beloved and to blind oneself to his or her human failings and is far different from authentic conjugal love, dies. Fidelity in marriage, a key to its happiness and central to the "good of the spouses," in particular when disappointments occur, is the "taking of one another without regard for future contingencies." It is a will "to accept the true self of one's beloved, a choice of this one in preference to any other – even in preference to any false self which may have to pass away. Fidelity is the will to become the person one will have to become if communion is to last and become more perfect."[38]

If a spouse is ever tempted to think that he or she ought not to have married his or her spouse but rather someone else, such a spouse should regard this temptation as an occasion of sin and immediately repel it by thanking God for the spouse he or she has been given. Deliberately to entertain thoughts of this kind is gravely sinful matter and should be recognized as such.[39]

Marriage Exhortation

I can think of no better way to conclude this paper than by reading to you the beautiful "Marriage Exhortation" which in the United States was given to every couple, just before pronouncing wedding vows up until 1969. I think it eloquently speaks to us of the "good" that the Church now identifies as the "good of the spouses." This is the text:

Dear Friends in Christ:

As you know, you are about to enter into a union which is most sacred and most serious, a union which was established by God himself. By it he gave man a share in the greatest work of creation, the work of the continuation of the human race. And in this way he sanctified human love and enabled man and woman to help each other live as children of God, by sharing a common life under his fatherly care.

Because God himself is thus its author, marriage is of its very nature a holy institution, requiring of those who enter into it a complete and unreserved giving of self. But Christ our Lord added to the holiness of marriage an even deeper meaning and a higher beauty. He referred to the love of marriage to describe his own love for his Church, that is, for the people of God whom he redeemed by his own blood. And so he gave to Christians a new vision of what married life ought to be, a life of self-sacrificing love like his own. It is for this reason that his apostle, St. Paul, clearly states that marriage is now and for all times to be considered a great mystery, intimately bound up with the supernatural union of Christ and the Church, which union is also to be its pattern.

The union is most serious, because it will bind you together for life in a relationship so close and so intimate that it will profoundly influence your whole future. That future, with its hopes and disappointments, its successes and its failures, its pleasures and its pains, its joys and its sorrows, is hidden from your eyes. You know that these elements are mingled in every life and are to be expected in your own. And so, not knowing what is before you, you take each other for better or worse, for richer or for poorer, in sickness and in health, until death.

Truly, then, these words are most serious. It is a beautiful tribute to your undoubted faith in each other, that, recognizing their full import, you are nevertheless so willing and ready to pronounce them. And because these words involve such solemn obligations, it is most fitting that you rest the security of your wedded life upon the great principle of self-sacrifice. And so you begin your married life by the voluntary and complete surrender of your individual lives in the interest of that deeper and wider life which you are to have in common. Henceforth, you belong entirely to each other; you will be one in mind, one in heart, and one in affections.

And whatever sacrifices you may hereafter be required to make to preserve this common life, always make them generously. Sacrifice is usually difficult and irksome. Only love can make it easy, and perfect love can make it a joy. We are willing to give in proportion as we love. And when love is perfect, the sacrifice is complete. God so loved the world that he gave his only begotten Son, and the Son so loved us that he gave himself for our salvation. "Greater love than this no one has, that one lay down his life for his friends."

No greater blessing can come to your married life than pure conjugal love, loyal and true to the end. May, then, this love with which you join your hands and hearts today never fail, but grow deeper and stronger as the years go on. And if true love and the unselfish spirit of perfect sacrifice guide your every action, you can expect the greatest measure of earthly happiness that may be allotted to man in this vale of tears. The rest is in the hands of God. Nor will God be wanting to your needs; he will pledge you the lifelong support of his graces in the holy sacrament which you are now going to receive.

William E. May is the Michael J. McGivney Professor of Moral Theology at the John Paul II Institute for Studies on Marriage and the Family at the Catholic University of America in Washington, D.C., where he has been teaching since 1991. From 1971 through 1991 he taught moral theology at the Catholic University of America. He is the author of more than a dozen books, notably such titles as *Marriage: The Rock on Which the Family Is Built* (Ignatius Press, 1995) and *Sex and Chastity: Reflections of a Catholic Layman, Spouse, and Parent* (Franciscan Herald Press, 1981); he is the co-author (with the late Ronald Lawler, O.F.M. Cap., and Joseph M. Boyle, Jr.) of the authoritative *Catholic Sexual Ethics: A Summary, Explanation, & Defense* (OSV Press, 1985); and he is the translator or editor of other volumes such as *Principles of Catholic Moral Life* (Franciscan Herald Press, 1980). He has also authored over 200 articles. By appointment of Pope John Paul

II, Professor May served on the International Theological Commission from 1986 through 1997. He received the *Pro Ecclesia et Pontifice* medal in 1991 and, in 1980, the Cardinal Wright Award from the Fellowship of Catholic Scholars, of which he served as President in 1987–89. In September 2003, the Holy Father appointed Professor May to be a consultor to the Congregation for the Clergy. He is married to Patricia Keck May, and they are the parents of seven children and the grandparents of twelve grandchildren.

Notes

1. St. Augustine developed his teaching on the threefold good of marriage principally in his *De bono coniugali, De nuptiis et concupiscentia, and De genesi ad literam.*

2. On this see Ramón García de Haro, *Marriage and the Family in the Documents of the Magisterium: A Course in the Theology of Marriage,* trans. William E. May (San Francisco: Ignatius Press, 1993), pp. 118–129.

3. A helpful essay on this point is Augustine Reagan, C.Ss.R., "The Perennial Value of St. Augustine's Theology of the Goods of Marriage," *Studia Moralia* (1981) 351–377.

4. *Code of Canon Law,* canon 1055, par. 1.

5. *Catechism of the Catholic Church,* no. 1601.

6. Vatican Council II did use the expression "good of the spouses" in *Gaudium et spes,* no. 48, but *not* in the sense of an *end* of marriage. In no. 48 it declared: "for the good of the spouses, of the children, and of society, this sacred bond [*sacrum vinculum*] no longer depends on human decision alone."

7. John Paul II, Addess *"Ringrazio Anzitutto a la Curia Romana,"* December 22, 1981, in *Insegnamenti di Giovanni Paolo II,* 4/2 (1981) 1215–1216.

8. In fact, the expression "good of the spouses" (*bonum coniugum*) is not even mentioned in the following very excellent works on marriage, faithful to the Magisterium, published after the publication of the 1983 revision of the *Code of Canon Law:* Peter Elliott, *What God Has Joined: The Sacramentality of Marriage* (New York: Alba House, 1989); Agostino Sarmiento, *El Matrimonio* (Pamplona: EUNSA, 1998), Francisco Gil Hellin, *El Matrimonio y la Vida Conyugal* (Valencia: Edicep C.B., 1995)*;* Germain Grisez, Chapter 8. "Marriage and Sexual Acts," in his *Living a Christian Life,* a book-length treatment of marriage in vol. 2 of his *The Way of the Lord Jesus* (Quincy, IL: Franciscan Press, 1993), pp. 553–751; Ramón García de Haro, *Marriage and Family in the Documents of The Magisterium.* Some theologians, e.g., Antonio Miralles, identify the "good of the spouses" with the old good of "mutual assistance" and discuss it only very briefly. See his *El Matrimonio* (Pamplona: EUNSA, 1993), p. 102. This view, however, is hardly correct. Dominic Kimengich and Cormac Burke offer serious criticism of this opinion, also championed by many canonists.

9. Dominic Kimengich, *The Bonum Coniugum: A Canonical Appraisal* (Romae: Pontificium Athenaeum Sanctae Crucis, 1997).

10. *Ibid*, p. 204. Kimengich's thesis was directed by Cormac Burke, a canonist and theologian who has himself written extensively and well on the meaning of the "good of the spouses." See, for example, the following essays by Burke: "The *Bonum Coniugum* and the *Bonum Prolis*: Ends or Properties of Marriage?" *The Jurist* 49 (1989) 704–713; "Personalism and the *Bona* of Marriage," *Studia Canonica* 27 (1993) 401–412; "Marriage: A Personalist or an Institutional Understanding?" *Communio* 19 (1992) 278–304.

11. Pontificia Commissio per Interpretationem Codicis Iuris Canonici, *Codex Iuris Canonici* (Vatican City: Libreria Editrice Vaticana, 1989).

12. See Dogmatic Constitution on the Church, *Lumen Gentium*, chapter 5, nos. 39–42.

13. "Christian spouses help one another to attain holiness in their married life and in the accepting and rearing of their children." *Ibid.*, no. 11; cf. no. 41.

14. Vatican Council II, Pastoral Constitution on the Church in the Modern World, *Gaudium etSpes,* no. 48. See also the Council's Decree on the Apostolate of the Laity, *Apostolicam Actuositatem*, no. 11.

15. Pope Pius XII, Address to the Italian Union of Midwives," October 29, 1951; text in *Official Catholic Teachings: Love and Sexuality*, ed. Odile Liebard (Wilmington, NC: McGrath Publishing Co., 1978), p.116. *AAS* 43 (1951) 848–849.

16. Pius XI, Encyclical *CastiConnubii,* no. 23, in *Acta Apostolicae Sedis* 22 (1930) 548.

17. *Ibid.*, no. 24. In the official English text of *Casti Connubii* no reference to the *Roman Catechism* is given. The Latin text, however, refers to *Catechismus Romanus*, Part II, chap. VIII, 13; *AAS* 22 (1930) 548.

18. *The Roman Catechism*, trans. Eugene Kevane and Robert Bradley, S.J. (Boston: Daughters of St. Paul, 1993), p. 323; emphasis added.

19. On this see Vatican Council II, Pastoral Constitution on the Church in the Modern World, *Gaudium et Spes,* no. 48; *Code of Canon Law*, canon 1055.

20. On the role of conjugal love in establishing the marriage and in its living out see Ramón García de Haro, *Marriage and Family in the Documents of the Magisterium,* trans. William E. May (San Francisco: Ignatius Press, 1993), and Francisco Gil Hellin, "*El lugar propio del amor conyugal en la estructura del matrimonio segun Gaudium et spes,*" Annales Valentinos.

21. On this see St. Thomas Aquinas, *Summa contra gentiles*, Book III, ch. 122, "Why Simple Fornication Is a Sin and Why Marriage Is Natural."

22. I have sought to specify this complementarity in Chapter 2, "Marriage and the Complementarity of Men and Women" in my book, *Marriage: The Rock on Which the Family Is Built* (San Francisco: Ignatius, 1995). I owe much to the treatment of this issue by Robert Joyce, *Human Sexual Ecology: A Philosophy of Man and Woman* (Washington, D.C.: University Press of America, 1976). David L. Schindler offers an analysis of male-female complementarity inspired by Hans Urs von Balthasar's theology in "Catholic

Theology, Gender, and the Future of Western Civilization," *Communio* 20(1993) 200–239, and Angelo Cardinal Scola provides a much more ample view rooted in Balthasar in *The Nuptial Mystery*, trans. Michelle Borras (Grand Rapids, MI: Eerdmans, 2005), Part One, Man and Woman, forthcoming. Other helpful discussions are those of Mary Timothy Prokes, F.S.E., *Toward a Theology of the Body* (Grand Rapids, MI: Eerdmans, 1996), Walter Ong, *Fighting for Life: Contest, Sexuality, and Consciousness* (Ithaca, NY: Cornell University Press, 1981).

23. John Paul II presented his "theology of the body" in a series of Wednesday audiences from September 5, 1979, through November 28, 1984. These addresses, divided into six cycles, were published in English originally in four separate volumes: 1) Cycle One was published as *Original Unity of Man and Woman: Catechesis on the Book of Genesis* (1981); 2) Cycle Two as *Blessed Are the Pure of Heart: Catechesis on the Sermon on the Mount and the Teaching of St. Paul* (1983); 3) Cycles Three, Four, and Five as *The Theology of Marriage and Celibacy* (1986); and 4) Cycle Six as *Reflections on Humanae Vitae* (1985). All four of these volumes were published by the Daughters of St. Paul in Boston. All six cycles were later published by the Daughters of St. Paul as Pope John Paul II, *Theology of the Body: Human Love in the Divine Plan* (Boston: Pauline Books and Media, 1998), with an introduction by John Grabowski. The one-volume edition, unfortunately, does *not* include the paragraph numbers found in the original Italian text and in the four-volume English edition. Here I will have need of only the addresses in the First Cycle, found in *Original Unity of Man and Woman* because it is in this cycle that John Paul II takes up male-female complementarity. I will refer to texts of John Paul II by giving the number of the Audience, followed by a period and then the relevant paragraph number. Thus 2.3 refers to the second Address found in *Original Unity of Man and Woman*, number 3.

24. On this see Robert Joyce, *Human Sexual Ecology: A Philosophy and Ethics of Man and Woman* (Washington, D.C.: University Press of America, 1980), pp. 67–71; William E. May, "Marriage and the Complementarity of Male and Female," *Anthropotes: Rivista di Studi sulla Persona e la Famiglia* 8.1 (June 1992) 41–60. A shorter version of this essay was published as chapter two of May's *Marriage: The Rock on Which the Family Is Based* (San Francisco: Ignatius, 1995), pp. 39–66, at pp. 50–54.

25. When non-married males and females engage in sexual coition, they do not "give" themselves to each other or "receive" each other. Their act in no way expresses and symbolizes personal union precisely because they have refused to give and receive each other unconditionally as persons. In genital union, such individuals do not make a "gift" of themselves to each other; rather, they use each other as means to attain subjectivistically determined ends.

26. Robert E. Joyce, *Human Sexual Ecology: A Philosophy and Ethics of Man and Woman* (Washington: University Press of America, 1980), pp. 70–71.

27. Steven Clark, *Man and Woman in Christ: An Examination of the Roles of Men and Women in the Light of Scripture and the Social Sciences* (Ann Arbor, MI: Servant Books, 1980). In chapters sixteen and seventeen (pp. 371–466) Clark summarizes relevant material from the descriptive social sciences and experimental psychology bearing on the differences between males and females. Clark provides an exhaustive search of the literature, providing excellent bibliographical notes. See also Alice Schlegel, *Sexual Stratification: A Cross-Cultural View* (New York: Columbia University Press, 1977).

28. Congregation for the Doctrine of the Faith, "Letter to the Bishops of the Catholic Church on the Collaboration of Men and Women in the Church and in the World," July 31, 2004, n. 13.

29. Pope John Paul II, Apostolic Exhortation *Christifideles Laici,* 51. See also his Apostolic Letter *Mulieris Dignitatem,* 30: "The moral and spiritual strength of a woman is joined to her awareness that *God entrusts the human being to her in a special way.* Of course, God entrusts every human being to each and every other human being. But this entrusting concerns women in a special way – precisely because of their femininity – and this in a particular way determines their vocation."

30. Pope John Paul II, Apostolic Letter *Mulieris Dignitatem,* 18.

31. John W. Miller, *Biblical Faith and Fathering: Why We Call God "Father"* (New York: Paulist Press, 1989), p. 57.

32. Peter J. Wilson, *Man, the Promising Primate: The Conditions of Human Evolution* (New Haven: Yale University Press, 1980), p. 71.

33. John Paul II, Apostolic Exhortation *Familiaris Consortio,* 25.

34. Benedict Ashley, O.P., "Moral Theology and Mariology," *Anthropotes: Rivista di studi sulla persona e la famiglia* 7 (1991), 140.

35. Pope Pius XII, "Address to Italian Union of Midwives" (October 29, 1951).

36. Germain Grisez, "Fidelity Today," unpublished paper, p. 2 of ms. The seventh chapter of volume 2, *Living a Christian Life* (Quincy, IL: Franciscan Press, 1993), of this author's *The Way of the Lord Jesus*, offers a splendid theology of marriage.

37. Ibid., p. 5.

38. Ibid., p. 7.

39. On this see Grisez, Living a Christian Life, pp. 620–622.

Chapter 7: Catholic Marriage and Feminism

SR. MARY PRUDENCE ALLEN, R.S.M., PH.D.

"The bridegroom is here! Go out and meet him." Matthew 5:7

Introduction

The focus of this 27th Annual Convention of the Fellowship of Catholic Scholars, with its theme of the International Year of the Family, points back to the theme of the 22nd Annual Fellowship Convention with its related theme of Marriage and the Common Good,[1] because, as Karol Wojtyla reminds us in writing about "the Marriage Covenant," [t]he basis of the family is marriage."[2] Because marriage is the basis of the family, my particular approach as a philosopher will be to consider some essential characteristics of Catholic marriage, ponder how these characteristics have been evaluated by feminist authors of different philosophical orientations in western thought, and then offer some conclusions about the meaning of Catholic marriage for the contemporary Church. The work of Pope John Paul II will encircle this analysis – beginning with his pastoral teachings about Catholic marriage and ending with the philosophical foundations for his thought about the institution of marriage.

Since marriage is usually studied by theologians,[3] it may surprise many of you to learn that Catholic marriage is also a serious topic for philosophers. However, a glance at the history of philosophy reveals that several Catholic Renaissance philosophers engaged in serious dialogue about the meaning of marriage and that many contemporary Catholic philosophers such as Edith Stein, Dietrich and Alice von Hildebrand, Emmanuel Mounier, Jacques and Raïssa Maritain, Gabriel Marcel, Bernard Lonergan, and Karol Wojtyla also wrote about marriage. Moreover, between the Renaissance and the current contemporary period, philosophers of the Enlightenment and Post-Enlightenment period attacked one or more of the essential characteristics of Catholic marriage.

Philosophical discussions about the meaning of marriage have frequently been associated with various kinds of feminism. Although the words "feminism" and "feminist" did not come into use until after the nineteenth century when political movements advancing feminism began to occur, by using the following heuristic definition of feminism we can extend the time-frame of this analysis. If we say that feminism "is the organized thought and action which aims at removing obstacles for a woman to become (as a woman) what a human being or a human person really is and can become,"[4] we can then describe philosophers' positions retrospectively as feminist when they seek to remove obstacles for woman's full development in an organized manner at different times in history.[5]

There are several different ways to divide the very broad feminist movements into categories.[6] The following categories of feminism will provide the framework for our analysis: Renaissance feminism, Enlightenment feminism, Post-Enlightenment feminism, and Personalist feminism. Only some Renaissance feminists and some contemporary Personalist feminists have positions compatible with the essential characteristics of Catholic marriage. Especially significant for the Fellowship of Catholic Scholars is the elaboration since 1995 by Pope John Paul II of a "new feminism" in the Personalist tradition. This new feminism shares some of the goals of previous feminisms, namely to "overcome all discrimination, violence, and exploitation" towards women; but it also introduces a new goal, namely:

> ... to acknowledge and affirm the true genius of women in every aspect of the life of society...[and be] called to *bear witness to the meaning of genuine love*, of that gift of self and of that acceptance of others which are present in a special way in the relationship of husband and wife, but which ought also to be at the heart of every other interpersonal relationship.[7]

Contemporary Catholic marriage becomes the workshop for this new feminism, and the Church and the world reap the benefits of its extension to every aspect of the life of society. But we must ask: What is Catholic marriage?

What is Catholic Marriage?

Catholicism is a covenant with Jesus Christ and a sacred living bond among all its members. In being baptized we are plunged into an enduring relation with Jesus Christ. Even if we are unfaithful, God is never unfaithful. In becoming Catholic we are immersed into this covenant –

an inter-personal relationship that lasts forever. Some have noted an analogy between 1) the ancient ritual bath of a bride and the bath of baptism and 2) the ancient custom of the bridegroom taking the bride into his father's home and Jesus Christ, as Bridegroom, coming to take us at death into His Father's home in Heaven.[8] The eternal spousal covenantal bond has also been recently reaffirmed by the Congregation for the Doctrine of the Faith in its 2004 Letter On the Collaboration of Men and Women:

> ...While having an evident metaphorical dimension, the terms bridegroom and bride – and covenant as well – which characterize the dynamic of salvation, are much more than simple metaphors. This spousal language touches on the very nature of the relationship which God establishes with his people, even though that relationship is more expansive than human spousal experience.[9]

Thus far we have been discussing sacramental marriage as the model for Catholic marriage. *The Catechism of the Catholic Church* describes the spousal relation of *all* Catholics, as brides to Jesus Christ, the Bridegroom:

> The Theme of Christ as Bridegroom of the Church was prepared for by the prophets and announced by John the Baptist. The Lord referred to himself as the "bridegroom" (Mk 2:19). The Apostle speaks of the whole Church and each of the faithful, members of his Body, as a bride "bethrothed" to Christ the Lord as to become but one spirit with him (Mt 22:1–4; 25:1–13; 1 Cor 6:15–17).[10]

The ontological reality of this analogical identity of Catholic marriage was explored in the language of signs by Thomas Aquinas in or with his discussion "On the Sacrament of Matrimony" in his *Summa Contra Gentiles*: "As in the other sacraments, by the thing done outwardly a *sign* is made of a spiritual thing, so, too, in this sacrament, by the union of husband and wife a *sign* of the union of Christ and the Church is made..."[11] The persons who carry the sign must represent truly what it signifies: "Since, then, the union of husband and wife gives a sign of the union of Christ and the Church, that which makes the sign must correspond to that whose sign it is."[12] As John Deely demonstrates, for medieval philosophy the sign is *inseparately* an ontological and epistemological reality, with a *triadic* import that includes the interpreter, the sign carrier, and that reality to which the sign points.[13] While a wedding ring is an inanimate sign of marriage, the persons of husband and wife are *living* sign carriers of marriage. The reality pointed-to by the spousal bond we are considering here must be given by faith. Reason alone can think it, but not personally appropriate it.

Thomas, following the example of his predecessor Anselm of Laon, selects permanent endurance between a man and a woman as an essential characteristic of marriage: "The union of Christ and the Church is a union of one to one to be held forever."[14] Marriages of men and women on earth point to the primordial heavenly marriage of God and His People – to Christ and His Church. If we delineate further essential characteristics of Catholic marriage: being initiated by God, confirmed through rite, and called to be generatively fruitful, the following list of essential characteristics are key for our analysis:

1. An enduring covenental bond of love
2. Between two different kinds of persons:
   a. man and woman (sacramental marriage)
   b. Divine Person and consecrated person
   c. human person (priest) and collective person (Church)
3. Initiated by God and confirmed through a rite
4. Generatively fruitful
5. Serving as a living sign.[15]

While spiritual authors have, for centuries, written about an interior marriage of Christ and the soul, most persons baptized in the Catholic Church are called to one of three paradigmatic vocations. John Paul II reminds us in his 1996 apostolic exhortation *Vita Consecrata* that "[t]he vocations to the lay life, to the ordained ministry, and to the consecrated life can be considered *paradigmatic*, inasmuch as all particular vocations, considered separately or as a whole, are in one way or another derived from them or lead back to them, in accordance with the richness of God's gift."[16] Viewing sacramental marriage as appropriate to the lay state, the Church has also described Priestly Ordination and Consecrated Life as participating analogously in spiritual Catholic marriages.

Hans Urs von Balthasar, referring to the lay state, the priestly state, and the evangelical state, noted their relation to one another: "Every [Christian] state of life is a specific representation of something that is present also in the other states."[17] By applying this insight to sacramental Catholic marriage and to the spiritual marriages of Priestly Ordination and of Consecrated life, it is suggested that they each carry in the Church *a particular sign-value* of the primordial covenantal marriage of God and the world, Christ and the Church. The *married couple together* is a living sign of the *covenantal bond of eternal love*, the *priest* is a living sign of the *Bridegroom's love* for his bride, and the *consecrated person* is a living sign of the *bride's response* to the Bridegroom's love.

Each of the three paradigmatic vocations serves the Church by actualizing, in a unique and public way, the inner form of their vocation to be a living sign carrier of the eternal marriage of God to his people. John Paul II succinctly summarizes in *Vita Consecrata* the inner penetration of our complement vocations to Catholic marriage: "These vocations are also at the service of one another, for the growth of the Body of Christ in history and for its mission in the world."[18] Communities of persons – of married couples, priests with their assigned area of responsibility, and consecrated men and women in religious institutes or congregations – are called to serve effectively as living signs for one another in likeness to the Holy Trinity, as a loving Communion of Divine Persons. This philosophical analysis will concentrate on the meaning of this sign-value of marriage.

Let us briefly consider some passages in which the Church describes how the three paradigmatic vocations serve as living signs of essential characteristics of Catholic marriage.

The Sacrament of Marriage is described by John Paul II in *Familiaris Consortio* with the phrases "*real symbol* of that new and eternal covenant sanctioned in the blood of Christ;" "*real representation, by means of the sacramental sign,* of the very relationship of Christ with the Church;" and "a `*sign*' – *a small and precious sign*...of the unfailing fidelity with which God and Jesus Christ love each and every human being."[19]

St. Augustine emphasized consent of wills and mutual donation as two essential characteristics of marriage as a "sacred signification" leading to a "lived sacrament."[20] The conjugal act of sexual intercourse, a sacred moment of interpersonal encounter for the husband and wife, may be generatively fruitful: "Thus the couple, while giving themselves to one another, give not just themselves but also the *reality* of children, who are a living reflection of their love, a *permanent sign* of conjugal unity and a *living* and inseparable synthesis of their being a father and a mother."[21] Not only are the children a living sign for their parents but the relation of the parents serves as a living sign for the children: "Their parental life is called to become for the children the *visible sign* of the very love of God, 'from whom every family in heaven and on earth is named.'"[22] In his Letter to Families, the Holy Father observes that the generativity of sacramental marriage flows, in likeness to the Holy Trinity, into the communion of persons known as the family.[23]

Spiritual Marriage by Priestly Ordination is explained as follows by Denver Archbishop Charles Chaput, O.F.M., Cap., in a pastoral letter entitled "As Christ Loved the Church":

> ...[The priest] is – through the indelible mark conferred by the Sacrament of Orders, which leaves him forever configured to the celibate Christ – married to His Bride, the Church. As such, he becomes a *sign* to those in the married state of the radical love God asks of them. It is in recognition of his vocation as a husband to the believing community he serves that we traditionally call priests "father." In this way, we who are born into the Church through Baptism express our love for those who are wedded to our Mother the Church.[24]
>
> The priest is married to a collective person – the Church as a *collective sign*, different from the unique and singular sign of the bridegroom. In *Mulieris Dignitatem*, the Holy Father says: "...the bride *is the Church*, just as for the prophets the bride was Israel. She is therefore a *collective subject* and not *an individual person*. This collective subject is the People of God, a community made up of many persons, both women and men."[25] John Paul II emphasizes in *Pastores Dabo Vobis* that this enduring spiritual marriage bond is also exclusive: "[T]he Church, as the Spouse of Jesus Christ, wishes to be loved by the priest in the total and exclusive manner in which Jesus Christ her Head and Spouse loved her."[26]

The ontological nature of the priest's configuration to Jesus Christ, the Bridegroom, is found in his definitive identity as a male human being. The Congregation for the Doctrine of the Faith elaborated in *Inter Insigniores* the essential connection between these real analogates:

> The Christian priesthood is therefore of a sacramental nature: the priest is a *sign* that must be perceptible and which the faithful must be able to recognize with ease. The whole sacramental economy is in fact based upon natural signs, on symbols imprinted upon the human psychology: "Sacramental signs," says Saint Thomas, "represent what they signify by natural resemblance." The same natural resemblance is required for persons as for things: when Christ's role in the Eucharist is to be expressed sacramentally, there would not be this "natural resemblance" which must exist between Christ and his minister if the role of Christ were not taken by a man: in such a case it would be difficult to see in the minister the image of Christ. For Christ himself was and remains a man.[27]

Analogous to the conjugal act of a married couple, John Paul II states that "*The Eucharist is the Sacrament of our Redemption. It is the*

Sacrament of the Bridegroom and of the Bride.[28] He reaffirms that *"It is the Eucharist* above all that expresses *the redemptive act of Christ the Bridegroom towards the Church the Bride.* This is clear and unambiguous when the sacramental ministry of the Eucharist, in which the priest acts *'in persona Christi,'* is performed by a man."[29]

In our ensuing analysis of feminist arguments about marriage, we will discover that rejection of essential aspects of Catholic sacramental marriage will be connected to rejection of essential aspects of the priest's spiritual marriage as expressed in the sacrament of the Eucharist.

Consecrated Marriage by vows, according to *Vita Consecrata,* "is *at the very heart of the Church* as a decisive element for her mission, since it 'manifests the inner nature of the Christian calling' and the striving of the whole Church as Bride towards union with her one Spouse."[30] In the spiritual marriage of consecrated women, "they give themselves to the divine Spouse, and this personal gift tends to union, which is properly spiritual in character. Through the Holy Spirit's action a woman becomes 'one spirit' with Christ the Spouse (cf. 1 Cor 6:17)."[31] This covenantal bond of love is between two different kinds of persons – the Divine Person Jesus Christ and the human person who is consecrated.

John Paul II also explains that consecrated men and/or priests relate analogically to this spiritual marriage: "One cannot correctly understand ... a woman's consecration in virginity – without referring to spousal love. It is through this kind of love that a person becomes a gift for the other. Moreover, a man's consecration in priestly celibacy or in the religious state is to be understood analogously."[32] The consecrated person, man or woman, is a living sign for the collective person, the Church, bride of Jesus Christ, the Divine Bridegroom.

This spiritual marriage occurs through the rite of profession of vows of chastity, poverty, and obedience. The 1983 document entitled *Essential Elements in the Church's Teaching on Religious Life* issued by the Congregation for Religious and Secular Institutes describes its eschatological sign-value: "It is a consecration of the whole person which manifests in the Church a marriage effected by God, *a sign* of the future life. This consecration is by public vows..."[33] The core sign-value of consecrated marriage is so important that it is stated in the *Code of Canon Law* # 607: "Religious life, as a consecration of the whole person, manifests in the Church the marvelous marriage established by God as a *sign* of the world to come."[34]

Just as the sign-value of a husband and wife extends to the sign-value of the family as pointing to the Holy Trinity, the sign-value of consecrated life extends from the individual consecrated person to a religious community as "a *sign* of the Trinity"(#21) and "an *eschatological*

sign ... foreshadowing ... the future Kingdom" of communion of saints
(#26). In the 1978 document *Religious and Human Promotion*, religious
are called to be *"experts in communion"* and "communally a prophetic
sign of intimate union with God, who is loved above all things."[35]

By living bonds of spiritual marriage together, yet another document, *Fraternal Life in Community*, states that "...life in common, in a
monastery, is called to be a *living sign* of the mystery of the Church
(#11)." *Vita Consecrata* again elaborates further: *"*... fraternal life,
understood as a life shared in love, is an *eloquent sign* of ecclesial communion (#42); [l]ife in community is thus the *particular sign* before the
Church and society, of the bond which comes from the same call and the
common desire – notwithstanding differences of race and origin, language and culture – to be obedient to that call (# 92); "...life of communion in fact `becomes a *sign* for all the world and a compelling *force*
that leads people to faith in Christ'" (#46).[36]

When *Vita Consecrata* suggests that consecrated persons pray for
"being for the people of our time...*living signs* of the Resurrection and
of its treasures of virginity, poverty, and obedience (#111)," it indicates
that it is in the practice of a vow that a religious serves other vocations
to marriage in the Church. Religious life is not a sacrament as are the
sacraments of Marriage and of Holy Orders; yet its focal spousal act of
grace, analogous to the conjugal act and the celebration of the Eucharist,
is participatory acts of virginity, poverty, and obedience (in a common
life for religious) in marriage to the Bridegroom.[37] These acts are made
possible by the sacramental grace of the Church which holds their vows
in perpetuity. In our subsequent analysis of feminist arguments about
marriage, we will also have occasion to see that the loss of the sign-value
of living the vows in consecrated marriage is often accompanied by
rejection of essential characteristics of the institution of marriage, sacramental marriage, and priestly spiritual marriage.

Renaissance Feminism and Marriage

Our analysis of feminism will be limited to philosophical works
which directly try to remove obstacles for women to become fully
human as married. The earliest feminist texts were written by
Renaissance Catholic authors. Christine de Pizan (1363–1431), the
devout Catholic widow of a French humanist and mother of three,
responded to a plethora of satirical works, often written by Catholic
priests, against marriage and against women. The main obstacle for
women that she sought to remove was the negative opinions of men
about women's inferior nature and incapacity to sustain loyalty in mar-

riage. In her early courtly love debate poems, she defended loyalty in marriage, and in her written public debate on the satirical *Romance of the Rose (Le Roman de la rose)* (1401–1403), Christine de Pizan argued that women were virtuous in the marriage bond, and she challenged men to become the same.[38] In *The City of Ladies (Le Livre de la cité des dames)* (1405), she asks whether:

> …what so many authors testify is true – that life within the institution of marriage is filled and occupied with such great unhappiness for men because of women's faults and impetuosity ... [and that] in order to escape and avoid such inconveniences, many authorities have advised wise men not to marry, affirming that no women – or very few – are loyal to their mates.[39]

Her respondent answers: "Certainly, friend…I assure you that women have never done what these books say."[40] Christine de Pizan proves her feminist claims by bringing together several loyal married women, widows, and nuns under the recapitulated leadership of Mary, Queen of Heaven. In this way, Christine de Pizan's Renaissance feminism supported and enlivened the essential characteristic of enduring Catholic marriage in both its sacramental and consecrated forms.

The Italian humanist Francesco Barbaro (1390–1454), in *Directions for Love and Marriage,* defended the wife's relation with the husband: "Now let us speak of conjugal love, the great efficacy and dignity whereof (as worthy men assure us), in a manner expressing the pattern of a perfect friendship."[41] The German humanist Albrecht von Eyb (1420–1466) went even further in his *Little Book of Marriage*; he argued against the satirical view that men should not marry: "If both married man and woman have such love, will, and friendship towards each other, then what one wants, the other wants…[i]f good and evil are shared by both…praise and laud holy, worthy marriage…[a] man should marry."[42]

Two later Renaissance feminist authors argued that women were superior to men. The first author, German humanist Henricus Cornelius Agrippa's (1486–1535), in his *Declamation on the Nobility and Preeminence of the Female Sex* (1509), appealed to Scripture, history, and experience to prove that "the illustrious feminine stock is always infinitely superior to the ill-bred masculine race."[43] Not surprisingly, the Catholic Agrippa argued in his text *De sacramento matrimonii declamatio (Declamation on the Sacrament of Marriage,* 1526) that most men should marry; and he remarried after being twice widowed.

The second author, Lucrezia Marinella (1571–1653), in *The Nobility and Excellence of Women, and the Defects and Vices of Men*

(1599), responded to a severe devaluation of woman's identity by Giuseppe Passi in *The Defects of Women (Dei donneschi difetti)*. Passi argued that, because women destroy men, a man either should not marry, or, if he does, the wife should be completely subordinated – like an animal.[44] Marinella, in turn, refuted Passi in her several-hundred page text ironically using Aristotele's *Ethics* and *Politics* against the traditional polarity theory (man is by nature superior to woman).[45] Also drawing upon and exaggerating Platonic arguments in the *Republic*, Marinella says that: "My desire is to make this truth shine forth to everybody, that the female sex is nobler and more excellent than the male."[46] Marinella, a Catholic married woman, mother, and widow, argued that women's virtues were greater than men's virtues, and that men's vice were worse than women's vices.[47]

These early Catholic feminist arguments struggled to find philosophical foundations to overcome the devaluation of women by satirists and to defend the equal worth and dignity of women and men in marriage. While Christine de Pizan, Barbaro, and von Eyb kept the balance of complementarity, Agrippa and Marinella reacted to traditional polarity arguments for natural male superiority by sliding into a reverse polarity of female superiority. Christine de Pizan, Barbaro, Agrippa, and Marinella all were living signs of their vocation to Catholic marriage. Von Eyb was a living sign of the vocation to clerical celibacy, while supporting sacramental marriage; and Christine de Pizan supported her daughter's vocation to consecrated marriage as a Dominican nun, while spending the end of her own life in her daughter's monastery and writing a poem in support of Joan of Arc's uniquely celibate Catholic vocation.

The Spanish humanist Juan Luis Vives (1492–1540), who eventually married, addressed the relation between marriage and a practical moral education, drawing upon classical humanist sources, in *The Education of a Christian Woman: A Sixteenth-century Manual* (1528).[48] Vives, a close friend of the Renaissance humanist Thomas More (who is well known for educating his daughters at home), defended women against the derogatory attitudes of satirists. He divided his text into educating women during three stages of life: unmarried, married, and widowed. He supported her vocational call to sacramental marriage initiated by God: "Right now, from the beginning, good woman, prepare to join yourself in love to the one whom God has joined to you in the sacrament in such a way that the joining may become easy and light for you. Do not wish the bond to be dissolved or loosened..."[49]

Vives' text can only be considered feminist in its support for women's identity against the derogatory views of satirists, and for its partial support for simple, moral education. To the contrary, however, it strengthened another obstacle for women's full development in its rigid description of the relation of ruling and obedience between husband and wife in marriage:

> ...She becomes hated and abominable to all as if she were attempting to invert the laws sanctioned by nature, like a soldier demanding the right to give orders to a general, as if the moon were superior to the sun or the arm to the head. In marriage as in human nature, the man stands for the mind, the woman for the body. He must command, and she must serve, if man is to live.
>
> Nature herself has declared this by making the man more fit for governing than the woman....
>
> The author of this whole fabric of the universe, when the world was still new and inexperienced and he was establishing laws for the human race, said to the woman, "You shall be under the power of the man, and he shall have dominion over you." In these words it is worthy of note that not only is man given right and dominion over the woman, but also use and possession.[50]

Because Vives' text was immensely popular, translated, and reprinted many times in Spain, France, Germany, Italy, the Netherlands, and England,[51] and given to many women as preparation for marriage, it had a significant negative influence on subsequent feminist authors.

Toward the end of the Renaissance a new direction for feminist arguments about marriage began to emerge. Because nearly all universities accepted only male students, the lack of women's access to higher education started to be seen as the major obstacle for women's full development as human beings. Marriage was increasingly viewed as an obstacle to women's higher education.

In the effort to defend equal dignity, Marie le Jars de Gournay (1565–1645), nominally Catholic, chose not to marry but to live in the world as a single intellectual woman. Her writing about marriage limits itself to the question of why a wife should be subordinated to her husband, and she concludes that, for "the need of fostering peace in marriage," one of the two partners must "yield to the other;" and that it is simply easier for the woman to be the one.[52]

In 1622, De Gournay wrote, in *The Equality of Men and Women*, that: "Man and woman are so thoroughly one that if man is more than woman, woman is more than man...Now in those whose nature is one and the same, it must be concluded that their actions are so as well, and that the esteem and recompense belonging to these are equal, where the works are equal."[53] In a subsequent text, *The Ladies Complaint*, written in 1626, De Gournay appealed to Plato and others for a philosophical foundation for equality and a unisex theory (of no significant differences between men and women); she appealed to "the eternal decree of God himself, who made the two sexes as a single creation and, moreover, honors women in his sacred history with all the gifts and benefits he assigns to men, as I have more fully portrayed in *The Equality of Men and Women.*"[54] Anticipating developments in Protestantism, which will deny any spousal understanding of the Priest in the person of Christ, the head and bridegroom, De Gournay suggests that it is unjust to deny women the capacity to administer all the sacraments.[55]

At this point in history, these early Catholic feminist authors all appeared to support the five essential characteristics of marriage: an enduring bond of love, between two different kinds of persons, initiated by God and confirmed through a rite, called to be generatively fruitful, and serving as a living sign. Most of the authors either chose marriage or the clerical state. At the end of this period, however, one woman feminist chose to remain single, suggesting that the married state was beginning to be viewed as incompatible with an educated and intellectual life.

Enlightenment Feminism and Marriage

Cartesian feminists and Reason's Disciples[56] have philosophical roots in the mind/body dualism of René Descartes (1596–1650). In his *Meditations,* Descartes states: "I am therefore precisely nothing but a thinking thing, that is, a mind, or intellect, or understanding, or reason...I am not that concatenation of members we call the human body."[57] Even though Descartes was a Catholic philosopher, with his "turn to the subject," as a mind disengaged from the body, he ruptured the soul/body *composite* that had, in the Thomistic tradition, provided the ontological and epistemological foundation for the sign-value of all three forms of Catholic marriage.

The identity of mind and reason in man and woman, disengaged from the body, also provided a new philosophical foundation for the feminist argument that lack of education was an obstacle for women's full human development. Just as there had been truth in Renaissance feminist arguments that the satirical views of men harmed women's human development, so also there was truth in Enlightenment feminist arguments that lack of access to higher education harmed women's full development. However, the rejection of marriage on the grounds that it was a total impediment to education was an unfortunate side effect.

Anna Maria van Schurman (1607–1678), in *Whether a Christian Woman Should be Educated* (1659), argued that "it often befalls a woman (especially in the unmarried state) to be as free as possible from work, etc. Therefore...[unmarried women should be able to be educated]."[58] In her correspondence, van Schurman mentions both her familiarity with Marie de Gournay, and Lucrezia Marinella's texts on equality of men and women, and their views that unmarried women should be able to study.[59] A pattern begins to emerge, in which support for feminism (in this case, a claim to equal access to education) implies a rejection of marriage. Schurman herself chose to remain an unmarried woman. A second pattern connects Protestantism with this argument. A member of the Dutch Reformed Protestant Church in the Netherlands, van Schurman later joined a second reform group founded by a former Jesuit, Jean de Labadie.

Descartes' disciple, François Poullain de La Barre (1647–1723), in his lengthy *On the Equality of the Two Sexes,* reduced the soul to mind (and/or brain) and put forth a feminist argument for equality: firstly, "...The most exact Anatomy remarks to us no difference in this part between *Men,* and *Women,* their brain is altogether like to ours..."[60]; secondly, "In effect, we All (both *Men* and *Women*) have the same Right to Truth, since the Mind in all of us is alike capable to know it; and that we are (All) affected in the same manner, by the Objects that make Impression upon the Body;"[61] and thirdly, "This is sufficient to prove, That, in Respect of the Head alone, the Two Sexes are Equal."[62]

Appealing to isolated reason, Poullain begins to reject all traditions or customs. In his advertisement for the book, Poullain states clearly that "we acknowledge no other Authority here, but that of Reason, and good Sense."[63] The prejudice of men and the weight of social custom are viewed as the essential obstacles for women's full development as human beings. In this way, the Catholic tradition itself is rejected. Not surprisingly, Poullain de la Barre, a Sorbonne-educated Roman Catholic cleric, left the Catholic faith and his vocation to the priesthood to join Calvinism in Geneva and marry.

Calvin had reduced marriage to a simple remedy for concupiscence.[64] According to Hilaire Belloc, Calvin's *Institutes* also laid an intellectual groundwork for "an intense hatred against the Mass, the Blessed Sacrament, the whole transcendental scheme."[65] Poullain appeared to reject the transcendental sign-value of the male identity of the priest when he argued: "And if men were accustomed to see *Women* in a Pulpit, they would be no more startled thereat, than the *Women* are at the sight of men."[66] However, Poullain appeared to leave intact the sign-value of consecrated women serving in hospitals "according to the example of their lord and Husband (*de leur Epoux*)."[67]

Even though Henry VIII wrote a text defending marriage as a sacrament, his own life choices proved to redefine marriage in utilitarian terms. Subsequently, the Protestant Reformation in England (1559–1605) succeeded in destroying all three forms of marriage – sacramental, priestly, and consecrated – by redefining the meaning of sacrament, forbidding the Mass, confiscating all Church property, and imprisoning and/or executing all priests.[68] At the Council of Trent (1563), "the Fathers were aware that by defining marriage as the sacrament of the unbreakable union between Christ and his Church, sacramentality itself would be the surest defense against the Protestant denial of the indissolubility of Marriage."[69]

Mary Astell (1666–1731), a devout Anglican feminist, described marriage as primarily a utilitarian relationship. Focusing on the here and now and the difficulties that women experienced within marriage, heaven was described simply as a compensation for all the suffering that women had to go through in their marriages: "A Prospect of Heaven...is a true, and indeed, the only Consolation; this makes her a sufficient Compensation for all the Neglect and Contempt the ill-grounded Customs of the World throw on her; for all the Injuries brutal Power may do her..."[70] Astell was influenced by the empiricism of John Locke which described the object of knowledge as ideas rather than reality: "By ideas we sometimes understand in general all that which is the immediate object of the mind, whatever it perceives..."[71] According to John Deely, Locke's philosophy of sign is *dyadic* because it leaves out the thing-signified.[72] Accordingly, marriage is simply the idea in the mind of the person based on temporal experience. Mary Astell's understanding of the meaning of marriage follows the dyadic pattern of Locke's epistemology.

Marriage laws in England at the time viewed a woman as the property of her husband, and any property that she either brought with her or inherited was also viewed as his property instead. In Astell's *Some Reflections on Marriage (1700),* she states that the first thing that a man asks about a prospective wife are the utilitarian questions: "What will she bring? Is the first Enquiry: How many acres? Or how much ready Coin?"[73] The wife's position in marriage is likened to enforced servanthood, enslavement, natural subjection, and a state of tyrannous domination, and love is reduced to a passing feeling which leaves women desperate:

> ...What though a Husband can't deprive a Wife of Life without being responsible to the Law, he may, however, do what is much more grievous to a generous Mind, render Life miserable, for which she has no Redress...If all men are born Free, how is it that all Women are born Slaves? As they must be, if the being subjected to the inconstant, uncertain, unknown, arbitrary Will of Men, be the perfect Condition of Slavery?[74]

In "the most systematic feminist theorist of the later seventeenth century,"[75] *A Serious Proposal to the Ladies for their Advancement of their True and Greatest Interest*, Astell in 1694 sought to establish a school for women alone "who were either permanently or temporarily" separated from men. Pitting marriage against education, it is not surprising that Astell decided to remain single. Her school would be based on Cartesian methodology with its development in British empiricism: "As prejudice fetters the Understanding so does Custom manacle the Will... Custom cannot Authorize a Practice if Reason Condemns it..."[76] Thus, while Astell truly understood English marriage laws and lack of education as obstacles to women's full human development, she reduced marriage to a rigid temporal utilitarian model of interpersonal relationship, which allowed women who desired to be educated the option only of remaining single. Astell followed Cartesian and Lockean epistemology, which made the object knowledge ideas in the mind, rather than realities in the world; and the rich medieval triadic sign-value of marriage disappeared into a dyadic mental picture of temporal experience alone.

In France, a different sort of reaction to Cartesianism occurred. Salons in Paris, led by women and including clergy and lay men, often contained an undercurrent of rejection of marriage by encouraging amorous relations outside of the marriage bond. Recently published texts from women philosophers in the salons state nothing about a transcendental spousal dimension to marriage or consecrated life; rather, difficulties of obedience and austerities provide the common thread.[77] The personal lives of members of these salons reveal a struggle between hedonism and Catholic values. In an interesting reversal of the move to Protestantism by some Enlightenment feminists, there was a return to Catholicism by two of the more significant leaders of the salons – Madame de la Sablière, converted from Calvinist Huguenot Protestantism, Cartesianism, and a licentious life-style to Catholicism; and Mademoiselle de la Vallière, the mistress of Louis XIV who had a religious conversion and became a Carmelite nun.[78]

The turn to hedonism and nature was articulated by Jean-Jacques Rousseau (1712–1778) who in his *Émile* described man and woman's identity in marriage:

> ...In the union of the sexes each alike contributes to the common end, but in different ways. From this diversity springs the first difference which may be observed between man and woman in their moral relations. The man should be strong and active; the woman should be weak and passive; the one must have both the power and the will; it is enough that the other should offer little resistance. When this principle [the law of nature] is admitted, it follows that woman is specially made for man's delight.[79]

Rousseau revealed in his own *Confessions* his attraction to hedonism: although he was born into a Calvanistic family in Geneva, he was initiated at an early age into life-long licentious relations with several women. He converted to Catholicism in Turin in his youth, eventually had five children with a mistress (each child of whom was turned over to a foundling hospital), and eventually he turned away from the Catholic faith to join the Dutch Reformed Church.[80] Rousseau's description of marriage was bitterly attacked by the English feminist Mary Wollstonecraft (1759–1797) in *A Vindication of the Rights of Woman*. The entire Section I of Chapter V of her text is a direct critique of Rousseau's *Émile* and the hypocrisy of his lascivious life style.

Another effect of the Cartesian rupture between soul and body was the development of a theory of fractional complementarity (a man and a woman are significantly different and each provides only a fraction of a single human being). Thus, husband and wife each contribute a fraction of one person in marriage. Rousseau states: "The relation produces a moral person of which woman is the eye and man the hand, but the two are so dependent upon one another that the man teaches the woman what to see, while she teaches him what to do."[81] The Thomistic metaphysical foundation of two separate persons, a man and a woman, who in marriage enter into union but do not lose their individual identities, disappears in the Cartesian turn to the isolated ego. In fractional complementarity, which often contains a hidden polarity of the natural superiority of the male, the two add up to only one human being.

After quoting a passage from *Émile* in which Rousseau describes the difficulty a woman without reflection would have in educating her children, Wollstonecraft attacks Rousseau's fractional complementarity:

> ...How indeed should she, where her husband is not always at hand to lend her his reason? – when they both together make but one

moral being. A blind will, "eyes without hands," would go a very little way; and perchance his abstract reason, that should concentrate the scattered beams of her practical reason, may be employed in judging of the flavor of wine, descanting on the causes most proper for turtle; or, more profoundly intent at the card-table, he may be generalizing his ideas as he bets away his fortune, leaving all the *minutiae* of education to his helpmate, or to chance.[82]

Wollstonecraft identifies the underlying hedonism of Rousseau's romantic view of marriage and of his way of life. Rousseau had given considerable attention to a wife's obligation to constantly seek to delight her husband, and the simultaneous claim that men will always become bored and unfaithful. Wollstonecraft answers back: "After thus cramping a woman's mind, if, in order to keep it fair, he has not made it quite a blank, he advises her to reflect, that a reflecting man may not yawn in her company, when he is tired of caressing her."[83] With Rousseau's rejection of the possibility of an enduring covenantal bond of love initiated by God, and a turning to nature alone as the foundation for marriage, he fell into as much a utilitarianism as had the English model criticized by Mary Astell.

In later Enlightenment feminism, authors turn to address another obstacle to women's full development: it is lack of participation in building the public common good by voting and holding political office. The attempt of married women to secure food for their families by leading the storming of the Bastille raised their hopes for full participation in future French political life. With these hopes dashed, Mary Wollstonecraft states:

> But, if women are to be excluded, without having a voice, from a participation of the natural rights of mankind, *prove first*, to ward off the charge of injustice and inconsistency, *that they want reason* – else this flaw in your New Constitution will ever shew that man must, in some shape, act like a tyrant, and tyranny, in whatever part of society it rears its brazen front, will ever undermine morality.[84]

Several feminist women were guillotined along with men, leading Mary Wollstonecraft to observe in her 1793–94 text entitled *An Historical and Moral View of the Origin and Progress of the French Revolution and the Effect it has Produced in Europe*: "I tremble, lest I should meet some unfortunate being, fleeing from the despotism of licentious freedom, hearing the snap of the guillotine at his heels."[85] Tragically, Wollstonecraft herself experienced the destructive consequences of licentious freedom by entering into many different sexual liaisons while single, marrying, then twice attempting suicide during her husband's frequent infidelities, marrying a second time only to die in the childbirth of her second child.

The final phase of Enlightenment feminism is played out through the philosophy of Immanuel Kant (1724–1804), an unmarried German pietist. Kant continued the tradition of fractional complementarity with hidden polarity, when he identified man with reason and woman with taste.[86] In addition, he reduced marriage to a private *contract* between husband and wife under a law of domestic society: these persons [husband and wife] "are joined by a *de jure* relationship..."[87] The reduction of marriage to a civil contract had also been previously argued by a French jurist, J. Launoy (1603–1673), to the detriment of the Catholic understanding of its essentially sacramental identity, "leaving spousal morality to the State – the dilemma of Protestant society."[88] For Kant, signs are reduced to regulative postulates of reason, or to metaphors of the imagination originating in man. John Deely shows that Kant also has a dyadic view of signs such that his contract theory of marriage as initiated by the state simply undermines its transcendent spousal dimension.[89]

Kant's disciple, Theodor Gottlieb von Hippel (1741–1796), published a lengthy feminist text against his mentor in 1792, entitled *On Improving the Status of Women*.[90] Hippel, a lawyer, Director of the Criminal Court, and eventually Mayor of the city of Königsberg, remained a bachelor throughout his life. Because the French Constitution of 1791 failed to give women equal rights, in the 1792 version of his treatise on marriage, *Über die Ehe,* Hipple argued for the equality of husband and wife and for the full emancipation of woman within marriage.[91] Hippel argues: "Where freedom is suppressed, nothing worthy of the appellation 'human' can flourish. Without freedom the sacrament of marriage – the holiest and most important contract in society – becomes nothing more or less than the buying and bartering of goods; and "Had we forgotten already that marriage is an institution of equals, that authority in marriage is distributed equally, and that the man can only claim his wife as his own by means of an *expressed* agreement?"[92] Even with this development in defending the equality of women and men, von Hippel suffered the consequences of Cartesian fractional complementarity when he concluded that: "Man and woman together constitute a complete human being."[93]

In Protestant sections of Germany, Luther's understanding of marriage (1520) contributed to the reduction of its sign-value. He argued that even though "matrimony is a figure for Christ and the Church, yet it is not a sacrament of divine institution; it was introduced into the Church by men who were misled by their ignorance both of the subject and the record."[94] In a similar way, he dismissed the sacrament of Orders as a complete fiction "devised by the Church of Popes."[95] Luther argued that sacraments cannot be "'signs' of efficacious grace"; and he criticized Catholics because they "stick to the sign, and to the use of the sign, thus seducing us from...the word to the sign."[96] Religious consecration was also rejected by Luther, as men and women "were restricted by vows, and turned into prisoners..."[97] Ultimately in the Reformation in Germany monasteries were closed, taken over as "the loot of Church property, of shrines, of all that could be looted, by the [Protestant] gentry, large and small," and nuns and monks forced to marry.[98] Martin Luther abandoned his priestly celibacy to marry a nun who had forsaken her vow of chastity.

Nineteenth century philosophers perpetuated fractional complementary/hidden polarity views of the man/woman relationship: Schopenhauer argued that women live like children only in the present moment, while men integrate through past, present, and future.[99] Kierkegaard, in *Stages on Life's Way*, placed the wife in the aesthetic and religious sphere and the husband in the ethical sphere of duty,[100] while Nietzsche identified the woman with Dionysian energies and man with Apollonian reason.[101] None of these philosophers, neither Schopenhauer, nor Kierkegaard, nor Nietzsche, chose to marry.

Georg Friedrich Wilhelm Hegel (1770–1830) claimed that in marriage the husband and wife merge into a single person: "[Marriage's] objective source lies in the free consent of the persons, especially in their consent to make themselves one person, to renounce their natural and individual personality to this unity of one with one another."[102] The individual identities of the husband and wife disappear: "The identification of personalities, whereby the family becomes one person and its members become its accidents...is the ethical mind."[103] After an unsuccessful romantic attachment to a Catholic woman he could not marry, and after fathering a child out of wedlock with a housekeeper, Hegel did eventually marry with a Protestant understanding of the bond.[104]

Hegel argued against Kant's view of marriage as simply a contract, because contracts were concerned only with property and not with persons: "To subsume marriage under the concept of contract is thus quite impossible; this assumption – though shameful is the only word for it – is propounded in Kant's *Philosophy of Law* #24–27."[105] He nonetheless reduces marriage to a materialistic bond in the section "on marriage and the family" in *Philosophy of Right* where he concludes: "The family, as person, has its real external existence in property; and it is only when this property takes the form of capital that it becomes the embodiment of the substantial personality of the family."[106]

Enlightenment feminists rejected three of the essential characteristics of Catholic marriage: that it is initiated by God, that it serves as a living sign, and that it is a sign of God's enduring covenantal love for the world. Two others are still held by a thread for most Enlightenment authors: namely, that marriage is between two different kinds of persons and that it is called to be generatively fruitful. However, marriage is generally reduced to a utilitarian, hedonistic, or simple contract relationship in which woman is devalued. Consequently, several women Enlightenment feminists choose to reject the choice of marriage. The slow unraveling of sacramental marriage was joined with attacks on the priesthood, on the Mass, on the religious life, and on the vows. The loss of the living sign value of one kind of marriage led to the loss of the sign value of the other two. Once the identity of the family was reduced to its property, we are poised for the Post-Enlightenment feminist philosophers, who all will seek, in one way or another, to destroy marriage itself.

Post-Enlightenment Feminism and Marriage

Post-Enlightenment Feminism shifts from individual feminist authors working essentially on their own to feminist authors who lead political movements aimed at changing women's situation in the world. Our analysis will include three examples in which marriage is front and center in their critiques: Marxist feminism, Existential to Radical feminism, and Secular feminism.

Marxist Feminism

The Communist Manifesto of Karl Marx (1848) and *The Origin of the Family, Private Property and the State* of Friedrich Engels (1877)[107] sought to abolish private property which both authors believed had reduced the wife to a "mere instrument of production" and marriage to a utilitarian system for a "bourgeois" husband.[108] The Communist revolution would abolish "the present system of production [which] must bring with it the abolition of the community of women springing from that system, i.e., of prostitution both public and private."[109] Engels still allows for marriage "after the revolution," but it is simply based on feelings of "mutual inclination" and consequently has no endurance.[110]

Many Marxist feminists have followed the main lines of Marx's and Engel's theory while developing further nuanced positions with respect to woman's identity and political options. Early Marxist feminists focused on the husband-wife relation in marriage and the family. Emma Goldman (1869–1940) argued that the main obstacle to women's full development was the internal tyrant of her own attitudes supported by external tyrants in society; once these were overcome, then marriage could occur on a new unisex foundation that rejected all dualism between woman and man.[111] Evelyn Reed argued that the main obstacle to be overcome was "the long imprisonment of womankind in the home and family of class society;" and once the nuclear family was abolished women could recover their full dignity.[112]

More contemporary Marxist feminists considered generative aspects of marriage as the main obstacle to women's full development. Marlene Dixon, who focused primarily on the working poor, argued for the right to abortion on demand.[113] Maria dalla Costa and Selma James argued that, because family was the main obstacle to women's development, it should be abolished, or at least women ought to earn "wages for housework" for their pre-market labor. Saying that pregnancy was like an eighteen-year prison sentence, they also promoted abortion on demand.[114] The most extreme Marxist feminist argument against generativity was expressed by Shulamith Firestone, who perceived "the tyranny of reproduction and childbearing" itself as the obstacle for women's full development; she concluded that only when all babies will be gestated in test tubes and laboratories will women achieve full (unisex) equality with men.[115] Thus, in the development of Marxist feminism every essential characteristic of Catholic marriage was destroyed. The disappearance of the triadic sign-value of marriage into the dyadic structure of the enlightenment has led to the evaporation of the value of marriage in Post-Enlightenment marxism.

Existential to Radical Feminism

Simone de Beauvoir's (1908–1985) classical feminist text, *The Second Sex* (1949), ridicules marriage by applying Marxist, Freudian, and Existentialist arguments against it. She identifies as obstacles to women's full development: the female body, marriage, "feminine nature," and man as "the other." De Beauvoir reveals the rupture in Cartesian dualism of mind and body through a hatred for her own embodied gender identity: "Woman has ovaries, a uterus; these peculiarities imprison her in her subjectivity, circumscribe her within the limits of her own nature."[116] She twice refused marriage to Jean Paul Sartre, stating that her vocation as a writer was not compatible with it.[117] In a later candid interview, she reasserted: "I have escaped many of the things that enslave a woman, such as motherhood and the duties of a housewife."[118] De Beauvoir even argues that marriage as a career for women should even be against the law.[119]

In 1970 De Beauvoir signed a "Manifesto of 343" women stating that she had an illegal abortion. She began to lead demonstrations in favor of legalizing abortions in France; and she argued that "the embryo, as long as it is not yet considered human, as long as it is not a being with human relationships with its mother or its father, it's nothing, one can eliminate the embryo."[120] She states that nothing has an *a priori* identity: "The basis of existentialism is precisely that there is no human nature, and thus no "feminine nature." It is not something given."[121] In this situation, man has "proposed to stabilize her as object and to doom her to immanence."[122]

Even though Simone de Beauvoir, baptized Simone-Ernestine-Lucie-Marie de Beauvoir, devoutly practiced her Catholic faith as a young girl, she progressively moved away from it, saying, "I became more and more convinced that there was no room in the secular world for the supernatural life."[123] When challenged by a confessor about her behavior, she fled, and soon concluded: "I no longer believe in God."[124] Before long she came to a new conclusion: "I frankly detested the Roman Catholic religion."[125] Her feminist path moved from rejection of the Bridegroom, to rejection of marriage, to rejection of the bride.

Radical feminism is a direct offshoot of Simone de Beauvoir's existential feminism. For the United States, Mary Daly articulated the premises of radical feminism by arguing at first that the Catholic Church was the obstacle for women's full development. In her first book, *The Church and the Second Sex*, Daly recalls approvingly Simone de Beauvoir's rejection of her Catholic faith, and calling herself a "Post-Christian," she rejects her own Catholic baptism. She offers a scathing analysis of the Church, the Second Vatican Council, the religious life, and Jesus Christ himself in subsequent chapters entitled "The Case Against the Church" and "Radical Surgery Needed."[126] Daly argues that sacramental marriage should be changed into simple partnership; Holy Orders should not be reserved to men; and nuns, "a walking paradox," should emerge from the cloister and convent.[127] Daly says that she is "exorcizing" these three areas of the spousal bond in Catholic tradition.[128] In *Beyond God the Father: Toward a Philosophy of Women's Liberation*, Daly reduces the Catholic Church to a "sexist patriarchal institution": "The image of the church as the 'bride of Christ' is another way of conveying that it is 'the extension of the Incarnation,' since a bride or wife in patriarchy is merely an extension of her husband."[129] Later Daly posited men as the main obstacle to women's full development. In her satirical text, *Pure Lust*:

Elemental Feminist Philosophy, although the Church, the Holy Mass, and Pope John Paul II are ridiculed, ultimately Daly argues that women should be only "woman-identified." This radical feminist position leads inevitably to lesbian relations and worship of a female divinity.[130]

Radical feminism in France (1975–2004) also followed Simone de Beauvoir's existential feminism, as well as Freud and Marx, but it viewed language itself as the obstacle to women's full development. One French feminist Manifesto proclaimed the goal: "To destroy the differences between the sexes...at the same time as we destroy the idea of the generic 'Woman,' we also destroy the idea of 'Man.'"[131] Monique Wittag argued that gender itself should be destroyed: "Gender is an ontological impossibility because it tries to accomplish the division of Being. But Being as being is not divided ...Gender then must be destroyed."[132] Hélène Cixous summarizes the attack on marriage and the family: "It will be up to man and woman to render obsolete the former relationship and all its consequences, to consider the launching of a brand-new subject, alive, with *defamilialization.*"[133]

Ironically, language deprived of all its depth is viewed simply as something to use for political purposes as in Julia Kristeva's radical feminism:

> ...The belief that "one is a woman" is almost as absurd and obscurantist as the belief that "one is a man." I say "almost" because there are still many goals which women can achieve: freedom of abortion and contraception, day-care centers for children, equality on the job, etc. Therefore, we must use "we are women" as an advertisement or slogan for our demands. On a deeper level, however, a woman cannot "be," it is something which does not even belong in the order of *being.*[134]

The rejection of the substance, essence, and existence of a man or a woman *ipso facto* leads to the rejection of any bond of Catholic marriage between them.[135] Thus, Existential feminism and Radical feminism reject all five essential characteristics of Catholic marriage. In Radical feminism, the disappearance of the triadic sign-value of marriage into the dyadic structure of the Enlightenment has resulted in the evaporation of the human identities of a man and a woman; as Michael Foucault suggests, it is like "a face drawn in the sand at the edge of the sea."[136]

Secular Feminism

The foundational document of secular feminism, *The Subjection of Women* (1869), by John Stuart Mill (1806–1873), provided numerous systematic arguments against the lack of women's access to higher education, unjust marriage laws in England, and prohibitions against women's right to vote and participate in society.[137] Mill did not just write about the reform of law, for on May 20, 1867, Mill proposed and debated before the House of Commons that in the Reform Bill the word "man" be replaced by the word "person."[138] Although defeated, Mill's public proposal initiated the woman's suffrage movement in England.[139]

Mill supported laws for divorce on demand, believing that "all laws whatever regarding marriage should be done away. Inclination, not dependency should be the tie..."[140] Mill's own secular marriage to the widow Harriet Taylor occurred in 1851 by a local Registrar; he wrote a formal protest against the marriage laws in England stating: "I absolutely disclaim and repudiate all pretension to have acquired any *rights* whatever by virtue of such marriage."[141]

English feminist attempts to overturn laws prohibiting women's suffrage and divorce were joined in the United States by Elizabeth Cady Stanton (1815–1902) and Susan B. Anthony (1820–1906).[142] Soon laws prohibiting artificial means of birth control were identified as a further obstacle to women's full development in the here and now. Margaret Sanger (1879–1966), an American nurse, suffered while tending several women who died either from multiple pregnancies or in giving birth. In "The Right to One's Body" and "My Fight for Birth Control" she argued the "false alternative" of either artificial birth control or death of women.[143]

The philosophy of secular humanism took root in England through the Oxford philosopher Ferdinand Schiller (1864–1937) who considered all truths to be "man-made products." It spread to the United States through the educational philosophy of John Dewey and the pragmatism of William James (1842–1910), who claimed that truths "make themselves as we go."[144] Corliss Lamont identified further characteristics of American secular humanism, as follows: "The supernatural does not exist," and the goal of life is to "build an enduring citadel of peace and beauty upon this earth."[145]

Secular feminism sprang out of American secular humanism with a fury when it identified what it considered to be obstacles blocking women's fulfilment here and now. Betty Friedan, in *The Feminist Mystique* (1963), criticized marriage for keeping women in a child-like psychological state as housewives, "married to a house."[146] Organized religion became a secondary obstacle because it seemed to keep women in a perceived infantile state. When the Humanist Manifesto, which came out in 1973, rejected God and organized religion and advocated that "the right to birth control, abortion, and divorce should be recognized" by law on demand,[147] secular feminists turned the National Organization of Women (NOW) into a political movement aimed at changing the civil laws to meet these demands. How successful NOW was in achieving these aims in society at large has become only too evident in recent years. While initially NOW focused on economic discrimination, today the Website of the National Organization of Women expresses what it styles a "so-called pragmatic truth," namely, that one out of every two women will exercise their "right" to abortion.[148] Same-sex marriage, common bathrooms, military service for all, as well as so-called "gay" and lesbian "rights" complete the unisex theories of this liberal secular feminism. Its agendas, which are, of course, totally against the Catholic concept of marriage are also unfortunately supported by several consecrated women and priests.[149]

In this brief introduction to three post-Enlightenment developments of feminist arguments, we have seen the following similar consequences with respect to Catholic marriage. Rejection of God (the Bridegroom) is followed by rejection of the Church (the bride), and then by the rejection of each of the essential characteristics of Catholic marriage identified at the beginning of this paper: an enduring covenantal bond of love, between two different kinds of persons, initiated by God and confirmed by rite, called to be generatively fruitful, and serving as a living sign. The rejection of the marriage as a living sign-carrier of the love of God for the world, or the love of Christ for His Church, has ended with the internal self-destruction of marriage itself.

The Catholic Response: Personalist Feminism to New Feminism

Simultaneously with the above post-Enlightenment rejections of all of the essential characteristics of Catholic marriage, Catholic authors provided both theological and philosophical principles for engaging with these arguments. Popes Leo XIII, Pius XI, Pius XII, Paul VI, and John Paul II combined to author four papal encyclicals, two letters (one apostolic), three post-synodal documents, and several other documents directly addressing feminist critiques of Catholic marriage. Dietrich von Hildebrand, Edith Stein, Emmanuel Mounier, Jacques and Raïssa Maritain, Gabriel Marcel, Bernard Lonergan, and, finally, Karol Wojtyla, who became Pope John Paul II, all recovered new foundations for a philosophy of the person that overcame the rupture of Cartesianism and the multifarious developments in the feminisms identified above. In remainder of this paper, a brief description of these Catholic responses will be given.

In 1880, Pope Leo XIII's encyclical, *Arcanum* (On Christian Marriage), argued against both the contract theory of marriage (##17–18) and the naturalistic view of marriage (#19).[150] He reaffirmed the divine origin of the spousal bond, and restated the Catholic understanding that "Marriage, moreover, is a sacrament, because it is a *holy sign* which gives grace, showing forth an image of the mystical nuptials of Christ with the Church."[151]

In 1923, Dietrich von Hildebrand (1889–1977) gave a lecture on marriage to the Catholic Academic Association in Ulm, Germany; present at the lecture was Cardinal Eugenio Pacelli, the Papal Nuncio in Munich who would become Pope Pius XII.[152] This lecture and his subsequent book *On Marriage (Die Ehe)* (1929) captured von Hildebrand's conversion from an Evangelical Lutheran to a Roman Catholic understanding of natural marriage as a good which is elevated to supernatural marriage by being a sacrament, an image of the primordial marriage of Jesus Christ and the soul.[153]

Arguing against the "terrible anti-personalism" of the age, von Hildebrand stated that "love is the primary *meaning* of marriage just as the birth of new human beings is its primary *end.*"[154] Marriage occurs between a man and a woman, "metaphysically" complementary persons, and is exclusive, enduring, and "constituted only by a solemn act."[155] Von Hildebrand confirmed all the essential characteristics of Catholic marriage, as well as the spousal dimension of priestly ordination and consecrated life in this book of his, and he continued to emphasize and strengthen his position during his subsequent years as a Professor of Philosophy at the University of Munich, the University of Vienna, and Fordham University in New York.

In 1930, Pope Pius XI, in his encyclical *Casti Connubii (*On Christian Marriage*)*, reaffirmed the spousal dimension, enduring stability, and "nature and dignity of Christian marriage."[156] He added to the triadic sign-value of marriage the notion of "seeds of grace" and thereby opened a dynamic and living nature of the sign that needs to be actuated by the husband and wife (#40). Directly addressing the "fallacies" of the day, Pius XI criticized the views that marriage is simply due to "the will of man," "temporary," compatible with contraception and abortion, or that it demands blind obedience of the wife to the husband's commands.[157] Concluding that the post-Enlightenment feminist positions are "not the true emancipation of woman...[but] rather the debasement of the womanly character and dignity of motherhood," Pius XI proposed that "public authority [should] adapt the civil rights of the wife to modern needs and requirements, keeping in view what the natural disposition and temperament of the female sex, good morality, and the welfare of the family demands..." He added that the origin and final orientation of marriage as a movement from and towards God should be kept uppermost in mind.[158]

Bernard Lonergan, S.J., in "Finality, Love, and Marriage" (1942), elaborated on the theme of the final orientation of marriage in Pius XI's encyclical:

> Next, an account of the nature of love is attempted, and this opens the way for a discussion of the "primary reason and cause of marriage" mentioned in the papal encyclical, *Casti Connnubii.* Here the argument draws upon Aristotelian analysis, and it endeavors to formulate an ascent of love from the level of two-in-one-flesh to the level of the beatific vision....Its most excellent end lies on the supernatural level of personalist development.[159]

Lonergan describes the encyclical's approach to marriage as an active "ascent from Nature to Beatific Vision," because in Catholic marriage "there is a dispositive upward tendency giving a new modality to that high pursuit, for husband and wife are called not only to advance but to advance together...from the level of nature to the level of the beatific vision."[160] Lonergan elaborates the metaphysical and ethical aspects of this common consciousness in the common life of the married couple as they "realize in common the advance in Christian perfection that leads from the consummation of two-in-one-flesh to the consummation of the beatific vision."[161] For Lonergan, a married couple must together appropriate and incarnate this upward movement of the sign-value of their marriage at the same time as they point to the eschatological end of their mutual journey.

As early as 1928, Edith Stein (1891–1942), a Catholic lay woman, gave a public lecture in Bavaria on the strengths and weaknesses of secular feminism, concluding that: "The Suffragettes erred so far as to deny the *singularity* of woman altogether; thus it could hardly be a question of woman's *intrinsic value* as well."[162] Stein wrote of her own support for feminism: "During my years in the gymnasium and as a young student [at the university], I was a radical feminist. Then I lost interest in the whole question. Now, because I am obliged to do so, I seek purely objective solutions."[163] Using the phenomenological method, she proposed essential characteristics of woman's singular identity:

> Her *point of view embraces the living and personal* rather than the objective;...she tends towards *wholeness and self-containment* in contrast to one-sided specialization;...[with an ability] to become a *complete person* oneself...whose faculties are developed and coex-

ist in harmony; ... [who] helps others to become *complete human
beings*; and in all contact with other persons, [who] *respects the
complete human being...*Woman's *intrinsic value* can contribute
productively to the *national community* by her activities *in the
home as well as in professional and public life.*[164]

In 1930, Edith Stein wrote about her collaboration with Dietrich
von Hildebrand in giving a lecture on "The Ethos of Women's
Professions" in Salzburg, Austria. He agreed to give the original topic
assigned to her on "The Ethos of Christian Professions."[165] As early as
1914, Stein and von Hildebrand had been members of the Philosophical
Society, composed of students studying under Husserl and Scheler in
Göttingen (although her conversion from Judaism to Catholicism in
1922 followed later than von Hildebrand's in 1914).[166]

Stein's philosophy of woman is based on a renewed Thomistic metaphysics which affirmed the unity of the soul/body *composite,* but which
argued that the soul has priority in gender differentiation: "The insistence that the sexual differences are 'stipulated by the body alone' is
questionable from various points of view: 1) If *anima = forma corporis*,
then bodily differentiation constitutes an index of differentiation in the
spirit. 2) Matter serves form, not the reverse. That strongly suggests that
the difference in the psyche is the primary one."[167]

Edith Stein developed a new philosophy of the person as an embodied spirit/soul which is the *carrier* of a rational nature: "The *ego* not only
carries life, but the carrying itself is life, and to this life there pertains a
being inwardly aware of itself..."[168] In addition, the living person "is
never finished. It is forever on the way to its own self, but it bears within itself – i.e., within its soul – the power of forming itself."[169]
Consequently, in a vocation to Catholic marriage as a living sign of the
spousal bond of God and the world, or of Christ and the Church, the person becomes a carrier of life; and the carrying itself is new life to the
Church. This position accords with the Latin, who, as John Deely
observes in "From the Being of Sign to the Action of Sign," liked to say,
agere sequitur esse, 'action follows upon being,' 'follows logically, but
is temporally simultaneous therewith and necessary thereto.'"[170]

Following Pius XI, Edith Stein supported the essential characteristics of Catholic marriage against the post-Enlightenment attacks upon
them: "The Church expresses the *threefold purpose of marriage* in the
words *fides, proles,* and *sacramentum*. It is necessary today to preserve
this traditional conception of marriage against the pressure of public
opinion."[171] She also followed von Hildebrand in giving an extensive
analysis of love as the "mutual self-giving of persons."[172]

Edith Stein defended the spiritual marriage of a consecrated person, saying that women who follow the prototype of the Virgin Mary will live "a life of love, a life in which all faculties come to development. It will be a spiritual maternity because the love of the bride of God embraces all the children of God...This is the second ideal which we must preserve."[173] She accepted her own vocation to the consecrated life, and, as Saint Teresa Benedicta of the Cross, she wrote that her spousal consecration in virginity "is not only the symbol and instrument of bridal union with Christ and of the union's supernatural fruitfulness, but also participates in the union. It originates in the depths of the divine life and leads back to it again."[174]

In her last major work, *The Science of the Cross,* Teresa Benedicta of the Cross included three chapters on the spiritual marriage of Christ and the soul, according to St. John of the Cross. Her explanation of the profound depth and breadth of this call follows:

> ...in the *Canticle*, it [the bridal relationship] is the focal point for everything. This image is not an allegory...The relationship of the soul to God as God foresaw it from all eternity as the goal of her creation, simply cannot be more fittingly designated than as a nuptial bond. Once one has grasped that, then the image and the reality directly exchange their roles: the divine bridal relationship is recognized as the original and actual bridal relationship and all human nuptial relationships appear as imperfect copies of this archetype...[175]

Drawing out the analogy of the Bridegroom coming to take His bride to His Father's house, Saint Teresa Benedicta observes that "in order to lead the bride home, the Eternal Word clothed himself with human nature."[176] Then she links this carrying of the bride home to the passageway of the Cross: "So the bridal union of the soul with God is the goal for which she was created, purchased through the cross, consummated on the cross and sealed for all eternity with the cross."[177]

Before her entrance into Carmel, in 1932 Edith Stein met with Jacques Maritain (1892–1973) and Raïssa Maritain (1893–1960) at conferences for Catholic philosophers in France.[178] In 1936, Jacques Maritain wrote a didactic essay on "Love and Friendship" in which he distinguished different kinds of love. "A love of *dilection*...[is] that absolutely unique *friendship* between married people one of whose essential ends is the spiritual companionship between a man and a woman in order that they may help each other fulfill their destiny in this world."[179] Emphasizing the transcendent finality of the sign value of marriage pointing towards the heavenly homeland of husband and wife, Maritain analyzes the Song of Songs:...whose original purpose...was to sing of the nuptial love, the *amour fou* between God and His Church..."[180]

Maritain also defended the priestly vocation and the spousal aspect of consecrated life: "The vow of chastity, and the two other vows which it accompanies, constitute for those who consecrate themselves to the religious state...the hope of making their way here below toward perfection, under the regime of *amour fou* for God and for Jesus."[181] He exemplifies the phenomenon of persons who, in supporting the sign value of one kind of Catholic marriage, support the sign value of the other two paradigmatic vocations as well.

In the 1930s the Maritains joined other Catholic philosophers in Paris to begin a personalist review, *Esprit,* with Emmanual Mounier (1905–1950), soon married to a Belgian Catholic convert, Paulette Leclercq. By1936, Mounier heralded a new personalist feminism when he published an essay in *Esprit* entitled "Woman Is Also a Person."[182] In another essay, Mounier argued against utilitarian and secular feminist critiques of marriage: "Man and woman can only find fulfillment in one another, and their union only finds its fulfilment in the child; such is their inherent orientation towards a kind of abundance and overflow, not to an intrinsic and utilitarian end."[183]

Between 1939 and 1958, Pope Pius XII gave a series of addresses to newly married couples and other groups on the theme of Catholic marriage and woman's and man's identity, especially as wife and husband or mother and father. One by one, the Pope supports the essential characteristics of marriage in the modern world: "Marriage is not only a natural act, but it is also for Christians a great sacrament, a great sign of grace and of the sacred espousals of Christ with the Church."[184] Again: "Marriage is the union of one husband with one wife" and "on the single bond of matrimony is stamped the seal of indissolubility."[185]

In many respects, one can hear an echo of von Hildebrand's lecture on marriage here, which Pius XII had attended so many years before; and in another respect he addresses the increasingly antagonistic philosophies behind the modern attacks on marriage. In an address to the Italian Catholic Union of Midwives in 1951, Pope Pius XII offered principles for authentic generativity within Catholic marriage at the same time as he provides them for the precious vocation of midwives. No child is to be deemed "worthless life" and deliberately killed "as practiced a few years ago on many occasions."[186] – he seems to be speaking about the Third Reich. Pius XII further states that the "sublime mission of woman is motherhood," but he also argues that "there is no field of human activity which must remain closed to women; her horizons reach out to the regions of politics, labour, arts, sports..."[187]

A husband and wife should remain open to new life in the conjugal act, but be responsible about governing their passions and respecting one another in their sexual relations. Artificial insemination is contrary to human dignity in generation.[188] A new-born child should be placed immediately in the father's arms so that he will accept the new life entrusted to him by God.[189] In 1941, Pius XII had written about "The Mystery of Fatherhood,"[190] anticipating future explorations of this theme by both Gabriel Marcel, who in 1943, in "The Creative Vow as Essence of Fatherhood," explained how dynamic internal actions of a father (and a mother) are essential for authentically living the call to Catholic marriage and family in a secular world; and by Karol Wojtyla, who in 1964 wrote two plays, *Radiation of Fatherhood* and *Reflections on Fatherhood*."[191]

Gabriel Marcel (1889–1973), in "The Mystery of the Family" (1942) criticized the view of marriage simply as a contract which can be broken at will: "The more marriage is regarded as a simple contract, the more one must logically come to admit that it can be renounced by common accord, that it can even become no more than a temporary promise."[192] The growing practice of divorce means that marriage is not what it is meant to be, and "[t]hus, the family has been attacked in the double spring whence it derives its special vitality: fidelity and hope."[193] He argued against the reduction to a naturalist view of marriage: "...it is worth noticing how easy it is to slide from what professes to be a completely rational notion of marriage to the grossest form of naturalism which claims to remove all lines of demarcation between man and other living creatures, in order that he may enjoy all the license which goes with the natural state."[194]

Marcel offered a new approach to building an enduring bond of love in marriage: "In reality the truest fidelity is creative"; and although creative fidelity is not necessarily tied to Catholicism, "Christian dogma gives it a transcendant justification and adds infinitely to its splendor."[195] In his plays and in his book *Creative Fidelity*, Marcel continued to engage modern positions opposed to several of the essential characteristics of Catholic marriage.[196]

Karol Wojtyla Who Became Pope John Paul II

Karol Wojtyla is the most significant philosopher for Personalist feminism. He was a young seminarian in Cracow 1946, when Mounier traveled there to give a lecture on Personalism to an audience already familiar with his writings, which had been translated into Polish as early as 1934. After his priestly ordination, advanced studies in Rome, and travels in France, Karol Wojtyla began to work with Roman Ingarden, a Professor at the University of Cracow. Ingarden's close familiarity with Edith Stein's work was very likely shared with his young student. At any rate, Karol Wojtyla, in his book, *Love and Responsibility* (1960), directly engaged both Enlightenment and post-Enlightenment attitudes towards marriage:

> ...The principle of "utility" itself, of treating a person as a means to an end, and an end moreover which in this case is pleasure, the maximization of pleasure, will always stand in the way of love.
>
> The incompatibility of the utilitarian principle with the commandment to love is then clear: if the utilitarian principle is accepted, the commandment simply becomes meaningless.[197]

Karol Wojtyla introduced a new personalistic principle (always treat a person as an end in himself rather than a means) in order to measure the quality of the relationship between husband and wife marriage:

> ...ontologically, what happens in the marital relationship is that the man simultaneously gives himself, in return for the woman's gift of herself to him, and thus although his conscious experience of it differs from the woman's it must none the less be a real giving of himself to another person. If it is not there is a danger that the man may treat the woman as an object, and indeed an object to be used. If marriage is to satisfy the demands of the personalistic norm it must embody reciprocal self-giving, a mutual betrothed love.[198]

Wojtyla's philosophical views on marriage were reflected in the Second Vatican Council (1963–1965): "Fifteen years ago," he wrote, "in my book *Love and Responsibility*, I presented a personalistic interpretation of marriage – an interpretation that, it would seem, has found its way into Vatican II's Pastoral Constitution *Gaudium et Spes*."[199] This document had identified "The Dignity of Marriage and the Family" as one of five most urgent problems to be faced by the Church in the Modern World.

Directly following the Second Vatican Council, Dietrich von Hildebrand, now married and professor of philosophy at Fordham University in New York, published in 1966 *Man and Woman: Love and the Meaning of Intimacy*.[200] In this text he elaborated a philosophy of marriage in including such themes as: "Love affirms the person of the beloved," "Man and woman are complementary," "Spousal love aims at an irrevocable gift of love," "Sacramental marriage transforms love," "Procreation is the superabundant end of marriage," "The irreverence of artificial contraception," and The mission of men and women to each other."[201]

In 1969 Pope Paul VI in his Encyclical *Humanae Vitae* reaffirmed the primordial sign- value of Catholic marriage: "The marriage of those who have been baptized, is...invested with the dignity of a sacramental sign of grace, for it represents the union of Christ and His Church."[202] Pope Paul VI criticized a utilitarian contraceptive mentality for its inevitable devaluation of women:

> ...Another effect that gives cause for alarm is that a man who grows accustomed to the use of contraceptive methods may forget the reverence due to a woman, and disregarding her physical and emotional equilibrium, reduce her to being a mere instrument for the satisfaction of his own desires, no longer considering her as his partner whom he should surround with care and affection(#17).

This encyclical also criticized the reduction of Catholic marriage to civil unions..."determined to avoid [difficulties of the divine law] they may give into the hands of public authorities the power to intervene in the most personal and intimate responsibility of husband and wife"(#17).

The next year (1969), Karol Wojtyla published *The Acting Person*, in which he argued that persons needed to develop self-possession, self-governance, and integration of the passions to become fulfilled in communion with others. He observed that "nineteenth- and twentieth- century philosophy has rightly interpreted alienation as draining or sifting man from his very own humanness, that is, as depriving him of the value that we have here defined as 'personalistic.'"[203] He challenged his readers to follow the commandment "thou shalt love," based on the truth about the person as the "Rule of Being and Acting 'together with others.'"[204]

In "A Personalistic View of Conjugal Love," from "The Teaching of the Encyclical *Humanae Vitae* on Love" (1968) Cardinal Wojtyla elaborated on the "meaning and sign" of the conjugal act:

> ...Love cannot be simply identified with the conjugal act, but must be sought in the persons, in their awareness, choice, decision, and moral responsibility...It means both a special union of persons and, at the same time, the possibility (not the necessity!) of fecundity, or

procreation. *If, in acting jointly, this is precisely what they intend to signify by their activity, then the activity is intrinsically true and free of falsification.*[205]

When Karol Wojtyla became Pope John Paul II in 1978, his Wednesday audiences (1979–1984) began to explode with teachings about the dignity of woman in marriage. He also supported all three paradigmatic vocations to marriage: "Perfect conjugal love must be marked by that fidelity and that donation to the only Spouse (and also of the fidelity and donation of the Spouse to the only Bride), on which religious profession and priestly celibacy are founded."[206]

In 1988, in his apostolic letter *Muleris Dignitatem (On the Dignity and Vocation of Women),* John Paul II turned to a direct defense of woman's and man's fundamental equality of dignity and worth: *"Both man and woman are human beings to an equal degree;* and *[m]an is a person, man and woman equally so."*[207] This equality is manifested in both man's and woman's rational and free identity, and in their call to live in a communion of love as "a *sign* of interpersonal communion...marked by a certain likeness to the divine communion (*"communio"*)" of Persons in the Holy Trinity."[208]

Here we discover a recovery of the medieval *triadic* sign-value of marriage: the interpreter, the living sign-vehicle, and that which is signified.[209] The married couple, as an ontological living sign-carrier, opens up to an observer the epistemological dimension of knowledge and truth about God's marriage to his people. In fact, John Paul II argues that a marriage which manifests an inequality fails to follow this gospel innovation. Noting the threat of rupture in the marital relationship and woman's historical condition of subjection so bitterly contested by traditional feminists, he states:

> ...But this threat is more serious for the woman, since domination takes the place of "being a sincere gift" and therefore living "for" the other: "He shall rule over you." This "domination" indicates the disturbance and loss of the stability of that fundamental equality which the man and the woman possess in the "unity of the two": and this is especially to the disadvantage of the woman, whereas only the quality resulting from their dignity as persons can give to their mutual relationship the character of an authentic *"communio personarum."*[210]

A marriage of domination or inequality is a sign pointing in the wrong direction, or in the direction towards evil. Therefore, it cannot signify the community of persons in the Holy Trinity, the ontological reality of Good that should be the sign value of marriage.

In 1994, the Year of the Family, John Paul II wrote a "Letter to Families," in which he directly mentioned the Cartesian roots of the Enlightenment and its destructive role in Catholic marriage. First, he set forth the meaning of Catholic marriage for the family: "The family itself is the great mystery of God. As the 'domestic church,' it is the *bride of Christ.*"[211] Referring directly to Descartes' dualism, which led to the rupture of mind from body, and of consciousness from reality, the human person is reduced to the body, human sexuality to raw material "*for manipulation and exploitation*," and the mystery of eternity to "the *mere temporal dimension of life*" (#19). A husband and wife not living their vocation well become "counter-signs" to others: "a civilization inspired by a consumerist, anti-birth mentality is not and cannot become a civilization of love...; when it can easily fall prey to dangers which weaken it or destroy its unity and stability...families...can even become a negation of it, a kind of *counter-sign.*"[212]

This criticism of the Enlightenment and post-Enlightenment directions of society with regard to marriage is not extended to all aspects of feminist critiques. In his "Letter to Women," the Pope said that "the great process of women's liberation...has been a difficult and complicated one and, at times, not without its share of mistakes. But it has been substantially a positive one."[213] Specifically, Pope John Paul II agrees with many traditional feminist arguments:

> ... history which has conditioned us... has been an obstacle to the progress of women. Women's dignity has often been unacknowledged and their prerogatives misrepresented; they have been relegated to the margins of society and even reduced to servitude. This has prevented women from truly being themselves and it has resulted in a spiritual impoverishment of humanity.[214]

He regrets that some have in the Church done this as well:

> ...And if objective blame, especially in particular historical contexts, has belonged to not just a few members of the Church, for this I am truly sorry. May this regret be transformed, on the part of the whole Church, into a renewed commitment of fidelity to the Gospel vision. When it comes to setting women free from every kind of exploitation and domination, the Gospel contains an ever relevant message which goes back to *the attitude of Jesus Christ himself* (#3).

Woman's relation to Jesus Christ brings us back to the original spousal analogy of Catholic marriage, while engaging with its rejection by modern feminisms, many of which have roots in Cartesian rationalism. In the Holy Father's words in his "Letter to Families": "For rationalism it is unthinkable that God should be the Redeemer, much less *that he should be 'the Bridegroom,'* the primordial and unique source of the human love between spouses"(#19). He repeats this conclusion because of its crucial message: "The deep-seated roots of the 'great mystery,' the sacrament of love and life which began with Creation and Redemption and which *has Christ the Bridegroom as its ultimate surety* have been lost in the modern way of looking at things"(#19).

In his Encyclical *The Gospel of Life (Evangelium Vitae)* (1995), Pope John Paul II introduced the concept of a "*new feminism*" which shares several goals of previous feminisms, namely to "overcome all discrimination, violence, and exploitation; and introduces the new goal "to acknowledge and affirm the true genius of women in every aspect of the life of society" in which woman will "bear witness to the meaning of genuine love, of that gift of self and of that acceptance of others which are present in a special way in the relationship of husband and wife, but which ought also to be at the heart of every other interpersonal relationship."[215]

The genius of woman depends upon the principle of complementarity of men and women: "Womanhood and manhood are complementary *not only from the physical and psychological points of view,* but also from the *ontological.*"[216] In *Evangelium Vitae* (1995) the pope elaborates:

> ...Women first learn and then teach others that human relations are authentic if they are open to accepting the other person: a person who is recognized and loved because of the dignity which comes from being a person and not from other considerations, such as usefulness, strength, intelligence, beauty, or health. This is the fundamental contribution which the Church and humanity expect from women. And it is the indispensable prerequisite for an authentic cultural change.[217]

Catholic marriage is the workshop of this new feminism, and the Church and the world reap the benefits of its extension.

We have now come full circle. Beginning with Pope John Paul II's rich theological descriptions of the three paradigmatic kinds of Catholic marriage, we discovered how the married couple together is called to be a living sign of the eternal convenant of love between God and the world,

Christ and the Church; how the Priest is called to be a living sign of the love of Jesus Christ, the Bridegroom; and how the consecrated person is called to be a living sign of the bride, the Church's response to Divine Love. While early Renaissance feminism supported the essential characteristics of Catholic marriage, Enlightenment and post-Enlightenment feminisms eventually rejected every essential characteristic of all three paradigmatic vocations to Catholic marriage. Finally, Personalistic feminism, developed by several twentieth century Catholic philosophers, provided new and renewed foundations to defend essential characteristics of Catholic marriage. A cross-fertilization of theological and philosophical works engaged directly with errors in other theories and opened new avenues for a recovery of dynamic possibilities for Catholic vocations as complementary living signs of the primordial love of God for his people.

In conclusion, when all three primary vocations in the Church – to priestly, consecrated, and sacramental marriage – are filled with vibrant and attractive persons actuated as living signs of different aspects of the primordial marriage – of the Bridegroom, the bride, or the relation of Bridegroom and bride – then the civilization of love will pour forth its treasures on all who see and welcome the reality to which these signs so vibrantly and communally point.[218]

"The bridegroom is here! [Let us now go] out and meet him." Matthew 25:7

Sister Mary Prudence Allen, R.S.M., received her Ph.D. in philosophy in 1967 from the Claremont Graduate School in Claremont, California. She then taught philosophy at Concordia University in Montreal, Quebec, Canada, becoming Professor Emerita in 1996. From 1998 to 2003, she chaired the Department of Philosophy and is currently Professor in the same department at the St. John Vianney Theological Seminary in Denver, Colorado. Her areas of scholarly specialization include Existentialism, Personalism, the concept of the person in the history of philosophy, and the philosophy of woman. Sister Allen has published more than 40 articles in professional journals, and in 2003 she published her widely acclaimed two-volume work, *The Concept of Woman* (Grand Rapids, MI: Eerdmans).

Notes

1. See Kenneth D. Whitehead, Ed., *Marriage and the Common Good* (South Bend, Indiana: St. Augustine's Press, 2001).
2. Karol Wojtyla, *Person and Community: Selected Essays* (New York: Peter Lang, 1993), Part III: Marriage and the Family, 279–342, here 323.

3. For excellent work on early theology of marriage, see Glenn W. Olsen, "Progeny, Faithfulness, Sacred Bond: Marriage in the Age of Augustine" and "Marriage in Barbarian Kingdom and Christian Court: Fifth through Eleventh Centuries," in Glenn W. Olsen, ed., *Christian Marriage: A Historical Study* (New York: Crossroad Publishing Company, 2001), chapters 3 and 4: 101–212.

4. See Sr. Prudence Allen, "Can Feminism Be a Humanism,?" in Michele M. Schumacher, ed. *Women in Christ: Toward a New Feminism,"* (Grand Rapids: Eerdmans, 2004): 251–284, here 252.

5. See, for example, Beatrice Gottlieb, "The Problem of Feminism in the Fifteenth Century," *Women of the Medieval World: Essays in Honor of John H. Mundy*, eds. Julius Kirshner and Suzanne F. Wemple (Oxford: Basil Blackwell, 1985), 337–364.

6. See, for example, Allison Jaggar and Paula Stuhl, eds. *Feminist Frameworks: Alternative Theories of the Relations Between Women and Men* (New York: McGraw Hill, 1978).

7. Pope John Paul II, Encyclical Letter *Evangelium Vitae* ("The Gospel of Life") (Boston: Pauline Books and Media,1995), #99. Hereafter *EV*. His emphasis in italics as hereafter.

8. I am grateful to Fr. Ralph Drendel, S.J. for bringing this analogy to my attention. For further theological study of early Jewish and Christian marriage practices see Francis Martin, "Marriage in the Old Testament and Intertestamental Periods" and "Marriage in the Mew Testament Period," in Olsen, ed., *Christian Marriage*, chapters 1 and 2:1–100.

9. Congregation for the Doctrine of the Faith, Letter to the Bishops of the Catholic Church On the Collaboration of Men and Women in the Church and In the World (May 31, 2004), #9. For an excellent theological analysis of analogy, see also, Fr. Francis Martin, "Analogy, Images, Metaphors, and Theology" in *The Feminist Question: Feminist Theology in The Light of Christian Tradition* (Grand Rapids: Eerdmans, 1994): 221–264.

10. *Catechism of the Catholic Church* (New York: Image, 1995), #796.

11. Thomas Aquinas, *Summa Contra Gentiles: On the Truth of the Catholic Faith* (New York: Image, 1957). Book IV: Salvation, Question 78, art 3. My emphasis is in italics as in subsequent passages.

12. Aquinas, *Summa Contra Gentiles*, IV,78, 5.

13. See John Deely, "The Role of Thomas Aquinas in the Development of Semiotic Consciousness," *Semiotica* 152 (1/4) (2004), forthcoming. My emphasis.

14. Aquinas, *Summa Contra Gentiles*, IV,78, 5. See also Teresa Olsen Pierre, "Marriage, Body, and Sacrament in the Age of Hugh of St. Victor," in Olsen, ed., *Christian Marriage*, chapter 5: 217–220; E. Schillebeeckx, O.P., *Marriage: Human Reality and Saving Mystery* (New York: Sheed and Ward, 1965), 31–34; and John Paul II, *Familiaris Consortio: Apostolic Exhortation on the Role of the Christian Family in the Modern World* (November 22, 1981), #13

15. For a 1994–1995 articulation of these five essential characteristics see Karol Wojtyla, "The Teaching of the Encyclical *Humanae Vitae* on Love," "The Family as a Community of Persons," and "Parenthood as a Community of Persons," in *Person and Community* (New York: Peter Lang, 1993), 1: 307 and 323; 2: 324 and 330; 3: 304; 4: 324 and 332; and 5:308.

16. John Paul II, *Post-Synodal Apostolic Exhortation Vita Consecrata* (March 25, 1996), #31. My emphasis in italics.

17. Hans Urs von Balthasar, *The Christian State of Life* (San Francisco: Ignatius Press, 1983), 385.

18. John Paul II, *Vita Consecrata*, #31.

19. John Paul II, *Familiaris Consortio*, #13, 20, and 14. My emphasis. I am very grateful to Sr. Moira Debono, R.S.M.., S.T.D., who introduced me to the importance of these passages during a co-presentation we made to Newman Theological College on "Man-Woman Complementarity: The Catholic Inspiration," in Edmonton, Alberta, Canada (November 7–8, 2003).

20. Peter J. Elliott, *What God Has Joined: The Sacramentality of Marriage* (New York: Alba House, 1990), 79.

21. John Paul II, *Familaris Consortio*, #14. My emphasis.

22. John Paul II, *Familaris Consortio*, #14. Including reference #36 from the document. My emphasis.

23. John Paul II, *Letter to Families* (Boston: Pauline Books and Media, 1994), #6–8.

24. Archbishop Charles Chaput, O.F.M. Cap., *As Christ Loved the Church: A Pastoral Letter to the People of God of Northern Colorado on Forming Tomorrow's Priests"* (1994), #10. My emphasis. He also refers in this passage to CCC #1620 and to John Paul II, *Pastores Dabo Vobis* (March 25, 1992), #22.

25. John Paul II, *Muleris Dignitatem*, # 25. My emphasis.

26. John Paul II, *Pastores Dabo V obis,* #29.

27. Congregation for the Doctrine of the Faith, *Inter Insigniores*: Declaration on the Admission of Women to the Ministerial Priesthood (October 15, 1976), #5. The reference to Thomas Aquinas is from his commentary on IV Sentences, dist. 25, q 2, art 1, quaestiuncula 1a. My emphasis.

28. John Paul II, *Muleris Dignitatem*, #26.

29. John Paul II, *Muleris Dignitatem*, #26.

30. John Paul II, Post-Synodal Apostolic Exhortation *Vita Consecrata: On the Consecrated Life and Its Mission in the Church and in The World* (1996), #3.

31. John Paul II, *Muleris Dignitatem*, # 20.

32. John Paul II, *Muleris Dignitatem*, # 20.

33. Sacred Congregation for Religious and for Secular Institutes, *Essential Elements in the Church's Teaching on Religious Life as Applied to Institutes Dedicated to Works of the Apostolate* (May 31, 1983), Norm #4 and 14. My emphasis. See also *Lumen Gentium* :"[T]his consecration will be the more

perfect, in as much as the indissoluble bond of the union of Christ and His bride, the Church is represented by firm and more stable bonds *Lumen Gentium*, #44.

34. The eschatological sign value of consecrated life is constantly reiterated in Church documents. See Vatican Council II, *Perfectae Caritatis: Decree on the Adaptation and Renewal of Religious Life* (October 28, 1965)..."It reveals itself as a spendid *sign* of the heavenly kingdom," #1; and Congregation for Institutes of Consecrated Life and Societies of Apostolic Life, *Fraternal Life in Community* (February 2, 1994): "Thus, those who live consecrated celibacy recall that wonderful marriage made by God, which will be fully manifested in the future age, and in which the Church has Christ for her only spouse," #44 including a quotation from *Perfectatae Caritatis, #12.*

35. Sacred Congregation for Religious and for Secular Institutes, *Religious and Human Promotion* (April 1978), #24. My emphasis.

36. See also, John Paul II, *Vita Consecrata*, "...communities of consecrated life, where persons of different ages, languages, and cultures meet as brothers and sisters, are *signs that dialogue is always possible* and that communion can bring differences into harmony (#51).

37. I am grateful to Sr. Mary Judith O'Brien, R.S.M., J.D.C., for bringing this aspect of religious consecration to my attention.

38. For a detailed account of these works see Prudence Allen, R.S.M., *The Concept of Woman: The Humanist Reformation*, vol. II (Grand Rapids: Eerdmans, 2003), chapter 7, 537–658.

39. Christine de Pizan, *The City of Ladies* (New York: Persea Books, 1982), II, 13, 118.

40. Christine de Pizan, *The City of Ladies*, II.13, 118.

41. Francesco Barbaro, *Directions for Love and Marriage* (London: John Leigh, 1677), 68.

42. Albrecht von Eyb, *Das Ehebüchlein: Ob einem manne sey zunemen ein eelichs weyb oder nicht* (Berlin: Weidmann, 1890), 69. Translated by Robert Sullivan.

43. Henricus Cornelius Agrippa, *Declamation on the Nobility and Pre-eminence of the Female Sex* (Chicago: University of Chicago Press, 1993).

44. Lucrezia Marinella, *The Nobility and Excellence of Women and the Defects of Men* (Chicago: University of Chicago Press, 1999), introduction by Letizia Panizza, 17–18.

45. Marinella, *The Nobility and Excellence of Women and the Defects of Men*, 136–138.

46. Marinella, *The Nobility and Excellence of Women and the Defects of Men*, 39.

47. For a detailed analysis of the text see Prudence Allen, RSM, and Filippo Salvatore, "Lucrezia Marinelli and Woman's Identity in Late Italian Renaissance," *Renaissance and Reformation* XXVIII, 4 (1992): 5–39.

48. Juan Luis Vives, *The Education of a Christian Woman: A Sixteenth Century Manual* (Chicago: The University of Chicago Press, 2000).

49. Vives, *The Education of a Christian Woman,* Book II, chapter 1, #3, 176. Oddly, Vives described children as "an incredible burden and fatigue," and that it is a "great benefit" for a woman to be sterile., Book II, chapter 10, #124–127, 265–267.

50. Vives, *The Education of a Christian Woman,* Book II, chapter 3, #25–27, 194–195.

51. Charles Fantazzi, Prelude in Vives, *The Education of a Christian Woman,* 30–35.

52. Marie le Jars de Gournay, *Apology for the Woman Writing and Other Works* (Chicago: University of Chicago Press, 2002)*,* 95.

53. De Gournay, *Apology,* 87.

54. De Gournay, *Apology,* 105.

55. De Gournay, *Apology,* 91.

56. See Hilda Smith, *Reason's Disciples: Seventeenth-Century English Feminists* (Urbana: University of Illinois Press, 1982).

57. René Descartes, *Meditations on First Philosophy In Which The Existence of God And the Distinction of the Soul from the Body are Demonstrated* (Indianapolis: Hackett Publishing Company, 1993), second meditation, p. 19, #28.

58. Anna Maria van Schurman, *Whether a Christian Woman Should be Educated and Other Writings from herIntellectual Circle* (Chicago: University of Chicago Press, 1998), 29.

59. Van Schurman, *Whether,* 42, 44 and 55.

60. Poullain de la Barre, *The Woman as Good as the Man Or, the Equality of Both Sexes* (Detroit, Wayne State University Press, 1988), 103. For another translation see François Poullain de la Barre, *The Equality of the Two Sexes* (Lewiston: Edwin Mellon Press, 1989).

61. Poullain, *Equality,* 114.

62. Poullain, *Equality,* 128.

63. Poullain, *Equality,* 151.

64. John Calvin, *Institutes of the Christian Religion* (Grand Rapids: Eerdmans, 2001), vol. i, 348–350 and vol. ii, 646–649. Calvin, *Institutes,* ii.607. For a theological study of marriage in the Reformation see R.V. Young, "The Reformations of the Sixteenth and Seventeenth Centuries," in Olsen, ed., *Christian Marriage,* chapter 6: 269–301.

65. Hilaire Belloc *How the Reformation Occurred* (Rockford, Illinois: Tan Books, 1975), 90. Belloc also states that Calvin's *Institutes* "produced ...[an] enormous effect in its first few years...as throughout the Reformation, [by its] attack on priesthood." 81.

66. Poullain, *Equality,* 122. There is no mention of the priestly role in the celebration of the liturgy of the Holy Eucharist in this text, but his writings on the Eucharist brought him into conflict with the Church., 12.

67. Poullain, *Equality,* 86.

68. See Hilaire Belloc, *How the Reformation Happened* (Rockford Illinois: Tan Books, 1975), The English Sector, 110–115 and England, 154–161. "The policy of completely uprooting the Catholic Church from English soil suc-

ceeded. It succeeded mainly through the negative instrument of forbidding all action which could keep the Catholic Church alive: preventing children from receiving a knowledge of Catholic truth, hunting out the priesthood till this was reduced to a handful of wandering, concealed men in peril of their lives. But the capital agent of the change was the stamping out of the Mass," 110.

69. Peter J. Elliott, *What God Has Joined ...The Sacramentality of Marriage* (New York: Alba House, 1990), 103. See also James Hitchcock, "The Emergence of the Modern Family," in Olsen, ed., chapter 7:302–331.

70. Mary Astell, *Some Reflections on Marriage* (London: William Parker, 1730, rpt. New York: Source Book Press, 1970), 84.

71. Astell, *A Serious Proposal to the Ladies,* Part II, chap. 111, in Margaret Atherton, ed., *Women Philosophers*, 116, see also 105.

72. John Deely, *Four Ages of Understanding* (Toronto: University of Toronto Press, 2001): "A general notion of signs able to cover equally internal and external expressions of knowledge, 'words and ideas,' as Locke... put the matter...the dyadic semiological notion of sign as the external linkage the mind provides (through conventions) between vehicle and content, *signifiant* and *signifié,* we find that precisely what is missing...is the *significate,* in the sense of the object signified," 681–682.

73. Astell, *Some Reflections on Marriage*, 20.

74. Astell, *Some Reflections on Marriage*, appendix by Astell, 107.

75. Smith, *Reason's Disciples*, 117 and 131.

76. Astell, *A Serious Proposal to the Ladies,* 73.

77. See John J. Conley, S.J., *The Suspicion of Virtue: Women Philosophers in Neoclassical France* (Ithaca: Cornell University Press, 2002), and Madame de Maintenon, *Dialogues and Addresses*, ed. and trans. John J. Conley, S.J. (Chicago: University of Chicago Press, 2004), with dialogues "On the Drawbacks of Marriage," "On the Different States in Life," "Of Religious Vocations, and Of the Single Life."

78. See Conley, *The Suspicion of Virtue*, 79, 97, and 101.

79. Rousseau, *Émile* (London: Dent, 1984), 322.

80. Jean-Jacques Rousseau, *The Confessions* (The Bibliophilist Society, 1934), 24, 69, 74, and 355.

81. Jean-Jacques Rousseau, *Émile*, 340.

82. Mary Wollstonecraft, *A Vindication of the Rights of Woman* (New York: Norton, 1975), 89.

83. Wollstonecraft, *A Vindication of the Rights of Woman*, 88.

84. Wollstonecraft, *A Vindication of the Rights of Woman*, 5 (my italics).

85. See also Mary Wollstonecraft, *Historical and Moral View of the Origin and Progress of the French Revolution and the Effect it has Produced in Europe* in *The Wollstonecraft Anthology*, ed. Janet M. Todd (Bloomington: Indiana Press, 1977), 132.

86. Immanuel Kant, *On the Beautiful and the Sublime* (Berkeley and Los Angeles: University of California Poress, 1965), 79.

87. See Immanuel Kant, *The Metaphysical Elements of Justice (Part I of The Metaphysics of Morals)* (Indianapolis: Bobbs Merrill, 1965), 63. See also the translator's notes where he states that the detailed sections on the laws of domestic society and marital rights are left out of this English translation., 67.

88. Elliott, *What God Has Joined: The Sacramentality of Marriage*, 107–108.

89. Deely, *Four Ages of Understanding*, 553–570 and 681–683.

90. Theodor Gottlieb von Hippel, *On Improving the Status of Women* (Detroit: Wayne State University Press, 1979).

91. Timothy Sellner, introduction to Theodor Gottlieb von Hippel, *On Improving the Status of Women*, 27 and 39. In earlier versions of 1974 and 1975 he had argued against this principle of equality.

92. Theodor Gottlieb von Hippel, *On Improving the Status of Women*, 100 and 108.

93. Theodor Gottlieb von Hippel, *On Improving the Status of Women*, 167.

94. Martin Luther, "Marriage" from "Pagan Servitude of the Church," in *Selections from His Writings* (New York: Doubleday, 1951), p. 329. Note also: "There is no Scriptural warrant whatsoever for regarding marriage as a sacrament; and indeed the Romanists have used the same traditions, both to extol it as a sacrament, and to make it naught but a mockery," 326.

95. Luther, "Marriage" from "Pagan Servitude of the Church," 340.

96. Luther, "Marriage" from "Pagan Servitude of the Church," 300 and 301.

97. Luther, "An Appeal to the Ruling Class," in *Selections from His Writings,* #13, 447.

98. Belloc, *How the Reformation Happened*, 51.

99. Arthur Schopenhauer, "On Women," in *Essays and Aphorisms* (Harmondsworth: Penguin Books, 1970), 83.

100. Soren Kierkegaard, *Stages on Life's Way* (New York: Schocken Books, 1969), 61, 88, 98, 107, 163, and 280.

101. Sister Prudence Allen, RSM, "Nietzsche's Ambivalence About Women," in *The Sexism of Social and Political Theory: Women and Reproduction from Plato to Nietzsche*, eds. Lorenne M.G. Clark and Lynda Lange (Toronto: University of Toronto Press, 1979): 117–133.

102. *Hegel's Philosophy of Right,* #162, 111.

103. *Hegel's Philosophy of Right,* #163, 112.

104. See Gustav Muller, *Hegel: The Man, His Vision and Work* (New York: Pageant Press, 1968), 75–76, 211, 249–258.

105. *Hegel's Philosophy of Right* (Oxford: The Clarendon Press, 1958), 58 #74.

106. *Hegel's Philosophy of Right,* #169, 116.

107. Engels argued that "[t]he overthrow of the mother right [over their children] was the *world historical defeat of the female sex"* which resulted in the institution of monogamy so that husbands should pass their private property to their own sons, and women and children became the husband's property. See Frederick Engels, *The Origin of the Family, Private Property and the State* (New York: International Publishers, 1972), 120.

108. Karl Marx, *The Communist Manifesto* (Chicago: Henry Regnery Company, 1954), 47–48.

109. Marx, *The Communist Manifesto*, 50.

110. Engels, *The Origin of the Family*: "Full freedom of marriage can therefore only be generally established when the abolition of capitalist production and of the property relations created by it has removed all the accompanying economic considerations which still exert such a powerful influence on the choice of a marriage partner. For then there is no other motive left except mutual inclination.," 144. See also, 125–143.

111. Emma Goldman, "The Tragedy of Woman's Emancipation," in Alice S. Rossi, ed., *The Feminist Papers* (New York: Columbia University Press, 1973), 506–516.

112. Evelyn Reed, "Caste, Class or Oppressed Sex?" in Jaggar, *Feminist Frameworks*, 107–117.

113. Marlene Dixon, "We are Not Animals in the Field: A Woman's Right to Choose," in *The Future of Women* (San Francisco: Synthesis Publications, 1980): "Abortion on demand is the right of every woman. If we cannot end an unwanted pregnancy, if we are forced to bear a child against our will, then our right to self-determination has been completely denied to us," 124. See also "The Right of All Women to Control Their Own Bodies," 207–214.

114. See Maria Dalla Costa, *The Power of Women and the Subversion of the Community*, (Bristol, Falling Wall Press, 1973) and Selma James and Giuliana Pompei, *Wages for Housework* (Toronto: Canadian Womens Educational Press, 1974).

115. Shulamith Firestone, *The Dialectic of Sex: The Case for Feminist Revolution* (New York: Bantam Books, 1971), 225. She argues: "Machines thus could act as the perfect equalizer, obliterating the class system based on exploitation of labor," 201.

116. Simone de Beauvoir, *The Second Sex* (New York: Alfred Knopf, 1957), xv.

117. Simone de Beauvoir, *The Prime of Life* (Cleveland: World Publishing Co., 1962), 24 and 65–67. "My vocation likewise renounces the engendering of individual human beings," 67. For a detailed account of her life, see Deirdre Bair: *Simone de Beauvoir: A Biography* (New York: Summit Books, 1990).

118. Simone de Beauvoir in Margaret Simons, "Two Interviews with Simone de Beauvoir (1982)," *Hypatia* 3, no. 3 (winter 1989), 19.

119. Simone de Beauvoir, *The Second Sex, 482*: "The truth is that just as – biologically – males and females are never victims of one another but both victims of the species, so man and wife together undergo the oppression of an institution they did not create. If it is asserted that *men* oppress *women*, the husband is indignant; he feels that *he* is the one who is oppressed – and he is; but the fact is that it is the masculine code, it is the society developed by the males and in their interest, that has established woman's situation in a form that is at present a source of torment for both sexes. It is for their common welfare that the situation must be altered by prohibiting marriage as a "career" for women."

120. Simone de Beauvoir in Margaret Simons, "Two Interviews with Simone de Beauvoir (1982), 18–19.

121. Simone de Beauvoir in Margaret Simons, "Two Interviews with Simone de Beauvoir (1982), 19.

122. De Beauvoir, *The Second Sex*, xxxiv.

123. Simone *de Beauvoir, Memoirs of a Dutiful Daughter* (Cleveland: World Publishing Co., 1959), 77–79.

124. De Beauvoir, *Memoirs of a Dutiful Daughter*, 144.

125. De Beauvoir, *Memoirs of a Dutiful Daughter*, 327.

126. Mary Daly, *The Church and the Second Sex* (New York: Harper, 1968, 1975) .

127. Daly, *The Church and the Second Sex*, 28.

128. Daly, *The Church and the Second Sex*, 147–148.

129. Mary Daly, *Beyond God the Father: Toward a Philosophy of Women's Liberation* (Boston: Beacon Press, 1973), 139.

130. Mary Daly, *Pure Lust: Elemental Feminist Philosophy* (Boston: Beacon Press, 1984), 51, 57, 82–84, and 246–253.

131. "Common Themes," in *New French Feminisms* (New York: Schocken Books, 1981), 215.

132. Monique Wittag, "The Mark of Gender," *Feminist Issues (Fall 1985)*, 6.

133. Hélène Cixous, "Le rire de la méduse," in *New French Feminisms*, 261. My emphasis.

134. Julia Kristeva, "La femme, ce n'est jamais ça," in *New French Feminisms*, 137.

135. The ideas of radical feminism have begun to penetrate even moderate secular feminism so that in 1995 at the UN International Conference on Women, a proposal was put forward by the American women to introduce five categories of gender, differentiated by combination of sexual orientation and sexual identity. The Vatican delegation successfully challenged this radical proposal to reaffirm the central place of the two gender identities: man and woman.

136. Michael Foucault, *The Order of Things: An Archeology of the Human Sciences* (New York: Vintage Books, 1970), 387.

137. John Stuart Mill, "The Subjection of Women," in *Three Essays* (London: Oxford University Press, 1969): "The object of this Essay is to explain...[t]hat the principle which regulates the existing social relations between the two sexes – the legal subordination of one sex to the other – is wrong in itself, and now one of the chief hindrances to human improvement; and that it ought to be replaced by a principle of perfect equality," 427.

138. Michael St. John Packe, *The Life of John Stuart Mill* (New York: Macmillan Company, 1954), 492.

139. Packe, *The Life of John Stuart Mill*. Mill wrote to a friend: "The Women's question has been a most decided and important success, and it is truly astonishing how the right opinion is spreading among women and men

since the debate. We are now forming a society in London for the Representation of Women, and hope to get others formed in Edinburgh and Dublin, and elsewhere (there is already a most efficient one in Manchester, which obtained the majority of the 13,500 signatures to this year's petitions.", 492–493.

140. Packe, *The Life of John Stuart Mill*, 138.

141. Packe, *The Life of John Stuart Mill*, 348. In fact, Mill's marriage to Harriet Taylor was one of profound love between the two spouses, built on 20 previous years of chaste friendship, and lasting seven years until Harriet's death.

142. See Rossi, *The Feminist Papers*, 378–470.

143. See Rossi, *The Feminist Papers*, 517–536.

144. William James, "Pragmatism and Humanism," in *Pragmatism* (Cleveland: Meridian, 1963), 159 and "Humanism and Truth," 230. See also, Sr. Prudence Allen, R.S.M., "Can Feminism be a Humanism?" in Schumacher, *Women in Christ*, 272–276.

145. Corliss Lamont, *The Philosophy of Humanism* (New York: Frederick Ungar Publishing Co., 1982), 14–16.

146. Betty Friedan, *The Feminine Mystique* (New York: Norton 1963), 43 and 282.

147. Corliss Lamont, "The Humanist Manifesto of 1973" in *The Philosophy of Humanism* (New York: Frederick Ungar Publishing Co., 1982) appendix, 295.

148. See www.now.org/issues/abortion/rights-rep.html

149. See "An Open Letter from 3000 Roman Catholic Voters," in *The New York Times* (October 23, 2000) available on Catholics Speak Out www.quixote.org/cso or cso@quixote.org. For another example see (Sr.) Sandra Schneiders, *Beyond Patching: Faith and Feminism in the Catholic Church* (New York: Paulist Press, 1991).

150. Pope Leo XIII, *Arcanum (On Christian Marriage)* (February 10, 1880) in Claudia Carlen, *The Papal Encyclicals, 1887–1903* (The Pierian Press, 1990).

151. Pope Leo XIII, *Arcanum*, 29ff., #24.

152. Dietrich von Hildebrand, *Marriage: The Mystery of Faithful Love* (Manchester, New Hampshire: Sophia Institute Press, 1991), Introduction, xiv–xv. His wife Alice Jourdain von Hildebrand confirmed in her lecture to the Fellowship of Scholars in 1999, "Marriage: *Magna Res Est Amor*," that "the overwhelming experience of discovering the sublime teaching of the Holy Catholic Church opened his eyes to a totally new dimension of love and marriage," in Whitehead, ed., *Marriage and the Common Good*, 36.

153. Von Hildebrand, *Marriage*, 53–55.

154. Von Hildebrand, *Marriage*, xxv and 7. For theological discussion of Von Hildebrand, see also John M. Haas, "The Contemporary World," in Olsen, ed., *Christian Marriage,* chapter 8: 340–346.

155. Von Hildebrand, *Marriage*, 14, 21, and 13–15.

156. Pope Pius XI, *Casti Connubii* (Encyclical On Christian Marriage), (December 31, 1930), in Claudia Carlen, I.H.M., *The Papal Encyclicals 1903–1939* (MS: The Pierian Press, 1990), 391ff, #4, 26, and 37.

157. Pope Pius XI, *Casti Connubii*, #44–75.

158. Pope Pius XI, *Casti Connubii*, #76–77. He also criticized materialistic Communism which ruptured woman's relation to the family. See also the encyclical *Divini Redemptoris* (March 19, 1937) in *Papal Teachings: The Woman in the Modern World* (Boston: Daughters of St. Paul, 1958), 39–40.

159. Bernard Lonergan, "Finality, Love, and Marriage," *in Lonergan: Collection*, Vol. 4 (Toronto: University of Toronto Press, 1967): 16–52, here18–19.

160. Lonergan, "Finality, Love, and Marriage," 29. For a theological discussion of Lonergan's view of marriage see Haas, "The Contemporary World," in Olsen, ed., *Christian Marriage*, 350.

161. Lonergan, "Finality, Love, and Marriage," 37. For some contemporary engagement of feminists with Lonergan's philosophy of marriage see Cynthia Crysdale, ed., *Lonergan and Feminism* (Toronto: University of Toronto Press, 1994). Some of these essays do not accept the essential characteristics of Catholic marriage as elaborated in this paper.

162. Edith Stein, *Essays on Women*, Second Edition, Revised (Washington DC: ICS Publications, 1996), Outline of a Lecture given to Bavarian Catholic Women Teachers in Ludwifshafen on the Rhine, April 12, 1928. Her italics. The beginning of this passage reads: "In the *beginning of the feminist movement*, it would hardly have been imaginable to consider this theme [The significance of Woman's Intrinsic Value in National life]. At that time, the struggle for "Emancipation" was taking place; i.e., actually the goal aspired to was that of *individualism*: to enable women's personalities to function freely by the opening up of all avenues in education and in the professions." Introduction, 27–28.

163. Edith Stein, "Letter to Sister Callista Kopf, O.P., Speyer, August 8, 1931)" in *Self Portrait in Letters 1916–1942)* (Washington DC: ICS Publications, 1993), 99.

164. Stein, *Essays on Women*, Introduction, 38–39. Her italics.

165. Stein, "Letter to Sr. Adelgundis Jaegerschmid, O.S.B.," in *Self Portrait in Letters,* 64.

166. Edith Stein, *Life in a Jewish Family* (Washington DC: ICS Publications, 1986), 253–258.

167. Stein, "Letter to Sister Callista Kopf," in *Self Portrait in Letters,* 99.

168. Edith Stein, *Finite and Eternal Being: An Attempt and an Ascent to the Meaning of Being* (Washington DC: ICS Publications, 2002), 361.My emphasis.

169. Stein, *Finite and Eternal Being*, 274.

170. Deely, *Four Ages of Understanding*, 643, referring back to John Deely, *The Human Use of Signs ; or Elements of Anthroposemiosis* (Lanham, MD: Rowman and Littlefield, 1994), #3ff.

171. Stein, *Essays on Women*, Mission of the Catholic Academic Woman (1932 address in Switzerland). Her italics. The quotation continues: "It is a vital question for our nation and the entire human race that the Church's conception stay preserved. It can be preserved on no theoretical foundation other than the teaching of the Catholic faith," 267.

172. See Stein, *Finite and Eternal Being*, 453–459.

173. Stein, *Essays on Women*, 267–268. Her italics.

174. Edith Stein, Sister Teresa Benedicta of the Cross, *The Hidden Life: Hagiographic Essays, Meditations, Spiritual Texts* (Washington DC: ICS Publications, 1992) (Sept. 14, 1941), 103–104.

175. Edith Stein (Saint Teresa Benedicta of the Cross), *The Science of the Cross* (Washington DC: ICS Publications, 2002), 242.

176. Stein, *The Science of the Cross*, 272.

177. Stein, *The Science of the Cross*, 273.

178. Edith Stein, *Self Portrait in Letters 1916–1942* (Washington DC: ICS Publications, 1993), 116–117, 124–125 and 145–146.

179. Jacques Maritain, "Love and Friendship: A Marginal Note to the Journal of Raïssa," in *Untrammeled Approaches* (Notre Dame: University of Notre Dame Press, 1997), 184. His italics.

180. Maritain, "Love and Friendship," 191.

181. Maritain, "Love and Friendship," 194.

182. Emmanuel Mounier, "La femme aussi est une personne," *Esprit* (June 1936): 292–297.

183. Emmanuel Mounier, *Personalism* (Notre Dame: University of Notre Dame, 1952), 108.

184. Pope Pius XII, "The Inviolability Dignity of Marriage Which is One and Indissoluble," in *The Dignity and Happiness of Marriage* (London: Campion Press, 1959) (April 22, 1942), 79. See also Pope Pius XII *Speaks to Married Couples: Dear Newlyweds* (Kansas City, MO: Sarto House, 2001), 85–89.

185. Pope Pius XII, "The Inviolability Dignity of Marriage," 78 and 79.

186. Pope Pius XII, *Moral Questions Affecting Married Life* (Washington DC: National Catholic Welfare Service, 1951), #12, 6.

187. Pope Pius XII, "The Dignity of Woman" (October 14, 1956), in *Papal Teachings: The Woman in the Modern World,* 272–273.

188. Pope Pius XII, *Moral Questions Affecting Married Life*, #51–68, 19–23.

189. Pope Pius XII, *Moral Questions Affecting Married Life*, #15, 7.

190. Pope Pius XII *Speaks to Married Couples: Dear Newlyweds*, 170–174.

191. Gabriel Marcel, "The Creative Vow as Essence of Fatherhood," in *Homo Viator,* 98–124 and Karol Wojtyla, "Radiation of Fatherhood" and "Reflections on Fatherhood" in *The Collected Plays and Writings on Theater* (Berkeley: University of California Press,1987), 323–368.

192. Gabriel Marcel, *Homo Viator* (New York: Harper, 1962), 86.

193. Marcel, *Homo Viator*, 82.

194. Marcel, *Homo Viator*, 86–87.

195. Marcel, *Homo Viator*, 90 and 92.

196. See Gabriel Marcel, *Creative Fidelity* (New York: Fordham University Press, 2002).

197. Karol Wojtyla, *Love and Responsibility* (San Francisco: Ignatius Press, 1981), 40.

198. Karol Wojtyla, *Love and Responsibility* (San Francisco: Ignatius Press, 1981), 99.

199. Wojtyla, "The Family as a Community of Persons," 325.

200. Dietrich von Hildebrand, *Man and Woman: Love and the Meaning of Intimacy* (Manchester, New Hampshire: Sophia Institute Press, 1966).

201. Von Hildebrand, *Man and woman*, 13–15, 37–38, 42–45, 66–68, and 90–91.

202. Pope Paul VI, *Encyclical Humanae Vitae* (On the Regulation of Birth) (July 25, 1968), #8.

203. Karol Wojtyla, *The Acting Person* (Dordrecht: D. Reidel, 1979), 279.

204. Wojtyla, *The Acting Person*, 297–298.

205. Karol Wojtyla, "The Teaching of Humanae Vitae on Love: An Analysis of the Text," in *Person and Community*, 309. His emphasis.

206. John Paul II, "Marriage and Continence Complement Each Other," in *The Theology of the Body: Human Love in the Divine Plan* (Boston: Pauline Books, 1997), 277.

207. John Paul II, *On the Dignity and Vocation of Women* (Boston: Pauline Books, 1988), #6. His emphasis.

208. John Paul II, *On the Dignity and Vocation of Women*, #7.

209. See Deely, *Four Ages of Understanding*, 681–682. Deely attributes this "post-modern" recovery of the triadic notion of sign to the philosophy of Pierce 640–644.

210. John Paul II, *On the Dignity and Vocation of Women*, #10.

211. John Paul II, *Letter to Families* (Boston: St. Paul Books and Media, 1994), #19.

212. John Paul II, *Letter to Families*, #14. His emphasis. See also: "What shall we say of the obstacles which...still keep women from being fully integrated into social, political and economic life?...the gift of motherhood is often penalized...much needs to be done to prevent discrimination against those who have chosen to be wives and mothers...there is an urgent need to achieve...equal pay for equal work, protection for working mothers, fairness in career advancements, equality of spouses with regard to family rights, and the recognition of everything that is part of the rights and duties of citizens in a democratic state," #4.

213. John Paul II, *Letter to Women*, #6.

214. John Paul II, *Letter to Families*, #3. For a detailed discussion of his relation to different kinds of feminisms see Sr. Prudence Allen, R.S.M., "Philosophy of Relation in John Paul II's New Feminism," in Schumacher, *Women in Christ*, 67–104.

215. John Paul II, *Evangelium Vitae* #99 in *The Genius of Women* (Washington DC: US Catholic Bishops' Conference, 1997).

216. John Paul II, *Letter to Women,* #7. For a detailed analysis of these different levels of complementarity see, Allen, "The Philosophy of Relation in John Paul II's New Feminism," 93–104.

217. John Paul II, *Evangelium Vitae* #99 in *The Genius of Women.*

218. With gratitude to Mother Mary Quentin Sheridan, Superior General of the Religious Sisters of Mercy of Alma, Sr. Rita Rae Schneider, R.S.M., Ph.D., Sr. Moira Debono, R.S.M., S.T.D., John Deely, Ph.D., and members of the Philosophy Department and the Theological Faculty of St. John Vianney Theological Seminary in Denver for suggestions related to this paper.

Chapter 8: Can Feminism Acknowledge a Vocation for Women?
A Response to Sr. Mary Prudence Allen, "Catholic Marriage and Feminism"

LAURA L. GARCIA, PH.D.

Sr. Prudence Allen presents a beautiful portrait of marriage and its intimate relationship to the priestly vocation and the religious vocation. In her careful historical analysis of feminism, she makes a convincing case for the connection between a high view of marriage and a high view of two other human vocations, to the priesthood and to religious life. She also illustrates the way in which denigration of any one of these vocations leads to neglect or distortion of the others. Along with her helpful analysis of the central characteristics of marriage, Sr. Prudence develops a *complementarity* model of male/female relationships that avoids the morally disturbing versions of this model represented by Rousseau and J. S. Mill, among others. She presents the new feminism as the product of fruitful interchanges between philosophy and theology, proving that such exchanges are actually possible. The new feminism resists the possible abuses of the complementarity model because of its radical commitment to the dignity and equality of persons *as persons*.

Despite the obvious appeal of this new feminism, many thinkers (including some Christians) reject it in its present form, and precisely because of its commitment to complementarity. Resistance to the complementarity model of male/female relationships often stems from the fear that it will lock the woman into a specific "place" where she must remain, regardless of her own desires, interests, talents, education, and circumstances. This kind of "role-rigidity" is not logically implied by the complementarity model, however, even if it can be extended in that direction. In fact, just the opposite conclusion follows from a complementarity model that incorporates a deep commitment to the equal personal dignity of women and men.

Preserving this equal dignity implies: (1) the role of wife and mother should not be restricted exclusively to intra-domestic activities, but (2) the contributions of women to domestic activities must be deeply respected and properly rewarded. Pope John Paul II strongly endorses both of these claims. In *Familiaris Consortio* he writes:

> There is no doubt that the equal dignity and responsibility of women fully justifies women's access to public functions. On the other hand the true advancement of women requires that clear recognition be given to the value of their maternal and family role, by comparison with all other public roles and all other professions. Furthermore, these roles and professions should be harmoniously combined, if we wish the evolution of society and culture to be truly and fully human (#23).

More radically still, the "Letter to Families" claims that:

> The "toil" of a woman who, having given birth to a child, nourishes and cares for that child and devotes herself to its upbringing, particularly in the early years, is so great as to be comparable to any professional work. This ought to be clearly stated and upheld, no less than any other labor right. *Motherhood, because of all the hard work it entails, should be recognized as giving the right to financial benefits at least equal to those of other kinds of work undertaken to support the family during such a delicate phase of its life* (#17; emphasis mine).

One reason for a re-evaluation of work, including work in the home, is John Paul II's profoundly developed theology of work as an integral aspect of the human vocation, common to each one of us and inherently relational. Work enables men and women to participate in the creativity of God. "As man through his work becomes more and more the master of the earth, and as he confirms his dominion over the visible world, again through his work, he nevertheless remains in every case and at every phase of this process within the creator's original ordering."[1] The subject of work, the person, is more important than the object of work, the things produced by work. Work is for man, not man for work. The basis for determining the value of human work is not primarily the *kind of work* being done, but the fact that *the one doing it is a person.*"[2] Considerations such as these may lessen the tendency toward "workaholism" and promote greater appreciation of husbands for wives and vice versa. Work is for the good of persons, so that good must not be sacrificed to work. Further, we never carry out our work in complete solitude, but in collaboration with others. The collaboration between men and women, both in general terms and in the more specific vocation of marriage, is one important instance of this relational dimension of work.

If the work that is carried out more by women than by men can find new dignity and respect, there will be less reason for resentment regarding it. One positive public relations development in this regard comes from the increasing numbers of men who are stay-at-home dads. The visibility given to these men by the press and their reflections of their work has helped to raised the social consciousness about the demands and opportunities in the work traditionally assigned (almost exclusively) to women. But the more controversial question is this*: Do women have a special responsibility, a special vocation*, for creating a family atmosphere in the home and attending to the needs of the children? Or are men and women *equally responsible* for these? In one sense, of course, it is obvious that fathers and mothers bear the same moral responsibilities vis-a-vis their children; the phrase "equal responsibility" stands in here as an abbreviation for the anti-complementarity view, namely, the view that there is no activity or sphere with regard to family life that is especially entrusted either to women or to men. On the other hand, if there *is* such an area of entrusting, this does not mean that the other spouse is totally exempt from paying attention to it. Marriage is calls for genuine collaboration, not a fixed and inflexible division of labor.

To even *suggest* that there is a role in the home or in children's lives that is (usually) best filled by the mother is, by today's cultural lights, to promote a dangerous heresy. (To claim that fathers fill a unique and crucial role in children's lives is also a cultural heresy, in spite of the mounting evidence for its truth.) Current social and intellectual orthodoxy insists that there are *no significant differences between men and women as men and women.* Hence, there are no roles or tasks or areas of responsibility that might fall especially upon men or upon women. If this plank in the feminist platform gives way, many women fear that men will be excused from paying attention to the home and family, while women will be completely restricted to this sphere, or at least strongly discouraged from developing and pursuing their personal interests and talents. Adding the term "vocation" here ups the ante by implying that it is God's will that women should remain in their place, with domesticity as a one-size-fits-all vocation for them.

Is it possible to acknowledge differences between men and women, between mothers and fathers, without imposing (explicitly or implicitly) rigid social roles? Obviously this is at least a logical possibility, and the recent statement from the Congregation for the Doctrine of the Faith speaks of the collaboration of men and women as though it were a live option even in the practical realm. In spite of the nobility of the goals of that document, it has met with skepticism and even hostility in many quarters (not that this is a new experience for the Congregation for the Doctrine of the Faith!). It is simply assumed that to distinguish the vocations of men and women is inevitably to coerce them into "acceptable" social roles, defined more or less arbitrarily.

The British author Dorothy Sayers was regularly asked too provide the "woman's point of view" on various issues and controversies of her day. In one her essays she complains about this, noting that "what is repugnant to every human being is to be reckoned always as a member of a class and not as an individual person."[3] With respect to career choices, she urges that women (and men) should be judged with regard to their personal interests, talents, and abilities, leaving them free to pursue whatever jobs they wish. To bring home her point that women can excel in virtually any profession, Sayers tells us that "among [Queen Elizabeth's] most remarkable achievements was that of showing that sovereignty was one of the jobs for which the right kind of woman was particularly well fitted."[4] On the other hand, Sayers tell us that we should not expect to find the same number of male and female composers or mathematicians. "What we must not do," she says, "is to argue that the occasional appearance of a female mechanical genius proves that all women would be mechanical geniuses if they were educated. They would not."[5] Here Sayers shows a remarkable balance between *acknowledging differences* between women and men while leaving many different career options open for both – perhaps even for the stay-at-home dad.

However, as Sayers nears her conclusion I believe she overstates the case for individuality. From the (sensible) premise that the fundamental difference between men and women is "not the only fundamental difference in the world," she concludes that "a difference of age is as fundamental as a difference of sex; and so is a difference of nationality."[6] This conclusion does not follow from her premises, and would require much more support than she provides here. Her own comments on traits typical of men and of women might suggest a rather different conclusion. Age *is* an important consideration, of course, but one that does not directly impact the question of adult vocation, and race and nationality are irrelevant in a similar way. Clearly one's existence as male or female goes deeper than these more contingent (and sometimes changing) characteristics. Sayers fears that categories and classifications can be used (and have been used) to justify oppression. "To oppose one class perpetually to another – young against old, manual labor against brain-worker, rich against poor, woman against man – is to split the foundation of the State; and if the cleavage runs too deep, there remains no remedy but force and dictatorship."[7] (Prophetic words indeed in 1938!)

Personalist feminism or "new feminism" seeks a third way. To distinguish one group of persons from another is not necessarily to bring them into opposition. Still, when one insists that the male/female distinction is fundamental and that it has implications for the vocation of each group, the shields go up. If a vocation is a calling, *should* men and women be required or pressured (if not legally, then morally or emotionally) to stay within the limits of their vocation? How can one preserve a role for personal freedom and individuality within a model that finds separate vocations for women and men?

The response to this concern is two-fold. First, the vocation in question is one of *extreme generality*, since it flows from a very general trait. If women have a special role as trustees of humanity, for example, this can live itself out in countless ways, and in any task, job or profession. Second, fulfilling a vocation does not require that one personally undertake *every task* associated with that vocation. The vocations of men and women *overlap* significantly, especially for parents, and a given couple will decide how to manage the care of the children (the house, the laundry, the car, the bills, etc.), adjusting their plan as their circumstances change. Single parents must take on multiple aspects of both vocations, calling on outside reinforcements where needed (just as all parents do – taking advantage of help from relatives and friends, teachers and coaches, and anyone who cares about their children.)

In a recent exchange of views on women and the future of the family, Elizabeth Fox-Genovese courageously suggests that women might have to rethink current paradigms of family life in light of the needs of children; specifically, children's needs might best be met by mothers sacrificing some of their career potential (as well as income, of course) to spend more time focused on their children. I call this proposal courageous because in today's intellectual climate, offering such a view in the public market of ideas comes close to committing academic hara-kiri. As far as I know, no other leading woman intellectual has attempted it. Even those who believe that children *do* especially need their mothers want to downplay the notion that any real sacrifice involved, or that women might be called (in this arena) to a greater degree of sacrifice than men. While Pope John Paul II insists on the importance of the mother's role in nurturing children, he follows this immediately with the insistence that the financial sacrifices involved must be minimized and that the work of the home should be duly compensated, perhaps even economically. Interestingly, Sr. Prudence Allen describes Marxist-style feminism as the original impetus behind the wages-for-housework proposal, a proposal later championed by some of the first-wave secular feminists. As a move for justice, it has its appeal; as a political proposal, I'm afraid it is dead in the water. It also seems highly unlikely that the value of women's work can be restored by means of economic incentives alone.

In spite of these obstacles, we cannot simply place the vocational question on hold, given the disarray in our culture and its successive blows to the dignity of women. As Fox-Genovese points out: "Christian women are beginning to understand that the price of radical individualism is too high. But many continue to choke on the notion that they might be called to somewhat different roles and somewhat different sacrifices than men."[8] Assuming that Christian women *will* choke on this notion, many of those writing on married life and the vocations of men and women stay as far away from it as possible. One theologically conservative priest, writing on conflicts between family and career, insists that this conflict is basically the same for men and women; he then urges that "the family should be a shared responsibility, *distributing tasks equally* between wife and husband."[9] In this statement everything depends on what counts as an "equal distribution." Is each task to be shared in 50/50 by both spouses? If so, then women are *not* called to different sacrifices than men.

In a critical response to Fox-Genovese's essay, Margaret (Mardi) Keyes calls for a discreet silence on the subject of woman's vocation, since she thinks the Bible itself is largely silent on the matter. Keyes explains: "*Shared parenting* – or 'joint stewardship for children,' as Fox-Genovese puts it – is the biblical norm. This pattern was established at creation and confirmed throughout the Old and New Testaments...The apostle Paul exhorted older women to teach the younger women how to love their husbands and children; and he warned fathers not to exasperate, embitter, or provoke their children to anger, but rather to nurture them in the training and instruction of the Lord (Eph 6:4; Col 3:21)."[10] Keyes believes that the silence of the Bible on gender roles is "striking" and "intentional" and that, viewed rightly, "gender complementarity is not defined in terms of separate roles, responsibilities, activities, or attitudes...It is more holistic, mysterious and flexible."[11] (So mysterious and flexible, in fact, that it runs the risk of disappearing altogether in a cloud of pious smoke!)

While she references the Biblical passages on fathering, Keyes omits the citation for Paul's advice to women, taken from his pastoral letter to Titus. There Paul's silence is less evident, as he writes: "[The older women] are to teach what is good, so that they may encourage the young women to love their husbands, to love their children, to be self-controlled, chaste, good managers of the household, kind, being submissive to their husbands, so that the word of God may not be discredited" (Tit. 2: 3b–5). There is also a prior charge to the men: "Tell the older men to be temperate, serious, prudent, and sound in faith, in love, and in endurance" (Tit 2: 2). Interestingly, women are assigned a task that involves educating the next generation of women as well as the next generation of children – it is person-centered, while also incorporating the same moral and theological virtues enjoined on men.

It might turn out that Mardi Keyes' concern to preserve the Biblical silences is incompatible with Betsey Fox-Genovese's concern to preserve the children. If so, *is there a greater responsibility for women in raising children* (if not greater, at least *substantive* in its demands and *different* from the demands on men)? It would certainly seem so. Children need the mother's presence in a way different from their need for the father's presence; this different need may also vary in what it demands of mothers and fathers, and in what it demands at different times in the child's life. While acknowledging the need for women to develop their gifts and to impact the culture at every level, the Holy Father frequently reiterates the crucial role women play in the home and in the lives of children.

> While it must be recognized that women have the same right as men to perform various public functions, society must be structured in such a way that *wives and mothers are not in practice compelled to work outside the home*, and that their families can live and prosper in a dignified way even when they themselves devote their full time to their own family.
>
> Furthermore, the mentality which honors women *more for their work outside the home than for their work within the family* must be overcome. This requires that men should truly esteem and love women with total respect for their personal dignity, and that society should create and develop *conditions favoring work in the home.*[12]

The problem is not just that *men* fail to esteem women for their work in the home: many *women* have *obvious contempt* for this work. It is regularly dismissed in feminist writings as "servant's work" (more recently, by Naomi Wolf and others, even as "shit work"), and is compared to slavery or imprisonment.

Professor Fox-Genovese goes to the heart of the matter in calling for a reversal of today's self-centered values and a renewed commitment to moral and spiritual virtues, including those of service and sacrifice. "Today," she observes, "women are wresting themselves from the bonds of those virtues, and, as they do, the virtues are all but disappearing."[13] We need to recover these virtues, and that recovery program clashes with demands to be liberated from service and sacrifice. Obviously Christians must lead the way in this recovery movement – Christian *women*, perhaps, most of all. Women still know that there is joy as well as effort in the washing of little feet. And if women have a special responsibility for children, it is also clear that men have a special responsibility for women. Service and sacrifice are at the heart of Christian discipleship and the disciples are not above the Master. As long as the age of grace lasts, there is hope that men and women, at least Christian men and women, will learn to collaborate more fully and more fruitfully, supporting each other in that greatest of all human vocations–learning how to love.

Laura L. Garcia has a Ph.D. in philosophy from the University of Notre Dame, and is currently teaching in the philosophy department at Boston College. She has previously taught at Notre Dame, Calvin College, the University of St. Thomas in St. Paul, Minnesota, the Catholic University of America in Washington, D.C., as well as at Georgetown and Rutgers Universities. Her philosophical essays have appeared in various publications. Her essay on "Preserving Persons" is forthcoming in the volume *The Contribution of John Paul II to Medical Ethics* edited by Christopher Tollefsen. Her specialties include metaphysics and the philosophy of religion. Currently she is working with a group of scholars in an effort to define Personalist Feminism. She is a founding member of Women Affirming Life and University Faculty for Life and lectures widely on the life issues.

Notes

1. Pope John Paul II, encyclical Laborem Exercens,# 4 (September 14, 1981).
2. Ibid, 6.
3. "Are Women Human?" an address given to a Woman's Society in 1938, published in Dorothy Sayers, Unpopular Opinions: Twenty-One Essays (New York: Harcourt, Brace and Co., 1947), p.130.
4. Ibid, p. 136.
5. Ibid, p. 137.
6. Ibid, p. 139.

7. Ibid, p. 141.
8. Elizabeth Fox-Genovese, Women and the Future of the Family, with responses by Stanley J. Grenz, Mardi Keyes, Mary Stewart Van Leeuwen, ed. James W. Skillen and Michelle N. Voll (Grand Rapids: Baker Books, 2000), p. 44.
9. Bishop Javier Echeverria, Prelate of Opus Dei.
10. Keyes, Ibid, pp. 69-70.
11. Ibid, p. 70.
12. Pope John Paul II, apostolic exhortation Familiaris Consortio,# 23; emphasis mine.
13. Fox-Genovese, Ibid, p. 43.

Chapter 9: Pornography and the Communion of Persons

Whitney R. Jacobs, M.A.

Abstract

Pornography is a hugely lucrative industry and an increasingly integral part of Western popular culture. It has been studied extensively for its effects on a wide range of social outcomes, and has been the focus of intense debate in the legal and political arenas, not least for its effects on the family. Yet despite the attention given to pornography, researchers have lacked an adequate anthropology with which to view it, and have been stymied by the political agendas of their research. In this paper I step back from the political and legal implications of pornography and examine it in light of the relationality that undergirds human fulfillment. Drawing from Karol Wojty³a's personalism and (as Pope John Paul II) his analysis of love as gift, as well as from the dialogical theories of Gabriel Marcel and Martin Buber, I explore the essence of pornography, the attitudes it expresses toward its subjects, and the inner development of its users. I propose that pornography instrumentalizes other persons and leads to self-absorption, limiting its users' psychic and spiritual availability and impeding the personal growth that occurs through intimate relationships informed by true values. My interpretation challenges researchers to transcend their limited agendas and views of the human person, and to address the issue of forming and maintaining the family in a pornographic culture.

Introduction

In 2003, the New Zealand Office of Film and Literature Classification published an extensive review of literature from the English-speaking world on the effects of pornography use (Barwick,

2003). Having set out to determine what is scientifically known about exposure to porn, the investigators came to the conclusion that extant data on the subject are weak and conflicting, and that the research has been almost entirely defined by the agendas of three ideological camps.

The first and most dominant of these camps may be called "liberal," and holds both that standards of acceptability are socially constructed, and thus variable, and that individuals can choose rationally both what products they consume and how much they are affected by them. Because consensuality is the lodestar of liberal sexual attitudes, the primary concern of liberal porn researchers has been to show whether its use contributes to coercive practices such as rape and child sex abuse, which they measure in direct and demonstrable ways.

The second camp may be called "feminist," and holds that pornography, like other media, conveys to its consumers messages that can affect their attitudes and behavior. Feminists are most concerned about messages they consider degrading to women, such as that women are unequal to men, that they exist to serve men's pleasure, and that they do not mind being raped and battered. Feminist porn researchers analyze the content of pornography for themes of subjugation and violence, seek evidence of its effects on users' attitudes, and may consider as relevant not only laboratory data, but also the anecdotal testimonies of women affected by pornography.

The third camp may be called "conservative-moralist," and holds, like the feminist camp, that pornography is a powerfully effective means of influencing people's attitudes. The attitudes that conservative-moralists oppose, however, are those suggesting that sexual activity without commitment is an ideal, that all forms of sexual gratification are equally valuable, and that the responsibilities of marriage and family life are unfulfilling. Conservative-moralist porn researchers tend to look at whether exposure to pornography influences people's attitudes toward deviant sexuality and their willingness to marry and beget children, as there is a pro-family element in this camp. These researchers also tend to be concerned about the effects of porn's sexual explicitness.

In investigating pornography's effects, all three of these camps are onto something. None of them is wrong as far as it goes. Yet neither are they adequate, either alone or in combination, to understanding fully pornography's effects on the human person. What none of them addresses is the question of what it takes to fulfill the sexuality of human persons, whose product pornography is. Implicit in each of the camps is a view of human nature and of what constitutes its flourishing. Those who endorse pornography use certainly believe that it is humanly fulfilling in some way, or at least that it is neutral with respect to human develop-ment. Many who seek to suppress pornography as a product, on the other hand, do not address its implicit view of fulfillment, which remains at large in the culture and finds its way into other forms of media. Understanding and critiquing the worldview of pornography requires one to see it from a perspective more profound than what social science and experimental method can muster: a perspective that considers the nature of man, how his dignity is expressed in his sexuality, and how his choices about sex bring him closer to or farther from attaining his true good.

Asking those questions, and appraising pornography in light of their answers, are the tasks I have undertaken in this paper. My approach to the issue is by way of theology, metaphysics, and psychology. I hope to demonstrate that the effects of pornography use can only be understood in light of an adequate anthropology in which man's nature as a self-forming agent, fulfilled in love and called to self-donation, are seen and acknowledged. When the human person is appreciated in its fullness, I believe, pornography will be recognized as an impediment to true hap-piness. I propose that it encourages its users to see other people as objects for use, deforms its users' interior lives by disconnecting them from reality, and renders them incapable of true intimacy. I also argue that pornography use is inimical to the values of interpersonal commun-ion, and that it forms an impediment to the formation and survival of the family. I propose that the values it espouses, both openly and implicitly, deserve careful scrutiny and rebuttal on the basis of a fuller view of human potential.

Toward the Essence of Pornography

Definitions of the term "pornography" are highly contested, less because its subject is mysterious than because the term is seen as pejo-rative. No one wants his own tastes written off as trash. For this reason the term 'pornography' is often distinguished from the terms "obsceni-ty" and "erotica," the former by those who wish to rescue it from its pejorative connotations, the latter by those who are willing to sacrifice the term in exchange for a putatively more elevated one. "Obscenity," as Christopher Hunter (2000) has noted, is primarily a legal term whose parameters were defined by the 1973 U.S. Supreme Court decision in *Miller v. California.* Those parameters include an appeal to prurient interest as determined by community standards, the depiction of sexual conduct in a "patently offensive way," and the lack of "literary, artistic, political, or scientific value." "Erotica," meanwhile, is a term primarily championed by feminists, who have argued that, in contrast to pornography, it depicts sexual activity in a non-exploitative and egalitarian manner (Hunter, 2000).

While these labels may have non-trivial legal ramifications, most people who are not ideologically partisan in the matter would admit that the distinctions among pornography, obscenity, and erotica are questions of degree, rather than of kind. All three terms refer in a general way to material that is self-consciously sexually provocative. It is noteworthy that the definitions of pornography used by experimental researchers would also be applicable to obscenity and erotica. The authors of a major Italian meta-analysis on pornography's effects, for example, employed a fellow-researcher's definition, as follows: "Any commercial product in the form of fictional drama designed to elicit or enhance sexual arousal" (Oddone-Paolucci, Genuis, and Violato, 2000). The late psychiatrist Robert Stoller, an expert on sexual perversions, defined pornography as "that product manufactured with the *intent* to produce erotic excitement" (1985, p. 15). A number of researchers have also employed as their operative definition "those explicit sexual depictions whose purpose or effect is to bring about sexual arousal in the ordinary viewer or reader" (cited in Hunter, 2000).

The common element in these definitions, which seem to bridge the conceptual gaps among pornography, obscenity, and erotica, is that they all refer to a product whose purpose is to arouse its consumers sexually. The phrases "designed to elicit or enhance" and "manufactured with the intent to produce" in the first two definitions suggest that pornography has a hypothetical audience upon whom it is intended to have a certain effect (sexual arousal), and to which that audience is expected to respond with action (such as masturbation or coitus). That pornography carries an intent of this kind – i.e., that it not only expresses its author's mind but is an incitement, implies that it is not merely a product, but in effect an *act of will*. The third definition states, in addition, that pornography can also be defined as anything that *causes* sexual arousal, regardless of its intent. This implies that pornography is less about content than about one's attitude toward particular persons or objects. There is material that, by its nature, can be called pornographic; there is also a pornographic way of treating what was not intended for that purpose.

Whereas researchers have defined porn deductively, Steven Marcus took a more inductive approach. He examined the content and themes of a large body of Victorian pornographic writings and identified in them a number of common elements that he considered to be characteristic of pornography's "ideal type." While the works he examined are rather distant in both time and medium from the pornography of today, they are, at least historically, closer than today's pornography to the mid-eighteenth century in which Marcus located the origin of the genre's significance. His insights, derived from works rich in literary indicators of their authors' worldviews, provide a window into the workings of the pornographic mind. The following quotations were taken from Marcus's book, *The Other Victorians* (1960):

> 1. "...almost all pornography is written by men and for men...the point of view is entirely masculine. It concentrates upon this organ and what it can do: the organ becomes the person, and the woman ceases to be a woman and is transformed into an object" (p.213).
>
> 2. "...one important attribute of...the kind of sexuality celebrated in pornographic writing is expressed in its abstract and quantitative idea of itself. Sexuality in this conception consists of an endless accumulation of experiences" (p. 181).
>
> 3. "...the idea of pleasure in pornography typically excludes the idea of gratification, of cessation. Pleasure is thought of as endless and as endless repetition" (pp. 214–15).
>
> 4. "...the author [of pornography] is not actually seeking union with another person. He is seeking to fulfill or act out certain fantasies; and the success of such a project depends on the degree to which he can dominate or control his sexual partners, the degree to which he can turn them into objects" (p. 160).
>
> 5. "Its [pornography's] success is physical, measurable, quantifiable; in it the common pursuit of true judgment comes to a dead halt. On this side, then, pornography falls into the same category as such simpler forms of literary utterance as propaganda and advertising. Its aim is to move us in the direction of action..." (p. 278).
>
> 6. "...the tone of the majority of pornographic works of fiction is lighthearted, humorous, harmless in intention, and slightly scatterbrained. It is only when one goes beneath the surface that one finds the mechanical grimness, the frenzied repetition, the impotent quest for omnipotence" (p. 251).

Marcus's insights into pornography are very much in keeping with other researchers' definitions, while probing deeper into the intentions behind the product. As Marcus sees it, the pornographic "project" is an essentially masculinist one, in which male sexuality is totemized in the phallus and brandished over women in a primal act of power and self-indulgence. Beneath the practice of pornography, furthermore, Marcus finds an essentially impersonal and dualistic view of sex, as conscious pleasure lacking both fulfillment and any sense of purpose. He has identified – without naming the anthropological underpinning of pornography – the view that human beings stand apart from their sexuality and may use it as they please; their sexual activities are disconnected from their personal development and are ultimately incapable of shaping who they are. Behind this anthropology, Marcus detects the nihilism of addiction, the despairing suspicion that this thing so desired yet imperfect is all there finally is to ease the plight of man. In the pornographic mind, it would seem, the quest for transcendence has been replaced by a grasping self-justification, and the hope of fulfillment is trampled in the struggle for pleasure.

In his analysis of pornography's masculinist agenda, Marcus's assessment would find sympathy with feminists. They have often claimed that pornography can be considered an act (for a sample, see Hunter, 2000), emphasizing that by its very nature porn embodies certain attitudes toward women on the part of its creators, attitudes that its consumers may come to adopt. For these feminists, the problem with pornography is that it promotes values disrespectful of the freedom, dignity, and unique sexuality of women as feminists understand those things. Thus anti-porn feminists tend to prefer erotica, which can be said to share the same essential intent as pornography but to portray women as equal and uncoerced partners in the activities it describes. Though feminists are often greatly concerned about the content of pornography, they seem not to ask whether the very consumption of products whose purpose is sexual arousal might itself denote certain problematic attitudes that are not changed by merely altering its content.

Supplementing and extending the feminists' insight is the definition of pornography given by Karol Wojty³a: "Pornography is a marked tendency to accentuate the sexual element when reproducing the human body or human love in a work of art, with the object of inducing the reader or viewer to believe that sexual values are the only real values of the person, and that love is nothing more than the experience, individual or shared, of those values alone" (1994, p. 192). Wojty³a's definition shares the feminist insistence that, because pornography intends certain values, it can be viewed as both a product and an act. In claiming that pornography's object is to induce its users to adopt and act upon certain attitudes, Wojty³a seems to liken pornography to a type of propaganda, just as Marcus did. He probes deeper than the feminists, however, by identifying that pornography also implies a particular view of human fulfillment that is defined, less by the attitudes evinced in the specific acts it depicts, than by its detachment of the sexual act from the context of true values.

For Wojty³a, the values conveyed by the content of pornography cannot compensate for porn's fundamental omission of what he calls the "personalistic norm." This norm consists in recognizing the special dignity of the human person, specifically the existential value of his sexuality as the means by which new life is created. To depict sexuality without reference to this existential quality is to conflate love with the external values of sex, reducing to a biological function the urge whose rightful setting is the desire of another's true good. This conflation is made not only by creators of pornography, whose concern is nothing more than to produce arousal, but also by anyone who regards a person or the representation of a person simply as a means to sexual arousal. According to Wojtyla's definition, the essence of pornography is choosing to emphasize the sexually arousing qualities of a person or thing above its other aspects. This choice has the effect of reducing the value of that person or thing to those elements that serve the desire for sexual arousal. As a result of this reduction, both the personal subject of the pornography (that is, the individuals portrayed in it), and love itself – of which sexual pleasure is but one aspect among many – come to be seen as instruments for the user's enjoyment.

Here we reach the moral dimension of pornography in a significant way. Wojty³a has developed Kant's imperative, that "whenever a person is the object of your activity, remember that you may not treat that person as only the means to an end, as an instrument, but must allow for the fact that he or she, too, has, or at least should have, distinct personal ends" (Wojty³a, 1994, p. 28). To treat a person instrumentally, Wojty³a proposes, would be to deny that person's interiority, agency, and freedom of conscience, and to regard him, falsely, as of lesser dignity than oneself. Wojty³a's point in criticizing sexual objectification is not to claim that there is anything immoral about sexual arousal; he writes that "neither sensuality nor even concupiscence is a sin in itself, since only that which derives from the will can be a sin – only an act of a conscious and voluntary nature" (Wojty³a, 1994, p. 161). What he would argue, rather, is that sexual arousal exists in the service of love, and that this fact is denied by the attitude exhibited in pornography, which obscures any understanding of sex's purpose other than selfish pleasure.

Writing later as Pope John Paul II (1997), Wojty³a expands upon his earlier critique of pornography. He continues to emphasize the unique dignity of human persons, specifying that the crucial element in pornography is connected to its portrayal of the human body. Arguing from an interpretation of the Book of Genesis, he begins by proposing that the masculinity of man and the femininity of woman, manifested in their respective bodies, reflects their interiority and personal dignity. The naked human body, male and female, has the meaning of a gift of each sex to the other, a gift of each person's self that includes the totality of his or her being. When this gift is welcomed and sustained in acceptance by the other party, it forms a nuptial system that John Paul refers to as the communion of persons (*communio personarum*). This communion is the deepest form of human communication, and constitutes the foundation of family life through the fertility and mutual support it encompasses within its exchange of total self-giving.

John Paul argues that the dignity of human beings revealed in their naked bodies (which he notes, citing Genesis, were not created to be alone) creates an ethical obligation to portray them appropriately. He writes that "it is precisely this truth about man – the whole truth about man – that makes it necessary to consider both the sense of the privacy of the body and the consistency of the gift connected with the masculinity and femininity of the body itself, in which the mystery of man, peculiar to the interior structure of the person, is reflected" (1997, p. 224). In practical terms, one must consider, whenever the naked human body is portrayed, the question of how the gift that it represents will be received by other persons. Whenever the naked body is displayed in an anonymous way, he states, it is "suspended in the dimension of an unknown reception and an unforeseen response. Thereby it is in a way threatened in the order of intention, in the sense that it may become an anonymous object of appropriation, an object of abuse" (p. 225).

What John Paul is proposing, here, is that the pornographer is guilty, not only of promoting whatever values are instantiated in the content of his product (i.e., degrading, illicit, or unfulfilling sexual practices), but of threatening the very dignity of his subjects, whose bodies he has exposed to an uncertain fate in the hearts of those who may see them. For consumers of porn, on the other hand, John Paul suggests that the burden before them is to avoid the temptation to lust by maintaining a purity of both sense and intention when confronted by the naked human person. By this additional foray into theological anthropology, John Paul has furthered his previous analysis of pornography. He continues to regard it as both a product and an act – an act that intends or allows the degradation of persons by violating their privacy and disregarding the need for their nakedness always to be perceived in the mutual vulnerability of self-giving love.

Pornography and the Relational Self

In investigating what pornography is, I have already hinted at its effects on the person. Now I will examine those effects in a more detailed way. I previously suggested in passing that the sexual arousal pornography intends is expected to result in action. This action can take the forms of masturbation or of coitus (consensual or forced), which can each be accompanied by efforts to resist it. Sexual arousal can go no farther than titillation, and can be either rebuffed or frustrated anywhere short of orgasm by interruption, guilt, emotional impediment, or physical dysfunction. Pornography can be employed, by an exercise of the will, to bring its user to any one of these states, and no farther; it can even be used for entertainment without arousal. The arousal created by pornography can also be diverted away from the pornography itself toward a real sexual interaction, as when pornography is employed by both married and unmarried couples as a form of sex therapy – if not in clinical sex therapy – where it can produce the excitement necessary for intercourse in relationships in which that has waned. If the use of pornography results in a preference for the imagined partner over the real and present one, however, such use remains essentially masturbatory in that it is focused on a stimulus that originates in oneself, rather than on another person.

To understand why this is so, it is necessary to understand the phenomenon of intimacy. In an unpublished article, philosopher Kenneth Schmitz described several characteristics of the concept of intimacy that are relevant to the present discussion. The essential element in Schmitz's definition of intimacy is the "undemanding" sense of another's presence, which can persist even in the physical absence of the other. Contrasting it initially with *Eros*, he distinguished that endless, questing desire to possess another, with the experience of "relaxation in the trusted co-presence of another" (1999; p. 15) that can describe intimacy. By an etymological analysis, Schmitz went on to state that the term itself connotes an interplay of inwardness, depth, and proximity. He explained that intimacy is an inter-subjective relation that does not objectify the other, arguing that it consists not merely in knowing (or exchanging) information about another, but in valuing her for whom (rather than what) she is. He proposed that intimacy has no other purpose than to share in coexistence with another: to embrace the presence of the other as such. Conceiving transcendence as an act of "reaching out" aimed at the "enlargement of the individual," Schmitz summarized much of his position by stating that "intimacy is *transcendence transformed*, an opening out of the person toward a relationship that terminates in an other in such a way that it resists exhaustive analysis" (1999; p. 21; emphasis in the original). Elsewhere in the article, he noted that intimacy requires persons and can only occur between them.

Though the sexual function is often referred to as an "intimate" act, it seems clear that pornography leaves the criteria for intimacy wholly unmet. In an immutable sense, recourse to pornography is characterized by an emotional investment of the individual in an inanimate object – a representation – with which there can be no mutuality. The dynamics of pornography consumption are one-sided, in that the consumer's attention is directed to something that cannot respond, even if it represents a person who in reality would be able to do so. Instead of simply being drained away, however, the attention and emotional investment of the pornography user are turned inward, so that his awareness becomes focused, not on the behavior or emotional states of another person (which are elements of that "presence" referred to by Schmitz), but upon his own arousal and the factors contributing to it. The result of this process is absorption in one's own feeling states and emotional investment in a world of fantasy that is tied, not to real other persons, but to one's own mental caricatures of them. (Where I use the word "caricature" here in the sense of an exaggerated representation that emphasizes certain features, it is worth noting the existence of an entire genre of pornography that is literally caricature: namely, erotic animation. The existence of such material vitiates any sense in which pornography use might be considered intimate, for those works seek – often unsuccessfully – to induce sexual arousal by reference to objects that clearly do not resemble real human beings, even if those objects are intended as likenesses of some living persons. In animation, the person is wholly absent.)

In short, pornography takes its users out of the real world and locks them into a realm of their own devising, in which other persons – or at least those belonging to that class by which the pornography user is stimulated – are not related to so much as appropriated. This process suggests a profound narcissism, and leads one to suspect that pornography may be employed in many cases as a hedge against social anxiety, a way of protecting its users from the challenges of that social interaction of which sexual intercourse is a type. I now turn to the question of what effect this all has on the user of pornography.

Effects on the User of Pornography

The antithesis between relating to a person and appropriating her constitutes the central element in the "dialogical" philosophy of Martin Buber. Beginning from a distinction between the "basic words," "I-You" and "I-It," Buber (1970) unpacked a broad array of principles governing interactions between people. For our purposes, four are most illuminating. First and foundationally, Buber proposed that, in their status as basic words, I-You and I-It are spoken with one's being, but that the former can only be spoken with one's whole being, whereas the latter can never be spoken that way. What he asserted here is that addressing oneself fully to another person – being entirely engaged in relating to her – is a special type of interaction unlike addressing oneself either to a person less than fully, or to an object (between which Buber did not distinguish). Secondly, Buber claimed that experiencing (i.e., internally reflecting upon) is the opposite of relating, in that the former is not a form of participation, does not require a mutual relationship, and provides only superficial data about *things* – to which even human subjects of experience are reduced. The upshot of this point, which Buber also explained, is that experience can never adequately represent a relationship of total presence between persons, but can only analyze the relationship partner in terms of attributes or qualities. Third, Buber argued that all real living takes place in encounter, which is unmediated by prior knowledge, imagination, or instrumental goals, and that the I requires this encounter with the You in order to become a whole being. This is not to suggest that Buber supported a naïve view of presuppositionless perception, only that he reserved the term "encounter" for a very particular type of interaction, in which involvement is so intense that there is no room for the self-conscious ego or its devices; and in which the You "fills the firmament," not by exclusion but by radiance. Fourth and perhaps most crucially, Buber suggested that as the human capacities to experience and use (activities directed toward It) gain strength, the human capacity to relate (directed toward You) grows weaker. Because this ability to relate provides the only method of living in the spirit (which Buber claimed exists only between an I and a You), the possibility of spiritual life appears to derive in large part from our ability to relate to other people, as opposed to it being a technique or field of knowledge that one can learn by study.

With this very condensed and inexhaustive reading of Buber in mind, what can we say about pornography? Since we have already established that its use is not a relational activity properly so-called, we know right away that it does not involve one's whole being; indeed, far from it. While it is easy enough for many people to be deceived, in the satisfaction of masturbatory release, into believing that what they are expressing through their use of pornography is a part of themselves that is profoundly integral to their identity – namely, the grounds for their (subjectively powerful) sexual arousal – there is very little personal identity to be found in pornography consumption. Because the single-minded pursuit of arousing stimuli does not entail any self-giving, emotional risk, or sacrifice of desiderata, there is no potential in it for the person to share himself or grow in maturity. With no encounter taking place,

Buber would argue, the pornography user is not truly living, precisely at those moments when he may feel most alive. It can be no other way, for pornography depends upon prior knowledge, fantasy, and instrumental goals (the very ingredients of the I-it dynamic), through which the sensory experience of human encounter gets filtered into unreality. All that can ever be outwardly known about a pornography user, on the basis of that activity alone, is what he finds arousing. For the purposes of social life, this is vanishingly little to work with; from the standpoint of intersubjectivity, it is nothing at all. The pornography user is, in that capacity, not present to anyone, including himself. Pornography consumption is a virtually pure example of the triumph of experience and use over relation, according to Buber's conceptions of those things. As such, it is also a grave impediment to spiritual life.

Buber's analysis of human interactions offers an austere, yet striking perspective on pornography and its use. His is an investigation of the metaphysics of intimacy, couched in poetic language and rich with interpretive nuance. To those whose concerns are rightly more practical, however, it is helpful to supplement Buber's thought with that of a philosopher who looked more closely at the human mind. The existentialism of Gabriel Marcel is noteworthy for its attention (albeit with philosophical abstraction) to psychological processes and their spiritual effects. Marcel described the highest Christian virtue – charity – as a condition of "total spiritual availability," which he identified by the French word, *disponibilité* (Marcel, 1966, p. 39). Summarizing Marcel's elaboration of this term, which is rich with meanings, philosopher Joe McCown (1978) sought to define it in practical dimensions. On the negative side, he identified four "indices to unavailability" that serve to indicate the absence of charity, or *indisponibilité*, according to Marcel's thought: encumbrance, crispation, susceptibility, and moral ego-centricity. (Though these terms are all translations from Marcel's French, McCown notes the original terms only for encumbrance (*encombré*) and crispation – it is the same word in French.)

The first of these, encumbrance, is conceived as a preoccupation with some aspect of oneself – whether an emotional, material, or spiritual state – which has the double result of precluding responsiveness to the appeals of others, and of producing tremendous anxiety connected to the possible loss of something one holds of value. This condition, as Marcel conceived of it, arises from a tendency to confuse the categories of being and having, so that the living person *has* his life, the dead person has *lost* it, and all the attributes that characterize one's existence are possessions that must be kept, less wastage or exhaustion of resources ensue. To conceive one's personal attributes as possessions, or one's possessions as attributes of oneself, leads to an inability to make room in one's life for others and their needs, according to this line of thinking.

The second index to unavailability is what Marcel called crispation, which is a shriveling or contraction of the person into himself, so that he no longer lives in the world or is influenced by it. Guided by the image of a snail secreting a carapace, Marcel argued that the operative phenomenon in crispation is a solidification of the self within only one of its manifold possibilities, resulting in a radical limiting of the person's potential. He proposed that fanaticism derives from this process, in which the person closes off pathways to experience and lives on the settled positions he has already reached. Such a person is not present to himself and has no capacity to accept the presence of others; he has lost his sensitivity and sense of life's value. No longer availing himself of others, the crispated person is likewise no longer available to them.

Susceptibility, the third index to unavailability, McCown described as a type of anguish, rooted in a sense of helplessness from one's awareness of a growing emptiness that defies one's efforts to fill it. Marcel believed that as a result of this emptiness, the susceptible person develops an outsize need for the affirmation and high regard of others, which he longs to control to his own advantage. Intensely self-conscious and yet cycloptically focused on others' opinions, the susceptible person is rendered inaccessible to human contact by his preoccupation with the views he imagines others to hold of him. He has thus replaced the real other with an idea of his own making. As McCown pointed out, self-consciousness in Marcel's thought is not enlightening but obscuring, for the person's reliance upon concepts of the world closes him in upon himself, rather than leaving him open to the world as it is.

The fourth of Marcel's indices to unavailability is moral ego-centricity. As the term suggests, this is a process of viewing reality with oneself at the center, not only perceptually but in terms of value. Starting from the belief that he is grounded in himself, the morally ego-centric person comes to think that space and time extend outward from his own self-awareness, as McCown put it. Thus, whatever lies beyond immediate consciousness ceases to be of concern, and is denied any ability to make claims upon the person's presence. The challenge here, according to Marcel, is to eliminate those areas of one's life in which one is not present; this begins by rejecting the belief that one is grounded in oneself. Marcel argued that the self is, paradoxically, grounded in *other people*, and that it is in social exchange that we learn who we are and what we truly need. The morally ego-centric person, by focusing exclusively on himself, does himself a disservice in that he blocks out the love, understanding, and perspectives of other people, all of which might be considered forms of reality testing, and which carry the potential to enlighten the egoist and reveal to him his true good.

Marcel's four indices to unavailability, though one might question their conceptual distinctness, flesh out in combination a highly realistic portrait of the person for whom emotional engagement and intersubjective presence are drastically stunted. Do they help us to understand the effects of pornography use upon its consumers? The common theme in all four indices is a preoccupation with the contents of one's own mind, leading to an inability to relate to other people in realistic and fulfilling ways. This condition bears a striking resemblance to our previous discussion of the dynamics of pornography use. Though each bears further empirical study on actual pornography users, the four indices are each highly suggestive of the inner lives of such people.

Encumbrance, as both a preoccupation with some aspect of one's sexuality, personal potency, or appearance, and as an anxiety related to perceived shortcomings in those areas, often plays a role in the fantasy lives of pornography users. Robert Stoller's observation that, in pornography, every detail counts, and his theory that preferences for highly specific types of pornography are based in their user's experiences (as opposed, e.g., to being random neurological quirks), fits well within a Marcelian analysis. After all, one does not get from an early life experience to an adult fetish without maintaining some degree of preoccupation, by which time the object of that preoccupation may well have become integral to identity, and the fear of its loss a major source of anxiety. To what extent any of this arises from the confusion Marcel proposed, is a question for the philosophically minded psychotherapist who encounters the "encumbered" porn user. It is reasonable to think, however, that the effects of confusing having with being can be seen even among those who are not aware of the conceptual distinction. John Paul II, most notably, has pointed out that when "the values of being are replaced by those of having," life comes to be seen in terms of "economic efficiency, inordinate consumerism, physical beauty and pleasure, to the neglect of the more profound dimensions – interpersonal, spiritual and religious – of existence" (John Paul II, 1995, § 23). Pornography would seem to be a prime example of this trend.

The concept of crispation, as applied to pornography, is harder to identify. There is a basic sense in which recourse to pornography is a turning away from life in the world, in that, with its use for masturbation, one need not go to the trouble of maintaining relationships in order to find sexual pleasure. More suggestive, however, is Marcel's linking of crispation to fanaticism. The pornography user, like the fanatic, has a settled position that he is unable to modify – in this case his preference for certain imagery – which seals him off from the appeals of real people and the challenges they pose. McCown's proposal, that "the fanaticized consciousness remains numb and unsympathetic to 'everything to which its own compass needle does not respond'" (p. 13), is a perfect depiction of the porn user whose acclimation to specialized tastes narrows his sexual responsiveness to an unrealistic range. An example of this would be the men described by the 26-year-old businessman who told a CNN reporter that "all of my friends are so obsessed with internet porn that they can't sleep with their girlfriends unless they act like porn stars." (Legon, 2003). Such men, accustomed to the eager, sexually adventurous, and physically modified women depicted in pornography, are likely to remain perpetually dissatisfied with their real relationships, which they will invariably measure against an artificial standard.

McCown's rendering of the concept of susceptibility in Marcel's philosophy is based on a hypothetical thought process that can only be verified in particular clinical cases. But even though the feelings behind the condition are largely inscrutable, the characteristic state of the susceptible person is readily observable, precisely by applying the concept to pornography use. As anyone with passing familiarity with pornography may have noticed, a certain (seemingly large) percentage of it is crafted in second-person perspective, designed to address its consumers directly, whether as text or image. The purpose of this is clearly to appeal to the user's need for affirmation, specifically of his manhood, and to attract him with a glamorized vision of his own potential. Much of the second-person approach has a role-playing component in which the user is cast as a powerful, desirable, or otherwise significant individual, whose attributes are credited with gaining access to the situation depicted in the pornography. Part of the appeal of pornography is that it offers a means of controlling other people's views of oneself, by offering fabricated responses designed to assuage its user's insecurities. That its unreal assessment of the consumer isolates him, within his own imagination, from real people and their feedback, makes Marcel's analysis especially apt.

The phenomenon of moral ego-centricity can be applied to pornography use in at least two senses. First, there is the consideration from Catholic moral teaching on masturbation, which holds that such stimulation is a use of the sexual function contrary to its purpose, separating it from its proper context in a relationship of total self-giving with its attendant fidelity and openness to fertility (Catholic Church, 1995, p. 624). From this perspective pornography use is egocentric in that it redefines the standard of right conduct according to the individual's pleasure, or at least disregards preexisting standards. There is also a more psychological sense in which pornography use mirrors Marcel's description of the moral ego-centric as one who arrogates for himself special privileges that reduce others to instrumental roles, either as supports for an inflated self-image, or as "obstructions to be removed or circumvented" (McCown, 1978, p. 15). The human object of pornographic depiction is reduced to the binary status of either one by whom the user is aroused, or one by whom he is not. While members of the former category are held in comparatively high regard (though still treated instrumentally and thus not as full persons), members of the latter are banished to the margins of awareness. I propose that this distinction manifests itself, not only in the pornography user's fantasy life, but also in his interactions with living persons. In both applications of Marcelian moral ego-centricity to pornography use, the user's operative belief is that he is grounded in himself, either morally or socially. This is a possibility that Marcel would deny, and that the Church considers an inadequate understanding of the human person – who is created and sustained by love and does not exist outside of relationship at least with God.

Challenges to Researchers and Families

I would like to close with two points that touch on the family. First, I submit that the family is the missing link in pornography research. By this I mean that the family, as the fulfillment of human sexuality, should always orient the study of sexual behavior. The conclusions of the aforementioned New Zealand review article reveal that beneath the warring agendas of researchers lies a pervasive failure to recognize the human person as anything more than an isolated individual whose fulfillment is only incidentally related to his relationships with others. Even when the value of relationships is recognized, they are seen as existing to serve the individual's needs, not as potentially binding him into a larger unit that fundamentally changes and enriches his existence. The love that perfects and gives meaning to sexual desire is not visible so long as man is seen as existing primarily for himself. It is only in the communion of persons – mutual and totally self-giving, irrevocable, exclusive, and open to fertility – that the desires of human sexuality find their home. Psychologists and all who treat of human sexuality would do well to recognize this, and to connect the dots between the increasingly impressive body of scientific literature on human bonding, intimacy, and gender complementarity, and the vision of nuptial sexuality espoused by the Catholic Church and defended by many pro-family groups. One beneficial project for researchers would be to look at the effects of porn use on a wide range of relationships. Some damning research findings and clinical case data on its spousal effects already exists (such as Bergner and Bridges, 2002; but see also the studies examined in Oddone-Paolucci, Genuis, and Violato, 2000). It would be instructive to see if it also affects friendships and family bonds, as the philosophers I have cited would suspect that it does.

My second concluding point is that families and individuals discerning marriage face great challenges in our sexually provocative culture. There is experimental evidence to support the hypothesis that exposure to pornography reduces the desire of both sexes to marry and beget children – especially female children, who are seemingly recognized, even by those who use pornography, as its primary victims (Zillmann, 1989). This means that both the married and those discerning or preparing for marriage must be wary of pornography's appeal, both subtle and obvious, as they develop relationships with the opposite sex. If persons discerning marriage are not open to the appeal of that state of life, or if a couple already married begin to lose their devotion to one another, the results can be tragic. Avoiding pornography is thus a good way to strengthen the appeal of real relationships, which are both humanly fulfilling and a source of many graces. This is important not only for the deepest relationship, with one's spouse, but also for one's friendships and intimate relations within one's family of origin, all of which are vulnerable to deficits in intersubjective openness. The disposition to charity – or total spiritual availability, to use Gabriel Marcel's term – requires self-possession and vulnerability to the demands of other people. It requires both the ability and the willingness to sacrifice one's own comfort and security to serve another in his or her need. To desire the true good of another person is utterly incompatible with subjecting that person to one's own instrumental goals. There is no communion in one person using another.

The formation of the family requires an education in purity, of both the heart and the senses. In striving to temper their desires with chastity, the married and those discerning marriage must be on guard against the lustful gaze that pornography serves. Especially for men, in whom the sense of vision is the primary mode of sexual arousal, pornographic imagery must not be allowed to take root, even uninvited. To the extent that expectations from the disordered world of pornography are imported into the sanctity of the marital embrace, that embrace will not reflect true intimacy, but will be marked by preconceptions and preoccupation within oneself. Part and parcel of the beatitude of purity of heart is the need to beware the loss of sensitivity to the dignity of the human person that is revealed in the naked male or female body. When that body is exploited by impersonal exposure, and when its sexuality is objectified and commoditized as something other than an integral part of the person, it is subjected to a great indignity. Those who view it are not able to perceive the body as a gift, nor are they able to respond by giving themselves to the person whose body is held out to them.

In pornography both the nuptial meaning of the human body and the fulfillment of self-donation are obscured by a deracinated image that beckons its viewers to lust after it. Pornography consumption cannot plausibly make the marital bond seem more appealing, except perhaps when one sees marriage merely as an opportunity for certain sexual practices that porn inspires. This, of course, would be a profoundly misguided conception of marriage, one in which the desire to use another person would overshadow the relationship. Whatever spouses do to enliven their marital embrace must always be informed by true charity, which can admit nothing that would harm the dignity of the beloved. St. Jerome once wrote that "Nothing is baser than a husband loving his wife as though she were a prostitute," to which we might add, "or as though she were a porn star."

"Whitney R. Jacobs is completing a M.S. degree in clinical psychology at the Institute for Psychological Sciences in Arlington, Virginia. He holds and M.A. degree in theology from St. Mary's University in San Antonio, Texas. He converted to the Catholic Church from atheism in 1999.

References

Barwick, Helena (2003). *A Guide to the Research into the Effects of Sexually Explicit Films and Videos*. New Zealand Office of Film & Literature Classification. Internet publication accessed 9/23/04. <http://www.censorship.govt.nz/pdfword/research_document_2003.pdf>

Bergner, R. M. & A. J. Bridges (2002). "The Significance of Heavy Pornography Involvement for Romantic Partners: Research and Clinical Implications," in *Journal of Sex & Marital Therapy*, 28: 193–206.

Buber, M. (1970). *I and Thou*. New York: Simon & Schuster. (Original German edition published 1923.)

Catholic Church (1995). *Catechism of the Catholic Church*. New York: Doubleday.

Hunter, C (2000). "The Dangers of Pornography? A Review of the Effects Literature." Internet publication accessed /23/2004.http://www.asc.upenn.edu/usr/chunter/porn_effects.html>

John Paul II (1997). *Evangelium Vitae* (Encyclical Letter). Internet document accessed 9/22/04. <http://www.vatican.va/holy_father/john_paul_ii/encyclicals/documents/hf_jp-ii_enc_25031995_evangelium-vitae_en.html>

John Paul II (1997). *The Theology of the Body*. Boston: Pauline Books and Media.

Legon, Jeordan (2003). "Sex Sells, Especially to Web Surfers." CNN.com; online article accessed 7/31/2004. <http://www.cnn.com/2003/TECH/internet/12/10/porn.business>

Marcel, Gabriel. (1966). *The Philosophy of Existentialism*. New York: Citadel.

Marcus, Steven (1966). *The Other Victorians*. New York: Basic Books.

McCown, J. (1978). *Availability: Gabriel Marcel and the Phenomenology of Human Openness*. Missoula: Scholars Press.

Oddone-Paolucci, E., M. Genuis, & C. Violato (2000). "A Meta-analysis on the Published Research on the Effects of Pornography." In C. Violato, E. Oddone-Paolucci, & M. Genuis, eds., *The Changing Family and Child Development*. Aldershot: Ashgate.

Schmitz, K. L. (1999). "The Roots of Intimacy." Unpublished manuscript obtained from the author.

Stoller, R. J. (1985). *Observing the Erotic Imagination*. New Haven: Yale.

Wojtyla, K. (1994). *Love and Responsibility*. New York: Farrar, Straus and Giroux. (Original Polish edition published 1960.)

Zillmann, Dolf (1989). "Effects of Prolonged Consumption of Pornography." In Dolf Zillmann and Jennings Bryant, Eds., *Pornography: Research Advances and Policy Considerations*. Mahwah, NJ: Lawrence Erlbaum Assoc.

Chapter 10: Chastity as the Fruit of "Genuine Affirmation"

Reflections on the Work of Anna Terruwe, Conrad Baars, and John Paul II

PHILIP M. SUTTON, PH.D.

Abstract

This paper was written, in part, as a response to another conference paper, *Pornography and the Communion of Persons,* by Whitney R. Jacobs. Before John Paul II's election to the papacy, Catholic psychiatrists Anna Terruwe and Conrad Baars already had written on "affirmation" as a fundamental human need and that the crucial psychological, moral and spiritual crisis of our time was the lack of genuine affirmation being given to, and received by, modern youth. Just before Baars died 1981, Terruwe and Baars dedicated their last two books (*Feeling and Healing Your Emotions* and *Psychic Wholeness and Healing*) to Pope John Paul II, whom Baars described as "an excellent example of affirming living."

The present paper reviews Terruwe's and Baars' understanding of the nature of genuine affirmation and the consequences for individuals and societies when persons are un-affirmed or dis-affirmed. The affirming person and the writings of John Paul II, especially his "Letter to Families," are discussed, and parallels are drawn between his work and that of Terruwe and Baars. An understanding of unchaste behavior – including the use of pornography – as *pseudo*-self-affirming behavior is explored, as is growth in chastity as the fruit of genuine affirmation. Ways in which chastity may be taught and unchastity may be prevented or remedied, through genuine affirmation, also are considered, in light of John Paul II's writings, the Pontifical Council on the Family's "The Truth and Meaning of Human Sexuality," and the pastoral and therapeutic wisdom found in the Courage ministry, Twelve-Step groups, and the fatherhood movements.

Introduction

This paper is both a short paper in itself and a response to Whitney Jacob's paper. My paper began as an abstract submitted in response to the Spring call for papers for this conference which celebrates "The International Year of the Family" and the tenth anniversary of John Paul II's 1994 "Letter to Families." I had proposed a paper entitled: "Genuine Affirmation: *Sine-qua-non* for "Raising Catholic (or any) Children in a Secular Culture". I had intended to discuss parenting in light of the concept of "affirmation" as taught and practiced *explicitly* by Catholic psychiatrists Anna Terruwe and Conrad Baars and *implicitly* through the presence and teaching of John Paul II, especially in his "Letter to Families." Subsequently, I was invited to be the chairman of this session to present a paper as well as offer a response to Mr. Jacobs paper.

In agreeing to do so, I decided to write on the concept of affirmation with a focus on its relation to chastity and the problem of pornography use and other unchaste behaviors. Part I of my paper thus discusses the concept of "genuine affirmation" in the work of Baars and Terruwe, and Part II reveals how the person, presence, and writing of John Paul II, specifically his "Letter to Families," offer excellent examples of "affirming living." In Part III, I discuss the consequences for individuals who have been poorly affirmed or even dis-affirmed as persons of worth and dignity, and explore how the need to compensate for insufficient affirmation may motivate unchaste behavior, including the use of pornography, as *pseudo*-self-affirmation and inauthentic self-denial. Finally, in Part IV, I reflect on how chastity may be taught as the fruit of genuine affirmation and how compulsive participation in pornography – or any unchaste behavior – may be remedied or prevented through receiving genuine affirmation from oneself and others.

Before continuing, I offer some personal comments. Fifteen years ago, while helping to start the M.A. in Counseling program at the Franciscan University of Steubenville, I was introduced to three sources of wisdom and professional knowledge that continue to influence my present thinking on the problem of pornography. These influences included not only the Thomistic-inspired psychology of Anna Terruwe and Conrad Baars; but also the Courage apostolate, a support group for Catholics who experience homosexual attractions, yet who want to live chastely, as well as the work of the mental health professionals who eventually formed NARTH: the National Association for Research and Therapy of Homosexuality. Along with my pre-existing familiarity with the writing of John Paul II, these influences have continued to direct my professional and academic work ever since.

As a therapist, I spend a significant amount of time serving adults and young persons who experience unwanted homosexual attractions or behaviors, and/or their loved ones. I serve as the professional advisor and meeting facilitator for Courage in the Diocese of Fort Wayne-South Bend, Indiana. And as the supervising psychologist for a number of different therapists, I offer them counsel on how to assist clients who are struggling with the consequences of compulsive or addictive pornography use and masturbation, which commonly accompanies such use. These professional experiences form a practical background for what I have written here.

I. "Affirmation" in the Work of Anna Terruwe and Conrad Baars[1]

The late Catholic psychiatrists Anna Terruwe and Conrad Baars developed an approach to the prevention and treatment of emotional disorders that was inspired by their study of the psychology of Thomas Aquinas. First Terruwe, and then Baars as her student, colleague, and translator, studied, taught and used in therapy an applied Thomistic psychology. Much of their work focuses on the nature, maturation and – when disabled – healing and strengthening of the emotional life. The ecology of the emotions and the causes of and therapy for emotional repression are a major focus of their work, but time and space prevent a further discussion of these topics.[2] Another significant focus of their work was affirmation, or, as Conrad Baars tended to say in the last years of his life, "affirming living."

Terruwe's and Baars's understanding of affirmation may be summarized as follows. To mature emotionally, each person must experience being affirmed. *Affirmation* is the universal, "fundamental human need"[3] to be strengthened (confirmed) emotionally, intellectually, and morally. This occurs as one recognizes and "*feels*" his or her own goodness, worth, significance, and value as a person, through the presence, appearance, and actions of significant others, particularly our parents. *Being affirmed* involves persons' experiencing that they are loved and lovable simply for *being*, for who they *are* – instead of for what they may do, achieve, produce, or have. Although human beings never outgrow the need for affirmation, the experience of "being affirmed" occurs initially, and ideally, as parents and/or other significant persons are able to be present to their children "with the full attention of their whole being" and thereby are able to recognize and be moved with joy by their children's goodness, truth and beauty and compassion when such are undeveloped or lacking.[4]

Terruwe and Baars consider affirmation so fundamental that they call being affirmed a human person's "psychic birth" (meaning psychological). In *Psychic Wholeness and Healing*, they write:

> To be and feel accepted and approved by others constitutes *man's second birth, his psychic birth.* Just as the human being is unable to give birth to himself, so he is not able to accept and love himself without the prior love of others. We receive our unique and specific full humanity form others. It is from this affirmation that we receive the strength *to be authentically human*, i.e., to give others in turn their unique and specific humanity (emphases in original).[5]

For the affirmer, *acting* affirming is secondary to *being* affirming. The process of (what Baars calls the "ABCs") of *affirming living* involves first the *a*ttentive presence and *a*wareness of the affirmer, with and for the one to be affirmed. Such attentive awareness results in the affirmer's *b*eing moved by, and genuinely feeling, the reality and goodness of the other. Such heartfelt empathy with and for the other leads to a *c*ommunion between the affirmer and the other, as the former spontaneously reveals, nonverbally, a regard and care for the other. The other, as it were, "experiences his or her own truth, goodness, beauty, worth" and the potential for future flourishing, in and through the attentive presence of the affirmer.

As the needs of the other warrant, the affirmer may, or may not, say or *do* something with or for the other to express this caring explicitly. Intentional or habitual actions, gestures, or words may, or may not, be necessary for another to be affirmed. Explicit communication or action need not (but may appropriately) follow the affirmer's being moved with love and compassion for the one affirmed to *feel* this emotional strengthening. Affirmation, or affirming living, is fundamentally a state of *being*, not doing, and implicit communion is necessary, and perhaps sufficient, for our psychological birth to occur.

II. John Paul II as the "Pope of Affirmation"

"*The truth that we owe to man is, first and foremost, a truth about man.*"[6] This quotation comes from an address by Pope John Paul II at Puebla, Mexico, to Latin American bishops and clergy during the first visit of his papacy to the Americas in January. 1979. Baars uses this quotation in the Postscript of his 1979 edition of *Feeling and Healing Your Emotions*, and Anna Terruwe and he use it in 1981 in the Preface and the first chapter of their final co-authored book, *Psychic Wholeness and*

Healing.[7] Baars died in the Fall of 1981, having experienced only the first three years of John Paul II's pontificate. Within the first year of his papacy, Baars already had declared John Paul II to be "an excellent example of what affirming living is all about."

But Baars (with Terruwe) had met him before, in 1971, as Cardinal Karol Wojtyla, during a trip to the Vatican to discuss their Thomistic-inspired psychology. Baars recalled that at that meeting, he was impressed by the future pope's intelligence, openness to asking questions and fostering discussion, and ability to make them feel at ease. During the first year of his pontificate, Baars commented on the affirming way that John Paul II "moves persons by his love, and by his courage to speak as he should speak, even in the presence of his enemies." In a videotaped workshop, Baars shows and describes a cartoon of John Paul II who has "a big smile and love on his face" for his flock while hitting a communist in the face with the shepherd's crook in his left hand. Baars asserts: "This is really the man we need for our time!" [8]

In addition to being impressed by John Paul II's emotionally affirming person, presence, and demeanor, as above quotation suggests, Baars and Terruwe admired his intellectual and moral affirmation as well. I understate when I say that the writings and talks of John Paul II are full of genuinely affirming intellectual and moral truths. In keeping with the theme of this conference, "The International Year of the Family," and mindful of this being the tenth anniversary of the Holy Father's "Letter to Families," I offer a few quotes and comments from the Letter as examples.

In Chapter 15 of the Letter, which is entitled, "The Fourth Commandment: 'Honor Your Father and Your Mother,'" John Paul II expresses well the essence of what Terruwe and Baars mean by affirmation. The Holy Father writes that this commandment is a profound call to "mutual honor": for parents to honor their children and each other, as well as, more literally, for children to honor their parents. He explains: " 'To honor' means to acknowledge! We could put it this way: 'let yourself be guided by the firm acknowledgment of the person'...*an acknowledgment of the individual* simply because he is an individual, 'this' individual life." Honoring another, then "is essentially an attitude of unselfishness. It could be said that it is "a sincere gift of person to person," and in that sense honor converges with love."[9]

Prior to this, in Chapters 11 ("The Sincere Gift of Self") and 12 ("Responsible Fatherhood and Motherhood"), John Paul II restates and explains the teaching of the Second Vatican Council that man *"cannot 'fully find himself except through a sincere gift of self."* This apparent contradiction "is the magnificent paradox of human existence: an existence called *to serve the truth in love.* Love causes man to find fulfillment through the sincere gift of self. To love means to give and to receive something which can be neither bought nor sold, but only given freely and mutually."[10] Sincere self-donation is the necessary path to human fulfillment "because (man) has been created in the image and likeness of god and redeemed by the only-begotten Son of the Father, who became man for us and for our salvation"[11]

III. Pornography as the *Pseudo*-Self-Affirming Denial of the Person

In this section, I wish to respond more directly to the topic of Mr. Jacobs' paper. I will discuss how participation in pornography may be considered an example of "pseudo-self-affirmation" as understood in the work of Terruwe and Baars, and related thoughts in the writings of John Paul II. Truthfully, most of what I've written applies as well to other forms of unchaste – as well as nonsexual, compulsive or addictive – behaviors besides pornography or masturbation, its frequent attendant.[12] Mr. Jacobs discusses the negative *consequences* of pornography on the personhood of – and the "communion of persons" between and among – those who participate in its production, distribution, or consumption. Participation in pornography is justifiably characterized as an objectification, denial or depersonalization of those who participate in it. My contribution to his discussion is to consider the *motivation* for such participation, especially by compulsive or addicted consumers. Using the ideas of Baars, Terruwe, and John Paul II, I next explain the concept of *pseudo*-self-affirmation and how compensating for a significant lack of affirmation may be a strong motivation for participation in pornography.

In brief, a person may engage in the habitual use of pornography as a self defeating attempt to compensate for having been poorly affirmed or even dis-affirmed – denied – as a person of worth and dignity. Terruwe and Baars explain that the human need for affirmation is so fundamental that persons who are significantly un-affirmed or inadequately affirmed are likely to be emotionally underdeveloped and driven to seek the *experience* of being loved and loveable, and/or escape the experience of feeling unloved or unlovable, in a variety of self-defeating ways.[13] Terruwe and Baars call the self-defeating action, habit, or lifestyle of trying to make oneself feel affirmed is called "*self-affirmation.*"[14] Although wholesome self-affirmation is possible for persons who have been affirmed and are emotionally mature and may be learned and practiced by those who have not, Terruwe and Baars use the term "self-affirmation" almost exclusively to mean "*pseudo*-self-affirmation." I use this latter term to avoid confusion.

Pseudo-self-affirmation means "looking for love in all the wrong places." Pseudo-self-affirmers may seek the experience of being affirmed, and/or avoid the feelings of being un-affirmed or dis-affirmed in many ways: amassing financial wealth or material possessions, acquiring status symbols such as professional degrees or credentials, excessive striving to achieve occupational success or community involvement, seeking political power, becoming famous or associating with others who are famous, engaging in sexual promiscuity, or abusing mind-altering drugs or other substances. Under-affirmed persons who are very talented, attractive, or assertive may be particularly prone to pseudo-self-affirming lifestyles centered on seeking wealth, fame, power or pleasure.[15]

The lifestyles of pseudo-self-affirmers may be truly self-defeating "vicious circles." For, such attempts to create the experience of being loved or worthwhile only leave deeper feelings of being unloved or worthless, which may lead to additional and more intense self-defeating efforts.[16] Some pseudo-self-affirming habits may be accurately classified as "secondary or psychological addictions." In such cases, the unmet need for affirmation is the motivating force behind a person's inability to limit or stop the "addictive" behavior. Of course, with a drug or other substance addiction, a "primary" addiction may also exist. Sexual compulsions may be a secondary effect of a lack of affirmation, as well as a primary effect of emotional repression.

One characteristic of compulsive sexual behaviors is a selfish preoccupation which prevents the "sincere self-giving" which John Paul II and Vatican Council II describe as essential for human fulfillment. Sexual compulsions and addictions involve a degree of psychological "bondage" or slavery. People who act in a psychologically compulsive or addictive manner have lost a significant degree of freedom to choose otherwise. In the 14th Chapter ("Love is Demanding") of the Letter to Families, John Paul II emphasizes that making oneself a sincere gift "for others" is at "the very heart of the Gospel truth about *freedom*. The person realizes himself by the exercise of freedom in truth. Freedom cannot be understood as a license to do *absolutely anything*: it means a *gift of self*. Even more: it means an *interior discipline of the gift*."

In this context, the Holy Father contrasts genuine *personalism* with *individualism* which is antithetical to a sincere gift of self. He explains that in contrast to a person making a free and "sincere gift" of himself or herself:

Individualism presupposes a use of freedom in which the subject does what he wants, in which he himself is the one to "establish the truth" of whatever he finds pleasing or useful. He does not tolerate the fact that someone else "wants" or demands something from him in the name of an objective truth. He does not want to "give" to another on the basis of truth; he does not want to become a "sincere gift." Individualism thus remains egocentric and selfish.The real antithesis between individualism and personalism emerges not only on the level of theory, but even more *on that of "ethos."* The "ethos" of personalism is altruistic: it moves the person to become a gift for others and to discover joy in giving himself. This is the joy about which Christ speaks (cf. *Jn* 15:11; 16:20–22).[17]

In contrast to the ethos of personalism, the cultural ethos of individualism ultimately frustrates the human quest for joyful, self-fulfilling, self-giving. For individualism is rooted in "ethical utilitarianism" which is itself founded on "the continual quest for 'maximum' happiness. But this is a *'utilitarian happiness,'* seen only as pleasure, as immediate gratification for the exclusive benefit of the individual, apart from or opposed to the objective demands of the true good."[18] As such, the ethos of individualism provides significant individual and cultural support for unchaste behavior, including participation in pornography and the all too common attending practice of masturbation. These and all compulsions to unchaste behavior are caused by, and invariably cause to worsen, the persisting human tendency toward egocentrism and selfishness.[19]

John Paul II's further discussion of unchaste "free love" also has particular relevance to pornography and its attending behaviors. He writes that:

> ...the phenomenon of so-called *"free love"*; this is particularly dangerous because it is usually suggested as a way of following one's "real" feelings, but it is in fact destructive of love. How many families have been ruined because of "free love"! To follow in every instance a "real" emotional impulse by invoking a love "liberated" from all conditionings, means nothing more than to make the individual a slave to those human instincts which Saint Thomas calls "passions of the soul." "Free love" exploits human weaknesses; it gives them a certain "veneer" of respectability with the help of seduction and the blessing of public opinion. In this way there is an attempt to "soothe" consciences by creating a "moral alibi". But not all of the consequences are taken into consideration, especially when the ones who end up paying are, apart from the other spouse,

the children, deprived of a father or mother and condemned to be in fact *orphans of living parents.*[20]

Many children – and adults – were affirmed only partially or not at all because their parents or other significant adults were physically absent too often or at important times and/or were emotionally unavailable when physically present. As John Paul II writes above, such unaffirmed or dis-affirmed children rightfully may be called "orphans of living parents." Analogously, their physically or psychologically abandoned partners deservedly may be called "widows," or "widowers," of living spouses."

Children who are deprived of a mother or father's love may experience "many dire consequences." Emotionally, physically, or even sexually neglected or abused children – and adults – commonly experience "painful, fresh wounds…hidden" in their hearts.[21] Such wounds and bad examples, if not forgiven, healed or otherwise resolved, are likely to repeat themselves in multiple generations of poorly loved- and poorly loving- men, women and children. The emotional pain and sadness caused by such wounds often drives young persons to experiment with and then persist in self-comforting, self- soothing, emotional pain-anesthetizing unchaste behaviors. Persistent practice leads to habits carried into adulthood. Such pseudo-self-affirming habits not uncommonly develop into true compulsions and addictions, which involve a denial of the truth about oneself and others, and the diminished freedom and capacity for "sincere love."

Habitual or compulsive participation in pornography (and masturbation) often is motivated by an underlying psychological need for genuine affirmation that was lacking during a person's infancy or youth. When persons attempt to compensate for their unmet needs for authentic love through sexual vice, they commonly find that the unmet needs grow more intense. Just as a person who habitually assuages the legitimate hunger for nutrition with tasty but non-nutritious "junk food" winds up physically malnourished, so does the participant in pornography wind up emotionally and spiritually malnourished.

All pseudo-self-affirming behaviors, including those which gratify "lust" (i.e., the "disordered desire for or inordinate enjoyment of sexual pleasure [which] is morally disordered when sought for itself, isolated from its procreative and unitive purposes")[22] ultimately leave a person frustrated and unfulfilled. Pseudo-self-affirmation renders a person less able to receive or give love, sexually or otherwise. It also frustrates the genuine "communion of persons" which they intrinsically, if not consciously, need. In attempting to meet legitimate needs for affirmation, the "vicious cycle" of pornography use, etc., perpetuates itself unless the person is able to learn how to love him or herself, and to be loved by others, in genuinely affirming ways.

IV. Chastity: the Fruit of Genuine Affirmation

Genuine affirmation and growth in chastity are the means of preventing and remedying pseudo-self-affirming participation in pornography. Being taught and learning to become chaste in one's youth enables one to avoid becoming trapped in the habitual practice of pornography and other unchaste behaviors. Beginning to learn, or relearn, chastity after one has developed an unchaste habit is the simple, but not easy, path by which someone entrapped by unchastity may become free(r) to love himself or herself and others. Whether as education, prevention or remediation, genuine affirmation of oneself by others and oneself is a necessary condition for growth in chastity.

As the *Catechism of the Catholic Church* reminds us: "Chastity means the successful integration of sexuality within the person and thus the inner unity of man in his bodily and spiritual being. Sexuality…becomes personal and truly human when it is integrated into the relationship of one person to another, in the complete and lifelong mutual gift of a man and a woman" (# 2337). Chastity involves a growth "in self-mastery which is a training in human freedom. The alternative is clear: either man governs his passions and finds peace, or he lets himself be dominated by them and becomes unhappy" (# 2339). This self-mastery is a life-"long and exacting work" (#2342), which requires "self-knowledge, practice of an ascesis adapted to the situations that confront him, obedience to God's commandments, exercise of the moral virtues, and fidelity to prayer" (# 2337). "The virtue of chastity blossoms" and "is expressed notably in friendship with one's neighbor" whether "between persons of the same or opposite sex" (# 2347).

Prevention through Education and Formation in Chastity

From the perspective of Baars and Terruwe, the education (formation) of children in chastity invariably occurs, both implicitly and explicitly, if and as one is being genuinely affirmed. As stated above in Part I, being *af*firmed involves our being *con*firmed or strengthened, intellectually and morally, as well as emotionally. Emotional strengthening occurs as we experience (i.e., notice and are moved ourselves by) the visible, sensible, physical changes in the affirmer's face, posture and voice. Genuine intellectual and moral strengthening requires that a person be given and receive accurate intellectual, moral and spiritual truth. One's intuitive mind (*intellectus*) as well as one's thinking or logical mind (*ratio*), and one's will, require a balanced diet of timely truths. Baars writes of the need for:

> ...balance between emotional and intellectual affirmation, between the giving of emotional health food and intellectual truths...If one gives the emotional health food together with insufficient intellectual and spiritual food, the emotions are denied the necessary guidance and tempering. If, on the other hand, one gives an abundance of intellectual and spiritual truths together with emotional junk food, one offers only half-truths.[23]

In order for intellectual affirmation to occur, it is necessary for parents and other familial and social "educators" to teach rational, moral and spiritual truth in the right time and the right way. Children need to be taught according to their maturity and ability to understand; and they need to be challenged to know, be, and do all that of which they are capable. Children also need their parents (and other educators) not to give what the children are not ready to accept and not to demand or expect from their children what the latter are not ready or able to do or give. In addition, children need their educators to teach by their example as well as their words, to live the intellectual and moral truths that they teach. Genuinely affirming parents, their surrogates and all caretakers of the young need especially to refrain from any immoral behavior, whether toward children or in their presence. This requires "self-restraining love" from the parents.[24]

It is worth citing here a passage from the Pontifical Council for the Family's document: "The Truth and Meaning of Human Sexuality." While the document offers wisdom for teaching, educating, or forming children of all ages in chastity, guidance in forming teenagers is particularly noteworthy. In this document, the Pontifical Council asserts that "during the stages of adolescent growth," sexuality has a "positive significance" for the "personal harmony and development" of persons, especially during adolescence. Therefore, adolescents in particular must be lovingly persuaded "that the disordered use of sex tends progressively to destroy the person's capacity to love by making pleasure, instead of sincere self-giving, the end of sexuality and by reducing other persons to objects of one's own gratification. In this way the meaning of true love between a man and a woman (love always open to life) is weakened as well as the family itself"[25]

In line with Terruwe and Baar's understanding of "self-restraining," affirming parental love, "The Truth and Meaning of Human Sexuality" recognizes the importance of "friendships" during adolescence and that "adolescence is a time when young people enjoy more autonomy in their relations with others and in the hours they keep in family life." But this document also advises that "without taking away" the adolescent's "rightful autonomy, when necessary, parents should know how to say 'no' to their children and, at the same time, they should know how to cultivate a taste in their children for what is beautiful, noble, and true. Parents should also be sensitive to adolescents' self-esteem, which may pass through a confused phase when they are not clear about what personal dignity means and requires."[26]

Similarly, "The Truth and Meaning of Human Sexuality" also reminds parents that through their "loving and patient advice" they will be able to "help young people to avoid an excessive closing in on themselves. When necessary, they will also teach them to go against social trends that tend to stifle true love and an appreciation for spiritual realities," especially looking to Christ to "restore, establish, and strengthen" them in their efforts (1 Peter 5:8–10).[27]

The clinical wisdom of Terruwe and Baars also deserves to be heard and heeded. On the one hand, giving accurate information about the moral law to children before they are mature enough to understand it, and giving inaccurate information, have both led to emotional repression. For example, emphasizing moral behavior to younger children in a manner which suggests that "sinful behavior is always a sin" may result in children developing much irrational fear or restless striving about the moral law. Some sincere, sensitive and intelligent persons may develop emotional difficulties as a result of being taught moral truths prematurely, inaccurately or in an overly fearful manner. Scrupulosity or difficulties with obsessive compulsive behaviors may result if young persons come to believe mistakenly that it was wrong, or even sinful, for them to feel certain emotions and bodily feelings and thereby habitually push such feelings out of conscious awareness.[28]

On the other hand, a form of pseudo-affirmation or denial of the personhood of children and adults may occur when psychological and spiritual educators, including parents, lower moral standards by giving the message that a given "sin is not a sin."[29] This may be communicated directly, in words or writings, or indirectly, through indifference, too permissive or absent guidance, and bad example. Such "open-minded" neglect leads minor (and adult) children to believe that they are "too weak" to live the moral life, that the moral life is too difficult or that the joy of the moral life is not worth the effort that may be required. Such intellectual and moral denial also leaves children and adults at great risk of suffering psychological and spiritual harm as a consequence of immoral actions and lifestyles, such as participation in pornography.

I do not want to minimize the difficulty which parents and other "parental educators" have in teaching young persons the virtuous life. And I do not want to overlook the need that those who "educate" the young in virtue have to seek the same divine assistance for teaching that their young persons need for living chastity and all of the virtues. Thank God that in Him, all things are possible!

Remediation of "Interior Chastity" through Genuine (Self-)Affirmation

Someone who is caught in the habitual, compulsive, or even addictive use of pornography or other unchaste behaviors may find freedom through growth in chastity. Courage founder, Fr. John Harvey, O.S.F.S., exhorts Courage members, and indeed all who struggle with living chastely, to pursue "interior chastity" according to the "Twelve Step" model. Unlike "white-knuckled" chastity[30] – what Twelve Step groups like Alcoholics Anonymous or Sexaholics Anonymous call sobriety or abstinence – interior chastity is peace of mind and joy of heart as well as the self-discipline of sexual behavior (continence). Twelve Step language calls this "serenity." Achieving serenity requires such spiritual disciplines as submission and conversion to God's will, repentance and confession of wrongdoing, giving and receiving forgiveness and making amends for one's actions, peer accountability, prayer and service.[31] Such steps are implicitly and genuinely self-affirming.

Genuine Affirmation

Un-affirmed or dis-affirmed persons may help themselves break a self-defeating cycle like the compulsive use of pornography by seeking the presence of mature, emotionally, morally, and intellectually affirming adults. Those who are authentically living the affirming life are able to recognize and be moved with compassion by the goodness and suffering of those who have not been affirmed. Hopefully, any therapists, counselors, pastoral caregivers or even wise friends who are sought for help are authentically affirming persons capable of self-restraining love. This means, in the words of Adrian van Kaam, that the caregivers are able to answer the sufferer's fundamental need and appeal: "Please be *with* me and *for* me" (emphasis added).[32] A genuine affirmer is one who can be fully present to the sufferer and love him or her unconditionally. An affirmer is a person in whom "kindness (or mercy or love) and truth meet" and "justice and peace embrace" (cf. Psalm 85: 11). The un-affirmed who are trapped in sexual compulsion need the loving presence of someone who neither condones unchastity nor condemns someone for being unchaste.

Genuine Self-Affirmation

According to Baars and Terruwe, the first step which un-affirmed persons may need to take to ready themselves for the authentic affirming presence of others is to stop or avoid any pseudo-self-affirming behaviors (such as the chronic use of pornography). This is easier to do if they already have begun to experience an emotionally affirming person who truly cares for them with self-restraining love. Another step is learning to lead a calmer, less hurried, and more patient lifestyle so that they may become more present to others and recognize better the goodness in others and themselves. A third step typically involves becoming more assertive. This includes their stopping trying to please everyone and risking "hurting other's feelings" while doing what seems right. Other steps include practicing "positive imagination" and self-restraining love. Baars encourages the un-affirmed – and also those who are learning to feel emotions that previously were repressed – to be gentle with themselves and their feelings that seem so "child-like." Patience is necessary to allow previously undeveloped or repressed emotions to "grow up" in their own way and at their own pace, according to the "law of gradualness." Emotional maturity also involves a season of "trial and error," as well as success, in learning whether, when and how to express or choose to act under the influence of awakening emotions.[33]

Along with the wisdom of Twelve Step Groups, the experience of modern fatherhood movements such as the St. Joseph Covenant Keepers and Promise Keepers offer men who struggle to be chaste and who were poorly affirmed growing up a healthy measure of challenging support. Men who grew up without experiencing genuine affirmation from their fathers tend to have trouble with knowing what it means to be "a man," with commitment in relationships, and with chastity (self-disciplined sexual behavior).

Overcoming the effects of physical or emotional paternal absence – and perhaps corresponding maternal over-involvement – typically involves helping men to make peace – through grieving and perhaps psychotherapy – with the memories, leftover emotions and ongoing relationships with their fathers, and sometimes their mothers; to seek the support of and to share mutual accountability with men who share their goal; to experience some form of surrogate fathering or mentoring (pastoral, therapeutic, etc.); to work toward sexual self-discipline aimed at serenity (peace of mind and joy of heart) and, if married, fidelity to their spouses and appropriate involvement with their children; and to use appropriate spiritual and religious activities as resources for change and growth.[34]

Humility

I recall that when asked what were the three most important virtues for living a holy life, St. Bernard answered: "Humility, humility, humility!" Fundamentally, receiving or giving genuine affirmation and growing in chastity requires humility, which is the fruit of a prayerful and charitable life. Realistic self-understanding and self-acceptance that are the heart of humility are the basis for genuine affirmation of self and others.

Two traps often faced by those who are un-affirmed and who struggle with sexual compulsion are the extremes of pride or of despair and presumption. The un-affirmed may be stuck on, or vacillate between, believing or living as if they *won't* or *can't* be loved (as if they are undeserving or unlovable) and as if they *don't need* to be loved. Those "imprisoned" by sexual compulsion often are stuck between condemning themselves as unforgivable or worthless and condoning their behaviors as "not (too) bad" after all. With humility, it is possible to realize and accept the possibility, as well as the difficulty, of being loved as well as loving authentically. This includes embracing both the challenges and hopes for living a serenely chaste life, free of compulsions like pornography.

Humble self-affirmation by those who have significant difficulties being chaste requires that they discern: "Whatever is true, whatever is honorable, whatever is just, whatever is pure, whatever is lovely, whatever is gracious, if there is any excellence, and if there is anything worthy of praise" (Phil 4: 8) about their compulsions and behaviors. Such compulsions often are triggered by unmet, genuine needs that are disguised or felt as "sexual." Some needs are relational, such as seeking to be affirmed in the present and/or compensate for not having been affirmed in the past. Others are more psychological, coping with unpleasant emotions or feelings or biological needs.[35]

My experiences within the Courage ministry and providing therapy to persons with unwanted homosexual (same sex) attractions or behaviors (SSAs) offer an example. SSAs are understood as ways of seeking the "3As": attention, affection, and affirmation" from significant, same gender persons. Commonly, SSAs are rooted in healthy needs for attention, affection, and affirmation that were met poorly in parental and peer relationships while growing up. Such legitimate needs also typically coexist with unresolved, and often repressed, sadness, anger, and emotional pain leftover from neglectful, abusive, and/or otherwise emotionally traumatic (i.e., un- or dis-affirming) parental and peer relationships. Humble, self-affirmation involves recognizing and taking steps both to satisfy healthy same gender needs and to forgive, otherwise resolve, and heal the offenses and wounds from the past that remain so powerfully influential in the present.

Genuine Forgiveness

On the one hand, the forgiveness process properly *understood* and *practiced* enables one who has been offended to set himself or herself free of the offense and the offender, even while continuing to cope with unchangeable difficulties resulting from the offense.[36] On the other hand, genuine forgiveness includes facing and feeling one's unresolved anger and the underlying pain, the personal and relational consequences of that anger, and one's possible co-responsibility for one's present life difficulties. For example, men with SSAs commonly have "experienced" same gender emotional deprivation or even traumatic dis-affirmation. This experience may be but need not be *objectively* "neglectful or abusive." Children who are more temperamentally sensitive, intelligent, and imaginative than the average may find outwardly "unremarkable" treatment from fathers, siblings, or peers so *subjectively* distressing that they react as if the (mis-)treatment was severe. If the treatment is objectively un- or dis-affirming, such children will "feel" it to have been more distressing than the average. Protecting oneself from further distress is at the origin of SSAs.[37]

Such men grew up "defensively detaching" from their fathers or other significant males. This means that they self-protectively withdrew from and habitually came to avoid future intimate encounters with the salient males in their lives, including peers, as a way of preventing further perceived rejection or abandonment. In overcoming the compulsive sexual behaviors which are rooted in such self-protective repression, these men must realize that "the true damage was done not by the father (or peers, etc.), *but by his own defensive detachment from him* (or them)." Overcoming the simultaneous need and aversion for male contact may be possible only if the man works to understand and ultimately accept (i.e., forgive) his "father for who he is, with his limitations, including his (past and perhaps present) limited ability to demonstrate love, affection, and acceptance."[38] Understanding and accepting sibling or peer dis-affirmers may also be necessary if one is to overcome unchaste habits which are motivated by such unresolved hurts and resentments. Finally, forgiving others may require recognizing the need for, and learning to forgive, oneself for having been co-responsible for or a co-participant in one's avoidance of potentially affirming contacts with others.

Prayer

Prayer is an excellent means of genuine self-affirmation. Prayer also is fundamental way for those who seek to overcome the difficulties of both sexual compulsion and emotional deprivation (having been poorly, un- or dis-affirmed). Whether one follows the wisdom of the Twelve Steps, the Christian Men's Movements, or Baars and Terruwe, daily meditation helps us to "be still, and know that I am God" (Ps 46:10). Those who "are still before the Lord" and who "find their delight in Him" find that the Lord reveals and ultimately satisfies the genuine "desires of their hearts" (Ps 37: 4, 6).

As Fr. John Harvey often reminds those attending Courage conferences, "prayer of the heart leads to chastity of the heart." Meditative or contemplative prayer opens a person up to the genuinely affirming and loving moral truths of God and to the grace that follows them. Psychiatrist Richard Fitzgibbons has written about the use of Catholic spirituality for overcoming SSAs and healing the hurts which cause and result from SSA behaviors.[39] Fitzgibbons readily refers his audiences to Harvard psychiatrist Herbert Benson's empirical study on the use of relaxing meditation for the resolution of a number of psychological problems, including compulsive behaviors.[40]

Throughout their writings and talks, Baars and Terruwe consistently advise their clients about both the spiritual and psychological benefits of regular religious practice. They encourage the practice of contemplative, as well as meditative, prayer and scripture reading in order to come to know God better so that we can love Him more with our "heart," our humane emotions and intuition, as well as with our rational mind and will.[41] They regard contemplative prayer as a way to develop and nurture our ability to love our neighbors and ourselves in more affirming ways. Baars also composed meditation tapes based on scripture to aid in learning both self-relaxation and contemplative prayer.[42] Baars and Terruwe likewise encouraged their clients to practice "natural" contemplation through the experience of both divinely created and humanly engendered beauty.

The contemplation of religious art, especially icons and statues, may be particularly helpful to those who struggle with pornography. Total abstinence from future pornography does not erase from visual or auditory memory, pictures, films or other media already experienced. Persons trying to resist remembered pornography can find that intentionally experiencing religious or natural beauty at moments of temptation to remember or fantasize about past pornography may help them overcome such temptations. Meditation on authentic beauty, whether natural or religious, gives an alternative focus for one's attention and imagination. It also affords, with time and practice, an awareness of and detachment from any emotions or feelings that are seeking indirect satisfaction or expression through the use of pornography. One who struggles with sexual compulsions may, with realistic hope, seek increasing freedom from such compulsions and a measure of peace and joy (serenity) through the contemplation of truth and beauty in genuine literary and musical art, as well.

Concluding Thoughts

I began Part II of the section on "John Paul II as the 'Pope of Affirmation'" with the following quotation by John Paul II: *"The truth that we owe to man is, first and foremost, a truth about man."* This quotation continues:

> *Perhaps one of the most obvious weaknesses of present-day civilization lies in an inadequate view of man.* Without doubt, our age is the one in which man has been most written and spoken of, the age of the foremost of humanism and the age of anthropocentrism. Nevertheless it is paradoxically also the age of man's deepest anxiety about his identity and his destiny, the age of man's abasement to previously unsuspected levels, the age of human values trampled on as never before. How is this paradox explained? We can say that it is in the inexorable paradox of atheistic humanism; it is the drama of man being deprived of an essential dimension of his being, namely, his search for the infinite, and thus faced with having his being reduced in the worst way. *Thanks to the Gospel...the truth about man...is found in an anthropology...whose primordial affirmation is that man is God's image."*

In commenting on the entire quotation, Baars states that the Holy Father's "words underscore the meaning and spirit of what I consider my task and that of every Christian psychiatrist" – and indeed, every scholar, researcher, and practitioner in the psychological arts and sciences – "to assist the Church and all Christians in knowing more about man as the image of God, to lessen his abasement, and to bring order and strength to his psychic life for optimal receptivity to God's healing grace." [43]

John Paul II's use of the word "affirmation" expresses an important dimension of affirming living. Human beings are made "in love, for love and to love." Experiencing the fullness of life, peace, joy, and freedom *of* the Truth, and *from* His "truth about man," is the created and recreated "birthright" of every human person. For Baars and Terruwe, genuine affirmation includes *speaking* and *living* the truth in love (cf. Eph 4: 15, 25). Authentic self-affirmation likewise requires *hearing* and living the truth in love, which includes hearing and living the love in the truth about the moral law.

Growth in the virtue of chastity – which may involve the struggle of stopping or avoiding pornography, masturbation and other unchaste behaviors – is essential to embracing and fulfilling our human destiny. To flourish as persons, the human race, whether as individuals and as pluralities, must hear and heed the love of those who speak the truth to us, whether expressed in actions, words, or gestures. This is the essence of giving and receiving affirmation and the means by which the genuine emotional, intellectual, moral and spiritual strengthening, growth and fulfillment of every person may occur.

It is good to realize that embracing the call or calling another to conversion and to growth in chastity really is "good news." As John Paul II explains in *Reconciliation and Penance*:

> "Conversion and contrition…for the purpose of bringing about a radical change of life…are (not just unpleasant self-denial but) even more a *drawing near to the holiness of God* (which means becoming more able to know the truth and to love and be loved) a *rediscovery of one's true identity*, which has been upset and disturbed by sin, *a liberation in the very depth of self* and thus a *regaining of lost joy*, the joy of being saved (cf. Ps 51:12), which the majority of people in our time are no longer capable of experiencing (emphasis added)."[44]

Teaching or learning chastity, like preventing or escaping unchastity, is a daunting task. I am comforted by the reality that growth in virtue and genuine affirmation is divinely willed, directed and empowered for all. Sharing a few quotations from the last section of "Letter to Families" (entitled: "Strengthened in the Inner Man") seems a fitting way to end this paper. In closing his Letter, John Paul II writes as follows:

> I bow my knees before the Father, from whom every fatherhood and motherhood is named, "that he may grant you to be strengthened with might through his Spirit in the inner man" (Eph 3:16). The family is the first human setting in which is formed that "inner man" of which the Apostle speaks. The growth of the inner man in strength and vigor is a gift of the Father and the Son in the Holy Spirit. …

Genuine affirmation of one human person by another – and, properly done, *of* oneself *by* oneself – is the ordinary means by which the Lord enables the "inner man" – the unique personhood – of every human being to grow "in strength and vigor." Such growth in "virtue" is both prevention and remedy for pseudo-self-affirming behaviors like pornography. No matter how gratifying unchaste behaviors may "seem" in the short term, they always and ultimately dis-affirm, deny, and "weaken" the personhood and family life of those who practice them.

John Paul II reminds us implicitly of the Christian truth about affirming living within the family and its relation to growth in chastity, when he writes about the need for family members to be "witnesses" of holiness.[45] ...

> I speak with the power of his truth to all people of our day, so that they will come to appreciate the grandeur of the goods of marriage, family and life; so that they will come to appreciate the great danger which follows when these realities are not respected, or when the supreme values which lie at the foundation of the family and of human dignity are disregarded. May the Lord Jesus repeat these truths to us *with the power and the wisdom of the Cross*, so that humanity will not yield to the temptation of the "father of lies" (Jn 8:44), who constantly seeks to draw people to broad and easy ways, ways apparently smooth and pleasant, but in reality full of snares and dangers. May we always be enabled to follow the One who is "the way, and the truth, and the life" (Jn 14:6).[46]

Philip M. Sutton earned a B.A. in philosophy at the University of Notre Dame (1973), an M.S. in clinical psychology from Purdue University (1980), and a Ph.D. in marriage and family therapy, also at Purdue (1983). He was the inaugural director of the M.A. in Counseling program at the Franciscan University of Steubenville (1989-91). He has taught at Purdue, the College of St. Francis in Joliet, Illinois, Indiana University at South Bend, and Notre Dame. As a licensed clinical and school psychologist, clinical social worker, and marriage and family therapist, he provides professional services for two Catholic schools as well as for the Marriage Tribunal and the local Courage chapter in the Diocese of Fort Wayne-South Bend. He has lectured widely and has published various articles as well as a monograph entitled *Fathers, Become Who You Are!* (1999).

Notes

1. This and the following sections summarize or include selected portions of an earlier paper by the author entitled: "Personalist Themes in the Applied

Thomistic Psychology of Anna Terruwe and Conrad Baars," in James DuBois (ed.), *The Nature and Tasks of a Personalist Psychology* (Lanham, MD: University Press of America,1995), 113–139. This was an expanded version of "Personalist Themes in the Work of Conrad Baars and Anna Terruwe," a paper presented at the Institute for Personalist Psychology (IPP) conference in October, 1994, at the Franciscan University of Steubenville.

2.   In addition to the paper by the author cited above, other sources of information about a Thomistic understanding of the emotions include: Aquinas, Thomas. *Summa Theologica*, I-II, QQ, 22–48; Baars, Conrad W. *Feeling & Healing Your Emotions* (Revised Edition.) Suzanne Baars and Bonnie Shayne (eds.). Gainesville, FL: Bridge-Logos, 2003; *Catechism of the Catholic Church,* Second Edition. Washington: United States Catholic Conference- *Libreria Editrice Vaticana*, 1997; # 1762–1775; Groeschel, Fr. Benedict, C.F.R., *The Reform of Renewal* (San Francisco: Ignatius, 1990).Cf. Chapter Five: "The Conversion of the Emotions."; Ripperger, Fr. Chad, F.S.S.P.. *Introduction to the Science of Mental Health: Philosophical Psychology* (Vol. 1), published by author; Terruwe, Anna & Baars, Conrad. *Psychic Wholeness and Healing.* New York: Alba House, 1981; Vogt, Fr. Emmerich, O.P., *The Passions: A Guide for Understanding Your Feelings & Emotions.* Portland, OR: *The 12-Step Review*, # S-2, 2000.

3.   Conrad Baars and Anna Terruwe, *Healing the Unaffirmed: Recognizing Deprivation Neurosis* (New York: Alba House, 1976), 204.

4.   Baars, *Feeling and Healing*, 153.

5.   Terruwe and Baars, *Psychic Wholeness*, 24.

6.   *Feeling and Healing Your Emotions*, 283–284; *Psychic Wholeness and Healing*, 3.

7.   This was a revised edition of the first English translation of Terruwe's doctoral thesis: *The Neurosis in the Light of Rational Psychology (*1960.)

8.   Conrad Baars. *Affirming Living & Healing* (1979). Video (VHS) of Graduate Theology Workshop, Catholic Charismatic Bible Institute, St. Mary's University, San Antonio, Texas (Boston: Daughters of St. Paul, 1992.)

9.   Pope John Paul II (1994), "Letter to Families" (Boston, MA: Pauline Books and Media), # 15.

10.   *Ibid*, # 11.

11.   *Ibid*, #12. I think that an unfortunate contemporary meaning of the word "sincere" may prevent an accurate understanding. The truth that self-fulfillment comes through sincere- and ideally mutual-self-giving means more than doing so with "good intentions" or in "good faith." The truth of this statement by the Council and its reassertion by John Paul II's hinges on the meaning of sincere as not just a quality of intention or of process, but of reality. A "sincere" gift in the full sense means one that is "genuine," "real," or "valid," one that is free of "hypocrisy, deceit or simulation" (*Funk & Wagnalls Standard Desk Dictionary,* NY: Harper & Row, 1984*).* I often have wondered if the assertion that man does not "*fully find himself except*

through a sincere gift of self" might be rendered better by "except through a sincere and *wise* gift of self."

12. *The Catechism of the Catholic Church* (1997, Second Edition; Washington: United States Catholic Conference- Libreria Editrice Vaticana, 1997) describes *"pornography"* as a behavior which: "consists in removing real or simulated sexual acts from the intimacy of the partners, in order to display them deliberately to third parties. It offends against chastity because it perverts the conjugal act, the intimate giving of spouses to each other. It does grave injury to the dignity of its participants (actors, vendors, the public), since each one becomes an object of base pleasure and illicit profit for others. It immerses all who are involved in the illusion of a fantasy world. It is a grave offense" (# 2354). Jacobs cites the *Catechism* description of *"masturbation."*.

13. Terruwe and Baars, *Healing the Unaffirmed*, chapters 1–2.

14. *Ibid.*; Terruwe and Baars, *Psychic Wholeness*, 25; Baars, *Born Only Once*, 73–80.

15. Cf. Baars, *Born Only Once*.

16. *Ibid*, 92.

17. John Paul II, *Letter to Families, #* 14.

18. *Ibid.*

19. "The Truth and Meaning of Human Sexuality: Guidelines for Education within the Family" (Pontifical Council for the Family. Boston, MA: Pauline Books and Media, 1996).This document talks about the need to always to bear in mind that human sexuality is affected by original sin. Specifically, "when teaching Catholic doctrine and morality about sexuality, *the lasting effects of original sin* must be taken into account, that is to say, human weakness and the need for the grace of God to overcome temptations and avoid sin" (# 122–123).

20. John Paul II, "Letter to Families," # 14.

21. *Ibid.*

22. *Catechism* # 2351.

23. Baars, *Feeling and Healing*, 234.

24. Baars and Terruwe, *Healing the Unaffirmed*, 185–189.

25. "Truth and Meaning of Human Sexuality," # 105.

26. *Ibid* # 107.

27. Ibid # 108.

28. Baars, *Feeling and Healing*, 120.

29. *Ibid.*, 41–42.

30. I have heard Fr. Harvey speak about "interior" vs. "white-knuckled" chastity on numerous occasions.

31. Cf. *The Twelve Steps: A Spiritual Journey* (Curtis, WA: RPI Publishing, 1994), xii–xiii.

32. Adrian van Kaam, *The Art of Existential Counseling* (Denville, NJ: Dimension Books, 1966), 33.

33. Baars, *Born Only Once*, 81–99.

34. Cf. Philip Sutton. *Fathers Become Who You Are! Social Science and Magisterial Teaching on What Causes Fatherlessness and How to Strengthen the Fatherhood of All Men.* Privately printed, 1999.

35. Common Twelve Step wisdom advises a person not to become "too tired, hungry, angry, or lonely" in order to avoid triggering an attraction to the addictive behavior one is trying to overcome. A more complete description of emotions or feelings states to be managed in order too avoid behavioral relapse is, to avoid becoming ASPHALTED: too Anxious, Sad, Pained, Hungry, Angry, Lonely, Tired, Elated, or Discouraged. I have in mind Uncle Remus' B'rer Rabbit, who had a self-defeating (asphalting) encounter with the Tar Baby when the latter would not behave as Rabbit wished.

36. Robert Enright, *Forgiveness is a Choice* (Washington: APA, 2001); Robert Enright & Richard Fitzgibbons, *Helping Clients Forgive* (Washington: APA, 2000); cf. International Forgiveness Institute, web-site: www.forgive-ness-institute.org.

37. In an audio-taped talk (Boston, MA: Pauline Books and Media) at the 1994 Courage Conference entitled: *Shattered Hearts- Whole Spirits*, psychiatrist Jeffrey Satinover explains the concept of the "childhood vow." In response to emotional distress which a child perceives as "intolerable," the child "vows" not to allow himself to be distressed again. Such a "decision," often a product of inexperience and immature judgment and made subconsciously, is one explanation for what other therapists who treat SSAs call "defensive detachment."

38. Joseph Nicolosi, *Reparative Therapy of Male Homosexuality: A New Clinical Approach (Northvale, NJ: Aronson, 1997)*, 161.

39. Richard Fitzgibbons, "The Origins and Healing of Homosexual Attractions and Behaviors," In John F. Harvey, O.S.F.S. , *The Truth About Homosexuality* (Ignatius Press, 1996), 307–343. Cf. *Homosexuality & Hope*: Statement of the Catholic Medical Association (2000, website: www.cathmed.org); and *Homosexuality & Hope* (Question and Answer Pamphlet- 2003; website: www.cmalansing.org) of which Fitzgibbons is primary author.

40. e.g., Herbert Benson, M.D., *Beyond the Relaxation Response: How to Harness the Healing Power of Your Personal Beliefs* (NY: Berkley, 1984).

41. Baars, *Feeling and Healing*, 243–244.

42. Conrad Baars. Audiotapes: "Fear is Useless – What Is Needed Is Trust"; "Don't Look at the Waves – Look at Jesus"; "Speak Lord – An Aid to Meditation"; and "Be Still – An Aid to Contemplation." (Cf. www.conrad-baars.com).

43. Conrad W. Baars, *Feeling & Healing Your Emotions* (Revised edition.) Suzanne Baars and Bonnie Shayne (eds.) (Gainesville, FL: Bridge-Logos, 2003, 283–284).

44. John Paul II, *Reconciliation and Penance* (1984), # 29. In *Veritatis Splendor (*Boston, MA: Pauline Books and Media, *1993)*. John Paul II like-wise reminds us that "it is the Gospel which reveals the full truth about man

and his moral journey, and thus enlightens and admonishes sinners; it proclaims to them God's mercy, which is constantly at work to preserve them both from despair at their inability fully to know and keep God's law and from the presumption that they can be saved without merit.God also reminds sinners of the *joy of forgiveness*, which alone grants the strength to see in the moral law *a liberating truth, a grace-filled source of hope, a path of life* (n. 112)."

45. Concerning such "witnesses," elsewhere in this section, John Paul II writes: "As Pope Paul VI observed, 'contemporary man listens more willingly to witnesses than to teachers, and if he listens to teachers it is because they are witnesses.' In the Church, the treasure of the family has been entrusted first and foremost to witnesses: to those fathers and mothers, sons and daughters who through the family have discovered the path of their human and Christian vocation, the dimension of the "inner man" (Eph 3:16) of which the Apostle speaks; and thus have attained holiness. *The Holy Family is the beginning of countless other holy families.* The Council recalled that holiness is the vocation of all the baptized. In our age, as in the past, there is no lack of witnesses to the "gospel of the family," even if they are not well known or have not been proclaimed saints by the Church," Letter to Families, # 23.

46. *Ibid.* Bill Saunders mentioned the "Letter to Families"in his opening remarks to the conference. What didn't get actually quoted, though, nevertheless bears repeating here: "The history of mankind, the history of salvation, passes by way of the family. In these pages I have tried to show how the family is placed at the center of the great struggle between good and evil, between life and death, between love and all that is opposed to love. To the family is entrusted the task of striving, first and foremost, to unleash the forces of good, the source of which is found in Christ the Redeemer of man. Every family unit needs to make these forces their own so that...the family will be 'strong with the strength of God' (cf. 1 Cor 7:1–40; Eph 5:21–6:9; Col 3:25; 1 Pet 3:1–7.

Chapter 11: K-12 Catholic Schools & the Revival of the Catholic Family in American Culture: An Appraisal

DENNIS PURIFICACION, ED.D.

Introduction

Some of the more seasoned members of this august Fellowship of Catholic Scholars may find among some of the younger members of the Fellowship a handful of teachers who have had the honor of having attended at least one World Youth Day. At the Denver WYD vigil Mass in 1993, Pope John Paul the Great said: "The family is under attack"! He then departed from his prepared text and repeated with an even stronger and more vigorous tone in his all-too-familiar Polish accent: "...is under attack"! Perhaps he said this twice to underscore the urgency of the message.

A year later in his "Letter to Families," the Holy Father again repeated his message on the situation of the family. He said:

> The Church's constant and trusting prayer during the Year of the Family is *for the education of man*, so that families will persevere in their task of education with courage, trust, and hope, in spite of difficulties occasionally so serious as to appear insuperable. The Church prays that the forces of the 'civilization of love,' which have their source in the love of God, will be triumphant.[i]

Both his addresses cited here form the *point de départ* of this paper's title and content. The proposed title, "K-12 Catholic Schools and the Revival of the Catholic Family in American Culture: An Appraisal," assumes the existence of systematic affronts undermining the Catholic family unit. It also presupposes that the Catholic family is, in fact, in need of renewal, and that K-12 Catholic schools play some type of positive role *vis-à-vis* the revival of the Catholic family. This author acknowledges and accepts previous assessments of the Fellowship concerning the state of the Church in the United States.[2]

Summary

The author of this paper appraises K-12 Catholic schools in the pastoral care of Catholic nuclear families in American society.[3] Just as a house appraiser sets a price on a home, I will try to set some value to Catholic schools over the past ten years (1994–2004). The three main areas of this paper are patterned after a three-fold approach of the U.S. Catholic bishops' document entitled "In Support of Catechetical Ministry" (2000).[4] In sum, the plan is to: (1) identify the good; (2) strengthen the weak; and (3) develop creative means for growth.

Apropos, I will here place a value on our Catholic schools by first identifying the good that has emerged from K-12 Catholic schools, given their historically limited resources. Second, I will appraise K-12 Catholic schools by proposing possible weak areas in need of pastoral attention by both bishops and educational leaders, given the current culture of death in which we find ourselves. Finally, where pertinent, I will suggest some possible areas for improvement so that K-12 Catholic schools can continue in its task of building a culture of life. Throughout these three parts, particular themes will be addressed in light of sensitive pastoral situations identified by the educational documents of the ordinary and universal magisterium.

Appraisal: Strengths and Weaknesses

The Holy Father is intent on building a civilization of love. In the United States, K-12 Catholic schools have been influential educational institutions that have impacted on the building and sustaining of a civilization of love and a culture of life.[5] There are five key areas around which I am framing my appraisal that merit further discussion and analyses:

A) Faith and Morals

The first and foremost of the Catholic school contribution to Catholic family life is in the area of preserving and promoting faith and morals. K-12 Catholic schools continue to provide some type of spiritual and moral formation to our young. The Congregation for Catholic Education (CCE) observed the positive course of Catholic schools over the past decades.[6] These included (1) the contribution that Catholic schools have made to the evangelizing mission of the Church and (2) the responsibilities that Catholic schools have assumed in providing social and economic development.[7]

Evangelization of Non-Catholic Population in Catholic Schools

In the area of evangelization, the CCE noted that in many instances Catholic schools were involved in areas in which no other form of pastoral work was possible. In a sense, Catholic schools provided the necessary beachhead that other ministries of the Church (such as health care and social services) could not directly penetrate on the front lines of evangelization. Let us first consider the non-Catholic population being served before considering the Catholic population being served. Bear with me as I cite two simple cases: I recall that in my early years as a rookie Catholic school teacher a good number of the student body at our school was Jewish. The Jewish families in that particular locale presumably trusted and revered the local Church through her educational institutions, and this was reflected in the student body enrollment numbers at this school. Did these Jewish students hear of the saving love of Jesus? Yes, they did. What became of this I cannot say, but I hope the point is clear enough. But for Catholic education, what other significant inroad would the Catholic Church ever have made into this particular Jewish neighborhood and community?

Similarly, there is a story of a young Muslim student at a Catholic grade school who lost both her parents in an accident. The first person to whom she ran in her grief was not her next of kin. Rather, she literally ran to the nun who was her teacher in school. Now take these two cases of Jews and Muslims and read in any non-Catholic community present in our pluralistic culture. Of course, countless stories abound, and I do not want to belabor the point with my examples here; but I think this underscores a valuable approach that the Fellowship and the Catholic school community can take in advising the bishops concerning our Catholic schools relative to the broader culture.[8] This approach is that Catholic schools remain an asset in contributing to the two-pronged mission of the Church in both (a) evangelization and (b) human development.

Evangelization of the Catholic Population in Catholic Schools

For our Catholic students, the Catholic student body is afforded, in many cases across the country, easier access to sacramental practice outside of weekly Sunday Mass. For example, Catholic students have availed themselves of the sacrament of Reconciliation during retreats and other moments offered. Even if this sacrament is offered only once a year, say, during Lent, it assists families at the bare minimum to meet the canon law requirement of going to annual Confession (CIC, 1983,

¶989). For younger grade school levels, First Holy Communion preparation is guaranteed; while in the upper levels many Catholic schools assist
in the preparation of the sacrament of Confirmation.[9]

Furthermore, student Masses are typically offered on a monthly
basis, and Catholic school administrators and campus ministers are com-
mendably cognizant of scheduling monthly Masses during the academic
year so that they sometimes coincide with Holy Days of Obligation
and/or the school patron's feast day. Also, Easter week is taken seriously and Stations of the Cross services are provided. All of these are examples of the Church's sacramental administration in K-12 education that
lie outside the Sunday obligation, not to mention the contribution
Catholic schools make to families inside the religion class. For now, let
us say that the Church is present to our young Monday thru Friday during the week; and, for the most part, year-round through the year.
Institutionally, then, there is some type of Catholic culture that they
experience. Bishop Paul S. Loverde, interviewed as the chairman of the
U.S. Conference of Catholic Bishops (USCCB) vocations committee,
confirmed findings that Catholic school graduates were more likely than
graduates of public schools to consider the priesthood and that those
vocations are nurtured in the Catholic identity and Catholic environment
of the school.[10] He also stated that both Catholic schools and parishes
form Catholic identity, particularly in active youth groups, and that
young people involved in parish and/or youth ministry are more likely to
consider a vocation, especially if youth ministry involved contact of
young people with a priest. In view of this, I add that during the upcom-
ing Year of the Eucharist, perhaps Catholic schools can do more to promote vocations through greater Eucharistic adoration.

Implementing the *Catechism of the Catholic Church*

In the Religion class, students receive education in the faith. While
there is still a lot of work to be done in this area, I am pleased to cite the
"Conformity List of Catechetical Texts and Series" of the USCCB Ad
Hoc Committee to Oversee the Use of the *Catechism*. The Summer,
2004, edition of *Catechism Update* listed 32 elementary series, 14 sacramental preparation texts, 5 high school series and 13 high school texts
all in conformity with the *Catechism*.[11] Parents now enjoy the value of a
list of choice textbooks with the comfort of knowing that a panel of bishops reviews texts for "completeness of doctrinal content" (p. 2).
Hopefully, the list will grow as time progresses.

While it has been twelve years since the *Catechism of the Catholic
Church* was promulgated, and 10 years since the English translation was

published, it is not too early to provide a brief appraisal of the situation. An increasing number of Catholic people (not just Catholic school students) are thirsting for substance and moral guidance. We are seeing among the young adults and youth a glimpse of the New Springtime of Faith prophesied by the Pope John Paul II; among these one finds some Catholic school students. For example, many of these youth and young adults find Eucharistic devotion an exciting discovery.[12] The self-anointed JP2 Generation, defined in this paper as the youth who grew up with only one pope, is making its resurgence in ecclesial life. The *Catechism* will surely help them in this task. Some teachers even require reading of the *Catechism* as a primary text, which exposes students to ecclesial documents. I remember as a junior in high school reading *Humanae Vitae* on my own and finding it written in very beautiful and understandable language. While there is a pedagogical need to articulate esoteric theological concepts in the language of children, I do not think it unreasonable to consider having older teenagers read the *Catechism* directly in religion class, particularly in their junior and senior years. It may be an insult to their person to suggest that they do not have the intellectual stamina to read the *Catechism*. And we might want to consider having 9th and 10th graders read the *Catechism* in their religion classes, too. Students, as much as some may rebel, like the moral structure and are very open to meeting high challenges. They like to be corrected and told that what they did was wrong. They are thirsting for it, in fact. Chastity speaker Molly Kelly lectured that if we treat students like animals, then they will behave accordingly, but if we tell them of their worth and ability, with God's grace, to follow the Commandments, then they will rise to the occasion. We need to tell them that they can comprehend their *Catechism* lessons and live the demands of the Christian life, and they will act accordingly.

Sex Education in Catholic Secondary Schools

This is particularly true in the area of the sex education minefield. My main comment for this part of the paper centers on the consistency with which Catholic school students receive some type of chastity education and introduction to Natural Family Planning in secondary Catholic schools.[13] Many families expect Catholic school teachers to perform this task. Although this may be the case, it should be emphasized that parents cannot abdicate their responsibility here. During a four-year course of study, students typically take courses on areas such as introductory theology, the Bible, social justice, world religions, maybe a philosophy class, the sacraments, Church history, and Christian marriage. In the introductory theology class, students receive a week or two of sexual morality, depending on the texts, curriculum, and teacher. Chastity education (and maybe NFP) is covered a few weeks out of the entire year. The Bible and social justice classes may dovetail chastity education and sexual morality for a few weeks, again depending on the teacher and curriculum. And certainly in a Christian marriage or a sacraments class, chastity education is reviewed for a while.

The question posed here is: Is this adequate? I take the position that promotion of chastity education itself is a great strength of secondary Catholic education, but that there are levels of chastity education that are currently not adequate enough. Chastity education needs to be strengthened and taught consistently. Students need to hear a consistent moral message, whether chastity or otherwise, during their impressionable high school years. The proposed inadequacy identified here is multifaceted, but I posit that it may be rooted in two critical areas of secondary Catholic education. The first, as addressed above, pertains to the four-year curriculum structure. The second, and arguably more important, pertains to the caliber of the religion instructor who is charged with the grave duty of transmitting the moral teachings of the Church.

Secondary Catholic School Curriculum

Let us first consider the high school curriculum structure. Do we simply need more chastity education (i.e., quantity), or do we simply need better curriculum plan (quality)? The answer may lay in both. Some practical guidelines contained in the document "The Truth and Meaning of Human Sexuality" (PCF, 1995) include recognizing chastity education which is in accordance with one's parents' values as a right, always with due regard for the child's stage of development. Elsewhere, John Paul II stated that even when parents entrust these responsibilities to schools, parental presence ought to continue to be "constant and active."[14]

What of the parental education role in sex education? Are Catholic school parents really talking to their kids about chastity? While this task of sex education belongs primarily to parents, many parents nevertheless shy away from this solemn duty of giving adequate sex education to their teenagers. If our Catholic youth, in Catholic schools and in CCD programs are constantly bombarded with the media's definition of sex and love, year-round, 24 hours a day, why do we only teach chastity education a few times a week during the year? To use business language, our competitors seem to be buying us out. Cardinal Trujillo (1996) wrote:

> Families sometimes leave this task to silence, to the indirect, but
> often unhealthy influence of chance, the television, or the school,
> because of the objective difficulty the delicate subject entails, or
> out of a kind of neglect passed on from the preceding generation.[15]

His Eminence also acknowledged that both children and couples are being led astray, particularly by the sexual revolution. I think parents who abdicate this role simply need to be offered examples from other parents who take their task seriously. Those of us involved with chastity education must address the phenomenon of the sexual revolution and forcefully demonstrate its abysmal failure. Perhaps a practical strategy might be to seriously consider establishing chastity clubs *en masse* in our Catholic schools.

Religion Teacher Preparation

This second diagnosis begs the issue of a religion teacher's qualifications and moral theological formation. One cannot always assume that the religion teacher is comfortable enough to address chastity as understood by the magisterium – not merely abstinence education-à-*la*-secular-humanism – and that teachers have studied and can introduce students to NFP as the alternative to contraception in their future family lives. Granted, the sound theological and moral formation of the secondary school religion teacher is imperative; however, these teachers find themselves in the middle of the culture of dissent found in Catholic higher academia that has trickled down to the classroom of the child.[16] This culture of dissent has exacerbated any perceived or real deficiencies in the sex education curriculum, and in teacher preparation, and has caused untold damage to the spiritual formation of children, even before high school graduation. Given all this, the main consideration to accentuate is that the local ordinary enjoys the juridical right to name or approve religion teachers and likewise to remove or to demand their removal under Canon 805.[17] This canon is mentioned here not to make heads roll, so to speak, but to simply reiterate that norms concerning secondary religion classrooms exist and can be utilized. But I suspect that, until Catholic higher academia accepts the norms of John Paul II's *Ex Corde Ecclesiae*, greater episcopal oversight on secondary Catholic education teachers may temporarily remain on the administrative backburner.

What do all of these strengths and weaknesses have to do with renewing the family scene? Even amidst internal challenges, the civilization of love is being built through Catholic schools, irrespective of the presence of the culture of death. In other words, Catholic schools are engaged in an already proactive way of spreading the Gospel and involved in the grave task of making disciples, although faced with internal challenges. During the 1960s and 1970s there was a notable decline in Catholic education enrollment and some Catholic school leaders wondered whether the mission of Catholic education merited substantial change in orientation.[18] This time was a moment of truth for Catholic education, but many Catholic educators stayed the course of teaching the Catholic faith among our children and assisting Catholics. I would add that, with the increasing non-Catholic student body rate, the main shift in the mission of Catholic schools is that it now benefits both Catholics and non-Catholics alike, whereas these schools benefited primarily Catholic students prior to the Second Vatican Council.[19]

Such difficulties remain, but such internal difficulties do not overshadow the Gospel preached within the classrooms of K-12 Catholic education. The tone is thus one of qualified optimism.

B) Parents as First Educators of Their Children

The educational role of parents is a constant theme of the magisterium's teaching on parents. These parents laudably sacrifice to send their children to Catholic schools in the face of increasing tuition. They volunteer and provide other services in many unseen ways. At the parochial school level, parents assist at co-curricular functions and even help raise money for the schools. Before continuing to sing the praises of the Catholic parents and the parental involvement of parents who are involved in the education of their children, however, I have to confess that the heart of my appraisal of the role of parents in education consists in a reflection on the current state of new young parents as marital role models for their children. The Church's evangelization efforts were identified above for the students, but what of the parents, whom the Church consistently calls the first educators of their children?

Broken Family Situations and Catholic Schools

I once heard a grade school teaching nun remark that, sometimes, it is the little students themselves who bring their parents to Sunday Mass each week! I may be generalizing with this anecdote but this may verify that, more often than not, it seems pedagogically easier to impart the life of discipleship for kindergarten through six grade students than for adults. "Unless you become like little children," Our Lord said.[20] Let us take this nun's statement as our focal point and identify yet another serious pastoral issue. Over the years, Catholic writers have tracked, and have sometimes preached in the wilderness, that the family unit was falling apart. Divorce rates and out-of-wedlock pregnancies skyrocketed over the years and numbers of young adults cohabiting multiplied.[21] Where are those thousands and hundreds of thousands of out-of-wedlock children or children of divorced and illicitly remarried adults now that they are a few years older? If we can indeed find some of them in our Catholic schools, it is imperative that our Catholic schools take care of irregular and even unusual pastoral situations.

Many Catholic schools deal with students who come from broken homes, with divorced and remarried parents, single mothers, abusive parents, older siblings (and parents) who cohabitate and contracept, et cetera. I am sure that many teachers can testify to these situations. My simplistic answer to students from broken homes has been: "I'm not here to talk about your parents right now, but when *you* get married, here is the way it should be…" In the beginning, it was not so. Maybe the students mention the Church's marriage teaching to their parents and siblings in irregular cases, maybe they do not. But it was a break-the-circle-of-divorce-somewhere approach and we-have-to-start-somewhere in their family line. From a certain point of view, the enrollment of students in this capacity may be categorized as a strong opportunity for K-12 Catholic education, considering that the Church, in her great mission of spreading divine mercy, wants to reconcile such situations to the Gospel. Their souls come before their grades. How are we ministering to these impressionable little ones so that they will someday raise a renewed Catholic family in the third millennium, not according to the values of the children of the sexual revolution, but according to Christ's teaching on marriage and family? Do we make concerted efforts to reach out to parents of our Catholic school students?

Perhaps one strategic priority should be to catechize the young student first and follow, if possible, with the parents.[22] Although this risks downplaying the parental education role, pastoral care of children of irregular family situations is where our pastoral energies, family renewal, books, and research must focus; to phrase a stereotypical platitude of politicians, on the notion that: "It's for the children…the children…the children!" There are ministries for divorced and remarried Catholics, but what of children who have suffered the scourge of divorce? What of the healing that needs to be done to their social and psychological damage? We certainly do not want our next generation of Catholic school graduates thinking, for example, that their oldest brother's de facto union (or even divorced daddy's new de facto union for that matter) with his newest girlfriend is the norm of Christian courtship. We have to engage them, and even sound nosey if necessary. Let us cast our nets out into the deep.[23] No *Walden Pond*s in Catholic education please!

Remote Marriage Preparation in Catholic Schools

John Paul's apostolic exhortation on the family distinguished between three phases of preparation for marriage: remote, proximate, and immediate. Since this paper focuses on Catholic school students, I would categorize the above situation as part of the *remote* preparation needed to revive the Catholic family. The Pontifical Council for the Family also called for adequate marriage preparation for youth coupled with a sound anthropological vision of man.[24] We cannot wait until many of these children of broken family life enter secondary and higher education levels or wait until young adults are in immediate stages of getting married. Let us get to them in the "remote" stages of preparation: teach them while they are young. (I leave the other two stages of preparation aside for now.)

To respond to the Pontifical Council for the Family's question, "Are the persons contracting marriage really prepared for it?" (2000, p. 43), I would set a conditional answer and reply that it depends on who is teaching the kids. It depends. If parents, who have the "original, primary and inalienable"[25] right to educate their children, have fallen away from the practice of the Faith as regards marriage, then in the area of remote preparation Catholic school students are not being properly prepared and there is need to strengthen this remote area. On the other hand, if parents received appropriate marriage catechesis, then in the area of remote preparation Catholic school students are receiving adequate preparation precisely because it is their parents themselves who bear witness to marriage in their lives. This is remote preparation *par excellence*. It is important to recognize that when stating that parents are the first educators of their children, we should ask: *How* can they adequately fulfill this task if they themselves received poor catechesis as children in the period that followed the Second Vatican Council through the appearance of the *Catechism of the Catholic Church*?[26] To support the magisterium's teaching on the parental education role, it is therefore incumbent on us to engage in a strategy of re-evangelizing these two generations of families (both the young parents and their children) rather than for the young parents to cede this role entirely to any school.[27]

The "New Poor" in K-12 Catholic Schools: Two Generations of Broken Homes[28]

As regards those Catholic families not in irregular situations, they must be commended and not neglected lest these children think that the plague of divorce is the norm among their classmates. But if it is true that over half to sixty percent of all marriages end in divorce, some, if not most, Catholic schools have a student body with broken families that may well reflect these numbers. Or, better phrased: We cannot always assume that a majority of our Catholic school students' parents have the blessings of a regular marriage situation. Catholic schools must sustain and nourish what the Church teaches about family life. This is an area where it is an asset for building a culture of life. The strategy is two-pronged: nourish Catholic families while at the same time tend to the broken families – preserve and promote. It is not novel, really, for the Church has always done this: take what is good and attempt to "baptize" what is not. The New Evangelization entails catechizing the kids *and* the new young parents. I have heard a principal acquaintance of mine say that, sometimes, principals have to be pastors. This was an epithet, of course, and I am not proposing that it be the norm for future pastoral action, since the parish is the normal center for pastoral care. Rather, what I am modestly proposing is some institutional policy of proactively rectifying irregular marital situations of young families in our Catholic schools.

C) Quality Education & Right to Quality Education

There are two main strengths I would like to identify in the area of educational quality. The first is the area of quality education itself. Quality education is defined here as the best learning and instructional system of the day. The second is that the very presence of Catholic schools in America itself is a human right conferred not by the state but as justice demands.[29]

Regional Accreditation and Local Governance of Catholic Schools

Catholic education meets secular standards in self-improvement methods and institutional self-evaluation. I am of course referring to regional accreditation, towards which the general Catholic school leadership is nationally moving. As such, secular standards are being met without substantial compromise of Catholic identity. At this point in history, the secular process for accrediting most, if not all, K-12 Catholic educational institutions does not in theory usurp the local self-governing rights of the school. The school can decide for itself the best means for providing quality education without direct government interference. The National Catholic Education Association (NCEA) would surely cry foul the moment regional accreditation process became more a matter of governance of Catholic schools rather than an educational quality issue.[30]

Equal Justice Denied in Catholic Education

Interestingly enough, however, while Catholic schools share some goals with their public school colleagues, they are denied equal justice in the matter of the right to a quality education. Denying equal rights to parents is inconsistent with American principle of equal justice under the law and even with the intent of America's founding fathers. The Second Vatican Council taught in its Declaration on Religious Liberty *Dignitatis Humanae*, as follows:

> Every family, in that it is a society with its own basic rights, has the right freely to organize its own religious life in the home and under the control of parents. These have the right to decide in accordance with their own religious beliefs the form of religious upbringing which is to be given to their children. The civil authority must therefore recognize the rights of parents to choose with genuine freedom schools or other means of education. Parents should not be subjected directly or indirectly to unjust burdens because of this freedom of choice. Furthermore, the rights of parents are violated if their children are compelled to attend classes which are not in agreement with the religious beliefs of the parents or if there is but a single compulsory system of education from which all religious instruction is excluded.[31]

The Second Vatican Council, then, not just the Republican Party platform, insisted on parental choice. Thus, educational choice itself is a basic human right, just as the right to life is a fundamental human right. The president of the National Catholic Education Association, Dr. Michael Guerra, identified two pressing areas of need for Catholic schools in this regard: First, the impact of U.S. national education reform on Catholic schools; and, secondly, the affordability of Catholic education for parents who choose to send their children to a Catholic school.[32] Regarding the first point, the federal government's education reform efforts explicitly involve increased parental involvement in their children's education.[33] And although increased parental education involvement is a shared educational goal between Church and State, the principle to underscore here is that the parental education role is a moral, and not just a partisan or political, position. Additionally, human rights language entails constitutional considerations and economic implications.

D) Constitutional Clarification & the Economic Question

The fourth major area of our concern flows from the previous discussion on the right to education. This area involves the issue of the so-called wall of the separation between Church and State. What precisely does this phrase mean? The common man on the streets cites this mantra any time religion is mentioned in connection with the public square. It is a common doctrine to which some judges, legislators, and even intellectuals appeal when dealing with such areas such as God, the Ten Commandments; or, when the Church speaks on a moral matters in the American public forum. However, the doctrine of the wall of separation of Church and State appears nowhere in the American founding documents of the Declaration of Independence and the U.S. Constitution with its Bill of Rights. What, prey tell, does this mean, and, even more to the point, what does it mean for Catholic education?

The Second Continental Congress in the First Amendment to the Constitution establishing the Bill of Rights mandated that:

> Congress shall make no law respecting an establishment of religion, or prohibiting the free exercise thereof; or abridging the freedom of speech, or of the press; or the right of the people peaceably to assemble, and to petition the Government for a redress of grievances.[34]

Where does this say anything about the separation of church and state? This church-state separation doctrine evolved as an interpretative theory of the Constitution, not as a founding principle – somewhat in the same way as the *Roe vs. Wade* mis-interpretation of the Constitution. The doctrine of the separation of church and state must be addressed by Catholic scholars and the Catholic school community. This is a watershed maxim because public law and human rights issues then translate into discussions of an ethical economic distribution of wealth. Along the ideological spectrum, the very presence of Catholic education itself enhances the diversity of the American people. Arguments are advanced that, in the name of promoting diversity, one must appeal to pluralism, but when it comes to mentioning the Catholic Church or her schools in public, they who normally advance this line of reasoning in favor of pluralism suddenly do not appeal to pluralism, but rather to the separation of church and state doctrine.[35] We need to demonstrate to the American public that the Catholic Church or Catholic education need not be feared.

The Congregation for Catholic Education has stated that the correct relationship between state and school – and not only a Catholic school – was based not so much on institutional relations as on the right of each person to receive a suitable education of his own free choice; and that this right should be acknowledged according to the principle of subsidiarity. The principle of subsidiarity constitutes a basis where one can ground theological and philosophical foundations for constructive dialogue with the state.[36] There must be a change in how the church-state separation theory is applied in American society. We need to continue to articulate clearly those educational areas that properly belong to the state and those that properly belong to the Church. When and where does the state intervene? When and where does it not?

Given these scenarios, one strength of Catholic education is its institutional insistence on the promotion of economic justice for all, Catholics and non-Catholics alike. The very presence of Catholic schools in a pluralistic culture and a constitutional republic requires discussions on equal justice in taxation. Justice warrants keeping the public debate open. At the outset of Catholic education in the United States, Catholic families have been burdened with excessive taxation. Nineteenth century Bishop John Hughes of New York, a staunch advocate of Catholic schools, argued that lack of public money to care for Catholic schools subjected parents who sent their children to a Catholic school to a second tax. I think one can almost look at this as a type of punishment for whatever reason: being Catholic, having kids, not supporting public education with the rest of the country, et cetera. Fathers Virgil Blum, John Courtney Murray, and Peter M. J. Stravinskas – contemporary U.S. Catholic school supporters – have argued that direct federal money for Catholic schools was constitutionally justifiable and a matter of justice.[37] However, the human rights and economic issues have been recently addressed in our own time, though primarily at the state level. For example, states such as New York, Ohio, and Florida have made recent headlines over the voucher issue. In my own State of California, from where I hail, Proposition 38, a measure that would have provided vouchers to Catholic schools, was recently defeated by the electorate. Regardless of the circumstances, the issue must be defined primarily as a matter of justice, treated as a measure to assist the poor, and resolved as a non-partisan issue at both the federal and state levels.[38]

E) The Witnesses of the Messenger & the Witnesses' Message

Tuition will continue to increase, given the market and given the fact that lay teachers need to be provided with just family wages. This means that economic resources are needed more than in the past. And barring any major increases in the number of teaching religious, Catholic laity will continue to staff our Catholic schools. With this decline in teaching religious sisters and clergy, the increased presence of the laity itself is a gift to Catholic education.[39] Typically, however, Catholic school teachers earn less than public school teacher colleagues. Perhaps it cannot be measured in empirical figures, but many Catholic school teachers are unsung evangelists in their day-to-day contact with the students. Sometimes, they can be exposed to their students more than their students' parents. Even with less economic resources, studies show that Catholic schools educate students up to half the cost of public institutions.[40] Reflecting on the life of Socrates, one learns that in order to be a teacher at any time period of history, one seems inevitably to suffer. I am not advocating the perpetuation of injustices or the human suffering incurred by teachers, but it seems that in order for us to advance the Kingdom and the civilization of love and life, Catholic education as well as those involved in this apostolate will undergo suffering, specifically on behalf of the family. Catholic education's strength, understood correctly, lies in its institutional martyrdom.

A fortiori, Dr. William E. May has written that Catholic school teachers have a special vocation to holiness.[41] Thus, teachers must themselves be saints in order to produce numerous saints and future teachers/doctors of the Church. What is therefore incumbent on Catholic schools is the proper spiritual formation of teachers. The unsung sacrifices of so many Catholic school teachers, administrators, and staff contribute to both individual sanctity and institutional progress in advancing the Kingdom.

The strategic recipe, therefore, for utilizing Catholic schools for family renewal is the living out of the universal call to holiness among Catholic school personnel, combined with their human suffering, and just the right flavor of replacing the unjust social sins of the culture of death. Social policy, such as school choice reform policy, must be based on a sound family policy.[42] And unless school choice is implemented in public policy, the economic strain will continue to haunt Catholic education in the foreseeable future. The holiness of the teacher will mysteriously entail a form of personal economic martyrdom.

Finally, this brief reflection on the person of the messenger in Catholic education prompts a reflection on the message itself. One of the greatest contributions Catholic education has given to both Church and American culture is the actualization of the view that every human person has worth, irrespective of background. By contrast, the lingo in *Goals 2000*, which could be perceived as a fruit of American pragmatism, is the production of students so that they eventually enter the workforce and contribute to a healthy American economy. It is vocational education-à-la-*Brave-New-World* as opposed to the Catholic education philosophy based on human dignity. As such, liberal education becomes merely utilitarian. Education is undertaken to build a democratic society.[43] But its methodology stops short of addressing the spiritual nature of the person.[xliv] Morality becomes mere positivistic and relativistic. Catholic education engages American culture by focusing on man and his dignity; in this case, on the human child's dignity. If indeed man is the way of the Church, as affirmed in *Redemptor Hominis*,[45] then the child-centered emphasis in U.S. education is not altogether evil. There is room for dialogue with American culture, but with a proper caveat, of course. In other words, secular humanism can be met with Christian humanism in educating our youth.[46]

Moreover, our message includes the moral formation of our young in virtue. In the almost four decades that have elapsed since the close of the Second Vatican Council, a gradual moral decline brought the United States to a state of a moral crisis.[47] In the realm of education, we are also in a state of crisis in education.[48] Consequently, the engagement of Catholic education with American culture brings the teaching of moral virtue to the public forum. Even American statesman and common school proponent Horace Mann advocated the need to teach morality and virtue in the classroom, although he frowned on parochial education.[49] In pluralistic America, there is still hope to revive the teaching of virtue in all our schools. The root of the message of the messenger then is that of the dignity of all human persons through one's moral choices. While it is true that we are experiencing moral decay and a crisis of faith, hope remains. We are at the same time seeing the seeds of moral renewal blossom among our youth.

Perhaps we could recover moral instruction in our schools by telling stories, as Alasdair MacIntyre advocated in *After Virtue*.[50] After all, Our Lord Himself told stories and parables. That, in fact, leads us to the final appraisal of Catholic education in this paper. It is this: Catholic schools institutionally proclaim that Christ reveals the dignity of man to himself.[51] Let us tell Christ's story, then, for all children love to hear stories. In the end, the greatest strength of Catholic education is that, day to day, it continues the kerygmatic proclamation of the person of Jesus the

Teacher in fulfillment of the Great Commission to teach and make disciples of all nations.

Conclusion

To summarize, we have examined the contributions of K-12 Catholic education in the revival of the Catholic family in American culture (a) through its teaching of faith and morals; (b) through its emphasis on the parental education role; (c) through a reflection on quality education and the right to education; (d) by briefly looking at the constitutional issues and their corresponding economic implications; and finally (e) through the witness of Catholic education itself and its message, which in the end is the very person of Christ. The current culture wars have impacted elementary and secondary Catholic education. It is thus necessary for Catholic educational leaders and scholars to identify these new, sensitive, and sometimes difficult areas in order adequately to respond to pastoral needs, promote the civilization of love, and help revive the family.

One key general approach to be emphasized in all this is reflected in the motto of the new University of Sacramento, founded by the fast-growing Legionaries of Christ.[52] The motto of the University of Sacramento is *Vince in Bono Malum* – Conquer Evil with Good. Once one has called an evil an evil and a good a good, and once one has removed the evil harmful to the human person, then one must replace the evil taken away with something good. And not only must we replace the evil with a good for the moment, but it is replaced with a perpetual good that endures and lasts. Any good that temporarily replaces the evil (whether educational or otherwise) and merely alleviates a problem only to later return is like building the foundations of a house on sand. Finally, persons who seek the demise of evil and exaltation of the good must seek this goal with a strong, passionate, and deliberate intent to win against the apparently prevailing evil. It is done with a conquering attitude. In a sense, this reechoes John Paul II's prayer about the culture of life being *triumphant* over the culture of death that I cited at the beginning of this paper. Thus, *Vince in Bono Malum* is the general recommended approach to develop concrete strategies to build a civilization of love and justice.

In closing, if one were to capture in a flashy media sound bite the final exhortation of this paper, it would be this: In spite of the confusion that followed Vatican II, *Don't Scuttle Catholic Education! Catholic Schools Work!* In spite of the declines in the Church in the United States over the past four decades, let not the evil that has emerged eclipse the good that has been done. May Our Lady guide our Catholic schools so that, in John Paul the Great's words, the civilization of love, which has its source in the love of God, will be triumphant.

Dennis Purificacion coordinates the M.A. in Education Program at the new University of Sacramento and manages student enrollment there. He has been involved in the youth apostolate for two decades; this included several years as a Catholic high school theology teacher; he was also a regular contributor to *YOU!* magazine. A one-time pro-life candidate for the California state legislature. who ran on a platform of moral renewal, he has also taught philosophy at California State University at Sacramento and was a student member of the Fellowship of Catholic Scholars from 1993 through 2003. However, he recently earned a doctorate in education from the University of San Francisco (where he completed research on educational reform in the USCCB *vis-à-vis* U.S. national educational reform efforts). Dr. Purificacion has studied at the Catholic University of America and at the former St. Ignatius Institute, as well as for a brief time at the John Paul II Institute. He is newly married to Tove Ann, after having proposed to her at World Youth Day 2002, while Pope John Paul II was in Toronto, Canada.

Dedication: This paper is dedicated to the memory of Father Francis E. King, S.J., the writer's former theology professor who inspired him to join the Fellowship. Rest in peace, priest of God!

Notes

1. See Pope John Paul II, "Letter to Families" (Boston: St. Paul Books & Media, 1994), p. 60.
2. See, for example, the official statement of the Fellowship of Catholic Scholars, *Vatican II: Promise and Reality – The Catholic Church in the United States Twenty-five Years After Vatican II*, September 20, 1990. For in-depth critiques specifically on the status of Catholic religious education since Vatican II, see Eamonn Keane, *A Generation Betrayed: Deconstructing Catholic Education in the English-Speaking World* (New York: Hatherleigh Press, 2002) and Michael J. Wrenn, *Catechisms and Controversies: Religious Education in the Postconciliar Years* (San Francisco: Ignatius Press, 1991).
3. "That school is considered to be Catholic which ecclesiastical authority or a public ecclesiastical juridic person supervises or which ecclesiastical authority recognizes as such by means of a written document" (*Code of Canon Law,* 1983, 803.1). Strictly speaking, in this paper, Catholic education consists of those educational institutions under the auspices of the Catholic Church that, at minimum, bear the name "Catholic." The same *Code of Canon Law* also placed a pre-eminent role on the rights of parents

in providing a suitable Catholic education for their children (cf. Can. 793, 797–798). As such, Catholic education in this paper, when broadly considered, consists of all those educational endeavors of Catholics under ecclesial leadership to provide an education suited to Catholic parental needs and values (e.g., home schooling, independent Catholic schools, non-sectarian private schools, and even recourse of Catholic parents to local Protestant schools, etc.). Thus, given the wide scope of educational initiatives that constitute or what one may construe to constitute Catholic education, and given these two norms from the *Code of Canon Law* as cited above, this paper simply denotes Catholic education in its broadest sense and meaning. However, given the scope of this paper limited to K-12 Catholic schools, and given that the author had access to data primarily for K-12 Catholic schools recognized by the National Catholic Educational Association, the educational population of this paper was delimited to K-12 Catholic schools as recognized by competent ecclesial authority.

4. See U.S. Catholic Bishops, Department of Education, "In Support of Catechetical Ministry: A Statement of the U.S. Catholic Bishops," in which the then-NCCB/USCC wrote that in their roles as chief catechists, the U.S bishops wanted to affirm all that was good in catechetical ministry, they committed themselves to strengthening that which was weak, and they looked forward to developing effective ways to reach all those in need of God's saving Word (Washington, D.C.: United States Catholic Conference, June 16, 2000). The text was approved for publication by the full body of bishops at their June 2000 General Meeting and authorized for publication by the General Secretary Msgr. Dennis M. Schnurr.

5. One need only review a history of Catholic education in the United States in building the Catholic Church to find a rich history of Catholic school graduates significantly influencing American culture. Catholic school graduates became societal entrepreneurs, assumed sensitive leadership positions, raised healthy families, and produced many bishops and saints. Now, at this turning point in history, as the Church calls all her institutions to bring to bear the full weight of their service to the world, K-12 Catholic education finds itself in the midst of the culture wars in Western civilization. See also George A. Kelly, *Catholics and the Practice of the Faith* (Washington, D.C.: Catholic University of America Press, 1946) and Andrew M. Greeley and Peter H. Rossi, *The Education of Catholic Americans* (New York: Doubleday, 1968).

6. Cf. Congregation for Catholic Education, *The Catholic School on the Threshold of the Third Millennium* (Boston: Pauline Books & Media, 1997).

7. In *The Catholic School on the Threshold of the Third Millennium*, the human development aspect of Catholic education was identified by the Congregation for Catholic Education (1997) as "genuine human and communitarian progress" (no. 5). A brief word then should be mentioned with respect to Catholic school contribution to the secular culture. I would sug-

gest that herein lay the respectability and credibility of Catholic schools as an institutional force to be reckoned with. One of the chief lessons from history for Catholic school leaders today is that Catholic education helped Catholic immigrants (a) preserve the faith in the new American republic under the then-leadership of our separated Protestant brethren; and (b) ascend the American social ladder by assimilating immigrants into the American mainstream of politics, economics, and business. Education was – and remains – the great means for the upward mobility for all of our Catholic school graduates, Catholic and non-Catholic, immigrant and non-immigrant. In California from where I hail, Catholic schools continue the service to immigrant communities from all over the world. As a self-described son of working immigrant parents from the Philippines, I credit many, if not all, of my social mobility to the Catholic Church and her educational institutions and I personally can testify to Catholic education's benefit for the social advancement of the poor in my own life.

8. One may call the non-Catholic presence in K-12 Catholic schools the "no-brainer" approach to re-evangelization or the New Evangelization. But this simplicity in approaching the non-Catholic population in Catholic schools should not be taken lightly considering that, in the United States, the non-Catholic student body is a new phenomenon in K-12 Catholic education. The phenomenon of the non-Catholic presence in our schools is about four decades in existence. Catholics were the primary beneficiaries of these schools. Instead of the Catholic Church approaching non-Catholics, non-Catholics, for whatever motives, literally come to our Catholic institutions and in doing so are exposed to the Church's evangelical message, even if only in its nascent stages.

9. The U.S. Catholic Conference (1972), in its document "To Teach as Jesus Did," likewise listed greater accessibility to student participation in liturgy and sacraments as a value.

10. See the USCCB Secretariat for Vocations and Priestly Formation, "Interview with Bishop Paul S. Loverde," at http://www.usccb.org/vocations/ordination/loverde.htm.

11. See USCCB Ad Hoc Committee to Oversee the Use of the Catechism, "Developments in Regard to High School Materials," *Catechism Update*, Summer 2004 at www.usccb.org/catechism/update/spring2004.htm.

12. For evidence of a revived Christian orthodoxy among young adults born between 1965 and 1983, see Colleen Carroll, *The New Faithful: Why Young Adults Are Embracing Christian Orthodoxy* (Chicago: Loyola Press, 2002).

13. Natural Family Planning (NFP) education at the secondary level is understood here as (a) proximate preparation for marriage that is age-appropriate and (b) as the great alternative to artificial contraception *in marriage* with which Catholic school teenagers can (and should) avail themselves when they later enter immediate preparation for marriage and eventually receive the Sacrament of Holy Matrimony. They need to know the good options that exist as alternatives to the evil of the contraceptive mentality. It is no secret

that NFP is not taught at a majority of Catholic universities. Absent the small minority of Catholics who practice NFP, and absent diocesan marriage preparation programs, there are no existing structures to prepare Catholic school students for NFP education. Consequently, this author premised that NFP education is necessary at the secondary level.

14. See John Paul II, "Letter to Families" (Boston: St. Paul Books & Media, 1994), n. 16.

15. Alfonso Cardinal Lopez Trujillo, *Commentary on the Truth and Meaning of Human Sexuality: Guidelines for Education within the Family* (The Wanderer Press & Human Life International, 1996), p. 26.

16. Dr. David Schindler (1996) lectured in a class at the John Paul II Institute that the spiritual battle now taking place in Western civilization is over a little child. This battle over the child is reflected in Herod's seeking to destroy the Child Jesus, in our contemporary debates over abortion and the moral status of the fetus, and in Revelation 12. I am taking his insights here and observing a similar symptom in the school classroom.

17. In practice, the ordinary generally demurs and/or delegates hiring religion teachers to the school principal.

18. See Timothy Walch, *Parish School: American Catholic Parochial Education from Colonial Times to the Present* (New York: The Crossroad Publishing Company, 1996). See also Andrew M. Greeley, William C. McCready, and Kathleen McCourt, *Catholic Schools in a Declining* Church (Kansas City: Sheed & Ward, Inc., 1976), pp. 302–312. Greeley *et al.* (1976) attributed the decline of the Catholic Church in the United States to Pope Paul VI's *Humanae Vitae* (1968), and noted the impact of demographic changes on the Catholic school population.

19. The issue of the non-Catholic student body in U.S. Catholic schools has raised questions outside the scope of this paper: To what extent should Catholic schools only serve the needs of Catholic youth? In other words, should we not take care of our own Catholic families first before taking care of non-Catholic students and their families? The general trend in NCEA is that Catholic schools serve all students, regardless of religion. See Administrative Committee, "Principles for Educational Reform in the United States" (Washington, D.C.: United States Catholic Conference, 1995).

20. See Mark 10:15. For the sense and meaning of "childhood" in this paper, see Hans Urs von Balthasar, *Unless You Become Like This Child*, trans. Erasmo Leiva-Merikakis (San Francisco: Ignatius Press, 1991).

21. See, for example, data provided by Dr. W. Bradford Wilcox, "Social Scinece and the Vindication of Catholic Moral Teaching," address to the 27th Anniversary Convention of the Fellowship of Catholic Scholars, 2004.

22. Somewhat similar to law school professors who use legal cases to illustrate the law, let us take the anecdotal case of children bringing their parents to Mass and identify one approach that has been made to re-evangelize parents (Figure 1). While it is well-intended and noble that children should

bring their parents to Sunday Mass, the risk in this approach is that it may
not respect the magisterium's insistence that parents are the first educators
of their children.

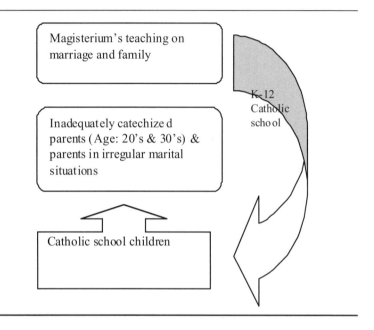

Figure 1.   Diagram Illustrating Approach #1 to Re-Evangelize Inadequately-
Catechized Parents.

23. Luke 5:4.
24. See John Paul II, Apostolic Letter at the Close of the Great Jubilee of the
     Year 2000 *Novo Millennio Ineunte*, in which he concluded, "*Duc in Altum!*"
     (nos. 58–59).
25. Pontifical Council for the Family, *Family, Marriage, and "De Facto"
     Unions* (Boston: Pauline Books & Media, 2000); Pontifical Council for the
     Family, "The Truth and Meaning of Human Sexuality" (The Wanderer
     Press & Human Life International, 1996).
25. See Holy See, *Charter of the Rights of the Family*, October 22, 1983,
     Article 5.
26. Perhaps the question can be best addressed by distinguishing between gen-
     erations of parents. Excluding present company, we may be looking at a
     new generation or two of parents who do not have the wherewithal to trans-
     mit the deposit of faith to their children (and I am thinking primarily of the
     younger 20-something, 30-something year-old parents). At the same time,
     we must adhere to the Church's teaching that parents remain the first edu-

cators of their children. (Grandma can only go so far to hand on the faith to her grandchildren.). We must continue stronger catechetical and reconciliatory efforts in our schools to parents themselves.

27. Figure 2 depicts parents as primary educators and K-12 Catholic schools as secondary educators. This model respects the primordial parental education role as the "domestic church" which receives the teachings of the ordinary and universal magisterium, which are then transmitted to children. Moreover, and perhaps more importantly, the K-12 Catholic school is thus viewed as only a vessel with the role to faithfully transmit the teachings of the magisterium. (Figure 2 does not seek to provide a collaborative system

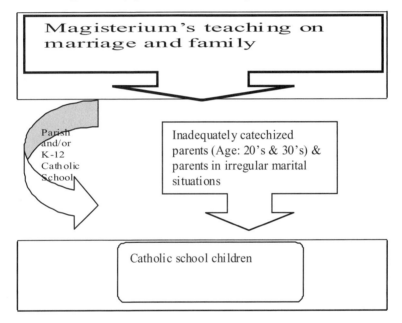

for parents to keep the Catholic school in check.)

Figure 2. Diagram Illustrating Approach #2 to Re-Evangelize Inadequately-Catechized Parents.

28. The Congregation for Catholic Education would call these students the "new poor" (no. 15). In this paper, the "new poor" in Catholic schools are denoted as the 20-something and 30-something year-old parents who were themselves products of broken homes and watered-down catechesis.

29. These are strong facets of K-12 Catholic education to be harnessed in the service of the culture of life. With the respect of individual Catholics (and Catholic schools) comes respect for the Catholic Church. Catholics schools are also appreciated and respected for the non-religious, secular education

they impart.
30. Catholic educational leaders and teachers have, in the interest of professionalizing their teaching force, maintained their own commitment to quality education (CCE, 1977; NCCB, 1972). Public education leaders like Diane Ravitch (1995) even acknowledged that Catholic schools provided models of academic excellence to the rest of the nation. Thus, Catholic schools share some similar academic goals with the rest of the nation. Compare http://www.ed.gov/legislation/GOALS2000/ for the national goals of *Goals 2000: Educate America Act* with Administrative Committee, *Principles for Educational Reform in the United States* (Washington, D.C.: United States Catholic Conference, 1995).
31. Second Vatican Council, Declaration on Religious Liberty *Dignitatis Humanae* (1965), no. 5; see also Declaration on Christian Education, *Gravissimum Educationis* (1965).
32. As cited in *The Catholic Herald*, "Association Sees Tuition, Reform as Major Issues" (January 25, 2003), p. 11; see also Michael J. Guerra, "Catholic schools and the national education goals," *Momentum* 26 (1995), pp. 8–9.
33. See http://www.ed.gov/legislation/GOALS2000/ for the national goals of *Goals 2000: Educate America Act*.
34. See the Second Continental Congress, *Bill of Rights*, 1791, ¶1.
35. See, for example, Joseph A. Varacalli, "Multiculturalism, Catholicism, and American Civilization" from http://www.catholilceducation.org/articles/multiculturalism/mu0001.html.
36. See also Jacques Maritain, *Man and the State* (Washington, D.C.: The Catholic University of America Press, 1951), and Jacques Maritain, *Integral Humanism: Temporal and Spiritual Problems of a New Christendom*.
37. Virgil C. Blum, *Freedom in Education: Federal Aid for All Children* (Garden City, NY: Doubleday & Company, Inc., 1965); Virgil C. Blum, *Freedom of Choice in Education* (New York: The Macmillan Company, 1958); John Courtney Murray, *We Hold These Truths: Catholic Reflections on the American Proposition* (New York: Sheed & Ward, 1960); Peter M. J. Stravinskas, *Constitutional Rights and Religious Prejudice: Catholic Education as the Battleground* (New York: Bookmasters Publishing Company, 1982).
38. This is how the voucher system works: Currently, local public schools (or government schools, if you like) are funded primarily by local tax money of homeowners. As such, tax paying residents and parents send their money to their local public school that, in theory, pays for a public school student's education. Now when the same parents send their children to their local Catholic school, they pay tuition to the Catholic school in addition to local taxes. In effect, said parents end up paying for their own kid's tuition as well as the per pupil expenditure of someone else's kid. I submit that the economic justice statement is the strongest argument because it is an ethical

argument, followed by constitutional arguments unless the doctrine of the separation of church and state is adequately addressed. One can almost call this an appraisal of Catholic schools vis-à-vis the state and culture. Another way of looking at this is that it is the economics of funding a culture of charity and justice. Again, the main consideration here is the appeal to justice. Granted, money can only go so far to address social ills and educational ailments, but as the circumstances in American culture stand, the double taxation of parents who choose to send their children to an alternative school needs to be alleviated. Interestingly, Dr. Bruno Manno of the Annie E. Casey Foundation refers to vouchers as public scholarships. For him, the word 'vouchers' connotes highly emotional images of taking money away from scarce public resources and reallocating them to religious schools. Thus, the public can perceive this as a violation of the U.S. Constitution. Then, at this point, anti-school-choice proponents would build up their straw man case and appeal to the red herring doctrine of the separation of church and state. Perhaps our choice of words should be language of school choice and public scholarships. For the USCCB, one public policy approach to Congress focuses on parental rights to choose the school for their children (see http://www.usccb.com). Finally, at the risk of addressing an issue outside the scope of this essay, I briefly mention the role of charter school education in the renewal of public education, advocated in Finn, Manno & Vanourek, *Charter Schools in Action: Renewing Public Education* (Princeton: Princeton University Press, 2000). Much like its Catholic school counterpart, charter schools in theory and practice promote greater self-government of each respective school as well as public accountability. But unlike Catholic schools, charter schools fall directly within the economic auspices of the public. Either way, an alternative system is provided to the existing education infrastructure. Like the right to life, the right to education is not just a "Catholic issue."

39. See also Congregation for Catholic Education, *Lay Witnesses in Schools; Witnesses to Faith* (*Les laïcs Catholiques*), 1982, in *Vatican Council II: More Postconciliar Documents* (Boston: St. Paul Editions, 1982).

40. As cited in *The Catholic Herald*, "Study Cites Benefits for Voucher Students" (June 15, 2002), p. 11.

41. See William E. May, "The Vocation of a Catholic Teacher/Scholar," *Fellowship of Catholic Scholars Quarterly* (Spring 2001), vol. 24, no. 2, pp. 8–16.

42. See Carl A. Anderson, "Criteria for Policies on Marriage, Family, and Life," in *Marriage and the Common Good: Proceedings from the Twenty-Second Annual Convention of the Fellowship of Catholic* Scholars, Kenneth D. Whitehead, ed. (South Bend, IN: St. Augustine's Press, 2001); see also John Paul II, Encyclical Letter on the Inviolability of Human Life *Evangelium Vitae* (Boston: Pauline Books & Media, 1995).

43. Cf. John Dewey, *Democracy and Education: An Introduction to the Philosophy of Education* (New York: The Free Press, 1944).

44. See Harold A. Buetow, *The Catholic School: Its Roots, Identity, and* Future (New York: Crossroads, 1988); and Harold A. Buetow, *A History of United States Catholic Schooling* (Washington, D.C.: National Catholic Education Association, 1985).

45. John Paul II, Encyclical Letter on the Redeemer of Man *Redemptor Hominis*, 1979.

46. For a philosophy of Integral Formation, see Marcial Maciel, *Educating Our Youth* (Hamden, CT: Center for Integral Formation, 1996). See also Jacques Maritain, *Man and the State* (Washington, D.C.: The Catholic University of America Press, 1951), and Jacques Maritain, *Integral Humanism: Temporal and Spiritual Problems of a New Christendom.*

47. Some leading indicators to measure this claim involve increased rates of crime, out-of-wedlock births, and decreased academic performance, as cited in William J. Bennett, *The Index of Leading Cultural Indicators: American Society at the End of the Twentieth* Century (New York: Broadway Books, 1999). Also, the greatest American statesman and Catholic politician of our time, Dr. Alan Keyes claimed that abortion is the ultimate expression of the moral crisis in America. For him, an abortion-saturated civilization cannot truly value children; see Alan Keyes, *Our Character, Our Future: Reclaiming America's Moral Destiny*, Geroge Grant, ed. (Grand Rapids: Zondervan Publishing House, 1996).

48. Daniel McInerny, ed. *The Common Things: Essays on Thomism and Education* (Washington, D.C.: The Catholic University of America Press, 1999). Also, John A. Haas has affirmed that our schools have failed us, particularly in the teaching of virtue. See "Building the Culture of Life Through the Family" in *Is a Culture of Life Still Possible in the United States?: Proceedings from the Twentieth Convention of the Fellowship of Catholic Scholars,* Anthony J. Mastroeni, ed. (South Bend, IN: St. Augustine's Press, 1997).

49. Horace Mann, "Twelfth Annual Report," (1848) in L.A. Cremin (ed.), *The Republic and the School:Horace Mann on the Education of Free Men* (New York: Columbia University, 1957), pp. 79–112.

50. Alasdair MacIntyre, *After Virtue: A Study in Moral Theory, Second Edition* (Notre Dame: University of Notre Dame Press, 1984). The American Founders told stories to instill virtue in their young; see, for example, William J. Bennett, ed., *The Book of Virtues: A Treasury of Great Moral Stories* (New York: Simon & Schuster, 1993).

51. As the Congregation for the Clergy (1997) stated in the *General Directory for Catechesis*, the center of all Catholic education and catechesis is Christ. See also Carlo Caffara *Living in Christ: Fundamental Principles of Catholic Moral Teaching*, Christopher Ruff, trans. (San Francisco: Ignatius Press, 1987); and John Paul II, Apostolic Exhortation *CatechesiTradendae*, 1979.

52. For more information on the Legionaries of Christ, visit www.legionariesofchrist.org. See also Jesus Colina, *Christ is My Life: Jesus Colina*

Interviews Marcial Maciel (Manchester, NH: Sophia Institute Press, 2003); and see also Angeles Conde and David J.P. Murray, *The Legion of Christ: A History* (Camden, CT: Center for Integral Formation, 2004). For more information on the spirituality of the lay movement known as *Regnum Christi,* visit www.regnumchristi.org. For more information on the University of Sacramento or the Legionary charism in higher education, visit www.universityofsacramento.org.

Chapter 12: Raising Catholic Children in a Secular Culture
The Importance of a Sound Vision of the Person in a Sexually Permissive Culture

THERESA H. FARNAN, PH.D.,
AND WILLIAM THIERFELDER, PH.D.

Introduction

One of the most difficult challenges Catholic parents face is raising children with the proper understanding of the gift of love. We live in a culture with a shallow understanding of love, in which love is defined by the physical, material, and emotional gratification two persons gain from a relationship. Many children who grow up in broken and/or blended homes never get to see their mother and father living in a relationship of sacrificial, generous love. Consequently, they have no role models who could offer an alternative to our culture's celebration of materialism and individualism in relationships.

In this paper, we will discuss the effect of philosophy on culture, specifically as it impacts the family. We will begin by describing some of the problematic cultural trends today and analyzing how they spring from the influence of modern philosophy on our culture. We will argue that an effective way to counter these trends is through personal formation grounded in an authentic philosophy of the person that includes an account of how virtues shape and guide the person. We will describe how a sound vision of the person enables us to form our children to be chaste and generous.

Finally, we will analyze the means we use to counter the prevailing cultural trends. Currently the favored method of teaching chastity is through classroom based human sexuality curricula and abstinence education curricula. We will argue that this approach is inherently flawed because it does not provide the kind of personal formation that is needed for the virtue of chastity. We will then offer suggestions for formation in chastity and other virtues that respect the dignity of the children involved and the relationship between parents and child.

The Effect of Philosophy on Culture

As we identify certain trends in Western society today, we can see several philosophical beliefs shaping how our culture reacts to sexuality. First is the belief in yourself as an autonomous individual, answerable to no one else for your actions. This manifests itself in certain attitudes – a resentment of criticism, a lack of commitment and will-power, aversion to sacrifice for the sake of others, and the single-minded pursuit of personal, self-centered goals and ambitions. We see this individualism exhibited concretely in diverse ways, but most especially in the breakdown of the family and the embrace of the culture of death.

Other beliefs pervading our cultural view of sexuality also come from philosophy as seen through the lens of popular culture. A materialist philosophy causes men and women to seek only self-gratification and physical pleasures from relationships. Relativism and pragmatism reflect not so much what we think of sexuality, but rather what we think about the truth of sexuality. A relativist denies that it is possible to know and assert the truth about human sexuality, especially regarding the actions of others. A pragmatist, on the other hand, does not worry about the truth of sexuality, especially regarding his own actions.

Finally, we would like to discuss two more ideas that are powerfully shaping how we and our children think of sexuality. The first is the denial of any real and meaningful differences between men and women. According to this perspective, the traditional roles of men and women – with women being the nurturing heart of the family, concerned primarily with caring for the immediate needs of children, and men being the provider and protector of the family – originate from cultures that repressed and oppressed women. According to this view, gender is a social construct, and men use the biological fact that women can bear children to prevent them from realizing themselves in any meaningful way.[1]

Originally the argument of radical feminists, this argument was quickly adopted by others who sought to change how we view sexuality as a whole. For if biology has nothing to do with how we express our relationships to others, then homosexuality and bisexuality, indeed anything imaginable, are all equally valid ways of acting and relating to others.[2]

The second idea shaping our culture's response to human sexuality is the rejection of Judeo-Christian morality and the natural law as the source of truth about sexual morality. This is not merely a form of relativism, for those who reject the truth of Judeo-Christian morality present their own claims as the truth. Their first claim is that morality is essentially a matter of ensuring freedom of choice. Secondly, they claim that morality based on the truth of Judeo-Christian morality is essentially irrational. Finally, Judeo-Christian morality is not only irrational but is also immoral because it excludes certain choices as wrong. As advocates of radical feminism and homosexuality have identified traditional Judeo-Christian morality as an obstacle to the goal of legitimizing alternative lifestyles in Western Europe and the United States, they have launched an attack on traditional Judeo-Christian morality, using a variety of media to marginalize Christian beliefs and end any discussion of sexual morality.

Of course, few people would characterize themselves as holding rigidly to any of these ideologies. In our culture today, people often adopt bits and pieces of various philosophies to create their own particular ideology. This can make it very difficult to offer philosophical arguments against these ideologies, for you cannot argue systematically against something that has not been adopted as a system. Moreover, it is difficult to offer philosophical arguments to people who do not realize that they have adopted an eclectic philosophical approach that justifies the cult of the self.

In the attempt to prevent sexual activity in young people, many educators have attempted to argue against these flawed beliefs one at a time. Educators also have been in a defensive posture, reacting to the influences of this permissive culture, trying to anticipate which attitudes and behaviors their students will be exposed to through television, music, print media, and the internet. Although this may be helpful in addressing a particular problem, ultimately it is a losing strategy. Focusing on one error often leads to neglecting the other erroneous attitudes and beliefs the student holds to be true. In addition, the Church's teachings are not presented coherently and positively. If Catholics remain in a defensive posture, the Church will lose a tremendous opportunity for active evangelization, based on our firm conviction that we have the truth, a truth so powerful and beautiful that it will change your life both here and hereafter.

We are at a crucial point in addressing this problem. Today, children in Catholic schools and religious education programs are the second generation of children in crisis. In many cases, their parents don't understand fully what the Church teaches about human sexuality, due to years of classroom-based sex education and neglected catechesis. In the light of this crisis, we must reconsider the content and methodology used to convey the truth and meaning of human sexuality to children and their families.

An Authentic Philosophy of the Person

Let us first consider the content of any instruction on human sexuality. In *Love and Responsibility,* Karol Wojtyla makes the point that there is a real difference between the sexual activity of animals and the sexual activity of human beings. Human beings choose to engage or not engage in sexual intercourse. The physical act is the result of a spiritual decision, a decision involving the intellect and the will. In this act we see the unity of the person, body and soul cooperating in the free action. Because sexual activity is the free action of a person, we can and must consider sexual morality, just as we would consider the morality of any freely chosen action. This means that we should evaluate each act as an expression of life-giving love and challenge the morality of sexual activity that is separated from life and love.[3]

Indeed the expression of love in any way is an act of the whole person, body and soul, as we demonstrate our love for others through the actions we perform.[4] In its fullest sense, love requires and completes the integration of the person. We as human beings in the unity of body and soul are able to utilize, direct and enjoy our bodies. The actions we perform with our bodies express the truth about ourselves and others. Moreover, the actions we perform with our bodies affect us spiritually, as through repeated action we become more virtuous or more vicious. This indicates to us the extremes which must be avoided in any kind of discussion of human love, namely a materialist approach or a purely spiritual approach. Either of these extremes misses some of the most important points about love and human sexuality as an expression of that love.

In addition, we must be aware of the implications of sexual activity that occurs before the person has reached a certain level of integration. Children who are sexually abused or become sexually active suffer spiritually, emotionally and physically. Imposing premature sexual information on children "tends to shatter their emotional and educational development and to disturb the natural serenity of this period of life."[5] Prior to puberty, children are unable to integrate the biological, affective and moral dimensions of sexuality.[6] Information about human sexuality must be imparted in a way that is sensitive to the unique development of each individual child. Education about human love must be carried out in a *personalist* way, that is, it must respect the individuality of each child, taking care not to disturb the tranquility and serenity of the years of innocence.[7]

In order to convey the full dimensions of the marital act as a life-giving expression of love, it is necessary to use a philosophy of the person that emphasizes the integration of the person as a unity of body and soul, a process that begins with the child's relationship with his parents and others and is facilitated by the moral and theological virtues. Instilling habits of virtue enables the child to master his emotions and direct his actions toward the good. In particular, the virtue of chastity is vital for the self-mastery that enables one to express love in a generous and responsible way.

Authentic Formation in Chastity

For children, formation in Christian chastity should include two elements, a philosophy of the person compatible with Christian anthropology and training in virtue. The philosophy of the person can be organized around four simple themes: person as image of God, the dignity of the person, person as relation, and person as gift. Using concrete examples helps children to internalize and apply these somewhat abstract ideas. While a child may not understand the phrase "person as gift," he can certainly appreciate the importance of giving, especially to those in need. Again, a child may not understand the phrase "person as relation," but even an infant can identify mother and father, sister and brother. "Dignity of the person" can be emphasized in a very concrete way by not allowing the child to harm another. As part of teaching children that each person is made in the "image of God", we can convey that God made us to know the truth and seek the good by teaching them to tell the truth and to do what is right. At each stage of formation, the child should learn that virtues make it easier to do what is right, and learn which virtues will help him with different actions.

Methodologies and Programs

In order to form the child in chastity, we need to clarify the methodology we are proposing, as well as our criteria for success. First, however, we would like to consider which methods of instruction are incompatible with a *personalist* approach to chastity formation. Let's briefly consider the goals and methods of three different deficient types of programs – sex education, abstinence education and Catholic family life programs designed for classroom use.

Sex education consists primarily of information about anatomy, its goal is to prevent pregnancies and sexually transmitted diseases, and success is measured by fewer teen pregnancies. It is based on the premise that knowledge ensures that children will avoid "risky behaviors"

Abstinence programs consist primarily of information about the importance of abstinence for one's own physical and emotional wellbeing, as well as reasons why to abstain from premarital sex despite a young person's curiosity and desire for physical pleasure and emotional gratification. The primary goal is to prevent sexual activity at an early age, and success is measured by students refraining from sexual activity.

Since the publication of "The Truth and Meaning of Human Sexuality," several Catholic programs have been published for classroom use that give a positive presentation of the Church's teaching on sexuality. These Catholic programs are designed to lay the foundation for the proper understanding of the theology of the body, including information about the dignity of the person, the importance of respect for life and the virtues, especially chastity and modesty. These programs diverge from the approach stipulated in the "Truth and Meaning of Human Sexuality" by requiring that parents should impart sensitive biological material on *all* aspects of human sexuality to their children by fifth or sixth grade.

Unfortunately, the methodology of any classroom-based program, even the better Catholic programs, has aspects that are incompatible with a personalist approach. Human sexuality is a topic that is so profound and so personal that it requires maturity, sensitivity and reverence for any discussion of sexual morality. Requiring that all children be informed of the biological facts by fifth or sixth grade fails to respect the child who may be immature, or whose period of latency lasts longer than others. Some may object that early education is necessary because of the cultural influences to which these children are subject. However, in these instances, "The Truth and Meaning of Human Sexuality" notes that the "parents will have to begin to give carefully limited sexual information, usually to correct immoral and erroneous information or to control obscene language."[8] Clearly the appropriate response to a child receiving premature sex information is a personal response, involving dialogue between the child and the ones who know and love him best, his parents.

Furthermore, detailed in-class discussions of sexual morality before all students involved have reached a certain level of maturity leads to a breakdown of modesty, a virtue that is crucial for any kind of chastity formation. Finally, because instruction is not personalized, it is not tailored to each child's individual needs. One result may be that the child whose parents do not allow him to watch sexually explicit movies and TV shows is exposed to this information prematurely. On the other hand, a student who has been exposed to sexual materials, including pornography, might not be getting the guidance proportionate to that level of exposure.

These problems reflect the difficulty of classroom instruction in a matter that should be personalized. In addition they indicate a lack of clarity both as to purpose and methodology. We suggest re-examining how we define success and the method for achieving it. This requires a clear understanding and articulation of Catholic education, our roles as educators, and our roles as parents.

"One Soul at a Time"

The Catholic education of our children should build the kingdom of God one soul at a time. That is, a Catholic school should be a place where children are informed about their faith and formed in virtue, so that as adults they may continue to persevere in the life of grace, love God wholeheartedly here on earth and someday be united with Him in heaven. In light of this goal, we should help our children cultivate a personal relationship with God and relationships with others that are founded on our love for God. In addition, we arm our children for the struggle ahead by helping them cultivate virtues, both by repeatedly practicing acts of virtue and by being open to the grace of God through which we are fortified in human virtues and are given the theological virtues. Specifically, the end of any Catholic chastity formation program should be to form our children to live their personal vocation chastely and joyfully, motivated by a generous love of God and others and in conformity with the teachings of Christ. Given the current estimates of the number of Catholics using contraceptives,[9] chastity formation since the publication of *Humanae Vitae*, has been stunningly unsuccessful.

In truth, the transmission of the Church's teaching on human sexuality since the early 1970's has been woefully deficient. Proper education in Catholic schools must go beyond basic transmission of certain information to students. Simply stating moral positions or facts about abstinence, for example, is insufficient. Virtuous living is a matter of the will as well as the intellect, and without grace, we cannot live a truly virtuous life. We see vividly exemplified in the writings of St. Augustine how difficult it is to overcome vices using human effort alone. We also see in the lives of saints like Maria Goretti, Domenic Savio, and Saint Gianna how the conscious cultivation of virtues in one's life can enable one to choose the good, even in the face of evil.

Education in Chastity a Matter of Formation Not Information

In short, education in chastity in the Catholic schools cannot be treated as any other subject, and must not be approached as a matter of information. Rather, education in chastity must be approached as a matter of formation, a process in which the intellect and the will are formed, while spiritually the soul is open to the opportunities to receive grace made available through prayer and frequent reception of the Sacraments. In the past, education in schools was supported by the formation at home by stable families and a culture that was grounded on the Judeo-Christian ethic. Now, however, we need a concerted program of formation for both the parents and children, all of whom are being exposed to a culture that is in many ways, antithetical to Christian virtue. This is vitally important, because without formation in virtue, children will be de-formed into vice.

In some ways, this is nothing new. Anyone who has spent time with children can attest to the importance of formation in the moral life. Children do not spontaneously develop perfect virtue. For all children, the guidance and discipline their parents give them are indispensable for their moral development. Parents should know their children better than any one else, especially in the primary years. The watchful guidance of their mother and father instills in children trust and love, an awareness of their own dignity and the dignity of others, and a sense of responsibility toward others and for their own actions. On a personal level, children learn the qualities of motherhood and fatherhood from their parents. Parents provide for children the first concrete examples of motherhood and fatherhood, without which understanding one's vocation becomes very difficult. As children undergo physical changes associated with sexual maturity, they should be encouraged to see their parents as role models.

Parents the Primary Educators

Accordingly, any chastity formation should be done through and with the parents for two reasons. First, it offers an unparalleled opportunity to form the parents themselves. Giving parents explanations of concepts and providing them with the appropriate language to explain those concepts can shape how the parents too view their gift of sexuality. For example, constantly referring to the gift of life can be a reminder to the parents that each child is precious. In addition, explaining why marital acts must always be open to life and love affirms the church's teaching on contraception. Further, such a program can provide parents with concrete examples of what to say to their children (words to use or not use, how to broach a subject, how to gently probe for misinformation) and how to address specific problems and concerns.

The second reason that chastity formation should be accomplished through the parents is that, on a more profound level, formation in chastity should take place in the context of a relationship of trust and love.[10] Children experience love and learn how to trust others within their families, primarily through their relationship with their parents. Sacrifice and generosity, two key concepts for formation in Christian chastity, take on greater significance for each person in light of his own experience, particularly the example of his parents. On a practical level, it goes against common sense to introduce a third party into this relationship at a time when communication between parents and child is essential for building trust and love.[11] Catholic educators should not see themselves as arming children against their parents or somehow circumventing parents. Instead, we must respect and nurture the relationship between parents and their children, while conveying catechesis on morality at the appropriate age.[12]

Parents are blessed with the unique privilege of being primarily responsible for the example and formation of their children in the virtues, including chastity. They do this from an example of holiness in their marriage where they effectively guide their children in the pursuit of holiness and prepare them to fulfill authentically their future vocation. How then, on a personal level, should parents prepare themselves to do this? The most effective way to teach children to love and live chastity is by loving and living a chaste marriage. This necessarily includes having an authentic understanding of marriage and the gift of sexuality, and cherishing purity.

An Authentic Understanding of Sex in Marriage

A husband and wife who have an authentic understanding of marriage are not focused on "having sex" but "becoming one." Actually, it is impossible in a chaste marriage to "have sex" because they "have each other." In a chaste marriage, the couple has the pleasure of physical intimacy, the happiness of spiritual unity, trust and confidence in each other's inviolable fidelity, the peace of following God's will, and the new life that springs from their union whether or not God grants them their own biological children.

When love and/or life are excluded from marital intimacy, "having sex" limits pleasure to the physical aspect of the person, but precludes the possibility of becoming "two in one flesh" (Mt. 19:6) and the happiness, trust, confidence, peace, and life that comes from Trinitarian unity.

"Having sex" is an appropriate term for any form of sexual activity outside of God's will for sacramental marriage. Married couples are "having sex" when contraceptives are used since the couples' relationship excludes the possibility for new life making the "two in one flesh" reality impossible. Married couples are "having sex" when their relationship lacks faithfulness or love for each other, even when their physical union may be open to new life.

In a chaste marriage, when the couple is joyfully obedient to God's plan for them, accepting crosses and suffering with trust, being open to life, and serving each other with respect, acceptance and loving affection, "becoming one" ensures the greatest possible sanctity, happiness, and pleasure for the whole person: body, mind, heart, and soul.

Although a young child is not normally aware of the parent's intimate relationship, the beauty and security of a chaste marriage is evident to the child in many visible ways. The specific words used and actions performed by the husband to express his love, respect, service, and sacrifice for his wife teaches the child about the love of Christ.[13] Likewise the wife's words and actions in expressing her love, respect, service, and sacrifice for her husband teaches the child about the "yes" and humility of Mary.[14]

As an essential part of living a chaste marriage, the husband and wife must individually and as a couple hate impurity, avoiding it through their words and actions, and taking care to avoid any occasion of sin. In order to be able to judge correctly whether or not a situation presents an occasion of sin, it is essential to cultivate a love of purity. The love of purity comes from and deepens one's relationship with God.[15] At the heart, then, of the love of purity, is love for God himself, for only one who truly loves God will order all of his desires and affections toward what is truly good and pure.[16] St. Francis de Sales insists that the one and only means to regain purity once it is lost is perfect devotion, which consists of perfect love of God.[17]

If love of God is the foundation for living a chaste marriage, which in turn is the foundation of a child's chastity formation, how should parents become open to receiving the grace of perfect charity? Parents must strive to cultivate the virtues of obedience, chastity, and humility in themselves first, then in their children.[18] This requires vigilance, perseverance, and grace.[19]

Prayer and Religious Practice

The most efficacious means of acquiring all the virtues that lead to perfect charity is through prayer.[20] The daily practice of prayer and the frequent reception of the Sacraments are the most efficacious means for forming our children in true devotion to God. Prayers, devotions, and the Sacraments are the means through which we enjoy an affectionate relationship with Jesus Christ. Many families choose devotion to Our Lady by praying the Rosary, which enables the family to "reproduce something of the atmosphere of the household of Nazareth."[21]

The devotion of the parents can often be the means through which children learn profound truths about God. For example, a parent who makes a short visit to the church to adore the Blessed Sacrament impresses upon the child that Christ is truly present in the Eucharist. Children can be taught to love the unique relationship with Christ in the Sacrament of Penance by observing their parents waiting to go before Sunday Mass each week. Parents can teach children to love the Holy Sacrifice of the Mass both by their own attitude of love and reverence and by following Sunday Mass with a celebration, such as a special family breakfast afterwards. Children learn the importance of intellectually seeking the truth about God when their parents read and discuss spiritual readings with them.

Prayer, while the most efficacious weapon, is not the only one. Parents are responsible for creating a culture in the home in which virtue can flourish through careful and prudent screening of television, movies, music, the internet, and print media. For instance, parents should refuse to allow television shows into their home that undermine marriage and the parent-child relationship and portray children as a burden, rather than the "supreme gift" of marriage. Parents should also impress upon their children the importance of demonstrating respect for God, oneself, and others.

The steps which parents take depend to some extent on the ages of their children. For instance, many parents of young children drive their children to school to avoid having their six year-old learn four letter words and their meaning on the bus. Mothers of pre-teen and teenage girls may spend hours at the mall with their daughters trying to find a modest, attractive outfit. Many fathers avoid James Bond movies and NFL half time shows, if they watch TV at all, and become expert at changing channels at lightning speed to avoid racy commercials and other corrupting influences.

Obedience and Humility: Necessary Virtues

It may help parents to see themselves as "coaching" their children to help them acquire the virtues that enable them to be open to the gift of charity. We will highlight the two virtues that help children become more coachable: obedience and humility. Every effective coach knows that the first virtue a player must learn is obedience, for through obedience children learn to defer to the wisdom and prudence of those who guide them.[22] Teaching cheerful prompt obedience is worth the daily repetition and time it takes to form the habit in young children. This can be done by following some basic principles. First, the parent must lovingly insist on obedience in even small matters, for virtue is formed in the mundane matters of daily life. Parents must communicate effectively by listening to their children, making eye contact and insisting that their children do the same. Parents must correct attitudes as well as actions, reminding children that the way they carry out an action is important too. Finally, parents should insist on an apology if the child disobeys, then tell the child that he is forgiven with an affectionate smile and hug.

Parents must also coach their children in the virtue of humility and seek to cultivate it in themselves. The virtue of humility enables us to see ourselves in relation to God as we really are. It involves an authentic understanding of our own gifts and flaws and ultimately enables us to be open to grace.[23] In a culture that values self-esteem, the importance of humility is often neglected. A child who is taught to focus on building his own self-esteem, may lack an awareness of his relation to God and focus only on himself. This can lead to a distorted view of the self as either better or worse than the child actually is.[24] A better approach would be for the parent to substitute the terms "self-knowledge," and "confidence in God" for "self-esteem," emphasizing to the child the importance of seeing himself as he really is, a child of God.

Parents should make use of education, athletics, and other extracurricular activities to enhance virtue rather than compromise it. Through these activities, the child prepares his intellect and will and practices the intellectual and moral virtues.[25] Finally, the child's participation in family life trains him to see the importance of behaving virtuously toward others. As children experience the joys and responsibilities of family life, they learn the importance of "relationships marked by respect, justice, dialogue, and love."[26] While children must be continually instructed in manners until they become automatic, their parents' affection and courtesy towards each other make it much easier to teach children to behave lovingly and respectfully toward others and ultimately enables them to have successful friendships and marriages. In family life they learn to work for the common good and become aware of the needs of others, especially the most helpless members of society.

As these examples illustrate, it is possible to incorporate formation in virtue in every aspect of one's daily life. We have focused on obedience and humility as two virtues that foster openness to formation in the child from an early age. Other virtues that are important for formation in Christian chastity, including modesty rooted in temperance, fortitude, and generosity, may be instilled using similar methods.[27] Parents and educators alike, by paying attention to the child's behavior in small matters, are laying the foundation for virtuous behavior in greater matters. Loving insistence on virtuous behavior conveys to the child the respect he should have for God, for himself, and for others, as well as his responsibility to them and for them. Insisting on virtuous behavior allows the child to develop a loving and generous personality and ultimately enables him to live a holy life.

Conclusion

A final note: up to this point, we have argued for a kind of personal formation based on a model of an integral family, with father and mother both present and involved in the upbringing of their child. Unfortunately, many children grow up with one or both parents physically or emotionally absent to them. The temptation may be to implement classroom programs in order to reach these children, based on the rationale that a deficient formation is better than no formation at all and motivated by the legitimate desire to prevent children from engaging in sexual activity. However, these children desperately need the kind of personal formation that we are arguing should be the norm. These are precisely the children who need attention on an individual basis from an adult with whom they can develop a relationship of trust, who is familiar with their situation, who can answer their concerns, and who can clarify any misunderstandings they may have. Unfortunately, this kind of personal, focused formation is nearly impossible in a group setting. In situations involving parents who are absent either physically or emotionally, it is important to strive for formation that is grounded in an authentic vision of the person and is carried out in a personal way. In situations in which the family is not intact, the parent who is present should turn to other trusted individuals, especially those who are naturally related to the child, as well as to the parish for assistance in formation of his/ her children.[28]

Theresa H. Farnum has an M.A. and a Ph.D. in Medieval Studies from the University of Notre Dame and is currently on the faculty of the Mount Saint Mary's Seminary in Emmitsburg, Maryland, where she teaches courses in the pre-theology program and serves as a formation advisor. She is also a member of several committees on education for the

Diocese of Harrisburg, Pennsylvania, where she has collaborated with other parents, educators, and physicians in drawing up a diocesan curriculum for formation in chastity. She has lectured frequently on the personalism of Pope John Paul II as well as on St. Thomas Aquinas and the virtues. She and her husband Michael are the parents of seven children.

William K. Thierfelder was recently appointed president of Belmont Abbey College, a small Catholic and Benedictine liberal arts college in North Carolina. Prior to this appointment, he was president of the York Barbell Company in York, Pennsylvania. He is a former Olympian, National Champion, and two-time All American who received his masters and doctoral degrees in sports psychology and human movement from Boston University. He is a licensed psychologist, and has presented more than 350 lectures, seminars, and workshops to professionals in mental health, sport, medicine, and business. He and his wife Mary are the parents of nine children.

References

Congregation for the Doctrine of the Faith, "On the Collaboration of Men and Women in the Church and in the World," May 31, 2004.

Feeney, Robert, *A Catholic Perspective: Physical Exercise and Sports.* Aquinas Press, 1995.

St. Francis de Sales, *Philothea, or An Introduction to the Devout Life.* Tan Books, 1994.

Pontifical Council for the Family, "The Truth and Meaning of Human Sexuality," 1996.

Pope John Paul II, *Mulieris Dignitatem.* August 15, 1988.

Pope John Paul II, *Familiaris Consortio.* November 22, 1981.

Pope John Paul II, *Rosarium Virginis Mariae.* 2002.

St. Teresa of Avila, *Interior Castle*, Image Books, 1961.

St.Thomas Aquinas, *Summa Theologica.* Benziger, reprinted by Christian Classics, 1981.

St. John Vianney, *The Little Catechism of the Curé of Ars*, Tan Books, 1987.

Wojtyla, Karol, *Love and Responsibility*, Ignatius Press, 1993.

Notes

1. See John Paul II, *Mulieris Dignitatem*, 10. The Holy Father notes that discrimination against women, which is a very real consequence of original sin, should never be the occasion for denying the essential differences between men and women, lest we lose the richness of the feminine nature

and the complementarity between men and women that is essential for rich interpersonal relationships.

2. In recent years, the United Nations conferences on women have been marked by concerted efforts to deny the link between gender and biology in order to impose a radical feminist agenda on developing nations. At the same time, secular sex education materials sympathetically present gay and lesbian lifestyles as valid and morally praiseworthy choices. "On the Collaboration of Men and Women in the Church and in the World,"published by the Congregation for the Doctrine of the Faith, May 31, 2004, paragraph 2.

3. The Pontifical Council for the Family, "The Truth and Meaning of Human Sexuality" (TMHS) 3.

4. For example, a parent comforting a child, a priest administering sacraments.

5. TMHS 83.

6. Ibid.

7. Ibid, 78.

8. Ibid, 84.

9. Of those who use any kind of family planning, only 3% use natural family planning. See Kippley, John, "How Many Couples Use Natural Family Planning?" http://www.ccli.org/articles/howmany.shtml; see also http://www.usccb.org/prolife/cmrwin99.htm.

10. TMHS 129.

11. In fact, the current model of sex education teaches the child that in this area other adults know more than his mother and father and are more trustworthy.

12. Even in a situation in which parents are not living a sacramental Catholic marriage, it is important not to destroy or damage that relationship.

13. "Husbands love your wives as Christ also loved the Church" (Eph 5:23).

14. "Let women be subject to their husbands, as to the Lord." (Eph 5:22).

15. "Nothing is so beautiful as a pure soul. If we understood this, we could not lose our purity…My children, we cannot comprehend the power that a pure soul has over the good God. O my children, a soul that has never been stained by this accursed sin obtains from God whatever it wishes…Our Lord showed one [a pure soul] to St. Catherine; she thought it so beautiful that she said, "O Lord, if I did not know that there is only one God, I should think it was one." St. John Vianney, *Little Catechism of the Curé of Ars,* 23–24.

16. St. Thomas Aquinas specifically states that no true virtue is possible without the virtue of charity, which directs us to our principal good. *Summa Theologiae*, II-II, 23,8.

17. ". . .Chastity which is as yet no way wounded or hurt may be preserved in many ways, but having once been meddled with, nothing can preserve it except a perfect devotion…" St. Francis de Sales, *An Introduction to the Devout Life,* 152. True living devotion…implies the love of God. Indeed it is itself a true love of Him in the highest form, for whereas divine love

enlightening our soul is called Grace, and makes us pleasing to His sight; so giving us power to do good, it is called Charity; and when it reaches that point of perfection wherein it not only causes us to do good, but to do it earnestly frequently and readily then it is called Devotion...Devotion consists in perfect charity...*Ibid.*, 2. Consider Jacobs ladder (which is a faithful representation of the devout life): the two sides between which we ascend, and which support the steps, are prayer, which brings the love of God, and the sacraments which confer it; the steps are but the various degrees of charity by which we advance from virtue to virtue, either descending in action to the aid of our neighbor, or ascending in contemplation to a loving union with God."*Ibid.,6*. See also, St. Thomas Aquinas, *Summa Theologica* II-II, 151,1 and 4, in which St. Thomas describes the relationship between chastity and charity, and describes purity as that part of chastity that regulates the external expressions of sexuality.

18. "The three great means of attaining charity are obedience, chastity, and poverty. Obedience consecrates our hearts, chastity our body, and poverty our worldly means to the love and service of God. These are the three branches of the spiritual cross and all have their foundation in the fourth which is humility..."St. Francis de Sales, *Introduction to the Devout Life*, 148.

19. As for our children, "virgins have need of a very simple and tender chastity, banishing all manner of curious thoughts from their hearts, and despising all impure pleasures with absolute contempt. St. Francis de Sales, 152.

20. "...Prayer brings the love of God and the Sacraments confer it." St. Francis de Sales, 6.

21. Pope John Paul II, *Rosarium Virginis Mariae,* 41.

22. St. Thomas notes that the virtue of obedience prompts one to obey his superior, and points out that virtue "ingrafts and protects" the other virtue. While he mentions the obedience of a son for his father in the conduct of his life, he does not specify the role of obedience for those who lack prudence. It is our contention that in those who lack prudence, especially children who lack the requisite maturity for prudence, obedience enables them to order their lives correctly. See *Summa Theologica* II-II 104, 1 and 3. See also *Summa Theologica* II-II 48 15, in which St. Thomas specifically says that prudence belongs to older persons, because of their long experience and because they have mastered their passions.

23. *The Catechism of the Catholic Church* defines humility as "the virtue by which a Christian acknowledges that God is the author of all good. Humility avoids inordinate ambition or pride, and provides the foundation for turning to God in prayer. *Catechism of the Catholic Church,* Glossary; see also 2559. See also St. Thomas, *Summa Theologica* II-II 161,5 in which St. Thomas describes humility as the "first step in the acquisition of virtue."

24. St. Teresa of Avila puts it bluntly: "...it is absolutely true to say that we have no good thing in ourselves but only misery and nothingness; and anyone who fails to understand this is walking in falsehood. He who best under-

stands it is most pleasing to Sovereign Truth because he is walking in Truth. May it please God, sisters, to grant us the grace never to fail to have this knowledge of ourselves. Amen." St. Teresa of Avila, *Interior Castles*, p. 196.

25. One way to focus a child's attention on virtue rather than himself is to ask him to memorize the following quotation and recite it before every practice and before and after each competition: "Sport, properly directed, develops character, makes a man courageous, a generous loser, and a gracious victor; it refines the senses, gives intellectual penetration, and steels the will to endurance. It is not merely a physical development then. Sport, rightly understood, is an occupation of the whole man, and while perfecting the body as an instrument of the mind, it also makes the mind itself a more refined instrument for the search and communication of truth and helps man to achieve that end to which all others must be subservient, the service and praise of his Creator." Pope Pius XII, "Sport at the Service of the Spirit," July 29, 1945, as quoted by Robert Feeney in *A Catholic Perspective: Physical Exercise and Sports,* p.36.

26. Pope John Paul II, *Familiaris Consortio,*43.

27. As children mature, parents can guide them in developing prudence, which ultimately enables them to choose the correct means of becoming virtuous. See Note 23 above.

28. One can imagine circumstances in which the grandparents, an aunt or an uncle, or another trusted person could assist the parents both in conveying information to the child and, more importantly, in serving as a model of fatherhood or motherhood. Similarly, in parishes with many at risk children, one can envision mentoring programs (like the Big Brother/ Big Sister programs), that would also provide children with an adult model of fatherhood or motherhood.

Chapter 13: Empowering Catholic Children to Live in a Secular Via the Theology of the Body

HANNA KLAUS, M.D.

Today's culture is awash in vulgarity, pornography, and pragmatism. While a strong, two-parent family is the bulwark against the onslaughts of the above forces, parents often so seek help to meet particular challenges when their children enter adolescence. As adolescence is the time for beginning to separate from the parents and parental worldviews on many subjects, including religion and sexuality, many parents welcome the assistance of Church and school in order to preserve their children's chastity into adulthood. As one who has long worked in the field, I welcomed the opportunity to chair this session, to introduce our various speakers, and to react, very briefly, to their presentations.

Dr. Dennis Purificacion offered a variety of suggestions on tackling the overall problems at many points of insertion. Drs. Theresa H. Farnan and William Thierfelder feel that very few, if any, programs currently offered in Catholic schools to pre-publertal children teach what is needed, as the primary, undisputed educator for children in matters of sexuality, as in most other topics, are the parents. When parents' personal practice differs from Church teaching, however, dilemmas arise. Our speakers offered useful approaches to balance these lacunae. However, it cannot be denied that a huge problems remain about which the Church and Catholics can only be very concerned.

Realizing that the physical aspects of sexuality can appear dominant if not overwhelming at the age when the youngster begins to live with the onrush of their hormones, I represent a program designed to integrate the physical with the emotional, social, intellectual, and spiritual aspects of the person, leading to a holistic, integrated sexuality. The program, delivered in developmentally appropriate curricula for early, middle, and late adolescence, has proved to be a practical way of teaching the Theology of the Body. Thankfully, it has continued to show a positive impact on teens' behavior. This whole area is one which will continue to occupy our attention.

Hanna Klaus, M.D., F.A.C.O.G. (Sr. Miriam Paul) is a Medical Mission Sister who directed the Departments of Obstetrics and Gynecology at Holy Family Hospital Rawalpindi, Pakistan, in 1961–66, and in Dhaka, Bangladesh in 1966–68. Currently she is the Executive Director of the Natural Family Planning Center of Washington, D.C., as well as of the Teen STAR Program. She is a gynecologist who has conducted use-effectiveness research and training of teachers of the Billings Ovulation Method for over 30 years, and the Teen STAR Program since 1980. Teen STAR, "*Sexuality Teaching* in the context of *Adult Responsibility*," is an international pro-active sexuality education program for teens which currently operates *in* 27 countries. Holistic Sexuality is a program for college students offered either as a credit course, or an elective.

Born in Vienna, Austria, she is a graduate of the University of Louisville and the University's Medical School; she served residencies in pathology at Massachusetts General Hospital, Boston, and in Obstetrics and Gynecology at Barnes and Allied Hospitals, St.Louis, Missouri.. After a year as a teaching fellow at Peter Bent Brigham Hospital, Boston, and Harvard Medical School, she joined the Medical Mission Sisters. Upon her return from seven years in Pakistan, she taught at Washington and St. Louis Universities, St. Louis. Until 1998, she was an Associate Clinical Professor of Gynecology and Obstetrics at the George Washington University Medical Center. As past president and current medical consultant of the Billings Ovulation Method Association of the U.S., she assists in the training and continuing education of the teachers and consults on problem cases for them, and many other of the NFP teachers on the Internet. She has been a consultant for Natural Family Planning seminars and projects for USAID in the Philippines, Kenya, and the Teen STAR program at the Pontifical University in Santiago, Chile. She serves as a periodic consultant to the Diocesan Development Program for Natural Family Planning of the USCCB, and she authored the Science Notes for NFP teachers while President of the Billings Ovulation Method Association. She has published 60 scientific articles, and 42 popular articles, many concerned with natural family planning and the Teen STAR program. She is a Fellow of the American College of Obstetricians and Gynecologists, a Diplomate of the American Board of Obstetrics and Gynecology, a member of the Endocrine Society, American Society for Reproductive Medicine, the Society for Adolescent Medicine, the Catholic Medical Association, University Faculty for Life, the National Abstinence Coalition, the Institute for Theological Encounter with Science and Technology, and the Fellowship of Catholic Scholars. When not traveling, she makes her home in Bethesda, Maryland.

Chapter 14: Homosexuality: How Relevant Are Experience and Science to Theology and Pastoral Practice?

PAUL FLAMAN, S.T.D.

Introduction

The traditional Christian understandings of the conjugal family and of marriage as a union of one man and one woman are being challenged by advocates of same-sex marriage and alternate forms of family, including lesbian and "gay" couples adopting children or having them by using means such as artificial insemination and surrogate mothers. Some who advocate these practices support their claims by appealing to experience and science. Some of these advocates who hold gay theological views say that the magisterium of the Catholic Church and others who support traditional theological understandings of marriage and the family are not listening to the experiences of gays and lesbians (Keenan, 2003). On the other hand, some who argue against same-sex couples getting married, adopting children, and so forth, support their case by appealing to empirical data and/or human experience including the experiences of ex-gays and ex-lesbians (cf., e.g., Family Research Council and Exodus International).

With regard to homosexuality, this paper focuses on the question: "How relevant are experience and science to theology and pastoral practice?" Some consider such a question pertinent to theological approaches in particular that appeal not only to revelation but also to reason and the natural moral law (Farley in Olyan and Nussbaum,1998, 106). I hope that my paper will contribute in a small way to the "integration of knowledge" called for by Pope John Paul II in *Ex Corde Ecclesiae* (nn. 16–17). I conclude in part that experience and science properly interpreted can be integrated with Catholic teaching and pastoral practice on homosexuality.

My paper has three main parts: 1) What Challenges do Science and

Experience in the Area of Homosexuality Present to Theology and Pastoral Practice?; 2) A More Critical Examination of Science and Experience with Regard to Homosexuality; and 3) Some Ways that Experience and Science Properly Understood can Contribute to an Authentic Development of Theology and Pastoral Practice.

1. What Challenges do Science and Experience in the Area of Homosexuality Present to Theology and Pastoral Practice?

In the past developments in certain sciences such as astronomy and evolutionary biology posed some serious challenges to Christians including Church leaders. Consider, for example, the cases of Galileo and Darwin. The initial responses of some within the Church were to reject scientific developments from such men. Some popes, however, such as Pius XII (1950) and John Paul II (1996), have more recently shown a genuine openness to and appreciation for genuine scientific developments in these areas. At the same time they have critiqued certain ideologies contrary to the Christian faith such as materialism, which often are associated with scientific theories. While some have seen a conflict between certain findings of the natural sciences and Christian faith, others including many Christian scientists conclude that the genuine findings of these sciences really do not undermine basic Christian beliefs such as God as the Creator, human sinfulness, the Incarnation and God's salvation. Indeed, many who become familiar with sciences such as modern physics, astronomy, paleontology, evolutionary biology, genetics, and neuroscience, for example, find that these sciences actually help them to appreciate the greatness of God as Creator and the beauty of God's creation even more (Polkinghorne 1998).

In recent years, there have been reports of certain scientific studies, for example, by Simon LeVay (1991) and Dean Hamer (1993), which have suggested that homosexuality may be biologically determined by hormones before birth which affect brain development and/or by certain genes. Within a number of professional organizations, beginning with the American Psychiatric Association in 1973, there have also been moves towards the "normalization" of homosexuality. Among other things, for example, an article on the American Psychological Association's official website, "Lesbian and Gay Parenting," by openly lesbian activist Charlotte Patterson, summarizes a number of studies and concludes that:

> ...there is no evidence to suggest that lesbians and gay men are unfit to be parents or that psychosocial development among children of gay men or lesbians is compromised in any respect relative to that among offspring of heterosexual parents. Not a single study

has found children of gay or lesbian parents to be disadvantaged in
any significant respect relative to children of heterosexual parents.

Today the experiences shared by many gays and lesbians are presenting serious challenges for Christians in various denominations.
Many Christians personally know one or more people living a gay or lesbian lifestyle. Some gays and lesbians are raising children and many
have entered partnerships, some of which have lasted many years
(Lofton and Croteau, 2004). Some of them have publicly claimed that
they have always felt different, that same-sex erotic relationships and
genital relations are "natural" for them, that being homosexual is an
unchangeable condition, and that their love and relationships are equal
to those of heterosexual couples (CMA, 2004, Introduction; and Court
of Appeal for Ontario, 2003, n. 94). With regard to this claim, consider
the movement to legalize same-sex civil marriages in Canada, the United
States, and elsewhere. Some churches, for example, the Metropolitan
Community Church (MCC), and some pastors within mainline Christian
churches, have already provided "blessing" ceremonies or religious
"marriages" for gay and lesbian couples (ELCIC 2003).

Some who hold gay theological views within a number of churches,
including the Catholic Church, say that the magisterium of the Catholic
Church and others who do not accept the goodness of committed and
loving gay and lesbian relationships are not listening to the experiences
of gays and lesbians (Keenan, 2003). They call on the churches to listen
to the experiences of gays and lesbians and to revise their theology,
teaching, and pastoral approach accordingly. In the light of publications
by such scientists as LeVay and Hamer, some theologians have been convinced that homosexuality is biologically "natural," and that Christians
should not resist science as a source for correcting our understanding of
Scripture and revelation (Keenan 2003, 140).

With regard to homosexuality and human experience, we can also
note that issues such as the ordaining of gays and lesbians and the celebration of "blessings" or church "marriages" for same-sex couples have
been very divisive in a number of churches, for example, in the United
Church of Canada and churches connected with the Church of England.
These deep divisions present a real challenge to Christians in the light of
Jesus' prayer for the unity of his disciples (see Jn 17:21).

2. A More Critical Examination of Science and Experience with Regard to Homosexuality

The claims that the homosexual orientation is biologically determined and unchangeable, that gay and lesbian relationships and partner-ships are equal to heterosexual marriages, and that children of lesbian and gay parents experience no significant disadvantages compared to children of heterosexual parents are undermined by a more critical examination of the related science and experiences.

a) Is the Homosexual Orientation Really Biologically Determined and Unchangeable?

First of all, studies such as those by LeVay (1991) and Hamer (1993) which have suggested that homosexuality may be determined by hormones before birth causing some brain differences and/or certain genes have not been replicated.(CMA 2004, I.1) A number of scientists critically reviewing such studies have pointed out their limits and/or deficiencies. Such studies cannot prove that anyone is "born gay" due to the complexity of factors involved in human sexual and brain develop-ment (Looy 1995; Satinover 1996, Part 1; and Nicolosi and Nicolosi 2003, Chs. 1–7).

Studies of identical twins, who share the same nuclear DNA, have found that many of them are not identical in their sexual attractions. Besides genes, identical twins would in general also share very similar early environments, both in the womb and their family. Nevertheless, identical twins also experience events unique to each twin. For example, in some cases only one of the twins may have experienced certain unique events such as seduction, sexual abuse, or a sexual encounter when young. Case histories where one twin later has a homosexual orientation and the other a heterosexual orientation "frequently reveal environmen-tal factors which account for the development of different sexual attrac-tion patterns..."(CMA 2004, I.1; also Satinover 1996, Ch. 5; and Neil Whitehead, "The Importance of Twin Studies," NARTH 2004).

The experiences of many ex-gays and ex-lesbians undermine the view that the homosexual orientation is unchangeable:

> There are...numerous autobiographical reports from men and women who once believed themselves to be unchangeably bound by same-sex attractions and behaviors. Many of these men and women...now describe themselves as free of same sex attraction, fantasy, and behavior. Most of these individuals found freedom through participation in religion-based support groups, although some also had recourse to therapists (CMA 2004, I.5; one can also read many accounts of such experiences on Exodus International's website; see also Morrison, 1999 and the Portraits of Courage videos, 2001).

There is also a large body of literature on the successful treatment of homosexuality and surveys of therapists. A number of therapists including psychiatrists and psychologists "have written extensively of the positive results of therapy for same-sex attraction...Reviews of treatment for unwanted same-sex attractions show that it is as successful as treatment for similar psychological problems: about 30 percent experience a freedom from symptoms and another 30 percent experience improvement."(CMA 2004, 1.5 – the percentages in the quotation are modest averages based on a number of studies and reports referred to in the statement's endnotes). For a couple of balanced reviews, which outline a number of specific secular and religious approaches to therapy, see, for example, Harvey (1996, Ch. 4) and Satinover (1996, Chs. 11–13).

In spite of the experiences of many ex-gays and ex-lesbians and the large body of literature on the successful treatment of homosexuality, the Catholic Medical Association points out that: "Unfortunately, a number of influential persons and professional groups ignore this evidence, and there seems to be a concerted effort on the part of 'homosexual apologists' to deny the effectiveness of treatment of same-sex attraction or to claim that such treatment is harmful..."(CMA 2004, I.5). For example, some say that reorientation therapy internalizes homophobia in homosexuals. Although they may claim to be cured, they are really deceiving themselves. At best such "cures" are only temporary and never last for more than five years. Some people with a homosexual orientation have spent thousands of dollars on such therapy without experiencing any change of orientation, have been disillusioned with it, and have returned to a gay or lesbian lifestyle (Besen 2003; Spitzer 2003, 403–5).

With regard to such criticisms, consider a recently published study (October, 2003) by Robert Spitzer, M.D. He is a respected psychiatrist at Columbia University. Of interest in the early 1970s, when the prevailing professional view was that homosexuality was a mental disorder, he sympathetically listened to the experiences of many gay and lesbian people. He was one of the leaders within the American Psychiatric Association seeking to have "homosexuality" removed as a mental illness from the DSM (Diagnostic and Statistical Manual). More recently, however, he has listened sympathetically to the experiences of many ex-gays and ex-lesbians.

Spitzer's study involved in-depth interviews of 200 men and women who reported that they were exclusively or predominantly homosexual before therapy; that they became predominantly or exclusively heterosexual, at least in part with the help of therapy; and that they have remained so for more than five years. 11 percent of the males and 37 percent of the females in his study reported a complete change, that is, from having an exclusively homosexual orientation to later having an exclusively heterosexual orientation. Individuals who had been at the extreme on homosexual measures had a prevalence similar to the entire sample with regard to an outcome of good heterosexual functioning at post, that is, 61 percent.(411). Spitzer concludes, for many reasons, that "the participants' self-reports were by-and-large credible. Thus, there is evidence that change in sexual orientation following some form of reparative therapy does occur in some gay men and lesbians."(403). Many of these people are now in normal, healthy heterosexual marriages. With regard to assessing this, Spitzer used the Spanier 1976 Dyadic Adjustment Scale, a validated instrument. There was no evidence of harm of the therapy for any of the participants, some of whom often reported other benefits as well. For example, 87 percent reported feeling more masculine (males) or more feminine (females) and 93 percent reported developing intimate nonsexual relations with persons of the same sex. (412).

Spitzer (2003) recommends further research into the efficacy of sexual reorientation therapy. Among other things, he concludes: "Many patients, provided with informed consent about the possibility that they will be disappointed if the therapy does not succeed, can make a rational choice to work toward developing their heterosexual potential and minimizing their unwanted homosexual attractions. In fact, the ability to make such a choice should be considered fundamental to client autonomy and self-determination" I agree." (414).

A number of experienced therapists and counselors think that the healing of homosexual attractions and behaviors is in general more effective when the best insights from psychotherapy are combined with good spirituality. For example, psychiatrists Richard Fitzgibbons and Jeffrey Satinover understand homosexual attractions and related behaviors as a symptom of certain emotional conflicts and pain or inner "psychic traumas." In both sexes, this may be related to such things as an emotional mismatch between the child and either the same-sex or opposite sex parent, sexual abuse, or being rejected by same-sex peers and a lack of bonding with them during the developmental years. In males this may be related to such things as alienation from or feeling abandoned by the father in early childhood, which later unconsciously led to seeking to fulfill the emptiness for father love in homosexual behavior; an overly protective or needy or demanding mother; mistrust of female love; and poor body image. In females, this may be related to such things as mistrust of male love connected with being sexually abused by a father or another male; a lack of maternal affection which led to a deep longing for female love; or to other things such as weak female identity related to such things as dislike for one's body.

Not all children who experience "external" traumas such as sexual abuse develop same-sex attractions, since the inner subjective experience or "psychic trauma" may be different in different children. Although it is clear that homosexuality is not biologically determined like eye or skin color, for example, Satinover and some other experts nevertheless think that there may be some biological predispositions in some cases. For example, a boy who is poor in sports and very much afraid of rough-and-tumble play is more likely to be rejected by same-sex peers. If he also has an emotionally sensitive temperament, he is likely to experience a greater "psychic trauma" due to such rejection. Such a boy is at a greater risk of developing a homosexual orientation. Other boys with the same biological predispositions may not develop a homosexual orientation, for example, because their parents helped them to develop a healthy masculine identity, and they had one or more good same-sex peer relationships in their childhood.

Associated with "psychic traumas" or being hurt are often feelings of anger, resentment, sadness, and so forth. Adults with same-sex attractions may have forgotten about or even suppressed memories of these negative experiences, which may have occurred many years earlier. Nevertheless, being healed of these bad memories, letting go of past resentments, and forgiving those who hurt one are important aspects of the healing process. Letting go of past resentments and forgiving can seem impossible to some people until they become open to God's healing power and transforming love. Related to this, Satinover says that finding the love of God makes it possible to lay down old defenses and face fearlessly the wounds that have inflicted so much pain and distorted so much of one's life over so many years.(1996, Chs. 13 and 15; for Fitzgibbons, see Harvey 1996, Appendix I, and Portraits of Courage 2001, 2; also Maria Valdes in Harvey, 1996, Appendix II; Brodner; Nicolosi and Nicolosi 2002; and CMA, 2004). We can note here that some experienced professionals speak not only of therapy and healing with regard to homosexuality, but also of "prevention" with regard to children who are at a higher risk of developing a homosexual orientation (see, e.g., Nicolosi and Nicolosi, 2002; and CMA, 2004, I.3). Among other things, Satinover also says:

> I have been extraordinarily fortunate to have met many people who have emerged from the gay life. When I see the personal dif-

ficulties they have squarely faced, the sheer courage they have displayed not only in facing these difficulties but also in confronting a culture that uses every possible means to deny the validity of their values, goals, and experiences, I truly stand back in wonder...It is these people – former homosexuals and those who are still struggling – who stand for me as a model of everything good and possible in a world that takes the human heart, and the God of that heart, seriously. In my various explorations within the worlds of psychoanalysis, psychotherapy, and psychiatry, I have simply never before seen such profound healing (1996, 249).

With regard to healing and homosexuality, Father John Harvey distinguishes spiritual and psychological healing (1992). He is a Catholic priest who has been involved for many years with men and women who are struggling with same-sex attractions and who are striving to live according to the Catholic Church's pastoral teaching on homosexuality. He is also the founding director of Courage, a Catholic spiritual support group. Courage does not focus on a change of orientation but on spiritual healing, that is, on growing in living a Christ-centered and chaste life. Nevertheless, in his many years of counseling, Fr. Harvey says he has witnessed many people with a homosexual orientation who have also experienced psychological healing. Many people he has known have experienced a diminishment of same-sex desires and have been able to develop their heterosexual potential in varying degrees. Among other things, Fr. Harvey recommends more empirical research on the effectiveness of various forms of therapy.(1996, Ch. 4). For further reading on research and therapy of homosexuality, see, for example, the many articles by professionals on NARTH's website.

As a believing Christian and Catholic theologian, I think it is helpful to consider homosexuality and healing in the broader context of the mysteries of sin and redemption. Not only people with a homosexual orientation, but all of us have been wounded in various ways by the sins of ourselves and others. We all are in need of God's redemption, healing power, and transforming love. If we cooperate with God's love and grace, God will heal us. This healing of our whole person, body and soul, however, will only be fully completed with our entry into eternal life and bodily resurrection. It seems to me that psychological healing in this life is generally a long process. Our incomplete psychological healing in this life, with its associated trials, can help motivate us to be humble and to keep turning to God. This is very important if we are to keep growing spiritually.

b) Are Gay and Lesbian Partnerships Really Equal to Heterosexual Marriages?

The claims by some gay and lesbian couples that their love, relationships and partnerships are equal to that of heterosexual couples and marriages have been challenged by some statistics, the experiences of many ex-gays and ex-lesbians, and the interpretations of some therapists. Since there seem to be some significant differences between gay and lesbian couples, they will not be lumped together here.

Very few male same-sex couples are sexually exclusive or faithful in the long-run. In a serious sociological study, *The Male Couple*, David McWhirter and Andrew Mattison studied 156 couples who had been together from one to thirty-seven years. 75 percent had assumed that their relationship would be sexually exclusive. Only seven couples, all of whom had been together for less than five years, were totally sexually exclusive. After five years, all of the couples concluded that some outside sexual relationships had to be accepted for the survival of the relationship. They viewed emotional stability with each other as more important than sexual fidelity (Harvey, 1996, 234; and Dailey, 2003). Although some heterosexual men are quite promiscuous, in general homosexual men are much more promiscuous than heterosexual men. For example, Laumann et al. (1994) found that in the United States since the age of eighteen, homosexual men have had an average of 44.3 partners, and heterosexual men have had an average of 6 partners (also Swenson, 2004). Dailey (2003) summarizes a number of studies in the United States published between 1994 and1997 which found that between 75–81 percent of married men reported that they never had sexual relations outside marriage. A study in the Netherlands, the first country to legalize same-sex civil marriage, found that the average male homosexual partnership lasted only one and a half years, which is much lower than heterosexual marriages, 57 percent of which last fifteen years or longer (Sprigg, 2004, 95–97; for more details, see Dailey 2004).

Speaking mainly of males, although some of this also applies to females, Gerald van den Aardweg, from his research and long clinical practice concludes that homosexual men feel inferior as men and come to admire, idolize, and attempt to contact other men as a passionate attempt to possess what they think they lack. Although many homosexual persons regard their homoeroticism as the deepest and purest love, Aardweg sees it as self-centered sentimentality, infantile romanticism, and seeking to be loved and accepted (Harvey, 1987, 49–60).

In an article, "The Homosexually Oriented Man's Relationship to Women," psychologist and therapist Dr. Joseph Nicolosi says in part:

Homoerotic orgasm provides a temporary, tension-relieving connection with the male sex, from which the gay man has defensively detached himself. Heroin also provides an intense, exciting high, but it depletes the person, leaving him emotionally drained and depressed and in need of another "fix." This same emotional dynamic is described by many homosexuals in reference to sex...A good measure of what is "right" is the feelings one is left with after sex. Men with a homosexual background who have married describe a qualitative difference in their sexual experiences with their wives. While these experiences are of less intensity, they are richer, fuller, and more emotionally satisfying. These men describe a feeling of "rightness" and a natural compatibility. As one married man said: "When I compare my intimate experiences with my wife to my homosexual experiences, it seems like we were little boys playing in the sandbox (NARTH, 2004; also, many testimonials of ex-gays on Exodus International's website).

Lesbian relationships generally are not as promiscuous as gay relationships. Homosexual women and lesbians, however, in general have significantly more sex partners than heterosexual and married women. For example, Laumann et al. (1994) found that in the United States since the age of eighteen, homosexual women have had an average of 19 partners, whereas heterosexual women have had an average of 4 partners, that is, almost 5 times as many (also more than three times as many as the average heterosexual man [6], see above). Blumstein and Schwartz (1983) found that after 2–10 years together, 38 percent of lesbians have had other partners, and 19 percent were not monogamous in the past year.(also Swenson 2004). Compare this to women in heterosexual marriages. For example, in a number of studies in the U.S. published from 1994–1997, between 85–90 percent of wives report that they never had sexual relations outside marriage (Dailey 2003).

According to a number of experts, lesbian relationships generally involve excessive emotional attachment and enmeshment, insecurity, and jealousy. For example, psychotherapist Diane Eller-Boyko, a married ex-lesbian, sees the lesbian as having a wounded feminine psyche. This may be related to such experiences as being sexually abused, feeling inferior as a woman, having a mother who did not honor the feminine in her, or a father wishing she had been a boy. Her falling in love with another woman is really seeking something of the feminine missing within her (Nicolosi and Nicolosi, 2002, 151; *ibid.,* Ch. 7; Andria L. Sigler-Smalz, "Understanding the Lesbian Client," NARTH, 2004; and many testimonials of ex-lesbians on Exodus International's website; also Harvey 1996, Ch. 10).

With regard to the above, some may point out that heterosexual marriages also have their problems; and that the significant average differences presented above with regard to homosexual men and women and gay and lesbian couples compared to heterosexual men and women and marriages do not necessarily apply to every individual and couple. I agree. There is, however, one fundamental difference that applies to every case. Many Catholic documents with regard to same-sex couples, including a few recent ones, have pointed out that they lack the natural complementarity of the sexes (Cere and Farrow, 2003; Sprigg, 2004, Ch. 4; CDF, 2003; CCCB, 2003; and USCCB, 2003). This is obvious on the biological level. In the light of common human experience and science, it is clear that the sexual organs of a man and a woman are designed for each other and together for procreation. In the light of the unity of human beings, male and female, as embodied persons (e.g., phenomenology regarding human experience and neuroscience), some have also presented strong arguments that the complementarity of man and woman includes not only the biological dimension of persons but also other dimensions including the psychological and spiritual (e.g., the related works of Dietrich von Hildebrand, Sr. Prudence Allen, and John Paul II, 1997).

c) Do Children of Lesbian and Gay Parents Really Experience no Disadvantages?

Do children of gay or lesbian parents really experience no disadvantages in any significant respect relative to children of heterosexual parents, as Patterson claims (Part 1 above)? Timothy Dailey, in an article, "Homosexual Parenting: Placing Children at Risk" (2003), points out serious deficiencies in the studies referred to by Patterson and others who make such claims. These deficiencies include "reliance upon inadequate sample size, lack of random sampling, lack of anonymity of research participants, and self-presentation bias." He also refers to many other studies which would support the view that in general children raised by gay or lesbian parents are not as likely to do as well as in traditional heterosexual marriages and families (also Sprigg, 2004, 98–101, which includes a summary of some related scholarly research as well as some testimonies of adults who were actually raised by homosexual parents).

With regard to parents with a homosexual orientation, I think we need to distinguish those who already are parents, perhaps even in or from a heterosexual marriage, from would-be parents by adoption or other technological means, such as donor insemination for lesbians and surrogate motherhood for gays. A Vatican document (CDF, 1987) considers donor insemination and surrogate motherhood to be an immoral means to create a child for anyone, not only for lesbian and gay couples, but also for heterosexual married couples. It affirms that a child has a right to be conceived and raised by his or her father and mother in a heterosexual marriage. Many, including many bioethicists, agree that there is something tragic when a child is not raised by both his or her biological mother and father. Consider, for example, the cases of a child where one or both biological parents die, or where a child is conceived and born of parents who are too young and immature to be good parents. In tragic cases, which already exist, when the biological parents are unable to raise their child, many agree that the best response is often adoption. But when couples, whether heterosexual or homosexual, have recourse to heterologous means such as donor insemination (also surrogate motherhood for gay couples), they are acting to bring a child into existence who does not yet exist and they plan to raise the child without one of its biological parents. This means creating a tragic situation that did not exist before.

With regard to adoption by same-sex couples, another recent Vatican document says:

> As experience has shown, the absence of sexual complementarity in these unions creates obstacles in the normal development of children who would be placed in the care of such persons. They would be deprived of the experience of either fatherhood or motherhood. Allowing children to be adopted by persons living in such unions would actually mean doing violence to these children, in the sense that their condition of dependency would be used to place them in an environment that is not conducive to their full human development. This is gravely immoral and in open contradiction to the principle, recognized also in the United Nations Convention on the Rights of the Child, that the best interests of the child, as the weaker and more vulnerable party, are to be the paramount consideration in every case (CDF, 2003, n.7).

With regard to the importance of children of both sexes having both a father and a mother, consider the following by Robert Knight and Daniel Garcia: "In a homosexual household, children miss out on seeing three important relationships between: mothers and fathers, men and women, and husbands and wives, not to mention personal relationships both sexes have with the children. Children need role models of both sexes in order to have the best chance to develop healthy, confident sexual identities."(2001,10). Joseph and Linda Nicolosi also write on how having healthy relationships with both a father and a mother helps a child of either sex to develop a healthy sexual identity. For example, a daughter who feels love and positive regard from her father will generally feel worthy of another man's love, and a son who has a healthy relationship with his mother will generally learn to trust female love. The development of a homosexual orientation is often related to a child's unmet needs for love and affirmation from his or her same-sex parent (2002, Ch. 4, "All in the Family."; also, for some of the views of other experts summarized above with regard to the development of a homosexual orientation, see Kirkey, 2000 and Sprigg, 2004, 98–101).

d) Some Additional Comments

In this part of my paper I have not attempted to provide a comprehensive analysis of all the phenomena of human experience involved, nor of all that various scientists have said with regard to homosexuality. This would be humanly impossible. Rather, I have attempted to provide a critical examination of some of the simplistic or erroneous claims with regard to homosexuality, which are often used as a basis to attack or to call for a radical revision of the traditional Christian understanding of marriage and the family and the Catholic teachings related to marriage and the family. Some who support these claims point to certain "scientific" findings and call on others to listen to the experiences of gays and lesbians (see Part 1 above). Many of these people, however, are either unaware of, or have failed to consider seriously, scientific findings which would undermine their views. Many are also unaware of, or have failed to listen to, the experiences of ex-gays and ex-lesbians. With regard to this, I would suggest that they follow the lead of the respected psychiatrist Robert Spitzer, who has listened to the experiences of both gays and lesbians as well as of ex-gays and ex-lesbians (see above under 2.a). I think we should try to be open to listening with profound respect to everyone, including those men and women with a homosexual orientation who have never been identified with any of these labels.

In concluding this part, I would like to make a few general observations with regard to science and theology. Research in the natural and social sciences is never purely "objective." Science, as well as philosophy and theology, is done by human beings who each have their limited perspectives of reality. Concerning this, some have used the analogy of "lenses" or "filters" through which we each perceive and understand reality. To illustrate this, one can take pictures of the same objects, for example, an apple and an orange with cameras using different lenses or filters. The pictures of the same objects can appear very different in certain aspects, for example, color. The reality of homosexuality, however, is very much more complex than apples and oranges. It is understandable that different people, including scientists and theologians with their different backgrounds and temperaments, have interpreted the related human experiences and scientific data in different ways (cf. Caramagno 2002). With regard to this, see, for example, *Homosexuality and the Politics of Truth* by psychiatrist Jeffrey Satinover. Among other things, he says: "The deep complexity of the scientific research into homosexuality is easy for people to misinterpret and easier still to misuse"(1996, 27).

As a Catholic theologian, a married man and a father of three adopted children, I realize that I also view and interpret the complex data of human experience and science through my own"lens." As a believing Catholic Christian, I try to understand homosexuality in the light of God's revelation. I see Jesus, the Incarnation of God in human flesh, as our hermeneutical key. Among other things, to have an integral vision of homosexuality, I think we need to consider it in the light God's love and plan for human beings, including his plan for human sexuality and redemption, as well as Jesus' call to conversion, forgiveness, and the love of one another as he loves us. Although I think the analogy of "lenses" can help people who disagree to grow in understanding each other, I do not think it should be used to argue for relativism, including moral relativism. While it is true that we human beings have limited perspectives and limited knowledge (see 1 Cor 13:12–13), I think we can, nevertheless, say many things that are true, that correspond to reality (Von Balthasar, 2000, III.B.2). This true also with regard to the complex reality of homosexuality.

It is important to respect the legitimate methods and limits of the various sciences as well as philosophy and theology. For example, although empirical science is a valuable tool, it cannot by itself determine what is "normal," moral, or immoral; nor can it tell lus the meaning of life (Nicolosi and Nicolosi, 2002, 168; and Satinover 1996, 146). With regard to these questions, good philosophy and theology have very important roles to play. In our scientific culture, some may think that theology and faith in God's revelation do not really contribute to genuine human knowledge. With regard to this, however, consider the following court case, which I witnessed as a member of the jury. A young girl testified (revealed) that a certain man (the accused) had sexually assaulted her. A medical doctor who had examined the girl stated that his findings were consistent with her being sexually assaulted, but that it could not be proved scientifically that the girl had been sexually assaulted, let alone by the accused. Nevertheless, a jury of twelve people was convinced "beyond a reasonable doubt" that the young girl's testimony was credible and that the accused had in fact sexually assaulted her. A lot of human knowledge, not only theological knowledge, is related to personal revelation and faith. Often we can be more certain of such knowledge than we can be of knowledge in the natural and social sciences, where many hypotheses over the years have been falsified. As we have seen above, this includes in recent years a few hypotheses and related claims with respect to homosexuality. Nevertheless, scientists and others can make real contributions to the growth of human knowledge by trying to develop hypotheses or theories that do not suppress any data but rather take into account all of the data of human experience and the various sciences.

With regard to the relationship of science and theology, Pope John Paul II in *Sapientia Cristiana* (1979) says in part:

> In fact, new sciences and new discoveries pose new problems that involve the sacred disciplines and demand an answer. While carrying out their primary duty of attaining through theological research a deeper grasp of revealed truth, those engaged in the sacred sciences should therefore maintain contact with scholars of other disciplines, whether these are believers or not, and should try to evaluate and interpret these latter's affirmations and judge them in the light of revealed truth...Revealed truth must be considered also in connection with contemporary, evolving, scientific accomplishments, so that it can be seen "how faith and reason give harmonious witness to the unity of all truth".(from the Foreword, III, par. 3; and Article 68, respectively).

3. Some Ways that Experience and Science Properly Understood Can Contribute to an Authentic Development of Theology and Pastoral Practice

Jesus promised his disciples that he would send the Holy Spirit to lead them into a fuller understanding of the truth (Jn 16:12). With regard to this many theologians, for example, Yves Congar, as well as Catholic teaching, speak of a genuine development of doctrine, not in the sense of denying truths that were understood before but in the sense of a development in understanding and articulating truth. Many of these developments have occurred in response to people experiencing new challenges, including those posed by certain developments in the human sciences.

For example, some developments in moral theology and Catholic moral teaching have happened in response to new ethical questions posed by developments in science and technology such as with regard to organ transplants, new reproductive technologies, and genetics. Many developments in the philosophy and theology of the natural moral law have been related to further reflection on various kinds of human experiences including moral dilemmas. Some significant developments in spiritual theology have been related to the spiritual experiences, as well as the reflections on these, of many saints (e.g., Augustine of Hippo, Teresa of Avila, John of the Cross, Thérèse of Lisieux and others). In the field of pastoral theology and practice, one sees many developments, often in response to various problems or other experiences, beginning with the New Testament itself – for example, parts of the Pauline and other Pastoral Letters. Use of the phenomenological method to carefully describe and analyze human experience has also contributed to developments, for example, with regard to the development of the theology of human sexuality, marriage, and the body (John Paul II,1997; and related works of Dietrich von Hildebrand).

a) The Contribution of the Experience of Many Ex-Gays and Ex-Lesbians

With regard to homosexuality and how human experience and science can contribute to an authentic development of theology and pastoral practice, let us begin with the experiences of many ex-gays and ex-lesbians. Many men and women have left the gay or lesbian lifestyle, experienced the love and healing power of God, and have shared their experiences of gaining a better understanding of themselves, experiencing diminished same-sex temptations and attractions, and growing in living chaste lives. Many of these same people have also experienced in varying degrees the development of their heterosexual potential living celibate lives or by entering or remaining in satisfying heterosexual marriages (see above under 2a). It seems to me that this can help us all to appreciate the wonder of God's love, grace, and healing presence. For many, these "experiences" lend credibility to, and help them to appreciate better, the Good News of Jesus Christ and the Church's teaching on homosexuality (see, e.g., Morrison 1996 and 1999). If we are humble and honest, this can help those of us who never struggled with same-sex attractions and temptations to be inspired in our own struggle with other temptations and to realize our own need for God's grace and healing. With regard to sexuality, for example, we must consider not only those who are sexually compulsive or addicted to pornography, but those who are married people struggling to overcome selfishness and grow in true self-giving love. All of us "have departed from God's ideals in the arena of sexuality. Who for example has not had lustful thoughts?"(Brown in Bradshaw, 138). Many of us could benefit from a healing of certain memories (cf. 2a above) in the sexual as well as other areas of our lives (Linn, 1978).

b) Experience and Science Properly Understood Exclude Some Theological Views

It seems to me that a critical examination of human experience and science with regard to homosexuality excludes a few interpretations or theories, including some theological views and pastoral approaches. First of all, some revisionist theology views the homosexual orientation itself as good, as a gift of God and part of God's wonderful creation (UCC, 2003; and some of the views summarized by Keenan, 2003). In the light of the many ex-gays and ex-lesbians who have experienced a profound healing of certain bad memories, various "psychic traumas" related to such things as experiencing sexual abuse, rejection by same-sex peers, and/or a lack of adequate love by one or both parents – and related to this have experienced a diminishment of same-sex desires and a development of their heterosexual potential in various degrees (see 2a above) – how can one possibly view the homosexual orientation as created good by God?

This is not to deny in any way that men and women with a homosexual orientation are gifted by God in many ways. For example, many men with a homosexual orientation are emotionally sensitive and have remarkable aesthetic gifts. A boy with such gifts who is also poor in sports is more likely in our culture to be ridiculed by his same-sex peers and experience "psychic traumas" which may contribute to the development of a homosexual orientation. Boys with the same gifts and limits, however, can be spared such "psychic traumas" and fulfill their heterosexual potential especially if they have some good same-sex peer relationships growing up and loving parents who help them to appreciate that "real" boys and men can have such gifts and do not have to be good in sports (2a above). Some experts think that too rigid stereotypes of masculinity and femininity are actually part of the problem (Nicolosi and Nicolosi, 2002; and CMA 2004, I.3).

Some Christians view homosexuality as simply caused by demons to be exorcized (Caramagno, 2002, Ch. 10). Some hold the view that if a homosexual orientation is not already healed completely it is simply because the person does not have enough faith in God. Such simplistic "theological" interpretations are not supported by sound biblical exegesis. The first is excluded by the actual journeys of healing of many ex-gays and ex-lesbians. The second is excluded by many persons who have a very deep faith and prayer life, but who still experience same-sex attractions (Brown in Bradshaw, 2003, 142; and Harvey, 1992, 94; as well as parts of 2a above). Other views held by some, including some Christians, that are excluded by a proper understanding of experience and science are that the homosexual orientation is a simple choice or that one can simply will it away. Such views have led to some very unfair judgments.

It seems to me that a proper understanding of experience and science also excludes the revisionist or proportionalist view held by a number of theologians that same-sex genital acts can be moral in a committed loving same-sex partnership. Some who hold this view see such partnerships and genital acts as falling short of the ideal of heterosexual marriage, but as a "lesser evil" than sexual promiscuity or as morally good for proportionate reasons.(some of the authors summarized by Keenan, 2003). Commenting on such views, Fr. John Harvey says that some hold that for the sake of psychic intimacy "one may violate the physical structures [and inherent meanings] of heterosexual intercourse, as it is meant to be, a physical union of man and woman, through penetration of the vagina by the penis, and the pouring in of the seed of the man...This is *dualism*, i.e., the failure to recognize the essentially composite structure of the human person which makes the psychic and the physical inseparable"(1996, 104). This critique of Fr. Harvey, it seems to me, is supported not only by revelation but by sound natural moral law reasoning with regard to the purposes of human sexual relations. The profound unity of human beings, male and female, as embodied persons, is supported by good phenomenological descriptions of human experience (Wojtyla, 1979), as well as by the findings of neuroscience with regard to the profound links between mind and brain or body and soul (Jeeves 1997).

In *Veritatis Splendor* (1993, nn. 47–53), Pope John Paul responds to accusations that Catholic teachings on sexual ethics including homosexuality are "physicalist." With regard to this, he says in part:

> To call into question the permanent structural elements of man which are connected with his own bodily dimension would not only conflict with common experience, but would render meaningless *Jesus' reference to the "beginning,"* precisely where the social and cultural context of the time had distorted the primordial meaning and the role of certain moral norms (cf. Mt 19:1–9). This is the rea-

son why "the Church affirms that underlying so many changes, there are some things which do not change and are *ultimately founded upon Christ*, who is the same yesterday and today and for ever." Christ is the "Beginning" who, having taken on human nature, definitively illumines it in its constitutive elements and in its dynamism of charity towards God and neighbor (n. 53).

A number of experts in the area of homosexuality also think that the view that genital acts are justified in an "exclusive" same-sex partnership is naïve especially with regard to male couples who are almost never sexually exclusive in the long run.(see 2b above). Moreover, Satinover, a psychiatrist and expert in the area of homosexuality, argues that:

> ...abstinence is a precondition for successful change...[and healing. This is] one of the basic principles of psychodynamic psychotherapy...So long as people allow themselves the habitual, compulsive, self-soothing behavior...they will have an escape from the underlying emotional distress that prompts the repeated acting-out in the first place. When they give up the behavior...the distress remains...Only under these...conditions can they now acquire *alternative* means of dealing with the distress. They learn to turn to others or to God instead of alleviating the distress with alcohol, orgasm, or indeed any form of solipsistic, self-centered soothing.(1996, 198; this view is related to Satinover's view regarding "psychic trauma" and homosexuality summarized in 2a above).

This view of Satinover is confirmed by the experiences of many ex-gays and ex-lesbians who have experienced profound healing (Exodus International; and Portraits of Courage, 2001). As just one example, David Morrison had lived in a gay partnership for a number of years. When he first became a Christian, he accepted the arguments of "gay theology" and continued to be sexually active with his partner. When, however, he decided to surrender himself, including the sexual area of his life completely to Christ, he came to realize that the sexual acts with his partner were "not so much love as utility. Each made the other, with their consent, a means to an end. But that is not love. And it contrasts sharply with my experience after committing myself to chastity." To the surprise of himself and his former partner their friendship improved after they stopped having sex (1992 and 1999); and Portraits of Courage).

With regard to authentic unity and communion of persons, I agree with Dietrich von Hildebrand that this requires us to subordinate our seeking of the merely subjectively satisfying to morally relevant values such as the dignity of persons, justice, the sacredness of human life and procreation, truth, self-giving, and faithful love; this theme is found in many of his writings including his classic *Christian Ethics*; also, there is Aristotle's distinguishing "sense goods," which both humans and other animals pursue, and "rational goods" which humans as "rational animals" pursue. Then there is Aquinas' *bonum delectabile* and *bonum honestum*, as well as Pope John Paul II regarding "personal goods"(1993, n. 79). It seems to me that one can not choose same-sex genital acts and properly respect at the same time the full truth of the language of the human body, male and female, as well as the inherent total-giving/receiving and procreative meanings of human sexuality and related "personal goods."

In the light of the above, with regard to homosexuality we can, therefore, conclude that experience and science properly understood do not contradict Catholic teaching and pastoral practice (CDF, 1986). Rather, they can be fully integrated.

c) Experience and Science Can Contribute to a Balanced Pastoral Approach

It is beyond the scope of this paper to present all the ways that a proper understanding of experience and science with regard to homosexuality can contribute to a balanced pastoral approach that is consistent with correct doctrine (cf. Tit 2:1) and to the development of pastoral theology. For a fuller treatment than is possible here, see the writings of Fr. John Harvey (e.g., 1987 and 1996). He writes not only out of his own very good knowledge and understanding of Catholic teaching and moral theology, but also out of his many years of ministerial involvement with homosexual men and women and their families, as well as out of his wide reading of the relevant literature. In parts of his writings, Fr. Harvey provides a careful and balanced response to theologians who dissent from Catholic teaching and pastoral practice on homosexuality.

In the following, I intend only to outline briefly a number of pastoral recommendations in the light of a proper understanding of experience and of the science in this area. The main concern of the great pastor, St. Francis de Sales, was how to lead people to the love of God and to the following of Jesus Christ. I think this should be our main concern too in the area of homosexuality. For example, how can we help others, including persons with a homosexual orientation, to believe more deeply in a God of infinite love and to entrust or surrender themselves completely including the sexual dimension of their lives to God? In this regard, the experience of David Morrison (1996 and 1999, summarized above and here) is pertinent. When he was immersed in the gay lifestyle he was not convinced that his behavior was wrong by good arguments from Scripture, although he later came to appreciate the value of good biblical exegesis (see, e.g., Gagnon 2001) and theology. His pastor asked him to surrender his life, including in the sexual area, completely to God before he was baptized. After Morrison did this, he came to see for himself that his same-sex genital acts were not expressions of loving as Jesus loves, which includes taking up one's cross and following Jesus.

How can we help others to believe that if we love God, he will work out everything for the good? (see Rm 8:28). I believe this "everything" can include things such as the struggle with same-sex attraction. God can bring good even out of our past sins if we truly repent and turn to God (cf., e.g., the lives of the Apostle Paul, Augustine of Hippo, and many other saints).

I also agree with Pope John Paul II that although people generally grow morally in stages, both in understanding God's will for them and in incarnating it in their lives, this does not mean that we should promote a "gradualness" concerning God's moral law. All people are called to follow God's moral law, which includes the call to grow in holiness and in living the virtue of chastity (1981, n.34). How can we grow in the virtue of chastity ourselves and help others to do so? We must heed Matthew 7:1–5 and Luke 6:42, where Jesus teaches us to remove the log from one's own eye first, then we will see clearly to remove the speck from the eye of our brother, so that one can see better how to help others. People are often inspired to do good more by the humble good example of others than by words which can ring empty or hypocritical if the speaker is not trying to live what he or she advocates.

An insight of Jean Vanier, based on his experience of living for many years with people with mental disabilities while maintaining his faith in Jesus, I think, can be applied to homosexuality in an analogous way. Vanier thinks that persons with the greatest needs such as young children in a family and the mentally disabled, are in a certain sense the most important members of a community because they call others to grow in love, which is what is really most important. He considers pride to be the greatest handicap because it is the greatest obstacle to growing in love. Many people with a homosexual orientation, including many former gays and lesbians who are now Christians, say that many Christians and Christian communities have not responded to their needs very well (cf., e.g., some of the experiences shared in Portraits of Courage). If Christians treat homosexual men and women in a judgmental, condemnatory, homophobic, or indifferent way, this will tend to turn many of them away from the Church and the Christian community. If their basic human needs – for real love, friendship, to be profoundly respected and affirmed as valued persons (Note: genital relations are not a need of individuals but a need of the continuation of a species) – are not met in the Christian community, they will be tempted to look elsewhere.

We need to show persons with same-sex attractions real concrete care, warmth, and compassion; and listen to them and their experiences with genuine interest. This does not mean that we should agree with any sinful behavior, which would be sinful formal cooperation on our own part and would not really help them in any case. But by being real friends of homosexual men and women, by loving them as Jesus loves them, we can help them to turn to the Christian community and to God to have their needs for friendship and love met; and, if they are engaged in any sinful behaviors and/or unhealthy relationships, to become free of them. The issue of homosexuality is a major challenge for Christians today. Responding to this challenge properly can help us all to grow in love.

Growing in knowledge and a proper understanding of homosexuality, including the related science and human experience, can help one to respond to the needs of others in this area more sensitively, compassionately, and effectively. For example, knowing something about the complexity of the related science and experience can help one to avoid making erroneous statements, to speak in a more balanced way, and to correct some of the more common erroneous claims and misconceptions about homosexuality. Among other things, this can help to remove certain obstacles for some people in the way of accepting the Good News of Jesus Christ and Catholic moral teaching and pastoral practice in this area. Having a good knowledge and understanding in this area can help us to provide others with the relevant information they may need to form their consciences properly and to have free and informed consent. Depending on the person's needs, this can include such things as: accurate information on Catholic teaching; the science, including the possibility of change, healing, and/or prevention (Note: these need to be presented in a realistic way without hiding the difficulties and noting that psychological healing in this life is often incomplete); and their options including the availability of good therapists, Christian ministries, resources and support groups such as Exodus International, Homosexuals Anonymous, Courage and Encourage.(for a good evaluation of some of these, see relevant parts of Harvey, 1987 and 1996).

We can also note here that many people with same-sex attractions prefer not to be categorized as "homosexual." There is so much more to a person than this aspect. It is better to "identify" as a person created in the image of God, a brother or sister of Jesus, and so forth (Nicolosi and Medinger in Harvey and Bradley, 2003, 25–32 and 170–89). In this sensitive area, we need to be careful not only that what we say is true but also that our choice of language is helpful.

In line with the overarching theme of this convention, which the speakers are addressing in various ways, we also need to all support wholesome and healthy family life. With regard to the divisiveness of the issue of homosexuality in society and among Christians (Part 1 above, last paragraph), we who are Christians, followers of Jesus, should try to do our part to contribute to the building of true unity. Among other things we can do this by joining in Jesus prayer (see Jn 17:21), and by our own continued conversion and growth in loving God and all people as Jesus loves them and in living the Christian virtues. We can also build unity by making ourselves one with others as Jesus did. Consider how God in Jesus in the Incarnation made himself one with us in all things except sin. With regard to this, consider also how the Apostle Paul made himself "all things to all people" that he might "by all means save some...for the sake of the gospel..."(1 Cor 9:22–23 NRSV). Today many people in various Christian denominations also find the writings of Chiara Lubich helpful; they provide many insights on building unity. The following prayer by St. Francis of Assisi has also provided inspiration for many:

> Lord, make me an instrument of your peace; Where there is hatred, let me sow love; Where there is injury, pardon; Where there is discord, unity; Where there is doubt, faith; Where there is error, truth; Where there is despair, hope; Where there is sadness, joy; Where there is darkness, light. O Divine Master, Grant that I may not so much seek to be consoled, as to console; to be understood, as to understand; to be loved as to love. For it is in giving that we receive. It is in pardoning that we are pardoned. It is in dying that we are born to Eternal Life.

Conclusion

In this paper, I have attempted with regard to homosexuality to address the question: "How relevant are experience and science with regard to theology and pastoral practice?" I realize that much more could be said on this topic. Nevertheless, within the space limits of this paper and its three parts, I have tried to offer some real contributions in response to this whole general question. I think it is a very relevant question today. Besides what is already written by others that is relevant to responding to the question, I hope that more contributions will be made to developing a fuller response.

Paul Flaman teaches moral and spiritual theology, including classes in bioethics and the theology of human sexuality and marriage, at St. Joseph's College in Edmonton, Alberta, Canada, an institution affiliated with the University of Alberta. He co-teaches an interdisciplinary course, "Neuroscience, the Person, and Christian Theology," which received a 2001 Templeton Science and Religion award. He holds an S.T.B. (1979), and S.T.L. (1981), and an S.T.D. (1985) from the Pontifical University of St. Thomas Aquinas in Rome (Angelicum). His publications include various articles and two books: *Genetic Engineering, Christian Values, and Catholic Teaching* (Paulist Press, 2002) and *Family Unity: A Christian Perspective* (St. Peter's Press, Sask., 1986). He is married to the former Maggie MacPhee and they have three adopted children.

References

American Psychological Association website, "Lesbian and Gay Parenting," by Charlotte J. Patterson with link to "Empirical Studies on Lesbian and Gay Parenting." Retrieved 7 Nov. 2003 from www.apa.org/pi/parent.html

Besen, Wayne R.(2003). *Anything but Straight: Unmasking the Scandals and Lies Behind the Ex-Gay Myth.* New York: Harrington Park Press.

Blumstein, P., and P. Schwartz. (1983). *American Couples: Money, Work and Sex.* New York: William Murren and Company Inc.

Bradshaw, Timothy, ed. (2003) *The Way Forward? Christian Voices on Homosexuality and the Church* (Second Edition), London: SCM Press.

Brodner, Wanda, Ph.D., in Christian Counseling (2003). Personal conversation.

Caramagno, Thomas C. (2002). *Irreconcilable Differences: Intellectual Stalemate in the Gay Rights Debate.* Wesport, CT: Praeger Publishers.

[CCCB] Canadian Conference of Catholic Bishops (2003, Sept. 10), "Marriage in the Present Day," Ottawa: Author.

[CDF] Congregation for the Doctrine of the Faith (1986, Nov. 13), "The Pastoral Care of Homosexual Persons," *Origins: NC Documentary Service*, Vol. 16, No. 22, 377–82.

[CDF] Congregation for the Doctrine of the Faith (1987, Mar. 19), "Instruction on Respect for Human Life in Its Origin and on the Dignity of Procreation," *Origins: NC Documentary Service*, Vol. 16, No. 40, 697–711.

[CDF] Congregation for the Doctrine of the Faith (2003, June 3), "Considerations Regarding Proposals to Give Legal Recognition to Unions Between Homosexual Persons." English translation available from the Vatican website: www.vatican.va.

Cere, Dan; and Farrow, Douglas (2003, June 18), "Don't Kiss off Marriage" (A defense of the traditional definition of marriage signed by a number of university professors, family experts, and representatives of a number of different Christian denominations and religions), *Toronto Globe and Mail Update*. Retrieved 4 June 2004 from www.globeandmail.com.

[CMA] Catholic Medical Association (2004, retrieved Jan. 5), *Homosexuality and Hope*, statement online: www.cathmed.org.

Court of Appeal for Ontario (2003, June 10), *Halpern v. Attorney General of Canada* [re same-sex marriage]. Retrieved www.canlii.org/on/cas/onca/2003/2003onca10314.html.

Dailey, Timothy, Ph.D. (2003), "Homosexual Parenting: Putting Children at Risk (2003). Retrieved 3 Nov. 2003 from <www.frc.org>.

Dailey, Timothy, Ph.D. (2004), "Comparing the Lifestyles of Homosexual Couples to Married Couples." Retrieved 17 Sept. 2004 from <www.frc.org>.

[ELCIC] Bishops of the Evangelical Lutheran Church in Canada (2003, July), A Pastoral Letter on Same Sex Marriage; and a Letter to the Bishops by a Number of Pastors (2003, Aug.). I received copies of these documents from the Lutheran chaplain at the University of Alberta.

Exodus International. For more information on this umbrella organization which promotes "Freedom from homosexuality through the power of Jesus Christ," see their website: <www.exodus-international.org>.

Family Research Council. For more information on this pro-family center, see their website: <www.frc.org>.

Gagnon, Robert (2001), *The Bible and Homosexual Practise: Texts and Hermeneutics*. Abingdon. For a good summary, see his interview on <www.zenit.org> 21 and 28 March 2002.

Hamer, Dean et al. (1993, July 16), "A Linkage between DNA Markers on the X-chromosome and Male Sexual Orientation," *Science*, Vol. 261, No. 5119, 321–27.

Harvey, John (1987). *The Homosexual Person: New Thinking in Pastoral Care*. San Francisco: Ignatius Press.

Harvey, John (1992, Sept.). "Sexual Abstinence for the Homosexual Person," *Fellowship of Catholic Scholars Newsletter*, 92–94.

Harvey, John (1996). *The Truth About Homosexuality*. San Francisco: Ignatius Press.

Harvey, John; and Gerard Bradley; eds. (2003). *Same-Sex Attraction: A Parent's Guide*. South Bend: St. Augustine's Press.

Jeeves, Malcolm A. (1997), *Human Nature at the Millenium: Reflections on the Integration of Psychology and Christianity*. Grand Rapids: Baker Books.

John Paul II (1979), Apostolic Constitution on Ecclesiastical Universities and Faculties, *Sapientia Cristiana*. English translation available from the Vatican website: <www.vatican.va>.

John Paul II (1981). Apostolic Exhortation on the Role of the Christian Family in the Modern World, *Familiaris Consortio*. Ottawa: Canadian Conference of Catholic Bishops.

John Paul II (1990), Apostolic Constitution on Catholic Universities *Ex Corde Ecclesiae*. English translation available from the Vatican website: <www.vatican.va>.

John Paul II (1993). Encyclical Letter Regarding Certain Fundamental Questions of the Church's Moral Teaching, *Veritatis Splendor*, Ottawa: Canadian Conference of Catholic Bishops.

John Paul II (1996), "Message to Pontifical Academy of Sciences on Evolution," *Origens: CNS Documentary Service,* Vol. 26, No. 25, 414–16.

John Paul II (1997), *The Theology of the Body: Human Love in the Divine Plan*. Boston: Pauline Books & Media.

Keenan, James F., S.J. (2003), "The Open Debate: Moral Theology and the Lives of Gay and Lesbian Persons," *Theological Studies* 64, 127–50.

Kirkey, Sharon (2000, Oct. 26), "Ethicist Questions Wisdom of Gay Couples Having Children," *Edmonton Journal*. The ethicist featured is Margaret Somerville, a founding director of McGill University's Centre for Medicine, Ethics and Law.

Knight, Robert H.; and Daniel S. Garcia (2001), "Homosexual Parenting: Bad for Children, Bad for Society," Washington, D.C.: Family Research Council.

Laumann, E., R. Michael, J. Gagnon and S. Michaels. (1994), *The Social Organization of Sexuality: Sexual Practices in the United States.* Chicago: The University of Chicago Press.

LeVay, Simon (1991, Aug. 30), "A Difference in Hypothalamic Structure between Heterosexual and Homosexual Men," *Science*, New Series, Vol. 253, No. 5023, 1034–37.

Linn, Matthew; and Dennis Linn (1978), *Healing Life's Hurts: Healing Memories Through Five Stages of Forgiveness*, New York: Paulist Press.

Lofton, Steve; and Roger Croteau (2004, Sept. 20), "The Lofton-Croteau Family." Retrieved from <www.lethimstay.com/loftons.html>.

Looy, Heather (1995), "Born Gay? A Critical Review of Biological Research on Homosexuality," *Journal of Psychology and Christianity*, Vol. 14, No. 3, 197–214.

Lubich, Chiara. For more information on her writings as well as the writings by some others on building unity today see <www.newcitypress.com> and <www.focolare.org>.

[MCC] Metropolitan Community Churches website: <www.mcc-church.org>.

Morrison, David (1996, Oct. 26), "Love that Speaks Its Name," *The Tablet*, 1390.

Morrison, David (1999), *Beyond Gay,* Huntington: Our Sunday Visitor.

[NARTH] National Association for Research and Therapy of Homosexuality (2004). There are many articles on their website: <www.narth.com>. This site has a good search engine so in the text I have referred to each article only by author and title. All the articles from this site that are referred to in this paper were retrieved in 2004.

Nicolosi, Joseph, Ph.D., and Linda Ames Nicolosi (2002), *A Parent's Guide to Preventing Homosexuality.* Downers Grove: InterVarsity Press.

Olyan, Saul M., and Martha C. Nussbaum (1998). *Sexual Orientation and Human Rights in American Religious Discourse,* New York: Oxford University Press.

Pius XII (1950), Encyclical *Humani Generis*, in *The Church Teaches: Documents of the Church in English Translation*, prepared by John Clarkson et al. Rockford: TAN Books and Publishers, Inc.

Polkinghorne, John (1998), *Science and Theology: An Introduction*, Minneapolis: Fortress Press.

Portraits of Courage videos (2001). Part 1: Into the Light; and Part 2: The Cry of the Faithful. New York: Courage Ministries. Produced by Fr. John Harvey.

Satinover, Jeffrey, M.D. (1996), *Homosexuality and the Politics of Truth,* Grand Rapids: Baker Books.

Spitzer, Robert (2003, Oct.), "Can Some Gay Men and Lesbians Change Their Sexual Orientation? 200 Participants Reporting a Change from Homosexual to Heterosexual Orientation"; and "Reply: Study Results Should not be Dismissed and Justify Further Research on the Efficacy of Sexual Reorientation Therapy," *Archives of Sexual Behavior,* Vol. 32, No. 5, 403–417 and 469–472.

Sprigg, Peter (2004), *Outrage: How Gay Activists and Liberal Judges Are Trashing Democracy to Redefine Marriage.* Washington, D.C.: Regnery Publishing, Inc.

Swenson, Don, Ph.D. (2004), "Same Sex Marriage: Biosocial and Sociological Refelections," Power Point presentation and references sent to me by email.

[USC] United Church of Canada (2003, retrieved Nov. 4). "Chronology of Marriage and Equality Rights in the United Church of Canada," 2000. Retrieved 4 Nov. 2003 from <www.united-church.ca>.

[USCCB] United States Conference of Catholic Bishops (2003, Nov. 12), "Between Man and Woman: Questions and Answers About Marriage and Same-Sex Unions," Washington, D.C.: Author.

Vanier, Jean. In 1964 he founded *L'Arche,* an international organization which provides homes and community for people with mental disabilities. He has published several books, including *Man and Woman: He Made Them* (New York: Paulist Press, 1984); and *Becoming Human* (New York: Paulist Press, 1998).

Von Balthasar, Hans Urs (2000), *Theo-Logic, Vol. 1 Truth of the World,* San Francisco: Ignatius Press.

Wojtyla, Karol (1979), *The Acting Person,* Boston: D. Reidel Publishing Company.

Chapter 15: The Human Family as a Type of the Family of the Trinity:
An Analysis of the Seven-Fold Family of God

KELLY BOWRING, S.T.D.

Introduction

There are obvious comparisons between the human family of father, mother, and child and God's divine Family of Father, Son, and Holy Spirit. While the Holy Trinity is not literally a father, mother, and child humanly speaking, this analogy is a profound insight into the relation between the human family and the Family of the Trinity. This analogy in comparing the human family with the divine Family expresses a deep spiritual insight, one I will pursue further through speculative theology, discussing herein the *seven-fold* Family of God in stages, corresponding to the three-fold work of the Triune God in the sacramental economy, namely, creation, redemption and sanctification (see the corresponding chart which highlights this discussion with diagrams).

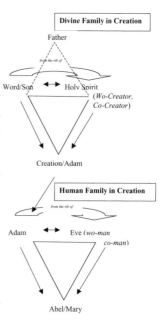

The Divine Work of Creation

1. The Human Family in Creation: A Type of the Family of God

As the Holy Trinity is a community of Persons united in love, the human family of father, mother, and children is also a communion of persons united in a biological union of love. In the spiritual, allegorical sense (cf. *Catechism of the Catholic Church* 117), the human family was from the beginning intended by God to be a sign and type of the Trinity. The Book of Genesis lays the foundation for this allegory. First, the Three Persons of God created man "in [Their] image, after [Their] likeness…male and female He created them" (Gen 1:26–27). God created man and woman in His image and likeness; and in His image and likeness, He created man as man and woman. Neither human person alone was able to fully image God. God endowed the two with a distinct and complementary sexuality so that Adam and Eve could love each other as God the Father and God the Son love Each Other.

Adam and Eve together in their communion, with the fruitful potentiality of offspring, constitute the full image of the Trinity. They are created, distinct in their sexuality, for one another. According to the Congregation for the Doctrine of the Faith: "From the very beginning therefore, humanity is described as articulated in the male-female relationship. This is the humanity, sexually differentiated, which is explicitly declared 'the image of God'…his capacity to love – reflection and image of God who is Love – is disclosed in the spousal character of the body, in which the masculinity or femininity of the person is expressed…From the first moment of their creation, man and woman are distinct, and will remain so for all eternity."[1]

Man and woman were made for love; they exist "for the other," both in covenant with God and in relation with each other (cf. CCC 357). John Paul II summarizes this two-fold communion in *Mulieris Dignitatem*:

> The fact that man "created as man and woman" is the image of God means not only that each of them individually is like God, as a rational and free being. It also means that man and woman, created as a "unity of the two" in their common humanity, are called to live in a communion of love, and in this way to mirror in the world the communion of love that is in God, through which the Three Persons love each other in the intimate mystery of the one divine life. This "unity of the two," which is a sign of interpersonal communion, shows that the creation of man is also marked by a certain likeness to the divine communion (*communio*).[2]

The pope continues elsewhere: "It is this sublime and fundamental truth concerning the human person – created male and female in the image and likeness of God – which constitutes the immutable basis for all other anthropological truths."[3] To clarify here, it is not in their sexuality itself that they are in God's image, but in the unitive *and* generative component of their sexuality, as Genesis discusses.

God commands Adam and Eve to "be fruitful and multiply" (Gen 1:28); in other words, to procreate, thus cooperating and participating in the divine creative power, so as to have a child, and thus to become a triune family of love, a living reflection of the Trinity. In their love for each other, God calls them not only to be unitive and thus to become one, but He also calls them to be always open to fruitful, generative offspring that is in character procreative, even if there are in some cases non-behavioral conditions that do not allow for conception. As one theologian puts it: "The body in its masculinity and femininity has a nuptial meaning – the capacity to express love. This consummate communion, expressed most completely in the one-flesh union, constituted original happiness. God blessed this communion with the gift of a child."[4] Genesis reveals that Adam and Eve had children, and that as they were created in God's image, so too, their children were begotten in Adam's image and likeness as well (Gen 5:3).

In co-operating with God's plans, Adam and Eve became an earthly image of His eternal Triune communion of love. John Paul remarks in his 1994 "Letter to Families," writing that:

> Human fatherhood and motherhood, while remaining biologically similar to that of other living beings in nature, contain in an essential and unique way a "likeness" to God which is the basis of the family as a community of human life, as a community of persons united in love (*communio personarum*). In the light of the New Testament it is possible to discern how the primordial model of the family is to be sought in God himself in the Trinitarian mystery of His life. The divine "We" is the eternal pattern of the human "we," especially of that "we" formed by the man and the woman created in the divine image and likeness.[5]

Thus, as Father, Son and Holy Spirit are united in the Family of God in eternity, so likewise Adam, Eve and Abel – Cain notwithstanding – as the original human family, are a type of the Triune God's reflection and image within creation. Scott Hahn summarizes: "The Trinity is the eternal and original covenant family. As Pope John Paul II writes: 'God in His deepest mystery is not a solitude, but a family, since He has in Himself fatherhood, sonship, and the essence of the family, which is love.'"[6] God is Three in Union – the Lover, the Beloved, and Love, as Fulton Sheen describes Him, a communion of love, Each existing eternally for the Others.

In the divine creation and guidance of humanity from the beginning, there was a two-step process in establishing marital union and offspring in the divine image. First the Lord God created Eve from Adam's rib, and then He intended that the first parents would enter into union with each other (and with Him) in love, and that their love would bear the fruit of a child. Genesis states that God "caused a deep sleep to fall upon the man, and while he slept took one of his ribs and closed up its place with flesh; and the rib which the Lord God had taken from the man he made into a woman" (Gen 2:21–22) to be a vital helper, partner, and lifelong companion fit for him. Scripture tells us that the reason she is called *woman* is because "she was taken out of Man" (Gen 2:23). First, Eve comes forth from Adam's rib, and then she becomes his wife. She was first conceived from his body, then he entered into union with her, and together they became one flesh. The Hebrew word for *flesh* is "*basar*," which here means *the male sexual organ* united in sexual union with the woman, and the oneness of their flesh with the fruit of a child. This word implies first, a personal union; second, a sexual act; and third, a child. This three-fold meaning of *one flesh* cannot be separated, as magisterially confirmed in Pope Paul VI's encyclical *Humanae Vitae, On Human Life*.

In creating man and woman in His image and likeness, God endowed them with sexuality so that *through the use of their sexual faculties* in covenantal union, they would become a communion of persons; and, in forming a family, would become the likeness of the Triune God Himself. The principal reason God created the two sexes is because man and woman, "created as a 'unity of the two' in their common humanity, are called to live in a communion of love, and in this way to mirror in the world the communion of love that is in God."[7] God first formed Eve from Adam's body, then Adam entered into union with her, and together they became one flesh. Their procreative union of love then bore fruit in the form of a child.

Eve's relationship with Adam is thus bi-relational. Her relationship with Adam entails both a *conception from* (Eve conceived from Adam's rib, or man from man) and a generative/procreative interpersonal *communion with* (Adam and Eve becoming husband and wife). In the first instance, the prefix *wo* is attached to *man* to designate that she came from him, thus being called *wo-man* ("*ish*" – man, and "*isha*" – woman, in Hebrew, from root words which mean "strong" and "delicate"). In the second, for the sake of our discussion, we will attach the prefix *co* to *man* to designate that she then entered into co-union, or communion (*communio*), with him, thus being in relationship with Adam as *co-man* (woman joined together with the man). In this two-step process, Eve is both *wo-man* and *co-man* in relation with Adam.

2. The Divine Family in the Work of Creation

As we continue to examine an analysis of family in relation to the Trinity, we will utilize this *wo-* and *co-* bi-relational analogy in regard to the divine work of creation itself. Creation was the work of the Triune God, particularly of the Word and the Spirit. The *Catechism* explains: "In the beginning was the Word...and the Word was God...all things were made through him...The New Testament reveals that God created everything by the eternal Word, his beloved Son...The Church's faith likewise confesses the creative action of the Holy Spirit, the 'giver of life,' 'the Creator Spirit'...The Old Testament suggests and the New Covenant reveals the creative action of the Son and the Spirit, inseparably one with that of the Father...The universe [was] created in and by the eternal Word" (CCC 291–2, 299). The Father creates all things through the Word (John 1:3, 10). For John says, "In Him was life" (John 1:4), as if to say He is the source of life with the Father. John states that the children of God are born from the Word of God (John 1:12–13). This may be understood in a natural sense in creation and in a spiritual sense in the Redemption.

But as the Word does not work alone with the Father in the work of creation, so too is creation the work of the Holy Spirit, as, again, the *Catechism* discusses: "The Word of God *and* his Breath are at the origin of the being and life of every creature" (CCC 703). In this context, the Word of God is the impetus of creation, while He unites with the Spirit, the latter Who comes forth from the Word, figuratively as His "rib." In this, the Holy Spirit proceeds from the Word, together with the Father, as Eve first came from Adam, also by the power of the Father. In the work of creation, the Word and the Breath of God, as God's two Hands, act in union to bring forth the offspring of all of creation, particularly Adam. M. J. Sheeben explains: "As Eve can, in a figurative sense, be called simply the rib of Adam, since she was formed from the rib of Adam, St. Methodius goes so far as to assert that the Holy Spirit is the *costa Verbi*...'By the rib,' says St. Methodius, 'we rightly understand the Paraclete, the Spirit of truth...[is] quite properly called the rib of the *Logos*.'"[8]

In this sense, the Spirit is *Wo-Creator* proceeding from the Creator Word, with the Father, and as well, then *Co-Creator*, in union with the divine Word in the work of creation. From this bi-relational union of both the Word with the Holy Spirit and of Adam with Eve, God's family in creation has its origins and existence. This two-leveled family is also paralleled by the Family of God in the work of the Incarnation and Redemption, and on three distinct levels. We will now discuss these next three levels of the Family of God in more detail, and the two-layered typology of *wo-man* and *co-man* in particular.

The Divine Work of Redemption

3. The Family of God in Eternity

The original human family resembles the eternal divine Family of the Father, the Son, and the Holy Spirit. God's Son, the Word, has eternally come forth from the Father, as similarly, Eve came forth from Adam in time. Church teaching from the Council of Toledo (675 A.D.) states: "The Son was born, but not made, from the substance of the Father, without beginning, before all ages."[9] As the first woman came forth from the rib of Adam, so too similarly is God the Word eternally generated from the Father God, and thus He came forth from the Father. In comparison with *wo-man* (man from man), we may refer to the Son as *Wo-God* (God from God). The Council of Toledo, again, states: "We must believe that the Son is (eternally) begotten or born, not from nothing or from any other substance, but *from the womb of the Father*,"[10] which is here analogous to His "rib." Thus, as Eve is man (in the general sense of being human) from the man Adam, so too the Son is God from the Father God.

Likewise, as Adam and Eve are equal in dignity, so too in all things the Father and the Son are equal; and They are one in Being, the same except in the distinction of their relation. In this analysis, the *wo-man* and the *Wo-God* are parallel, such that Eve is a type of the Word of God.

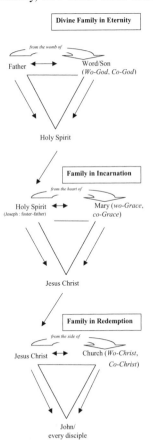

Perhaps a digression is in order here. In investigating the analogy between Eve and the divine Son, this does not mean that the Word, as *Wo-God*, is understood literally in a human feminine way. It is important to remember the comparison here is *allegorical* and not literal, and that while some things are alike in allegory, many things remain unalike. In His divinity, God is Spirit; He belongs to the numinous – a category of supernatural being that transcends the material realm of creation, though He is at the same time immanent in creation. He encompasses *both* the masculine and feminine qualities of man in His divine nature. The *Catechism* clarifies: "…we must humbly cleanse our hearts of certain false images drawn 'from this world.'…The purification of our hearts has to do with paternal or maternal images, stemming from our personal and cultural history, and influencing our relationship with God. God our Father transcends the categories of the created world. To impose our own ideas in this area "upon him" would be to fabricate idols to adore or pull down" (CCC 2779).

Returning to our discussion, we have seen how the parallel between the first woman and the Word is allegorical. We have already discussed how Eve is from Adam (*wo-man*) in a similar way as the Word is from the Father (*Wo-God*). Let us now go to the next step in our analogy. While Adam and Eve, as man and *co-man*, enter into union to conceive Abel, so too, the Father and the Son, as God and *Co-God*, have from eternity existed in spousal-like love, and with this, have eternally spirated the Holy Spirit as the fruit of Their love for Each Other. To analyze this comparison further, first Eve came forth from Adam, and then, they entered into generative union, albeit in a sexually procreative way. And by their union, Adam and Eve brought forth Abel. In an allegorical way in relation to God, the Son too came forth from the Father from eternity, and They are eternally in union. And by Their divine union, the Father and the Son bring forth, though in a non-sexual way, the Holy Spirit in an eternal spiration of love. Thus the human child Abel is a type of the Holy Spirit in the first level of the Family of God.

There are a couple other dimensions of this analogy that would benefit from explanation here. First, the Father is the sole origin of the Son *and* the Holy Spirit[11] in like manner as Adam is the sole human originator, via monogenism, of the whole human race;[12] secondly, the Holy Spirit eternally proceeds from the Father *and* the Son (*Filioque*), and from *both* at once, as Their uncreated Love-Gift and as the personal expression of Their Self-giving Love. In regard to this second dimension, so too does the unitive and procreative love between Adam and Eve imitate the love of the Father and the Son, such that nine months later they, having united together, give the fruit of their love a name as a separate child.

In a fuller sense, we may also say that in varying degrees every family, and most fully the Holy Family, is a living sign of the divine Family. It may be interesting to note here that in most traditional marriages, the woman upon marrying her husband, takes his name as her own, signifying her new identity or her new life born from him, as a *wo-man* from her husband, at the same moment she becomes *co-man* in union with him. And the children to come from this "one flesh" are also one in the body with this family, all sharing the same last name of the husband/father, the origin of the family. The wife, in her unique charism of receptivity, having a unique *capacity to accept the other*, "makes the tastes of her husband her own, she gives way to his habits, adopts his ways, even his thoughts…And her children bear the features of one and the other."[13] Thus, the human family of father, mother, and child is in allegorical relation to divine Family of God, of the Father, the Son, and the Holy Spirit.

4. The Family of God in the Incarnation

As I have discussed, the fruit of the love of the Father and the Son, Who is the Holy Spirit, is analogous to a child in a human family. Taking our discussion to the next level, within the human family, as the boy grows to adulthood, he becomes a candidate for marital husband/fatherly love himself, such that the cycle of family life continues to a new level, to the next generation. Thus, in our discussion, Abel the child-son in the first generation family potentially becomes Abel the husband-father in the second generation, on down to the Blessed Virgin Mary. So too then, the Holy Spirit *allegorically* takes on the role of child-become-husband-become-father in this generational level of the Family of God. Within this level, the Holy Spirit, as the eternal "uncreated Immaculate Conception" (St. Maximilian Kolbe), unites Himself with Mary, the "created Immaculate Conception," from the first instance of her existence. Mary is both the natural, biological, human child of Sts. Ann and Joachim and, in some mysterious way, the created one in the fullness of grace by the power of the Holy Spirit, from His "heart" of grace and love spiritually speaking, or better still, from His "rib" allegorically speaking. Here it is important to maintain that in Mary's relationship with the Holy Spirit, her human nature and person remains totally distinct from the Holy Spirit, as in the case with any two spouses who become one while remaining distinct. With her life-long, perpetual *fiat* of humility and obedient love, Mary was perpetually full of the gratuitous gift of the

Holy Spirit's grace and love. As "Max Thurian affirmed, immaculate conception means that in Mary everything is grace from the beginning."[14]

While the Holy Spirit is the *divine* Personification of Grace, so too, by association, Mary is the *human* personification and quasi-incarnation of grace, or *wo-Grace* (created grace from uncreated Grace) as Luke 1:28 describes her at the Annunciation. M. J. Sheeben speaks of Mary being the "rib" of the Spirit in this way: "Mary is the *organ* of the Holy Spirit, who works in her in the same way that Christ's humanity is the instrument of the *Logos*."[15] St. Maximilian Kolbe agrees: "The Holy Spirit is in Mary after the fashion, one might say, in which the Second Person of the Blessed Trinity, the Word, is in his humanity. There is, of course, this difference: in Jesus there are two natures, divine and human, but one single person who is God. Mary's nature and person are totally distinct from the nature and person of the Holy Spirit. Still, their union is so inexpressible, and so perfect that the Holy Spirit acts only by the *Immaculata*, his spouse."[16] She is one with the Spirit, Whom she is part of, through her mysterious Immaculate Conception.

Mary is not only perpetually full of grace by the Holy Spirit from her conception; she is also invited to enter into generative, though non-sexually procreative, communion with Grace Himself to become spiritually the spouse of the Holy Spirit, as *co-Grace* (Mary in union with the Holy Spirit). In this level of the Family of God, the Holy Spirit enters into union with Mary such that they together bring forth offspring, the Incarnation of the God-Man, Jesus Christ. Thus, by the power and spiritual "fatherhood" of the Holy Spirit and through the biological maternity of Mary, the Word-became-Man is both Mary's Child while also remaining *Wo-God* Himself. Through the spiritually unitive and procreative love of the Spirit and His Bride (cf. Rev 22:17), the Father's Son became the Son of Mary (Son of Man). In this, Mary truly is the Daughter of the Father, Spouse of the Holy Spirit, Mother of the Son, and as we will discuss, Handmaid of the Church.

Another digression is offered here. While the unitive spousal love of the husband and wife is well established, the filial unitive love of the parents with their child deserves some consideration here. Is not the Holy Spirit united to the Father as the Son is, and to both equally as They are to Each Other? Certainly this is so as we profess Three Persons in the One Being of God. So too then is the child of the human family united to his parents, in another form of *co-* relationship, one that is unitive without being sexual (generative and procreative). In this second level of the Family of God, this point is clear in Mary's relation with her Son,

Jesus. Mary is one with her Spouse the Holy Spirit in the Incarnation, but she is also one with her Son in the Redemption, as *co-llaborator* with Christ in the Redemption. As a type of Eve, Mary is the New Eve, such that St. Jerome stated: "Death through Eve, life through Mary." While Eve was the *co-peccatrix* (female who is one with the sinner Adam) in the Original Sin, which upset and darkened God's original plan for the couple and family but did not abrogate it altogether, Mary is the *co-redemptrix* (female who is one with the Redeemer) in the work of Redemption.[17] St. Albert the Great discusses how Mary is united with her Son such that she too suffers a *co-passion* with His Passion:

> To [Mary] alone was given this privilege, namely, a communi-
> cation in the Passion; to her the Son willed to communicate the
> merit of the Passion, in order that He could give her the reward; and
> in order to make her a sharer in the benefit of Redemption. He
> willed that she be a sharer in the penalty of the Passion, in so far as
> she might become the Mother of all through re-creation even as she
> was the adjutrix of the Redemption by her *co-passion*. And just as
> the whole world is bound to God by His supreme Passion, so also
> it is bound to the Lady of all by her *co-passion*.[18]

Thus, Mary is both Spouse of the Holy Spirit and Mother of the Son, both together in an inseparable co-union of love with the Father.

5. The Family of God in the Redemption

As we progress to the next generational level of the Family of God, here, the divine Child of the previous level of God's Family grows up to become the Bridegroom at this generational level. Within the history of salvation, the Christ Child grew to adulthood and then entered into spir-itual union with His Offspring-become-Bride the Church, and together they begot children in love. This marriage of Christ and the Church is, according to St. Paul in Ephesians, "a great mystery" (5:32). St. Ambrose describes this relationship as follows:

> The Holy Church is immaculate in her marital union, fruitful in
> her births and virgin in her chastity, notwithstanding the children
> she generates. Therefore, we are born of a virgin, who conceived
> not by the power of man but by the power of the Spirit. We are born
> of a virgin not in physical pain but in the jubilation of the angels.
> Our virgin nourishes us not with milk from the body but with that
> of which the Apostle speaks, when he says that he nursed, in their
> tender age, the adolescent people of God.

> What married woman has more children than the Church? She
> is virgin by the holiness she receives in the sacraments and mother
> of peoples. Her fruitfulness is attested also by Scripture, which
> says: "For more numerous are the children of the deserted wife
> than the children of her who has a husband" (Isaiah 54:1; Galatians
> 4:27). Our mother does not have a man, but a spouse, because *both
> the Church in the peoples as well as the soul of each
> individual...are married to the Word of God* as to an eternal
> spouse.[19]

At the moment of the fullness of time, Jesus exchanged covenantal vows with His Bride the Church at the Last Supper (cf. Mt 26:28) and spiritually consummated (cf. Jn 19:30) with her from the Cross, so that she would be His Witness to the ends of the earth. This covenantal union of marital love is now renewed until the end of time at every Mass through the co-union of Eucharistic Holy Communion. Scott Hahn confirms, stating: "The Eucharist is the sacrament of the consummation of the marriage between Christ and his Church."[20]

As Eve came forth from Adam, the Son from the eternal Father, and Mary from the Holy Spirit, St. Augustine sees the Bride of Christ, the Church, coming forth from Jesus' side (rib) while He slept on the Cross, through the Centurion's lance: "Here was opened the door of life, from which the sacraments of the Church have flowed out... Here the second Adam with bowed head slept upon the cross, that thence a wife might be formed of him, flowing from his side while he slept."[21] The CDF agrees, stating: "This messianic wedding (of Christ with humanity) is accomplished on the Cross,"[22] and the whole Christian life is essentially the living out of this nuptial mystery. Thus, as Eve is *wo-man*, the Spirit is *Wo-Creator*, the Word is *Wo-God*, and Mary is *wo-Grace*, so too the Church is *Wo-Christ* (Mystical Body of Christ from Christ) in this level of the Family of God.

Tradition refers to the Church as the Body of Christ. This may be understood here in two ways. First, the Church is the Body of Christ through the Lord's spiritual conception of *her* as *Wo-Christ*, as already discussed. Second, Paul's First Epistle to the Corinthians declares that a wife's body belongs to her husband (7:4) and visa versa, so that in this allegory, the Church's Body belongs to the Lord as His own Body. Thus, the Church, as the Body of Christ, is also, through a mystical marital communion, *Co-Christ*; she is one with and yet distinct from Christ. Jesus "in a certain sense [entered] into a mystical marriage with the whole human race,"[23] according to Leo XIII, expressing what took place at the Incarnation (and Redemption). In a certain sense, the whole human race together, and each person individually, make up the Spouse of Christ, the Church. For as St. Augustine said: "All men are one man in Christ." Through the unitive and spiritually generative love of Jesus and His Bride the Church, they together generate "child" disciples, new creatures in Christ and His Church through Baptism. This is represented by the Apostle John at the foot of the Cross when Jesus stated to Mary His Mother, "Woman, behold your son!" (Jn 19:26). On the literal level, the *woman* is Mary (in relation also to Gen 3:15, Jn 2:4, and Rev 12:1); and on the allegorical level, the woman is also the Church, the mystical Bride of Christ; and the *son* is not only John, but also every disciple of Christ.

Those who receive Baptism are re-born into God's Family of love as both the children of God and the children of the Church. The *Catechism* states, "Becoming a disciple of Jesus means accepting the invitation to belong to *God's family*" (CCC 2233). As disciples of Christ, we declare, not only to Mary, but also to the Church, "Behold, [our] Mother"!

The analysis of the Family of God as has been analyzed here is one that is not segregated or dissected, but is instead united and layered, such that together all the levels make up only one Family of God. The various triangles representing each bi-relational *wo-* and *co-* relationship, with corresponding mutual offspring, should only appear to be superimposed on one another to the point where they seem to be undistinguishable, but are in reality distinct and without confusion, forming one tri-united, multi-layered matrix, in a way reflective of the unity and diversity proper to God. Our relationship is with Each Person of God and with All at once. So too are there various layers of the Family of God, though only one Family of God. This explains why Jesus is both our Brother and our Bridegroom, and in some ways, and why the Father of Jesus is our Father (*Abba*) too. Perhaps our relationship with Jesus Christ is the most layered among the Three Persons of God. We are Jesus' Brothers through our adoption to the Father, we are His Bride through membership in His Church, and we are His Body in that we are transformed into Him via re-generation in Baptism and Holy Communion. We were spiritually conceived from His side on the Cross – distributed to us via the regeneration of faith and Baptism – as *wo-Christ*, and we were united with Him in an eternal marital communion of love – via the spiritual, mystical marriage of the Eucharistic life – as *co-Christ*.

This also explains why Mary and the Church are both our spiritual Mothers (and why Mary is not our grandmother). Its no wonder the Church teaches: "One could say metaphorically that Mary is a mirror placed before the Church, in which the Church is invited to recognize her own identity"[24] This is because Mary was our Mother before the Church was. We are born from the side of Christ and His Church, and also, according to St. Pius X, from "the womb of Mary" with the Holy Spirit, and she is our Mother in the order of grace.[25]

In a related point, we might be able to say as well in some ways that the Holy Spirit is figuratively our "Mother" together with Mary and the Church, for He was united with the Word in bringing forth all creation. The Holy Spirit is a sort of Mother of all Creation and Life, as Eve was. The *Catechism* perhaps allows such a metaphor when it states: "God's parental tenderness can also be expressed by the image of motherhood, which emphasizes God's immanence, the intimacy between Creator and creature" (CCC 239). This is again allegory, just as Christ spoke of Himself as the Good Shepherd, the Bread of Life, and Living Water, so too we speak of the Spirit as Mother in this way. Just as Eve is Mother of the Living, so too are the Holy Spirit, the Word, Mary, the Church, and all disciples in some ways *Mothers* of all life.

So we may say allegorically here that the Father "mothers" the Son from all eternity and fathers the Holy Spirit with the Son Who is Mother-like; that the Word "mothers" the Holy Spirit, and then fathers creation and Adam with the Spirit Who is Mother-like; that Adam "mothers" Eve from his rib and then fathers Abel with her as Mother; that the Holy Spirit first "mothers" Mary in grace, and then fathers Jesus with her who is His Mother; and that Jesus first "mothers" the Church from His side and then fathers every disciple with her who is our Mother; that the Holy Spirit "mothers" every disciple by the power of grace and then fathers the Word with them who are "mothers" of the Word by faith and good deeds of love.

But still, many have discussed how, or even whether, God may be understood in a feminine way, particularly citing Scripture, which alludes to Lady Wisdom. The Old Testament theme of Wisdom bears some consideration here. The ultimate personification of Wisdom is Jesus Christ, Who as the eternal *Logos* became the Word Incarnate. Jesus, the Son of God, is the "wisdom of God" (1 Cor 1:24) who became man, or Wisdom Incarnate. But, as the *Catechism* states, the Holy Spirit is also the Wisdom of God, Who together with the Word created all things (see CCC 292). The Son and the Spirit are both the Wisdom of God. As we examined the Word within eternal Family of God, we proposed that the Word is Mother-like in relation to the spiration of the Holy Spirit, and also that in turn, the Holy Spirit, acting in union with the Word, is Mother-like in relation to creation. In this sense, Both are archetypes of Lady Wisdom. In Genesis 1, God creates things through His

Word by the power of the Spirit in complements – light and darkness, day and night, land and sea, earth and sky, and man and woman. These complements are a reflection of God Himself. We may say that creation occurs by the Word, Who with the Father impregnates the Spirit to bring forth creation. In this way, might both the Second and the Third Persons of God be both respectively Lady Wisdom *and* He Who is divine Wisdom?

But some hold that support for identifying Lady Wisdom with God does not arise from the inspired text, especially when examining Proverbs 1–9. They argue that Lady Wisdom is not to be properly understood as God's feminine side or a feminine co-deity.[26] She is the personification of Wisdom, who is brought forth, and daily the Lord's delight (cf. Prov 8:22–31). Who might she be then? Most scholars point to Lady Wisdom as a type of Mary. Tradition calls Mary the *Seat of Wisdom*,[27] as the *Logos* is enthroned within her womb and upon her lap. While I agree that the Lady Wisdom of Proverbs is not literally a feminine counterpart to the Father God as if there were two gods, perhaps in the context of this discussion, Lady Wisdom is in some ways, the divine Word, the Spirit, and the Blessed Virgin Mary, and as we shall see later the Church as well. All these in some ways epitomize Lady Wisdom.

In all this theological speculation, it may be concluded that the divine Word is Mother-like on one level of the Family of God; though on another level when incarnated in Mary and impregnated in all disciples, He is Son; while on another level, He is analogous to being a father in relation to creation and to the Church. Likewise, the Holy Spirit is Mother-like in the work of creation, Child-like as the spiration of the love of Father and Son, and Husband -like in relation to Mary in the Incarnation and in relation to all disciples in the work of sanctification. In this, the Son and the Holy Spirit are an archetype of father, mother, *and* child.

The Divine Work of Sanctification & Glory

6. The Family of God in the Work of Sanctification

In Baptism, we are given new life in Christ, Who in turn gives us His Gift of love. Jesus gives us the gift of His Holy Spirit, "and [together] their mission is conjoined and inseparable" (CCC 743), though also distinct. The Holy Spirit has His specific mission in the economy of salvation. Looking at this with the spiritual moral sense, like with Mary in the work of the Incarnation, each Christian in Baptism is *first* born by the power of the Spirit (uncreated Grace). The Holy Spirit thus "mothers" Christian disciples from His "rib" as *wo-grace* (Christian re-created with grace from uncreated Grace). J. Chalassery, in *The Holy Spirit and the Christian Initiation in the East Syrian Tradition*, seems to agree with this hypothesis, stating: "The Holy Spirit acts as mother in the life of Christians.... Aphrahat, in his Demonstration *On Virginity*, says... 'In the rite of Christian Initiation, it is the Holy Spirit who gives birth to Christians in the Church through the womb of Baptism. As a mother the Spirit prepares spiritual food for *her* children.'"[28] This work of the Spirit in re-creation is similar to the Spirit's work as "Mother" in creation. The Father and the Son are present in us as graced persons, however, not because Father and Son are sent, but because the Spirit is sent, distinctly from the Son. Then each Christian disciple enters into union with the Spirit to bring forth the offspring of the Word as *co-grace* (union of Christian with Holy Spirit). In this bi-relation, we then unite with the Spirit in a spiritual marriage-like union and are thereby *impregnated*, by the power of the Holy Spirit, with the Word of God. When *we* receive God's Spirit, like Mary our Mother, according to John Paul II, *we* are "impregnated by [the] Word" and are changed with grace into new creatures in Christ.[29] Connecting Mary to the Spirit's work of generating the Word, St. Louis de Montfort confirms: "The Holy Spirit, the more He finds Mary His dear and inseparable spouse in any soul, the more active and mighty He becomes in producing Jesus Christ in that soul."[30] With this understanding, we might say that each of the faithful, as man and woman, is "Mother" of the divine Word by the power of the Spirit's grace, and that the Word comes forth through us, *quasi-incarnated* through faith, good deeds, and the fruit of love, in a similar though less complete way as He did through Mary.

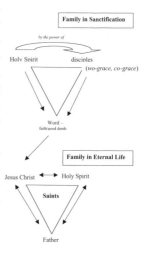

7. The Saints in the Family of God in Eternal Life

After the divine work of sanctification in the Family of God, there remains a final stage of the Family of God, which exists for man through natural death into communion with the Trinity in eternal life. This final stage is really the goal of the previous stages and their fulfillment. At this stage, those that die in grace and friendship with God, are born into eternal life as a sort of *wo-God* from God, deified by Him; and there is a final joining together of the Christian disciples-become-Saints with the Holy Trinity in an eternal communion of love, each Saint as a sort of *co-God* with God, though with no new offspring.

Seeing the original human family in an allegorical sense in relation to every family, each human person is created by God to become saints, such that in the spiritual moral sense, as the *image of God*, each of us in some ways becomes also *wo-God* (created by God through His Word), *wo-Grace* (restored to life in God via the grace of the Sacraments), and *wo-Christ* (made to be another Christ) in the Family of God; and as well, we are called to become in some ways *co-God*, *co-Grace*, and *co-Christ* (cf. Col 1:24) in the *likeness of God* through prayer and an active sacramental life of love in relationship with Him and other persons.

As we consider the human family at this stage in a spiritual anagogical sense in relation to the Triune Family of God, the *Catechism* reminds us that: "The ultimate end of the whole divine economy is the entry of God's creatures into the perfect unity of the Blessed Trinity" (CCC 260), so as to be united within the Family of God for eternity. Each member of the Church enters into Christ and dying in Christ, each is promised a share in the divinity of Christ, each becoming "partakers of the divine nature" (2 Pet 1:4), to live in loving communion with the Triune God for eternity as Saints in the Communion of Saints. God has adopted "us as his children in his only Son: by Baptism, he incorporates us into the Body of his Christ...he [then sanctifies us and] makes us other 'Christs'" (CCC 2782).

We who enter into union with the Holy Spirit, to become impregnated by the Word, are soon transformed into the Word ourselves. As Paul says: "It is no longer I who live, but Christ who lives in me" (Gal 2:20), and thus are prepared for the glory of the Saints in eternal life, through our final *transitus* of natural death, into the eternal Family of God. This is the Revelation of Christ, in that "He became man so that we might become God" (St. Athanasius),[31] so that we may enter into an eternal oneness of communion with the Three Persons of God, while at the same time remaining distinctly our own selves in the dimension of each of our unique human personages.

This is the mystery of the Communion of Saints in Heaven. Marriage does not exist between one man and one woman in Heaven because all the saints are "married" to the Triune God and to each other in eternal mystical union. The saints are also brothers and sisters in Christ with each other in God's Family of love, as Tobias prefigures by calling his wife also his sister (Tobit 8:4, 7).

In a certain sense, the whole Church's destiny, and that of each of her members individually, is to be welcomed into communion with the Trinity as a type of "fourth person" in God's Family. It is interesting that in the Nicene Creed, we profess faith not just three times in each of the Persons of God, but a fourth time as well: We believe in the Father, the Son, the Holy Spirit, *and* we believe in the Church. All four are one in the Family of God. Even as John Paul II states: "For the family of God includes everyone: not just those who through Baptism become God's adopted children, but in a certain sense all mankind, since Christ has redeemed all men and all women and offered them the possibility of becoming adopted sons and daughters of the Eternal Father."[32] Heaven belongs to all who die in God's grace.

Toward Some Practical Applications

At this point, some may be asking what practical application all this speculative theology may have. I will suggest just a few. The first concerns flawed attempts to label the three Persons of God in variation with a husband, a wife, and a child in a literalistic way, and with this the attempt to feminize God in a literal way.

The second practical application concerns the identification of the Holy Spirit with the wife/mother of the family, the latter of which is the topic in a recent popular book on the Trinity and the Family by Scott Hahn, entitled *First Comes Love*.[33] This hypothesis in his book, though supported by sources including M. J. Scheeben, Louis Bouyer, Jean Corbon, Benedict Ashley, F.X. Durrwell, and others, has received much unwarranted criticism from other theologians, especially from three *New Oxford Review* articles, who have themselves attempted to retain a overly-restricted view of the dynamism of the Trinity and each divine Person's relationship with the Other and with humanity. This paper, however, has attempted to establish a cohesiveness between the critics' popular view of the Holy Spirit as Bridegroom of Mary in the Incarnation *and* Hahn's view with the Holy Spirit as Mother figure of man in relation to creation and in relation to man's re-birth from His 'rib' as disciples in Baptism. Hahn's critics may want to re-evaluate their hasty and, dare I say, flawed critiques of his hypothesis, for this paper I think has dispelled these critiques from a new vantage point as perhaps could not have been possible until this new research was investigated, proposed, and now published.

The third practical application concerns the implications of homosexual unions. Recent theories attempting to obscure the difference or duality of the sexes intending to promote prospects for equality of women through liberation from biological determinism have "in reality inspired ideologies which, for example, call into question the family, in its natural two-parent structure of mother and father, and [attempt to] make homosexuality and heterosexuality virtually equivalent, in a new model of polymorphous sexuality."[35] So judged the Congregation for the Doctrine of the Faith in its newest document, "Letter to the Bishops of the Catholic Church on the Collaboration of Men and Women in the Church and in the World," issued in May of this year (2004). However, according to a statement of Archbishop Angelo Amato, secretary of the Congregation for the Doctrine of the Faith, a few months before this document was promulgated: "*...there is no principle whatsoever to assimilate or establish analogies between homosexual unions and God's plan for matrimony and the family*" found anywhere in God's Revelation. The analogies discussed herein certainly confirm Archbishop Amato's declaration.

While homosexual unions may on some levels be unitive, they cannot by nature be generative and procreative, and thus do not fit the criteria of marriage neither as God models it in Himself nor in His relationship with humanity. As I stated earlier, it is not in our sexuality that we are in God's image, but in the unitive *and* generative component of our sexuality. And this is confirmed on all three levels of the Family of God, including the first in the relationship of the Father and the Son. While the Father as Spirit is in relation with the Word His Son, their union of love may not be identified as homosexual. It is not because it is spiritual, but more importantly because it is generative. This is something no homosexual union can imitate, even potentially. Thus, this paper has presented one argument to sustain that homosexual unions cannot be considered legitimate or true marriages because they cannot succeed in resembling the relational unity within the Family of God.

It's All About Family Communion & Love

Both on her earthly pilgrimage and in her heavenly destiny, "The Church is nothing other than 'the family of God'" (CCC 1655). Marital and family love is a reflection of the inner life of the Trinity. We were first created and then brought forth by the Father *through* the Son, Mary, and the Church in Baptism, by the power of the Holy Spirit, so as to then enter into intimate communion with Him for eternity. We are all together invited into a bi-relational (*wo-* and *co-*) familial bond of love with God, all of us living as *mutual* (freely-given, total, unconditional, faithful) and *fruitful* (reciprocal) self-gifts to each other. This paper has utilized Scripture and Tradition within speculative theology to attempt to explain and reconcile every credible analogy of the Trinity and the family to synthesize them all into one full spectrum of the multi-dimensioned Family of God. This paper only attempts to be an introduction, and which in itself recognizes the cross-spectrum of new implications it offers to theologians of the various theological disciplines, including Trinitarian theologians, biblical exegetes, feminist theologians, Christologists, pneumatologists, Mariologists, and ecclesiologists. If they should find that this paper's hypothesis is plausible and even credible, may they continue the work of critically analyzing it and drawing out its implications for the good of the development of doctrine and the advancement of theological science.

In the end, however, this *analogy* of the human family in relation to the Trinity, with God's seven-fold family plan from eternity, to the creation of Adam, to the creation of the first human family, to the Incarnation, to the Redemption, to our sanctification, to God's Family with the Saints in eternal life, pales and flounders perhaps in ways similar as the divine surpasses the human. Nevertheless it has at any rate been proposed here as the paradigm of God's Family of love.

Kelly Bowring, S.T.D. who received his doctorate in sacred theology from the University of St. Thomas Aquinas in Rome – and a *mandatum* to teach theology from Cardinal Adam Maida Of Detroit – has been an Associate Professor of Sacred Theology at St. Mary's College of Ave Maria University in Orchard Lake, Michigan. He has published articles in the *National Catholic Register*, *Our Sunday Visitor*, *The Catholic Faith* and *Magnificat* Magazines, and has also published several catechetical and prayer books with the W. J. Hirten Company. He has been a presenter at various conferences, including with University Faculty for Life and the Steubenville Catechetical Conference, and has also been a guest on programs including EWTN's "The Choices We Face."

Notes

1.   Congregation for the Doctrine of the Faith, "Letter to the Bishops of the Catholic Church on the Collaboration of Men and Momen in the Church and in the World" (May 31, 2004), 5, 8, 12.
2.   John Paul II, *On the Dignity & Vocation of Woman* (*Mulieris Dignitatem*) (1988), 7.
3.   John Paul II, Address to Donald Smith, the New Ambassador of Canada to the Holy See (September 6, 2004).
4.   Mary Shivanandan, Zenit Interview, September 2, 2004.
5.   "Letter to Families," 6.

6. Hahn, Scott, *A Father Who Keep Promises* (Ann Arbor: Charis, 1998), 36; with citation from an address that the pontiff gave at the Puebla conference in 1979.

7. John Paul II, *On the Dignity & Vocation of Women*, 7.

8. M. J. Sheeben, *The Mysteries of Christianity* (St. Loius: Herder, 1946), 185, citing *Convivius decem virginum* III.C.8; PG, 18:73. See also Hahn, Scott, *First Comes Love* (NY: Doubleday, 2002), endnote 'Page 135' on pg. 203–4.

9. The Eleventh Council of Toledo Symbol of Faith (675) in J. Neuner, S.J. and J. Dupuis, S.J., *The Christian Faith* 7ᵗʰ ed. (New York: Alba House, 2001), 309. *The Christian Faith* is cited hereafter as ND.

10. *Ibid.*

11. John Paul II, Homily 6/29/95; Pontifical Council for Promoting Christian Unity, "Clarification Regarding the Procession of the Holy Spirit," 9/13/95, cited in ND 339.

12. Cf. Pius XII, *Humani Generis*, cited in ND 420.

13. Jesus to Sr. Mary of the Holy Trinity, *Words of Love*, compiled by B. Gottemoller, OCSO (Tan: Rockford, 1985), 82.

14. Jesús Castellano Cervera, *History and Significance of Dogma of Immaculate Conception*, Interview: Zenit News Service (7/18/04). Thurian was a Protestant convert to Catholic priest of Taizé, France.

15. M. J. Scheeben, *Mariology*, tr. T. Geukers, St. Louis, Herder, 1946, v. II, 185.

16. St. Maximilian Kolbe, Letter to Fr. Salezy Mikolajczyk, 28 July 1935, as found in Manteau-Bonamy, *Immaculate Conception and the Holy Spirit*, tr. by Richard Amandez, F.S.C., from the French original, *La Doctrine Mariale du Pere Kolbe, Esprit-Saint et Conception Immaculee*, Libertyville, II, Franciscan Marytown Press, 1977, 41.

17. Mark Miravalle, *Mary Coredemptrix, Mediatrix, and Advocate* (Santa Barbara: Queenship, 1993), 7–8.

18. *Mariale, Opera Omnia*, v. 37, q. 150, 219.

19. St. Ambrose, *The Virgins*, I,31: Saemo 14/1, pp. 132–133, italics added.

20. Hahn, *A Father Who Keeps His Promises*, 255.

21. *In Ioann. Evang.*, 120, 2.

22. CDF, "Letter to the Bishops of the Catholic Church on the Collaboration of Men and Women in the Church and in the World," 10.

23. Leo XIII, *Octobri Mense*, cited in ND 710.

24. CDF, "Letter to the Bishops of the Catholic Church on the Collaboration of Men and Women in the Church and in the World," 15.

25. LG 62; CCC 969.

26. Cf. William E. Mouser, Jr., "Who Is Lady Wisdom? A Case of Mistaken Identity Explored," online at http://www.fiveaspects.org/booklets/ladywisdom.html.

27. Litany of the Blessed Virgin; John Paul II, Address 11/8/01; CCC 721.

28. See Hahn, *First Comes Love*, endnote "Page 135," pg. 202–3; citing J. Chalassery, *The Holy Spirit and Christian Initiation in the East Syrian Tradition* (Rome: Mar Thoma Yogam, 1995), 188.

29. John Paul II, apostolic exhortation *CatechesiTtradendae* (On Catechesis in Our Time), 1979, 20.

30. St. Louis Marie Grignion de Montfort, tr., F. Faber, *True Devotion to Mary*, ns. 20,35; cf. also ns. 21,25.

31. See CCC 460.

32. John Paul II, "Letter to Priests for Holy Thursday 1995" (April 7, 1995).

33. Hahn, *First Comes Love*. Hahn attempts to provide one context for the Holy Spirit's identity as a mother within the Family of the Trinity. He proposes that the Holy Spirit "fits [his wife] Kimberly to a tee," such that he encourages his children to know their mother as "the Holy Spirit of [their] home" (*Ibid.*, 130). He concludes his analysis by stating that his view of the Holy Spirit as bride and mother "serves to reinforce the Holy Spirit's motherly role...[such that] what a mother does in the natural order, the Holy Spirit accomplishes in the supernatural order" (*Ibid.*, 130–131). His views have been widely criticized, including recently in *New Oxford Review* articles (September 2002, May 2003, June 2004).

34. CDF, "Letter to the Bishops of the Catholic Church on the Collaboration of Men and Women in the Church and in the World, 2.

Chapter 16: On Allegory and Metaphysics in the Language of Sexuality: A Response

DAMIAN P. FEDORYKA, PH.D.

Kelly Bowring's central focus is on the "likeness" of the human fatherhood and motherhood to God, who in the Trinitarian mystery is the primordial model of the family. In his reflections, Bowring focuses on the unitive and generative components of the spousal dimension as a reflection of the Trinitarian mystery. I do not take issue with this.

However, I do wish to seek clarification on another aspect, namely, the ambiguity of the term "sexuality" as often used in the discussions of the issue in general and of the theology of the body in particular. The clarification of this ambiguity is, in my judgment, necessary to bring out the metaphysics of the spiritual or personal foundations of the human dimension as incorporated in the body and the spousal act that expresses the *communio personarum* of human spousal love.

The persistence of this ambiguity leads to what in my judgment is a temptation, if not a flaw, in the discussions of the spousal and family structures, namely, a tendency toward literalism in the analogies or allegories used. Despite the interesting use of the allegory of "woman" in Bowring's paper, I have some problems in understanding its use, even allegorical, in reference to some of the individual Persons of Trinity.

If we are to understand correctly the family as a type of the Trinity, it seems we must focus on the *spiritual* dimension of the type. Bowring correctly quotes the CDF in its affirmation of the spousal dimension of the body as an expression of masculinity and femininity. But the quoted passage allows us, at least from its verbal level, to note that the body as male and female is an *expression* of masculinity and femininity. In this respect, masculinity and femininity are prior to the body. This seems to indicate that the proper meaning of masculinity and femininity, even in its human dimension, risks obscurity if one attempts to articulate this meaning in terms of its human embodiment. In the words of the pope's "Letter to Families," the biological similarity of fatherhood and motherhood to other living beings may obscure their essential and unique likeness to God. If the body is an expression, or a sign and symbol of masculinity and femininity, its meaning rests on a prior understanding of masculinity and femininity in their metaphysical spirituality. They are to be explained from above, not from below.

I choose this focus for my comments because it also allows me to apply the distinctions I will propose to the problem of homosexuality, the topic of the other paper by Paul Flaman during this session. In this area we find not simply a risk or a danger. We seem to have, on the part of the defenders of homosexuality as a legitimate "expression of sexuality," an approach that considers the problem from "below," with a heavy emphasis on the bodily and psychological dimension. Here again, in my judgment, the problem itself is obscured because one fails to take into consideration the *metaphysical* dimension of masculinity and femininity as spiritual characteristics of a personal being. Such an approach will distract even the supporter of Church teachings in this matter, shifting the focus and discussion to secondary considerations.

I. The Language of Sexuality

I begin with a brief terminological distinction. The term "sexuality," when signifying a human dimension, is ambiguous. It can refer variously to any of the three following dimensions either singly or in combination:

> a) "Sexuality" can refer to the "life bearing" or *genital* dimension of *bodily* existence. In this respect it bears a similarity to the "sexuality" of animals. The words "male" and "female" can be used in this connection.
>
> b) "Sexuality" can also refer to the *psychic and psychological* dimensions, ranging from the outspoken "dynamic" aspect of sexuality that is akin to the instinct and drive in the animal to the specific way in which the human spirit experiences itself as "united" with a body.
>
> c) "Sexuality" can refer to the specifically *spiritual* characteristics of masculinity and femininity. It is in this sense that we can refer to sexuality as belonging to the deepest core of the person. When secularizing authors invoke the notion that sexuality belongs to the deepest core of the person, they do not mean it in the spiritual sense, but rather in the first two meanings above, the bodily and the psychological.

It seems to me that the above distinctions in the use of the term "sexuality" are particularly important for Catholic thinkers if we are to profit from the development that has been initiated by Vatican II and the teaching of Pope John Paul II.

II. Characteristics of Masculinity and Femininity

I restrict myself, next, to a brief mention of what, in my mind, are the essential characteristics of masculinity and femininity from the perspective of a metaphysics of personal being:

a) Receptivity as Feminine

I begin with a question in St. Paul: what do we have that we have not received? As creatures, we have all *received* our existence. But that means we are all more than creatures simply. We have also received our existence from God. In other words, we have been given our existence *as a gift*, which we are obliged to receive and to reciprocate with a gift of self. The spiritual nature of receiving is an essential attribute and capacity of persons. It is also an essential state of the created person. In this regard, every created person stands in the relation of receptivity, of which femininity is a type with respect to its Creator. The essentially *feminine articulation* of receptivity is also the metaphysical precondition for every created human soul, "male and female" being called to become the "bride" to Christ's "groom."

b) Spontaneity as Masculine

The etymological root "*sponte*" as in *sua sponte* accurately indicates that which proceed from a being and is not caused by something other than the being in question. Spontaneity is the characteristic of a *response* to what is received. We respond with our word to what is given to us, to what we have received. If in receiving something is given to us, in the response we give something of our own, ultimately of ourselves.

In giving man the gift of existence, God gives Himself in the gift. In this sense of spontaneity, he "gives himself" – he *transmits Himself* and His life: He is Father, not merely creator. In the created order, neither receptivity nor spontaneity can be initiated by man. Both are possible only "by virtue of a gift received" from God, who, as St. John reminds us, "loved us first."

c) The Human Articulation of Masculinity and Femininity

Every person, human, angelic, or divine, has the capacity to receive from another and to "go out of" itself to the other. Receptivity and spontaneity are spiritual capacities and belong to every person as person. In terms of the above, therefore, every human has these personal capacities that can be articulated as "feminine" and as "masculine."

The woman, who has both of these capacities, is articulated with an "emphasis" on, or perhaps more correctly, in a receptive "tone." She is a symphony written in the "key of femininity." The man too, is spiritual, called to open himself in receptivity in order to respond adequately to what is given. But the man, in turn, is permeated by the dominant note of spontaneity. He is a symphony written in the "key of masculinity." All the other characteristic of the human person, including the way he receives the world, resonate in harmony with the dominant tone.

III. The Hermeneutics of the Gift

The above notions of femininity as receptivity and masculinity as spontaneity are well known. But if they are not to be reduced to an androgynous polarity, with the feminine and masculine as sociologically and culturally determined variations, they must be interpreted by a hermeneutics of the gift, as John Paul II terms it. If these traits are to be understood in their specific *spirituality* they must be understood in the context of the reciprocity of the gift: the receiving of the gift and the response of a gift of self. At the same time, the notion of the gift brings into focus *complementarity* of the spiritual traits of receptivity and spontaneity both in the interior dimension of the human person and in the interpersonal relation between man and woman.

a) Intrapersonal Complementarity and Unity

Within the interiority of the individual person, the act of receiving can be completed only when it is followed by an act of responding in gratitude. In the cognitive and affective dimensions, the responses are spontaneous and cannot be willed into existence. They are *engendered* by the gift received and evoked by it in a movement in which the individual is drawn to the giver of the gift. In the act of the will, the individual can appropriate and make "his own" this movement of the soul that we can generically call "love" – a movement that is itself a gift received.

Within the individual person, the receptivity and spontaneity of receiving and giving complete each other in a way that *integrates the individual, actualizing an inner unity*. The extent and depth of one's self-giving is a function of one's inner unity and self-possession. A refusal to accept the gift and, therefore, a failure to "go out of oneself" in the response of gratitude manifest themselves in an inner rupture within the person and a loss of self-possession. Union with the other becomes difficult and incomplete, if not impossible.

b) Interpersonal Complementarity and Unity

One of the central truths about the person, constantly repeated and presupposed by the Holy Father is "being for the other." It is an essential mark of the person as person. The communion of persons that finds its highest realization in the nuptial unity, if we follow the indications of language, is a sharing of the gift, of the *munus,* a *com-munio.*

The metaphysical structure of interpersonal relations, of being-for-the-other, is a mutual giving and receiving. As John Paul notes in his encyclical *Evangelium Vitae,* each human being is a gift to every other human being. Each is called to receive the gift of the other; each is called to respond with a sincere gift of self.

Man and woman, as persons, have both the capacitites of receptivity and spontaneity. In addition to this and in a marvelous fashion, each is articulated in a dominant "key," either feminine or masculine, that allows for a complementarity not simply between the aspects of femininity and masculinity abstractly conceived, but for a complementarity of two persons, feminine and masculine, in the reciprocity of giving and receiving.

Of direct significance for our discussion is that the traits of femininity and masculinity are specifically *human* articulations of receptivity and spontaneity as *metaphysical* traits of personhood. A human articulation of receptivity as femininity may include, for example, motherhood. But this is not yet a justification for attributing motherhood, even spiritual motherhood, as a property of personhood. On the other hand, the metaphysical status of the creature that has received its existence form God allows us to speak of every created human person as called to be a "bride." Fatherhood (or parenthood), by way of contrast, can be attributed as an essential property of God, who "transmits" himself in the gift of self to the Son and the Spirit, each of whom "receives" the gift, without, for all of that, becoming "feminine." Just as the status of the feminine can be attributed to humanity, so also, motherhood is a specific articulation of parenthood in the human order. Even though all fatherhood (parenthood) on earth comes from God, it does not follow that motherhood, as the creaturely participation in parenthood, is attributable to God.

IV. The Rejection of the Gift

The theme of *complementarity* is a central element in the Church's teaching on marriage between man and woman and its rejection of homosexual unions. A proper understanding of the complementarity grounding the unity man and woman presupposes that each achieve as certain measure of inner unity. This inner integrity of the human person depends on his or her receiving the gift given and completing the reception by a "sincere" gift of self.

a) Sin as the Appropriation of the Gift

John Paul II identifies the contrary of such a receiving as an *appropriation* of what is given, which rejects the giver and his love. One keeps the gift and oneself, refusing to reciprocate in gratitude. The culture of death, therefore, consists in this, that "man refuses to accept the gift of life." On a more fundamental level, he tells us in his talks on the "Unity of Man and Woman" that such an "extortion of the gift" constitutes the structure of sin. And sin causes a fourfold rupture: the rupture between man and God, the rupture within man himself, the rupture between man and woman, and the rupture between man and the world of nature.

b) Lust or Concupiscence

John Paul II goes on to identify the specific disruptive consequences of lust or concupiscence for both the *experience* and the *understanding* of femininity and masculinity. Basically, lust is the attitude in which man pursues as his end and motive the satisfaction connected with the sexual dimension. I note three of these consequences in this context.

First, lust produces a constitutive difficulty in the individual's experience of identity with his own body. Rather than experiencing an inner unity with his body, man experiences it as something in opposition. In the act of lust, man alienates himself from his body and experiences what is metaphysically an intimate part of his being human as a tool or a means. He experiences the *degradation of his body*. In pursuing sexual satisfaction, man yields to his "desire" and consequently loses possession of himself. He experiences the *degradation of his soul*. Lust, therefore, not only turns the other into a means of what the Pope calls an "object," but it also makes self-giving difficult or impossible.

Second, lust or concupiscence turns the difference between man and woman from a mutually enriching one to one of hostility and opposition. This occurs on the level of lived experience. Because lust turns the other into a means and a tool for one's own sexual satisfaction, it violates the other in his or her dignity as a person. The relation of using and dominating excludes the relation of self-giving and service.

Third, implicit in the above is the existential distortion of femininity and masculinity in their essential traits. The attitude of lust *distorts the respective traits of femininity and masculinity* shaping the very experience and perception of them. These distortion produced by lust are the material for many of the *caricatures* of femininity and masculinity. The pope notes that lust results in the "sexualization" of the human condition of embodiment.

Again, I restrict myself to two essential distortions. Femininity, as the articulation of receptivity and its openness to reality and the Other, is perverted by lust into the act and posture of consuming. With a twist of the wrist, the posture of receptivity with its open hand turned palm up is turned into the grasping claw, palm down. The woman becomes the predator, capable of only one word: "Mine." Masculinity, as the articulation of a spontaneity which ventures forth from itself in order to serve in an act of self-giving, is also perverted into a predatory venture that goes out into the world to seek a domination that is achieved by the deconstruction of creation and its restructuring into a brave new world of which the man too can only say: "Mine." The essential difference between femininity and masculinity vanishes into their quintessential opposite, the predator.

With regard to our discussion, allegory or metaphor that use human sexuality in the attempt to express the dimension of the spirit must beware of the fact that experience of our own femininity and masculinity may already be "sexualized," if not in the blatant and lurid hues of pornography and vulgarity, then in its more sophisticated relative, the elegance and charm of *eros*. The actual human condition of fallenness requires us to be aware that on the level of experience there is already operative a "hermeneutics of lust" that casts the perception of our own sexuality as mode of appropriation rather than the embodiment of a total gift of self.

V. The Metapysics of Homosexuality

Whatever the moral dimension and implications of lust as sin, apart from the question of moral guilt, it bears upon the metaphysical dimension. Lust is a way in which the person exercises his "act of being a person."

If the intimate union of body and soul manifests itself in the sphere of sexuality by virtue of the fact that the latter is *not merely the expression* of a spiritual act of spousal love, but its *metaphysical embodiment,* then lust implies a disembodiment, a dis-identification of oneself with one's body.

The metaphysical status of homosexuality as a lived personal experience is marked not only by the structural dissociation from one's body and the experience of it as something hostile to the individual, but is marked also marked by an inner *hostility* of the subject *toward the body and his embodiment in it.* This seems to be the case regardless whether this inner rupture occurred as a trauma caused by the lust of another or because of the individual's own pursuit of sexual satisfaction.

The paradox of an inner metaphysical spiritual hostility to the "same" gender to which one is psychologically attracted – a paradox which, incidentally, is also present in the phenomenon of "sexiness" as found in heterosexual attraction – can be explained by the structure of lust and its connection to pride. Lust seeks satisfaction and uses the sexuality of the other as a means for this satisfaction. It may be combined with pride which seeks domination over the other, a domination which is facilitated by the tremendous psychic power of the sexual dynamism that is awakened in the other.

Homosexuality in its metaphysical structure does not seek union with the other, but rather the intimacy that can *dominate*, punish, and destroy the other *from within*. Similarly, lust as the pursuit of sexual satisfaction, does not seek union with the other, as much as its seeks that intimacy in which the other's sexual dissolution is as much a source of one's own sexual satisfaction as it is evidence of one's domination over the other at the very core of his personal being. One can understand that a consistent pursuit of sexual pleasure can intuitively shun the opposite sex. For it is the opposite sex that in a special way, by its very nature as "complementary" can become the vehicle of a gift. Through the embodied sexuality of the other, one can be touched, awakened and *drawn* to the other as a gift which demands to be received and reciprocated. In this respect, the attraction of the complementary sex in all of its charm is in some sense a real "risk" to the subject in as much as it can initiate a real movement towards union. The real but mysterious nature of the "opposite" sex is the source and origin of the experience of being touched, moved and "captivated" by the "magic" of the other's beauty, as expressed in his or her embodiment. Lust, as consistent pursuit of the erotic may lead one to reject this risk and choose the same gender. In its own way, homosexual sex is "risk free." But precisely as lust, it retains the dominating hostility toward the other that is characteristic of all lust, even if in this case the limp wrist disguises the implacable aggression delivered by the mailed fist.

What interests us here is the *metaphysics* of homosexuality, which is not an identification with one's own gender, with the same sex, nor even simply the experience of one's own sexuality as something that opposes the subject, but rather the subject's active hostility towards his own gender. More important than the spiritual aggression towards the other, as embodiment of the same gender, is the aggression against one's own being. Active homosexuality is not only homicidal but also suicidal.

If we consider the homosexual "attraction" as it originates in the trauma of abuse, the victim is "given" to himself as degraded. The specific form of the spiritual trauma that can result is the belief that the abuse is the proper and fitting response evoked by some flaw or evil in the victim. At the deepest core of his being, the victim is "given" to himself as bad. And the fitting response to what if flawed or bad is to reject it. At that depth level of his sexuality, where, as John Paul II notes, is to be found the "point" of union between body and soul, the victim rejects and punishes his embodiment. This seems to be the case notwithstanding the equally deeply grounded "need" for affirmation that has its source in an original and fundamental self-experience in the interpersonal context: the discovery that I am a gift given to the other and that the other is a gift given to me. By virtue of the gift status, I discover myself worthy to be received by the other; and I discover the other as a gift that is beautifying. The disappointment of the initial promise of such an experience creates an inner emptiness that is spiritually painful, a terrible wound that demands is own negation.

As a consequence of the abuse of the human soul, the victim's body becomes the embodiment, the "sacrament" – both symbol and actualization – of his or her degradation. The interpersonal structure of personal consciousness, its vocational orientation towards the other, accounts for the fact that the wounded desire for affirmation focuses on the embodied existence of another, the domination of whom becomes a form of a paradoxical self-affirmation by destruction.

If the above sketch of a metaphysics of homosexuality is correct, it provides a key to a therapy which must be focused on healing the inner spiritual wound or rupture. The retrieval of self-worth and dignity calls for a reconstitution of that fundamental personal status of being-for-others. In this instance it calls for a forgiveness for the wound, if it is caused by others. Or, if it is the result of one's own lust, it calls for a disavowal, an inner separation from the dynamism of sexuality to which one has yielded. In both cases, it involves the regaining of self-possession.

But the hermeneutics of the gift indicates that the above is not enough, or rather, that it becomes possible only to the extent that *an other* affirms the homosexual. The latter finds himself affirmed in his human worth and dignity precisely when he is received as a gift. In the loving affirmation by the other, the homosexual finds himself given to himself as endowed with an intrinsic preciousness and in that love can begin regaining possession of himself.

If lust in general implies a hostility to love as a receiving and self-giving even in heterosexual relations, the inner logic of homosexuality demands a consistent rejection of the essence of marriage as involving man and woman exclusively. At the same time, the inner logic of homosexuality demands a hostile rejection of the spiritual difference between femininity and masculinity as articulations of receptivity and spontaneity. Femininity and masculinity are therefore radically sexualized and interpreted "from below" in terms of the first two meaning of "sexuality" outlined above. A defense of marriage, therefore, cannot be simply asserted by the invocation of the physical and psychological difference between and complementarity of the sexes as willed by God and taught by the Church. Such a defense will not be able to withstand the onslaught which invokes the "personal" dimension of a "freedom" to choose satisfaction, namely, lust. Only the intuition of the metaphysical foundation of the difference between man and woman as spiritual can provide a confirmation of the truth accessible to the intellect but obscured by specious reasoning and a culture of lust.

Damian P. Fedoryka is currently a professor of philosophy at Ave Maria College in Ypsilanti, Michigan. Formerly he taught at the Franciscan University of Steubenville, Ohio. Prior to that he was president of Christendom College in Front Royal, Virginia. Dr. Fedoryka has degrees from the University of Louvain, Fordham University, and the University of Salzburg. His main interests are ethics and the philosophy of the person, and, in particular, the thought of Dietrich von Hildebrand and Karol Wojtyla/Pope John Paul II. He has made many public appearances before many audiences on the topics of sexual morality, abortion, and education. He has also lectured and worked extensively with youth in Austria and Ukraine. Dr. Fedoryka and his wife Irene, a graduate of the Juillard School of Music and currently director of choirs at Ave Maria College, have ten children, all home-schooled but subsequently all college graduates.

Session IV: The Future of Marriage and Family
in the United States

Chapter 17: The Future of Marriage and Family in the United States
Some History Lessons

Allan Carlson, Ph.D.

For several decades now, I have tried to explore and explain the historical context for our contemporary "family crisis," our "war over the family," our "culture war." Today, I will present what I see as six lessons to be learned from this history, with a special emphasis on the Roman Catholic angle, and with an eye to the future.

Lesson One: The Family Issues Never Change or, at Least They Haven't for 215 Years.

It is said that the Chinese Communist leader Chou En-Lai, when asked what the impact of the 1789 French Revolution on human affairs had been, replied: "it's too soon to tell."

Actually, it is unclear to whom and just when Chou said this. One source says it was to Archduke Otto von Hapsburg in 1948; another source says to Richard Nixon in 1972; another to Tony Benn in the mid-1970's; and still another to a French journalist in 1989: the latter could be called miraculous, for Chou had been dead for thirteen years by then.[1] Perhaps Chou, living and dead, has simply prattled this observation out to every Westerner that he has met.

In any case, his answer *rings true*. The revolutionaries of 1789 unleashed passions and ideas that continue their work up to our time. Many of them directly target natural family relations, including the leveling idea of equality; the divorce revolution; secular liberalism; sexual freedom; state-centered education; communism; even the "creative destruction" of modern capitalism. The "family issues" are a legacy of these continuing revolutions. Take, for example, this peculiar story:

Jack was sitting before the hearth fire, darning his working's wife's sock. A tear lay in his eye. "No," the wretched man said in a thick Yorkshire accent, "there is plenty of Wark for Wemen and Bairns [children] in this quarter but very Little for men – thou may as well go try to finde a hondred pounds, as go to find wark abouts heare – but I hed not ment neather thee nor eneyone els to have seen me manding t'wife's stockings, for it's a poar job."

Jack wiped away the tear. "I do not [k]now what is to become of us," he whimpered, "for she as been't'man now for a long time, and me t'woman – it is hard wark." When he had married, Jack said, he held a fine job and the couple "'gat on very well – we got a firnished Home…I could wark for us boath. But now 't'world is turned upside down. Mary has to turn out to wark and I have to stop at home to mind Bairns – and to Wash and Clean – Bake and mend." At that point, Jack lost control and wept violently declaring over and again his wish that he had never been born.[2]

Who wrote this lament about gender roles turned upside down? Was it some early version of Beverly LaHaye? Or perhaps an ancestor of Phyllis Schlafly? No, it was the proto-Communist Friedrich Engels, in his 1844 book, *The Condition of the Working Class in England*, a powerful indictment of industrial capitalism's social effects.

Indeed, we can see the non-Marxist labor movement of the 19th and early 20th centuries as seeking, in large part, to rebuild traditional family life within a world torn asunder by the industrial principle, a principle that dictated the radical separation of work and home. The labor movement's central strategy was to secure a "family wage." This meant that the industrial sector could have one, but only one family member: the father. Leo XIII's *Rerum Novarum* implied the necessity of a "family wage." A more forceful articulation came from Father John Ryan of the USA in 1916:

> …The laborer has a right to a family Living Wage because this is the only way in which he can exercise his right to the means of maintaining a family, and he has a right to these means because they are an essential condition of normal life.[3]

Pius XI directly endorsed the family-wage idea in *Quadragesimo Anno*. In a long commentary on this document, the Jesuit author Oswald von Nell-Brenning emphasized the radical consequences of the "family wage":

> …It will be absolutely necessary to see to it that female labor is kept from the labor market, something that will have to be attained by prudent and clear-sighted measures. Everyone knows that this

cannot be accomplished by decree but requires a far-reaching reconstruction of the entire economic system.[4]

In the United States, at least, a somewhat less rigorous version of this "family- wage" economy did exist between 1900 and 1965. It rested in part on public policy (more on that later) and in part on a culturally enforced form of conscious, open job discrimination: the phenomena of so-called "men's jobs" (marked by higher wages and salaries and long-term tenure) and "women's jobs" (oriented to lower pay and the short term).[5] However, the revolutionary principle of pure gender equality, embodied in Title VII of the Civil Rights Act of 1964 and Title IX of The Education Amendments of 1972, shattered this system. The real wages of men fell; and the flow of young mothers into the workforce resumed.

Today, no one in America really talks about the "family wage," except for equity feminist historians who still, with great ritual, regularly dance on its grave. And yet, the underlying problems posed by families living in an industrial milieu are still very much with us. There are, for example, muddled campaigns in our day for a "living wage," although they are marked by intentionally ambiguous normative goals. Does a modern "living wage" assume one, or two earners per household? Never a clear answer. Contemporary complaints over a lack of quality day care; mounting talk of a "care- giving deficit"; the growing "elder care" crisis; so-called "work/family conflicts"; even the push for "gay marriage": all still derive from the disorders created by the industrial revolution.

Lesson Two: While the Underlying Family Issues Never Change, the "Pro-Family" Political Party Does.

The politicization of America's family crisis does not begin during, say, the late 1960s. In fact, it goes back at least one hundred years, to the presidency of Theodore Roosevelt. The scourge of divorce (the Reno divorce mills were up and running by then); the immorality of birth control; the dangers of equity feminism; the peril of shrinking family size and depopulation: between 1900 and 1919, all drew Mr. Roosevelt's frequent and often eloquent commentary. Roosevelt also crafted his own ideology of the hearth, resting on the political and legal equality of women and men, their necessary complementarity in function. Indeed, he equated traditional *familism* with *Americanism*:

> ...[I]n all the world there is no better and healthier home life, no finer factory of individual character, nothing more representative

of *what is best and most characteristic in American life*, than that which exists in the higher type of family; and this higher type of family is to be found everywhere among us.[6]

And yet, among early 20th century Republican leaders, Roosevelt was nearly unique. The dominant spirit in the GOP came from the great bankers, financiers, and manufacturers who made up the corporate-financial wing of the Party. Its views on the family were very different. In 1904, the National Association of Manufacturers adopted resolutions designed to subvert the "family wage," including this: "No limitation should be placed upon the opportunities of any person to learn any trade to which he *or she* may be adapted."[7] When equity feminists, led by Ellen Paul, formed the National Woman's Party in 1917, they too pushed for equal work and equal pay for women outside the home. There is even evidence to suggest that the manufacturer's Association secretly funded the National Woman's Party. So, when this party drafted its proposed Equal Rights Amendment in 1923, it came as no surprise that the NAM immediately endorsed it and that Republicans served as its chief sponsors in both the U.S. House and Senate. The Republican Party also was the first to endorse the ERA in its Platform. The common goals of the equity feminists and of big business – hostility to the "family wage," the inclusion of all women, especially young mothers, in the labor market, the commodification of all human activity – made this a strong political alliance. Once the Birth Control League of America cleverly changed its name to Planned Parenthood, this movement too found a compatible home in the GOP; indeed, by the 1950s, Planned Parenthood was a favored charity among Republican women's clubs.

The Democrats, meanwhile, consolidated their legacy of "Rum, Romanism, and Rebellion;" that is, as the party of cultural pluralism, northern Catholics, Southern agrarians, small property, and the trade unions. Between 1913 and 1933, moreover, the Democratic Party became the favored home of the "social feminists," or the *maternalists*, as some now call them: women including Julia Lathrop, Florence Kelley, Frances Perkins, Grace Abbott, Mary Anderson, Frances Kellor, and Molly Dewson. Relative to gender, these women believed in the *equality of rights, difference in function*. The *first* duty of *all* women, they held, was the defense of home and infant life. And they believed that a *career outside the home* was *incompatible* with good mothering.[8] The maternalists – backed in all cases by Democratic votes – were responsible for creating the U.S. Children's Bureau in 1912, for the provision of federal subsidies for *homemaking* classes for girls in 1917, and for passage of the Sheppard-Towner Act in 1921. This latter measure, the first universal "entitlement" ever approved by Congress, focused on "baby saving" – what a nice description for a federal program – "baby saving" through programs aimed at reducing maternal and infant mortality. Of course, the American Medical Association fiercely opposed Sheppard-Towner, calling it "sob stuff."[9]

The Democrats' "New Deal" of the 1930s also represented a triumph for the maternalists. One current sign of this is the *uniform loathing* of the New Deal shown by all recent equity feminist historians.[10] Why this reaction? Simply this: *every* New Deal domestic program either *openly built on* or *assumed* a "family wage" model. The Democrats' ideal social order was a nation composed of family homes with *breadwinning fathers, stay-at-home mothers, and flocks of children*. All economic, welfare, and social insurance measures adopted during the 1930s aimed at strengthening this modest patriarchal order. For example, the largest relief program – the Works Progress Administration or WPA – was limited to one breadwinner per family: 85 percent of the 4.5 million enrollees were men. Even those women *who were* in the program found themselves assigned to "sewing rooms" and to classes in child care, home health, and cooking. Or consider the Social Security Amendments of 1939, the crown jewel of the New Deal, which gave to working men (but *not* to working women) new, family-oriented benefits: an extra pension for homemaking wives; and survivors benefits to widows (but not to widowers) and their children.

In short, by 1940, it would be fair to label the Democratic party as *the party of the traditional family*. The close alliance between ethnic Catholics and the Party of Jefferson and Jackson made sense. And this lasted until a fateful day – February 8, 1964 – when American political coalitions underwent a seismic shift. Under debate was the Civil Rights Act of 1964.[11] The Southern Dixiecrats, with their backs to the wall, turned to a desperate strategy. Howard Smith, Democrat of Virginia, rose and proposed adding "sex" to the list of prohibited discriminations under Title VII, dealing with employment issues. He and his Southern colleagues saw this, it appears, as a killer amendment; or perhaps as a way to push aside the intended beneficiaries of Title VII – black males – by turning legal attention to the job claims of vastly more numerous white females. In any case, the equity feminists in the Republican Party – including Representatives Katherine St. George of New York and Catherine May of Washington state – rallied behind their at times whimsical, at times bewildered Dixiecrat colleagues. A remarkable debate ensued, where traditional New Deal Democrats opposed to the amendment mounted maternalism's "last stand." Emanuel Cellar – liberal Democrat, Manhattanite, Jewish, and Chairman of the House Judiciary Committee – defended in this debate the natural *inequality* of woman and man:

> You know, the French have a phrase for it when they speak of women and men…"*vive la différence*." I think the French are right. Imagine the upheaval that would result from the adoption of blanket language requiring total equality. Would male citizens be justified in insisting that women share with them the burdens of compulsory military service? What would become of traditional family relationships? What about alimony?

Prescient questions all. Representative Edith Green, Democrat of Oregon, insisted that the real "biological differences" between men and women needed to be recognized in employment. And so on through this last iteration of the classic maternalist case in defense of the "family wage" regime. In the end, the segregationist Dixiecrats and the Republican equity feminists carried the day: on a vote of 166 to 133. As the Civil Rights Act was implemented over the next several years, the carefully constructed social and legal order of the maternalists entered into crisis…and eventual collapse.

Also in 1964, of course, a Catholic wife, mother, and lawyer named Phyllis Schlafly leapt onto the public stage with her book on Barry Goldwater: *A Choice, Not an Echo*. Over the next 16 years, she sparked a massive realignment of the political parties. Groups attached to the traditional family, blue collar Catholics worried about the spread of abortion, and Southern evangelicals all migrated from the Democratic to the Republican Party. Meanwhile, equity feminists and Planned Parenthood backers largely moved into the Democratic Party. The old, morally grounded industrial and trade unions faded away, or were transformed into "public sector" unions logically committed to the equity feminist agenda.

All the same, this new alignment remains unstable. On the Democratic side, wealthy, white equity feminists and population-control enthusiasts actually have little in common with the real interests of ethnic minorities. On the Republican side, the "Fortune 500" and "the autonomous family" have sharply conflicting agendas, which no amount of "fusionist" wishful thinking can bridge. The very treatment of social conservatives at this year's Republican Convention – locked up out of sight in the party's attic just like slightly lunatic children – underscores the fragility of this coalition. It is unlikely to last.

Lesson Three: "Social Engineering" Can Be Done the Right Way.

The first direct Federal interventions into elementary and secondary education were The Smith-Lever Extension Act of 1914, which launched the 4-H movement, and The Smith-Hughes Vocational Training Act of 1917, which used federal dollars to pay for home economics teachers. There were technical sides to these initiatives, but the real spirit of this federal experiment is ably captured by two songs from the Department of Agriculture's Extension Service's *4-H Songbook of 1928*. For boys, there was "The Plowing Song":

> A growing day in a waking field
> And a furrow straight and long
> A golden sun and lifting breeze,
> And we follow with a song.
> Sons of the soil are we,
> Lads of the field and flock.
> Turning our sods, asking no odds;
> Where is a life so free?
> Sons of the soil are we,
> Men of the coming years;
> Facing the dawn, brain ruling brawn.
> Lords of our lands we'll be.

And for the girls, there was the song "Dreaming" (here, the third verse):

> My home must have its mother,
> May I grow sweet and wise;
> My home must have its father,
> With honor in his eyes;
> My home must have its children,
> God grant the parents grace –
> To keep our home through all the years
> A kindly, happy place.

Again, this neo-agrarian, generically Christian, pleasantly patriarchal vision represented federally engineered education in 1928. It is a far cry from the spirit of today's Title IX. Indeed, it rises out of an alternate moral universe.

All the same, this family-building experiment worked, at least for a time. The family-farm was not saved, but the ethos of homemaking thrived. In 1945, the U.S. Department of Agriculture created Future

Homemakers of America, and this high-school club soon claimed over 600,000 members. As noted earlier, New Deal programs such as Social Security undergirded the breadwinner-homemaker-child-rich family model. So did a string of housing programs, which together mobilized massive capital to provide newly married couples with their own homes. Tax reforms implemented in the 1940s reinforced marriage and full-time homemaking through the policy of "income splitting" on joint returns. These same tax reforms encouraged larger families through generous per-capita exemptions for children.

The results were striking. For the first time in over 100 years, three things happened in America at once: the marriage rate rose; the divorce rate fell; and the marital birth rate soared. These were the celebrated "Marriage" and "Baby" Booms of the 1945–64 era, a time unique in American history. I believe that Federal policies favoring the breadwinner/homemaker/child-rich family model – helped to *create the material conditions* which made this family renewal possible.

Lesson Four: Roman Catholicism in the American Setting Has Been, But Is Not Now, Culture-Shaping.

American Catholics in the 1900 to 1940 period had behaved increasingly like their Protestant neighbors, at least relative to family formation and fertility. There was a convergence of Protestant and Catholic birthrates in America, perhaps a sign of the victory of social and economic pressures over the influence of belief. At the doctrinal level, though, there was a growing divergence in these years. While some Protestant groups – the Anglicans, the old Federal Council of Churches – toyed with birth control, the Catholic hierarchy labored to shore up orthodoxy on family-related questions. Pius XI issued *Casti Connubii* in 1930, which reaffirmed historic Catholic teachings: procreation and the rearing of children as the primary purposes of marriage; marriage as an indissoluble sacrament; limitation of family size only for licit reasons; periodic abstinence as the only licit means of birth control; total abstinence from sexual activity as the rule for the unmarried; and the married woman serving in the home as wife and mother.

In some ways, in fact, the Catholic emphasis on family life was extended. The large Catholic family received explicit theological affirmation somewhat later. As Pius XII declared: "Large families are most blest by God and specially loved and prized by the Church as its most precious treasures."[12]

Witnessing, it seems, to this steadfastness in doctrine, the 1945–64 era produced a "heroic" flowering of Catholic family life in America. Although fertility rose for all American religious groups, it rose far more rapidly and continued longer among Catholics. Indeed, there are signs that the American "Baby Boom" was largely "a Catholic thing." Allow me a couple of numbers here. The total marital fertility rate for non-Catholics averaged 3.15 children born per woman in the early 1950s and 3.14 in the early 1960s; essentially unchanged. For Catholics, the respective figures were 3.54 and 4.25. More dramatic was the return of the large Catholic family: in a survey conducted in the early 1950s, only 10 percent of Catholics under age 40 reported having four or more children, a figure very close to the 9 percent for Protestants. By the late 1950s, the Protestant figure was unchanged, but the proportion of Catholics with four or more children had more than doubled, to 22 percent.

Still more surprising was the nature of this postwar resurgence in Catholic fertility. Violating a law of sociology (namely, the more education a woman receives, the fewer children she has), large families flourished among the best educated. Catholic women who had attended college were bearing more children than Catholic women without a high school degree. We also find increased fertility primarily among younger parents: through 1965, each new cohort of parents was more pro-natalist in its attitudes than the group before. And it had a clear religious focus: more frequent attendance at Mass was related to more births. Indeed, the Catholic family ethic resting on devotion to church teachings seemed to be reaching new highs in the mid-1960s.[13] Among the American laity, at least, there was no apparent crisis of faith.

Within ten years, though, all of these qualities had collapsed. There seems little doubt that the currents of ideas affecting Catholicism in the mid-1960s – challenges to traditional practices and hierarchical authority during Vatican II, debate on the contraceptive question followed by the stunning reaffirmation of orthodoxy in the encyclical *Humanae Vitae*, and the impact of feminist and neo-Malthusian ideas on key Catholic elites – lay behind this shift. Dissent gained some legitimacy. It appears that the laity may simply have followed the easiest of several disputed paths of obedience.

Indeed, changes in lay Catholic attitudes and behavior concerning the family can be traced to the specific years 1967–71. In their study of Catholic fertility in Rhode Island, Bouvier and Rao found that average expected family size among Catholics fell from 3.3 children to 2.8 during those four years, a substantially greater decline than seen among Protestants. This fall in expected fertility was sharpest for the better educated: among Catholic women with some college education, the decline was from 3.7 to 2.7 children: again, in just four years. Moreover, frequency of attendance at Mass no longer proved to be related to fertility. Even the large family ideal vanished: in 1967, 28 percent of "devout" Catholics planned to have five or more children; by 1971, only 6 percent did.[14]

Lesson Five: Fertility Decline Is the Great Issue of Our Day.

One book disorienting the Roman Catholic laity during the late 1960s was *The Population Bomb*, Paul Ehrlich's notorious case for radical measures aimed at population control. While the American "Baby Boom" and falling *mortality* rates in the Developing World could be used to project frightening scenarios of a globe swarming with over 50 billion people, it is now clear that falling human fertility has been the real long-term story, and poses the real danger. Already in 2004, 80 nations record below-replacement, or negative-growth, fertility. The global population, it appears, should peak in 2050 at a little over 8 billion souls, and decline thereafter, as nation after nation falls into the "age trap" described in Phillip Longman's new book, *Empty Cradle*: too few children to sustain the elderly.[15]

What caused this radical shift? There actually appear to be two distinct fertility transitions. The first one accounts for a shift from a "natural" level of fertility, seven to nine children born per couple, down to two. The best explanation for this, I believe, comes from the Australian demographic historian, John Caldwell.

Looking at the Western world, Caldwell attributes part of this decline to a "spectacular growth in capitalist" production and gadgets that overwhelmed residual home production; and part to Europe's egalitarian streak, a legacy of the French Revolution. Yet the real spoiler, Caldwell insists, was *mass state education*, which indoctrinated new generations against the old family morality rooted in Christian faith. The new government schools, introduced in the 19th century, not only reduced the potential for child labor around the house and raised the cost of items such as children's clothing. They also became for the children involved the new *focus-of-loyalty* and *advocate-for-the-future*, displacing the family. As Caldwell shows: "...[the schools] made citizens of those whose horizons had been largely confined to the family, and taught the immorality of putting family first." State schools so "destroy[ed] the corporate identity of the family," attacking parental authority in particular, and fertility tumbled. What was true for Europe and America, soon became true for the whole world. As Caldwell concludes: "It seems improbable – and has yet to be demonstrated – that any society can sustain stable high fertility beyond two generations of mass schooling."[16]

Testing this theory in the U.S., researchers found the spread of state schooling to be closely related to fertility decline in the 19th and early 20th centuries. Indeed, even in rural school districts, each additional *month* of a public school year resulted in an average fertility decline of .23 children: the state schools literally consumed children.[17]

The second fertility transition is from a level of two children per couple, down to *.85* of a child, which one European analyst considers the natural "floor" of fertility. What might be the cause here?

The very pervasiveness of this "second" transition points to certain explanations. David Coleman notes that remaining pockets of high fertility in Europe – such as in the rural regions of Switzerland – all disappeared after 1964. So did pockets of higher "Catholic fertility" still to be found in Spain and Portugal.[18] Dirk Van de Kaa reports that *97 percent* of 21-year-old Danish women now report having had pre-marital sex, essentially marking the full collapse there of the old sexual ethic.[19] Belgium demographer Ron Lesthaeghe shows that only 20 percent of all European Community citizens above age 18 have some link to organized religion; among young adults, the figure is closer to 10 percent.[20] Ronald Inglehart cites the *sharp* decline in votes for religious political parties in Europe starting in 1964 as a sign of what he calls "the silent revolution" in European values.[21]

As Lesthaeghe concludes, recent changes in family formation and marital fertility are nothing new. They merely continue the "long-term shift in the Western ideational system" *away* from the *values* affirmed by Christian teaching (specifically "responsibility, sacrifice, altruism, and sanctity of long-term commitments") and *toward* a militant "secular individualism" focused on the self.[22]

Can the Europeans turn their situation around? It is highly unlikely. To begin with, the "momentum" of demographic change in the EU shifted to the negative side in the year 2000.[23] The very age structure of the population now makes fertility decline much more likely than during the prior four decades, when it was already sharp and sustained. Moreover, most European policymakers are simply *clueless* regarding the driving roles of *statism* and *secularism* in the changes they now confront. They commonly embrace materialistic explanations of cause, welcome the disappearance of motherhood as a vocation, dismiss the Christian religion as a superstition of the past, and place all their hopes in the Swedish model. Specifically, they call for full gender equality, the priority of the work line over the family, and generous day care, paid parental leave, child allowances, and other welfare benefits as their policy solutions. However, such reforms actually lock post-family, anti-child values into place.

Lesson Six: American Exceptionalism is Real; Social Creativity Remains Possible Here.

Europe is dying; so is Japan, also being done in by a broad rejection of children. However, unlike forty years ago when America was leading the global retreat from marriage and children, something different is now happening here. The United States is the *only developed nation* in the world which recorded an increase in its total fertility rate between 1981 and 2000: from 1.81 in the former year to 2.13 in 2000, an increase of 18 percent, to a point slightly above the replacement or zero-growth level. This was not, as some suggest, only a function of a rising number of births out-of-wedlock. Between 1995 and 2000, even marital fertility rose by 11 percent, the first sustained increase in that number since the mid 1950s. Nor was this a function of America's greater ethnic diversity. Fertility among Americans of European descent actually climbed by 21 percent after 1981, to a total fertility rate of 2.114 in 2000. As *The Economist* magazine recently summarized, "demographic forces are pulling America and Europe apart…America's fertility rate is rising; Europe's is falling. America's immigration outstrips Europe's… America's population will soon be getting younger. Europe's is aging."[24] By 2050, *The Economist* calculates a U.S. population of up to 500 million, compared to an EU in demographic freefall, with barely half as many people.

The best explanation for America's greater fecundity – this openness to children – is the higher degree of religious identification and behavior shown by Americans. Forty-five percent of Americans in the year 2000 reported attending religious services during the prior week; in Europe, it was about ten percent. And believers usually do have more babies. Alas, outside of recent Hispanic immigrants, overall Catholic numbers *today* are not impressive here. But "white fundamentalist Protestants" who attend church weekly show a fertility rate that is 27 percent above the national average.[25] To choose another example, the fertility of active American Latter-Day-Saints, or Mormons, is about double the national average.

America's resilience can also be seen in that most unexpected, but successful, American folk movement of the last thirty years: home schooling. Probably numbering fewer than 20,000 children in 1975, there are probably two million home educated children in America today: a hundred-fold increase. The last fifteen years have witnessed a surge in the number of Catholic families so engaged. And fertility is affected as well. Remember John Caldwell's thesis: state-run mass schooling drives fertility down. Well, as would be predicted, home-schooling families reverse this relation. Sixty-two percent of home-educated children come from families with three or more children, compared to 20 percent of non-homeschoolers. Over 33 percent of home-schooling families have four or more children, compared to but 6 percent of those in state and private schools.[26]

And so, I offer you again my six lessons from history:

* *The family issues never change.*
* *The identity of the "pro-family" political party does.*
* *"Social engineering" can be done the right way.*
* *Roman Catholicism in America has been in the past, but is not now, culture shaping.*
* *Fertility decline is the great issue of our day.*
* *And, American exceptionalism is real.*

Allan C. Carlson is President of The Howard Center for Family, Religion & Society in Rockford, Illinois, and Distinguished Fellow in Family Policy Studies at The Family Research Council in Washington, DC. He received his Ph.D. in Modern European History at Ohio University. His books include: *From Cottage to Work Station: The Family's Search for Social Harmony in the Industrial Age* (Ignatius); *The "American Way": Family and Community in the Shaping of the American Identity* (ISI Books); and *Fractured Generations: Toward an American Family Policy in the 21st Century* (forthcoming). He is editor and publisher of the Howard Center's highly respected publication, *The Family in America.*

Notes

1. Quotations collected at: http://shamrockshire.yi.org/2002/10/20021025.html (8/02/04).

2. Adapted from: Friedrich Engels, *The Condition of the Working Class in England*, trans. W.O. Henderson and W.H. Chalover (New York: Macmillan, 1958 [1844]): 162–63.

3. John A. Ryan, *Distributive Justice: The Right and Wrong of Our Present Distribution of Wealth* (New York: Macmillan, 1916): 374–76.

4. Oswald von Nell-Brenning, S.J., *Reorganization of Social Economy: The Social Encyclical Developed and Explained* (New York: Bruce, 1939): 176–77.

5. The mechanisms behind this system are described in Vernon T. Clover,

Changes in Differences in Earnings and Occupational Status of Men and Women, 1947–1967 (Lubbock: Department of Economics, College of Business Administration, Texas Tech University 1970): 4, 17–21, 26–27, 36, 43, 50–51.

6. Theodore Roosevelt, "The Man Who Works With His Hands," Address at the SemiCentennial Celebration of the Founding of Agriculture Colleges in the United States, Lansing, MI, May 31, 1907; in *The Works of Theodore Roosevelt: Memorial Edition, Vol. XVIII* (New York: Charles Scribner's Sons, 1924): 188. Emphasis added.

7. Albion Guilforn Taylor, "Labor Policies of the National Association of Manufacturers," *University of Illinois Studies in the Social Sciences* 15 (March 1928): 38.

8. On the maternalists, see: Molly Ladd-Taylor, *Mother-Work: Women, Child Welfare, and the State, 1890–1930* (Urbana: University of Illinois Press, 1994): 75–88.

9. Molly Ladd-Taylor, "My Work Came Out of Agony and Grief: Mothers and the Making of the Sheppard-Towner Act," in Seth Koven and Sonya Michel, eds., *Mothers of a New World: Maternalist Politics and the Origins of the Welfare State* (New York: Routledge, 1993): 321–28.

10. For example, see: Lois Scharf, *To Work and to Wed: Female Employment, Feminism, and the Great Depression* (Westport, CT: Greenwood Press, 1980): 111, 129; Mimi Abramovitz, *Regulating the Lives of Women: Social Welfare Policy from Colonial Times to the Present* (Boston: South End Press, 1988): 235; Gwendolyn Mink, *The Wages of Motherhood: Inequality in the Welfare State, 1917–1942* (Ithaca, NY: Cornell University Press, 1995): 171; Alice Kessler-Harris, *Out to Work: A History of Wage-Earning Women in the United States* (New York: Oxford University Press, 1982): 251; Suzanne Mettler, *Dividing Citizens: Gender and Federalism in New Deal Public Policy* (Ithaca, NY: Cornell University Press, 1998); 214; and Winifred D. Wandersee, *Women's Work and Family Values, 1920–1940* (Cambridge, MA: Harvard University Press, 1981): 101.

11. The full debate is recorded in: *The Congressional Record: Proceedings and Debates of the 88th Congress, Second Session* (Vol. 110, Part 2), February 8, 1964: 2577–87.

12. Pius XII, "The Large Family Address to the Association of Large Families of Rome and Italy, Jan. 19, 1958," in *The Pope Speaks* 4 (Spring 1958): 363–64.

13. See: William D. Mosher, David P. Johnson, and Marjorie C. Horn, "Religion and Fertility in the United States: The Importance of Marriage Patterns and Hispanic Origin," *Demography* 23 (Aug. 1986): 367–69; Gerhard Lenski, *The Religious Factor: A Sociologist's Inquiry* (New York: Doubleday, 1961): 203, 215–18; and Lincoln H. Day, "Natality and Ethnocentrism: Some Relationships Suggested by an Analysis of Catholic-Protestant Differentials," *Population Studies* 22 (1968): 27–30.

14. Leon Bouvier and S.L.N. Rao, *Socio-religious Factors in Fertility Decline* (Cambridge, MA: Ballinger, 1975): 1–4, 84–91, 156–58; Charles Westoff and Larry Bumpass, "The Revolution in Birth Control Practices of U.S. Roman Catholics," *Science* 179 (Jan. 12, 1973): 41–44; Andrew Greeley, *The American Catholic: A Social Portrait* (New York: Basic Books, 1977): 189; and Charles F. Westoff and Elise T. Jones, "The Secularization of U.S. Catholic Birth Control Practices," *Family Planning Perspectives* 9 (Sept.-Oct., 1977): 203–07.

15. Phillip Longman, *The Empty Cradle: How Falling Birthrates Threaten World Prosperity (And What to Do About It)* (New York: Basic Books, 2004).

16. John C. Caldwell, *Theory of Fertility Decline* (London & New York: Academic Press, 1982): 305; also pp. 158–63, 168–72, 175–76, 302, 311, 324.

17. Avery M. Guest and Stewart E. Tolnay, "Children's Roles and Fertility: Late Nineteenth Century United States," *Social Science History* 7 (1983): 355–80.

18. David Coleman, ed., *Europe's Population in the 1990's* (Oxford: University Press, 1990): 45–47.

19. Dirk J. Van de Kaa, *Europe's Second Demographic Transition* (Washington, DC: Population Reference Bureau, 1987): 11.

20. Ron Lesthaeghe and Dominique Meekers, "Value Changes and the Dimensions of Familism in the European Community," *European Journal of Population* 2 (1986): 259.

21. Ronald Inglehart, *The Silent Revolution: Changing Values and Political Styles Among Western Publics* (Princeton, NJ: Princeton University Press, 1977): 216.

22. Ron J. Lesthaeghe, "A Century of Demographic and Cultural Change in Western Europe," *Population and Development Review* 9 (1983): 411–35.

23. Wolfgang Lutz, Brian C. O'Neill, and Sergei Scherbov, "Europe's Population at a Turning Point," *Science* 299 (March 28, 2003): 1992.

24. "Half a Billion Americans?" *The Economist* (Aug. 22, 2002).

25. F. Althaus, "Differences in Fertility of Catholics and Protestants Are Related to Timing and Prevalence of Marriage," *Family Planning Perspectives* 24 (Sept./Oct. 1992).

26. Lawrence M. Rudner, "Scholastic Achievement and Demographic Characteristics of Home School Students in 1998," *Education Policy Analysis Archives* 7 (March 23, 1999): 7–8, 12.

Chapter 18: Towards a Catholic Ethos of Family, Work, and Culture

Rev. Msgr. Stuart W. Swetland, S.T.D.

Dr. Allan Carlson's lecture and his historical work on the "American Way" of family life is both *interesting* and *challenging*.[1] It is interesting because it brings together a tremendous body of research (historical, sociological, psychological, philosophical, and theological) to paint a fascinating episodic portrait of America's historic efforts to support, protect, and defend a traditional, family-centered community life. It is challenging because it demonstrates just how quickly this remarkable consensus concerning the centrality of the family as the building block of society evaporated in the latter part of the twentieth century. In fact, in very short order, an outright hostility to all that the traditional family represented and contained seems to have become the norm, at least among the cultural elites.

His thesis is also of particular interest and challenge to the Fellowship of Catholic Scholars because of the role played by Catholics in this history. If Dr. Carlson's views are correct (and I think that they generally are), Catholics contributed to both the rise and albeit temporary victory of the "maternalist view" and Catholics (especially Catholic theologians and other influential Catholics in the cultural elite) played a significant role in the abandonment and dismantling of this world view.

The evidence for this shift is widespread. Its devastating affects on children and society are well documented. We need to look no further than the Family Research Council's *The Family Portrait* for proof.[2] Other works (i.e. William Bennett's *Broken Hearth*) amply document the numerous "shadows" plaguing marriage and family life today.[3] Time does not permit an exhaustive cataloging here. Only a couple of examples are necessary to demonstrate how far we have strayed from the ideal.

For example, there was a time when everyone understood and accepted the centrality of children in marriage. The main reason for marriage (or at least one of the main reasons) was the begetting and rearing of children. But this is not so today. Not only has the DINK (double-income no kids) household become Madison Avenue's favorite family form, but studies show that even families with children are not necessarily child-focused. For example, psychologist and educator Dr. Francine M. Deutsch of Mt. Holyoke College (no friend of the traditional family) has demonstrated that less than one third of families in modern America are child-centered families. In an extensive study of 150 families in the Boston area, Deutsch discovered that only 41 could be called child-centered. The remaining 109 would have to be labeled "career-centered" families. This meant that career-centered families give priority to work outside the home and career advancement rather than having their primary focus on the rearing of the children.[4] Gary Martin and Vladimir Kats of the Division of Foreign Labor Statistics in the Bureau of Labor Statistics have done extensive research on family and work relationship internationally focusing on the United States, Canada, Japan, Denmark, France, Germany, Ireland, Italy, Netherlands, Spain, Sweden and the United Kingdom. They summarized their results in 2003:

> Profound changes in family structure and employment patterns took place in 12 developed countries during the last two decades of the 20th century, continuing earlier trends. The traditional nuclear family unit, a married couple with children, declined steadily as a proportion of all households. Married-couple households without children maintained a generally stable share. By contrast, the proportion of single-parent and one-person households rose in all of the countries studied. The United States had the highest proportion of single-parent households throughout the period, but some countries had larger increases. The one-person household became the dominant living arrangement in Denmark and Sweden.
>
> Accompanying and interacting with these trends in household composition were continued demographic shifts and changes in the work-family relationship. Fertility rates, already low by historic and world standards in 1980, fell further in most of the countries studied, but rose and then leveled off in the United States. U.S. marriage and divorce rates remained the highest in the developed world, but other countries were narrowing the difference. The proportion of children born outside of marriage rose in all of the countries examined, with the two Scandinavian countries maintaining the highest percentages throughout the period. The United States was among a group of countries joining Sweden with a lower average age of women at first birth than at first marriage.
>
> Women of childbearing and child-rearing ages entered the labor force in greater numbers, and the proportion of working mothers with very young children rose rapidly in the last decade, except in

Sweden, where the proportion declined, but remained the highest among the countries studied. U.S. single mothers had much higher rates of employment than most of their European counterparts.

In a comparison (limited to eight countries) of the working patterns of couple families with very young children, the United States was the only country in which the predominant pattern was for both parents to work full time. In the mid-1980s, the traditional pattern of the husband working full time and the wife not working outside the home was clearly dominant in the United States, as well as in the other seven countries. Although declining since then, this traditional pattern remained the most frequent arrangement in France, Germany, Ireland, Italy, and Spain...[5]

The results of this drastic shift away from a traditional family-centered community include numerous social pathologies associated with what some have called the "parenting deficit."[6] In light of this recent history, I cannot help but agree on the whole with the six "lessons" presented by Dr. Carlson.

One, the family issues never change.

Two, the identity of the "pro-family" political party does.

Three, "social engineering" can be done the right way.

Four, Roman Catholicism in America has been in the past, but is not now, culture shaping.

Five, fertility decline is the great issue of our day.

Six, American exceptionalism is real.

Of particular interest in this context is Dr. Carlson's fascinating review of the pro-maternalist viewpoint that was enshrined in the various social programs associated with the Progressivism and the New Deal. Equally interesting, and very disquieting, is how quickly this "maternalist consensus" seemed to unravel in the social upheaval of the late 1960s and early 1970s. Sadly, a significant contribution to this unraveling was played, in my opinion, by the widespread disquiet and dissent associated with the issuance of *Humanae Vitae* by Pope Paul VI in 1968. If Catholics, especially our academic and pastoral leaders, had been more willing to take a stand with Paul VI in 1968, much of what followed might had been avoided. Now one can only look back to Paul VI's warning of what would result from a widespread acceptance of the "contraceptive mentality" and recognize just how profoundly prophetic this seemingly tormented man was.

The mention of dissent though brings me to one point of minor disagreement with Dr. Carlson's paper. In it he states, "Today, no one talks about the 'family wage,' except for equity feminist historians who still routinely denounce it."[7] I believe that this is unfair to another heroic man who has spoken and continues to speak eloquently on behalf of the family wage: John Paul II. In fact, I believe that it is still dissent – or deliberate ignorance or willful neglect (to the same effect) – this time from Catholic social teaching that is at the heart of Dr. Carlson's fourth lesson: "Roman Catholicism in the American setting has been, but is not now, cultural-shaping."

John Paul II has placed work at the very center of the social question.[8] I believe that it is our attitude towards work as much as anything else that has fundamentally skewed our vision about marriage and family. Clearly in his social teaching, John Paul II has championed the family wage. In *Laborem Exercens* #19 he writes:

> Hence, in every case, a just wage is the concrete means of *verifying the justice* of the whole socioeconomic system and, in any case, of checking that it is functioning justly. It is not the only means of checking, but it is a particularly important one and, in a sense, the key means.
>
> This means of checking concerns above all the family. Just remuneration for the work of an adult who is responsible for a family means remuneration which will suffice for establishing and properly maintaining a family and for providing security for its future. Such remuneration can be given either through what is called a *family wage* – that is, a single salary given to the head of the family for his work, sufficient for the needs of the family without the other spouse having to take up gainful employment outside the home – or through *other social measures* such as family allowances or grants to mothers devoting themselves exclusively to their families. These grants should correspond to the actual needs, that is, to the number of dependents for as long as they are not in a position to assume proper responsibility for their own lives.[9]

John Paul II also reminds us of the need for balance, rest, and leisure in the workers' lives, going so far as to call the right to rest a fundamental human right. Is it not here that we have one of our greatest social pathologies? Quite frankly, almost all Americans are working too much. The statistics are startling:

> 1) Results of Harris Polls have shown the average work week for most Americans is rising. In 1973, the average work week was 40.6 hours. By 1980 it rose to 46.9. By 1994 it topped 50 hours per week and by 1997 it stood at 50.8 hours.
>
> 2) Another way of looking at this is hours worked per year.

When comparing Canada, Great Britain, Germany, Japan, and the United States, every country but ours decreased their working hours between 1990 and 2000. Ours went up to 1,979 hours per year. We now, by this study on average work 49 ½ weeks. That is 3 ½ weeks per year more than the Japanese; 6 ½ weeks more than the British and an astonishing 499 hours (12 ½ weeks!) more than the Germans. While we were pushing the fifty hour mark per week, places like France and Belgium were reducing their work weeks to 35 or less hours. Not surprisingly, all this work has made us the most productive workers on earth. But we are not the most productive per hour worked. Despite all of our technological innovations, the French and Belgium worker is more productive per hour worked.[10]

3) The picture gets bleaker when one looks at working couples. In 1977, the combined work hours of all couples (dual and single earners) was 70. By 2002 it had increased to 82. If couples have children, it gets even worse. In 1977 the combined working hours of dual-earner couples with children was 81. By 2002 it had reached 91.[11] No wonder John Paul II has talked of the growing phenomena of children growing up "orphans of living parents."[12]

4) The polls also show that all this work has not made us happier. It is really not surprising that, in a 2003 poll, 57% of workers consider themselves overworked and 80% were not happy with their work/life balance. But what is astonishing is that an amazing 83% of workers (almost 5 of 6) are not satisfied with their jobs despite spending so much of their lives at them.[13]

Many more statistics could be cited, but I think it is clear that, for many Americans, they are so busy making a living that they do not have time to have a life. For example, unsurprisingly, time for leisure has significantly declined in this period. In 1973, Americans had on average 26.2 hours per week of leisure. Today that number is below twenty at 19.5.[14]

I believe that almost everyone in this room agrees with the thesis of Josef Pieper that leisure is the basis of culture. And it is the question of culture that forms my last critique of Dr. Carlson's presentation. Here, I do not have so much a disagreement as a distinction to make. Dr. Carlson has made much of the effects of the change of law such as the "sex equity" philosophy embedded in the Civil Rights Act of 1964 and also in Title IX. But how much of this change in law (*de jure*) was merely a reflection of what in fact (*de facto*) was already occurring in our culture? I believe we all accept the educative nature of law, but could these laws have passed and been widely accepted without deeper forces at work in our culture already undermining and corroding our family-centered focus?

This, I believe, is vital because we will not effect change in these areas until we recognize and unmask a powerful force at work in our culture that is undermining every and all efforts to "shore up" family and family life. I believe there is an implicit "theology" at work in American culture and society that is not fully consistent with any robust form of Christianity (especially not with Catholicism). In fact, I would propose that our workaholic tendencies mentioned above are a reflection or symptom of this deeper, more profound, more subtle, more dangerous ideology.

Of course this point is not unique to me. Professor David Schindler has written extensively and eloquently about it. And as early as the midpoint of the twentieth century, the power of this underlying theology in America was being noted by sociologists. It became the theme of Will Herberg's famous essay in religious sociology, *Protestant-Catholic-Jew*.[15] This work was a study of the so-called "third generation," meaning by this, the third generation after immigration to America. They were the grandsons and granddaughters of immigrants. Herberg noticed a general "return" of this generation to the religious practices of their ancestors, rejecting their parents' rejection of religion. But he also noted that despite this religious revival, the "trend towards secularism"[16] in ideas, beliefs and practices had not been abated. In fact, despite their religious difference, Americans seemed to profess a certain uniformity of belief that Herberg calls "the American Way of Life":

> It seems to me that a realistic appraisal of the values, ideas and behavior of the American people leads to the conclusion that Americans, by and large, do have their "common religion" and that that "religion" is the system familiarly known as the American Way of Life. It is the American Way of Life that supplies American society with an "overarching sense of unity" and conflict. It is the American Way of Life about which Americans are admittedly and unashamedly "intolerant." It is the American Way of Life that provides the framework in terms of which the crucial values of American existence are couched. By every realistic criterion the American Way of Life is the objective faith of the American people.[17]

Herberg describes this American Way of Life as individualistic, dynamic, pragmatic, humanitarian, generous, and optimistic.[18] Its spirituality is a "certain kind of idealism," and "it stresses incessant activity."[19] It has a belief in progress, education and self-improvement.[20] Herberg believes that it is best characterized by the word "democracy." Herberg explains:

> ...If the American Way of Life had to be defined in one word, "democracy" would undoubtedly be the word, but democracy in a peculiarly American sense. On its political side it means the Constitution; on its economic side, an egalitarianism which is not only compatible with but indeed actually implies vigorous economic competition and high mobility.[21]

Herberg summarizes his argument by stating emphatically that the "secularization of religion could hardly go further."[22] Herberg, of course, was writing in 1955 about the paradox of great numbers of religious adherents whose actual religion had "lost much of its authentic Christian (or Jewish) content."[23] Barry Kosmin and Seymour P. Lachman return to this paradox in their study of American religion, *One Nation Under God*. Their work is an analysis of the results of a 1990 survey of 113,000 people across the continental United States called the "National Survey of Religious Identification" (NSRI).[24] Kosmin and Lachman's study shows that Herberg's main thesis is still valid for America. They write, "While America may be among the most religiously diverse nations, one can observe a process of Americanization at work on all its religions."[25] In Kosmin and Lachman's opinion, this trend is most "vividly portrayed" among American Catholics who were closer in many beliefs to their fellow citizens than they were to their bishops.[26] They point to an underlying syncretism at work in America. This process means that the "minority religions" become Protestantized and the Protestant churches become Americanized. In addition, there is in American society a powerful civil religion at work.[27] They write:

> A corollary problem of contemporary American society is that despite his or her more frequent church attendance, the thoughts and values of the average churchgoer are less often derived from religious sources than from secular ones. Gerhard Lanski wrote that this is an example of a "transcendental faith...gradually being transformed into a cultural faith." A generation ago this was truer of Protestants than of members of other faiths, but Catholics and Jews are now moving in this direction, too. What is there in American history and the American environment that propels this movement?

Kosmin and Lachman cannot fully answer this vital question by statistical methods or by sociology. However, in their conclusion they attempt to venture an opinion. They believe that in the United States, secularism and religion each use and are reinforced by the other:

> In other nations, in countries as different as Italy and Algeria, the tension between religion and secularism is more pronounced than it is in the United States, where secularism and religion regularly use and redefine each other. Religion in the United States frequently sanctifies the goals of a basically secular society, and the secular society affects and influences the very meaning of religious identification and association. It is therefore not surprising that America appears to be growing more secular precisely at a time when religious identification is highly pronounced.[28]

The best example of this mutual reinforcement, Kosmin and Lachman argue, is the American understanding of religious liberty. Americans have a tendency to believe that religious liberty applies not just to the state ("Congress shall make no laws...") but also to one's own relationship with one's own religious organization. For example, eight out of ten Americans believe that their religious beliefs should be independent of organized religion.[29] Kosmin and Lachman write, "Our democratic society breeds the notion that if all creeds can co-exist, then they must be fundamentally similar."[30]

Kosmin and Lachman notice that there is in modern American society a backlash against the trend towards secularization among some religious groups – most noticeably among the so-called "fundamentalist." Even in the more mainline denominations there exists among a significant minority a desire for more traditional values and religious practices. But even this traditionalist movement is up against very powerful "countervailing trends" that are undermining it. These trends, according to Kosmin and Lachman, are mainly economic in origin. Economic pressures require great mobility that undermine community life and break down close-knit extended families. Economic necessity requires most families to have two wage earners, taking mothers away from their traditional role as primary caregiver to their children. Competition in the marketplace ensures an ever-expanding search for innovation, new ways, and new consumer goods. These goods and services must be marketed, which usually means being sold by advertising that further undermines family values and stability.[31] Kosmin and Lachman note:

> These opposing forces create the paradoxical nature of American religion to which we have often referred. There appears to be a collective schizophrenia whereby the public says one thing, with apparent sincerity, in answer to public-opinion polls and acts

quite differently. The modern and the traditional become both
seductive and repulsive simultaneously. America's market-oriented
religion bears a similarity to the rest of society in its hopeful and
optimistic tone and its unwillingness to face certain uncomfortable
realities.[32]

They conclude their study by stating that the trends that they noted
show no signs of abating in the near future. In fact, they believe that the
"Protestantization of American Society" will most likely accelerate as
the general pace of society accelerates.[33] In fact, I believe there is a "theology" at work in American society although often implicit. It is a theology that while attempting to be value-free is in fact imbued with a particular sense of reality – the symbol of the free market. Michael Novak,
now a proponent of a system he used to criticize, discussed this embedded theology in *Ascent of the Mountain, Flight of the Dove*:

> To put the matter more harshly, however, we might notice that
> present American institutions *do* embody a sense of reality, stories,
> and symbols. These are, radically, the symbol of the "free market
> place" – an impersonal mechanism designed to allow a maximum
> of private space to individuals. That symbol dominates American
> economics, "value free" universities, pluralistic political arrange-
> ments, and even that part of church life which appeals to the pri-
> vate heart and the private mind of each individual. The story
> Americans are encouraged to live out is that of "economic growth"
> (for the sake of growth), ethical *laissez-faire* ("Do whatever you
> wish – I don't care – so long as you don't injure others"), and pri-
> vate freedom from coercion or disturbance by others. American
> society is built upon a flight from others. Americans try to have as
> little to do with others as possible. Mechanical procedures (ticket
> windows, subways, girls at cash registers, passengers on planes
> who do not speak to one another, automobiles that search for
> deserted beaches and quiet mountain retreats, etc.) are designed to
> allow Americans in most transactions to be as little "present" to
> other human beings as possible. That is real which is private.[34]

This theology of the market place can at times tend, as liberation
theologians have noted, to a "total market mentality" where everything
and everyone is weighed and measured by the dynamics of the marketplace. I believe many are beginning to recognize this underlying theology with its tendency towards consumerism and materialism.

In other words, I believe we must take very seriously the call of John
Paul II's social teaching towards "changes in established lifestyles"
(*Centisimus Annus* #73). This call, dismissed by too many as a "rhetori-
cal mistake," is a call to find "an authentic theology of integral human

liberation" (*Centisimus Annus* #26). To this end, the Holy Father wrote in *Centisimus Annus*: "The Church has no models to present; models that are real and truly effective can only arise within the framework of different historical situations, through the efforts of all those who responsibly confront concrete problems in all their social, economic, political and cultural aspects, as these interact with one another. For such a task, the Church offers her social teaching as an indispensable and ideal orientation, a teaching which…recognizes the positive valve of the market and of enterprise, but which at the same time points out that these need to be oriented towards the common good" (*Centisimus Annus* #43).

We must take Catholic social teaching seriously as an authentic guide to conscience. In a particular way, the lay faithful must be the "salt" and "light" they are called to be in the midst of the world. But if the laity is to be the "leaven" that they are called to be – "raising the whole mess up" – they will need to be formed with a truly Catholic ethos.[35] We must challenge secularism, consumerism, and materialism. For example, we must recapture the ideals of rest and leisure especially the idea of the Sabbath rest.[36]

If what I stated above is true, then the challenge ahead is not so much to change laws as to change a culture. Here, I believe, Dr. Carlson and I are in agreement. The task ahead then is a transformative one. It is the task of inculturation of the gospel of Jesus Christ.[37] I have written elsewhere that what I believe we need to cultivate is a "receptive ethos" more grounded in the contemplative dimension than the active that, I believe, is best captured by the concept of spiritual childhood.[38]

In summary, the Church in America must be counter-cultural because the culture in America embodies an implicit theology at odds with authentic faith. Our task is not one of standing aloof, apart or even "over-against." It is to immerse ourselves in the midst of the world-having previously "set out in the deep" encountering and being encountered by the mystery of Christ, to act as agents of transformation, "leaven in the dough, raising the whole mess up." In this task, we Catholic Scholars have a great friend and ally in Dr. Allan Carlson. His historic work on the American way of being family-centered has rightly been praised by no other than our dear friend and colleague Fr. James Schall as "the most counter-cultural book of the year." Well earned praise indeed and for this work and your other efforts on behalf of marriage and family, we thank-you.

Rev. Msgr. Stuart W. Swetland, S.T.D., was ordained a priest in 1991 for the Diocese of Peoria, Illinois. He received his undergraduate degree in physics from the United States Naval Academy and was selected as a Rhodes Scholar in 1981. Raised a Lutheran, he became a Catholic while studying at Oxford. He has a B.A. and M.A. in politics, philosophy, and economics from Oxford; an M.Div. and an M.A. from Mt Saint Mary's Seminary; and an S.T.L. and an S.T.D., from the John Paul II Institute for Studies on Marriage and the Family. He currently serves as director of the Newman Foundation and chaplain to Catholic students at the University of Illinois in Urbana-Champaign. He is also an adjunct associate professor in the program of religious studies at the university. At the same time he serves as vicar for social justice for the Diocese of Peoria. The story of his conversion was recently published in the *Surprised by Truth* series edited by Patrick Madrid. He is also currently serving as the executive secretary of the Fellowship of Catholic Scholars.

Notes

1. Cf. Allan Carlson, *The "American Way": Family and Community in the Shaping of the American Identity*, (Wilmington, Delaware: ISI Books, 2003).

2. Bridget Maher, ed., *The Family Portrait* (Washington, D.C.: Family Research Council, 2004).

3. Cf. William Bennett. *The Broken Hearth: Reversing the Moral Collapse of the American Family* (New York: Random House, Inc, 2001).

4. Francine M. Deutsch, *Halving It All: How Equally Shared Parenting Works* (Cambridge, MA: Harvard University Press, 1999).

5. Gary Martin and Vladimir Kats, "Families and Work in Transition in 12 Countries, 1980–2001," *Monthly Labor Review* (September 2003): 3.

6. Council of Economic Advisors, "The Parenting Deficit: Council of Economic Advisors Analyze the 'Time Crunch'," (May 1999).

7. Allan Carlson, "The Future of Marriage and Family in the United States: Some History Lessons" (Paper delivered at the Fellowship of Catholic Scholars, Pittsburgh, PA, 24–25 September 2004).

8. *Laborem Exercens*, 2

9. *Ibid.*

10. "We Aren't Whining, We Do Work Too Much," *Seattle Post* (September 1, 2001).

11. Stephanie Armour, "Workers Feel Burn of Longer Hours," Business Section *Kentucky Journal* (December 21, 2003).

12. John Paul II, "Letter to Families."

13. Stephanie Armour, "Workers Feel Burn of Longer Hours," Business Section *Kentucky Journal* (December 21, 2003).

14. Merrill Goozner, "Are Americans Working Better-or Just More?" Chicago Tribune (June 22, 1998).

15. Will Herberg, *Protestant-Catholic-Jew: An Essay in American Religious Sociology* (Chicago: University of Chicago Press, 1983). Herberg's work was initially published in 1955.

16, *Ibid.*, p. 1.

17. *Ibid.*, p. 75.

18. *Ibid.*, pp. 78–79.

19. *Ibid.*

20, *Ibid.*, p. 79.

21. *Ibid.*, p. 78.

22. *Ibid.*, p. 83.

23. *Ibid.*, p. 3.

24. Barry A. Kosmin and Seymour P. Lachman, *One Nation Under God* (New York: Harmony Books, 1993), p. 1.

25. *Ibid.*, p. 10.

26. *Ibid.*

27. *Ibid.*, pp. 11–12.

28. *Ibid.*, p. 280.

29. *Ibid.*

30. *Ibid.*, p. 11.

31. *Ibid.*, p. 282.

32. *Ibid.*

33. *Ibid.*, p. 283.

34. Michael Novak, *Ascent of the Mountain, Flight of the Dove* (New York: Harper & Row Publishers, 1978), pp. 136–137.

35. Cf. Matthew 5:13–16; 13:33.

36. Cf. John Paul II, *Dies Domini.*

37. Cf. Francis Cardinal George, *Inculturation and Ecclesial Communion* (Rome: Urbaniana University Press, 1990).

38. Stuart W. Swetland, "Towards the Civilization of Love? Theological Reflections on the Social Teaching of Michael Novak" (Ph.D. diss., Lateran University, John Paul II Institute, 1997).

Chapter 19: Social Science and the Vindication of Catholic Moral Teaching

W. Bradford Wilcox, Ph.D.

It is no secret, in the wake of *Humanae Vitae,* that the Catholic Church largely lost her ability to successfully convince the American laity of the truth and beauty of her moral teaching on matters related to sex and marriage. The historical, sociological, and intellectual factors that account for this failure are familiar. Let me name just two.

First, *Humanae Vitae* came at the worst possible moment in history. The encyclical arrived in the wake of Vatican II, just after the Church had thrown open her windows to the modern world. Unfortunately, the modern world was then succumbing to the siren song of the sexual revolution, and was awash in a pervasive anti-authoritarianism. As Emory University theologian Luke Timothy Johnson has observed, "American Catholics truly became American at [precisely the] moment when America itself was undergoing a cultural revolution."[1]

In the aftermath of John F. Kennedy's ascendancy to the presidency, and their own dramatic increases in educational and economic attainment, Catholics in the U.S. were coming into their own as independent-minded Americans. With their newfound status, they were less inclined to extend undue deference to the opinions of "Father," and the Church more generally, especially on matters that would require them to sacrifice their cherished American aspirations to upward mobility and material success – sacrifices often associated with having a large family. For all these reasons, most Catholics in the late 1960s and 1970s rejected *Humanae Vitae.*

Secondly, and just as ominously, this rejection led many of these same Catholics to call into question their commitment to the whole fabric of Catholic moral teaching on sex-related matters. If the Church is wrong on birth control, the thinking went, she is probably wrong on divorce and remarriage, premarital sex, and so on. As Johnson, himself a critic of *Humanae Vitae*, observes: "The birth control issue finally initiated many American Catholics into the hermeneutics of suspicion,"[2] a hermeneutics that made them skeptical of all pronouncements regarding sexual morality from Holy Mother Church. Indeed, the controversy surrounding *Humanae Vitae* was, as Fr. Andrew Greeley pointed out, "the occasion for massive apostasy and for [a] notable decline in religious devotion and belief"[3] as many Catholics concluded the Church had fallen out of touch with the modern world.

To make matters worse, the mistaken view that the Church is hopelessly out of touch, hopelessly inflexible, and hopelessly bereft of compassion on matters related to sex and marriage has been and continues to be advanced by Catholic intellectuals with substantial public platforms. The pronouncements of Andrew Greeley and Richard McBrien and other like-minded Catholic theologians and social scientists have only added to the confusion, dissent, and scandal that swirls around Catholic moral teaching. In various ways, and with varying degrees of clarity and honesty, the dissenters argue that the Church must accommodate her morality to the ways of the world if she hopes to speak in an authentic way to the experience and concerns of modern men and women. They also argue – and this is important – that the most compassionate route forward for the Church is one which leads to changes in Church moral teaching. Law must give way to grace, rules must give way to experience, and the pope must give way to the people.

However, there are numerous problems with this accommodationist approach. I will focus on two in today's talk.

The first problem is that the accommodationist approach is based on bad social science. When most of these intellectuals were in their prime, the best social science suggested that the ideal posture of the Church to "family change," as it was euphemistically called, was one of acceptance and support. But contemporary social science on the contentious issues of our time – such as contraception, divorce, and cohabitation – suggests just the opposite conclusion. The shifts in sexual and familial behavior that these dissenters would like the Church to accommodate herself to have been revealed in – study after study – as social catastrophes.

Let me be perfectly clear: the leading scholars who have tackled these topics are not Catholics and most of them are not conservatives. They are, rather, honest social scientists willing to follow the data wherever it may lead. And the data have, as we shall see, largely vindicated Catholic moral teaching on sex and marriage. So the intellectual foundation for dissent on moral matters is collapsing.

The second problem with their dissenting agenda has been and is that its moral laxity is most disastrous for the most vulnerable members of our society: the poor. The poor have paid and continue to pay the largest price for the cultural revolution that Greeley, McBrien, and others would like the Church to baptize.

Let me now offer a summary of the social scientific research on contraception and divorce that illuminates the problems with the dissenting agenda.

Contraception

In *Humanae Vitae,* Pope Paul VI warned that the widespread use of contraception would lead to "conjugal infidelity and the general lowering of morality"; he also warned that man would lose respect for woman and "no longer [care] for her physical and psychological equilibrium"; rather, man would treat woman as a "mere instrument of selfish enjoyment, and no longer as his respected and beloved companion." Why? By breaking the natural and divinely-ordained connection between sex and procreation, women and especially men would focus on the hedonistic possibilities of sex and cease to sex as something that was intrinsically linked to new life and to the sacrament of marriage.

As you well know, in the United States, *Humanae Vitae* was the object of unprecedented dissent. Let me summarize the argument of one dissenter on this subject, Father Greeley. First, Greeley argues that Catholic teaching on contraception does not appreciate that married Catholics rely on sex for bonding, and they should not have to worry about always bringing a baby into their lives when they bond. Secondly, he claims that the hierarchy is more concerned about keeping its power, by blindly following Church tradition on contraception, than with helping ordinary people. "[T]he problem is the arrogance of power that makes many church leaders insensitive to the problems of ordinary people and heedless of their needs – and of the Holy Spirit speaking through their experiences."[4] He even goes so far as to suggest that "[messing] around with the intimate lives of men and women to protect your own power is demonic."[5]

So there we have it. The efforts of the popes and bishops to uphold the Church's constant teaching on artificial contraception is legalistic, unrealistic, and demonic. But on this topic, as on others, Greeley does not reconcile his polling data with what he knows the data says about the consequences of widespread contraception in the U.S. What does the data tell us? Well, scholars from Robert Michael at Greeley's own University of Chicago to George Akerlof at the University of California at Berkeley argue that contraception played a central role in launching the sexual and divorce revolutions of the late 20th century. Michael has written that about half of the increase in divorce from 1965 to 1976 can be attributed to the "unexpected nature of the contraceptive revolution" – especially in the way that it made marriages less child-centered.[6] Akerlof argues that the availability of first contraception and then abortion in the 1960s and 1970s was one of the crucial factors fueling the sexual revolution and the collapse of marriage among the working class and the poor.

I will focus on Akerlof's scholarship. George Akerlof is a nobel-prize winning economist, a professor at Berkeley, and a former fellow at the Brookings Institution; he is not a conservative. In two articles in leading economic journals, Akerlof details findings and advances arguments that vindicate Paul VI's prophetic warnings about the social consequences of contraception for morality and men.[7]

In his first article, Akerlof begins by asking why the U.S. witnessed such a dramatic increase in illegitimacy from 1965 to 1990 – from 24% to 64% among African-Americans, and from 3 percent to 18 percent among whites. He notes that public health advocates had predicted that the widespread availability of contraception and abortion would reduce illegitimacy, not increase it. So what happened?

Using the language of economics, Akerlof points out that "technological innovation creates both winners and losers."[8] In this case the introduction of widespread effective contraception – especially the Pill – put traditional women with an interest in marriage and children at "competitive disadvantage" in the relationship "market" compared to modern women who took a more hedonistic approach to sex and relationships; the contraceptive revolution also reduced the costs of sex for women and men, insofar as the threat of pregnancy was taken off the table – especially as abortion became widely available in the 1970s.

The consequence? Traditional women could no longer hold the threat of pregnancy over their male partners, either to avoid sex or to elicit a promise of marriage in the event that pregnancy resulted from sexual intercourse. And modern women no longer worried about getting pregnant. Accordingly, more and more women gave in to their boyfriends' entreaties for sex.

In Akerlof's words, "the norm of the premarital sexual abstinence all but vanished in the wake of the technology shock."[9] Women felt free or *obligated* to have sex before marriage. For instance, Akerlof finds that the percentage of girls 16 and under reporting sexual activity surged in 1970 and 1971 as contraception and abortion became common in many states throughout the country.

Thus, the sexual revolution left traditional or moderate women who wanted to avoid premarital sex or contraception "immiserated" because they could not compete with women who had no serious objection to premarital sex, and they could no longer elicit a promise of marriage from boyfriends in the event they got pregnant. Boyfriends, of course, could say that pregnancy was their girlfriends' choice. So men were less likely to agree to a shotgun marriage in the event of a premarital pregnancy than they would have been before the arrival of the Pill and abortion.

Thus, more of the traditional women ended up having sex and having children out of wedlock, while more of the permissive women ended up having sex and contracepting or aborting so as to avoid childbearing. This explains in large part why the contraceptive revolution was associated with both an *increase* in abortion and illegitimacy.

In his second article, Akerlof argues that another key outworking of the contraceptive revolution was the disappearance of marriage – shotgun and otherwise – for men. Contraception and abortion allowed men to put off marriage, even in cases when they had fathered a child. Consequently, the fraction of young men who were married in the U.S. dropped precipitously. Between 1968 and 1993, the percentage of men 25 to 34 who were married with children fell from 66% to 40%. Accordingly, young men did not benefit from the domesticating influence of wives and children.

Instead, they could continue to hang out with their young male friends, and were thus more vulnerable to the drinking, partying, tomcatting, and worse that is associated with unsupervised groups of young men. Absent the domesticating influence of marriage and children, young men – especially men from working class and poor families – were more likely to respond to the lure of the street. Akerlof notes, for instance, that substance abuse and incarceration more than doubled from 1968 to 1998. Moreover, his statistical models indicate that the growth in single men in this period was indeed linked to higher rates of substance abuse, arrests for violent crimes, and drinking.

From this research, Akerlof concludes by arguing that the contraceptive revolution played a key, albeit indirect, role in the dramatic increase in social pathology and poverty this country witnessed in the 1970s; it did so by fostering sexual license, poisoning the relations between men and women, and weakening the marital vow. In Akerlof's words:

> ...Just at the time, about 1970, that the permanent cure to poverty seemed to be on the horizon and just at the time that women had obtained the tools to control the number and the timing of their children, single motherhood and the feminization of poverty began their long and steady rise.[10]

Furthermore, the decline in marriage caused in part by the contraceptive revolution "has intensified...the crime shock and the substance abuse shock" that marked the 70s and 80s.[11]

One pair of statistical trends illustrates the way in which the social pathologies of late 20th century fell disproportionately on the poor. About 5% of college-educated women now have a child outside marriage (little change since 1960s) and about 20% of women with high school education or less now have a child outside marriage (up from 7% in 1960s).

Why, you might ask, were family decline and attendant social pathologies concentrated among poor and working class Americans? Think of marriage as dependent upon two pillars: socioeconomic status and normative commitment. The poor have less of an economic stake in marriage, so they are more dependent on religious and moral norms regarding marriage. Middle and upper class remain committed to marriage in practice because they continue to have an economic and social stake in marriage. They recognize that their lifestyle, and the lifestyle of their children, will be markedly better if they combine their economic and social resources with one spouse.

So the bottom line is this: the research of Nobel-Prize winning George Akerlof suggests that the tragic outworkings of the contraceptive revolution were sexual license, family dissolution, crime, and poisoned relations between the sexes – and that the poor have paid the heaviest price for this revolution. This research suggests that the Church's firm commitment to the moral law in the face of dramatic and widespread dissent from within and without is being vindicated in precincts that are not normally seen as sympathetic to Holy Mother Church. This research also suggests that the dissenting agenda advanced by people like Fr. Andrew Greeley amounts to a false compassion. Greeley may be right to claim that the Holy Spirit sometimes speaks through people's experiences; but a sober look at our experience with contraception reveals that it is in fact contraception – not the magisterium – that is not in men, women, and children's best interests.

Divorce

We have talked for a while now about one of the most controversial moral teachings of the Church. I now turn to the issue of divorce and remarriage, where once again the Church offers a sign of contradiction to the modern world. The *Catechism of the Catholic Church* aptly summarizes the Church's teaching on divorce and remarriage:

> *Divorce* is a grave offense against the natural law. Divorce is immoral … because it introduces disorder into the family and into society. This disorder brings grave harm to the deserted spouse, to children traumatized by the separation of their parents and often torn between them, and because of its contagious effect, which makes it truly a plague on society. (CCC 2384 –2385)

The *Catechism* is making two central points here: (1) divorce harms children and (2) divorce is an infectious social plague that hurts the commonweal. For these reasons, among others, divorce is condemned and remarriage is prohibited.

The Church's seemingly inflexible position on divorce also comes in for serious criticism from the dissenters. Fr. Richard McBrien, for instance, argues that the Church's position makes no allowance for individuals whose marriage falls apart "despite the best efforts of all concerned." He further argues that this pope does not encourage "the way of compassion" in dealing with Catholics who have divorced and remarried, and does not acknowledge the "traditional Roman principle that laws are ideals to strive for and not standards one can realistically expect to achieve on a day-to-day basis." Such is McBrien's argument, which echoes the arguments of mainline Protestants in the early 20th century; it boils down to this: The Church should dispense with the moral law in an effort to be more compassionate to people in difficult situations.

But what we have, once again, is false compassion.

This becomes clear when we take a careful look, once again, at the data. Numerous scholars – from Leora Friedberg at the University of Virginia to Nicholas Wolfinger at the University of Utah – have shown that divorce does in fact function as a social plague. Friedberg shows, for instance, that passage of no-fault divorce laws in the 1970s accelerated the pace of divorce by about 17 percent between 1968 and 1988.[12] Wolfinger shows that a parental divorce increases children's chance of divorce by more than 50 percent, and is by far one of the most potent predictors of divorce. So we can see that Pope John Paul II is right when he says that divorce "has devastating consequences that spread in society like the plague."

But I would like to focus on the other aspect of the Church's teaching, namely, that divorce brings grave harm to children. Here, I am going to focus on the research of Sara McLanahan, a professor of sociology at Princeton (one of my advisors at Princeton). Sara is also no conservative. In the 1970s, as a divorced, single mother she set out to show that the negative effects of divorce could be attributed solely to the economic dislocation caused by divorce. But after spending 20 years researching the subject, she came to the conclusion that the social and emotional consequences of divorce also played a key role in explaining the negative outcomes of divorce. She also found that remarriage was, on average, no help to children affected by divorce.

McLahanan argues that the intact, two-parent family does four key things for children. First, children benefit from the economic resources that mothers and particularly fathers bring to the household through work and sometimes family money. Second, children see their parents model appropriate male-female relations, including virtues like fidelity and self-sacrifice. Third, because both parents are invested in the child, they spell one another in caring for their children, and they monitor one another's parenting. This reduces stress, helps to insure that parents are not too strict, or too permissive, and makes it much more likely than other family arrangements to forestall abuse. Finally, fathers often serve as key guides to children seeking to negotiate the outside world as adolescents and young adults. Fathers introduce them to civic institutions, the world of work, and provide them with key contacts in these worlds.

McClanahan also argues that stepfathers do not have the history, the authority, and the trust of the children to function – on the average – as well as biological fathers. She writes:

> ...From the child's point of view, having a new adult move into the household creates another disruption. Having adjusted to the father's moving out, the child must now experience a second reorganization of household personnel. Stepfathers are less likely to be committed to the child's welfare than biological fathers, and they are less likely to serve as a check on the mother's behavior.[13]

So what does McClanahan find? Children from divorced families are about twice as likely to drop out of high school. Data from the National Survey of Families and Households showed that children in divorced families had a 17% risk of dropping out of school, compared to a 9% risk for children in married families, even after controlling for parents' education and race. Other surveys found similar results.[14] Girls raised in divorced families are almost twice as likely to have a non-marital birth as teens. In the National Survey of Families and Households, the risk for children in divorced families is 15% compared to 9% for those with married parents. Again this survey is typical.[15] McLanahan also finds that boys raised outside of an intact nuclear family are more than twice as likely as other boys to end up in prison, even controlling for a range of social and economic factors.[16]

McLanahan also explored whether children in step-families did better than children in single-mother families. Bear in mind that by the time she was conducting this latest round of research, she had remarried. Here is what she found: "Remarriage neither reduces nor improves a child's chances of graduating from high school or avoiding a teenage birth."[17] In other words, remarriage *does not* mitigate the devastating social effects of divorce.

The final point I would like to make about the divorce revolution is that it has fallen, once again, disproportionately on the shoulders of the most vulnerable members of our society. My own research with the National Survey of Families and Households indicates that married couples with a high school diploma or less education have a 19% higher risk of divorce than married couples with a college degree. Other studies show that poor and working-class married couples are much more likely to divorce than are middle- and upper-class married couples.

So, after spending 20 years researching the effects of family structure on children, McLanahan came to this conclusion with her colleague Gary Sandefur at the University of Wisconsin:

> If we were asked to design a system for making sure that children's basic needs were met, we would probably come up with something quite similar to the two-parent ideal. Such a design, in theory, would not only ensure that children had access to the time and money of two adults, it also would provide a system of checks and balances that promoted quality parenting. The fact that both parents have a biological connection to the child would increase the likelihood that the parents would identify with the child and be willing to sacrifice for that child, and it would reduce the likelihood that either parent would abuse the child (McLanahan and Sandefur 1994: p. 38).

This, of course, sounds quite similar to the perennial wisdom of the Catholic Church, as articulated by figures as various as Pope John Paul II and St. Thomas Aquinas.

Conclusion

The portrait I have painted is sobering. But I would like to conclude on two hopeful notes.

First, there are signs that our family freefall is coming to a close. The dramatic and devastating decline we witnessed in the institution of the family in the U.S. has largely halted in the last decade or so. In the late 1990s, divorce rates continued a decline begun earlier, the percentage of children in two-parent families increased slightly, and, for the first time in years, opinion polls indicated that more married Americans report being "very happy" in their marriages. Not surprisingly, we have also seen dramatic reductions in juvenile delinquency, youth suicide, and child poverty in the last decade.

Secondly, as my comments suggest, we are beginning to see a new openness among intellectuals to the importance of marriage and to the perils of divorce. For a long time intellectuals were not willing to acknowledge the importance of marriage for children. But the intellectual tide is now turning towards a refreshing willingness to grapple with our children's toughest social problems in a probing and open-minded manner. Besides Akerlof and McLanahan, scholars like Linda Waite at the University of Chicago, Robert Lerman at the Urban Institute, Belle Sawhill at Brookings Institution, and Norval Glenn at the University of Texas have all underlined the importance of marriage in recent years. Their willingness to speak up on behalf of the unvarnished truth – the truth written on our hearts, and the truth evident for all to see in our statistical models – suggests that the intellectual foundations of dissent are crumbling before our very eyes.

Faithful Catholic scholars need to seize this moment, and underline the intellectual power and coherence of Catholic moral teaching to our colleges and universities, our parishes, our pastors, and in the public square. Above all else, we need to drive home the point that social justice cannot be divorced from the Church's moral teaching. More than anyone else, the poor have been devastated by the outworkings of the sexual revolution of the last 40 years. We must make it crystal clear that the Church's commitment to the poor requires nothing less than a vigorous proclamation of the Church's true and beautiful teaching about sex and marriage. In other words, we must make it clear that the preferential option for the poor begins in the home.

W. Bradford Wilcox, Ph.D., an assistant professor of sociology at the University of Virginia, studies religion, fatherhood, marriage, and parenting. He is the author of *Soft Patriarchs, New Men: How Christianity Shapes Fathers and Husbands* (University of Chicago Press, 2004). Wilcox has published numerous articles. He has previously held research fellowships at the Brookings Institution, Princeton

University, Yale University, and the University of Pennsylvania. Professor Wilcox's research on religion and the family has been featured in the *Los Angeles Times*, the *Washington Post*, the *Washington Times*, *USA Today*, and numerous NPR stations. Dr. Wilcox is married and the father of three children.

Notes

1. Luke Timothy Johnson. 2001. "Abortion, Sexuality, and Catholicism's Public Presence." *Commonweal* Fall 2001 Colloquium. New York: Union Theological Seminary.
2. *Ibid.*
3. Andrew Greeley, *The Catholic Myth*. New York: Collier Books, 1990.
4. Andrew Greeley. *The Catholic Myth*. p. 99.
5. *Ibid*, p. 96.
6. Robert Michael, Talk at Emory University family conference in March, 2003.
7. George Akerlof, Janet L. Yellen, and Michael L. Katz. 1996. "An Analysis of Out-of-Wedlock Childbearing in the United States." *The Quarterly Journal of Economics* CXI: 277 –317. George A. Akerlof. 1998. "Men Without Children." *The Economic Journal* 108: 287 –309.
8. Akerlof *et al.*, p. 279.
9. *Ibid.*, p. 309.
10. *Ibid.*, p. 313.
11. Akerlof, p. 289.
12. See Linda Waite and Maggie Gallagher, p. 179. Margaret F. Brinig and F.H. Buckley. 1998. "No-Fault Laws and At-Fault People." *International Review of Law and Economics* 18: 325 –40.
13. Sara McLanahan and Gary Sandefur. 1994. *Growing up with a Single Parent*. Cambridge, MA: Harvard University Press. p. 29.
14. *Ibid.*, p. 41.
15. *Ibid.*, p. 53.
16. Cynthia C. Harper and Sara S. McLanahan. 1998. "Father Absence and Youth Incarceration." Annual Meeting of the American Sociological Association (San Francisco).
17. McLanahan and Sandefur, p. 71.

Chapter 20: The Global War against Baby Girls
An Update

Nicholas Eberstadt

Over the past three years the American public has received regular updates on what we have come to call "the global war on terror." A no-less significant global war – a war, indeed, against nature, civilization, and, in fact, humanity itself has also been underway in recent years. This latter war, however, has attracted much less attention and comment, despite its immense consequence. This world-wide struggle might be called "The Global War Against Baby Girls." It is a conflict of astonishing and ever more dismaying dimensions. Whatever one's personal estimate of our progress to date in the global war on terror, what remains beyond dispute is that humanity has been faring much more poorly in this other war. Herewith, my friends, an update on this global war's many different fronts.

For the entirety of human inquiry – and no doubt, since the beginning of time – there has been a clear and steadily observable biological regularity to the distribution of male and female offspring in those species that have just males and females. That regularity has been equally apparent for the human species. In fact, the earliest findings of demographers investigating the rhythms and regularities of human populations included the discovery of slight but constant and almost unvarying excess of baby boys over baby girls born in any population. This excess was so regular that it led early demographers like Johan Peter Suessmilch and others to believe that there was a natural intention in it.

Regardless of intention, this slight surfeit of baby boys over baby girls is a proven biological and historical fact, so predictable and sure as to qualify as a rule of nature. What is called the "sex ratio at birth" by demographers – the number of baby boys born for every hundred baby girls – has been found in all settings and at all observed times to fall in a very narrow range: on the order of 103, 104, or 105 (and in rare cases, 106 or just a bit over).

The U.S. sex ratio at birth, which is tabulated fairly well, and is quite stable over time, offers an illustration of this regular disproportion.

Sex Ratios at Birth, All Races: United States, 1940–2002

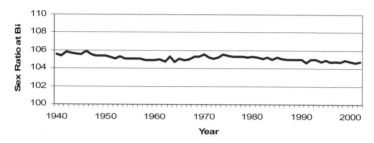

Source: Derived from U.S. National Center for Health Statistics, *Vital Statistics of the United States*, 1978 –2002 editions, Volume I.

These sex ratio differences can be observed in any ordinarily constituted population. For reasons not yet well understood, sex ratio variations on the basis of ethnicity can also be observed; even then they are fairly small and quite stable over time.

Sex Ratio at Birth by Ethnicity, United States: 1984
Total: 105.0
White: 105.4
Black: 103.1
American Indian: 101.4
Chinese: 104.6
Japanese 102.6

Source: Derived from U.S. National Center for Health Statistics, *Vital Statistics of the United States*, 1984 edition (1988), Volume I, Table 1 –53.

Differences in sex ratio at birth also seem related to birth order and the age of parents. Again, these differences are small and fairly stable over time.

Sex Ratio at Birth, by Birth Order and Ethnicity, United States: 1984 Live Birth Order

	1	2	3	4	5	6	7	8+
All Races	105.4	105.0	104.8	104.6	103.8	100.6	101.2	100.9
White	105.8	105.3	105.2	104.8	105.3	102.3	101.5	101.4
Black	104.0	103.2	102.7	102.9	99.9	98.4	100.8	101.9

Source: Derived from U.S. National Center for Health Statistics, *Vital Statistics of the United States*, 1984 edition (1988), Volume I, Table 1 –58.

Sex Ratio at Birth, by Birth Order and Ethnicity, United States: 1993

	1	2	3	4	5	6	7	8+
All Races	105.4	104.9	104.8	103.7	103.4	105.4	104.3	103.0
White	105.7	105.4	105.3	104.2	103.7	106.1	105.3	104.4
Black	103.8	102.3	102.0	102.1	103.3	103.5	99.9	100.2

Source: Derived from U.S. National Center for Health Statistics, *Vital Statistics of the United States*, 1993 edition, Volume I.

However, in the last generation the sex ratio at birth in some parts of the world has become completely unhinged. The first evidentiary exhibit we may present for this unsettling new phenomenon comes from the People's Republic of China. Bearing in mind that the regular sex ratio at birth is in the order of 103, 104, 105, or a bit higher, let us explore China's November 2000 census, which reported sex ratios at birth by individual provinces. In the table below the red lines indicate where the customary expectations of human populations.

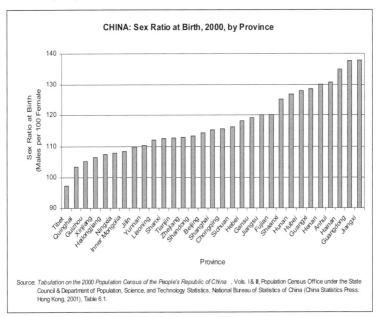

CHINA: Sex Ratio at Birth, 2000, by Province

Source: *Tabulation on the 2000 Population Census of the People's Republic of China*, Vols. I & II, Population Census Office under the State Council & Department of Population, Science, and Technology Statistics, National Bureau of Statistics of China (China Statistics Press: Hong Kong, 2001), Table 6.1.

Clearly, there are only a few provinces in China that report a sex ratio at birth in the year 2000 under, or even as low as, 110. By contrast, in a number of provinces with populations of tens of millions of people, the reported sex ratio at birth ranges from over 120 boys for every 100 girls to over 130 boys for every 100 girls.

A number of factors must be considered when accessing this type of data. For one, the calculations or tabulations could be wrong. As the Chinese government does not actually tabulate the vital statistics for its entire population on a year to year basis, playing "catch-up" with huge national population counts might possibly lead to some deviations in statistical data. Another reason for doubting these numbers could be China's longstanding program of population control, the notorious "one-child norm." If there is an existing preference for sons, as one might expect in a highly Confucian society where sons continue the family line, people might try to "game the system" by hiding baby girls to try for another "shot" at a son.

There are also some notable discrepancies in the Chinese demographic data. Daniel Goodkind of the Census Bureau, for example, has brought to light the fact that hospital birth numbers have regularly displayed a lower sex ratio at birth than the ones reported by the Census statistics. Even if we allow for the fact that hospital births tend to be more frequent in urban centers where the reported sex ratio disparity is smaller, the reported sex ratio disproportion in recent years is still highly anomalous.

Sex Ratio at Birth Data in China: Reported Statistics vs. Hospital Records, 1988 –1995

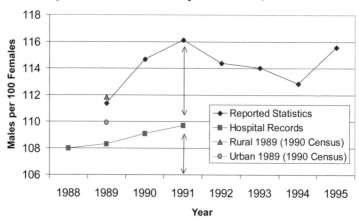

Sources: Zeng, et al., 1993; Population Census Office and State Statistical Bureau, Department of Population Statistics, 1993; National Bureau of Statistics, Department of Population and Employment Statistics, 1991, 1992, 1994, 1995, and 1997; Gu and Roy, 1995.

Courtesy of Daniel Goodkind, U.S. Census Bureau, from his paper, *Recent Trends in the Sex Ratio at Birth in East Asia*, June 2002.

Moreover, Chinese Census statistics display a fairly high degree of internal consistency. For example, the 1990 census, which reported a ratio of almost 112 for babies under the age of one, corresponds with the 2000 census, which shows nearly the same ratio for 10-year-olds, ten years later. The consistency in data indicates that the statistics are not a mere artifact. Clearly, a highly unusual and utterly abnormal demographic process has been taking place in the world's largest population.

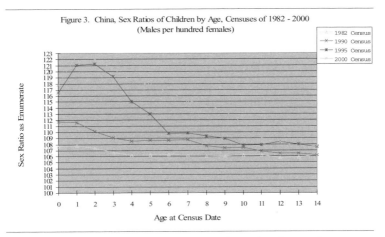

Figure 3. China, Sex Ratios of Children by Age, Censuses of 1982 - 2000
(Males per hundred females)

Source: Judith Banister, "Shortage of Girls in China Today: Causes, Consequences, International Comparisons, and Solutions," 2003

To understand the process that is perverting modern-day China's secondary sex ratio, it is necessary to examine the sex ratio at birth in

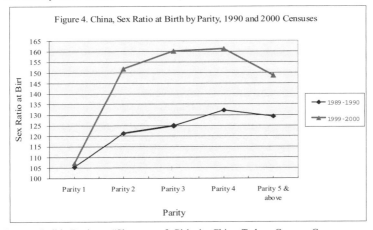

Figure 4. China, Sex Ratio at Birth by Parity, 1990 and 2000 Censuses

Source: Judith Banister, "Shortage of Girls in China Today: Causes, Consequences, International Comparisons, and Solutions," 2003

China according to the different parities and to birth order. A table prepared by Judith Banister, formerly of the Census Bureau, gives us significant insight into the developing demographic trends in China. For parity one, for first births, the sex ratio in China in 1990 and 2000 stood at just about 105 – an unexceptional ratio in any ordinary human population. The second, third, fourth and fifth order parities, however, display significant aberrations from the ordinary. For higher-order births, the most recent Chinese census displays sex ratios at birth of 150 boys and higher for every hundred baby girls – a phenomenon utterly without natural precedent in human history.

To emphasize the obvious, these anomalies are the reflection of the advent and rapid proliferation of inexpensive prenatal sex determination technology and the rampant use of abortion as a gender determination tool. At the very minimum, half of all second-order (or higher) female pregnancies in China are terminated on a gender-selective basis.

It would be heartening to think that the rapid modernization of the People's Republic of China would do away with the vestiges of "backward thinking" that are manifest in these dramatic demographic ratios. Unfortunately, the data currently available does not allow for any such optimism.

CHINA: Sex Ratio (Children Ages 1-4) vs. Female Illiteracy Rate by Province, 2000 China Census

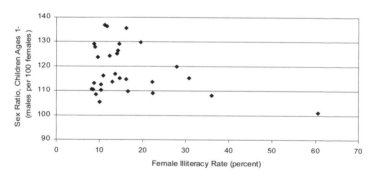

ɔurce: *Tabulation of the 2000 Population Census of the People's Republic of China* , Vols. I & II, Population Census Office under the State Council & Department of Population, Science and Technology Statistics, National Bureau of Statistics of China (China Statistics Press: Hong Kong, 2001), Tables 1.7 and 6.1.

Not only is there no positive correlation between literacy rates and lower sex ratio at birth, but also in actuality there is negative correlation between the two. To the contrary: available data suggests that the higher the literacy rate in a given Chinese province, the higher the disproportion between baby boys and baby girls at birth that can be expected there.

Sex Ratio at Birth vs. GDP per Capita: China, 1953 –1999

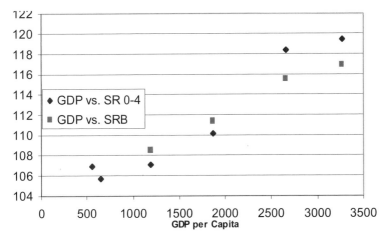

Sources: Lavely, William. *First Impressions of the 2000 Census of China.* Available electronically at http://csde.washington.edu/pubs/wps/01-13.pdf, accessed 10/15/02. Maddison, Angus. *The World Economy: A Millennial Perspective.* OECD: 2003.

The correlation between income levels and sex ratios at birth by province does not offer reason for optimism, either. The steady increase in China's income level tracks directly with a steady rise in the disproportion between baby boys and baby girls at birth. Over the past two decades, recall, China's linkages with the outside world – through trade, investment, and communication – have also grown steadily. Evidently, "Globalization with Chinese characteristics" is not inconsistent with an extraordinary and still-increasing imbalance between baby boys and baby girls.

Although the People's Republic of China is notorious for its gruesome involuntary population control program, the data from other parts of East Asia do not afford us the happy presumption that China's aberrant demographic trends are the product of a single oppressive regime. Demographic reports from South Korea, Taiwan, Hong Kong, and the Chinese ethnic groups in Singapore yield disturbingly similar results.

Although all four of East Asia's "little dragons" have implemented anti-national population programs at one time or another, none of them has been coercive. In addition, each of these places is significantly more educated and significantly more affluent than the population of the Chinese mainland, taken as a whole. Nevertheless, since the 1980s, all of these populations have exhibited biologically impossible sex ratios at birth.

Males per 100 Females, Three-Year Averages 1980 –2001

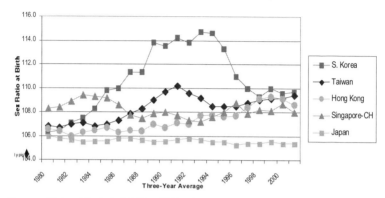

Sources: National Statistical Office, 2002; Directorate-General of Budget, Accounting and Statistics, 1992 and 2000; Ministry of the Interior, 2001; Singapore Department of Statistics, 1990, 1996, 1998, 1999, 2001a, 2001b; Census and Statistics Department, 1983 and 2000; National Institute Of Population and Social Security Research 2002.

Taiwan shows sex ratio at birth according to parity or birth order very similar to those observed in China. In fact, for higher order births, the disproportion in Taiwan has been even more pronounced in certain recent periods.

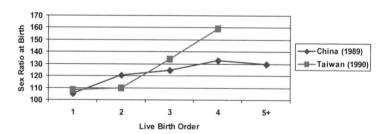

Sex Ratio at Birth by Birth Order, China and Taiwan
Source: Park and Cho, *Population and Development Review*, Volume 21, No 1 (March 1995).

As with China and Taiwan, South Korea's statistics from the 1990s reflect the advent and proliferation of prenatal gender-determination technology.

Sex Ratio at Birth by Birth Order, South Korea: 1980 vs. 1992

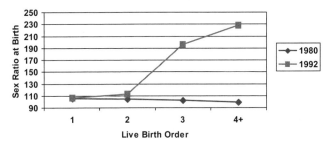

Source: Park and Cho, *Population and Development Review*, Volume 21, No 1 (March 1995).

The next figure shows similar parental decision-making dynamic at work in Hong Kong.

	Previous Birth		
	Male	Female	Total
Sex Ratio Second Birth	105	116	110

	Previous Births			
	Male-Male	Female-Female	Male Female	Total
Sex Ratio Third Birth	94	137	92	109

The data from the East Asian Tigers warrant a revision of the hypothesis that the war on baby girls is limited to China – and is a consequence simply of and Beijing's coercive "one-child norm" population policy. Population control programs could surely be exacerbating gender imbalances, depending upon local norms – but just as clearly; they are not the driving force behind this phenomenon on the East Asian rim. Instead, it would seem to be due in these locales to a collision of three powerful factors: enormous and enduring son preference, the use of rapidly spreading prenatal sex determination technology for gender-based abortion, and the rapid drop in fertility in different populations, making the gender outcome in each birth all the more portentous for parents. However, there is much more to the global war on baby girls than is visible in East Asia alone.

Despite all the billions of dollars spent on population programs around the world, it is extremely hard to find population surveys indicating gender preference for a next child among potential parents. Fortunately in the case below, the Indian Government did ask its people: "What is your preference for the gender of your next child?" The following is the result of a recent survey from the late 1990s. It shows that for married women as a whole, the preference is over four to one for a boy.

Fertility and Child Gender Preference Among Married Women, India: 1998–1999
Number of Living Children

	0	1	2	3	4+	Total
Desires an additional child	89.0	76.4	23.0	11.3	5.5	30.3

Preferred Sex of Addition Child

Boy	34.8	40.3	60.2	74.5	72.0	46.9
Girl	2.5	15.9	14.4	9.0	6.8	11.0
Number of respondents	7,620	13,631	20,836	18,359	23,202	83,649

Source: "National Family Health Survey (NFHS-2): 1998–99," (Bombay: Institute for Population Sciences, October 2000).

As the numbers for India are an arithmetic average, there are significant differences between its various states. The data from the state of Punjab, for example, a prosperous state up in the north, presents a startling extreme. For married women, in the year 1993, the reported Punjabi preference for boys as opposed to girls was over ten to one.

Fertility and Child Gender Preference Among Married Women, Punjab, India: 1993
Number of Living Children

	0	1	2	3	4	5	6+	Total
Desires an additional child	92.7	82.4	21.0	7.4	2.5	1.9	1.3	24.9

Preferred sex of additional child

Boy	38.3	51.0	80.8	96.6	*	*	*	58.9
Girl	0.6	6.1	12.6	1.7	*	*	*	5.6

*: Percentage not shown, less than 25 respondents

Source: "National Family Health Survey (MCH and Family Planning): Punjab 1993," (Bombay: Institute for Population Sciences, September 1995).

How have India's strong preferences for sons translated into demographic results? The figure below provides some indication. These data, drawn from the latest Indian census are not for the sex ratio at birth, but rather for the ratio of boys and girls under the age of seven. Nevertheless, these numbers can be taken as a fairly serviceable proxy for sex ratio at birth since we have no great reason to think that they have been hugely affected either by sex-selective migration or by other post-birth, sex-selective mortality patterns. Clearly, in India that there are a number of states, which hit or exceed the biologically impossible sex ratio of 110 to 100. Note, by the way, that Punjab in the year 2001 counted 127 little boys for every 100 little girls.

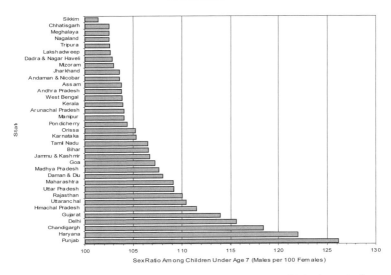

INDIA: Sex Ratio Among Children Under Age 7
By State, 2001

Source: Census of India, 2001, accessed 15 October 2002, available electronically at http://www.censusindia.net/results/provindia2.html.

As with China and the other Asian Tigers, there is not much evidence from India's population census that education in India is vitiating the problem. The next graphic compares literacy rates for women and the disproportion between little boys and little girls in different states of India. Educational levels vary greatly among the states of India today. But to judge by this cross-section, literacy levels do not appear to have any immediate bearing on the reduction of gender disproportion.

Female Literacy Rate vs. Sex Ratio Ages 0–6: Indian Provinces, 2001

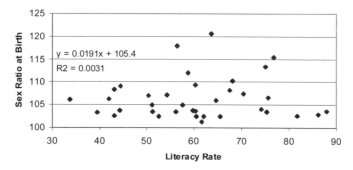

Sources: http://www.censusindia.net/results/provindia2.html, accessed 9/14/04; Census of India, 2001: Chapter 7, Statement 32, http://www.censusindia.net/data/chapter7.pdf accessed 9/14/04.

Sex Ratio of the Population Under Age 1: Azerbaijan, Armenia, and Georgia, 1990–2001

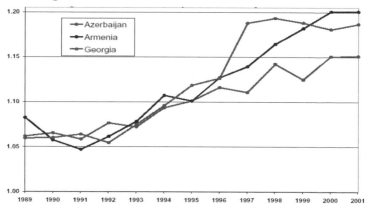

Source: "Surprising Sex Ratios in the South Caucasus: Son Preferences in the Former Soviet States of Armenia, Azerbaijan, and Georgia," Dennis Donahue and Jennifer Fortado. International Programs Center, U.S. Census Bureau, May 2003.

China and India, of course, are the world's two most populous states, together accounting for nearly two fifths of the current human population. But our tour of battlefronts in the global war against baby girls is by no means yet concluded. I'm indebted to Dennis Donahue of the Census Bureau, who alerted me to the huge upsurge in the ratio of baby boys to baby girls in Azerbaijan, Georgia, and Armenia in the period since the end of the Soviet Union. Again, it is impossible to propose that natural biological processes would have caused such gender disproportions. Rather, the end of the Soviet regime ushered in an era of technological advance: including the advent of prenatal gender determination technology, which in turn made possible the practice of gender-selective abortions on a massive scale. In Armenia, Georgia, and Azerbaijan, these gender aberrations are approaching what one may call the "Chinese gold standard of gender disproportion."

Most of the population of Third World countries does not live in areas where governments track birth and death records on regular, comprehensive and reliable annual basis. There are preciously few countries in different parts of the world where annual vital registration data are accurately updated each year. Yet the limited data at hand reveal what are historically aberrant and, in any large national population, biologically impossible ratios in various countries around the world, including Europe and Latin America.

International Sex Ratios At Birth Over 107, Based On Vital Registration Data: Recent Years

Bulgaria	1997	108	Cuba	1998	109.4
Estonia	1997	107.8	"	1996	118.0
Greece	1998	107.2	El Salvador	1998	107.1
"	1995	108.0	Venezuela	1998	107.5
Luxembourg	1998	109.9	"	1996	107.5
Macedonia	1999	108.4			
"	1997	108.7			
"	1995	110.7			
Yugoslavia	1999	107.2			

Source: UN Demographic Yearbook, 1997 through 2000 editions.

Of the countries in Europe, Luxembourg is a possible statistical exception because of its extremely small annual number of births (under 6,000 a year in the late 1990s). Macedonia, however, cannot claim the same exemption from the laws of sampling error, and in Yugoslavia, it becomes clear, *ethnic* cleansing is not the only national demographic sport.

Again, in East Asia, Macau follows the echoes of the Chinese mainland and nearby Hong Kong. In largely Muslim Malaysia, the Philippines, and in Singapore, too, the gender ratios are abnormally high. It is worth noting that Singapore's national ratio is higher than the Chinese ethnic ratio, which suggests that local Malaysian and Indian populations have even higher sex ratios at birth than the local Chinese population.

International Sex Ratios At Birth Over 107, Based On Vital Registration Data: Recent Years, Continued

Macao	2000	111.7	Cyprus	1998	107.1	Cape Verde	1990	107.5
Malaysia (Peninsular)	1998	107.1	Kyrgyzstan	1996	107.2	Egypt	1995	108.7
Philippines	1993	108.7	Pakistan	1997	107.7	"	1990	109.3
Singapore	2000	109.2	"	1994	110.9	Libya	1996	108.5
			"	1993	110.0	Tunisia	1995	107.3
			Qatar	1992	107.2			

Source: UN Demographic Yearbook, 1997 through 2000 editions.

Preferred Sex of Next Child: Pakistan, 1990–91

	Gender Preference					
Son	Daughter	No Preference	Missing/ Other	Total	Number of Women
No children	31.7	0.2	67.6	0.5	100.0	512
One child	49.5	4.3	46.2	--	100.0	548
Two children	47.5	11. 0	41.5	--	100.0	417
Three children	63.9	7.0	29.1	--	100.0	329
Four children	62.8	6.4	30.6	0.2	100.0	193
Five children	59.3	4.5	36.2	--	100.0	175
Total	49.1	5.2	45.6	0.1	100.0	2174

Note: Figures in parentheses are based on 25 to 49 unweighted women – less than 0.05 percent. Source: http://www.measuredhs.com/pubs/pdf/FR29/08Chapter8.pdf accessed 9/15/04.

Moving toward the African continent Egypt, Libya, and Tunisia, that is to say, most of the countries of the Maghreb, display notable gender irregularities. And in Western Asia, anomalous gender imbalances are reported in Qatar, Kyrgyzstan, Cyprus, Pakistan (which does not have comprehensive vital statistics registration, but records large numbers of births on a regular basis).

One may wonder: what are the prospects for the war against baby girls in the globe's vast Muslim expanse? As it happens, one of the few countries in the Third World that *does* ask about gender preference for the next birth is the government of Pakistan. Just as in many parts of India, a preference for boys over girls in the order of ten to one is evident.

Another rare survey on parental gender preference for a next child exists for the country of Yemen. The graph below clearly shows the preference of parents for boys over girls to be many fold.

Preferred Sex of Next Child: Yemen, 1997

	Gender Preference						
	Son	Daughter	No preference	God's will	Missing/ Other	Total	Number of Women
No children	28.3	13.1	44.2	14.2	0.3	100.0	770
One child							
No sons	56.6	3.2	28.6	10.7	0.8	100.0	367
One son	8.0	51.2	29.1	11.7	0.0	100.0	366
Two children							
No sons	72.4	1.4	13.3	12.8	0.0	100.0	146
One son	28.1	9.5	41.1	20.5	0.9	100.0	271
Two sons	5.4	66.9	20.5	7.2	0.0	100.0	156
Three children							
No sons	76.4	0.0	7.0	16.6	0.0	100.0	65
One son	47.3	1.9	36.1	13.9	0.8	100.0	134
Two sons	14.7	35.3	36.9	12.7	0.4	100.0	181
Three sons	(0.0)	(83.4)	(11.3)	(5.3)	(0.0)	100.0	66
Four children							
No sons	82.6	2.9	12.7	1.8	0.0	100.0	38
One son	61.2	5.4	21.2	12.0	0.2	100.0	89
Two sons	28.4	6.3	41.0	24.3	0.0	100.0	99
Three sons	15.7	46.8	25.0	11.6	1.0	100.0	83
Four sons	12.4	64.1	11.4	12.1	0.0	100.0	19
Five children+							
No sons	86.4	0.0	10.6	3.0	0.0	100.0	25
One son	73.0	0.7	11.8	14.6	0.0	100.0	65
Two sons	39.2	2.2	40.4	18.3	0.0	100.0	110
Three sons	29.2	19.4	33.6	17.9	0.0	100.0	139
Four sons	20.3	26.4	43.7	8.5	1.1	100.0	104
Five sons or more	16.1	53.2	22.6	7.1	1.1	100.0	76
Family composition							
No living children	28.3	13.1	44.2	14.2	0.3	100.0	770
All boys	6.4	60.0	24.0	9.6	0.0	100.0	622
All girls	64.9	2.4	21.3	11.0	0.4	100.0	641
Boys = Girls	27.9	8.5	42.1	21.0	0.5	100.0	430
Boys > Girls	16.1	38.1	33.0	12.0	0.8	100.0	460
Boys < Girls	51.9	3.1	30.1	14.6	0.2	100.0	447
Total	32.6	21.2	32.4	13.3	0.3	100.0	3,369

Note: Figures in parentheses are based on 25 to 49 unweighted women – less than 0.05 percent.
Source: http://www.measuredhs.com/pubs/pdf/FR94/06Chapter06.pdf accessed 9/15/04.

The Palestinian Authority also collects survey information on gender preference. For women in the West Bank in Palestine, the preference for a boy over a girl as next birth is almost three to one. For men it is over five to one. This even more exaggerated preference for boys on the part of prospective fathers should be kept in mind. After all the role of men in determining family outcomes in a traditional Islamic setting is not exactly incidental.

Sex Preference for Next Child Among Palestinian Women and Husbands Who Want More Children: West Bank, 2001

	Women (n=424)			Husbands (n=513)		
	Boy	Girl	Up to God	Boy	Girl	Up to God
Total	27.5	10.6	61.9	35.7	6.9	57.3
Sex composition of living children						
No boys	35.8	6.7	57.5	36.2	8.6	55.2
No girls	16.3	20.5	63.2	22.9	14.6	62.4
Boys > girls	7.0	26.1	67.0	27.9	10.4	61.7
Boys = girls	21.3	8.5	70.1	22.7	9.4	68.0
Boys < girls	49.7	0.7	49.7	55.1	1.7	43.3
Source: client exit interview						

Source: http://www.hdip.org/reports/php_baseline.htm#tab7, Table 7, accessed 9/15/04.

Taken together the data assembled above presents compelling evidence that the war against baby girls is, indeed, a war of truly global proportions. It encompasses East and West Asia, the Indian subcontinent, North Africa, parts of Europe and the western hemisphere.

Are There Any Leading Indicators for *Future* SRB Imbalances?
• Possibly, death rates for ages 1-4.
• Male rates are normally always higher
• If death rates for little girls are higher, this may be evidence of existing deadly discrimination practices
• We can determine child mortality rates from national "life tables" published by WHO and UNPD

Data on parental preferences for next birth would be most useful in predicting the development of the global war on baby girls. A second best indicator would be information on death rates for little girls and little boys. Just as there is a biological regularity to the number of baby boys and baby girls born in any normal population, there is also a biological regularity to mortality schedules. At any given age, in a normal population, the death rate for males is a little higher than that for females. This can be seen over time, in different settings, different ethnicities, and different countries. It is an occurrence so regular, that it again may be taken as a rule.

Nevertheless, there are places in the world where the death rates for little girls, on an episodic or on a regular basis, are higher than those for little boys. If we take those abnormal and highly unusual distortions as a sign of extreme son preference, we should examine how the imbalance between sex ratios at birth corresponds with those peculiar patterns where death rates for little girls are higher than those for little boys. It is worth investigating what countries remain in these regions where, so to speak, the sex-ratio-at-birth "shoe" had not yet been dropped.

Key To Following Charts

Boldface: history of deadly discrimination *plus* existing SRB imbalance

No boldface: history of deadly discrimination against little girls but not SRB imbalance yet detected

Asterisk*: population over 25% Muslim

The chart below identifies five places in East Asia where historically there have been higher death rates for little girls than for little boys, and where today we see impossible sex ratios at birth. It should be noted, however, that there are as yet many other places in East Asia where there have been reports of higher death rates for little girls than for little boys – but where the sex ratio at birth has not yet risen to biologically impossible levels.

The Shape of Things To Come? East Asia & Pacific

China	Democratic People's
Hong Kong	Republic of Korea
Peninsular Malaysia*	Mongolia
Republic of Korea	Myanmar
Taiwan	Nauru
Brunei*	*Sabah**
Burma	*Sarawak**
Cambodia	*Thailand*

Note: Italicized countries rely on data from the U.N. Population Division life tables; Regular font indicates data from World Health Organization life tables.

Sources: World Health Organization Life Tables, available online at http://www3.who.int/whosis/life_tables/life_tables.cfm?path=evidence,life_tables&language=english accessed 9/15/04; United Nations Population Division Life Tables.

South Asia has a history of prejudicial death rates for little girls. Thus far, the sex ratios at birth in India and Pakistan have felt the effect of this prejudicial treatment. There is a reason to wonder whether the "fertile ground" in Bangladesh, Bhutan, Maldives, Nepal and Sri Lanka will be plowed in the same manner in the years ahead.

The Shape of Things To Come? South Asia	
India	Maldives*
Pakistan*	Nepal
Bangladesh*	*Sri Lanka*
Bhutan	

Note: Italicized countries rely on data from the U.N. Population Division life tables; Regular font indicates data from World Health Organization life tables.

Sources: World Health Organization Life Tables, available online at http://www3.who.int/whosis/life_tables/life_tables.cfm?path=evidence,life_tables&language=english accessed 9/15/04; United Nations Population Division Life Tables.

Three large countries in Europe (Greece, Macedonia, and Yugoslavia) betray some hints of prejudicial death rates for little girls in the post-war period. These differentials, should be emphasized, are not enormous – to the contrary, they are very small – but are nonetheless curious and unusual. Three other European countries (Italy, Luxembourg, and Norway) have seen strange and noteworthy increases of imbalances in sex ratio at birth, but have not yet reached biologically impossible levels.

The Shape of Things To Come? Europe	
Greece	Italy
Macedonia*	Luxembourg
Yugoslavia	Norway

Note: Italicized countries rely on data from the U.N. Population Division life tables; Regular font indicates data from World Health Organization life tables.

Sources: World Health Organization Life Tables, available online at http://www3.who.int/whosis/life_tables/life_tables.cfm?path=evidence,life_tables&language=english accessed 9/15/04; United Nations Population Division Life Tables.

The Shape of Things To Come? Latin America/Caribbean	
El Salvador	Dominican Republic
Venezuela	Guatemala
Antigua and Barbuda	Haiti
Bahamas	*Honduras*
Barbados	*Mexico*
Bolivia	Nicaragua
Chile	Peru
Columbia	*Puerto Rico*
Costa Rica	*Uruguay*

Note: Italicized countries rely on data from the U.N. Population Division life tables; Regular font indicates data from World Health Organization life tables.

Sources: World Health Organization Life Tables, available online at http://www3.who.int/whosis/life_tables/life_tables.cfm?path=evidence,life_tables&language=english accessed 9/15/04; United Nations Population Division Life Tables.

In the western hemisphere, Venezuela and El Salvador both have unnatural death rates for little girls and now also display unnatural sex ratios at birth. The rest of the countries in the list warrant careful observation in the future.

With the exception of Armenia, there are significant Muslim populations in all of the other countries in the table below. Four of those countries (Cyprus, Egypt, Libya, and Tunisia) have already reported both adverse death rates for little girls and abnormal gender imbalances in sex ratio at birth. The rest of the countries listed may demarcate a field of concern for the future. Note, incidentally, that the Palestinian population in the West Bank – whose preference for sons is so strongly ratified in health and demographic survey data – happens to be one of those showing abnormal death ratio for little girls.

The Shape of Things To Come? Middle East/North Africa/West Asia	
Armenia	Iraq*
Cyprus*	*Israel (non-Jewish pop)* *
Egypt*	Jordan*
Libya*	*Kuwait* *
Tunisia*	Lebanon*
Afghanistan*	Oman *
Algeria *	Syria*
Bahrain *	Tajikistan*
Djibouti*	Yemen*
Iran*	

Note: Italicized countries rely on data from the U.N. Population Division life tables; Regular font indicates data from World Health Organization life tables.

Sources: World Health Organization Life Tables, available online at http://www3.who.int/whosis/life_tables/life_tables.cfm?path=evidence,life_tables&language=english accessed 9/15/04; United Nations Population Division Life Tables.

In sub-Saharan Africa there apparently there as yet no indications of abnormal gender imbalances at birth. But estimated life tables for almost every country in the sub-Sahara are imprinted with discriminatory discrepancies between death rates of little girls and little boys. The absence of any indications as yet of unnatural sex ratios at birth in the sub-Sahara may have to do with wise parental decisions. On the other hand, it might simply speak to the lack of prenatal sex determination technology in those areas of the world – so far.

The Shape of Things To Come? Sub-Saharan Africa		
Angola	Ethiopia*	Mozambique
Benin	Gabon	Namibia
Botswana	Gambia*	Niger*
Burkina Faso*	Ghana	Nigeria*
Burundi	Guinea-Bissau*	Reunion
Cameroon	Kenya	Rwanda
Central African Republic	Lesotho	Sao Tome
Chad*	Liberia	Senegal*
Comoros	Madagascar	Sierra Leone*
Congo	Malawi	Somalia*
Cote d'Ivoire	Mali	Sudan*
Dem. Republic of the Congo	Mauritania*	Swaziland
Equatorial New Guinea	Mauritius	Tanzania*
Eritrea*		Togo
		Uganda
		Zambia
		Zimbabwe

Note: Italicized countries rely on data from the U.N. Population Division life tables; Regular font indicates data from World Health Organization life tables.

Sources: World Health Organization Life Tables, available online at http://www3.who.int/whosis/life_tables/life_tables.cfm?path=evidence,life_tables&language=english accessed 9/15/04; United Nations Population Division Life Tables.

Perhaps this portrait of a war that is apparently unfolding on practically every continent outside North America around the world should make us happy we live in the United States. Unfortunately, the situation

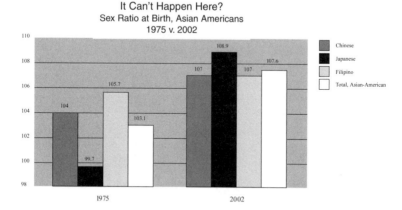

It Can't Happen Here?
Sex Ratio at Birth, Asian Americans
1975 v. 2002

Note: Total 1975 births for each population are as follows: Chinese, 8413; Japanese, 7442; Filipino, 11233. Total 2002 births for each population are as follows: Chinese, 33673; Japanese, 9264; Filipino, 33016.

Source: Derived from U.S. National Center for Health Statistics, *Vital Statistics of the United States*, 1975 and 2002 editions, Volume I.

is not necessarily rosy in "the land of the free." Some of the changes in reported sex ratios at birth in the United States over the past generation are deeply disturbing. There has been a notable and substantial increase, for example, in sex ratios at birth for the Chinese-American population, the Japanese-American population, and the Filipino-American population, as well as for the Asian-American population as a whole. All of these American ethnicities now exhibit sex ratios at birth that could be considered biologically impossible.

By the same logic that led us to remove Luxembourg from immediate suspicion in a previous graphic – i.e., low sample size – we may wish similarly to exempt our Asian-American populations. An argument could be made that these statistical data cannot be accorded too much confidence, because there are relatively few Asian-Americans in our midst, because Asian-Americans have relatively low fertility levels, and because we are looking at relatively small numbers of total births in any given year.

Such arguments, unfortunately, do not withstand scrutiny, under ordinary application of the techniques of statistical inference. In 1975 Asian-American births totaled roughly 130,000 to 140,000. In 2002 their numbers exceeded 200,000. These are not small "sample sizes". Under a "normal distribution" we can calculate just how likely would be the Asian-American 1975 and 2002 birth rates presented in the graph were chance discrepancies: those odds work out to about 1.5 in a billion. To make the odds even smaller, we could "pool" data: adding together the figures on births and sex ratios at birth for recent years, and then comparing those results to the corresponding figures from the early 1970s. Viewed from this perspective, the odds against seeing the recently SRBs reported by Asian-American communities as an artifact of pure chance would rise into the tens of billions.

"It can't happen here"? Think again: quantitative data and applied statistical reasoning provide us with unavoidable evidence beyond any reasonable doubt that *it is happening here.*

How will the global war against baby girls unfold in the years immediately ahead? At the dawn of the 21st century, sex preference for boys is prevalent in many parts of the world. Prenatal gender determination technologies are becoming increasingly accessible and inexpensive. And as my colleague Ben Wattenberg points out in his book *Fewer: How the New Demography of Depopulation Will Shape Our Future*, fertility trends all around the world are dropping rapidly, and lower than ever before: at this juncture, approximately half the world's population lives in countries where sub-replacements levels of fertility currently prevail.

If my hypothesis above is correct – that is to say, if the freakish SRBs we are now beginning to witness around the world are the consequence of a by the fateful collision between overweening son preference, the use of rapidly spreading prenatal sex determination technology for gender-based abortion, and the low or dramatically declining fertility levels – then it may well be, as the late President Ronald Reagan said in a very different context, that "You ain't seen nothing yet"!

Nicholas Eberstadt holds the Henry Wendt Chair in Political Economy at the American Enterprise Institute in Washington, D.C., and is senior adviser to the National Bureau of Asian Research in Seattle, Washington. For over twenty years Mr. Eberstadt served as a member of Harvard University's Center for Population and Development Studies, and he continues to serve as a member of the Visiting Committee for the Harvard School of Public Health. Mr. Eberstadt regularly consults for governmental and international organizations and is often invited to offer expert testimony before Congress. Mr. Eberstadt has published over three hundred studies in scholarly and popular journals and has authored over a dozen books and monographs. Mr. Eberstadt lives in Washington, D.C., with his wife, Mary, and their four children. (He offers thanks to Ms. Assia Dosseva and Ms. Courtney Richard for research assistance with the present paper.)

Session VI: Theological Developments Regarding the Family since Vatican II: As Nuptial Body and As Domestic Church

Chapter 21: John Paul II and the "Nuptial Attribute" of the Body
The Family and the Future of Humanity

DAVID L. SCHINDLER, PH.D.

This session of the Fellowship of Catholic Scholars Convention on "The International Year of the Family" is assigned the task of reflecting on theological developments regarding the family since Vatican II, treating in particular the topics of the "nuptial body" and the "domestic Church." Our division of labor gives Professor Atkinson the main burden of developing the latter notion. My own focus is on what Pope John Paul II, in his Wednesday audiences on *The Theology of the Body*, terms the "nuptial attribute" of the body. This notion, to which the Congregation for the Doctrine of the Faith's recent – and wonderful – letter on the collaboration of men and women,[1] goes to the heart of the ecclesial and cultural achievements of the papacy of John Paul II. It is perhaps the true key to understanding the contrast between what the pope terms the "culture of life" on the one hand and the "culture of death" on the other. He states in his apostolic exhortation *Familiaris Consortio* that "the future of humanity passes by way of the family."[2] My proposal, in the name of the Holy Father, is that the nuptial attribute of the body is fundamental for understanding the relationships proper to the family, and that recovery of an understanding of the body as nuptial is therefore indispensable if the humanity that passes through the family is to have a viable future.

This centrality of the notion of the nuptial body and, further, of the nuptial relations proper to the family, implies that the most crucial problems of our time bear on the sexual difference and the nature of marital-familial love. My thesis is thus a double one: coming to terms with the nuptial nature of the body is necessary for any civilization that would be human (let alone Christian); and issues in biotechnology – since it is in biotechnology (or reproductive technology) that the nuptial nature of the body is most directly challenged – indicate what are the most serious problems needing to be faced in the current cultural situation. To be sure, we cannot minimize the brutality of terrorism, the constant threat of which now hovers over us. It nonetheless suffices here to insist simply that the problems indicated – which is to say, matters such as same-sex unions, *in vitro* fertilization, and cloning – signify the gravest threat emergent from within, as endemic to, American civilization. It is precisely these issues that take us most directly and profoundly to the crisis in the *humanum* in its properly Western liberal form.

Given the limitations of the present forum, the argument takes the form of rapid statements of theses in three steps:

> 1) First, I will discuss some texts from the present pontificate showing forth the meaning and centrality of the notion of the nuptial body and thereby of the nuptial relations proper to marriage and the family;
>
> (2) Secondly, I will show how phenomena such as same-sex unions, IVF, cloning, and the like undermine at its heart the nuptial view of the person and the sense of being as gift that the pope sees as bound up with the idea of nuptiality;
>
> (3) Thirdly, and in conclusion, I will comment briefly on the shape of the cultural task that is presupposed in and by the foregoing arguments.

I.

Man is created by God, who is love, as we are told in the first letter of St. John. The Holy Trinity, Father, Son, and Holy Spirit, is the communion of three distinct Persons who live in the eternal oneness of love. The love of God is not a static, inert union, but an eternally dynamic act of self-giving and gratitude shared in distinct ways by the Father, the Son, and the Holy Spirit. The loving self-gift that the Holy Trinity *is* is so abundant that God freely extends the gift of himself to creation, and creation bears traces of God's own nature as gift. These traces of the divine nature are present in a distinct and particularly profound way in human beings: we are made by God in his image, *imago Dei*. Being-gift is thus at the heart of our identity as beings made in the image of the God. Our imaging the Holy Trinity comes to expression not only in each of us as individuals but also and especially in the human communion of persons, whose primary expression in the order of creation is the community of self-giving love we call the family.

The doctrine of *imago Dei* finds its scriptural basis in the first chapter of Genesis: "God created man in his image; in the divine image he created him; male and female he created them" (v. 27). Here, contained in the primary reference to man as created in God's image, is a reference to gender difference, that is, to that fundamental characteristic of mankind most evident in our *bodiliness*. Man "as a person [is thus] one who, even in all his corporality, is similar to God."[3] The human person, in his body-soul unity, is what the Holy Father calls a "primordial sacrament":

> Thus…a primordial sacrament is constituted, understood as a sign that transmits effectively in the visible world the invisible mystery hidden in God from time immemorial. This is the mystery of truth and love, the mystery of divine life, in which man really participates…The sacrament, as a visible sign, is constituted with man, as a body, by means of his visible masculinity and femininity. The body, and it alone, is capable of making visible what is invisible: the spiritual and the divine. It was created to transfer in the visible reality the mystery hidden since time immemorial in God, and thus be a sign of it.[4]

Integral to the body's revelation is the specification of every human person as either male or female. The pope teaches us that the sexual difference is no superficial trait like height or eye color, nor even ethnic difference: Scripture does not, for example, read "in the image of God he made him, American and Chinese he made them." Our sexuality reaches to the core of our person, to the very heart of our identity, and situates our identity in relationality, in *aptness for love*. The (gendered) body itself, the "expressive sign of the whole person,"[5] is apt for love; the pope names this aptness the "nuptial attribute" of the body: "The human body, marked with the sign of masculinity or femininity, 'includes right from the beginning the nuptial attribute, that is, the capacity of expressing love, that love in which the person becomes a gift and – by means of this gift – fulfills the meaning of his being and his existence' [*Theology of the Body*, 63]."[6] The pope writes further:

> So the very sacramentality of creation, the sacramentality of the world was revealed in a way, in man created in the image of God. By means of his corporeality, his masculinity and femininity, man becomes a visible sign of the economy of truth and love, which has its source in God himself and which was revealed already in the

mystery of creation...The sacrament of the world, and the sacrament of man in the world, comes from the divine source of holiness, and at the same time is instituted for holiness."[7]

Notice the key notions that are linked together here. The body in its
very physicality as such, in its nature and shape *as* a body, is apt for
expressing the love in which the person becomes a gift and thereby fulfills the meaning of his being and existence. The body expresses the
form of love, even as love takes form in the body, (also) *as* a body. The
body, in its masculinity and femininity, reveals a dual unity, a communion of persons who are different at once in and as the unity of their
humanity. It is this dual unity of man and woman, this communion of
persons who are a unity-in-difference, that images the trinitarian God.
The body is not a mere instrument of love; the body is not simply
employed by lovers as a means to communicate a strictly spiritual love.
Rather, the body is itself an expression and sign of self-gift, called,
already in the mystery of creation, to express and exist in the communion of persons in the image of the trinitarian God.

But further, in terms of the argument proposed here: the body
reveals love, not just in a general way, but in a nuptial way. What does
this mean, and why is it significant? Let us turn our attention at greater
length to the nuptial relations – paternity, maternity, and filiality – that
mark the primary human communion of persons: the family. The Holy
Father asks us to deepen our awareness of "procreation as a unique event
which clearly reveals that human life is a gift received in order then to
be given as a gift. In giving origin to a new life, parents recognize that
the child, 'as the fruit of their mutual gift of love, is, in turn, a gift for
both of them, a gift which flows from them.'"[8]

This "summary" of love in procreation is paradigmatic: it discloses
to us the nature of all authentic love. In the first chapter of Genesis, we
find God blessing the man and woman he has created, commanding
them to "be fruitful and multiply" (v. 28). It is through an act of human
love, the "one-flesh" union of our mother and father, that we receive our
origin as a tiny zygote in the body of our mother. The act of procreation
is an answer to God's first command, revealing that our purpose and destiny is to give and receive love. The physical expression of love between
a man and a woman discloses something essential about the communion
of persons: fruitfulness. No love between two persons is complete until
it issues in a third – and this is not simply a matter of biology.[9] Rather,
the biological order and physical fruitfulness reveal, because they participate in, the structure of love, the mutual self-gift that most deeply characterizes human being.

The teaching of twelfth-century monk and theologian Richard of St. Victor, while it does not take up the significance of gender in the unity-in-difference of spouses, is nonetheless illuminating. He wrote that love does not consist in two persons' turning in on themselves in a mutual absorption that effectively isolates them from others; rather, love in its mutuality is precisely *open:* two who love always in some sense procreate a third who transcends both. Both share this third; both love the third. Love is complete only in openness and generosity, in generativity. This is true both in the physical order and in the spiritual order, in spiritual motherhood and fatherhood. In the case of married love, the embodied union of husband and wife bears fruit in the bodily generation of a third person, a child whose conception crowns the communion of persons that was the couple and now is the family.

The conception of a child is always a gift from God, who works through the primary initiative of the father, on the one hand, and the primary receptivity of the mother, on the other hand. Here we see that generativity, or fruitfulness, requires not just two, but the unity of the two *in their difference*. The maleness and femaleness of human beings bodies forth the two *different* forms necessary for the full sense of self-gift. Man and woman are each constituted in-oneself-for-the-other, *differently*. Each is ordered toward fruitfulness in relation to the other, *differently*.

When the union of the two spouses results in the conception of a child, their physical act of self-giving is extended through time and space in the pregnancy of the woman, who gives over her body for the sake of their little one, patiently and generously making space for the new person within, as her husband shares her waiting and preparation in a different way, from a greater distance, from without. The unity and difference of the spouses is clear, translated beyond the brief act of physical union into further acts and dispositions of a shared love of one another and of their child, specified by their sexuality (gender). The import of gender difference reaches through the relation of man and woman to one another into their relation to their child. We see that gender difference can be characterized most fully as the man's aptness for paternity and in the woman's aptness for maternity. Fatherhood and motherhood are the destiny of the maleness or femaleness that the body expresses. To be a father or to be a mother, however, is no "mere" biological destiny but rather the very form of human love in its two irreducible expressions. Or, better, the biological reality of fatherhood or motherhood, precisely in its biology, participates in the structure of being as gift, as love. A man's love is fatherly in that he gives but receives precisely in his giving; a woman's love is motherly in that she receives but gives precisely in her receiving.

Let us reflect at greater length upon the mother's pregnancy, which beautifully exemplifies her giving receptivity in an extension into time and space of the conjugal union and its fruitfulness. During the nine months of gestation a mother welcomes the child with her whole self. Gestation is not so much a constructive act on the mother's part as a continuously patient act of "making space" for the child that gives him his form, and in turn forms her. The mother, in a sense, makes herself obedient to the child, who himself is dependent upon her obedience. This making space is a kind of embodied *fiat*: "let it be done." "Let this child be and become." The example of pregnancy offers us a paradigm for the whole of our relation to reality, in relation to God: as creatures, we become who we are in activity that is always first a patient (contemplative) attention. Both men and women have to body forth the Marian *fiat*, differently, each according to the gendered mode of being human given at conception.

As a man or a woman, each of us possesses an aptness for either fatherhood or motherhood into which we must mature, if we are to attain the fulfillment of the meaning of our lives as creatures for love. But another relational identity is concurrently ours: our own first role as child. This role is perhaps more difficult for us to identify with. It has been a long time since each of us was a child in the womb, and we have no memory of our early weeks and months of nearly absolute dependency. Nor do we even recall our first year, when, although we could breathe on our own, we could not do much else. Over the years, through the care and instruction of both parents, we grew and became more and more able to care for ourselves and to do things independently of our mother and father. But we did not, and never will, become truly independent. We cannot. We remain beings who are *from others*. Once again, our bodies affirm this point, not just in our physical origins from our father and mother, but even in our dependency upon an environment to sustain us, which is continuous throughout our lives. In our most basic physical processes, breathing and metabolism, we are dependent upon what is beyond our ability to generate or sustain, upon the very stuff of creation. Above all, we remain totally dependent – in our very "independence" – upon our divine origin. Always, we are children before God. A fundamental challenge for us as adults is to learn to cultivate a childlike posture before God.

Theologian Hans Urs von Balthasar wrote an extended reflection on the Gospel scene in which Jesus welcomes the little children over his disciples' protests. Balthasar reminds us of Jesus's insistent message: "Amen I say to you: whoever does not receive the Kingdom of God like a child will not enter into it" (Mark 10:15). But how do we do this child-like receiving? As adults, and especially in modern America, we are trained to value our independence and our own initiative, we are accustomed to the weight of the responsibility of providing for ourselves and our loved ones, and we know the necessity of calculation just to make ends meet. It is difficult for us to imagine living as a child, just as it was difficult for Nicodemus to imagine what he thought Jesus meant by being "born again": "How can a man be born when he is old? Can he enter a second time into his mother's womb and be born?" (John 3:4).[10] But the Father does not demand a new physical birth from us, but rather incorporation into his child Jesus, whose very body we become through baptism by "water and the Spirit" (John 3:5). Jesus is a child because he received his whole being from his Father – from his "Abba" – in a twofold way: he is the second Person of the Holy Trinity, the "only Son of the Father" who eternally receives the Father's complete self-giving; and in our own worldly history "he was conceived by the Holy Spirit and born of the Virgin Mary," as we confess together each Sunday. And Jesus is the child who in a sense never grew up, who never ceased to be the Son before his "Abba," even, as Balthasar says, "as he was entrusted with the difficult, superhuman task of leading the whole world back home to God."[11] Jesus shows us what our response must be to the one who is twice our Father (in a different twofold way: that is, in the generation of our natural life through our conception in our mother's womb and in our regeneration to supernatural life through baptism into Christ). The response that Jesus teaches us is one of wonder, confident surrender, and gratitude. A child has eyes wide open to receive the wonder of each new day, each new experience. In the Gospels we find Jesus rising to meet each new moment of his public mission. He surrenders himself to the Father in every encounter and every prayer, even in the Garden of Gethsemane, where he accepts the cup of sorrows at the hand of the Father whose love he trusts. He teaches us to "give thanks always," as St. Paul will repeat.

In fact, Jesus not only gives thanks, he *embodies* his thanks: his existence is thanksgiving to his Father. We learn this of Jesus definitively in the Upper Room on Holy Thursday, when he offers himself to the Father and to us in the bread and wine he consecrated before he died. He commanded us to repeat this meal in his memory. Like the disciples, we receive the Eucharist, which renews our incorporation into Christ, the Son. *Eucharistia* is Greek for thanksgiving. The Eucharist is a sacrifice of thanksgiving, made by Jesus in response to the Father's eternal generosity. It is the source of our life in Christ, and our identifying characteristic as children of the Father and members of Christ's body. At Mass the priest prays: "Father, it is our duty and our salvation always and everywhere to give you thanks." This is a way of saying that thanksgiving is who we *are*, if we are true to the identity God has given us in Christ. Thus, when we teach our children to say "please" and "thank you" when asking for the salt and pepper, we are not just teaching them how to get along nicely. Rather, we are teaching them how to be who they are[12]: little ones who first receive everything they are and may have confidence that they will also receive all they need. If children do not learn these acts, they cannot recuperate the meaning of their existence.

Thus far I have traced the contours of a notion of the human person that situates the person's existence in a creation that is gift. Man is made in the image of the triune God, a communion of Persons eternally enacting self-gift. As a "sacrament" of the human person, the human body, in its two gendered forms, makes visible the structure of reality as gift, most evidently in the unity-in-difference of man and woman and its fruitfulness in the family. The family bodies forth the nuptial relations (paternity, maternity, and filiality) that are fundamental for every love, and these relations extend beyond the family and give shape to human work and human culture. I would like now briefly to sketch the ways in which this anthropology is undermined and indeed contradicted by the dominant liberal culture.

The modern liberal notion of the person centers upon the individual self, abstracted from *constitutive* relations to the body, to others, to God. In liberalism, these relations are not denied but rather are *added* to this abstract individual, and as additions are just so far assumed not to be as deep as what constitutes the individual as such. While there are many varieties of liberalism, I am aware of none that does not presuppose something like this abstract individual self. In this abstraction, the "sacramental" character of the body is obscured, its form reduced to a "premoral" instrument of the will in the fashion criticized by *Veritatis Splendor*: "…human nature and the body appear as presuppositions or preambles, materially necessary for freedom to make its choice, yet extrinsic to the person, the subject and the human act" (n. 48). An abstract, disembodied notion of the person implies the "unisex" attitude that permeates our culture: The gender difference is seen as external to the meaning of the self, as not intrinsically related to the form of human action or to love itself. Liberal anthropology construes relations with others and with God as stemming first from an exercise of human freedom, rather than as constitutive of the person and thus always anteriorly formative of that (always embodied) freedom.

It is logically (ontologically) impossible, given these assumptions, to assign a decisive normative significance to the originary meaning of the human being as differentiated in and through the nuptial relations (the person's constitutive aptness for paternity or maternity and for being always filial), or to see these differentiating relations as fundamental to the identity of the person, and indeed of civilization in its entirety, *as human.* The pervasive assumptions of a liberal culture yield a logical vulnerability to current trends that threaten the authentic humanity of our fundamental relationships and our civilization. Among the most difficult of the problems with which we are currently confronted are legally recognized, culturally normalized homosexual unions and *in vitro* fertilization. In both of these cases, drawing out the implications of John Paul II's notion of the nuptial attribute of the body is immensely helpful in identifying the ontological falsehood at the heart of the moral problem.

II.

Homosexual "marriages" deny the nuptial attribute of the body and the destiny of the human person to spousal love. To call a homosexual relationship a "marriage" does violence to the word, for the true sense of union that characterizes an authentic nuptial communion of persons is unity-*in-difference.* As we have discussed, the gender difference that is manifested in our bodies speaks to a fundamental difference in the character of love as it is offered by a man or offered by a woman, a difference that can never be bracketed or overcome but rather can only be given and accepted as a gift. There is no authentic marital union without the irreducible, spiritual-corporal difference that is gender. There is, to be sure, an identity shared by a man and a woman: both are human persons with the full dignity of being made in the image of God. However, it is their difference – the man's capacity to receive precisely in his fundamental act of giving, and the woman's capacity to give precisely in her fundamental act of receiving – that draws them together and *makes possible* the real unity of the two, the complete mutual self-gift that affirms the difference of the two precisely as it establishes their unity. It is not by accident that a homosexual relationship cannot generate a child, that is, cannot attain to the fullness of love: fruitfulness. In the order of procreation, man's fatherhood is only possible through spousal union with a woman, whose motherhood is possible only through her spousal union with the man. There is no generic, unisex aptness for "parenthood," abstracted from the specific modes of love of the man/father and the woman/mother. Just so, there is no generic spousal union of "partners"

whose gender is indifferent. Interestingly, contraception, another fragmentation of the nature of authentic spousal unity-in-difference, is also
a denial of gender difference, for it impedes the full expression of either
the man's masculinity or the woman's femininity in their union. In order
to avoid fruitfulness, contraception blurs the gender difference that
enables the complete union of man and woman. Rowan Williams,
Anglican Archbishop of Canterbury, has commented that a Church that
accepts the logic of contraception – as his Anglican Church does – has
no has no warrant for proscribing homosexual behavior.

In vitro fertilization is a degradation of human persons and a dissolution of nuptial relations. IVF brings to the fore the insufficiency of
subjective intention to humanize an objectively dehumanizing process.
The intention of the couple, often happily married, often could not be
more hospitable to a child or more desirous that fruitfulness characterize their union. What is not recognized or acknowledged, however, is that
a child is the spontaneous, God-given fruit of the *embodied* love of
spouses, not a product to be made at will. We do not first make, but
receive, children. The nuptial attribute of the body is integral to the conception of a child, whose own body is a sign of the love of his parents.
The child comes to be and begins to mature in a physical environment
that is essentially loving: the womb of his mother, whose body is structured to welcome and nurture him. In the practice of IVF, the conjugal
act is circumvented and the spouses isolated as mechanical parts in a
process that is no longer "procreation" but "reproduction." The spouses
are no longer lovers who give themselves wholly, body and soul, to one
another, but rather are reduced to donors of materials that are manipulated in a petri dish to form the new person. This does violence to the
spouses, for it is their embodied act of loving union – not individual
body cells, first isolated and then brought together by a third party apart
from either of them – that is meant to bear the fruit of children and that
indeed identifies them as spouses. But it also does real, even if not
empirically measurable, violence to the child, whose origin is meant to
be in the embodied love of his parents and in the nurturing environment
of the womb, and not in a mechanical process that transpires in a laboratory dish. The contrast can be rightly illustrated with reference to the
difference between the loving warmth of a home and the sterility of a
hospital room, and the effect of this difference on a convalescing person.
How much more important is the effect of environment on the new life
at conception and the beginning of gestation!

The list of problems goes on in a similar vein with the development
of cloning techniques and the willingness to experiment on embryos for

the sake of finding cures for certain diseases. In every case there is a denial that, independent of any act or intention, the human body – in its origin and in its generative capacity in both genders – is meant to be a sign and expression of nuptial love.

III.

We have highlighted elements of a "culture of death" that are pernicious because they obscure and threaten the very meaning of our life, our sense of who we are: embodied creatures called into existence by, through, and for love. In response, we need to develop the habits of being that correspond to who we are, and we need time and space in which to do this. We need an environment, a *culture* of life to counter the intensifying threats that together amount to a "culture of death." How can we build a culture of life in the face of death, as the Holy Father exhorts us? The pope gives what seems a surprising answer. While he acknowledges that "[s]ervice of the Gospel of life is...an immense and complex task,"[13] the first step is "to foster, in ourselves and in one other, a contemplative outlook."[14] He goes on to describe what he means:

> ...Such an outlook arises from faith in the God of life, who has created every individual as a "wonder" (cf. Ps 139:14). It is the outlook of those who see life in its deeper meaning, who grasp its utter gratuitousness, its beauty and its invitation to freedom and responsibility. It is the outlook of those who do not presume to take possession of reality but instead accept it as a gift, discovering in all things the reflection of the Creator and seeing in every person his living image (cf. Gen 1:27; Ps 8:5). This outlook does not give in to discouragement when confronted by those who are sick, suffering, outcast or at death's door. Instead, in all these situations it feels challenged to find meaning, and precisely in these circumstances it is open to perceiving in the face of every person a call to encounter, dialogue and solidarity.[15]

The proposition that our *first* task in building a culture of life is conscientiously to receive our very being as described above and to reflect on it is truly a remarkable teaching, offered to a world that recognizes visible, vocal action such as protests and law suits. It is who we are that tells us first and fundamentally what to do. And we have an example to follow in the mode of response to which the Holy Father exhorts us: Mary, the mother of Jesus, who "kept all these things, pondering them in her heart" (Lk 2:19). The mysteries of her experiences since the angel's message form her as she keeps them, meditating upon them. This calls to mind the image of the pregnancy of a woman, who both receives and gives the child within, and, in patience and love, both forms and is formed by this new life, on a physical and a spiritual level. In the Year of the Rosary given to us by John Paul II, he asked all of us, men and women alike, to enter the "school of Mary," contemplating the face of Christ, whom we receive as Mary did, though in sacramental form. We can be sure that Jesus himself learned at this school. He exemplifies patient prayer and contemplation, spending thirty years of his life in the home at Nazareth before commencing his public ministry. On the surface this may seem to us a waste of time, given the world of the sick and the sinful who needed him.[16] But in his wisdom and attention to the Father's timing, Jesus was content to set aside these years to mature as his Son-made-man, and to extend the love of this relationship to those intimate people around him. This time of contemplation bore fruit in the three years that followed.

When we consider the hidden life of the Holy Family, who received and radiated the love of God in the quiet of their home and home town, it becomes perhaps even more clear why the Holy Father has stated that the future of civilization passes through the family. Throughout the years of child-rearing, the initial bodily self-gift of the parents that brought each child into existence extends through time and space to create an environment of love – we could say, a miniature culture – in which the small persons may develop to maturity, growing like the child Jesus "in wisdom and in stature, and in favor with God and man" (Lk 2:52). For it is not only natural life that the family fosters. Because the family's role is as the home not only of physical life but also of spiritual life, the Second Vatican Council and the pope refer to the family as a "domestic Church." It is in the context of the family that most of us are incorporated into Christ through baptism. Just as we are given life without our own consent or prior planning, so too most of us receive the gift of new life in Christ through the representation of our parents when we are infants. The gift of baptism, like the gift of life, is nurtured in the family. The mother has a special role in the formation of a small culture of life within her family and beyond it, for, as the Holy Father explains:

> "...Motherhood involves a special communion with the mystery of life, as it develops in the woman's womb...This unique contact with the new human being developing within her gives rise to an attitude towards human beings not only towards her own child, but every human being, which profoundly marks the woman's personality" [*Mulieris Dignitatem,* 18]. A mother welcomes and carries in herself another human being, enabling it to grow inside her, giving it room, respecting it in its otherness. Women first learn and then

teach others that human relations are authentic if they are open to accepting the other person: a person who is recognized and loved because of the dignity which comes from being a person and not from other considerations, such as usefulness, strength, intelligence, beauty, or health. This is the fundamental contribution which the Church and humanity expect from women. And it is the indispensible prerequisite for an authentic cultural change.[17]

A mother, often referred to as the "heart of the home," has a great capacity for generating culture by giving physical form to the love she bears her family. A simple example of this is a home-cooked meal. There is no comparison between a meal prepared by Mom and a fast food experience, even if similar ingredients are used. A mother's attention and care in preparation makes a qualitative difference in the food, which she makes her gift to us. The small details that define a well-prepared meal and a beautifully set table are attended to in love, and they invite the special way in which we partake in the meal together, a way that nourishes us in spirit as well as in body.

A meal is not the only example of the embodiment of love that makes a home and, by extension, makes a culture. Other social forms could be cultivated, extending from the family into the community. The practice of "calling on" one another has died out completely, in favor of more casual and spontaneous get-togethers. Courtship forms have dissolved into the amorphous phenomenon of dating, which often has little to do with the families of the young man and the young lady, and as often as not has little to do with marriage. We have dispensed with habits associated with mourning (wearing black for an extended period of time, withdrawing from social engagements for a period following the death of a loved one), which served to acknowledge the depth of the pain of separation and the time required for healing. While it is not necessary or even perhaps advisable to resurrect these social forms according to some previous historical expression, mothers, fathers, families, circles of friends, must seek ways to mark the time and space in which we live with the form of love. We are encouraged in *Evangelium Vitae* to incorporate into our lives the wealth of rites and rituals the Church offers us, as well as these non-liturgical forms, in order to be ourselves the seeds of a "civilization of love":

> "...While the urgent need for...cultural transformation is linked to the present historical situation, it is also rooted in the Church's mission of evangelization. The purpose of the Gospel, in fact, is "to transform humanity from within and to make it new" [*Evangelii Nuntiandi*, 18]. Like the yeast which leavens the whole measure of

dough (cf. Mt 13:33), the Gospel is meant to permeate all cultures and give them life from within [*EN, 20*], so that they may express the full truth about the human person and about human life.[18]

All of the little habits and details that create culture require time, and they require bodily presence. Time is one of the things we seem to have the least of. But how ironic: it is the medium of our life – how can we not have it? It is God's gift; how can we not return it to him attentively? And presence is something that is also easily sacrificed: the "I am my office" mentality can trick us into thinking that availability by phone or by email is enough. It may seem incongruous, to say the least, to critique the hectic pace of our lives, the cell phones and the email that invite perpetual intrusiveness, in the same breath as homosexual marriage and IVF. To be sure, these technological devices are not intrinsically evil, in the way that the latter are. But they do change our sense of space and time and their meaning. It does seem to become increasingly difficult to make time for rest, for play, for contemplation. And yet, as the pope teaches so eloquently in the apostolic letter *Dies Domini*, absent this contemplation, this rest in our Origin, the work we try to accomplish – even on his behalf – cannot bear fruit as it ought. Our response to the crisis we face consists most basically in recuperating the habits of being implied in the beautiful words of St. Bernard of Clairvaux:

> [T]he fact that man was created gratuitously, out of nothing – and in such dignity – makes the duty of love still clearer ...If I owe all that I am in return for my creation, what am I to add in return for being remade [redeemed]? "What then shall I give the Lord for all that he has given me?" In the first act he gave me myself; in the second, he gave himself; and when he did that, he gave me back myself. Given, and given again, I owe myself in return for myself, twice over"(*De Diligendo Dei*).

The task of Christians in our time is above all to ponder the meaning of these words over and over again, in their implications for all that we are, do, and make, in private and in public. John Paul II's theology of the "nuptial body" presents us with a key for such pondering.

David L. Schindler is the academic dean and the Edouard Cardinal Gagnon Professor of Fundamental Theology at the John Paul II Institute for Studies on Marriage and Family in Washington, D.C. He holds a Ph.D. in religion from the Claremont Graduate School. Formerly a Weaver Fellow and a Fulbright Scholar in Austria, Professor Schindler taught four years at Mount St. Mary's College and Seminary and for thirteen years in the Program of Liberal Studies at the University of Notre Dame. Since 1982, he has also been the editor-in-chief of the North American edition of *Communio: International Catholic Review*, a group of journals founded in 1972 by Hans Urs von Balthasar, Joseph Ratzinger, Henri de Lubac, and other European theologians. He serves as editor of the series "*Ressourcement*: Retrieval and Renewal in Catholic Thought" with the Eerdmans Publishing Company. He has published over sixty articles in the areas of metaphysics, fundamental theology, and the relation of theology and culture. His latest book bears the title: *Heart of the World, Center of the Church* (T & T Clark and Eerdmans). His most recent edited collection (with Doug Bandow) is *Wealth, Poverty, and Human Destiny* (ISI). Professor Schindler is a consultor for the Pontifical Council for the Laity.

Notes

1. Congregation for the Doctrine of the Faith, "Letter to the Bishops of the Catholic Church on the Collaboration of Men and Women in the Church and in the World." See also the recent document of the International Theological Commission, "Communion and Stewardship: Human Persons Created in the Image of God."
2. Pope John Paul II, apostolic exhortation *Familiaris Consortio*, 86.
3. *The Theology of the Body*, 47.
4. *Ibid*, 76.
5. "Address to the Faculty of the Pontifical John Paul II Institute for Studies on Marriage and Family," August 27, 1999.
6. "Letter to the Bishops of the Catholic Church on the Collaboration of Men and Women in the Church and in the World," 6, fn. 7: John Paul II, *The Theology of the Body* (Boston: Pauline Books and Media, 1997), 63.
7. *The Theology of the Body*, 76.
8. Pope John Paul II, encyclical *Evangelium Vitae*, 92.
9. Cf. "Letter to the Bishops of the Catholic Church on the Collaboration of Men and Women in the Church and in the World," 8.
10. Cf. Hans Urs von Balthasar, *Unless You Become Like This Child* (San Francisco: Ignatius Press, 1991),
11. Cf. *Ibid*., 44.
12. Cf. *Ibid*., 49.
13. *EV*, 91.
14. *EV*, 83.
15. *EV*, 83.
16. Cf. Peter Henrici, "The Mystery of the Everyday," *Communio International Theological Review* (Spring 2004): 4–7.
17. *EV*, 99.
18. *EV*, 95.

Chapter 22: Family As Domestic Church:
Developmental Trajectory, Legitimacy, and Problems of Appropriation

JOSEPH C. ATKINSON, PH.D.

It is impossible to deny that there has been a serious, fundamental, and sustained theological development of the family since Vatican II. For the first time, beginning with the conciliar debates, the family itself was taken up as a separate theological topic and surprisingly, at that time at least, within terms of ecclesiology. At the heart of this process was the recovery of the family as the *domestic church*. With the promulgation of *Lumen Gentium* in November, 1964,[1] this ancient patristic concept of the baptized family was reinserted into modern theological parlance. However, this re-introduction was done with little or no explanation and, it should be noted, with no developed theological grounding.[2] Because the modern history of this term is so short, one can easily trace the trajectory of its development in three stages.

In the first stage, the term domestic church was only tentatively re-appropriated at Vatican II.[3] At that point the family could only be understood in relationship to the Church in an analogous manner. The second stage came immediately after the Council when the theological development of this term (as well as its usage) was nothing short of meteoric. During this phase, the fundamental categories of Vatican II (Christocentricism, personalism, and universal holiness) which controlled the Council, now acted as a hermeneutical catalyst by which the nature of the family could be fruitfully examined and articulated. With the publication of the *Catechism of the Catholic Church* (1992) came the third stage. In an observable development of doctrine, the domestic church moved from an *analogous* position to an *ontological* relationship with the Church. This brought the first part of its developmental trajectory to a conclusion. The question which confronts us is not about the existence of such development, but rather to what extent this development has been carried out and whether or not it is legitimate. The purpose of this paper will be to examine how this development has proceeded and to show its continuity with, and its deepening of, the seminal idea in Scripture and the Church Fathers. By way of conclusion, we will examine some of the problems which face the acceptance and legitimization of this term.

Prior to Vatican II

In some ways, the present Holy Father, himself, represents the extent of the development that has taken place concerning the family. Prior to the Council, he wrote a critically important book on marriage and family entitled *Love and Responsibility*. At this point, he could only define the family as "an educational institution within the framework of which the personality of a new human being is formed." [4] Elsewhere, in the same book, he referred to the family as "a small society, and the existence of all large societies – nation, state, Church – depends on it"[5] or "an institution based on marriage."[6] Arguably, this prosaic presentation has not the slightest intimation of the family as a domestic church or of its fundamental ecclesial nature. It will only be *after* Wojtyla's experience of Vatican II, that he begins his radical[7] investigation of the family and becomes personally responsible for the securing of the ecclesiological dimension of the family (as constitutive) in the Church's consciousness.

Perhaps nothing exemplifies this theological shift more than the exchange which took place on the floor of the Vatican Council on November 23, 1962. It many ways, this was the watershed moment from which all progress can be marked. The draft on the nature of the Church – *which listed all the constitutive parts of the Church* – was being discussed. Bishop Fiordelli of Prato, Italy, who had worked in the Christian Family Movement, rose and made the following observation:

> ...But these drafts, it painfully seems to me (in my humble opinion), that in all of the documents nothing is to be found by way of a special chapter which concerns another state in the Church which is of the greatest nobility and sanctity...namely the state of sacramental marriage.[8]

As Fiordelli began to draw out the implications of what he has said, the president objected and stated that these ideas were *"extra ordinem huius schematis"*[9] – outside the realm of the schema. This reaction is quite understandable even though, around the time of the Council, a reevaluation of the nature and role of the family was being explored by a few people (such as Fiordelli and Paul Evdokimov). However, these ideas were not yet a part of the Church's consciousness – as clearly seen from this objection raised to Firodelli's presentation. At this point, the intrinsic relationship between Church and family was not grasped.

Given the post-conciliar advances in theology, it is perhaps difficult for us to appreciate the *functional* understanding of marriage and family that obtained prior to the Council. While the sacramentality of marriage was officially affirmed, nonetheless, there was a hesitancy to see the positive, grace-filled aspects of marriage and family and its position as a state of holiness. Historically, this can be traced amongst other things to a) a certain uneasiness with certain aspects of human sexuality and b) the dominance of a monastic and celibate lifestyle as a model for Christian perfection.

It took the Church about a millennium to define formally the sacramentality of marriage. This was the case precisely because it was difficult for theologians to accord the physical realities of marriage a truly spiritual effect. Also, fallen human sexuality is deeply wounded and problematic. It would be sheer naïveté to refuse to acknowledge this. Still, an overemphasis on the negative can ultimately prevent us from seeing gender and sexuality for the gifts they are, especially when redeemed by grace. With the edict of Constantine and the ushering of the worldly masses into the Church, many sought to perfect their Christian life within monastic settings. For many centuries, this became normative in the pursuit of Christian perfection and unfortunately (and erroneously) caused marriage and family to be accorded a second class status within the Church, at least at a perceptional level. Again, as John Paul II has himself affirmed in *Familiaris Consortio*, the Church has always and unhesitatingly "defended the superiority of this charism (i.e., celibacy) to that of marriage."[10] But this has never been to denigrate or even question the value of married life. Indeed, scripturally speaking, it is the marital state which has the iconic value of showing to the world the love of Christ for His Church. In reality, each of these states of life informs the other.[11]

Bishop Fiordelli, wanting to correct these improper and limiting perceptions, addressed the assembled bishops, asking that the Council formally acknowledge the essential goodness of marriage and legitimate it as a way of holiness. "For today, it seems by many that a special place in the Mystical Body of Christ *must* be given to those who are situated in the state of Christian marriage."[12] He wished to emphasize that the marital state was indeed "a sacramental (state)…(and) not purely a formality."[13] The novelty of these ideas, and the perceived threat they posed, clearly can be seen in the speeches at that time and the caution that

Bishop Fiordelli exercised when introducing anything positive about marriage. He was careful to show that anything positive about the familial state does not thereby denigrate the celibate state. These types of reactions (i.e., the fears and the caution) are instructive inasmuch as they show the degree to which the true nature of marriage and family had been obscured at that time in the thinking of people.

Foundations for Theology of the Family

It is in the debates of Vatican II, rather than in the actual documents, that we find the seminal ideas which have informed and structured the renewal of the theology of the family. In his second speech, Bishop Fiordelli, surprisingly, yet logically, laid bare the theological structure of the family:

> ...It seems to me that this would be the true structure of the Church of Christ...Is the parish the ultimate division of the Church? No. The parish is further divided into so many holy cells, which are *Christian families*, which we can call, following the example of the Holy Fathers, tiny churches.[14]

His desire was to show the organic connection of the family with the Church; and to make clear that the parish is not its smallest articulation, but rather the family is the Church's smallest organic cell. He then showed how the family possesses a legitimacy with regards to the Body of Christ which goes beyond even that of the parish since the family proceeds *"ex voluntate ipsius Christi"* – out of the will of Christ, Himself – and is therefore *"iuris divini"* – of divine law.[15] Then, in a perhaps novel contribution, Fiordelli extended the spiritual reality of marriage to the whole of family life. Christ "has made sacramentally the institution of the family holy.[16]

Finally, in his 1963 submission, Bishop Fiordelli brought his last three precisions to his understanding of the domestic church. He first proposed that families be seen not only as members of the Church but also as organs and communities of Christ's Body.[17] Secondly, he not only applied Ephesians 5:32 to marriage but he now extended it to the family which proceeds out of marriage. He stated: "It is possible to refer to the Christian family as a small church possessing in itself a sharing (communication) of the very mystery of the union of Christ with the Church."[18] Thirdly, he spoke of parents being, as it were, consecrated (*consecrati*) to their roles."[19] To clench his argument, Bishop Fiordelli then quoted from both Sts. Augustine and Chrysostom who directly develop the idea of domestic church and use either that language exactly (Augustine) or approximate it (Chrysostom).[20] In both these Fathers, we find a prolonged understanding of the unique episcopal-like role of the father as head of the family, who is responsible for its religious education, and who is called to become a Christ-like servant to his family, and thereby serve Christ.

These principle ideas of Bishop Firodelli's became, as it were, the fundamental building blocks out of which the theology of the family as domestic church was built: the family as the smallest organic cell of the Church; familial life as a way of holiness; the sacramental nature of the family; the fundamental ecclesial nature of the family, and its sharing in the mission of Christ. Family, like marriage, came to be considered part of the great *mysterion* of Ephesians 5:32; and parents to be *consecrated* for their roles, thus living out their "priesthood" in a uniquely familial manner. The problem, however, is that while these intuitions and assertions appear to be correct, they were not theologically grounded. In some ways, it is amazing that such a radical re-evaluation of marriage and family was accepted without further theological investigation. By the end of the debates, Bishop Fiordelli's position was essentially accepted, but only in a cautious and limited manner. Only in *Lumen Gentium* 11 is the term used explicitly and only in an analogous manner. It states that: "In what might be regarded as the domestic Church (*"In hac velut Ecclesia Domestica..."*), the parents, by word and example are the first heralds of the faith with regard to their children."[21]

The importance of *Lumen Gentium*'s inclusion of domestic Church is *not* that it endorsed a systematic theology of the family or affirmed all that was said during the debates, for it did not. What it accomplished was to begin the process of re-evaluating the place of the family within theology and, by the affirming the phrase "domestic Church," *Lumen Gentium* provided the critical hermeneutic by which the family could be studied. From this point onward, the family was to find its identity and theological center in its ecclesial nature. Thus, the theological development of the family was not left victim to the theological vicissitudes and vagaries of the modern age but was grounded in a Patristic and ecclesiological framework. Clearly, the term had to be unpacked- but at least now, it was once again a part of the Church's consciousness – something that had not occurred for approximately 1,500 years – and criteria for its authentic development was established.

Post-Vatican II Development

It is an arguable point, that the concept of the family as a domestic church would have remained an interesting but dormant footnote in the history of the Council had it not been for the pontificate of John Paul II.

While Paul VI[22] and John Paul I[23] briefly mention the term, it is only with John Paul II that a systematic analysis is attempted and a "theology of domestic church" is sketched out. His achievement is that he not only secured a permanent place for this concept in the Church's magisterium, but established it as the dominant hermeneutic by which the family was to be understood. Most importantly, he did not allow this newly recovered construct to free-float theologically. Rather, he provided a definitive interpretative framework by which the domestic Church is to be understood, and established that the family must be understood through the prism of its ecclesiological and Christological identity. In an amazing statement, John Paul II states that "families...will manifest to all people the Savior's living presence in the world, and the genuine nature of the Church" (*Familiaris Consortio* 50). Would that statement have been possible prior to the Council?

In this apostolic exhortation, *Familiaris Consortio*, the "summa of the Church's teaching on family,"[24] JPII begins with the fundamental call of the Gospel, conversion to Christ.[25] Then in a deft move, to prevent mere moralism from developing, or an extrinsicism in regards to the life and activity of the family, John Paul II clearly unites being and mission, ontology and praxis. "The family finds in the plan of God...not only its identity...but also its mission...The role that God calls the family to perform in history derives from what the family is...family become what you are" (*FC*: 17). As we will see shortly, this principle will become increasingly important in the ensuing debates over the "nature" of the domestic Church.

John Paul II situates the identity of the family along two axes: Christ and the Church. In sections 17–49, the bulk of the document, *Familiaris Consortio,* defines the family's essence and role as being "to guard, reveal and communicate love. But, once again, this is not merely an amorphous phrase. It is further defined by its interior reference to Christ. "This is a...real sharing in God's love for humanity and the love of Christ the Lord for the Church His bride" (*FC*:17). What I propose is that this reveals the ecclesiological nature of the family. John Paul II then divides this into four constitutive aspects: (1.) forming a community of persons; (2.) serving life; (3.) participating in the development of society; and, (4.) sharing in the life and mission of the Church. These are marks of the Church and of the family; if it truly shares in the life of the Church, the family cannot be separated from the Church but must be inserted into her very reality – if the family is to be true to its nature.

Immediately following this presentation, John Paul II begins to develop the second axis of the family: its relationship to Christ Himself. He says that to understand the "substance" of the family, we must do so "in reference to Jesus Christ as Prophet, Priest and King" (*FC* 51). This is further expanded in terms of the family being (a) a believing and evangelizing community [prophetic nature]; (b) a community in dialogue with God [priestly nature]; and (c) a community at the service of man [kingly nature] (*FC*:50). *This means that the nature of the family is to be found in the nature of Christ.*

Now, we must begin by admitting that this is not a self-evident statement; by all estimations, it is rather an astonishing one. We can easily draw the parallel between the family and the Church, inasmuch as both have a community-like structure and purpose. But with the injection of this Christological dimension, we are truly entering into the realm of the *mysterion*. John Paul II grounds this in the sacrament of matrimony and later will refine this further by saying that marriage "makes specific the sanctifying grace of Baptism" (*FC* 56). While this is adequate for his presentation, it is here that the greatest work has to be done. John Paul II has given us the hint, but until there is a recovery of the profound reality of baptism and its effecting not only transformational *but* also ontological change (i.e. our being indwelt by Christ), the Christological nature of the family will forever remain not only the mystery (in the sense of *mysterion*) that it truly is, but it will forever be wrapped in a Churchillian enigma. It is the inner reality of baptism which unlocks the mystery of the domestic church.

The power of this analysis is somewhat Pauline because it cuts through the exterior layers and shows the sacramental nature of reality, in this case the family. In the famous passage of Ephesians 5, Paul, drawing from the order of creation, is at pains to show how husbands and wives are to live out their marriage and are involved, not in a culturally conditioned relationship, but in a sacred order (which is the root meaning of *hierarchy*). He shows how headship means that the husband must lay down his life for his wife, for he is head "as Christ also is head of the Church." That is, the Lord, out of his love for His Bride, dies for her. By verse 32 Paul wakes up, as if it were, to the reality of what he is really taking about: "In talking about the prosaic reality of marriage, I really am speaking about the mystery of Christ's love for the Church." Similarly, John Paul II, through the prism of domestic church, reveals to us the profound (and we should underline, *hidden)* mystery of the family – its ecclesial and Christological nature.

Thus, at this point in history: (1) the term "domestic Church" has been recovered as a dominant hermeneutic of the family; and (2) its development, to be authentic, *must* be rooted in Scriptural and Patristic categories; and (3) its nature cannot be subjectively determined, but is grounded in its ecclesial and Christological ontology,[26] which is ultimately revelatory of the Church, herself, of which it is an organic part. The task before us now is to prevent this term from being co-opted for any ends that we may choose. This can only be done by discovering the God-given, constitutive structure and nature of domestic church; and this, in turn, will provide it with its own adequate theological grounding.

The Problems

First Problem: Epistemological

There are serious problems regarding the authentic reception of this doctrine. The first is the nature of modern consciousness. In "Letter to Families," John Paul II points out that the mystery of Christ as the Bridegroom lies at the heart of marriage and family, and it is precisely this which is rejected by modern rationalism. It cannot perceive of God as the Bridegroom. The pope writes:

> ...Saint Paul uses a concise phrase in referring to family life: it is a "*great mystery*" (Eph 5:32). Husbands and wives thus discover in Christ *the point of reference for their spousal love*. The family itself is the great mystery of God. As the "domestic Church", it is the *bride of Christ*. Unfortunately, Western thought, with the development of *modern rationalism*, has been gradually moving away from this teaching. Within a similar anthropological perspective, the human family is facing the challenge of a *new Manichaeanism*, in which body and spirit are put in radical opposition. Modern rationalism *does not tolerate mystery*. It does not accept the mystery of man as male and female. The deep-seated roots of the "great mystery"...have been lost in the modern way of looking at things. The "great mystery" is threatened in us and all around us (*FC*19).

Unless we can successfully challenge this type of thinking, and show the reality of the symbolic (i.e. sacramental) value of that which is concrete, the world will be trapped in a materialist worldview which is incapable of comprehending, or even perceiving, the spiritual.

Second Problem: Legitimacy

The question needs to be raised as to how legitimate is this development of the family as domestic Church. It is clear that the use of the domestic Church as a hermeneutic for the family flows directly from the Church's patrimony and is an outgrowth of the reality of baptism. But little solid work has been done in grounding this concept theologically. John Paul II has sketched out a theology for us, but further and extensive grounding of this is a necessity. From initial work that has been done, it

is clear there first needs to be a recovery of the Old Testament understanding of the family on which the New Testament understanding is
predicated. Here we will find that the family can be defined in its formal aspect as, what I have termed, "the carrier of the covenant. Essential
to its grounding is the understanding of baptism (alluded to by John Paul
II) and the theology of creation (alluded to by St. Paul), as well as the
recovery of the Semitic concept of corporate personality.[27] We must be
careful to understand that the reality of the family as the ecclesial unit
(domestic Church) is found in the New Testament not by the mere existence of the term (which in the Vulgate is problematic) but more importantly, it emerges from the New Testament understanding of baptism.
This is given particular witness by household baptisms.[28] The family in
the New Testament now becomes what I have come to call *the sphere of
eschatological reality*. Finally, in our own day, we have witnessed a genuine development of doctrine. Vatican II could only use analogous language about the family and Church: "In what might be regarded as the
domestic Church." With the publication of the *Catechism of the Catholic
Church*. the Church now begins to employ ontological language: "The
Christian family constitutes a specific revelation and realization of
ecclesial communion, and for this reason it can and should be called a
domestic Church" (2204).[29]

Third Problem: Problematic Appropriation

The greatest threat to the domestic Church lies elsewhere. There is
a real danger that the concept of the domestic Church may become an
empty theological tag, used without due regard for its constitutive theological nature. This, in the end, can only seriously confuse or even
wound the authentic nature of the family as the *domestica Ecclesia*.
Indeed, this is a danger for any theological concept. This may be done
out of a misplaced compassion, as people seek to be inclusive. "*Define
family any way you are comfortable with and you are Church*." But is
this legitimate? Some find the ecclesial and Christological dimension of
family too limiting, and prefer to see family principally as a sociological
unit which can effect its own self-definition. For some, the domestic
Church (as Christologically or ecclesiologically defined) might appear
too restrictive or possibly judgmental. One modern theological writer,
who brings up these themes, writes:

> Given the current state of our Church and society, it is easy to
> see that the guiding beliefs of domestic church might not be uni-
> versally accepted. In an age where families are broken apart for a
> variety of reasons, and where many individuals do not experience

a healthy family life, it is important to consider how this concept can be well-utilized in the Church to-day...First there is considerable debate about the meaning of the term "family"...The official teaching of the Roman Catholic Church, for example, insists that the Christian family must spring from Christian marriage...This raises a question as to what happens in families where kinship springs from a relationship that is not marriage, for example, the single mother who chooses to raise her child outside of marriage. According to social scientists, this would be a family, but in the eyes of the Church, would this relationship constitute domestic church? Some would say no; domestic church occurs in a family formed from Christian marriage. I prefer a definition of domestic church which respects the ideals presented in <u>Gaudium et Spes</u>, but which recognizes the diversity in which contemporary families are formed...[30]

One appreciates the dangers of an overly legalistic approach. The problem here, however, is that a non-objective approach edges closely to denying that the family in Christ, precisely *as* domestic Church, has any specific *constitutive* dimensions, and that it is *uniquely* defined by the created and salvific order. It restricts the formative power of the baptized family's ecclesial nature from being determinative. The counterbalance to this self-defining approach is the argument that only in its salvific and ecclesial identity does the family find the full truth of its being. This cannot be manipulated but must be received as a gift. The danger is that "domestic Church" can become a "concept" into which any one of us can pour own "content": we can then have preferences as to its meaning. The non-objective approach leads inevitably to restructuring the very identity of the family (with implications for the salvific order) which no longer has any objective definition. This would be unfortunate as the concept of domestic Church could then "filled" with any content and become merely a tool to be used for whatever end one was pursuing. In effect, it would be only an empty label. This denies there is a fundamental reality which constitutively transforms a family giving it a new ontological reality and thereby an essential specificity which is not negotiable.

There must be some boundaries. It is clear that differences can be a good thing. However, when diversity is of such a nature that it attacks the constitutive structure of an entity, it cannot then be said to participate properly in that reality. As long as any specific diversity is not contrary to the fundamental structure of the family in Christ, there is no problem. When it is, it becomes destructive of this reality. The critical and important issue of legitimate boundaries which define the essence of the domestic Church has received scant attention but needs to be addressed. It can only be answered as we uncover more fully the authentic theological foundation on which the family as domestic Church is built.

At the heart of the Church is the Person of Christ. To be in Christ, to be part of His Body, is to encounter the salvific power of Christ and to be converted by Him, choosing to be His disciple. To choose Him means to seek to be formed by, and in Him, not as an ideal but in our own actual historical reality. Surely, any reality which mitigates or is intrinsically opposed to Christ and His expressed will cannot be said to participate in Him. Can the domestic church be construed in any other terms?

Conclusion

One of the critical functions of the term domestic church is that it serves as the hermeneutic by which we come to know the truth about marriage and the family. Understood aright, the domestic Church is the end for which marriage and the family were created. The reality (to which the Scriptures and the core of Jewish-Christian tradition attest) is that the salvific family (i.e., the domestic Church) is not a free-floating construct, awaiting the informing principles either of theologians or of a modern secular society. Rather, it is grounded in the Person of the Word of God, is part of His revelation, and is a critical part of the salvific plan of God for all humanity. In fact, it is a sign of contradiction. In becoming part of His body, our bodies become part of Him. When, in love, we give ourselves bodily to another in covenantal terms, our two bodies become one flesh in Christ, the fruit of which is the procreation of other bodily realities made in the image of God. The mystery of the baptized family is that we are called to be an organic part of the body of Jesus Christ, to participate in His nature and His salvific mission to the world. Only here do we find our true identity and purpose as individuals, as families, and as the domestic Church.

Dr. Joseph Atkinson, Ph. D., is assistant professor of Scripture at the John Paul II Institute for Studies on Marriage and Family. His work includes foundational research in developing the biblical and theological basis of the domestic Church. He has authored several articles including "Nuptiality as a Paradigmatic Structure of Biblical Revelation," "Paternity in Crisis: Biblical and Philosophical Roots of Fatherhood," and most recently (co-authored) in *Logos*: "Person As Substantive Relation and Reproductive Technologies: Biblical and Philosophical Foundations."

Notes

1. To this can be added the later *Apostolicam Actuositatem* (November, 1965) which adds (indirectly) to the concept of the family as the domestic Church.

2. Maurice Eminyan states: "And yet it seems to be a fact that a theology of the family has to this day not yet been worked out...a systematic treatise on the theology of the family, has to my knowledge, still to be written." *Theology of the Family* (Malta: Jesuit Publications, 1994) 8–9).

3. Its inclusion in the document caused little stir, but it has taken time for the family as domestic Church to find its place in the theological consciousness of the Church.

4. Karol Wojtyla, *Love and Responsibility* (London: William Collins & Sons, 1982), 242.

5. *Ibid.*, 217.

6. *Ibid.*, 217.

7. In the sense of *radix* , the Latin word which refers to the fundamental roots.

8. "*Sed his praemissis, humiliter, mihi dolendum videtur, quod in toto schemate nullum inveniatur speciale caput quod agat de aliquo statu in Ecclesia, qui est maximae nobilitatis et sanctitatis et – ad incrementum Mystici Corporis Christi – maximae fecunditatis: sel de statu sacramentali matrimonii.*" Bishop Fiordelli, *Acta Synodalia Sacrosanctii Concilii Oecumenici Vaticani II*, Vatican City, 1960–1989 (henceforth called *Acta Synodalia*) vol. 1, pars 4, 309. (All translations are by the author and are purposely literal.)

9. *Acta Synodalia*, vol. 1, pars 4, 309.

10. "It is for this reason that the Church, throughout her history, has always defended the superiority of this charism to that of marriage, by reason of the wholly singular link which it has with the Kingdom of God" (*FC* 16). At this point, *FC* gives the footnote: Cf. Pius XII, encyclical *Sacra Virginitas*, II: AAS 46 (1954), 174 ff.

11. "Virginity or celibacy for the sake of the Kingdom of God not only does not contradict the dignity of marriage but presupposes it and confirms it. Marriage and virginity or celibacy are two ways of expressing and living the one mystery of the covenant of God with his people" (*FC*16).

12. *Acta Synodalia*, vol. 1, pars 4, 309. "*Plurimis enim hodie videtur quod specialis locus in Mystico Corpore Christi tribuendus sit iis qui in statu matrimoniali christiano positi sunt.*"

13. *Acta Synodalia*, vol. 1, pars 4, 309–310.

14. "*Mihi videtur quod haec sit vera structuratio Ecclesiae Christi...Nunc autem: estne paroicia ultima divisio Ecclesiae? Non. Paroecia ulterius dividitur in tot cellulas sanctas, quae sunt familiae chritianae, quas vocare possumus, exemplum Sanctorum Patrum, velut minusculas Ecclesias.*" *Acta Synodalia*, vol. 1, pars 4, 310–311.

15. *Acta Synodalia*, vol. 1, pars 4, 311.

16. "*Sanctum immo sacramentale fecit ipsum institutum familiare.*" (*Acta Synodalia*, vol. 1, pars 4, 311).

17. "*Quod si praeter membra, in Ecclesia, etiam organa et communitates...considerentur...familiae christianae.*" (*Acta Synodalia*, vol. 2, pars 1, 794–5.) "What if more than just members the family was considered even as organs and communities in the Church?"

18. "*Minusculam ecclesiam familiam christianam vocare possumus, in se habentem communicationem ipsius mysterii unionis Christi cum Ecclesia.*" (*Acta Synodalia*, vol. 2, pars 1, 794.

19. *Acta synodalia*, vol. 2, pars 1, 795.)

20. "*Cum tota domestica vestra ecclesia,*" Augustine, *De Bono Viduitatis* (*PL* 40,450); "*Domum... vestram non parvam Christi ecclesiam deputamus,*" Augustine *Ep. 188,3* (*PL* 33, 849); "*Domum tuam ecclesiam fac.*" Chrysostom, *In Gen* 6,2 (PG 54, 607).

21. *Lumen Gentium* 2,11, *Vatican II: The Conciliar And Post Conciliar Documents*, Flannery, A., ed., (North Port, N.Y.: Costello Publishing Co., 1975) 362–363. "*In hac velut Ecclesia Domestica parents verbo et exemplo sint pro filiis suis primi fidei praecones, et vocationem unicuique propriam...foveant oportet*": Michael Faye, "The Christian Family as Domestic Church at Vatican II," *Concilium* Fall 94/5, 89.

22. Pope Paul VI, *Marialis Cultis*: 52,53 *AAA* 66(1974) 13–168.

23. John Paul I to a group of Bishops from the United States given on Sept 21, 1978: *The Christian Family: A Community ofLlove* in *L'Osservatore Romano*, 28 September 1978 (p.11). "The Christian family is so important and its role is so basic in transforming the world and in building up the Kingdom of God that the Council called it a "domestic Church" (*Lumen Gentium*)."

24. John Paul II, address "*La Chiesa Rinnova il Dialogo con il mondo per Favorire La Comprensione Tra I Popoli*" Dec 22, 1981, in *Insegnamenti di Giovanni Paolo II*, 4/2 (1981) 1215. "*...mendiante la recentissima Esortazione Apostolica "Familiaris Consortio", resa pubblica una settimana fa, che vuol essere una "summma" dell'insegnamento della Chiesa sulla vita, I compiti, le responsabilita, la missione del matrinio e della famiglia nel mondo d'oggi.*"

25. "The Church once again feels the pressing need to proclaim the Gospel...to all those who are called to marriage...The Church is deeply convinced that only by the acceptance of the Gospel are the hopes that man legitimately places in marriage and in the family capable of being fulfilled" (*FC:*3). "We must all set ourselves in opposition through a conversion of mind and heart, following Christ Crucified by denying our own *selfishness"FC:*9).

26. This is an important area of study and is precisely where the development of doctrine lies and which must be explored further. It is clear that papal statements clearly move in this direction. In his "Letter to Families," JPII states that: "As the "domestic Church," it is the *bride of Christ*" (LtoF:19). This further develops the CCC's assertion that the family can and should be called the domestic Church (2204).

27. Only by such a recovery can passages such as 1 Corinthians 7 be explained properly.
28. Act 11:13ff; 16:15; 16:33; 1 Cor 1:16.
29. As noted above, in LtoF, John Paul II asserts that "as the 'domestic church', [the family] is *the bride of Christ*"(LtoF:19).
30. Joanne Heaney-Hunter, "Domestic Church: Guiding Beliefs and Daily Practices" in *Christian Marriage and Family: Contemporary Theological and Pastoral Perspectives*, edited by Michael Lawler and William Roberts (Collegeville: Liturgical Press, 1996) 60.

Session VII: Defending the Family at the United
Nations: 10 Years Since Cairo

Chapter 23: The International Jujitsu of the Sexual Vanguard

AUSTIN RUSE WITH DOUGLAS A. SYLVA, PH.D.

There is a sexual vanguard at work. They operate quite openly in places where most of us scarcely look and so most of us have missed them. What this vanguard seeks to spread and otherwise institutionalize is a small bundle of radical social policies, mostly related to millennial-long understandings of sex, that find their purest oxygen in women's studies departments and other exotic locales, like the United Nations, the European Parliament, some parts of the U.S. State Department, and increasingly the U.S. Supreme Court.

What this vanguard found – what they always find – is that they get little traction beyond university towns. They find little democratic support anywhere, in fact, and so – no surprise – they seek less than democratic means to advance their agenda. Hence they have washed up on the shores and found succor and sustenance at the least democratic institutions on the planet. And it is from these perches, behind closed doors, in quiet and carpeted rooms, that they go about their work.

What do these people find so attractive in the UN system, the European Union, or the International Criminal Court? To them, these structures appear like a never-ending constitutional convention, where laws are elastic and jurisdictions swell over national boundaries. If the revolutionaries can control this juridical process, they can control the laws that will regulate a multinational system that resembles evermore closely the foundations of a transnational government.

In fact, the kind of expansion they desire is taking place so quickly that critics have not been able to keep pace. For instance, those worried that the International Criminal Court may seek to prosecute American generals have barely noticed that the ICC's own top prosecutor, Luis Moreno-Campo, has announced that he now has the authority to prosecute *business* leaders for complicity in crimes against humanity.

Other useful characteristics include: the billions of dollars at stake in international development programs; a willingness on the part of the UN to shift funds from basic humanitarian relief to more controversial (and less quantifiable) pursuits under a feminist framework called "gender mainstreaming;" a strong habit within the international community to find "rights-based" solutions to development problems (these create legal obligations for governments); a new type of legislation, in the form of international "consensus" documents, far removed from individual citizens or their directly-elected representatives; and, finally, an increasingly complex international legal vocabulary, which instantly becomes the domain of specialists and legal experts.

So who belongs to this vanguard, and what is their plan? This vanguard certainly includes members of governments, mostly in the European Union, but also in the U.S. State Department as well. It also includes the elites in many targeted developing countries as well as many of those who describe themselves as the international civil servants who work for Kofi Annan. This vanguard is also – and most alarmingly – composed of leftist non-governmental organizations (NGOs) and legal advocacy groups. Their plan is to create a body of international "law" that can be imposed upon nations and peoples that otherwise disagree with it.

Perhaps the best example of the vanguard is the Center for Reproductive Rights (CRR), a Washington D.C.-based group founded in 1992 by lawyers formerly associated with the American Civil Liberties Union (ACLU). In the fall of 2003, the staff and allies of the CRR held a secret conference to assess the organization's progress in achieving its extremely ambitious goal: to establish a right to abortion on demand for women and girls in every nation on earth. In the course of their meetings, they examined the general strategy – revolution without the masses – in exquisite detail. They kept meticulous notes (even if they did not do an equally good job of keeping track of all of the copies). One day a copy appeared on my desk. Here, then, are the finer points of their magisterial strategy:

1) The Need for Secrecy

The notes envision an on-going multi-year "stealth" effort to create an international right to abortion that will be binding on all nations. It must be secret, because the goal is to impose this right upon pro-life nations – what the CRR labels the "hard countries." According to the CRR: "The gradual nature of this approach ensures that we are never in an 'all-or-nothing' situation, where we may risk a major setback…there is a stealth quality to the work: we are achieving incremental recognition of values without a huge amount of scrutiny from the opposition. These lower profile victories will gradually put us in a strong position to assert a broad consensus around our assertions." In other words, the CRR hopes to present the international right to abortion as an established fact.

2) While Working for This "Consensus," Never Admit That It Does Not Already Exist

When advocates for fisheries management seek new international fishing regulations, they lobby for an international conference on the subject. Likewise, the CRR acknowledges that an international conference on abortion rights, resulting in a new international legal instrument, would "offer strong, clear and permanent protections of women's reproductive rights." In the memos, however, CRR explicitly rejects calls for such a conference. Why? The CRR is most interested in creating the perception that international law *already* recognizes abortion rights. According to the memos: "Embarking on a campaign for a new legal instrument appears to concede that we do not have legal protections already, making failure potentially costly…As a matter of public perception, does pursuing a new instrument – without any assurance of success – undermine current claims regarding the existence of reproductive rights"? The CRR seems to believe that if it can alter perceptions – if it can convince enough countries that abortion is already an internationally recognized human right, then it will be so.

And thus it that the CRR seeks to propagate a fiction, a deliberate lie, really, about international law. In the memos, memos which were intended only for its own colleagues and collaborators, the CRR readily admits that there are profound "gaps" in current international law relating to reproductive rights. The memos state flatly that "there is no binding norm that recognizes women's rights to terminate a pregnancy." However, in the very next sentence, the CRR begins to explore how "to argue that such a right exists…"

3) Change the Interpretation of Longstanding International Law to Include the Right to Abortion, No Matter How Incongruous This Might Seem.

The CRR intends to reinterpret almost every major internationally recognized human right to include a right to abortion, and *then* fight for that reinterpretation to become the definitive one, thereby creating a legal obligation for the "hard countries" to comply with it. According to the CRR: "Reproductive rights advocates, including the Center, have found guarantees of women's rights to reproductive health and self-determination in longstanding and hard international norms (including the Universal Declaration of Human Rights, the International Covenant on Civil and Political Rights, the International Covenant on Economic, Social and Cultural Rights, and the Convention on the Elimination of All Forms of Discrimination Against Women [CEDAW])."

In fact, The CRR "finds" reproductive rights everywhere it looks: "We and others have grounded reproductive rights in a number of recognized human rights, including: the right to life, liberty, and security; the right to health, reproductive health, and family planning; the right to decide the number and spacing of children; the right to consent to marriage and to equality in marriage; the right to privacy; the right to be free from discrimination on specified grounds; the right to modify traditions or customs that violate women's rights; the right not to be subjected to torture or other cruel, inhuman, or degrading treatment or punishment; the right to be free from sexual violence; and the right to enjoy scientific progress and to consent to experimentation."

According to the CRR again: "This approach involves developing a jurisprudence that pushes the general understanding of existing, broadly accepted human rights laws to encompass reproductive rights." But that is understating the case, because the strategy amounts to rewriting carefully crafted international norms, sometimes decades after they were negotiated, to include things never intended by the countries that ratified them.

4) Create New "Customary" International Law That Is Binding on All Nations.

The "hard norms" plan is complemented by a "soft norms" strategy. Soft norms are second-tier international norms, norms that do not have the binding force associated with treaty provisions. These international norms are created by "human rights treaty committees, rulings of international tribunals, resolutions of inter-governmental political bodies, agreed conclusions in international conferences, and reports of special rapporteurs." The rulings of these groups, especially treaty monitoring bodies, although "soft" in legal terms, are essential to the CRR's strategy for the very simple reason that these rulings often count as the authoritative interpretations of established hard norms. Make the right soft norms and you can transform the hard norms that really matter. Thus, for the CRR, a "principal option is to develop 'soft norms' or jurisprudence (decisions or interpretations) to guide states' compliance with binding norms." The CRR knows that this strategy works, since it has already worked: "It is possible to secure favorable interpretations. Indeed, the Center has begun to do so." Not surprisingly, the CRR and its pro-abortion allies have had the most success in the monitoring body established to assess states' compliance with the UN women's rights convention, CEDAW. Although the CEDAW document in no way calls for the expansion of abortion services, or the legalization of abortion, or the recognition of an international right to abortion, the CEDAW Committee now acts as if it did all of these things, telling numerous countries that they must legalize abortion-on-demand to remain in compliance with the treaty.

Additionally, the CRR believes that a soft norm, repeated often enough, may become a hard norm, may, through its "customary" use, become a binding international law. The possible creation of pro-abortion "customary" law is especially attractive, since it implies that this norm is now the standard view of the world community. In fact, the CRR even believes that new customary international law can therefore become binding on recalcitrant countries, those "hard countries" that have not played along with the reproductive rights agenda. In this regard, the gradual accumulation of soft norms may result in an international hard norm even harder than treaty provisions, since only the states that ratify a specific treaty are bound to respect its provision.

5) Undermine Democratic Decision-making

In the memos, the CRR discusses how to protect abortion rights from "hostile majorities." There is little mention of typical democratic action such as voter registration drives or the formation of political parties and coalitions. The strategy here is to use international law to ensure that the will of "hostile majorities" is never reflected in actual governance. Since the goal is not to persuade, but to impose, CRR concludes that "litigation" remains "the most effective strategy for protecting the right to choose abortion in hostile political climates."

6) Undermine National Sovereignty

According to the CRR: "Our goal is to see governments worldwide guarantee women's reproductive rights out of recognition that they are bound to do so." And so the CRR works for the strengthening of international governmental structures at the expense of national sovereignty, since the "international *fora* with a quasi-juridical character arguably offer the most promising venues for securing justice and interpretations that actually change governments' behavior."

7) Undermine the United States

In the memos, it is clear that the CRR holds a special animus towards the United States, on account of its well-organized and influential opposition to CRR's agenda: "Since the decision of the United States Supreme Court in *Roe v. Wade*, there has existed an ongoing political, legal, and social movement in the United States to overturn *Roe*, prohibit abortion, and protect fetal life from the moment of conception." This opposition is certainly reflected in the policies of the administration of President George W. Bush, leading the CRR to lament: "What good is all our work if the Bush administration can simply take it all away with the stroke of a pen, by, for example, enacting the federal partial-birth abortion ban that we are currently fighting?" What is more, as the actions of the Bush administration at the United Nations have made clear, the U.S. can use its immense international influence to pursue a worldwide counter-revolutionary agenda on reproductive rights.

And so the CRR has elaborate plans for the United States. First, the Center seeks to isolate the United States from the rest of the international community: "In order to counter opposition to an expansion of recognized reproductive rights norms, we have questioned the credibility of such reactionary yet influential international actors as the United States and the Holy See." Even more importantly, the CRR hopes that its customary law strategy will simply wrest power away from the U.S. to govern itself on issues relating to abortion. In court papers filed against the Bush administration in 2001, the CRR (then known as the Center for Reproductive Rights and Policy, CRLP), asserts that "...generally recognized international legal norms may, if endorsed and accepted by the vast majority of nations, become part of customary international law and thus binding on the U.S. even if it does not ratify or endorse those norms." In fact, the suit admits that the CRR and its allies are preparing "for the eventuality that *Roe* may be overturned by the United States..." by advancing customary international law.

8) Create Enforcement Mechanisms

The CRR knows that there must be teeth in these laws: "Because we wish not only to set standards for government behavior, but also to ensure that governments understand that they are bound to those standards, our success depends on some focus on enforcement of international law." But here, too, the CRR has problems: "Gaps in substance of human rights instruments are accompanied by weaknesses in mechanisms for enforcing even the most accepted norms." The CRR uses the "quasi-judicial" institutions that now exist to test, and, it hopes, temper, international enforcement mechanisms, bringing cases in front of the Inter-American Commission on Human Rights and the UN Human Rights Committee. The CRR holds out special hopes for the enforcement potential of the International Criminal Court and a strengthened and expanded form of the CEDAW Convention.

But a less formal enforcement mechanism is also essential, namely: the courting of "fellow travelers" on national supreme courts, including the U.S. Supreme Court: "Jurists are aware of how legal questions have been resolved by their peers in other *fora*. Arguments based on the decisions of one body can be brought as persuasive authority to decision-makers in other bodies."

Four current U.S. Supreme Court justices have now signaled their willingness to accept the decisions of foreign and international human rights committees and tribunals when adjudicating U.S. disputes. The majority decision to overturn Texas's sodomy law, for instance, relied on judicial rulings made in Europe and at the United Nations. In the majority opinion, Justice Anthony Kennedy cited a "Friend of the Court" brief submitted in the case by Mary Robinson, former UN High Commissioner for Human Rights. Robinson asserts that the U.S. must accede to certain international beliefs on this topic in order to avoid being shunned: "To ignore these [pro-homosexual rights] precedents virtually ensures that this Court's ruling will generate controversies with the United State's closest global allies."

And in the recent Supreme Court decision striking down the death penalty for crimes committed under the age of majority, they majority opinion again cited so-called international legal standards. Specifically mentioned was the Convention on the Rights of the Child, a UN document the U.S. has neither signed nor ratified. They also cite Article 6(5) of the International Covenant on Civil and Political Rights (ICCPR) which forbids such executions. While the U.S. has signed and ratified the ICCPR, the U.S. filed a specific reservation on that paragraph.

This is little more than a judicial game of three-card-Monte. Yes, our elected representatives can know the red king is *right there*, but the Supreme Court and the UN always manage to palm it. No matter what, we lose.

This is also adjudication through international peer pressure. And how can the U.S. Supreme Court join the club? Robinson provides the answer: simply accept the hard norm reinterpretations of groups like the

CRR and its allies within international bodies: "Five of the six major UN human rights treaties have been interpreted by their respective supervisory organs to cover sexual orientation discrimination." Of course, none of the UN treaties cited by Robinson actually mentions sexual orientation.

Supreme Court Justice Sandra Day O'Connor has promised that the Supreme Court will rely "increasingly on international and foreign courts in examining domestic issues." And, perhaps most significantly for the CRR, in a 2003 decision on affirmative action, Justice Ruth Bader Ginsburg cited CEDAW, the CRR's most beloved document, a document upon whose compliance committee the CRR has had the most influence in its "reinterpretations," and a document that the U.S. government has steadfastly refused to ratify. In a speech a few weeks after the decision, Ginsburg admitted that "sadly, the United States has not ratified" CEDAW. Yet her decision shows that she is willing to act as if it had.

The CRR acknowledges that the strategy it has chosen is a difficult one: "The major disadvantage is that developing a customary norm is a slow process and it is difficult to know when you have accomplished your goal. Very few norms that are currently considered accepted and mainstream can be attributed to recent deliberate campaigns. While the standard for creating a customary norm is open to some scholarly debate, most such norms can be traced to centuries of practice and belief. In addition, although we are talking about undertaking a campaign of sorts, it is a difficult one to explain to non-lawyers and it is not very sexy."

However, the documents are punctuated with optimism: "The substantive reproductive rights of adolescents are not 'hard' (yet!)."

So what is the current status of this legal revolution, this international revolution without the masses? The CRR has successfully courted allies within the realm of international nongovernmental organizations. The International Planned Parenthood Federation (IPPF) and the International Women's Health Coalition (IWHC) are working towards the same reinterpretations of "hard" norms, as well as towards the creation of the same new "soft" norms. The CRR has successfully cultivated allies within the governments of many nations, especially the European Union countries and Canada; they routinely introduce reproductive rights language into international documents, no matter how tangential such rights might appear to the topic under discussion. The CRR has also successfully secured favorable interpretations of international norms by UN compliance committees, most notably the CEDAW committee and the Committee on the Rights of the Child. But, so far, there is no evidence that any nation has legalized abortion "out of recognition" that it is "bound to do so." However, all we have to do is wait.

Austin Ruse is president of the Catholic Family & Human Rights Institute, a non-governmental organization that monitors international social policy. Ruse is also president of the Culture of Life Foundation, which focuses on domestic social policy. Both organizations play important roles in today's pro-life and pro-family movements.

Douglas A. Sylva, Ph.D., was until recently vice president of the Catholic Family & Human Rights Institute, and remains a senior fellow there. He earned a doctorate in political theory from Columbia University, where he was also an instructor. Dr. Sylva has been published widely, including in the *New York Times*, the *Washington Times, National Review Online, Insight,* and the *National Catholic Register*. He and his wife, Susan, are the parents of two children.

Chapter 24: The International Year of the Family

WILLIAM L. SAUNDERS

Several important events, bearing on the health of the family, occurred ten years ago. First, the United Nations declared that the nations of the world were invited to observe 1994 as "the International Year of the Family." This was a development that the Holy See welcomed – at least, in principle. However, it soon became clear that the forces set on undermining the natural family would try to use the year to advance their agenda. This sparked the second significant event of 1994 – the Holy Father, John Paul II, issued his highly important "Letter to Families." The third event was the convening of the Conference on Population and Development by the UN in Cairo, Egypt (which I will hereafter refer to simply as "Cairo" or the "Cairo conference").

Hopes treasured by many, including the Holy See, that 1994 would offer a significant opportunity to support the natural family were dashed, when, at the Cairo conference, the Clinton administration and its allies tried (a) to undermine the normative notion of the natural family and (b) to promote an international "human right" to abortion. While they failed to win a complete victory (due the valiant efforts of the Holy See, many Latin American nations, and most Muslin countries), they did succeed in having ambiguous language (such as "reproductive health care") inserted in the text of the statement issued at the end of the Cairo conference.

As Cardinal Lopez-Trujillo notes in the paper he delivered to our convention, one problem that came up ever since the beginning stages of the preparation for the Year of the Family [in 1994], was the attempt to consider "families," in the plural, and thus to avoid the use, in the singular, of "the family." The goal was to impose an unacceptable interpretation that evades the model of the family willed by God, a natural institution that should be recognized without reluctance and with all the consequences that flow from it as the basic unit of society.

In the ten years since Cairo, pro-abortion and anti-family advocates have been relentless in trying to win what they failed to win at Cairo through the creation of an international right to abortion and homosexual marriage *under customary international law*. Their strategy has involved a two-step process – first, by repeating the ambiguous language from Cairo in as many international conferences, statements, and documents as possible; and, secondly, by arguing that such language is really not ambiguous at all; rather, it actually *means* "abortion" – and "homosexual marriage"! While this may appear to common sense to be an absurd claim, there is more plausibility in it than at first appears.

There are two kinds of international law–treaty and custom. Treaties are like contracts – words on paper, which the parties negotiate. Thus, the "content" (the meaning) of a treaty is clear and fixed. If a nation signs onto the treaty, it is bound by its terms.

Customary international law – the second kind of international law – is a much more malleable concept. Customary international law is, simply, the custom of nations, i.e., what nations do. Since customary international law, unlike treaties, is not *written*, it must be "found," by a court, through an examination of the behavior of nations. Historically, to become customary law, customary practices must have been followed by *all* nations for a *long period of time*.

It is important to understand that, under widely-accepted legal doctrines, international law – both treaty and custom – *is* the law in the United States. It is true that it does not trump, or overrule, the Constitution, but it can trump federal statutes and regulations. Thus, it is not the irrelevancy many conservatives often imagine it to be.

The threat to the family today comes from a combination of this powerful legal principle – customary international law – with a relaxation (for leftist ideological reasons) of the stringent legal standards ordinarily employed to "find" customary international law, along with the emergence, over the past thirty-five years, of an activist U.S. judiciary prepared to go along with the new "customary" findings. Judicial activists do not understand their role to be limited to applying the law as written (and as passed by the people through their elected legislatures). Rather, they see themselves as "champions," empowered, under a "living Constitution," to do justice, as they see it. We have seen the terrible fruit of judicial activism in Supreme Court decisions such as *Roe v. Wade*. We have also seen it in the recent case of *Lawrence v. Texas* effectively legalizing consensual sodomy.

In *Lawrence*, in 2003, the U.S. Supreme Court overturned established legal precedent and struck down anti-sodomy laws. Why? Because, in part, such laws did not, in the Supreme Court's view, reflect the "common values" of the civilization the United States shares with

Europe. This is a striking evidence of a growing trend in the federal courts to use non-U.S. norms to advance a leftist agenda.

Sexual liberationists could never win the agreement of the nations of the world to be bound by a written agreement – a treaty – to recognize homosexual marriage and abortion. Thus, they try to achieve by sleight of hand and maneuvering what they cannot do openly. Leftist legal academicians urge activist U.S. judges to "find" that the nations of the world – by endlessly repeating ambiguous terms – have demonstrated a "custom" accepting homosexual marriage and abortion.

All of this is, however, merely prologue to my main point. The UN has declared 2004 to be the second Year of the Family. Some pro-family advocates and lawyers decided that during this, the second, International Year of the Family, we would cease playing defense and would go on the offensive. We decided that this year we would put into place the legal facts that would defeat the left's claim that customary international law recognizes homosexual marriage and abortion.

To do so, we began "the Doha process." Several of us serve on the NGO (non-governmental organizations) organizing committee for a series of international pro-family meetings which took place around the world during 2004. The first took place in Mexico City in March. Others took place in June in Stockholm and in August in Geneva. There will be another meeting in Kuala Lumpur, Malaysia, in October. At each of these meetings, scholars – social scientists, lawyers, philosophers, and others – from around the world have gathered to discuss, and to present papers affirming, the importance of the natural family and marriage.

In November, there will be an inter-governmental meeting in Doha, Qatar. The government of Qatar serves as president of what is called the Group of 77 at the United Nations. The G-77 is composed of the nations we previously designated as "the non-aligned nations" (i.e., neither with the U.S. or with the U.S.S.R. during the Cold War years). These are mostly the nations of the "developing world," i.e., the nations of Africa, Asia, and the Middle East. They constitute an important voting bloc at the UN.

At the meeting in Qatar, these nations will adopt a document affirming the importance of the family. The document – the Doha Declaration – will repeat important pro-family language from previous international documents such as the Universal Declaration of Human Rights. This is important because when contentious issues are involved (unfortunately, because of the leftists, "the family" is a contentious issue), the UN operates by relying on "consensus language", i.e., by repeating language used in previous UN documents (thus, no country can complain that anything "new" is being foisted upon it). By repeating language from previous documents, we brunt any legitimate objection from the leftist European nations – this is, after all, merely "previously agreed-upon" language.

And the good news is that the language about the family in the "old" UN documents, such as the Universal Declaration on Human Rights from 1948, is always better than any language we could negotiate today. This "previously agreed consensus language" was adopted at a time long before anyone contended that homosexual marriage or abortion were human rights. Thus, the Doha Declaration, using this "old" language, will affirm the importance of marriage, the right of men and women to marry one another, marriage as the foundation of the family, the family as the foundation for society, the right to life of every human being, and so on.

After the Doha Declaration has been adopted in Qatar, it will then be taken to the United Nations and introduced in the General Assembly in December to be accepted as the last UN event of the International Year of the Family. We think the General Assembly will accept it since (a) it is built around "previously agreed consensus language" and (b) because it will have the sponsorship of the over 100 nations of the G-77.

And, here, finally is the important point: if the Doha Declaration is adopted by the UN, it becomes an official UN document that can be cited in any court case in which the left claims that "customary international law" supports abortion or homosexual marriage. And it is decisive evidence against that claim. Recall that the left asserts that the *custom of the nations* has converged to recognize abortion and homosexual marriage. The Doha Declaration, *by itself*, will be evidence that no such anti-life, anti-family consensus exists among the nations of the world, for the nations will, in the Doha Declaration, have asserted to the contrary.

If this happens, it will be a tremendous victory. It will mean that 2004 was, indeed, worth commemorating as the International Year of the Family after all.

William L. Saunders, Jr., a graduate of Harvard Law School, is Senior Fellow and Director of the Family Research Council's Center for Human Life & Bioethics. Bill also writes a column twice a year for the *National Catholic Bioethics Quarterly* discussing major developments in the bioethics field. He was appointed by President George W. Bush to serve on the United States delegation to the UN Special Session on Children in 2001/02. He was pleased to be the drafter of a statement in support of the Holy See at the United Nations, which formed part of the "Holy See Campaign," launched by Austin Ruse and the Catholic Family and Human Rights Institute to defend the Holy See's role at the UN. Again in 2004, Bill served on the International Secretariat for the Intercultural Dialogue on the Family in support of the pro-family declaration introduced by developing nations at the UN in 2004.

Chapter 25: Remarks on Receiving the Cardinal Wright Award

SISTER PRUDENCE ALLEN, R.S.M., PH.D.

Thank you very much for this great honor of the Cardinal Wright Award given "to a Catholic adjudged to have done outstanding service for the Church..." I would like to take a few minutes to invert this relation and acknowledge the great service that the Church has done for us.

The Catholic Church opened to us graces of the sacramental life; educated our intellects with many truths of the faith; called and formed us in our vocations; and provided ways for us to inherit eternal life. This universal Catholic Church has, "with outstanding service," nourished us beyond all hopes and expectations.

How can we ever thank the Catholic Church and Our Lord sufficiently for these wonderful gifts of the sacraments and intellectual and religious formation? By offering them back in service to the Church and the world – as the Statement of Purpose of the Fellowship of Catholic Scholars so beautifully says: "...to serve Jesus Christ better...by putting our abilities more fully at the service of the Catholic faith"; and "to Him we give thanks for our Catholic faith and for every opportunity He gives us to serve that faith."[1] Of course, we all do this according to our specific vocations – serving one another in the Church and in the world as consecrated religious, ordained priests, sacramentally married, or as single persons.

In *Vita Consecrata*, Pope John Paul II says that "[t]he experience of recent years widely confirms [what Pope Paul VI first observed in *Ecclesiam Suam*[2]] that `dialogue is the new name of charity.'"[3] Let us consider together how dialogue as the new name of charity applies to two different aspects of our Fellowship: first, to the family as the focus of this year's annual convention, and second to our interaction with one another in interdisciplinary studies.

Technology offers new challenges to dialogue in the family. For example, with the advent of television and the internet many parents no longer read to their children; and with the use of the microwave and hectic life-styles many families no longer eat common meals together.

Catholic philosophers have noticed the potentially devastating effects of the extensive use of these technologies on children's capacities to participate during Mass in the Liturgy of the Word and the Liturgy of the Eucharist.[4] A child who has never experienced on-going dialogue in listening and responding to significant words read to them or shared with them during meals at home, may be unable to dialogue with God in hearing the Sacred Word or in receiving the Eucharist in Holy Communion.[5]

A true parent/child dialogue is a new form of charity. The family is called, as the "domestic church" to provide the foundation for the spiritual fertility of the diocesan church and the universal Church. During the coming Year of the Eucharist perhaps one way parents could serve their mission to build the Body of Christ is through providing real opportunities for genuine dialogue within their own families.

For Catholic scholars, participating in interdisciplinary dialogue in the search for truth is another way to build up the Body of Christ. Dialogue is enhanced by adherence to the Church's magisterium, and interdisciplinary dialogue is central to the mission of this organization of Catholic scholars. What characteristics should our dialogue have in order to fulfill this mission?

Several characteristics of dialogue recently articulated by the Holy Father in his encyclical *Ut Unum Sint* have analogical application to discussing the mission of the Fellowship of Catholic Scholars. To begin: "Dialogue is not simply an exchange of ideas. In some way it is always an 'exchange of gifts.'"[6] Dialogue should occur between competent experts, who are seeking truth in conformity to the dignity of the human person (##31–32).

John Paul II further states that dialogue is related to a "personalist way of thinking" because it is "an indispensable step along the path" towards self realization of the individual person and of "every human community" (#28). Furthermore, although it "might appear to give priority to the cognitive dimension, all dialogue implies a global, existential dimension" (#28). It involves each one of us entirely. Authentic dialogue "serves as an examination of conscience" (#34), as we are challenged by others from different disciplines, states of life, and points of view. Dialogue has "a primarily vertical thrust, directed towards the One...Redeemer of the world and the Lord of history...(#35)," as we incarnate our call to serve one another as living signs of the love of Jesus Christ for His Bride, the Church, and of the Bride's response of love to being loved.

Returning to the theme of "dialogue as the new name of charity," the Holy Father repeats that "there must be charity towards one's partner in dialogue, and humility with regard to the truth which comes to light and which might require a review of assertions and attitudes (#36)." In my years of research in the history of the philosophy of integral complementarity of woman and man, it has been a joy to discover moments when dialogue fulfilled its name of charity. The search for communion of persons through authentic interdisciplinary dialogue achieves one of its purposes in a living likeness to the Divine Persons in the Holy Trinity, who live in a Communion of Love and Knowledge.

May the Fellowship of Catholic Scholars continue to provide new opportunities for this wonderful way of service to the Church and the world. Thank you.

Notes

1. Fellowship of Catholic Scholars, Statement of Purpose, #1 and #2, in Kenneth D. Whitehead, ed., *Marriage and the Common Good: Proceedings from the Twenty-Second Annutal Convention of the Fellowship of Catholic Scholars* (South Bend, Indiana: St. Augustine's Press, 2001), 228.

2. Pope Paul VI, *Ecclesiam Suam:* Encyclical Letter On the Church (August 6, 1964), Section III.

3. John Paul II, *Vita Consecrata:* Post-Synodal Apostolic Exortation on The Consecrated Life and Its Mission in the Church and in the World (Boston: Pauline Books and Media, 1996), #74.

4. See Albert Borgmann, "Technology and the Crisis of Contemporary Culture," in *Philosophy of Technology: Proceedings of the American Catholic Philosophical Association Volume LLX* (Washington DC: Catholic University of America, 1996), 33–44. For example: "For a Catholic, however, it is but a short step from the culture of the word to the World of God and from the culture of the table to the breaking of the Bread," 40.

5. See Borgman, "Technology and the Crisis of Contemporary Culture," where he states: "Catholics cannot be unconcerned about the decay of the culture of the word and the thoughtless dismissal it is suffering at the hands of cyberspace enthusiasts"; "At the level of...parents it comes to affirming on Monday what has been professed on Sunday. If the sacrament of the Eucharist is not reenacted in the sacramental of the dinner table, the Breaking of the Bread has a precarious place in contemporary culture," 42.

6. John Paul II, *Ut Unum Sint*: Encyclical Letter on Commitment to Ecumenism (Boston: Pauline Books and Media, 1995), #28.

Chapter 26: Banquet Address on the Fellowship of Catholic Scholars

Most Reverend Anthony Fisher, O.P.

Scholars like to wear academic dress, at least for graduations. I have seen photos of children as early as preschoolers 'graduating' in academic gowns of various colors. Few realize that this dress originated in medieval clerical vesture, especially that of the friars, who were exploding onto the European ecclesial scene at exactly the time when the new universities were appearing, and who quickly dominated both the student body and faculty of those universities.

As a result their dress came increasingly to be identified with the academy; the Dominican cappa or black hood and cloak, worn over the white habit, for which we were known as the "black friars," is the origin of the basic black academic gown. For the Dominican friars, the black and white colors of their habit were about more than an evangelical poverty that resorted to the unbleached wool of white sheep for the habit and the undyed wool of black sheep for the cloak: the color also told of Order's motto: *Veritas*, Truth, which is black and white.

All that most people know about friars is Friar Tuck from Robin Hood and Torquemada from the Inquisition. Certainly many of us friars are fat and jolly like Tuck, and some of us do take an unseemly delight in sniffing out heresy. But the ruling passion of those first friars was *Veritas*. The first black-and-white friars had a fervid interest in contemplating the truth and communicating it to others. That sounds strange to our tolerant, relativist, nihilist world; it is alien to an age like ours where meaninglessness characterizes so much of politics and commerce, art and science; Dominic's plain motto *Veritas* is unfamiliar to an age more inclined to adopt Pilate's *Quid est veritas?* – "What is truth?" – as its motto.

Truth seems to many of our contemporaries too hard to know, to communicate, to agree upon. Worse still, truth makes its claims on us: it threatens, interrogates, cuts us to the quick, regarding our public structures, institutions, and policies, our private prejudices, ideologies, and behaviors. Truth demands a rethink, an intellectual, moral, and personal conversion; and it demands also to be lived – all of which sounds all too intimidating for our age.

Yet the first wearers of academic gowns were convinced that the truth is *good news*. Our past century, the century of Monsignor Kelly, perhaps better than any other, has seen how big lies hurt people: lies like Nazism, Communism, Secularism, Anti-Populationism, the Sexual Revolution, and, most recently, Terrorism – the big ideologies and systems built on lies that kill. And then there are the less systematic commercial lies we call consumerism, advertising, and credit beyond our means; the political lies like pragmatism and all-for-the-party; the social and sexual lies we call freedom and self-fulfillment. Then, too, there are lies like happiness through infidelity in our relationships, through aborting our babies, through abandoning our poor, sick, and elderly, through self-indulgences of a thousand different kinds.

Into such an age, as in every age, the Logos of God enters as liberation, God is the Truth that sets us free: from falsehood, superstition, and fear: from the mirages created by various interests and the illusions we create for ourselves. Truth disillusions, without making us cynical; it releases the heart from false anxiety; it unfetters the body from misuse and abuse; it liberates the mind from half-truths and the soul from inauthenticity; it frees the spirit from slavery to false gods.

The Fellowship of Catholic Scholars has for many years, unashamedly put its energy at the service of Christian truth, Catholic faith, divine wisdom. For the Fellowship the academic habit is not just for graduation dress-ups and photo opportunities. It is, rather, about that for which St Catherine of Sienna cried out to God: "Clothe me, clothe me round, O God, with your holy truth." We try to dress in the habits of truth-friars, truth-seekers, and truth-teachers, so that we can join Christ in his words: "To this end was I born, and for this I came into the world, that I should bear witness to the truth…For their sake I consecrate myself, that they might be consecrated in the truth" (Jn 18:37; 17:19).

Monsignor George Kelly, in his battles for the American Church and campus and soul, wrote often and with passion against "Catholic" scholars who publicly dissent from Catholic teaching. His passion was borne not of mere annoyance at disobedience or rank-breaking, but of a love for that Catholic truth which is guarded by the magisterium and which Catholic scholars are called to serve, a love ultimately for that God and those billions of souls that are served by that Truth. "If no Catholic Truth binds the minds, consciences or lives of allegedly believing Catholic members," he wrote, "then no reason exists to justify the existence of a

Catholic school, save as a propaganda mechanism for elites" to push their own inventions. "In a healthy environment," he suggested, "thinking with the Church, exemplifying the obedience of faith, having the mind of Christ, would be the normal attribute of the believing Catholic – even if he holds an advanced academic degree."

Well, this Fellowship which he helped to found has for nearly three decades been just such a healthy environment, a place where it is easy to be a Catholic and to be a scholar. I, for one, have so much enjoyed being at this 27th Annual Conference and with all of you. How different it feels to so many academic "communities" and "societies," even Catholic ones I have known, who often enjoy community about as real as a school of piranhas. Amongst you there is deep, genuine fraternity, common vision, and so I've felt very much at home here.

As a youngish bishop, friar, and scholar I also want to express my gratitude to the giants of Catholic scholarship who have been honored by this Fellowship over the years and tonight with prizes and eulogies, and who have offered fraternity to others engaged in the pursuit of Holy Truth. I join you all in congratulating Sister Mary Prudence Allen and in mourning the passing of Father Ronald Lawler and Monsignor George Kelly.

My thanks to you all for your scholarly contribution: as I look around this room I see so many whose words have fed my mind and soul for past decades, so many who have contributed in so many ways to the Church's intellectual mission. My thanks also for your fidelity, your witness, your martyrdom, especially in those times and places where other academics, other Catholics, some of the clergy, even some of the hierarchy, have seemed too enamored with the *Zeitgest*, or too foolish, or too cowardly, to stand by you and with you when they should have. You have fought the good fight: now there are many fruits of your work, many signs of hope (if challenges too).

Some people, I know, think the Ten Commandments were "ten suggestions"; they likewise interpret an apostolic constitution like *Ex Corde Ecclesiae* as an option to take or leave or as an obstacle course to be circumvented. Yet we see in that document the thoughts of a great Catholic scholar who is also our God-given teacher and who set out for us a vision of our vocation, a description of its essential outlines, and directions for its institutional execution. And so I would like to leave the last word to him.

I would like to recall his words in that constitution of reverence and thanks to Catholic scholars such as yourselves and your friends and collaborators: "I want to express my deep appreciation for your work. You give me a well-founded hope for a new flowering of Christian culture under the action of the Spirit of truth and of love…Beloved brothers and sisters, my encouragement and my trust go with you in your weighty daily task, ever more necessary, ever more urgent, of evangelizing the culture…The Church and the world have great need of your witness and contribution." Thanks be to God for you!

Chapter 27: Homily for the 27th Annual Convention of the Fellowship of Catholic Scholars

Most Reverend Donald W. Wuerl, Bishop of Pittsburgh

Before beginning these reflections on our liturgy and celebration today, I want to thank Professor Gerard Bradley, President of the Fellowship of Catholic Scholars, for his kind invitation to be with you today and to be the principal celebrant at this Eucharistic Liturgy. I also want to recognize Dean Bernard Dobranski, the incoming President of the Fellowship. In a particular way I want to express my gratitude to Monsignor Stuart Swetland, Executive Secretary of the Fellowship, for his great kindness in organizing all of this morning's activities. I would also like to acknowledge my brother priests, women and men in consecrated life, members of the Fellowship of Catholic Scholars and brothers and sisters in the Lord.

It is with particular attention and affection that we recognize in this liturgy today two of the founding members of the Fellowship and pray for their eternal rest and peace – Monsignor George A. Kelly and Father Ronald Lawler, O.F.M. Cap. I have fond memories of working with both Monsignor Kelly and Father Lawler in the early and mid-seventies when they together with others, some present at this Mass, forged the framework of the Fellowship of Catholic Scholars that has served the Church so well and continues to do so today.

Earlier this year at a gathering at Point Park where the Allegheny and Monongahela Rivers come together to form the Ohio River we initiated a celebration of the 250th anniversary of the first Mass celebrated west of the Alleghenies – in what is now the Diocese of Pittsburgh.

When a French expeditionary force arrived at what is now the Golden Triangle to establish the claim of France to this part of the new world, there traveled with them a chaplain, Father Denys Baron. On arrival on April 17, 1754, the first thing Father Baron did was celebrate the Eucharist – Holy Mass.

We commemorated the 250th anniversary of that event first at Point Park and then at Saint Paul Cathedral to reflect on our connectedness today in southwestern Pennsylvania with that great apostolic tradition that first came to our part of the world when Denys Baron celebrated Mass.

In an unbroken line we trace the apostolic tradition back through the centuries, through the arrival of Franciscan and Dominican Friars and Jesuit priests in the new world 500 years ago, on through the evangelization of Asia, Africa, and Europe by missionary religious and missionaries such as Saint Patrick, Saint Boniface, Saint Ignatius, Saint Francis Xavier, Saints Cyril and Methodius – all the way back to the apostles, Peter, Andrew, James and John and, ultimately, to the Last Supper. In the Eucharist which we celebrate today we are brought into a living communion – a vital union – a true connectedness with Jesus Christ, His Gospel, and His life-giving grace.

In his encyclical on the Eucharist, *Ecclesia de Eucharistia*, our Holy Father, Pope John Paul II, reminds us: "When the Church celebrates the Eucharist, the memorial of the Lord's death and resurrection, this central event of salvation becomes really present and 'the work of our redemption is carried out'…This is the faith which generations of Christians down the ages have lived" (#11).

The great living continuity, the great connectedness, that you and I have with Jesus Christ is not just through the wonder of his sacramental presence. It is also through the Gospel message – his teaching that answers for us the great questions of life. The perennial human questions which take many forms, and which are articulated in many ways, come essentially to these: How shall I live? What values shall guide my life? Where do I find answers to the truly great questions of life?

Today's liturgy and our gathering here tell us that we believe there is a wider context. That context helps us understand our human condition and helps us to answer the great questions about the meaning, the purpose and goal of life. No one lives life disassociated from everyone else – from human society, human history, or the human condition. No person is an island. Each of us seeks some context out of which we can respond to life and its joys, sorrows, challenges and wonders.

Today as we gather for this liturgy we are all reminded that this gathering of the Fellowship of Catholic Scholars continues its work with the celebration of the Eucharist as a clear reminder that we are all part of a living connectedness with Christ. It is ultimately in Christ that we find the meaning of life and the answers to life's great questions.

Many of us here at this 27th convention of the Fellowship of Catholic Scholars are associated with institutions of higher learning. In that capacity we have a particular connectedness with the teaching mission of the Church. Listen to these words and see if they strike a resonant cord in your life's journey. "By vocation, the university is dedicated to research, to teaching, and to the education of students, who freely associate with their teachers in a common love of knowledge."

Where do you think those words originate? Do they sound like something that the bishop might write to the president of a university? Do they sound like something that maybe Pope John Paul II today in our contemporary age would write to all the Catholic university leaders and those dedicated to scholarship throughout the world?

Actually, these words were addressed by a pope to a university. The pope was Alexander IV, the university was the University of Paris, and the date was 1255. It has always been a part of the Catholic intellectual, spiritual, and pastoral tradition to foster the joy "of searching for, discovering and communicating truth in every field of knowledge" (*Ex Corde Ecclesiae*, 1).

The Catholic intellectual initiative, the work of the Fellowship, has the privileged task "to unite existentially by intellectual effort two orders of reality that too frequently tend to be placed in opposition as though they were antithetical: the search for truth and the certainty of already knowing the font of truth." These last words were taken from a talk of Pope John Paul II in 1980 to the Catholic Institute of Paris – successor to the University of Paris.

Part of our connectedness, of our own identity, includes the spiritual dimension of human life with the moral values that follow on the realization that we do not live by bread alone. A profound part of the human experience is the search for truth, and the development of human wisdom, which includes: the recognition of God; the appreciation of religious experience in human history and life and the special truth that is divinely revealed – religious truth.

Our Fellowship helps to provide the environment where this connectedness is realized. Science without religiously grounded ethics, art without spirituality, technology without human moral values are only shadows, incomplete imitations, of what they as branches of learning are called to be.

Human experience includes religious truth. This is the message of today's Gospel. We cannot truly evaluate the purpose and meaning of life apart from God's Word. The revelation of the mystery of God with us is not incidental to the human enterprise. It gives life and light, direction and purpose to the struggle we call the human condition and the reality we call the human experience.

By definition the Catholic intellectual initiative in all of its manifestations brings to the whole educational effort a dimension that not only enriches our lives but helps us to understand who we are; how we relate to one another; how we relate to the world in which we live, and how we relate to God, the Author of all Creation.

Before us is the challenge of exploring and more deeply understanding the truth. With us is the living witness of the words of Jesus who is alive in His Church vivified in His Holy Spirit. We have both the challenge and the opportunity to integrate fully into our life the wisdom of God, the love of Christ and the power of the Holy Spirit.

Just as that first Mass celebrated 250 years ago symbolized and actually connected us with the great sacramental tradition of the Church, so this celebration of the Eucharist today; this outpouring of the Holy Spirit; this annual meeting of the Fellowship of Catholic Scholars; your participation in the work of the great Catholic intellectual effort connect you to a centuries old tradition.

A tradition that, as a pope said 800 years ago, is "…dedicated to research, to teaching, and to the education of students who freely associate with their teachers in a common love of knowledge."

May this year be a year of growth and grace for you, for all who work so hard to preserve and enhance Catholic thought, and for the whole Fellowship family.

Thank you.

Bishop Donald W. Wuerl was installed as the 11th bishop of Pittsburgh on February 12, 1988. A native of Pittsburgh, he was ordained a priest in 1966 and a bishop in 1986; both ordinations took place in Rome. He has an earned S.T.D. from the Pontifical University of St. Thomas, and is the recipient of nine honorary degrees. Bishop Wuerl is the spiritual leader of some 800,000 Catholics in 215 parishes throughout Southwestern Pennsylvania. In addition to his responsibilities as shepherd of the Catholic Church in the six counties that comprise the Diocese of Pittsburgh, Bishop Wuerl is involved in a wide range of community, ecumenical, and interfaith activities, joining with civic and business leaders in educational and community-service initiatives. These include the Christian Leaders Fellowship and its many ecumenical enterprises, the Extra Mile Education Foundation which is responsible for a number on inner-city parochial schools, the Urban League of Pittsburgh, and the United Way of Allegheny County.

To many, Bishop Wuerl is known from the television program "*The Teaching of Christ.*" The best-selling adult catechism of the same name, of which he is one of the co-authors, is now in its 28th year of publication, and has been translated into more than 10 languages. It is used throughout the world. He is the author of a number of other books, notably *The Fathers of the Church* (1975) and *The Church and Her Sacraments: Making Christ Visible* (1990). His most recent publication, *The Catholic Way: Faith for Living*, was published by Doubleday in September 2001.

IN MEMORIAM
REV. MSGR. GEORGE A. KELLY,
1916–2004

(Rev. Msgr. George A. Kelly was the principal founder of the Fellowship of Catholic Scholars, and served at various times as both president and secretary. He was the first recipient of the FCS Cardinal Wright Award in 1979. Throughout the first quarter century of the Fellowship, and up until his death, he was the principal moving spirit within the organization. It was not the least of his many accomplishments. Indeed his career as a priest would have had to be rated outstanding on any one of several different counts: his many published writings and academic achievements, the important archdiocesan offices he held at various times, and his steady work as a parish priest and pastor. But his work as founder and moving spirit of the Fellowship was both outstanding and indispensable, and we have thought it appropriate and, indeed, obligatory, to publish this tribute to Msgr. Kelly written by some of those in the Fellowship who knew and loved him best. A tribute to Msgr. Kelly's close friend and associate, Fr. Ronald Lawler, the first president of the Fellowship who preceded him in death was included last year in the "Proceedings" for the 2004 convention entitled The Catholic Citizen.*)*

The Leader of the "Resistance"
Patrick G. D. Riley

For members of the Fellowship of Catholic Scholars, the death of Msgr. George A. Kelly restores meaning to the term "end of an era." Many of us must wonder who else could have mid-wifed our organization and imparted the impetus to give it impact, even survival. But beyond that, and beyond question, he was a national figure, a foremost leader of the resistance to the decades-long retreat of Catholics from the obedience of faith.

During the past quarter-century and more since he founded the Fellowship, his word could be decisive for us. That was due in part to natural *pietas* toward the venerable founder, of course, but at least equally due to respect for his almost preternatural good sense and his unerring grasp of situations. He epitomized that rare charisma known as leadership in years when religious superiors and others responsible for the Church's well-being were invoking it as a substitute for authority.

His breakthrough book, *The Battle for the American Church*, published in 1979, a year after our foundation, cemented his unique prestige within the Fellowship, and established him throughout the country and abroad as a chronicler and interpreter of the Church's turbulent times.

He loved to quote Emerson's adage that an institution is the lengthened shadow of one man. Anyone writing a memorial of him could scarcely avoid mentioning it, or its obvious relevance to the Fellowship and to himself. If the Fellowship is feisty, intransigent, and fired with love of the Church, we can in large part credit George Anthony Kelly.

All of us who knew him, whether up close or from a distance, have savored the flavor of the man, and understand its uniqueness. Hard as it is to conjure up anyone for those who did not know him, I think it less difficult in the case of George A. Kelly. His conversation was always provocative and at times "outrageous – but he gets away with it," as another New York priest once remarked in astonishment. Its piquancy was "like mustard in the mouth of a young child," as was said of the great Dr. Samuel Johnson.

An admirer of his in the bureaucracy of the old National Conference of Catholic Bishops – there were some there, if they generally kept quiet about it – reported that when the name of George Kelly arose at high-echelon meetings "everybody starts foaming at the mouth" – unconscious praise indeed, and unwilling, but all the more sincere for all of that.

Before reminiscing more about Msgr. Kelly, I should offer some particulars of his life. For that purpose I'll reproduce an obituary which I wrote when he died, and I will give it entire for the very special reason that the *New York Times* and other media did not choose to publish it, although it was submitted in proper form through proper channels. As a prominent New York priest over more than half a century, who held various leadership positions in the archdiocese, Msgr. Kelly by any standard deserved more than the two inches of fine print that appeared in the obituary section of the *Times* on August 16, 2004.

Perhaps the *Times* was embarrassed by Kelly's unique success in marshaling outstanding scholars to oppose the kind of dissenting Catholic academics considered at once progressive and mainstream by major media. I hardly need mention that the *New York Times*, whose obituary page often has a plebeian flavor, had published lengthy obituaries of priests of far lesser achievement, if any. One of them, prominent in the

Midwest, Kelly thought doctrinally ambiguous and even a dissenter; another, who had once employed the wife of a *Times* religion reporter as a secretary, received an extensive obituary complete with photo, although he was practically unknown outside clerical circles. Be all that as it may, here is the rejected obituary:

Monsignor George A. Kelly

Msgr. George A. Kelly, who rose to leadership in the ranks of traditional Catholics a quarter-century ago by founding the Fellowship of Catholic Scholars and then publishing *The Battle for the American Church*, a documented account of dissent from Roman Catholic doctrine and discipline, died August 12. He was eighty-seven years of age, and had been ill with cancer for about a year. Msgr. Kelly was a priest of the Archdiocese of New York. He had been a pastor, diocesan administrator, and university professor, as well as the author or editor of some three dozen published books.

Edward Cardinal Egan, Archbishop of New York and a longtime friend of Msgr. Kelly's, celebrated the mass and preached the homily at Msgr. Kelly's funeral in his old parish church of St. John the Evangelist in the building of archdiocesan headquarters at 1011 First Avenue, Manhattan.

In 1978, while he was Flynn Professor in Contemporary Catholic Problems at St. John's University, in Jamaica, N.Y., Msgr. Kelly founded in the Fellowship of Catholic Scholars, whose more than 800 members in the United States and abroad include professors and writers in theology, philosophy, law, history, and science. Although fully committed to Vatican Council II and the legitimate authority of the pope and bishops, the Fellowship was founded to break what Msgr. Kelly considered was a stranglehold of dissenters over associations of Catholic theologians, scripture scholars, canonists, and academics, and to rally the Catholic loyalists among those disciplines to the genuine flag of the Church.

Msgr. Kelly often recalled how he came to found the Fellowship. Cardinal Gabriel Garrone, prefect of the Holy See's Congregation for Catholic Education, complained to him about the strongly dissenting character of Catholic scholarly associations in America, and asked in anguish: "Does nobody speak for Catholic scholars in America except Father Theodore Hesburgh and the Catholic Theological Society of America?"

Msgr. Kelly's 1979 *The Battle for the American Church* (Doubleday) is an account of rebellion against the authority of Rome and the bishops. Because of its detailed documentation, it remains a work of reference today, and it made him a national figure among Catholics of religiously orthodox and conservative bent. The more progressive Catholics saw him as an adversary of mettle.

Another of his three dozen published books, *The Catholic Marriage Manual*, earned him almost a quarter-million dollars in royalties, a princely sum in 1958 when the book was published. He donated the entire proceeds to the New York Foundling Hospital, a Catholic foundation.

Msgr. Kelly's published works on family life, and his decade as director of the archdiocesan Family Life Bureau (1955–65), brought him to Rome as a member of Pope John XXIII's Papal Birth Control Commission. He was one of the very few members who held to the traditional condemnation of contraception, which was reaffirmed in 1968 by Pope Paul VI in the hotly-contested encyclical *Humanae Vitae*. In 1984, Msgr. Kelly was made a consulter of the Holy See's Congregation for the Clergy, which is responsible for the welfare of Catholic priests and for the soundness of religious instruction throughout the world.

Although not a specialist in scriptural studies, he took on the foremost American Catholic biblical scholar, Father Raymond Brown, in a highly critical book: *The New Biblical Theorists: Raymond E. Brown and Beyond* (Ann Arbor:Servant Publications, 1983). International theologians such as Hans Urs von Balthasar and René Laurentin praised the book, even though it was not well received by most American biblicists. "They don't like it, but then they haven't read it," observed a former president of the Catholic Biblical Association, Rev. Neil McEleney, C.S.P.

Msgr. Kelly's readiness to take on all comers was appreciated by the late John Cardinal O'Connor of New York, who called him "that clerical Jimmy Cagney." Cardinal O'Connor's aides and predecessors also knew him as a man to be reckoned with. During the late 1960s, Coadjutor Archbishop John Maguire deputized him to visit U.S. Senator Robert Kennedy, who had asked to meet with a representative of the archdiocese. Senator Kennedy opposed legislation that would partially reimburse low-income parents for tuition at non-public elementary and secondary schools. He did not look up from his desk when Msgr. Kelly entered, but continued writing until he suddenly and abruptly challenged his visitor: "What has the Catholic Church done for the blacks of this country?" Msgr. Kelly shot back: "A hell of a lot more than you have, or your father." Then he listed the work of the archdiocese of New York for blacks, dating to early in the nineteenth century, and pointed out that *Ebony* magazine, three years running, had listed Catholic priests as the whites whom blacks trusted most.

Msgr. Kelly liked to point out that when he was secretary for education in the Archdiocese of New York, from 1966 to 1970, the Catholic school complex in the New York metropolitan area, comprising the archdiocese of New York and the diocese of Brooklyn, was the third-largest education system in the United States, behind only the public school systems of New York and Chicago.

In 1999, a colloquy in his honor was given in the auditorium of the archdiocesan center. It brought visitors from around the world, including Archbishop George Pell, now archbishop of Sydney and a cardinal. A *Festschrift* of the colloquy was published as *Keeping Faith: Msgr. George A. Kelly's Battle for the Church* (Christendom Press), with contributions by Joseph Varacalli, J. Brian Benestad, William E. May, James Hitchcock, Ralph McInerny, Kenneth D. Whitehead, Scott Hahn, the future Cardinal Pell, Gerard Bradley, Father Anthony Mastroeni, and Robert P. George.

George Anthony Kelly was born on September 17, 1916, at his parents' apartment in Good Counsel Parish, part of the strongly Catholic Yorkville section of upper East Side Manhattan. He was the eldest of six children of Charles Kelly from Athlone, Ireland, an employee of the New York subway system, and Bridget Fitzgerald Kelly from Offaly, Ireland. On leaving Catholic grammar school, he entered Stuyvesant High School but then switched to the archdiocesan minor seminary at Cathedral College. In 1942, on completing his philosophical and theological studies at St. Joseph's Seminary, in Yonkers, he was ordained by Archbishop Francis Spellman of New York.

He wrote in his autobiography, *Inside My Father's House* (New York: Doubleday, 1989): "What in hindsight is remarkable about the parish is that from 1918 to 1945 one, two, or three priests celebrated their first mass there every year." He recalled that this was not too rare in the New York of those years. Young Father Kelly then was sent to the Catholic University of America, where he obtained a Ph.D. in sociology in 1946. But he was not deeply impressed by the sociologists of his day. He wrote:

> ...It is fashionable nowadays to pay attention to sociologists and psychologists when they dissect the psyches of priests from a purely unbelieving point of view. Priests were firstborn, they say, or the only child, or dogmatic characters, or mother pets, or conformist types, or members of large families, and so forth, hardly suggesting a relationship of vocation to faith. Fortunately, none of us at the start knew we were any of those things.

Despite his doctorate he was first assigned to pastoral work. Until 1956 he was an assistant at St. Monica's parish in the Upper East Side.

Former parishioners hold that even as an assistant, he was the man to see. His last pastoral assignment was to St. John the Evangelist Church on East 55th Street. He oversaw its move into the ground floor of the archdiocesan headquarters, directing its internal design, and traveling abroad to find the most sumptuous furnishings. He directed that he be buried from it. He was buried in Calvary Cemetery in the borough of Queens, in a plot he had prepared to be near his parents.

He is survived by his sisters Beatrice Long of Whiting, New Jersey, and Delray Beach, Florida; Isabel Hoff of Valley Cottage, New York; and Margaret Bergin of Lynbrook, New York. He was predeceased by his sister Mae Comiskey and his brother Daniel.

Such was the kind of obituary that should have appeared. Thankfully, we are at least able to print it here.

Everyone who knew Msgr. George A. Kelly will agree that he was exceptionally single-minded. He would not be distracted. That may have been his salient characteristic, and what made him and his career so exceptional. He was fiercely focused on the Catholic Church, on what the Church means to the world, and above all on defending her. His enemies *par excellence* were her false friends, Catholics of every status who attacked her from within. If he couldn't help detesting them and what they stood for, they returned the compliment.

"Culture" in the narrow sense seemed to interest him little, although he had enjoyed and benefited from the excellent classical education provided to most New York priests of his generation. But if he wanted to make a vaguely remembered allusion from literature, classical or modern, he called upon one of the many experts who had flocked into his Fellowship of Catholic Scholars.

In middle life, his method of writing and editing was unusual if not bizarre. He would get fired up by an idea, and compulsively dash off page after page in his strong clear hand. Dr. William Kimmig, his first altar boy who referred to himself as Kelly's "anonymous amanuensis," would type up his manuscript and mail it to various friends for editing. Kelly's compulsiveness was such that he would phone a friend to say an article or a new chapter was on its way, and advise what to look for in the manuscript. A day or two later he might call the friend again to ask if it had arrived.

He once complained to me that one such victim was in the habit of rewriting rather than simply editing; that was too much for Kelly, who told me he had stopped sending him material. In editing his manuscripts, I rarely questioned his ideas, but I sometimes touched up his style for clarity, though only rarely for elegance, which he appreciated but did not strive for. He usually let the changes stand, and thanked me for them, but if he stuck by his original he would carefully explain why.

His talent for judging and improving the writing of others can be called prodigious. Though I had worked under some storied veterans at United Press International and elsewhere, I think he was the most perspicacious editor in my experience. He knew what had to be emphasized or expanded, and he cut ruthlessly. The result was not only more concise but also more forceful and more readable.

"Make damn sure it comes out clear as a bell," he barked when had persuaded me to tackle a book on contraception. "The average college person must understand every sentence." Even on this metaphysics-saturated question he seemed averse to mere theory, but I was to emphasize the factual and the human. "Talk about the father," he kept saying, and then made it clear he was talking also of our *heavenly* Father.

He often spoke of his own father. I saw him weep only once, when he told me of what he called "a high point in my life." As a young priest he was speaking at a Communion breakfast of the New York transportation workers' union when, at the end of his talk, he pointed to his father, a union official, saying how much he owed him. When father and son embraced in front of hundreds of other men, there was a standing ovation. At the memory of this, Msgr. Kelly broke down.

In the last years of his life he recalled his sense of awe as he had walked from his parents' flat to his parish church for his first Mass. He repeated for me – and here he spoke very slowly – the words he spoke over the host: *Hoc est enim corpus meum.*

He confessed that as a seminarian he was dismayed not to find himself among those chosen to go to Rome for theological study. He then applied himself strenuously, and upon ordination was sent to Catholic University for a doctorate. When he returned to New York for his first pastoral assignment, he declined a proffered posting to his home parish on grounds that his father would be too strong an influence. The chancery sent him to an adjoining parish.

His recollections of years as a curate and than as a pastor were warm, entertaining, and somehow managed to be edifying even when the incidents he was recalling might not be. His autobiography, *Inside My Father's House*, contains some luminous pages on the priesthood. They also glow with appreciation for his fellow priests – this was far from a pose, as anyone privileged to converse with him regularly will know.

His autobiography got a warm review from Gerald M. Costello, editor of the archdiocesan weekly *Catholic New York.* Mr. Costello was not in full accord with Msgr. Kelly on every issue, to understate the case, but he appreciated him as "an Irish storyteller with some good stories to tell." Gerry's summary: "The scrappy Msgr. Kelly hasn't mellowed out, not by a long shot. But he packs enough smiles in this book to last a long time."

Early in 2003 a precipitous decline in Msgr. Kelly's health became apparent. His voice, always vigorous, was suddenly weak and at times indistinct. He began to complain, "I'm so tired." In June his leg buckled beneath him on the way to a midnight visit to the bathroom, and he fell hard on his face. "There was blood all over the place," he reported.

He had been living alone in an apartment house in Rockaway Beach built over the cluster of summer cottages where his father and mother had brought the family every year until the Great Depression. Sobered (he said) by a reminder of mine that he was approaching ninety, he entered the Mary Manning Walsh Home in Manhattan on August 5, but in such poor condition that he was taken immediately to a hospital, and then to Our Lady of Consolation Residence for Clergy, a nursing home in Riverdale, a leafy section of the Bronx.

He had lost 50 pounds. Curled up in his bed in a quasi-fetal position, he looked shrunken. But he crowed that his blood tests showed that his cancer was losing ground. "What more do you want?" he asked with his customary defiance of the odds. He asked me to send him my notes for the book on contraception that he kept speaking about almost compulsively, as if it were his own.

Among his visitors were Edward Cardinal Egan of New York and Archbishop George Pell, not yet ordinary of Sydney and a cardinal. However, I was shocked when Msgr. Kelly said that he didn't want to receive an associate who had displeased him on the subject of contraception. I practically pleaded with him to relent, but he was adamant, saying in some agitation of this friend and another who had abandoned the project with him, effectively sinking it: "Don't they realize that contraception is at the root of the West's travail?"

(I was reminded of an evening two decades earlier when we were sitting in a car at Catholic University and he pulled his hat brim over his eyes to avoid meeting his old friend and mentor, the historian Fr. John Tracy Ellis, who he thought was giving aid and comfort to dissent.)

Hardly had he entered the nursing home than its director advised me to visit him at once. "He's in hospice care," she said, and would say no more to someone not of the family. Despite her guarded language, it was clear she thought he would soon die. Also in guarded language she made it known that she would not change her way of running the institution at his behest, so I realized he was not planning to die anytime soon. And when he answered by knock at his door with "Come in – if you're good-looking," I was sure he had plenty of life in him. In the dining room, where he was brought in a wheelchair, he paid little attention to the table conversation, and he once blurted out, "The question is: When do I get out of here?"

He told me that he had decided against asking for assignment as a curate because that "wouldn't be fair to the pastor." He explained: "I would soon be in charge." I suppose that anyone who knew him well would agree with that. Still, after a while he suggested to Cardinal Egan that he be posted to some parish as "senior priest" – a title, I believe, of his own invention. He said the Cardinal was "working on it." During his homily at Msgr. Kelly's funeral Mass, Cardinal Egan actually used those same words. In response to Kelly's request for such an assignment, he told him he was "working on it." He added that he expected to be forgiven for stretching the truth in such a worthy cause.

When Msgr. Kelly arrived at Our Lady of Consolation, a physician wanted to speak to his sisters about moving him to a hospital for the dying. That didn't happen. By October he had moved to the home of his sister Margaret Bergin in Lynnbrook, Long Island. He told me that he found the distress of his sisters at his condition a burden.

A month later, on November 6, 2003, his friend and collaborator Father Ronald Lawler, O.F.M. Cap., died. Mrs. Bergin thought he was too weak to be given that news, but she later realized a friend had told him. When he and I finally discussed Father Lawler's death two months later, he spoke in anguish.

He was still restless and eager to move, although his only excursions were around the block by wheelchair. By April, 2004, he was back in Manhattan at the Mary Manning Walsh Home. In June, when I wanted to arrange a motorized, self-righting scooter to make him mobile, he said, "I have a feeling I'll get out of this. Let's hold off for a few months."

I happened to phone him on Independence Day. Again urging me to get busy with the book on contraception, he returned to a favorite topic, the fatherhood of God – "to which all men owe fealty," he said. A book on contraception, he said, "could be the most important book of our time." Again: "Make a lot of fatherhood."

The week before he died, incapacitated by a stroke, his sister Peg Bergin said: "He can't speak, but he can still say *bullsh-t*." The old Kelly was still alive, even with death only days away.

Death came shortly after Mrs. Bergin found him gasping for breath, with two aides lifting him rhythmically to help him pull air into his lungs. She couldn't bear the sight of him struggling so, and ordered that he be allowed to die peacefully. She told me she and her sisters had had no idea of their brother's importance to the Church until they heard Cardinal Egan's homily at the funeral. "He would just say he was going on a trip," she said. This was the last thing I learned about him, and I confess it came as a surprise. He was modest.

When the funeral cortege got to the cemetery, the coffin was set down by the newly-dug grave, and the prayers of the Church were recited. The mourners – old-fashioned word, *mourners*, but how timelessly apt! – the mourners lingered to speak with one another, then slowly dispersed. The solemnity had vanished. Some drifted to the nearby grave where Msgr. Kelly had moved his father and mother, to be near them until the resurrection. The coffin, draped in baize, seemed forlorn, the body abandoned. We did not witness the burial. We could not watch the remains returning to that earth from which this great man had come. We could not sprinkle dirt on them. For a moment the figure of Antigone rose before me, and only with difficulty did I banish her.

Dr. Patrick G. D. Riley, a philosophy teacher as well as a longtime Catholic journalist and writer, is the author of *Civilizing Sex: On Chastity and the Common Good* (Edinburgh: T&T Clark, 2000). He was the editor of the *Festschrift* volume mentioned above, *Keeping Faith: Msgr. George A. Kelly's Battle for the Church* (Front Royal, VA: Christendom Press, 2000). For many years Dr. Riley was the correspondent in Rome for the Catholic News Service with a by-line that became familiar to many through their diocesan newspapers. Subsequently he completed a Ph.D. in philosophy and has since taught in a number of institutions, including the Catholic University of America. He is currently at work on a book on contraception.

"Look All Around You!"
Rev. Msgr. Michael J. Wrenn

Visitors to St. Paul's Cathedral in London may or may not admire the edifice itself, but they can hardly fail to admire the tribute to its architect, Christopher Wren, set into the pavement by his son. "If you want to find his monument," runs the Latin inscription, more famous than anything the father in his genius ever wrote, "then look all around you."

The best monument to a man is the one he builds himself. Speakers at the Second Annual Lucille Choquette Memorial Lecture, a two-day colloquy in honor of Msgr. George A. Kelly in 1999, were keenly aware of this, and they repeatedly drew attention to the books and briefer writings of this astonishing polymath. The colloquy, made possible by the bequest of a faithful Catholic woman, Lucille Choquette, enabled this writer to honor Msgr. Kelly and others. The extended remarks at the colloquy in question, constituting the volume *Keeping Faith: Msgr. George A. Kelly's Battle for the Church* (edited by Patrick G.D. Riley), deal for the most part with critical problems in the field of specialization of each speaker, such as Catholic social teaching, moral theology, or scriptural scholarship; but they repay reading also for the broad canvass they paint of the Church in the post-conciliar period. Nor do they neglect Msgr. Kelly's tremendous achievement in founding the Fellowship of Catholic Scholars, now filling a virtual vacuum in authentic Catholic scholarship.

It falls to me, however, to draw attention to his achievements not as an intellectual – and a genuine intellectual who never put on airs – but as a working parish priest and archdiocesan administrator. Perhaps I should preface that account by confessing that as a young priest dealing with Msgr. Kelly as a New York archdiocesan official, I failed utterly to appreciate him. To be frank, I didn't like this particular monsignor. How could a young man out to change the world not resent the bureaucrat who resisted his best ideas, no matter how eloquently they were urged? Who ever told him either shut up or get out? Anyone who met him could appreciate Ralph McInerny's later crack that if George Kelly had gone to Hollywood instead of Dunwoodie (the archdiocesan seminary), Jimmy Cagney would have spent his life tending bar. It was only when I saw the success that crowned Kelly's endeavors, when I saw the lucidity and suspected the profundity of his intellect, when I caught a glimpse of a zeal that eclipsed mine – even mine! – and of a charity beggaring mere human sympathy, it was only then that I began to appreciate this priest *par excellence*.

George Anthony Kelly was born in 1916 into Good Counsel Parish. In those days, as for the next half-century, New York Catholics tended to identify themselves by their parish. "What in hindsight is remarkable about the parish is that from 1918 to 1945 one, two, or three priests celebrated their first mass there every year," Kelly was to write in his autobiography, *Inside My Father's House*. "Somehow it was taken for granted that Good Counsel would ordain a new priest each year." Nor was that rare in the Catholic New York that nurtured men of Kelly's generation, and then of mine. Kelly, himself a social scientist of achievement, had little patience for the kind of condescending psycho-social analysis that explains away the world that made him. H wrote:

> ...It is fashionable nowadays to pay attention to sociologists and psychologists when they dissect the psyches of priests from a purely unbelieving point of view. Priests were firstborn, they say, or the

only child, or dogmatic characters, or mother's pets, or conformist types, or members of large families, and so forth, hardly suggesting a relationship of vocation to faith. Fortunately, none of us at the start knew we were any of those things. We did not even know we were part of a Catholic subculture and were using the priesthood as a stage in upward mobility for our entire ethnic group.

When we played saying Mass as kids, in a secret corner of our parents' flat, we were only copying the men in the neighborhood we admired most. And without being able to explain it, we sensed that the most important aspect of the priest was his ability to say Mass. Deeply imbedded in our being by this time – no older than ten or eleven – was the understanding that the most important task for a priest was saving other people's souls. So we fought to serve Mass, even at five-thirty on a dark wintry morning, disturbing our poor mothers who needed more sleep than we knew.

Tempting as it is to reminisce with George Kelly, whose account of his boyhood calls back long-silenced voices from my own, I must push on to his active life. It began when he prostrated himself on the altar of St. Patrick's Cathedral in the spring of 1942. The ordaining prelate was Francis J. Spellman, the "Spelly" of countless Kelly yarns, and the archbishop who was Kelly's boss until the silver anniversary of his priesthood, when the old man died. The new priest was immediately dispatched to the Catholic University of America in Washington, D.C., to earn a Ph.D. in social science.

Kelly's doctoral thesis, published as *Catholics and the Practice of the Faith*, drew on a summer-long census he conducted in Florida with the participation of two-thirds of the clergy of the St. Augustine diocese, which then covered practically whole state. The experience led to the conviction that every new priest should be an apprentice census-taker.

It is an enlightening commentary on the myths of institutional cruelty that have surrounded the Church of half a century ago, and the Spellman administration more perhaps than any other, that when young Father George Kelly returned to New York in the fall of 1945 for his first working assignment, he was offered a choice: work either in Catholic Charities, or as dean of the social sciences at a new archdiocesan high school, or in a parish. It is an enlightening commentary on the priesthood of that day that Kelly's response was: "Whatever you think." They thought a parish.

Not that Kelly was without his share of disappointments at the hands of officialdom. His comment on that was: the Church lives on obedience. If I may be permitted my own comment: nothing that George Kelly has contributed to the Church in this country over the past half-century may prove more constructive than the example of his obedience. Such obedience didn't keep him out of two of the major struggles of the Catholic Church in our times: to maintain Catholic education and to maintain Catholic marital morality. In fact, obedience thrust him into them. Moreover, the fact that his superiors would choose him to wage these particular battles says a good deal about the wisdom of the men in question, chiefly Cardinal Spellman, but also Co-adjutor Archbishop John Maguire (the man who ordained me), as well as others.

The reader of Msgr. Kelly's accounts of the struggles – political, ecclesiastical, theological – in these crucial fields of education and sexual morality would scarcely know the role he played in them. Modesty, a virtue that Kelly was too modest to pretend to, gets in the way of history here. But these two issues were the focal points of his inexhaustible energies.

The confidence that Cardinal Spellman eventually placed in Msgr. Kelly said a lot also about a largeness of soul that some would deny to the New York Cardinal – for as a young priest Kelly had found himself in Spellman's doghouse. It involved what was surely the biggest blunder the cardinal ever made, when he confronted striking gravediggers and their wives, and ordered his seminarians to bury the dead in their place. It was the bleak winter of 1949, and Kelly, less than seven years a priest, devoted his regular labor column in *The Catholic News* to the right of workingmen to form a union for the purpose of collective bargaining, even if they were working for a not-for-profit institution. Even though it was written before the gravediggers' strike, the union made much of it, and from that time on Kelly was no longer a columnist in *The Catholic News*. But he was not hindered from continuing his work with the labor unions.

Then, in 1955, Cardinal Spellman appointed him Family Life Director of the Archdiocese of New York. In Kelly's estimation, family life was the Church's most significant apostolate during the two decades between the end of World War II and the end of Vatican II. "It spread like wildfire," he recalls. "The couples themselves were on fire for all that the teachings of Christ and His Church could give to the family. They would go anywhere to spread the word, the enthusiasm. Msgr. Kelly commented:

> What an inspiring time of my life! The groupings of large families, the blessings of expectant mothers, of mothers after birth! I can't conceive of anything that I've done that gave me more happiness.

When I ran Family Life Day in St. Patrick's Cathedral and brought together the golden jubilarians in the presence of the cardinal, eight bishops of the archdiocese showed up, as well as 150 priests. They came without any pressure from anybody. I just sent out the invitations. The movement was so alive!

The Chicago priests did a good job but then they bought into contraception, and the bishops became co-conspirators. In the early days of the movement nobody fought the Church's teaching; they just went ahead and had another baby. I think the bishops letting Charlie Curran off the hook destroyed everything.

Father Charles Curran, of course, was a novice teacher of moral theology at Catholic University who, in the turmoil of the 1960s, was let go for unorthodox teaching on sexual morality. But after a widely-publicized protest strike by students and faculty which closed down Catholic University, he was re-instated by the bishop-trustees of the university, and given tenure to boot. Two decades later the university fired him at the insistence of the Holy See. He then took the university to court but lost his case in an American civil court.

In 1958, George Kelly published his *Catholic Marriage Manual*, which sold a quarter of a million copies and netted him almost a quarter-million dollars in royalties, every penny of which went to the New York Foundling Hospital. "Kids who hadn't benefited from marriage could at least benefit from a book on marriage" was a typical Kelly comment.Then came his *Catholic Family Handbook*, "which also did well." In 1960, his *Catholic Youth's Guide to Life and Love* came out and "did superbly well."

Dr. James Hitchcock, in the talk reprinted in *Keeping Faith*,, recounts Msgr. Kelly's role in Rome as a member of what came to be known as the Papal Birth Control Commission. He was one of the minority to stand fast for the Church's millennial teaching that contraception is an intrinsic evil. Some may think this was George Kelly's finest hour.

Then came Msgr. Kelly's entry into Catholic education. As he tells it: "After the close of Vatican II I was made Secretary for Education. My job was to create a department of education where every part of the system would be under the bishop. It would have taken five years to do it, but unfortunately Spelly died a couple of years later."

"The bishops never knew what was going on in education," Kelly comments. "That's why it ran away. By the time I got on the scene the religion textbooks were already bad."

Msgr. Kelly had only been in that office for a year when he met Father Joseph Cahill, C.M., the valiant President of St. John's University, in Jamaica, Queens, New York. St. John's had been one of the first major targets of the secularizers in Catholic education, but it was a prize that would escape them so long as Father Cahill had his say. It was amid that struggle that Cahill journeyed to Manhattan from his campus in the Brooklyn diocese for a meeting on threats to the Catholicity of Catholic higher education, and that he met George Kelly. The meeting proved momentous. Four years later, Father Cahill invited Msgr. Kelly to take the University's new chair in contemporary Catholic problems. Cardinal Cooke agreed, but at the same time gave Msgr. Kelly the additional job of pastor of St. John the Evangelist Church. (It is my own honor to have succeeded him in that task!)

By this time the reader may have begun to wonder why George Kelly was never made a bishop. To raise that question here is not the digression it may seem, for it leads naturally into the next chapter of the Kelly story. I couldn't begin to count the number of Catholics, clerical and lay, who have asked why this creative priest, this outstanding defender of the faith, this leader of men and women in the pews as well as the men and women in high academia, remained in the ranks of the clergy. In answer, an account of the Kelly colloquy published in the *Fellowship of Catholic Scholars Quarterly* ventured into the mind of Divine Providence, and claimed that Msgr. Kelly "might never have become the strategist and inspirer of Catholic intellectuals that he became had he been tied to the duties, and tied down by the caution, of a bishop." A more mundane answer can be found in the history of the Church since Vatican II. Priests of forthright, uncompromising orthodoxy were an embarrassment to the cautious authorities of the Church in America.

Perhaps calling them cautious is too kind. For a good two decades and more after the Council, many in high places at the conference of bishops actively fostered dissent by showing favoritism to dissenters and by countenancing the faint presentation of doctrine. Nobody has chronicled this tragedy, or outrage, more convincingly than Msgr. Kelly. His *Battle for the American Church* in 1979 brought this drama to the attention of American Catholics in meticulous and, for many of us, heartrending detail.

He continued his incisive chronicle in subsequent books, including the already-quoted *Inside My Father's House*. There, to cite but one example, he listed the dissenting theologians and other scholars enlisted by officials of the bishops' conference supposedly to explain "Catholic teaching" – chiefly on sex – to the nation's Catholics. He named names, quoted their dissenting positions verbatim, and then recalled the responsible roles given them by top bureaucrats in the bishops' conference.

Msgr. Kelly laid this all out in a chapter of his autobiography devoted to the Fellowship of Catholic Scholars, which he founded partly in order to offer the bishops' conference a pool of scholars of proven fidelity. Unhappily, those for whom this resource was designed have scarcely ever utilized it. Nonetheless, the Fellowship of Catholic Scholars will surely stand among Msgr. Kelly's outstanding achievements, along with his dozens of books and with the hundreds and perhaps thousands of Catholics who owe their faith, or their families, or their courage – so much of what they hold dearest – to this personally unpretentious priest. For his monument these men and women need not look *around* themselves but just *within* themselves.

Rev. Msgr. Michael J. Wrenn is the author of *Catechisms and Controversies* (San Francisco: Ignatius Press, 1991) and co-author (with Kenneth D. Whitehead) of *Flawed Expectations: The Reception of the Catechism of the Catholic Church* (San Francisco: Ignatius Press, 1996), as well as of many articles mostly on religious education or scriptural topics. He was for many years pastor of St. John the Evangelist Church in New York City – the same parish which earlier Msgr. George A. Kelly had headed. He was the founding head of the New York Archdiocesan Catechetical Institute, served as a special consultant on religious education to the late Cardinal John J. O'Connor, and did yet another stint as head of the Archdiocesan Catechetical Institute before retirement. He has organized a number of outstanding conferences and colloquia, including one in honor of Msgr. Kelly. He received the Cardinal Wright Award from the Fellowship of Catholic Scholars in 1998.

Priest and Founding Father
Rev. Msgr. William B. Smith

Monsignor George A. Kelly was born September 17, 1916, and he died August 12, 2004: a man for 87 years; a priest for 62 years; and our Founding Father for all of our 26 years in the Fellowship of Catholic Scholars..

One could speak of our first organizational meeting at the Kenrick Seminary as a gathering or our "Founding Fathers" (plural). But the truth was and is that it was the insight, the vision, and the sheer energy of

George Kelly that initiated this Fellowship of Catholic Scholars – Msgr. Kelly was truly our Founding Father.

Characteristic of George Kelly was that he cared very little whether he or anyone else got credit for the job, but he cared a great deal whether the job got done or not. As often as I asked him when or where he got the idea for the Fellowship, he attributed the initial spark to a Roman curial official who once asked him: "Are there no other voices in America?"

That was a post-Land O'Lakes question. The famous Land O'Lakes declaration of secular-academic independence, when a good number of highly placed names in Catholic higher education declared that their notion of "academic freedom" was so thoroughly secular and so thoroughly "American" that to render some things to God would have made it impossible for them to render important things to Caesar. In fact, as Ken Whitehead has pointed out more than once, a large number of Catholics in Catholic higher education rushed to render unto Caesar what Caesar had never even asked for.

And yet, when any official of the Congregation for Education in Rome asked about the Land O'Lakes shift, a steady chorus of trained voices all sang the same responsorial: U. S. Law requires this! U. S. funding requires that! Academic prestige requires something else! The Gospel, of course, is shorter, sweeter, and clearer on the one thing that really is required (Lk 10:41) and no choir of masculine Marthas running wild can camouflage that truth.

But all Rome ever heard from the U. S. was one very well-organized chorus – Land O'Lakes was the future, whereas canonical interference (yes: that is what it was called – "interference"!) was the supposed dead hand of the past. It was in that context, that the Roman official asked Msgr. Kelly: "Are there no other voices in America?" George Kelly thought that there *were* other voices – his own being not the least among them.

It was then he took it upon himself to visit old and new friends in six different dioceses throughout the U. S., just to test the air and test the water, and to assess whether there were "other voices" – men and women, teachers and scholars, administrators and professionals who were quite willing to render unto Caesar what is Caesar's, but first to render unto God what is God's. After that multi-site visit, Msgr. Kelly organized the organizational meeting at the Kenrick Seminary, with the knowing and kindly support of the late Cardinal John J. Carberry of St. Louis. The next year, he organized our first convention in Kansas City, Missouri. That was in 1978.

From that beginning, Msgr. Kelly was pretty much always the executive secretary of the Fellowship (although he also served two years as president). Mostly, he was the heart-and-lung machine of its internal organization. As a fellow New York archdiocesan priest, I can tell you that Msgr. Kelly held a number of senior and responsible positions in our archdiocese – together with at least 1000 stories of humor, irony, or clerical absurdity for each one. As he got older, many of those stories became "repeats"; he truly believed the maxim: *repetitio est mater studiorum*!

But I am not here to repeat stories of his or about him; I focus only on his steady voice: when the Catholic labor movement was troubled, he spoke with a steady voice; when the Catholic family movement was troubled, he spoke with a steady voice; and when Catholic higher education was troubled, and even internally traumatized, he spoke with a steady voice.

At George's funeral last month, Cardinal Egan quoted the late Cardinal O'Connor who wrote of George Kelly: Never in the 20 years since I first met George Kelly have I ever met him without thanking God that this erudite, streetwise prelate is on the Church's side" (*Catholic New York* (9/04), p. 56).

George was a churchman from the top of his head to the tip of his toes. He always insisted that every FCS convention must be open to the local bishop and be carried out only with his blessing. George had boundless energy, unlimited dedication to the priesthood, equally unlimited dedication to the Catholic faithful, and to the Catholic faith. His was a tremendous work ethic always at the service of the Church.

Over twenty-five years ago, a question was asked in Rome: "Are there no other voices in America?" It is with gratitude, deep and dear personal gratitude, that I feel that I can answer that question truthfully. The answer was and is "yes"! There was and is another voice, a steady voice, a thoroughly Catholic voice – the voice that called this Fellowship together, a voice, I hope, the Fellowship will honor and continue "to speak the truth in love" (Eph 4:15). For that voice, I thank God; I thank God's grace; and I thank George Anthony Kelly. May he rest in peace.

Rev. Msgr. William B. Smith, S.T.D., is a moral theologian and dean at the New York archdiocese's St. Joseph's Seminary at Dunwoodie in Yonkers, New York. He also conducts the regular monthly "Questions Answered" column on moral theology in the *Homiletic and Pastoral Review*. He is a past president of the Fellowship of Catholic Scholars (1981–1983) and the 1995 recipient of its Cardinal Wright Award. He was a long-time friend of and collaborator with Msgr. Kelly.

Remembering Monsignor Kelly
Ralph McInerny

The option represented by Martha and Mary could not be easily applied – even with appropriate gender inclusiveness – to Monsignor George A. Kelly, our dear friend who died in the fullness of his years on August 12, 2004. How could this bustling, active defender of the faith be thought of as a contemplative? Throughout his priestly life, he was a blur of activity: right hand man of Cardinal Spellman, deep in the apostolate to Catholic families, pastor of St. John the Evangelist Church, busy, in short, about "many things." But there was another side to Monsignor Kelly: the university professor, the author of a whole series of books, and (the role in which I primarily knew him), one of the founders and certainly the animating spirit of the Fellowship of Catholic Scholars. Martha or Mary? Both, and in the way St. Thomas Aquinas allows for in his discussion of the contemplative and active lives.

When one seeks the unifying core of this man's life, he finds it in his priesthood. George Kelly was quintessentially a priest. His priesthood was the one thing of which he was unequivocally proud, and of course it was a gift. I have had clerical friends throughout my life, but from the first time I met Kelly I was certain that I had never before encountered a priest who was more thoroughly settled and at ease in the vocation to which he had been called. To say that his was a clerical outlook seems too weak a description. He breathed the priesthood. He saw life through the lens of the priesthood. His small talk was inevitably clerical – memories of "Spelly" (Cardinal Francis J. Spellman of New York) and of his episcopal friends; gossip about the *Sturm und Drang* of life in the archdiocese of New York. It never occurred to him that a mere layman could be otherwise than enthralled by tales of what for him was the center of his life. And he was right, not least because as a raconteur he was without parallel.

Late night bibulous bull sessions in his hotel room at meetings of the Fellowship of Catholic Scholars were seminars on what was happening in the Church in the United States. It was his conviction that our bishops would rally and do what they ought to do as soon as they realized they had the support of such groups as the Fellowship. He was convinced that they had been cowed by dissenting theologians and the dread of negative press coverage. Only assure them that they had troops behind them and they would rally. Much of his reminiscing dealt with churchmen of the past who would have known how to act in the post-conciliar turmoil. That was the point of recalling the days of Cardinals Spellman and McIntyre.

His opening salvo had been his magnificent *The Battle for the American Church,* a detailed tour of the post-conciliar *monde* without a trace of morose delectation as he narrated the incredible tragedies that had followed the Second Vatican Council because of the radical distortion of its message. This massive book was meant to be a prelude. Only when one saw clearly the problem could a solution be found. It was the solution, not dwelling on the outrages, that interested Kelly. And increasingly the Fellowship loomed for him as a principal instrument in a return to order and orthodoxy.

Kelly ran the Fellowship in the manner of an Irish Catholic politician, whether or not he was president. And we took his lead. Better Boss Tweed than Tweedledum. There was absolutely no thirst for personal power in this. I came to think that Kelly was a prime example of a type of which I have seen several instances, the self-effacing egoist. It never occurred to him that his interlocutors could think differently than he did on issues before us. And he was usually right. The few times we failed to follow his advice usually led us into difficulties. But none of his energetic machinations was ever aimed at the aggrandizement of George Kelly. His primary love was the Church whose priest he was.

When Monsignor Michael J. Wrenn organized a tribute to Monsignor Kelly some years ago, the now Cardinal Pell was on the program. His topic was the priesthood. It was one of the most moving expositions of the nature of the priesthood I have ever heard, one which breathed its speaker's gratitude that he himself was a priest. One of the points of the talk was to capture the fundamental inspiration of the life and activity of George Kelly. Sometimes, as when reading his book on the role of the bishop, it occurred to one that Kelly might have nursed episcopal aspirations of his own. Perhaps, but I doubt it. He had a sense of the grace of the present moment, and of the demands of the situation in which he found himself. There was no question of day-dreaming about what he might do if he had another role. His chief interest lay in doing what had to be done here and now in the position in which he found himself. It is even a chilling thought to imagine how he might have been marginalized if he had been raised to"the hapless bench of bishops."

His writings were all aimed at the most neuralgic points of the post-conciliar confusion. I think of his book on scriptural scholarship. But I think most of how he was galvanized by the appearance of *Ex Corde Ecclesiae*. The growing distance between the ideal recalled by that document and the Catholic universities and colleges of the nation was palpable to him, and for a long time he nursed the hope that here was a campaign that the bishops as a body could not fail to wage. That hope was dashed, of course. The proposed implementation of *Ex Corde Ecclesiae* was attacked by those whose task it was to implement it, whereupon the bishops sat down with their critics and added more water to their already watery proposals. A lesser man than George Kelly would have been daunted. His conviction that the bishops would respond when they had orthodox support was refuted by events. But he did not repine.

Evelyn Waugh's Gilbert Pinfold recalled the saying, "It is later than you think," by adding: "It was never later than Gilbert Pinfold thought." There was none of that half-despairing resignation in George Kelly. He soldiered on. He fought the good fight.

There is perhaps no greater test of character than growing old. When Cicero wrote his *De Senectute*, he was of an age we would consider young. Born on September 17, 1916, ordained in 1942, George Kelly's long life ended on August 12, 2004. He had lived on by himself in his apartment at Rockaway Beach, but eventually he moved to a rest home, that penultimate step that has undone so many great spirits. But the long distance calls nevertheless continued. One picked up the phone to hear that distinctive voice already in full flight, speaking as if one were being let in on an ongoing conversation. Gradually, over the months, the voice altered. The contemplative side of George Kelly was now in the ascendant. He prepared for death with the ebullient faith that had carried him through his long life. Above Patrick G. D. Riley has written a moving account of those last days. His salty language did not desert him as he approached the end. And at last the end came. George Kelly, incredible as it seemed, was dead.

He would have been embarrassed by unctuous reminiscing. Old friends will seek consolation in his two volumes of memoirs. Those familiar with Irish crustiness are not surprised to find that, beneath that sometimes rough exterior beat the warmest of hearts. Every life is a mystery and it is not given to us to presume to pass a comprehensive judgment. But those who knew him thank God for the experience and pray that angels tended him to his final reward. May God have mercy on his immortal soul.

Renaissance man Dr. Ralph McInerny is the Michael P. Grace Professor of Medieval Studies at the University of Notre Dame and Director of the Jacques Maritain Center there. He is the author of many scholarly books including *St. Thomas Aquinas* (Notre Dame, IN: University of Notre Dame Press, 1977) and *A First Glance at St. Thomas Aquinas: A Handbook for Peeping Thomists* (Notre Dame, IN;

University of Notre Dame Press, 1990). He is also the prize-winning author of many works of fiction, including *The Priest* (Harper & Row, 1973) and *The Red Hat* (Ignatius, 1998), but also, especially, many mystery novels, including the well-known Father Dowling series. Dr. McInerny delivered the prestigious Gifford Lectures in Scotland in 2000. He is a past president of the FCS (1991–1995) and the 1996 recipient of its Cardinal Wright Award.

A Man of the Church
James Hitchcock

Msgr. George A. Kelly stamped his personality on the Fellowship of Catholic Scholars not only because he almost single-handedly brought it into being, via a cross-country trip through the United States in 1976 to enlist scholars in the project, but also because from the beginning, and long after it began to thrive, he continued to see to every detail – all the while pushing others into the spotlight. Not until the organization had been in existence for some years did he somewhat reluctantly accept the presidency.

His personality was also stamped on the organization because, for me at least, the annual conventions will always be associated with his striding energetically across a hotel lobby, a wide smile on his face, his voice booming as he was halted every few steps by the innumerable people crowding around to greet him. For some years, despite his usual habit of retiring early, there were little gatherings in his room after each day's proceedings – meetings that combined good fellowship with exchanges of the latest scuttlebutt and that were always enlightening experiences for many of us.

Msgr. Kelly was a man of the Church in every fiber of his being, both in the ultimate spiritual sense and in the institutional sense. No one ever had a better understanding of ecclesiastical dynamics, and for many years he navigated the often tricky waters of ecclesiastical politics, not to get anything for himself, but to promote the good of the Church. He was one of the first people to understand the depths of the crisis through which the Church was passing and to recognize how essential it was to deal with it decisively. Few people in authority ever thanked him for his deep concern, and in the end I think his confidence that the ecclesiastical machinery worked was disappointed. But no one ever made a more valiant effort. Well past the age when most people would have been content to take a well-earned rest in the sun, he continued to devote every bit of his energy to the good of the Church he had loved and served for so many years.

Dr. James Hitchcock is a professor of history at St. Louis University and the author of many books on the post-conciliar Church including the *Recovery of the Sacred* (New York: The Seabury Press, 1974) and *Catholicism and Modernity: Confrontation or Capitulation?* (New York: The Seabury Press, 1979). He has recently completed a major two-volume work entitled *The Supreme Court and Religion in American Life* published by the Princeton University Press in 2004. He also writes a syndicated column for the Catholic press. He is a past president of the Fellowship of Catholic Scholars (1979–1981) and winner of its 1981 Cardinal Wright Award.

A Good Fighter
William E. May

I was not a founding member of the Fellowship of Catholic Scholars, but I joined it as soon as I heard of it, and, in fact, gave a paper at its first annual convention in Kansas City, Missouri, in 1978. It was there, I think, that I met Msgr. George A. Kelly for the first time, and we immediately hit it off. I love a good fight and a good fighter, and George was a good fighter who loved a good fight.

At the time I was teaching moral theology at the Catholic University of America, where I had, thanks to divine providence been granted tenure by one vote in 1976; and where most of my colleagues at the time were very much opposed to magisterial teaching, particularly on questions of sexual and marital morality. A "hermeneutic of suspicion" regarding the teaching of the Church was regnant at CUA in those days. As a result, the academic climate in which I was working was, to say the least, somewhat inhospitable. Academic wars can be fierce, and subtle kinds of pressures can be and are employed to make life uncomfortable.

The Fellowship that George founded was thus for me a true gift from God, for it gave me – and many others in similar situations – a source of profound support and encouragement. But the one who above all was the embodiment of this support – a support rooted in the firm conviction that "we shall overcome," because of our commitment to the Rock on which Christ founded the Church – was Msgr. George A. Kelly himself. His wonderful good humor, his Irish wit, his dogged determination and spirit were simply fantastic. He was a marvelous general in the "Battle for the American Church," as his 1979 book was so aptly titled; he was undoubtedly a man whom God had chosen for this needed work at this time in history. One of my greatest joys is that Msgr. George A. Kelly – and Fr. Ronald E. Lawler, O.F.M. Cap. – were around during those post-*Humanae Vitae* years to "stand up" for the magisterium and to stiffen the backbones of so many others. May God rest the souls of both of them.

Dr. William E. May is a professor at the John Paul II Institute for Studies on Marriage and Family at the Catholic University of America. He is the author of many books including *Sex, Marriage, and Chastity* (Chicago: Franciscan Herald Press, 1981) and *Marriage: The Rock on Which the Family Is Built* (San Francisco: Ignatius Press, 1995). He served on the Church's International Theological Commission from 1986 through 1997. He received the *Pro Ecclesia et Pontifice* Medal in 1991. He is a past FCS president (1987–1989) and recipient of the Fellowship's 1980 Cardinal Wright Award.

George Anthony Kelly, R.I.P.
Gerard V. Bradley

Captain Jack Aubrey of H.M.S. *Surprise* delivers a short funeral oration about halfway through the movie, *Master and Commander.* The ship's "Jonah" – a ne'er-do-well midshipman named Hollum – is a recent suicide, having tossed himself overboard wrapped around a cannonball. Aubrey (played convincingly by Russell Crowe) looks at and closes the Good Book, opened for the occasion to the book of Jonah. He begins his extemporaneous eulogy with these words: "The sad truth is that some of us never become the men we once dreamed of becoming."

These words would be the last ones chosen for the funeral of George Anthony Kelly. He was born to be *exactly* what he became. Monsignor once told me that as a kid he practiced saying Mass in a corner of his bedroom. I never doubted it. He was 62 years a priest of the archdiocese of New York, every day of it a bundle full of blarney. He possessed all the virtues of an unrepeatable generation of clerics; he was first among a band of brothers, exemplar of (in Cardinal O'Connor's words) a "legion of indescribably faithful priests who have taught, preached, ministered, celebrated, and sacrificed for lifetimes of fourscore years and more."

No one was ever more in love with being an Irish Catholic priest than was George Anthony Kelly. That is saying a lot, given how numerous have been the competitors. And no one was more in love with his native city than was George Kelly with New York. He was not tall but he was broad-shouldered, and it is easy to imagine him striding the streets of the upper East Side, pastor of the local parish and (thus, in those days) boss of the neighborhood. No less an authority than *his* boss – John Cardinal O'Connor – likened Monsignor Kelly to a "clerical Jimmy

Cagney." Monsignor rather put me more in mind of Spencer Tracy. Either way, George Anthony Kelly was straight out of central casting. And he was right out of my own memories of the priests in my Irish neighborhood of Brooklyn, circa 1962.

I was reminded last Christmas of the breadth of Monsignor Kelly's achievements. My daughter had spent a semester studying in London, with frequent weekend trips to Ireland. She told me that my Christmas present that year was "something she picked up in a second-hand book-store in Limerick." I imagined a frayed copy of something by Joyce, or maybe by Yeats, at least something distinctive to the "old sod." Instead she handed me on Christmas morning a copy, signed by the author, of *Catholics and the Practice of the Faith: A Census Study of the Diocese of Saint Augustine.* This path-breaking sociological study of Catholic observance was submitted in 1942 to the faculty of the Catholic University of America, in satisfaction of the requirements for the degree of Doctor of Philosophy. Its author was described on the cover as a "Priest of the Archdiocese of New York" The author was George Anthony Kelly. It was the first of his publications – the rest too numer-ous to mention, but each one better and more influential, than the previ-ous one.

George Kelly was nothing if not feisty. And so it is fitting that prob-ably his best-known work is a book called *The Battle for the American Church.* (A more recent volume added the word "Revisited" to that orig-inal title and was published in 1995 by Ignatius Press.) They always said that Hubert Humphrey was the "happy warrior," and Hubie probably was. But no one was a happier warrior, enjoyed a good fight, or retained his sense of humor better during one, than Monsignor Kelly. He was occasionally earthy in his description of polemical adversaries or "weak sisters" in the Church. But he was never really crude or profane. He was also never much for liturgical dance, especially when it involved an over-weight nun or a willowy seminarian.

Our paths first crossed in 1993, when Monsignor conspired with Ralph McInerny to have me elected vice-president of the Fellowship of Catholic Scholars. I thus became the *Dauphin,* slated by Kelly to suc-ceed Ralph in the Oval Office. In due course, that is exactly what hap-pened. And thus began our years of close collaboration: Kelly the tire-less spirit of the Fellowship and my unerring counsel on all things involving the institutional Church; me, the avid learner and novice spokesman for the group which sprang from his mind and heart, and from his insatiable desire to serve Holy Mother Church.

Monsignor Kelly used to call the house almost every Saturday morning. It was a pretty routine procedure. One of the younger Bradley children would tear away from cartoons and grab the phone. Monsignor would charm whichever child it was; it didn't hurt that, notwithstanding my wife's Italian heritage, all our kids ended up with Irish-sounding names, from Brendan on up through Kevin, eight in all.). It was usually Mrs. Bradley's turn next to be beguiled by the Monsignor. After about twenty minutes of all this, the receiver was finally handed to me, the ostensible purpose of the call. We would then plot strategy for the next FCS Board meeting, or a mailing to the bishops, or a letter to the Vatican. Or we just talked. During the last difficult year of his life, some one of our kids would say his name during time for petitions at the family dinner table.

Sooner or later in almost all our conversations Monsignor Kelly about his childhood, the "cold-water" flat into which he was born, his sisters, and his father and mother – especially his mother. My wife Pam and I recognized the enormous influence Monsignor's mom was upon him, and that he obviously still loved her a great deal. Of his father he spoke much less frequently. "Charlie" Kelly worked for the city and one story Monsignor told about him goes like this: on the occasion (I think) of Mr. Kelly's retirement there was a grand Communion Breakfast, to which (then) Father George Kelly was invited. Before long it appeared to Father George from all the talk and intros and buzz that he – more so than his father – was becoming the center of attention. He was a young priest scholar, on his way to great things, Charlie's son and all that. When it was his time to address the communicants assembled, Father George Kelly had this to say: "I appreciate all your kindness. But I should like to say a few words about the best man it has been my privilege in life to know, my father Charlie Kelly".

In some ways Monsignor Kelly was about as clerical as one could be. His adult life was spent with priests and bishops, and he loved to tell stories about them; his chit-chat tended towards the waxing and waning of various episcopal wannabes, or the next assignment of some up and coming bishop. But in the most important ways Monsignor Kelly was spectacularly free of clericalism. He pioneered the Catholic family life movement in the fifties, a movement which we can see now anticipated the lay spirituality and lay vocations we now see so prominently in the Council documents. (I believe but am not certain that it was in connection with a family life workshop in Chicago that Monsignor befriended John and Eileen Farrell, longtime members of the Fellowship and benefactors responsible for our highest award, named for Cardinal John Wright.)

George Kelly promoted the work of Catholic laypersons without hesitation and this was strictly according to merit ("merit" included, of course, fidelity to the magisterium!). It was *his* idea to promote Ralph McInerny, and then me, as presidents of the Fellowship.He said more than once that the group needed to build bridges to the younger generation of Catholic scholars, and that it was best to do so with lay leadership. For the younger generation of scholars unfortunately included too few priests and religious.

In any collection of tributes to George Kelly most will say that he was one of a kind, a real corker, a maverick, a rare gem. He was. Most will also say that he was the perfect specimen of a genre which has all but passed away – the streetwise priest, Irish and urban down to his toes, a cross between Fr. Fitzgibbon (Barry Fitzgerald) and Fr. O'Malley (Bing Crosby), embodiments of the pre-Vatican II halcyon days of big families and bulging Sunday Masses – that he was a *type.* He was. But most importantly, George Anthony Kelly was a model of fidelity to his priestly vocation. We can thank the Council Fathers for renewing our attention to an undeniable fact of life: namely, that each one of us is called by Jesus to a unique life of works, a distinct and unrepeatable share in building His Kingdom. Monsignor Kelly is a model for all of us, for each one of us does have a personal vocation.

I suppose we should not be too grateful to George Kelly – or to anyone else – for being born when and where he was. As Ralph McInerny once wrote, what alternative does one have? But we can thank God for sending to us those who make our lives here richer, more edifying, and our salvation thereby just a little bit easier because we see that one *can* be cheerfully faithful to the end, steadfast and good, in season and out of season.

And so: thank you, Lord, for the life of George Anthony Kelly, priest.

Gerard V. Bradley is a professor of Law at the University of Notre Dame Law School. He holds a J.D. degree from Cornell University. He was formerly an assistant district attorney in New York City. He is co-editor of the *American Journal of Jurisprudence*, and has authored many articles, including a book, *Church-State Relations in America* (1987). With Fr. John Harvey, O.S.F.S., he recently edited the book *Same-Sex Attraction: A Parent's Guide* (St. Augustine Press, 2003). He is currently recognized as one of the national authorities on the question of so-called "same-sex marriage" and its implications for the law and society. The same thing is true with regard to his knowledge of the Catholic university situation in the light of Pope John Paul II's *Ex Corde Ecclesiae.* He served as president of the Fellowship of Catholic Scholars between 1995 and 2001 (and again, temporarily, in 2003). He and his wife Pam are the parents of eight children.

A Friend to Those in Need
Kenneth D. Whitehead

I first got to know Msgr. George Kelly in the late 1970s when he was a professor at St. John's University in Jamaica, New York, and director of the Institute for Advanced Studies in Catholic Doctrine there. Our relations were cordial but not close. He was very appreciative of a review I wrote for his 1979 book *The Battle for the American Church*, but I was not then involved – nor for a whole decade to come – in the affairs of the Fellowship of Catholic Scholars. My appreciation of him as a man and a priest, however, came in 1980 when I suddenly found myself out of work at age 50 with four children still to support.

To say that Msgr. Kelly was concerned when he learned of my situation would be an understatement. With a pastoral concern which I am sure was experienced by many others when he learned they were in trouble – but which he never talked about or took credit for – Msgr. Kelly worked tirelessly through his extensive network of friends and contacts to try to help me out. According to the reputation that he undeservedly acquired, at least in some circles, he was supposedly nothing but another "right-winger," unconcerned about the poor, jobless, and disadvantaged. In my experience, however, these were among the *first* of his priorities, and I am sure that the list of people he helped without fanfare is going to prove to be a long one when we get to heaven and find out about it (if we make it).

He actually wrote a book entitled *The Catholic Church and the American Poor* (Alba House, 1975) which he dedicated to a list of well-known "labor priests" including Msgrs. John A. Ryan and Paul Hanly Furfey who, in Msgr. Kelly's words, "on behalf of the Church were working for the poor before the rest of us knew there really was a problem." These labor priests were actually Msgr. Kelly's heroes and ideals and he spoke about them on not a few occasions. Like Joseph Ratzinger, who wanted to be an academic theologian, but was obliged by the vicissitudes of the times to work most of his life as a bishop and administrator, George Kelly really wanted to *be* a labor priest himself, but was obliged to devote most of his time to the defense of Catholic doctrine instead.

As it happened, the job I eventually found was not due to

Monsignor's efforts, but while I was out of work he was able to help tide me over by securing for me my first book translation contract from the same Alba House that had published his book on the American poor. It had never crossed my mind that the foreign language proficiencies I had acquired during study at the University of Paris and ten years abroad as a career Foreign Service Officer, including a tour of duty at the American Embassy in Rome, could actually be of any economic benefit; but it was Msgr. Kelly himself who actually helped launch me into a new part-time career which I continued after I was re-employed, and in the course of which I have since translated some twenty-odd books for publication from French, German, and Italian, most of them (though not all) of Catholic interest. The extra translation income that came from this new part-time career proved vital for paying college tuitions and the like.

The regular job that I soon got through other friends, some of them in the New York Conservative Party, was a political appointment as a manager in the U.S. Department of Education during the Reagan Administration. This meant a return to Washington and to working for the federal government, where I had already spent more than fifteen years working for the State Department and later the Smithsonian Institution. Somewhat to my surprise, I was in due course elevated in the Department of Education to be the Deputy Assistant Secretary for Higher Education Programs (and later by presidential appointment to be the Assistant Secretary for Post-secondary Education).

It was around this same time – the mid-1980s – that Fr. Theodore M. Hesburgh of the University of Notre Dame told the *New York Times* in an interview that the Catholic colleges and universities that had followed the Land O'Lakes model and secularized had *had* to secularize in this fashion; otherwise, Fr. Hesburgh claimed, they would no longer have been eligible for federal aid. Reading this interview, I had to rub my eyes and tell myself: "Wait a minute: you're *in charge of* federal aid to higher education in America, and what Fr. Hesburgh told the *Times* is simply not true."

Unlike the court-imposed ban on government aid to religiously-affiliated schools in America on the elementary and secondary levels, there has never been any such comparable ban on government aid to higher education. As everybody knows, or should know, the original G.I. Bill of Rights after World War II allowed students to study with federal loans and grants in religiously affiliated as well as in secular institutions. The same thing remains true up to the present day with the Higher Education Act of 1965 as Amended (many times). No doubt many thousands of students in the Catholic institutions that decided to secularize after the Land O'Lakes statement in 1967 were studying with the help of federal grants and loans, and this *cannot* have been something that Father Hesburgh was ignorant of when he claimed that Catholic institutions *had* to secularize in order to receive federal aid. The Catholic schools that secularized did so for no other reason than that they *wanted* to secularize. There were no government requirements or pressures of any kind involved.

I wrote an article pointing out the error of the Hesburgh claim that Catholic colleges and universities had somehow had to secularize. Much to my surprise, *America* magazine printed the article (impressed, perhaps, by the prestige of the high position I then held in the federal government). The editor of *America* very soon regretted his decision to print the article, however, since all the Catholic professional associations in Washington – such as the Association of Catholic Colleges and Universities (ACCU) and the Association of Jesuit Colleges and Universities (AJCU) – almost immediately came down on his head. In an editorial in a later issue *America* hastily backed away from the position it had seemed to endorse by printing my article. Some of the Catholic education association people in Washington also called upon Education Secretary William Bennett and presented him with a very severe bill of particulars directed against *me* (which Secretary Bennett then just simply handed on *to* me for reply).

I used this bill of particulars drawn up against me – which repeated the false claim that Catholic colleges and universities could not continue to affirm and maintain an integral Catholic character and still receive government aid – to write a point-by-point refutation of the original erroneous Hesburgh claim about this. This became my book *Catholic Colleges and Federal Funding* (Ignatius, 1988), which briefly caused a bit of a stir at the time. No sooner was this book published than Msgr. Kelly was on the telephone to me to invite me to present my thesis to the 1988 Fellowship of Catholic Scholars convention in Boston. This was my first real contact with the Fellowship. As a result of that meeting, I then began getting calls from Msgr. Kelly from time to time on a variety of subjects. These calls almost always came in the morning, usually quite early. Msgr. Kelly turned in early at night and got up early in the morning, and apparently was then regularly on the telephone on many mornings with a wide circle of friends, colleagues, and contacts (including, it seems, even a few friendly bishops!). His telephone bill must have been something!

It wasn't too long before Msgr. Kelly began insisting that I needed to participate more actively in the work of the Fellowship and even join the Board of Directors. Today FCS Board members are duly elected (except former FCS presidents who, at Msgr. Kelly's specific insistence, remain on the Board for life if they wish). I myself even helped draft the new FCS by-laws providing for the election of Board members. But in the old days, the founder seems just to have decided when and if he wanted somebody in particular on Board. It was in this fashion that I ended up serving on the Board through most of the 1990s (having been duly *elected* again after a hiatus in 2004!). I had initially tried to demur, protesting that I was not really a *scholar*, but merely a retired bureaucrat and writer and translator. But Msgr. Kelly would have none of that; once he had decided upon something, he tended to insist upon it in his own inimitable way – a way that made it hard if not impossible to refuse.

As a result, my years in the Fellowship have certainly been rewarding for *me*. As others have mentioned, many of us concerned about contemporary Church affairs just naturally did tend to look to him for leadership on many things – and leadership was precisely what he provided in abundance.

Some of us began to be aware that Msgr. Kelly was failing because the early morning telephone calls began to be more and more rare. Then, finally, there were no more calls at all, and we had to realize, sadly, that we would not soon see his like again. *Requiescat in pace!*

Kenneth D. Whitehead is a former career Foreign Service Officer who completed his federal government career as the Assistant Secretary of Education for Post-secondary Education under President Ronald Reagan. Currently he works as a writer, editor, and translator in Falls Church, Virginia, across the river from Washington, D.C. He is the author, most recently, of *One, Holy, Catholic, and Apostolic: The Early Church Was the Catholic Church* (Ignatius, 2000), and the co-author (with Msgr. Michael J. Wrenn) of *Flawed Expectations: The Reception of the Catechism of the Catholic Church* (Ignatius, 1996). His new book *What Vatican II Did Right: Forty Years after the Council and Counting* is forthcoming from Ignatius Press. He was a recipient of the FCS Cardinal Wright Award in 1998. He is married to the former Margaret O'Donohue, a parish director of religious education, and they are the parents of four grown sons.

Appendix
Fellowship of Catholic Scholars
Membership Information
For information about joining the Fellowship of Catholic Scholars, contact the Executive Secretary, the Rev. Msgr. Stewart Swetland at:

St. John's Newman Foundation
604 East Armory Avenue
Champaign, Illinois 61820

TEL: 217-344-1184 Ext. 305

E-MAIL: msgrswetland@newmanfoundation.org

Or visit the FCS website at:
www.catholicscholars.org

Statement of Purpose

1. We, Catholic scholars in various disciplines, join in fellowship in order to serve Jesus Christ better, by helping one another in our work and by putting our abilities more fully at the service of the Catholic faith.
2. We wish to form a Fellowship of Catholic Scholars who see their intellectual work as expressing the service they owe to God. To Him we give thanks for our Catholic faith and for every opportunity He gives us to serve that faith
3. We wish to form a Fellowship of Catholic Scholars open to the work of the Holy Spirit within the Church. Thus we wholeheartedly accept and support the renewal of the Church of Christ undertaken by Pope John XXIII, shaped by Vatican Council II, and carried on by succeeding popes.
4. We accept as the rule of our life and thought the entire faith of the Catholic Church. This we see not merely in solemn definitions but in the ordinary teaching of the pope and the bishops in union with

him, and also embodied in those modes of worship and ways of Christian life, of the present as of the past, which have been in harmony with the teaching of St. Peter's successors in the See of Rome.

5. The questions raised by contemporary thought must be considered with courage and dealt with in honesty. We will seek to do this, faithful to the truth always guarded in the Church by the Holy Spirit, and sensitive to the needs of the family of faith. We wish to accept a responsibility which a Catholic scholar may not evade: to assist everyone, so far as we are able, to personal assent to the mystery of Christ as made manifest through the lived faith of the Church, His Body, and through the active charity without which faith is dead.

6. To contribute to this sacred work, our Fellowship will strive to:

    *   Come to know and welcome all who share our purpose;
    *   Make known to one another our various competencies and interests;
    *   Share our abilities with one another unstintingly in our efforts directed to our common purpose;
    *   Cooperate in clarifying the challenges which must be met;
    *   Help one another to evaluate critically the variety of responses which are proposed to these challenges;
    *   Communicate our suggestions and evaluations to members of the Church who might find them helpful;
    *   Respond to requests to help the Church in her work of guarding the faith as inviolable and defending it with fidelity;
    *   Help one another to work through, in scholarly and prayerful fashion and without public dissent, any problem which may arise from magisterial teaching.

7. With the grace of God for which we pray, we hope to assist the whole Church to understand her own identity more clearly, to proclaim the joyous Gospel of Jesus more confidently, and to carry out it redemptive work to all humankind more effectively.

Member Benefits

All members receive four issues annually of the *The Fellowship of Catholic Scholars Quarterly*, which includes scholarly articles, important documentation, book reviews, news, and occasional Fellowship symposia.

All members are invited to attend the annual FCS convention held in various cities where, by custom, the local ordinary greets and typically celebrates Mass for the members of the Fellowship. The typical convention program includes: Daily Mass; Keynote Address; at least six scholarly sessions with speakers who are customarily invited to help develop and illustrate the theme of each convention chosen by the FCS Board of Directors; a Banquet and Reception with Awards; and a membership business meeting and occasional substantive meetings devoted to subjects of current interest in the Church.

Current members receive a copy of the "Proceedings" of each convention, consisting of an attractive volume with the title of the convention theme and containing the texts of the conventions speeches and other material of interest to the membership. Every three or four years all members receive a Membership Directory with current information on Fellowship members (addresses, telephone numbers, faxes, e-mails, etc.).

National Awards

The Fellowship grants the following Awards, usually presented during the annual convention:

The Cardinal Wright Award – Presented annually to a Catholic judged to have done outstanding service for the Church in the tradition of the late Cardinal John J. Wright, former Bishop of Pittsburgh and later Prefect for the Congregation for Catholic Education in Rome. The recipients of this Award have been:

1979 – Rev. Msgr. George A. Kelly
1980 – Dr. William E. May
1981 – Dr. James Hitchcock
1982 – Dr. Germain Grisez
1983 – Rev. John Connery, S.J.
1984 – Rev. John A. Hardon, S.J.
1985 – Herbert Ratner, M.D.
1986 – Dr. Joseph P. Scottino
1987 – Rev. Joseph Farraher, & Rev. Joseph Fessio, S.J.
1988 – Rev. John Harvey, O.S.F.S.
1989 – Dr. John Finnis
1990 – Rev. Ronald Lawler, O.F.M. Cap.
1991 – Rev. Francis Canavan, S.J.
1992 – Rev. Donald J. Keefe, S.J.
1993 – Dr. Janet E. Smith
1994 – Dr. Jude P. Dougherty
1995 – Rev. Msgr. William B. Smith
1996 – Dr. Ralph McInerny
1997 – Rev. James V. Schall, S.J.
1998 – Rev. Msgr. Michael J. Wrenn & Kenneth D. Whitehead

1999 – Dr. Robert P. George
2000 – Dr. Mary Ann Glendon
2001 – Thomas W. Hilgers, M.D.
2002 – Rev. J. Augustine DiNoia, O.P.
2003 – Prof. Elizabeth Fox-Genovese
2004 – Sr. Mary Prudence Allen, R.S.M.

The Cardinal O'Boyle Award – This Award is given occasionally to individuals whose actions demonstrate a courage and witness in favor of the Catholic Faith similar to that exhibited by the late Cardinal Patrick A. O'Boyle, Archbishop of Washington, in the face of the pressures of contemporary society which tend to undermine the faith. The recipients of this award have been:

1988 – Rev. John C. Ford, S.J.
1991 – Mother Angelica, P.C.P.A., EWTN
1995 – John and Sheila Kippley, Couple to Couple League
1997 – Rep. Henry J. Hyde (R.-IL)
2002 – Senator Rick Santorum (R.-PA)
2003 – Secretary of Housing and Urban Development, the Honorable Melquiades R.Martinez and Mrs. Kathryn Tindal Martinez
2004 – Rep. Christopher J. Smith (R.-NJ) and Marie Smith

The Founder's Award – Given occasionally to individuals with a record of outstanding service in defense of the Catholic faith and in support of the Catholic intellectual life. In 2002, the Award was presented to Fr. Joseph Fessio, S.J., and in 2003, to Fr. Ronald Lawler, O.F.M.Cap.

Presidents of the Fellowship of Catholic Scholars

2004 –   Dean Bernard Dobranski, Ave Maria Law School
2003 – 2004 Prof. Gerard V. Bradley, Notre Dame Law School
2002 – 2003 Dean Bernard Dobranski, Ave Maria Law School
2001 – 2002 Rev. Thomas F. Dailey, O.S.F.S., DeSales University
1995 – 2001 Prof. Gerard V. Bradley, Notre Dame Law School
1991 – 1995 Prof. Ralph McInerny, University of Notre Dame
1989 – 1991 Rev. Kenneth Baker, S.J., Editor, *Homiletic & Pastoral Review*
1987 – 1989 Prof. William E. May, John Paul II Institute on Marriage and the Family
1985 – 1987 Rev. Msgr. George A. Kelly, St. John's University
1983 – 1985 Rev. Earl Weiss, S.J., Loyola University

1981 – 1983   Rev. Msgr. William B. Smith, St. Joseph's Seminary
1979 – 1981   Prof. James Hitchcock, St. Louis University
1977 – 1979   Rev. Ronald Lawler, O.F.M.Cap., Diocese of
Pittsburgh